Ewald Geschwinde and
Hans-Jürgen Schönig

PHP and PostgreSQL

Advanced Web Programming

201 West 103rd Street, Indianapolis, Indiana 46290

PHP and PostgreSQL
Advanced Web Programming

International Standard Book Number: 0-672-32382-6

Library of Congress Catalog Card Number: 2001098213

Printed in the United States of America

First Printing: June 2002

05   04   03   02   4   3   2   1

Trademarks

Warning and Disclaimer

Acquisitions Editor
Shelley Johnston

Development Editor
Scott Meyers

Managing Editor
Charlotte Clapp

Project Editor
Carol L. Bowers

Copy Editor
Margaret Berson

Indexer
Ken Johnson

Proofreader
Linda Seifert

Technical Editors
Vince Vielhaber
Kenneth Kloeppel

Team Coordinator
Amy Patton

Multimedia Developer
Dan Scherf

Interior Designer
Anne Jones

Cover Designer
Aren Howell

Page Layout
Ayanna Lacey

Graphics
Stephen Adams
Tammy Graham
Oliver L. Jackson, Jr.
Laura Robbins

Contents at a Glance

Table of Contents

About the Authors

Ewald Geschwinde

Ewald Geschwinde was born on June 21, 1976 in Vienna, Austria. After primary school, he attended the high school for economics in Oberpullendorf. During this time he dealt with computers and extended the work in his favorite field while studying at the Technical University in Vienna.

A few months later he started working at the computer center of CA (an Austrian bank), where he was responsible for writing data converters and network solutions for backup systems.

In February 1999 he joined Synthesis, where he focused on scientifically monitoring the development of unemployment in Austria and generating reports using C, EFEU, LaTeX, and Perl. In his spare time he developed a database solution for business consultants.

After focusing on Oracle databases, he left Synthesis to found Cybertec Geschwinde & Schönig OEG—a company providing commercial support, training courses, tuning, and remote administration for PostgreSQL (`www.postgresql.at`) as well as LDAP (`www.openldap.info`).

Hans-Jürgen Schönig

On August 9, 1978 Hans-Jürgen Schönig was born in Knittelfeld, a small town 125 miles southwest of Vienna. After primary school he attended a private school in Seckau. After the high school final exam, he started studying "Economics of Information" at the Technical University and the University of Vienna where he met Ewald Geschwinde. Just for fun, Hans started working on various projects and was finally employed at Synthesis (an Austrian research company focusing on forecasting the Austrian labor market), in September 1998. There he was responsible for the scientific analysis of data provided by the Austrian social security insurance (dozens of millions of records). During his time at Synthesis, he worked with Unix systems and automated text production, using EFEU, LaTeX, and Perl. In addition, he taught Unix classes in an adult education program once a week.

In the summer of 2000 Hans and Ewald left Synthesis to found Cybertec Geschwinde & Schönig OEG (`www.cybertec.at`), focused entirely on PostgreSQL, LDAP, and Unix databases.

Dedication

On September 29, 2001, Ewald Gerhard Geschwinde married Christina Geschwinde (formerly known as Christina Szabo) in a gondola on Vienna's famous Ferris wheel ("Riesenrad") in an area called the "Prater."

This book is dedicated to Epi's wife Christina and their unborn baby son.

Acknowledgments

After months of hard work, this book has finally come true. This is a magical, emotional moment for us and we want to say thank you to all who have helped us to make this book happen.

Personally we want to thank Patricia G. Barnes who supported the development of the concept. She was the one who had the original idea for this book and got us started writing books. She worked on our first book (*PostgreSQL Developer's Handbook*) and we want to thank her for her work. Unfortunately she has left Sams. Pat, thanks for all you have done for us.

We were inherited by the most likable acquisitions editor we have ever dealt with. We want to say thank you to Shelley Johnston ("The Brain"—all of us are fans of "Pinky and the Brain"), who has supported us during the entire process. She is the one who makes things work—she is the key motivator in the entire team. We want to thank her for a personal and warm relationship that helps us to do our best. Let's hope that her son Alex (8 months old) will also be an acquisitions editor like her. Thanks, Shelley; we hope to meet some day.

Personal thanks goes to Vince Vielhaber, who has done a major part of the technical editing. Vince is one of the best PostgreSQL developers and provided a lot of experience as well as expertise.

We want to thank Erich Frühstück (see `http://efeu.cybertec.at`), who is the maintainer of the EFEU package. He is the person who taught us Unix and who showed us how to write proper programs, not just code. Erich is the best IT expert we have known in our careers. Thanks for all you have done for us. In a way you are the father of the technology that Cybertec (`www.postgresql.at`) can provide today.

Thanks to all our friends who have supported us during the past months and years.

Finally we want to say thank you to all those people involved in the process. Thanks to all of those who spent weeks and months to make this book come true. They are the people we will never meet personally, but they are also the people who play a major role. A book is not made only by authors. There are dozens of people involved who do all this wonderful work.

Tell Us What You Think!

As the reader of this book, *you* are our most important critic and commentator. We value your opinion and want to know what we're doing right, what we could do better, what areas you'd like to see us publish in, and any other words of wisdom you're willing to pass our way.

You can e-mail or write me directly to let me know what you did or didn't like about this book—as well as what we can do to make our books stronger.

Please note that I cannot help you with technical problems related to the topic of this book, and that due to the high volume of mail I receive, I might not be able to reply to every message.

When you write, please be sure to include this book's title and author as well as your name and phone or e-mail address. I will carefully review your comments and share them with the author and editors who worked on the book.

E-mail: opensource@samspublishing.com

Mail: Mark Taber
            Associate Publisher
            Sams Publishing
            201 West 103rd Street
            Indianapolis, IN 46290 USA

Reader Services

For more information about this book or others from Sams Publishing, visit our Web site at **www.samspublishing.com**. Type the ISBN (excluding hyphens) or the title of the book in the Search box to find the book you're looking for.

Introduction

Since we started working on our first Sams book, *PostgreSQL Developer's Handbook*, many things have changed. The people we started working with have become friends, and writing has become a key component of our daily life. PostgreSQL has been improved constantly and the development will certainly continue in the future. It is exciting to participate in a tremendous evolution and to see how a group of volunteers develops a database system that can hardly be compared to anything else on this planet. PostgreSQL is not just a database—it is a philosophy and it is magic. When reading this book, you might feel the enthusiasm we felt when writing the text and presenting solutions based on PostgreSQL to a wide audience.

You will see that PHP and PostgreSQL are a wonderful team for building powerful Web applications, and in this book you will learn about both platforms.

Why You Should Read This Book

This book is dedicated to all people who want to implement advanced database solutions. For all those among you who want to implement more than just lousy applications, this book contains all the information you need to write professional, database-driven programs.

When writing the sample code in this book, we tried to focus on the main idea of the examples so that they are easy to understand. In addition, we tried to avoid trash and components that are not useful for the reader. This way it should be possible to get the gist of an example quickly.

The goal of this book is to be a professional manual providing enough detailed information about both PHP and PostgreSQL, as a team and as individual packages, that you can implement any kind of application.

Finally

We hope that you will have fun reading this book and it will help you to improve your skills.

We are no fans of long, boring introductions, so it is time to get started with some real action.

Have fun!

PART I

Getting Started

IN THIS PART

1

Getting Started

Since the beginning of human history, people had to work with data. In the early days, data was stored on stones or on other ancient media. The idea was to store data in such a way that other people could use it. At first, simple pictographs were drawn to code various fragments of information. With the invention of the alphabet, storing data became easier and communication was constantly improved.

With the ability to store information, it was also possible to share knowledge with others and to have some sort of backup for the human brain. Looking at the process from a modern point of view, it was all about storing and retrieving data in such a way that people could work with the information. This is exactly what people are doing today. The "stone computers" have been replaced by highly sophisticated clusters or personal computers. Data is not transmitted on stones any more, but is sent across fiber cable networks within hundredths of a second. No matter which methods have been used or which methods are still used today, the basic ideas of IT are still the same: Storing, retrieving, and displaying data are still the fundamentals of every system, and I guess things won't change in the next few centuries. It is all about information and it still will be about information in the future.

With the invention of the alphabet and writing in general, it became possible to describe things. Using letters, it is possible to build words and phrases. Alphabets and languages are fundamental components that every culture relies on. For a long time humans have used language to interact with other humans. In recent times, it has become very popular to interact with computers. However, the way interaction is done is still the same. Characters are used to tell the partner what to do and what has happened.

Because computers cannot understand human languages, new forms of communications have been invented. Programming languages were developed for working with machines and telling them what to do.

With the arrival of modern technologies such as the Internet, more and more specialized and highly optimized languages have been developed. One of these languages is called PHP. PHP was designed for building Web sites. Of course, PHP can be used as an ordinary programming language, but the main purpose of PHP is to work in combination with network environments. The language is a child of the Internet and the father of many Web sites all around the globe. Millions of Web sites have been built with the help of PHP, and it has been installed on thousands of servers.

To store data efficiently, databases can be used. One of these databases is PostgreSQL, a flexible and easy-to-use platform for working with millions of pieces of information. PostgreSQL is a so-called object relational database, which means that it offers more features than a purely relational database.

1.1 Why Use PHP and PostgreSQL as a Team?

At the beginning of the Internet age, many Web sites were based on Perl applications, which were using the CGI interface. With the help of the CGI interface, it is possible to use every programming language for generating HTML code on-the-fly. The programming language Perl is optimized for building text processors, so it is a great tool for building Web sites. HTML code is based on text, so dynamic pages can easily be generated. However, Perl was not designed to be a Web language. Especially when running Perl, using the CGI interface is very common. Other programming languages such as PHP can have several advantages over Perl because PHP has been optimized for the Web. Of course, you can use mod_perl, but an increasing number of people rely on PHP.

Both PHP and PostgreSQL are open source, which means that the source code of PHP and PostgreSQL can be used and distributed freely. Using open source software has several advantages:

- **Costs**—You don't have to pay for the software, which helps reduce the total cost of your software projects.

- **Security**—Free software is said to be more secure than commercial software. In many cases security updates for free software are available quickly, so severe security problems will not last a long time.

- **Information**—When using commercial software, you might not know exactly what a certain component does. In this case free software will be helpful because you just have to look at the source code of PHP or PostgreSQL and you will find out what the code does.

- **Independence**—Free software helps you to gain independence from software manufacturers. This is important because you need not follow the update path proposed by a big player in the software business.

- **Quality**—In most cases free software contains high-quality code. People implementing open source are highly motivated, so free software offers stability as well as flexibility.

- **Freedom**—Free software offers the possibility to modify the software to your needs. Features can be added easily, and in addition, you can optimize the software for your application.

The last point especially is truly an important one. "Free software is not free beer"— this is what Richard M. Stallman, the father of free software, has to say about open source. Freedom means that nobody can force you to stick to a concept and nobody threatens your personal freedom. If you have no chance to modify your software, your mind is not free and this must be avoided.

Today a variety of free databases are available. Many developers rely on databases such as MySQL. MySQL offers a special version of SQL that is not ANSI-SQL–compliant. Especially when porting MySQL applications to other databases, MySQL's incompatibility is a real problem because you might have to rewrite or at least modify major parts of your SQL code. In addition, PostgreSQL provides highly sophisticated features such as inheritance, triggers, and embedded languages.

In contrast to MySQL, PostgreSQL is ANSI SQL-92–compliant. Therefore porting applications to PostgreSQL is an easy task, and it is also possible to switch from PostgreSQL to a commercial database such as DB2 or Oracle.

PHP provides an easy-to-use interface to PostgreSQL. PHP's programming interface is built on PostgreSQL's libpq library. This library is used by all important programming languages such as Python, Tcl, or Perl and provides all the features you will need to build powerful database applications.

1.2 What You Can Do with PHP and PostgreSQL

There are many reasons for using PHP and PostgreSQL as a team and in this section you will see some practical examples. You will see what you can do with PHP and PostgreSQL and you will learn about the most important features.

The first few chapters of this book focus entirely on PHP. First the installation will be discussed. You will see how PHP can be set up and how PHP interacts with the Web server.

When you know how to install the system, you can get started with PHP. Chapter 3, "PHP Basics," is an introduction to PHP where you will see how to implement and maintain simple applications. You will learn about the scope of variables, working with files, building packages, and working with forms, as well as debugging.

After this brief introduction, it is time to take a look at PHP's object-oriented capabilities. Chapter 4, "Object-Oriented PHP," is all about objects. Constructors, classes, inheritance, and so forth will be the topics of this chapter. Object orientation will help many of you to build more modular applications, and this will help you to reuse your code in many applications.

When you are familiar with PHP, PostgreSQL will be introduced. Chapter 5 will guide you through the principles of relational and object relational database theory. This will help you to gain an overview of working with databases and give you the fundamental knowledge you will need in this book.

Chapter 6, "Installing PostgreSQL," will be about the installation process of PostgreSQL. The chapter will focus on installing PostgreSQL on Unix and Windows-based systems.

As soon as PostgreSQL is up and running, you can take a look at SQL in Chapter 7, "Basic SQL." SQL is a structured query language whose only purpose is to interact with databases. Knowing the basics of SQL will enable you to implement simple database-driven applications.

Chapter 8 will definitely rock your boat. It is all about advanced SQL. For all of you who already are familiar with MySQL, this will be an avatar of advanced database technology provided by PostgreSQL. In the first part of the chapter we will discuss advanced data types you can use for storing network information or geometric data. Further sections of the chapter cover views, subselects, aliases, autojoins, constraints, and transactions, as well as object orientation. In a special section you will learn about rules. Rules are an extremely cool feature of PostgreSQL that enable you to redefine SQL commands to your needs.

For all who are migrating from Oracle to PostgreSQL, Chapter 9, "Embedded Languages," will be interesting. Most parts of this chapter are about PL/pgSQL, which is an embedded language similar to Oracle's PL/SQL. In this section you will also learn to write triggers.

An important topic when working with a database is its administration. Defining user rights and managing network security are only two parts of Chapter 10, "PostgreSQL Administration."

After all these fundamentals you will be ready for action, and it is time to get started with PHP and PostgreSQL as a team. Chapter 11 will guide you through the basics of working with simple database-driven applications. You will learn to insert and retrieve data from the database as well as learning about locking and inheritance.

For those of you who are working with huge files, Chapter 12, "Working with BLOBs," will be useful. You will learn how files can be stored inside a PostgreSQL database. Yes, you have understood correctly—files can be stored inside a database. There is no need to work with external files that are not consistent with the file-names in the database. This section is about file uploads as well. You will learn how files can be uploaded to remote Web servers safely.

Speed is an important issue in modern application development. Chapter 13 will give you a brief insight into working with persistent database connections. You will learn about dangers and benefits of persistent connections and you will focus on measuring performance.

Regular expressions are a powerful invention. For fuzzy matching and pattern matching, regular expressions are essential. Although they are said to be difficult, simple patterns are not that complicated to write. In Chapter 14, "Managing Regular Expressions," you will be guided through the fundamentals of regular expressions and you will get a closer look at Perl-style and POSIX-style regular expressions. You will also see how regular expressions can be used in SQL.

Have you ever built a Web site consisting of more than just one dynamic page? If you have already done that, you know that it is essential to pass information from one script to another. Session management, which is the topic of Chapter 15, is an essential task, and the more complex your Web site is, the more important session management will be. HTTP is not a connection-oriented protocol, so some sort of connection-oriented capabilities must be available on the application level.

For many years building dynamic Web sites was about generating HTML code. With the evolution of modern technologies, it became possible to generate images, sounds, movies, and documents on the fly, as explained in Chapter 16, "Working with Dynamic Documents, Images, and Movies." You can build systems that do not have static, predefined components any more. No matter what application you want to build, PHP and PostgreSQL will provide the right solution for you. Figure 1.1 shows an example of what can be done with PHP and PostgreSQL.

In combination with tools such as LaTeX, nice-looking documents can be generated. The content of the document is taken from the database and can be administered easily. It is possible to generate documents consisting of hundreds of pages fast and efficiently.

Dates and time have always been crucial. Unlike data such as integer values, dates and time cannot be processed that easily. The reason lies in the complexity of dates. Just think of months. A month can be 28, 29, 30, or 31 days long; in addition, it is not the same every year. You can easily imagine that this can be a problem.

In Chapter 17, "Working with Dates and Time," you will take a closer look at dates and time and we will try to present easy yet powerful solutions for the most common problems.

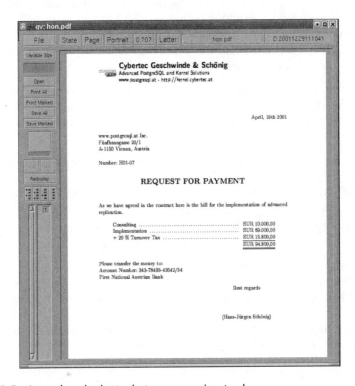

FIGURE 1.5   Just take a look at what we are going to do.

Speed is the drug of IT people. I am not talking about illegal substances but about performance tuning. It is all about speed, and every software developer wants to get the maximum performance out of his computer. In Chapter 18, "Tuning," you will learn to tune PostgreSQL and take a look at measuring performance in general.

Recently XML has become more and more popular. For exchanging data, XML is widely used for business-to-business (B2B) communication. The advantage of XML is that it is based on ASCII. This means that it can be read by every platform on every system available. An additional advantage of XML is that the definition of the structure of a document and the data itself need not be in the same file. This makes the creation of templates easier and helps you to gain flexibility.

Modern Web environments must be secure. Just think of a company's intranet where confidential data is transmitted, or think of a stock exchange where billions of dollars are managed. Security is an important issue. However, when building simple

Web sites, the main problem is still the same—how can these sites be made more secure? Chapter 20 focuses on security.

In Chapter 21, "Web Applications," you will see some prototypes of the most common applications. From Web shops to content management systems—from application servers to drawing stock charts—everything will be discussed in this chapter.

PostgreSQL is one of the most flexible databases available. It allows the user to implement simple extensions easily. Therefore, PostgreSQL can be the basis for every kind of application. The basic features of PostgreSQL are extraordinary, but when building your own extensions, the power of PostgreSQL can be even greater. Chapter 22 focuses on extending PostgreSQL as well as persuading the database to do things that are not core features such as building substring indexes or tolerant searching.

The topics of the two final chapters are high availability and migration. In the sections about high availability, you will learn about error-tolerant database structures. Just think of undoing transactions—this chapter is what you are looking for.

1.3 Web Sites Built on PHP and PostgreSQL

All around the globe people are using PHP and PostgreSQL. To encourage you to use the two products as a team, we will go on a quick tour to visit some Web sites around the globe running PHP and PostgreSQL. You will see what can be done and you will learn that even high-performance sites can be implemented safely.

Let's start our tour around the world.

Ecomtel offers online billing tools. Billing software is extremely security- and performance-critical, so it is necessary to use well-tested and fast applications such as PHP and PostgreSQL. High quality, high availability, and flexibility are the keywords, and that is exactly what PHP and PostgreSQL offer. The Web site of Ecomtel can be found at http://www.ecomtel.com.au/. Figure 1.2 gives you a look at the Web site of the company.

You can even see the logos "powered by PHP" and "powered by PostgreSQL" at the bottom of the Web site.

With PHP and PostgreSQL it is not only possible to run highly sophisticated applications; it is also possible to build simple, content-driven Web pages. One example of that can be found on the other side of the globe. A small town in the Czech Republic relies on PHP and PostgreSQL as you can see at http://www.karlovyvary.cz, which is shown in Figure 1.3.

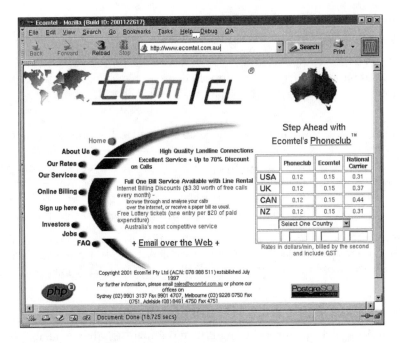

FIGURE 1.2   Ecomtel's Web site.

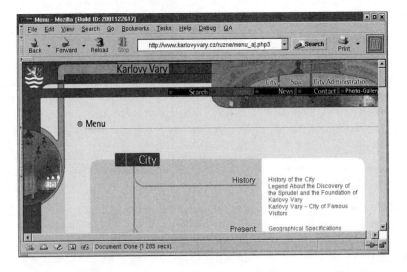

FIGURE 1.3   PostgreSQL and the Czech Republic.

Let's continue our world tour and make a stop at the University of Vienna. There we can find people building geographical databases and generating maps with the help of PHP and PostgreSQL. Because of PostgreSQL's wonderful interface for working with geometric data types, the database is a wonderful playground for scientists as well as for students.

At `http://www.gis.univie.ac.at/karto/` you can find the Web site of the institute running PHP and PostgreSQL.

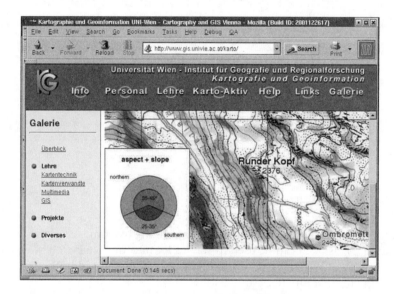

FIGURE 1.4   Geographic applications with PHP and PostgreSQL.

Let's finish our world tour in one of the homelands of PostgreSQL and visit one of the most popular and most useful PostgreSQL Web sites. `http://techdocs.post-gresql.org/` is a Web site for users of PostgreSQL. The site itself is built on PHP and contains a lot of useful information about PostgreSQL and software related to the database.

The site is maintained by Justin Clift and can be seen in Figure 1.5.

PHP and PostgreSQL are used by countless Web programmers and database administrators all around the globe. They are a playground for hackers as well as for ordinary programmers, and both products offer what you have been looking for. PostgreSQL is one of the most stable databases, and PHP can easily be used in combination with PostgreSQL. PHP and PostgreSQL are a perfect tool for beginners as well as for pros, and you will soon see why.

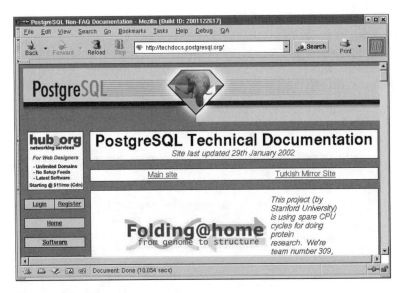

FIGURE 1.5   Technical documentation.

1.4 Summary

PHP and PostgreSQL are a fantastic team for building dynamic, database-driven applications. This team can be used to solve a lot of common as well as exotic problems. Any kind of Web site can be implemented efficiently, and both products offer the user a rich set of functions and features.

In this book you will see what you can do with PHP and PostgreSQL, and you will learn to use these two open source products in a professional way.

2

Setting Up PHP

In the first chapter of this book, you have seen what can be done with PHP and PostgreSQL. PHP and PostgreSQL are a powerful team that can be used to build a variety of sophisticated, fast applications.

The first step to becoming a really good PHP developer is to learn how to set up the language on your machine. This chapter will guide you through the installation process of PHP. The most important platforms will be covered.

2.1 About PHP

PHP is a language optimized for generating dynamic Web sites. Theoretically it can also be used as an ordinary programming language, but only a few people use PHP that way because this is not the purpose PHP has been optimized for.

Back in 1994 Rasmus Lerdorf was looking for an easy method to program his personal Web server. He called his first attempt "Personal Home Page Tools." As you can easily imagine, these tools were basically designed for satisfying his personal demands—at this early stage, nobody was thinking of something big like the PHP of today.

In 1995 these tools became more professional. A version called PHP/FI (Personal Home Page Tools/Form Interface) was released. This was the first version of PHP that really made sense and that was used by people other than Lerdorf.

After version 2 (PHP/FI), PHP was developed more rapidly, and in 1997 PHP3 was released. PHP3 was widely used and can still be found on many Web sites because it was a reliable and easy-to-program language. In contrast to many other platforms, PHP was written for the Web. Unlike Perl, PHP was designed for the Web from the ground up, so many things that are more difficult when using Perl can be done easily with the help of PHP. Of course, programming languages such as Perl have many other advantages and can also be used without a Web server, but for Web applications, PHP has become popular.

The most recent release of PHP is PHP 4, which is based on the so-called Zend engine. The Zend engine is significantly faster than any prior version of PHP because of the internal compiler.

Today PHP is a fast and reliable platform for developing Web applications. The development of PHP will continue, and many powerful features will be added to PHP just as in the past.

2.2 Installing Apache with PHP from Source

PHP can be run on multiple platforms and it can interact with various Web servers. However, the most widespread Web servers are Apache and Microsoft's IIS. In this section you will see how PHP can be compiled in combination with Apache.

2.2.1 Installing Apache with PHP on Unix

Installing Apache with PHP on Unix is not difficult. In contrast to installing binary packages, installing the sources has some advantages. The biggest advantage is most likely that you know exactly which flags have been enabled and which components have been compiled into your binaries. If you are planning to modify the core of Apache or PHP, you have to compile the source code; otherwise, there is no way to make the changes in your binaries.

One disadvantage is that it is a lot more work to install sources than to install binaries. An additional disadvantage is that you will most likely not have the knowledge of an experienced Linux or Unix distributor. In case of security problems or any other problems with a software package, your distributor will most likely know what to do best to get around a problem.

No matter what you like best in this section, you will learn to compile and to install the source distribution of Apache and PHP.

The first thing you have to do is to download the sources of Apache and PHP. Check out your local mirror sites or go to www.apache.org (for Apache) and www.php.net (for PHP).

On Unix machines the source code is usually stored in /usr/src. In this scenario we generate a directory called apache_php located in /usr/src. This directory will contain the sources of Apache and PHP as well as a shell script for compiling the sources. Download the sources to /usr/src/apache_php and extract the two packages using tar xvfz *packname* (for Linux; on other systems consider using tar -xvfz *packname*; Linux supports both statements) where *packname* is the name of a package (for example, apache_1.3.22.tar.gz). In the next step you can create two softlinks for making the script you are going to write more independently from the version of Apache and PHP being compiled. This can easily be done using ln:

```
[root@duron apache_php]# ln -s apache_1.3.22/ apache
[root@duron apache_php]# ln -s php-4.1.0/ php
```

If no errors occurred, two softlinks have been created that do not contain the version number of the two packages.

2.2.1.1 Configuring Apache

Before you see how to compile Apache and PHP as a team, it is time to take a closer look at the configuration parameters supported by Apache (in this case Apache 1.3.22). Enter the directory called apache and type **./configure --help** as shown in the next listing:

```
[root@duron apache]# ./configure --help
[hang on a moment, generating help]

Usage: configure [options]
Options: [defaults in brackets after descriptions]
General options:
  --quiet, --silent       do not print messages
  --verbose, -v           print even more messages
  --shadow[=DIR]          switch to a shadow tree (under DIR) for building

Stand-alone options:
  --help, -h              print this message
  --show-layout           print installation path layout (check and debug)

Installation layout options:
  --with-layout=[F:]ID    use installation path layout ID (from file F)
  --target=TARGET         install name-associated files using basename TARGET
  --prefix=PREFIX         install architecture-independent files in PREFIX
  --exec-prefix=EPREFIX   install architecture-dependent files in EPREFIX
  --bindir=DIR            install user     executables in DIR
  --sbindir=DIR           install sysadmin executables in DIR
  --libexecdir=DIR        install program  executables in DIR
  --mandir=DIR            install manual pages in DIR
  --sysconfdir=DIR        install configuration files in DIR
  --datadir=DIR           install read-only data files in DIR
```

```
  --iconsdir=DIR          install read-only icon files in DIR
  --htdocsdir=DIR         install read-only welcome pages in DIR
  --manualdir=DIR         install read-only on-line documentation in DIR
  --cgidir=DIR            install read-only cgi files in DIR
  --includedir=DIR        install includes files in DIR
  --localstatedir=DIR     install modifiable data files in DIR
  --runtimedir=DIR        install runtime data in DIR
  --logfiledir=DIR        install logfile data in DIR
  --proxycachedir=DIR     install proxy cache data in DIR

Configuration options:
  --enable-rule=NAME      enable  a particular Rule named 'NAME'
  --disable-rule=NAME     disable a particular Rule named 'NAME'
                          [DEV_RANDOM=default EXPAT=default   IRIXN32=yes ]
                          [IRIXNIS=no       PARANOID=no      SHARED_CHAIN=de]
                          [SHARED_CORE=default SOCKS4=no         SOCKS5=no  ]
                          [WANTHSREGEX=default                             ]
  --add-module=FILE       on-the-fly copy & activate a 3rd-party Module
  --activate-module=FILE on-the-fly activate existing 3rd-party Module
  --permute-module=N1:N2 on-the-fly permute module 'N1' with module 'N2'
  --enable-module=NAME    enable  a particular Module named 'NAME'
  --disable-module=NAME   disable a particular Module named 'NAME'
                          [access=yes      actions=yes     alias=yes      ]
                          [asis=yes        auth_anon=no    auth_dbm=no    ]
                          [auth_db=no      auth_digest=no  auth=yes       ]
                          [autoindex=yes   cern_meta=no    cgi=yes        ]
                          [digest=no       dir=yes         env=yes        ]
                          [example=no      expires=no      headers=no     ]
                          [imap=yes        include=yes     info=no        ]
                          [log_agent=no    log_config=yes  log_referer=no ]
                          [mime_magic=no   mime=yes        mmap_static=no ]
                          [negotiation=yes proxy=no        rewrite=no     ]
                          [setenvif=yes    so=no           speling=no     ]
                          [status=yes      unique_id=no    userdir=yes    ]
                          [usertrack=no    vhost_alias=no                 ]
  --enable-shared=NAME    enable  build of Module named 'NAME' as a DSO
  --disable-shared=NAME   disable build of Module named 'NAME' as a DSO
  --with-perl=FILE        path to the optional Perl interpreter
  --with-port=PORT        set the port number for httpd.conf
  --without-support       disable the build and installation of support tools
  --without-confadjust    disable the user/situation adjustments in config
  --without-execstrip     disable the stripping of executables on installation
```

```
--server-uid=UID          set the user ID the web server should run as [nobody]
--server-gid=GID          set the group ID the web server UID is a memeber of
[#-1]


suEXEC options:
--enable-suexec           enable the suEXEC feature
--suexec-caller=NAME      set the suEXEC username of the allowed caller [www]
--suexec-docroot=DIR      set the suEXEC root directory [PREFIX/share/htdocs]
--suexec-logfile=FILE     set the suEXEC logfile [PREFIX/var/log/suexec_log]
--suexec-userdir=DIR      set the suEXEC user subdirectory [public_html]
--suexec-uidmin=UID       set the suEXEC minimal allowed UID [100]
--suexec-gidmin=GID       set the suEXEC minimal allowed GID [100]
--suexec-safepath=PATH set the suEXEC safe PATH [/usr/local/bin:/usr/bin:/bin]
--suexec-umask=UMASK      set the umask for the suEXEC'd script [server's umask]


Deprecated options:
--layout                  backward compat only: use --show-layout
--compat                  backward compat only: use --with-layout=Apache
```

As you can see, the list of configuration parameters provided by Apache seems endless. The following list describes the most important of these parameters. For a complete reference of all flags, check out Apache's documentation:

- --quiet or --silent—Makes the system stop displaying messages.

- --verbose—Tells the system to display more debugging information.

- --prefix—Defines where Apache should be installed. If no other flags such as --exec-prefix, --bindir, and so forth are configured, all paths will be relative to the path defined by --prefix.

- --add-module—To add modules that are not included in the core distribution, the --add-module flag must be used to tell Apache where to find the additional module.

- --activate-module—To activate a module on-the-fly, this flag has to be set. The file containing the module has to be defined.

- --with-perl—Defining the path to the Perl interpreter can be important. Perl is one of the most important languages when working with Apache. If you have compiled Perl yourself, this flag might be essential.

2.2.1.2 Configuring PHP

Now that you have seen how to configure Apache, it is time to take a closer look at PHP. As you have already seen, PHP is not included in Apache's core distribution. PHP is an external yet powerful module that has to be configured independently.

In this section you will take a closer look at PHP's configuration parameters in detail. Again, the most important flags will be explained in detail.

After you have extracted the sources of PHP and entered the directory containing the sources, you can use ./configure --help to get a list of all configuration parameters of PHP (PHP 4.1):

```
[root@duron php]# ./configure --help
Usage: configure [options] [host]
Options: [defaults in brackets after descriptions]
Configuration:
  --cache-file=FILE       cache test results in FILE
  --help                  print this message
  --no-create             do not create output files
  --quiet, --silent       do not print `checking...' messages
  --version               print the version of autoconf that created configure
Directory and file names:
  --prefix=PREFIX         install architecture-independent files in PREFIX
                          [/usr/local]
  --exec-prefix=EPREFIX   install architecture-dependent files in EPREFIX
                          [same as prefix]
  --bindir=DIR            user executables in DIR [EPREFIX/bin]
  --sbindir=DIR           system admin executables in DIR [EPREFIX/sbin]
  --libexecdir=DIR        program executables in DIR [EPREFIX/libexec]
  --datadir=DIR           read-only architecture-independent data in DIR
                          [PREFIX/share]
  --sysconfdir=DIR        read-only single-machine data in DIR [PREFIX/etc]
  --sharedstatedir=DIR    modifiable architecture-independent data in DIR
                          [PREFIX/com]
  --localstatedir=DIR     modifiable single-machine data in DIR [PREFIX/var]
  --libdir=DIR            object code libraries in DIR [EPREFIX/lib]
  --includedir=DIR        C header files in DIR [PREFIX/include]
  --oldincludedir=DIR     C header files for non-gcc in DIR [/usr/include]
  --infodir=DIR           info documentation in DIR [PREFIX/info]
  --mandir=DIR            man documentation in DIR [PREFIX/man]
  --srcdir=DIR            find the sources in DIR [configure dir or ..]
  --program-prefix=PREFIX prepend PREFIX to installed program names
  --program-suffix=SUFFIX append SUFFIX to installed program names
  --program-transform-name=PROGRAM
```

```
                           run sed PROGRAM on installed program names
Host type:
  --build=BUILD            configure for building on BUILD [BUILD=HOST]
  --host=HOST              configure for HOST [guessed]
  --target=TARGET          configure for TARGET [TARGET=HOST]
Features and packages:
  --disable-FEATURE        do not include FEATURE (same as --enable-FEATURE=no)
  --enable-FEATURE[=ARG]   include FEATURE [ARG=yes]
  --with-PACKAGE[=ARG]     use PACKAGE [ARG=yes]
  --without-PACKAGE        do not use PACKAGE (same as --with-PACKAGE=no)
  --x-includes=DIR         X include files are in DIR
  --x-libraries=DIR        X library files are in DIR
--enable and --with options recognized:
  --enable-maintainer-mode enable make rules and dependencies not useful
                           (and sometimes confusing) to the casual installer
  --with-aolserver=DIR     Specify path to the installed AOLserver
  --with-apxs[=FILE]       Build shared Apache module. FILE is the optional
                           pathname to the Apache apxs tool; defaults to apxs.
  --with-apache[=DIR]      Build Apache module. DIR is the top-level Apache
                           build directory, defaults to /usr/local/apache.
  --with-mod_charset       Enable transfer tables for mod_charset (Rus Apache).
  --with-apxs2[=FILE]      Build shared Apache 2.0 module. FILE is the optional
                           pathname to the Apache apxs tool; defaults to apxs.
  --with-caudium=DIR       Build PHP as a Pike module for use with Caudium
                           DIR is the Caudium server dir, with the default value
                           /usr/local/caudium/server.
  --enable-force-cgi-redirect
                           Enable the security check for internal server
                           redirects.  You should use this if you are
                           running the CGI version with Apache.
  --enable-discard-path    If this is enabled, the PHP CGI binary
                           can safely be placed outside of the
                           web tree and people will not be able
                           to circumvent .htaccess security.
  --with-fhttpd[=DIR]      Build fhttpd module.  DIR is the fhttpd sources
                           directory, defaults to /usr/local/src/fhttpd.
  --with-fastcgi=SRCDIR    Build PHP as FastCGI application
  --with-isapi=DIR         Build PHP as an ISAPI module for use with Zeus.
  --with-nsapi=DIR         Specify path to the installed Netscape
  --with-phttpd=DIR
  --with-pi3web=DIR        Build PHP as a module for use with Pi3Web.
  --with-roxen=DIR         Build PHP as a Pike module. DIR is the base Roxen
                           directory, normally /usr/local/roxen/server.
```

--enable-roxen-zts	Build the Roxen module using Zend Thread Safety.
--with-servlet[=DIR]	Include servlet support. DIR is the base install directory for the JSDK. This SAPI prereqs the java extension must be built as a shared dl.
--with-thttpd=SRCDIR	Build PHP as thttpd module
--with-tux=MODULEDIR	Build PHP as a TUX module (Linux only)
--enable-debug	Compile with debugging symbols.
--with-layout=TYPE	Sets how installed files will be laid out. Type is one of PHP (default) or GNU
--with-config-file-path=PATH	
	Sets the path in which to look for php.ini, defaults to PREFIX/lib
--with-pear=DIR	Install PEAR in DIR (default PREFIX/lib/php)
--without-pear	Do not install PEAR
--enable-safe-mode	Enable safe mode by default.
--with-exec-dir[=DIR]	Only allow executables in DIR when in safe mode defaults to /usr/local/php/bin
--with-openssl[=DIR]	Include OpenSSL support (requires OpenSSL >= 0.9.5)
--enable-sigchild	Enable PHP's own SIGCHLD handler.
--enable-magic-quotes	Enable magic quotes by default.
--disable-rpath	Disable passing additional runtime library search paths
--enable-libgcc	Enable explicitly linking against libgcc
--disable-short-tags	Disable the short-form <? start tag by default.
--enable-dmalloc	Enable dmalloc
--enable-php-streams	Include experimental php streams. Do not use unless you are testing the code!
--with-zlib-dir=<DIR>	Define the location of zlib install directory
--with-zlib[=DIR]	Include zlib support (requires zlib >= 1.0.9). DIR is the zlib install directory.
--with-aspell[=DIR]	Include ASPELL support.
--enable-bcmath	Enable bc style precision math functions.
--with-bz2[=DIR]	Include BZip2 support
--enable-calendar	Enable support for calendar conversion
--with-ccvs[=DIR]	Include CCVS support
--with-cpdflib[=DIR]	Include cpdflib support (requires cpdflib >= 2). DIR is the cpdfllib install directory, defaults to /usr.
--with-jpeg-dir[=DIR]	jpeg dir for cpdflib 2.x
--with-tiff-dir[=DIR]	tiff dir for cpdflib 2.x
--with-crack[=DIR]	Include crack support.
--enable-ctype	Enable ctype support

```
--with-curl[=DIR]          Include CURL support
--with-cybercash[=DIR]     Include CyberCash support.  DIR is the CyberCash MCK
                           install directory.
--with-cybermut[=DIR]      Include CyberMut (french Credit Mutuel telepaiement)
--with-cyrus                Include cyrus imap support
--with-db                  Include old xDBM support (deprecated)
--enable-dba=shared        Build DBA as a shared module
--with-gdbm[=DIR]          Include GDBM support
--with-ndbm[=DIR]          Include NDBM support
--with-db2[=DIR]           Include Berkeley DB2 support
--with-db3[=DIR]           Include Berkeley DB3 support
--with-dbm[=DIR]           Include DBM support
--with-cdb[=DIR]           Include CDB support

--enable-dbase             Enable the bundled dbase library
--with-dbplus               Include dbplus support
--enable-dbx               Enable dbx
--with-dom[=DIR]           Include DOM support (requires libxml >= 2.4.2).
                           DIR is the libxml install directory,
                           defaults to /usr.
--enable-exif              Enable exif support
--with-fbsql[=DIR]         Include FrontBase support. DIR is the FrontBase base
                           directory.
--with-fdftk[=DIR]         Include fdftk support

--enable-filepro           Enable the bundled read-only filePro support
--with-fribidi[=DIR]       Include fribidi support (requires FriBidi >=0.1.12).
                           DIR is the fribidi installation directory -
                           default /usr/local/
--enable-ftp               Enable FTP support
--with-gd[=DIR]            Include GD support (DIR is GD's install dir).
                           Set DIR to shared to build as a dl, or
                           shared,DIR to build as a dl and still specify DIR.
--enable-gd-native-ttf     GD: Enable TrueType string function in gd
--with-jpeg-dir=DIR        GD: Set the path to libjpeg install prefix.
--with-png-dir=DIR         GD: Set the path to libpng install prefix.
--with-xpm-dir=DIR         GD: Set the path to libXpm install prefix.
--with-freetype-dir=DIR    GD: Set the path to freetype2 install prefix.
--with-ttf[=DIR]           GD: Include FreeType 1.x support
--with-t1lib[=DIR]         GD: Include T1lib support.
--with-gettext[=DIR]       Include GNU gettext support.  DIR is the gettext
                           install directory, defaults to /usr/local
```

```
--with-gmp              Include gmp support
--with-hyperwave        Include Hyperwave support
--with-icap[=DIR]       Include ICAP support.
--with-iconv[=DIR]      Include iconv support
--with-imap[=DIR]       Include IMAP support. DIR is the c-client install
prefix.
--with-kerberos[=DIR]     IMAP: Include Kerberos support. DIR is the
Kerberos install dir.
--with-imap-ssl[=DIR]     IMAP: Include SSL support. DIR is the OpenSSL
install dir.
--with-informix[=DIR]   Include Informix support.  DIR is the Informix base
                        install directory, defaults to nothing.
--with-ingres[=DIR]     Include Ingres II support. DIR is the Ingres
                        base directory (default /II/ingres)
--with-interbase[=DIR]  Include InterBase support.  DIR is the InterBase base
                        install directory, defaults to /usr/interbase
--with-ircg-config      Path to the ircg-config script
--with-ircg             Include ircg support
--with-java[=DIR]       Include Java support. DIR is the base install
                        directory for the JDK.  This extension can only
                        be built as a shared dl.
--with-ldap[=DIR]       Include LDAP support.  DIR is the LDAP base
                        install directory.
--enable-mailparse          Enable mailparse support
--enable-mbstring       Enable multibyte string support
--enable-mbstr-enc-trans   Enable japanese encoding translation
--with-mcal[=DIR]       Include MCAL support.
--with-mcrypt[=DIR]     Include mcrypt support. DIR is the mcrypt install
                        directory.
--with-mhash[=DIR]      Include mhash support.  DIR is the mhash
                        install directory.
--with-ming[=DIR]       Include ming support
--with-mnogosearch[=DIR]
                        Include mnoGoSearch support.  DIR is the mnoGoSearch
                        base install directory, defaults to
                        /usr/local/mnogosearch.
--with-msql[=DIR]       Include mSQL support.  DIR is the mSQL base
                        install directory, defaults to /usr/local/Hughes.
--with-muscat[=DIR]     Include muscat support.
--with-mysql[=DIR]      Include MySQL support. DIR is the MySQL base
                        directory. If unspecified, the bundled MySQL library
                        will be used.
```

```
--with-ncurses             Include ncurses support
--with-oci8[=DIR]          Include Oracle-oci8 support. Default DIR is
                           ORACLE_HOME.
--with-adabas[=DIR]        Include Adabas D support.  DIR is the Adabas base
                           install directory, defaults to /usr/local.
--with-sapdb[=DIR]         Include SAP DB support.  DIR is SAP DB base
                           install directory, defaults to /usr/local.
--with-solid[=DIR]         Include Solid support.  DIR is the Solid base
                           install directory, defaults to /usr/local/solid
--with-ibm-db2[=DIR]       Include IBM DB2 support.  DIR is the DB2 base
                           install directory, defaults to /home/db2inst1/sqllib
--with-empress[=DIR]       Include Empress support.  DIR is the Empress base
                           install directory, defaults to $EMPRESSPATH.
                           From PHP4, this option only supports Empress Version
                           8.60 and above
--with-empress-bcs[=DIR]
                           Include Empress Local Access support.  DIR is the
                           Empress base install directory, defaults to
                           $EMPRESSPATH.  From PHP4, this option only supports
                           Empress Version 8.60 and above.
--with-velocis[=DIR]       Include Velocis support.  DIR is the Velocis base
                           install directory, defaults to /usr/local/velocis.
--with-custom-odbc[=DIR]
                           Include a user defined ODBC support.
                           The DIR is ODBC install base directory,
                           which defaults to /usr/local.
                           Make sure to define CUSTOM_ODBC_LIBS and
                           have some odbc.h in your include dirs.
                           E.g., you should define following for
                           Sybase SQL Anywhere 5.5.00 on QNX, prior to
                           run configure script:
                               CPPFLAGS="-DODBC_QNX -DSQLANY_BUG"
                               LDFLAGS=-lunix
                               CUSTOM_ODBC_LIBS="-ldblib -lodbc".
--with-iodbc[=DIR]         Include iODBC support.  DIR is the iODBC base
                           install directory, defaults to /usr/local.
--with-esoob[=DIR]         Include Easysoft OOB support. DIR is the OOB base
                           install directory,
                           defaults to /usr/local/easysoft/oob/client.
--with-unixODBC[=DIR]      Include unixODBC support.  DIR is the unixODBC base
                           install directory, defaults to /usr/local.
```

```
--with-openlink[=DIR]      Include OpenLink ODBC support.  DIR is the
                           OpenLink base install directory, defaults to
                           /usr/local.  This is the same as iODBC.
--with-dbmaker[=DIR]       Include DBMaker support.  DIR is the DBMaker base
                           install directory, defaults to where the latest
                           version of DBMaker is installed (such as
                           /home/dbmaker/3.6).
--with-oracle[=DIR]        Include Oracle-oci7 support.  Default DIR is
                           ORACLE_HOME.
--with-ovrimos[=DIR]       Include Ovrimos SQL Server support. DIR is the
                           Ovrimos' libsqlcli install directory.
--enable-pcntl              Enable experimental pcntl support (CGI ONLY!)
--without-pcre-regex       Do not include Perl Compatible Regular Expressions
                           support. Use --with-pcre-regex=DIR to specify DIR
                           where PCRE's include and library files are located,
                           if not using bundled library.
--with-pdflib[=DIR]        Include PDFlib support. DIR is the pdflib
                           base install directory, defaults to /usr/local
                           Set DIR to shared to build as dl, or shared,DIR
                           to build as dl and still specify DIR.
--with-jpeg-dir[=DIR]       PDFLIB: define libjpeg install directory
--with-png-dir[=DIR]        PDFLIB: define libpng install directory
--with-tiff-dir[=DIR]       PDFLIB: define libtiff install directory
--with-pfpro[=DIR]         Include Verisign Payflow Pro support
--with-pgsql[=DIR]         Include PostgreSQL support.  DIR is the PostgreSQL
                           base install directory, defaults to /usr/local/pgsql.
                           Set DIR to shared to build as a dl, or shared,DIR
                           to build as a dl and still specify DIR.
--disable-posix            Disable POSIX-like functions
--with-pspell[=DIR]        Include PSPELL support.
--with-qtdom               Include QtDOM support (requires Qt >= 2.2.0).
--with-libedit[=DIR]       Include libedit readline replacement.
--with-readline[=DIR]      Include readline support.  DIR is the readline
                           install directory.
--with-recode[=DIR]        Include recode support. DIR is the recode install
                           directory.
--with-satellite[=DIR]     Enable CORBA support via Satellite (EXPERIMENTIAL)
                           DIR is the base directory for ORBit
--with-mm[=DIR]            Include mm support for session storage
--enable-trans-sid         Enable transparent session id propagation
--disable-session          Disable session support
--enable-shmop             Enable shmop support
```

```
--with-snmp[=DIR]           Include SNMP support.  DIR is the SNMP base
                            install directory, defaults to searching through
                            a number of common locations for the snmp install.
                            Set DIR to shared to build as a dl, or shared,DIR
                            to build as a dl and still specify DIR.
--enable-ucd-snmp-hack      Enable UCD SNMP hack
--enable-sockets            Enable sockets support
--with-regex=TYPE           regex library type: system, apache, php
--with-system-regex         (deprecated) Use system regex library
--with-swf[=DIR]            Include swf support
--with-sybase[=DIR]         Include Sybase-DB support.  DIR is the Sybase home
                            directory, defaults to /home/sybase.
--with-sybase-ct[=DIR]      Include Sybase-CT support.  DIR is the Sybase home
                            directory. Defaults to /home/sybase.
--enable-sysvsem            Enable System V semaphore support.
--enable-sysvshm            Enable the System V shared memory support
--with-vpopmail[=DIR]       Include vpopmail support.
--enable-wddx               Enable WDDX support

--disable-xml               Disable XML support using bundled expat lib
--with-expat-dir=DIR        XML: external libexpat install dir
--with-xmlrpc[=DIR]         Include XMLRPC-EPI support
--with-expat-dir=DIR        XMLRPC-EPI: libexpat dir for XMLRPC-EPI
--enable-xslt               Enable xslt support
--with-xslt-sablot          XSLT: Enable the sablotron backend
--with-expat-dir=DIR        Sablotron: libexpat dir for Sablotron 0.50
--with-yaz[=DIR]            Include YAZ support (ANSI/NISO Z39.50). DIR is
                            the YAZ bin install directory
--enable-yp                 Include YP support
--with-zip[=DIR]      Include zip support (requires zziplib >= 0.10.6).
                            DIR is the zziplib install directory,
                            default is /usr/local.
--enable-versioning         Export only required symbols.
                            See INSTALL for more information
--enable-experimental-zts   This will most likely break your build
--enable-inline-optimization   If you have much memory and are using
                                gcc, you might try this.
--enable-memory-limit       Compile with memory limit support.
--with-tsrm-pth[=pth-config]   Use GNU Pth.
--with-tsrm-st
--with-tsrm-pthreads        Use POSIX threads (default)
--enable-shared[=PKGS]      build shared libraries [default=yes]
```

```
--enable-static[=PKGS]  build static libraries [default=yes]
--enable-fast-install[=PKGS]  optimize for fast installation [default=yes]
--with-gnu-ld           assume the C compiler uses GNU ld [default=no]
--disable-libtool-lock  avoid locking (might break parallel builds)
--with-pic              try to use only PIC/non-PIC objects [default=use both]
```

Let's take a detailed look at the most important flags:

- `--prefix`—Defines the location where PHP has to be installed.

- `--with-aolserver`—If you want to run PHP in combination with the AOL Web server, this flag has to be set. Alternatively, you can use Apache or (almost) any other Web server.

- `--with-apache`—To run PHP with Apache, this flag can be used to tell PHP where the source code of Apache can be found.

- `--with-tux`—Recently Tux has become more and more popular. Tux is a Web server optimized for high performance, which can only be used in combination with Linux kernels.

- `--with-pear`—PEAR is a library for PHP. `--with-pear` defines where this library should be installed.

- `--with-openssl`—This flag is necessary if you want PHP to support OpenSSL, which is a layer for secure communication based on public-private key encryption.

- `--enable-bcmath`—bc is an arbitrary precision calculator language. bc is a standard tool on Unix machines and is often used in combination with shell scripts. If bcmath is enabled, PHP will also support this way of calculating.

- `--with-cpdflib`—This flag is required if you want PHP's PDF interface to be enabled. Therefore `cpdflib >= 2` is required. If the library is not installed on your system, you can download it from `http://www.pdflib.com/pdflib/index.html`.

- `--with-jpeg-dir`—For working with JPEG images, it is necessary to enable this flag. Especially for working with dynamically generated images, this flag is essential; otherwise, PHP won't be able to understand JPG files.

- `--with-gd`—The gd library is one of the standard libraries for processing images. If you are planning to modify images, this flag is necessary.

- `--enable-gd-native-ttf`—This flag enables support for TrueType fonts. In contrast to "pixel" fonts, TrueType fonts are much smoother. When working with dynamic images and text, this flag will be essential in order to generate high-quality images.

- `--with-freetype-dir`—For working with FreeType 2 (a rendering engine for TrueType fonts), this flag has to be enabled.

- `--with-ttf`—If you want to work with an old version of FreeType (versions 1.x), you have to use `--with-ttf` instead of `--with-freetype-dir`.

- `--with-imap`—IMAP (Internet Message Access Protocol) is a protocol for interacting with working with e-mail. IMAP is the counterpart of POP (Post Office Protocol) and supports a variety of sophisticated features. To work with IMAP and PHP, this flag must be enabled.

- `--with-kerberos`—Kerberos is a highly developed system for user authentication across networks.

If you need additional components such as support for DB2 or Oracle, you just have to use the flags in the listing generated by `./configure --help`.

2.2.1.3 Compiling Apache and PHP as a Team

Up to now you have seen which configuration parameters are supported by Apache and PHP. In the next step it is time to compile Apache and PHP as a team. Compiling the code is a crucial point because you have to know which components you are going to use and which components won't be interesting for you.

Recall that we have generated a directory called `apache_php` located in `/usr/local`. `apache_php` contains the source code of Apache and PHP as well as two softlinks called `apache` and `php` pointing to the directories generated by extracting the tar-archives. Many people install the sources in `/usr/local/src` or `/usr/src`. It's up to you where best to install the code.

To install Apache and PHP, it is useful to write a small shell script containing all commands needed to configure, generate, and install the binaries. In the next listing you can see a Korn shell script containing everything you need to install the two software packages. Let's take a look:

```
#!/bin/ksh

STARTDIR=$PWD
APACHEPREFIX=/usr/local/apache

print "Installation tool for Apache and PHP"
print "Configuring Apache ..."

cd apache
CFLAGS='-O3 -march=athlon' ./configure --prefix=$APACHEPREFIX \
```

```
print "configuring PHP ..."
cd ../php
CFLAGS='-O3 -march=athlon' ./configure --prefix=$APACHEPREFIX \
        --prefix=/usr/local/apache \
        --with-apache=../apache \
        --with-config-file-path=$APACHEPREFIX/conf \
        --enable-ftp \
        --enable-gd-native-ttf \
        --enable-mailparse \
        --enable-mbstring \
        --enable-memory-limit \
        --enable-sockets \
        --enable-sysvsem \
        --with-bcmath \
        --with-bz2 \
        --with-freetype-dir=/usr/include/freetype2/freetype \
        --with-gd \
        --with-jpeg-dir=/usr/include \
        --with-pgsql=/usr/src/postgresql-7.2 \
        --with-png-dir=/usr/include \
        --with-system-regex \
        --with-tiff-dir=/usr/include \
        --with-xpm-dir=/usr/include


sleep 10

print "building PHP ..."
make
make install

print "configuring and buidling Apache with PHP"
cd ../apache
CFLAGS='-O3 -march=athlon' \
        ./configure --activate-module=src/modules/php4/libphp4.a \
                --with-perl=/usr/bin/perl \
                --enable-module=php4
make
make install

print "copying and updating configuration"
cd ../php
```

```
cp php.ini-dist $APACHEPREFIX/conf/php.ini -v

if      [[ $(egrep -e '^( |\t )*AddType application/x-httpd-php .php' \
              $APACHEPREFIX/conf/httpd.conf) = '' ]]
then
        print "AddType not found - adding configuration"
        print "AddType application/x-httpd-php .php" >> \
              $APACHEPREFIX/conf/httpd.conf
else
        print "AddType found - no modifications necessary "
fi


cd $STARTDIR
```

At the beginning of the script, APACHEPREFIX is defined. This variable contains the location where you want to install Apache. Then you can go to the directory called apache. In this line you can see that it is useful to use a softlink and not the full name of the directory. If the version of your software changes, you can still use the same script and no changes have to be made. After that Apache is configured the first time, configure is called, which generates the makefiles needed to build Apache binaries. In this example, configure is called with some additional parameters that are optional: CFLAGS contains additional flags the C compiler should use to build the binaries. -O3 tells GCC to use the highest level of optimization. -march tells the compiler to optimize the binaries for AMD Athlon machines. Keep in mind that these flags are optional. It is not necessary to use CFLAGS, but in some cases, it can help you achieve minor improvements in speed. After running configure the first time, you can go to the directory containing the PHP sources. There you have to call configure again. In order to build powerful PHP binaries, many flags can be enabled. In this scenario many components of PHP such as support for GD, PostgreSQL, or FreeType are enabled.

In most parts of the book we will work with Red Hat 7.2's standard binaries of PHP. In real life most people will work with precompiled binaries, so we have decided to stick to this in most parts of the book. However, in some specific sections such as the section about PDF, we will use self-compiled binaries because the standard binaries do not support the PDF format. In sections where the standard packages of Red Hat are not used, we will mention that the self-compiled binaries have been used.

After configuring PHP, the compiler has to be started using make. make builds all binaries, and make install will copy these binaries to the appropriate location. If the binaries have successfully been configured and installed, Apache has to be compiled and a configuration file can be copied to the correct location. In case of PHP 4, this file is called php.ini-dist.

Finally the line shown in the next listing has to be added to `httpd.conf`, which is the file containing the configuration of Apache:

```
AddType application/x-httpd-php .php
```

As you have just learned, this line has to be added to the configuration file. However, this script does not just add this line to the file because this way the line could be added to the file more than once. Therefore the script checks if the line is already in the file, and if so, a message is displayed but no changes are made. Otherwise the line is added to the end of the file.

To check if the required line is in the file, `egrep` is used in combination with a simple regular expression.

Before running the shell script, don't forget to generate the directory called `apache` in `/usr/`**local**; otherwise, Apache cannot be installed. Make sure that you add execution rights as shown in the next listing:

```
[root@duron apache_php]# chmod +x compile.sh
```

2.2.1.4 Starting and Testing Apache

After compiling and installing Apache, you can start the daemon. You can go to the directory containing Apache's binaries:

```
[root@duron root]# cd /usr/local/apache/bin/
```

The command for starting Apache is called `apachectl`. This command starts various processes that will be used to handle the requests sent to the Web server. To find out how `apachectl` works, you can use the command shown in the next listing:

```
[root@duron bin]# ./apachectl --help
usage: ./apachectl (start|stop|restart|fullstatus|status|graceful|configtest|
help)

start      - start httpd
stop       - stop httpd
restart    - restart httpd if running by sending a SIGHUP or start if
             not running
fullstatus - dump a full status screen; requires lynx and mod_status enabled
status     - dump a short status screen; requires lynx and mod_status enabled
```

```
graceful    - do a graceful restart by sending a SIGUSR1 or start if not running
configtest  - do a configuration syntax test
help        - this screen
```

To start Apache, `./apachectl start` has to be used:

```
[root@duron bin]# ./apachectl start
[Mon Dec 31 01:06:20 2001] [alert] httpd: Could not determine the server's
fully qualified domain name, using 127.0.0.1 for ServerName
./apachectl start: httpd started
```

The warning is caused by a wrong default setting of Apache. The warning can easily be avoided by changing the directive `ServerName` to a useful value such as `localhost`. After starting the Web server, you can take a look and see if Apache is running. This step is highly recommended because it is the only reliable way to find out if the Web server has really been started successfully:

```
[root@duron bin]# ps ax | grep http
 5570 ?        S    0:00 /usr/local/apache/bin/httpd
 5571 ?        S    0:00 /usr/local/apache/bin/httpd
 5572 ?        S    0:00 /usr/local/apache/bin/httpd
 5573 ?        S    0:00 /usr/local/apache/bin/httpd
 5574 ?        S    0:00 /usr/local/apache/bin/httpd
 5575 ?        S    0:00 /usr/local/apache/bin/httpd
 5578 pts/3    S    0:00 grep http
```

Quite a few processes are running. Apache 1.3.x is a so-called preforking server, which means that there are usually spare processes in memory so that every request passed to the Web server can be processed easily.

After you have started Apache, you can check whether PHP works correctly. You can go to `/usr/local/apache/htdocs` and write a simple demo application in PHP:

```
<?php phpinfo() ?>
```

This line will make PHP display a lot of information about the installation. Figure 2.1 shows some information about the current PHP installation.

If information about the desired components.is listed, there should not be any problems when working with PHP. If a feature you need is not listed, something has gone wrong during compilation.

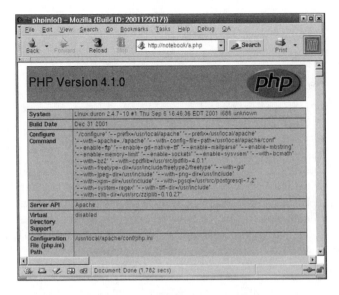

FIGURE 2.1   Information about the current PHP installation.

2.2.2 Installing the ApacheToolBox on Unix

Many people are fed up with installing Apache and a huge set of additional components manually all the time. Just think of the huge number of Apache modules and
interfaces that can be installed in combination with Apache. Installing the Web
server with support for PHP, mod_perl, Jakarta, Tomcat, and many other packages can
be painful and time-consuming.

To get around the problem, you can use a product called ApacheToolBox, which can
be downloaded from http://www.apachetoolbox.com.

Usually this package contains a recent set of all modules that are widely used.

After downloading the ApacheToolBox, you can extract the source code by using tar
xvfz Apachetoolbox-1.5.50.tar.gz. If no errors occurred, just enter the directory
that was created when extracting the directory and run install.sh:

```
[hs@duron Apachetoolbox-1.5.50]$ ./install.sh
```

The script will check some basic settings on your machine and an interactive menu
will be displayed. There you can select which components you want to be installed.
In Figure 2.2, you can see what the form looks like. Just follow the instructions and
Apache will be compiled.

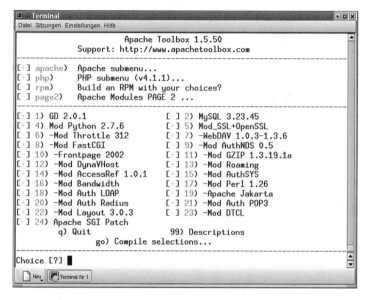

FIGURE 2.2   Installing the ApacheToolBox.

2.2.3 Installing Apache with PHP on Windows

Installing Apache with PHP and PostgreSQL is slightly more difficult than installing it on Unix machines. In this section you will be guided through all the important steps and you will see what has to be done.

The first thing is to install Cygwin. This package contains PostgreSQL binaries you will need to run PostgreSQL on Windows. Chapter 6, "Installing PostgreSQL," explains how to install Cygwin.

The next thing to do is to install Apache. Just download binaries for Windows from `http://www.apache.org/dist/httpd/binaries/win32/` and execute the EXE file. This will start an interactive wizard. Just follow the instructions and Apache will be installed almost automatically. Figure 2.3 shows what the interactive tool looks like.

After you have successfully installed Apache, it is time to test the Web server. If the installation was successful, Apache is already up and running. Therefore you simply have to access `localhost` as shown in Figure 2.4.

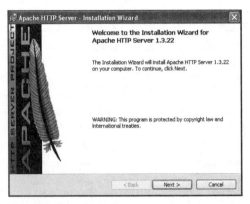

FIGURE 2.3   Apache's installation at work.

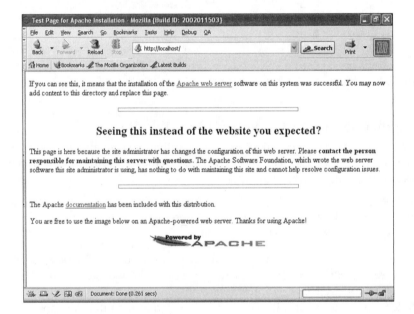

FIGURE 2.4   Testing Apache.

If the HTML page been displayed properly, Apache is up and running. In the next step you can shut down Apache again and you can start installing PHP. Go to your nearest PHP mirror or to www.php.net and download the PHP installer for Windows. Just start the EXE file and you will be guided through the installation as shown in Figure 2.5.

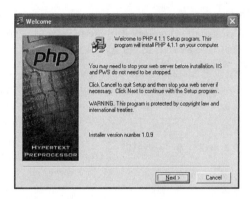

FIGURE 2.5 Installing PHP.

After installing PHP, you have to perform some basic modifications that you will need to run PostgreSQL on your Windows box. The first thing do to is to modify your php.ini file. In this file you can find a line like the one in the next listing:

```
;extension=php_pgsql.dll
```

Remove the leading semicolon and exit the file. After that you have to edit httpd.conf. The following line must be added to the file:

```
AddType application/x-httpd-php .php
```

The only thing that is still missing is the library responsible for interacting with PostgreSQL. This DLL can be found in a WinZip package you can download from www.php.net. Just unzip the file and create a directory called dlls located in the directory where you have installed PHP. Copy the DLL file called php_pgsql.dll to the newly created directory and restart Apache. Now Apache, PHP, and PostgreSQL are running as a team.

2.3 Installing Binaries on Linux

Installing binaries on Linux systems is an easy task. Two major packet-managing tools are available for Linux. In this section you will have a brief look at both systems.

2.3.1 RPM Packages

The RPM system was originally developed by Red Hat and is the most widespread management tool for binary as well as source packages.

To find out if PostgreSQL is already installed on your system, you can use `rpm -qva` to display a list of all packages installed on the system. To extract all core packages of PostgreSQL, grep can be used. The result might look like the one shown in the next listing:

```
[root@duron root]# rpm -qva | grep postgr
postgresql-libs-7.2.0
postgresql-python-7.2.0
postgresql-jdbc-7.2.0
postgresql-7.2.0
postgresql-odbc-7.2.0
postgresql-tk-7.2.0
postgresql-devel-7.2.0
postgresql-contrib-7.2.0
postgresql-perl-7.2.0
postgresql-server-7.2.0
postgresql-docs-7.2.0
postgresql-tcl-7.2.0
```

In this case many PostgreSQL 7.2 packages are installed on the system.

To install additional packages, you can use the following command:

```
rpm -Uvh names_of_packages
```

U tells RPM to update all existing packages. v stands for verbose, and h tells PHP to display 50 hash marks as the package archive is unpacked.

2.3.2 Debian Packages

Installing Debian packages is as simple as installing RPM packages. Simply use dselect to add or remove packages from the system. Using the package manager guarantees that all software packages PostgreSQL depends on are installed on the system.

2.4 Configuring PHP

After you have successfully installed PHP, you can start configuring the package. This is essential because the default setting will not always satisfy your demands. The configuration file of PHP is called `php.ini`. The location of this file depends on how and where you have installed PHP. If you are using Red Hat's standard packages, the file is located in `/etc/php.ini`.

In this section, you will take a closer look at this configuration file and all relevant settings will be discussed extensively. The various entries are described in the same order they occur in the configuration file of PHP 4.1:

- `engine`—To enable PHP to use it, this flag has to be set to `On`. The word `engine` refers to the Zend engine, which is the core of PHP 4.

- `short_open_tag`—If short tags are enabled, the Web server will accept `<?` and `?>` in addition to `<?php` and `<script>`. To make your scripts more portable, we recommend using `<?php` for defining the beginning of a PHP script because otherwise you might run into trouble if you want to run your script on a server where short tags are turned off.

- `asp_tags`—ASP (Active Server Pages; these are the ones many people use when working with IIS) supports `<% %>` tags, which have the same meaning as `<?`. In the default configuration this kind of tag is turned off.

- `precision`—PHP supports variable floating-point precision.

- `y2k_compliance`—Enforces Y2K compliance. This can cause trouble with non-Y2K–compliant browsers. The default value is `Off`.

- `output_buffering`—Output buffering allows you to send header lines after you send body content. By default this setting is set to `Off` in order to achieve higher performance.

- `output_handler`—The output of a script can be sent to a function. This way various operations such as filtering and compression can be done.

- `zlib.output_compression`—If this flag is set to `On`, transparent output compression will be used.

- `implicit_flush`—This flag tells the output layer to flush the buffers after every block.

- `safe_mode`—PHP's safe mode is an attempt to achieve a higher level of security. When working with safe mode, some PHP functions such as `system` for performing system calls and `pg_loimport` (responsible for working with binary objects stored in a PostgreSQL database) are disabled.

- open_basedir—This flag can be used to restrict all file operations outside the directory defined by this flag.

- disable_functions—Some functions that are still beta or that are a potential threat for your system can be disabled by this flag. The functions have to be defined as a comma-separated list.

- max_execution_time—To prevent problems caused by endless loops or scripts that take too long to execute, you can define the maximum time a script is allowed to run. As soon as the time limit is reached, a script will be terminated immediately.

- memory_limit—The memory consumption of PHP scripts can be limited by the size defined by the memory_limit script. The size is defined in megabytes. Every PHP script running may consume this amount of memory.

- error_reporting—Defines the way errors are displayed by PHP. Depending on how much debugging information you need, this flag can be modified to your needs.

- display_errors—Tells PHP whether to display errors. The default value of this flag is On.

- display_startup_errors—Errors can occur when PHP starts up. In the default configuration, these errors are not displayed.

- log_errors—For debugging purposes it is useful to set this flag to On because otherwise, errors won't be logged.

- track_errors—Stores the most recent error message in $php_errormsg.

- arg_separator.input—By default the arguments passed to PHP via a URL are separated using a &. This can be changed by modifying this setting.

- variables_order—Defines in which order GET, POST, cookie, environment, and built-in variables are registered. The default value is EGPCS.

- register_argc_argv—Defines whether variables passed to PHP via standard input should be registered.

- post_max_size—POST requests send data to a script. For security reasons, the maximum amount of data should be limited using the post_max_size parameter.

- default_mimetype—By default the header sent to the browser is text/html.

- enable_dl—dl is an important command. If you want to add extensions to PHP without recompiling the server, or if you want to try new versions of a component, shared objects can be included dynamically using the dl command. enable_dl tells PHP whether to support dynamic loading or not.

- `file_uploads`—File uploads are a potential security threat and they can easily be disabled by setting `file_uploads` to `Off`.

- `upload_max_filesize`—The maximum size of a file uploaded to the Web server can be defined in two ways. One way is to add a parameter to the HTML document. The second and more secure way to do the job is to tell PHP how big a file is allowed to be.

- `extension`—Windows extensions can easily be added to the server by adding an entry pointing to a DLL.

- `odbc.allow_persistent`—This flag tells PHP whether it is allowed to use persistent database connections in combination with ODBC.

- `odbc.check_persistent`—To find out if a persistent connection is still valid before reusing the connection handle, this flag must be set to `On`.

- `odbc.max_persistent`—Defines the maximum number of simultaneous persistent connections. `-1` means unlimited.

- `odbc.max_links`—Defines the total number of connections allowed (total = persistent + nonpersistent).

- `pgsql.allow_persistent`—This flag tells PHP whether it is allowed to use persistent database connections in combination with PostgreSQL.

- `pgsql.max_persistent`—Defines the maximum number of simultaneous persistent connections. `-1` means unlimited.

- `pgsql.max_links`—Defines the total number of connections allowed (total = persistent + non-persistent).

- `session.save_handler`—Tells PHP which handles are used for managing sessions.

- `session.save_path`—Defines the directory where session information is stored. The default value is `/tmp`.

- `session.use_cookies`—Defines whether to use cookies.

- `session.name`—Defines the name of the session.

If you make changes in the configuration file of PHP, it is necessary to know when the changes take place. Usually the configuration file is read when PHP starts up. If PHP is used as a module of the Web server, the file is read when the server is started. Therefore you have to restart your server in order to make changes that affect your system. With CGI scripts, the configuration is read every time a CGI script is started.

2.5 Summary

Installing Apache and PHP can be done in two ways. The easiest way is to install the precompiled binary packages of the software. The second way is to compile the packages yourself. This is more complicated than installing the binaries, but it will help you to gain flexibility.

PHP can be used in combination with a variety of Web servers on Unix and Windows.

3

PHP Basics

PHP is an easy language and you'll find it an easy task to get used to PHP. In this chapter you learn to write simple PHP applications. You learn the basics of PHP syntax as well as PHP's built-in functions.

3.1 Getting Started

In this section you learn to write simple applications. The basics of PHP's interpreter are also covered in detail.

3.1.1 "Hello World"

The first application you will find in most books about computer programming is "Hello World". "Hello World" is easy to implement in all languages because it does nothing except print a string on the screen, so it is a good start. Here is the easiest version of "Hello World" written in PHP:

```php
<?php
        echo 'hello world<br>';
?>
```

With just three lines of code, you can print a simple message on the screen. The first line of code tells the Web server that the next lines of code have to be executed by the PHP interpreter. ?> means that the code ends here. Using <?php is not the only possible way to tell the Web server that PHP code has to be executed. PHP provides three additional ways to escape from HTML:

```php
<?
        echo 'hello world 1<br>';
?>


<script language="php">
        echo 'hello world 2<br>';
```

```
</script>

<%
        echo 'hello world 3<br>';
%>
```

In the first three lines, you can see that it is not necessary to mention that the PHP interpreter has to be called. This method of escaping HTML is possible only when short tags are enabled (you can do this by setting the `short_open_tag` option in PHP's configuration file). However, to make clear which programming language is meant, we recommend using `<?php` instead of `<?`.

The third method can be used if Active Server Pages (ASP) tags are enabled. If ASP tags are turned off, `<%` and `%>` will be treated like ordinary text and the PHP code will not be interpreted. Therefore we recommend using either `<?php` or `<script language="php">` to tell the Web server what to do with the PHP code. In this book we will use `<?php` to escape HTML.

If you have put the file containing the code into the right directory (see the documentation and configuration of your Web server to find the right directory), you can execute the script by accessing it in your Web browser. If the file is called `hello.php` and if it is in the default HTML directory of your local machine, it can easily be accessed by using `http://localhost/hello.php`. You do not have to add execute rights to the file because the Web server only has to read the file.

If everything has been done correctly, PHP has been configured successfully, and your Web server has been started, `hello world` will be displayed on the screen.

Your first version of "Hello World" produces just text. However, the main target of a PHP program is to generate HTML code. In the next example, you will see a small script generating the HTML version of "Hello World".

```
<html>
<head>
        <title>Title of the site</title>
</head>
<body>
        <?php echo 'hello world<br>'; ?>
</body>
</html>
```

As you can see, the PHP code is included in the HTML code. `<?php` tells the server that the PHP interpreter has to be started here. In the example you can see that parts of the document are static and other parts of the document are created dynamically by PHP.

Another way to obtain the same target would be to generate the entire document dynamically. This will be slower than the version you have just seen, but in some cases it makes sense or is necessary to generate everything dynamically. Let's have a look at the following code:

```php
<?php
        echo '<html>
                <head>
                <title>Title of the site</title> '.
                '</head>';
        echo "<body>hello world<br></body></html>\n";
?>
```

The first echo command consists of two parts. The first three lines can be found between two single quotes. PHP recognizes that the command continues in the next line and does not end in the first line of the echo command. This way multiple lines can be treated as one command. Another way is to use a string operation as you can see at the end of line number 3 of the echo command. After the single quote, we use a point to tell PHP that the first string, which has just ended, has to be connected with the next string. In this case the second string is </head>. All components of the first echo command are passed to PHP in single quotes.

The second echo command contains the text we want to be displayed on the screen. This time we pass the text to echo using double quotes. Using single quotes or double quotes makes a significant difference: Single quotes are used to pass static text to PHP. Using double quotes allows you to use variables within the string. Knowing this difference is important because otherwise you might run into trouble. When executing the script you have just seen, the result will be a simple HTML document:

```html
<html>
                <head>
                <title>Title of the site</title>
                </head>
                <body>hello world<br></body>
</html>
```

The HTML is still not more than a simple "Hello World" application, but it is already HTML code.

3.1.2 Variables

Variables are a core component of almost every programming language available, and without variables it would be impossible to write useful applications. The idea behind variables is to have a language component that can have different values assigned to it. It is also possible to use variables as containers for storing data that is used in many different places in your application. Let's imagine an example where you want to display the same text on the screen twice:

```php
<?php
        $text="hello world";

        echo '<html><head><title>Title of the site</title></head><body>';
        echo "$text<br>";
        echo "$text<br>";
        echo '</body></html>';
?>
```

First, you assign the string you want to be displayed on the screen to the variable called text. In the next step some HTML code is generated and the variable is printed on the screen twice. Keep in mind that we have to use double quotes instead of single quotes; otherwise, the result would be:

```
$text
$text
```

With single quotes, variables cannot be used within a string, so the result is not what you want it to be.

Figure 3.1 shows what comes out when you look at the result using Mozilla.

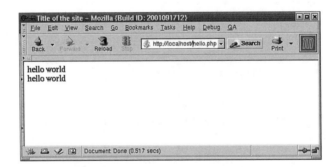

FIGURE 3.1   A more sophisticated version of Hello World.

3.1.3 Adding Comments

Documentation is nearly as important as the code of a program. Nowadays only 10% of all costs of producing a software product are used for writing the source code. The remaining 90% are used for maintaining the product (this information is provided by the University of Vienna). To reduce the costs of maintaining a product and to reduce the time required to become familiar with the source code, it is essential to add comments to your programs. PHP provides some simple ways to add comments to a program:

```php
<?php
        // this is a comment
        /* a C-style comment */
        echo 'hello world';
?>
```

In PHP comments can be added to the code as in C and C++. // tells the interpreter that the entire line should not be executed. /* */ is the old C style, which is also supported by PHP. C-style comments can be used to insert commands consisting of multiple lines:

```php
<?php
        /*
          a C-style comment
          which is longer than just one line.
        */
?>
```

We recommend making heavy use of comments to make your code clearer and easier to understand. Especially if you are not the only one who will have to work with the code, comments will make your daily life much easier.

3.1.4 Executing PHP from the Command Line

In many cases it is useful to execute PHP code from the command line instead of executing the script by starting it using a Web browser.

Let's return to the three-liner called hello.php that we discussed at the beginning of this chapter:

```php
<?php
        echo 'hello world<br>';
?>
```

To execute a script using a shell command, try the following:

```
[hs@athlon test]$ php ./hello.php
X-Powered-By: PHP/4.0.4pl1
Content-type: text/html

hello world<br>
```

As you can see, PHP produces more output than just "hello world". The additional information created by PHP defines which output has been created by PHP. In this case it is text/html. To make sure that the entire output is sent to standard output and not to standard error, we redirect all errors returned by PHP and see what comes out:

```
[hs@athlon test]$ php ./hello.php 2> /dev/null
X-Powered-By: PHP/4.0.4pl1
Content-type: text/html

hello world<br>
```

The result is still the same, and this shows that no errors have occurred.

PHP provides a lot of command-line parameters that can make daily life with the language much easier:

```
[hs@athlon test]$ php -h
Usage: php [-q] [-h] [-s] [-v] [-i] [-f <file>] | {<file> [args...]}
  -q              Quiet-mode.  Suppress HTTP Header output.
  -s              Display colour syntax highlighted source.
  -f<file>        Parse <file>.  Implies `-q'
  -v              Version number
  -c<path>        Look for php.ini file in this directory
  -a              Run interactively
  -d foo[=bar]    Define INI entry foo with value 'bar'
  -e              Generate extended information for debugger/profiler
  -z<file>        Load Zend extension <file>.
  -l              Syntax check only (lint)
  -m              Show compiled in modules
  -i              PHP information
  -h              This help
```

As you can see, PHP provides a lot of options you can use from the command line directly. Many developers use only a Web browser to build and to debug PHP applications. Using PHP's command-line parameters can make life much easier; we strongly recommend making heavy use of these features.

One of the most important command-line flags is the `-m` flag, which you can use to ask PHP which modules have been compiled. This is extremely important if you have not compiled PHP yourself or if you no longer know which modules you added at compile time:

```
[hs@athlon test]$ php -m
Running PHP 4.0.4pl1
Zend Engine v1.0.4, Copyright (c) 1998-2000 Zend Technologies

[PHP Modules]
imap
ldap
mysql
pgsql
zlib
yp
xml
wddx
sysvshm
sysvsem
standard
sockets
session
posix
pcre
gettext
gd
ftp
dba

[Zend Modules]
```

As you can see, the standard PHP distribution included in Red Hat 7.1 supports a lot of modules. You will learn about many of these modules in this book, which will guide you through the details of these modules. One module you will have a very close look at is the `pgsql` module, which is responsible for interacting with PostgreSQL databases.

An important command-line flag of the PHP interpreter is the `-i` flag, which can be used to generate information about PHP itself. To generate the result, you can use the following:

```
[hs@athlon test]$ php -i > /tmp/phpinfo.html
```

The HTML file that has been generated is very long, so it is not included here.

3.2 Control Structures and Operators

Usually programs need so-called control structures, which are used to decide at runtime what a program has to do. Flow control is an important part of every programming language and is essential for building applications. PHP provides a broad range of methods, as you will see in this section.

3.2.1 Operator and IF/ELSE/ELSEIF Statements

Use if to check whether a certain expression is true or not. If is supported by all commonly used programming languages such as C/C++, Java, Perl, and Python, and therefore it is a fundamental instrument of every computer programmer. To show you how conditions can be checked using if, we include a short example:

```php
<?php
    if      (2 > 1)
    {
            echo '2 is higher than 1<br>';
    }
?>
```

A message will be displayed on the screen because 2 is higher than 1. If the condition wasn't fulfilled, nothing would be displayed.

> **NOTE**
>
> If an empty document is returned by PHP, an error will be raised by some browsers.

Normally if is used to decide whether or not something has to be done. If a certain condition is fulfilled, PHP will execute the code in parentheses, but what has to be done if a condition is not fulfilled? If is very often used in combination with else. Every time an expression in the if statement returns false, the code of the else branch will be executed. Using if in combination with else is an extremely comfortable feature because it makes programming much easier and helps you to avoid bugs. In the next example you will learn how to use if and else:

```php
<?php
    $a=23;
    $b=34;

    if      ($a > $b)
    {
            echo 'a is higher than b';
    }
```

```
        else
        {
                echo 'b is higher than a';

        }
?>
```

First, we initialize two variables. $a is set to 23 and 34 is assigned to $b. In the next step we check if $a is higher than $b. If the expression returns true, a is higher than b will be displayed on the screen. Otherwise, b is higher than a will be the result of the program.

In the next example you will see what you can do if you want a message to be displayed if $b is higher than $a and $b is higher than 30:

```
<?php
        $a=23;
        $b=34;

        if      ($a > $b)
        {
                echo 'a is higher than b';
        }
        else
        {
                if      ($b > 30)
                {
                        echo 'b is higher than a and higher than 30.';
                }
        }
?>
```

$a is lower than $b, so PHP will execute the else branch. In the else branch you use a second if statement to find out if $b is higher than 30. It is an easy task to solve the problem the way it is shown in the previous example, but it is not the most elegant way:

```
<?php
        $a=23;
        $b=34;

        if      ($a > $b)
        {
                echo 'a is higher than b';
        }
```

```
        elseif  ($b > 30)
        {
                echo 'b is higher than a and higher than 30.';
        }
?>
```

Instead of using a second `if` statement in the `else` branch, it is also possible to use `elseif`, which is in most cases the shorter and more elegant way.

Sometimes it is necessary to find out if two or more conditions are fulfilled. Therefore multiple expressions can be combined using operators and parentheses. Assume that you want to check whether $a is higher than 10 but lower than 50:

```
<?php
        $a=23;

        if      ($a > 10 && $a < 50)
        {
                echo "$a higher than 10 and lower than 50";
        }
?>
```

You can use the `&&` operator to tell PHP that both conditions have to be fulfilled; otherwise, `false` will be returned and the `else` branch, which does not exist in our example, will be executed. `&&` is equal to and, so it does not matter if we use ($a > 10 and $a < 50) or ($a > 10 && $a < 50) in our example. Using `&&` instead of and is the more common way because `&&` is also supported by programming languages like C/C++ and Perl. If you execute the example, the result will be `23 higher than 10 and lower than 50`.

The counterpart of and is the or operator. If or is used, `true` will be returned if one expression returns true. Let's have a look at an example:

```
<?php
        $a=2;

        if      ($a > 10 || $a < 50)
        {
                echo "$a higher than 10 or lower than 50";
        }
?>
```

You want a string to be printed on the screen if $a is either higher than 10 or lower than 50. If one of those conditions is fulfilled, the string will be displayed. The number 2 is not higher than 10 but lower than 50, so we can find 2 higher than 10 or lower than 50 printed on the screen. Instead of || you can also use or.

Another important operator is the xor operator. False is returned if both values are the same; otherwise, the result is true. The next example demonstrates the usage of xor.

```php
<?php
        $a=18;
        $b=19;

        if      ($a xor $b)
        {
                echo '$a and $b are the same';
        }
        else
        {
                echo '$a and $b are not the same';
        }
?>
```

As you might have expected, $a and $b are not the same is returned by the script.

So far, you have learned to use &&, ||, and xor. Now it is time to use these operators as a team to build more complex expressions. Assume that you want a string to be displayed if $a is higher than 10 and lower than 20 or exactly 2. In this case it is necessary to group expressions:

```php
<?php
        $a=2;

        if      (($a > 10 && $a < 20) || $a == 2)
        {
                echo "$a higher than 10 but lower than 20 or exactly 2";
        }
?>
```

The first expression consists of two parts, which are connected using &&. If all expressions in parentheses are fulfilled, the first part will return true. If either the first or the second part of the entire expression returns true, the result will be true. In your case the second part of the expression is an exact match, so the entire expression is true.

Those among you who haven't done a lot of computer programming yet might wonder why == is used instead of = in the example you have just seen. It is not a typo. == is used to check whether two variables are the same. =, however, is used to find out whether a variable can be assigned to another variable. Let's have a look at a very simple example:

```php
<?php
        $a=18;

        if      ($a = $b)
        {
                echo '$a can be assigned to $b';
        }
        else
        {
                echo '$a cannot be assigned to $b';
        }
?>
```

First, a value is assigned to $a. In the next step you try to find out if $b can be assigned to $a. Therefore you have to use the = operator. Because $b hasn't been used yet, the else branch will be executed.

If statements can also be used to find out whether a variable has already been defined. As you will see in the section called "Working with Forms," later in this chapter, checking variables is essential for every PHP program. The next example shows how you can find out whether a variable has already been in use:

```php
<?php
        if      ($a)
        {
                echo '$a has already been defined';
        }
        else
        {
                echo '$a has not been defined yet';
        }
?>
```

In this case the result will be $a has not been defined yet because $a has not been used before.

3.2.2 WHILE **and** DO..WHILE

WHILE loops are very widespread in programming languages. Like almost all other programming languages, PHP provides WHILE loops, but what are WHILE loops good for? WHILE loops are used to execute a piece of code multiple times. Here is an example of a simple WHILE loop:

```php
<?php
        echo '<html><body>';

        $a=1;

        while   ($a <= 5)
        {
                echo "a: $a<br>\n";
                $a++;
        }
        echo '</body></html>';
?>
```

The numbers from one to five are displayed. First, some HTML code is generated. In the next step we set $a to 1 and start the loop. The code between the curly brackets has to be executed until $a is higher than 5. Every time the loop is processed, a: and the content of $a are displayed on the screen. After that $a is incremented by one. The ++ operator is very often used in languages like C and C++. As you can see, it is also available in PHP. $a++ is equal to $a=$a+1.

Let's have a look at what is displayed in the browser when we execute the script:

```
a: 1
a: 2
a: 3
a: 4
a: 5
```

As we have promised, the numbers from 1 to 5 are displayed. The HTML code you generated will not be displayed on the screen because it is used only by the browser.

The syntax that has just been described is the most commonly used way of using WHILE loops. However, PHP provides an additional way of using WHILE:

```php
<?php
        echo '<html><body>';

        $a=1;
```

```
while    ($a <= 5):
        echo "a: $a<br>\n";
        $a++;
endwhile;
echo '</body></html>';
?>
```

The code shown in the preceding listing is equal to the code you have seen before. The only difference is the way WHILE is used. In the second example you don't use curly brackets, so you have to tell PHP when the loop ends. This is done using endwhile.

If you are using loops, make sure that the condition that makes the loop stop will be false after executing the loop for the desired number of times; otherwise, the loop will run until one of the components (PHP, the kernel, the Web server, and so forth) stops the execution of the script. In your case you'd have an endless loop if $a was never incremented. Endless loops are very dangerous and you have to keep that in mind. PHP offers an option in php.ini to limit both the memory consumption and runtime of a PHP script. We highly recommend setting these options to a reasonable value.

Sometimes it is necessary to execute the code of a loop once and to check the condition for stopping the loop after that. For that PHP offers do..while loops:

```
<?php
        echo '<html><body>';

        $a=6;

        do
        {
                echo "a: $a<br>\n";
        }
        while    ($a <= 5);
        echo '</body></html>';
?>
```

First, 6 is assigned to $a, and then we start the loop using do. $a, which is 6, is displayed on the screen and you check if the loop has to be executed again. Because 6 is higher than 5, the echo command won't be executed again. In this case you are lucky because if $a was lower than 6, you'd run into an infinite loop. $a is not increased, so ($a <= 5) would always be true.

What can you do if you have to leave a loop in the middle of a block? PHP has the right solution for you. Break is a command that can be used to stop all kinds of loops in the middle of a block. Here is an example:

```php
<?php
        echo '<html><body>';

        $a=1;

        do
        {
                echo "a: $a<br>\n";
                $a++;
                if      ($a == 3)
                {
                        break;
                }
        }
        while   ($a <= 5);
        echo '</body></html>';
?>
```

You want to execute the loop as long as $a is lower than 6, but if $a is equal to 3, you want to exit the while loop.

If you execute the script, you can see the result in the browser:

a: 1
a: 2

Two lines will be displayed because the loop is interrupted after printing two lines on the screen.

Continue is another important keyword when dealing with loops. Continue is used to stop the execution of a block without leaving the loop. The idea is to ignore steps in the loop. Here is an example:

```php
<?php
        echo '<html><body>';

        $counter=0;
        $test=10;
        while ($counter < $test)
        {
```

```
        if      ($counter %2)
        {
                $counter++;
                continue;
        }
        echo "Current value of counter: $counter<br>";
        $counter++;
    }

    echo '</body></html>';
?>
```

The loop is executed until $counter is equal to $test. In the loop you try to find out if $counter can be divided by two. If the result is different from 0 (in your case if it is 1), increment the counter and use continue. The program will start to check the condition again and if it is still true, the block will be executed again.

The output of the script is not surprising:

```
Current value of counter: 0
Current value of counter: 2
Current value of counter: 4
Current value of counter: 6
Current value of counter: 8
```

One line is generated for every second number the loop is processed for.

Continue can also be used to leave more than just one loop. Let's have a look at the next example:

```
<?php
    echo '<html><body>';

    $counter=0;
    while ($counter == 0)
    {
            $counter++;
            $inner=0;
            while    ($inner == 0)
            {
                    $inner++;
                    continue 2;
                    echo "inner<br>";
            }
            echo "middle<br>";
```

```
        }
        echo "outer<br>";

        echo '</body></html>';
?>
```

You can see two while loops. Every loop is entered, but in the inner loop you call continue with a parameter to tell PHP how many loops have to be left. In this case you tell PHP to leave two loops, so the result is outer. Nothing else is displayed on the screen. Very efficient applications can be built by using continue with parameters, but this is also very dangerous because a programmer can easily lose the overview of the logic flow of the source code.

3.2.3 FOR

If a block has to be executed a fixed number of times, it is recommended to use for loops instead of while loops.

A for loop consists of a starting value, a condition that is checked every time the loop is processed, and an expression that is executed after every time the loop is processed. Let's have a look at an example:

```
<?php
        echo '<html><body>';

        for($i = 0; $i < 5; $i++)
        {
                echo "i: $i<br>\n";
        }

        echo '</body></html>';
?>
```

You want to display the numbers from 0 to 4 on the screen. Therefore a for loop has been implemented in the script. The loop starts with $i being 0 and it is executed as long as $i is lower than 5. The third parameter tells PHP to increment $i after every time the loop is processed. The output of the script shows what comes out when you start the program using a Web browser.

```
i: 0
i: 1
i: 2
i: 3
i: 4
```

Sometimes it is necessary to implement more powerful and more complex for loops. Just as in many other languages like C or C++, a list of conditions can be used in combination with for loops. This feature is very important because it allows you to implement complex features with little effort:

```php
<?php
    echo '<html><body>';

    for($i = 0, $j = 10; $i < 5, $j > 0; $i++, $j = $j - 2)
    {
        echo "i: $i --- j: $j<br>\n";
    }

    echo '</body></html>';
?>
```

All three parameters consist of a list of expressions used to process a certain variable. The text generated by the program shows what has happened to the variables in the program:

```
i: 0 --- j: 10
i: 1 --- j: 8
i: 2 --- j: 6
i: 3 --- j: 4
i: 4 --- j: 2
```

$i was incremented by one, whereas $j was reduced by two every time the loop was processed. Using the syntax you have just seen allows you to treat multiple variables using just one for loop. The list of operations used in the loop can easily be extended to the desired complexity.

Up to now, you have learned to use for loops with a list of expressions. However, in PHP, programmers are not forced to provide a list of at least one parameter because it is also possible to leave the list empty, as shown in the following example:

```php
<?php
    echo '<html><body>';

    $i=0;
    for     (; $i < 5; )
    {
        echo "i: $i<br>\n";
        $i++;
```

```
        }
        echo '</body></html>';
?>
```

The first and the third parameter of the `for` loop are empty. The result of the loop is still a list of all numbers from 0 to 4, but it has been generated differently. `$i` is initialized in the line before the loop starts and it is incremented after displaying the output on the screen:

```
i: 0
i: 1
i: 2
i: 3
i: 4
```

As you can see, there are many ways to solve the problem because PHP has a comparatively rich syntax. For those of you out there who are interested in writing very short and efficient code, the next example might be of interest:

```
<?php
        echo '<html><body>';
        for     ($i = 0; $i < 5;  print "i: $i<br>", $i++);
        echo '</body></html>';
?>
```

The output of the script is still the same, but we needed only one line to print the numbers on the screen. As you can see, PHP allows you to use any kind of expressions in a `for` loop, which makes that kind of loop extremely flexible.

3.2.4 SWITCH

To avoid long sequences of `if` statements, it is sometimes possible to use `switch` and `case` statements instead. `Switch` and `case` are often used to find the right piece of code that has to be executed from a list of possibilities. Let's have a look at the next example:

```
<?php
        $a=2;

        switch ($a)
        {
```

```
              case 1:
                      echo "case 1: \$a is $a<br>";
                      break;
              case 2:
                      echo "case 2: \$a is $a<br>";
                      break;
              case 3:
                      echo "case 3: \$a is $a<br>";
                      break;

      }
?>
```

First, 2 is assigned to $a. The switch statement checks all cases and if the right value is found, the branch is entered and PHP executes all the code until a break command is found. If you execute the script, one line will be displayed:

```
case 2: $a is 2
```

The same result can also be achieved by using if statements instead of switch and case:

```
<?php
      $a=2;

      if     ($a == 1)
      {
                      echo "case 1: \$a is $a<br>";
      }
      if     ($a == 2)
      {
                      echo "case 2: \$a is $a<br>";
      }
      if     ($a == 3)
      {
                      echo "case 3: \$a is $a<br>";
      }
?>
```

You can print the string $a on the screen. The $ character has to be escaped using a backslash because otherwise PHP would display the content of the variable $a instead of the string $a on the screen.

In the next step you will try to use switch and case without using break as well:

```php
<?php
    $a=2;

    switch ($a)
    {
        case 1:
            echo "case 1: \$a is $a<br>";
        case 2:
            echo "case 2: \$a is $a<br>";
        case 3:
            echo "case 3: \$a is $a<br>";
    }
?>
```

The result of the version using no break commands differs significantly, as you can see in the following example:

```
case 2: $a is 2
case 3: $a is 2
```

All of a sudden two lines are returned and that is definitely not the result you want. PHP searches for the right value and executes the code until a break command is found. In your case no break commands are in the code, so it is executed until the end. In some cases this might be the desired behavior of the program, but in most cases it is not.

Another feature of switch and case is the ability to handle default values. If no value in the list matches, PHP will execute the default branch. In the following example, you are looking for 9, but 9 is not listed in the switch statement:

```php
<?php
    $a=9;

    switch ($a)
    {
        case 1:
            echo "case 1: \$a is $a<br>";
            break;
        case 2:
            echo "case 2: \$a is $a<br>";
            break;
```

```
                default:
                        echo "the value couldn't be found<br>";
        }
?>
```

PHP will execute the default code because 9 has not been found in the list:

```
the value couldn't be found
```

As we have already mentioned, you can make a workaround using if statements instead of switch and case, but this can be far more complex especially when default values are involved and some of your branches do not contain break statements. Let's have a look at the next example. The target is to display 1 and 2 on the screen if the switch statement is called with $a being 1. In all other cases, only the value switch is called with should be displayed:

```
<?php
        $a=1;

        switch ($a)
        {
                case 1:
                        echo '1<br>';
                case 2:
                        echo '2<br>';
                        break;
                case 3:
                        echo '3<br>';
                        break;
                default:
                        echo 'default';
        }
?>
```

The task is easy because the only thing you have to do is to write a switch block where every entry but the first one contains a break command.

Switch and case constructions are a very flexible and powerful feature of PHP. It is possible to build sophisticated applications without having to use complex if/else constructs.

3.3 Data Types and Functions

In the previous sections you have already seen that PHP supports variables, but so far you have only learned to use numbers and strings. Just like control structures, data types are a core component of every programming language.

Like most other high-level languages, PHP works to a large extent without types and tries to recognize the data type of a variable by itself. However, PHP provides a set of different data types, as shown in Table 3.1.

TABLE 3.1   Data Types in PHP

Data Type	Description
Int, integer	Numeric values with no commas
Double, real	Floating-point number
String	A sequence of characters
Array	A pool of values
Object	A artificial, user-defined data type

In this section you will learn to use these data types efficiently.

3.3.1 Variables and Names

As you have already seen in the examples discussed in the previous sections, variables are marked with $ in PHP. Unlike Perl, PHP marks all variables with a $ and does not use @ and % as symbols.

In PHP the names of variables are case sensitive, which means that it makes a difference whether a name is written in capital letters. The name of a variable may start with a letter or an underscore. After the first character, all letters and numbers as well as underscores are allowed. However, we strongly recommend using only letters in the variable name because otherwise programs can be confusing and hard to understand, especially when people start mixing up variables written in either capital letters or lowercase letters.

The next example shows that $a is not equal to $A:

```
<?php
        $a = "I am a string";
        $A = "I am a string as well";

        echo "a: $a; A: $A<br>\n";
?>
```

As you can see, in the result, the two strings are not the same.

```
a: I am a string; A: I am a string as well
```

3.3.2 Automatic Data Type Recognition

When a variable has to be processed by PHP, the interpreter follows some predefined rules in order to recognize which data type a variable has:

- If a sequence of characters starts and ends with quotes, it will be treated as a string: $a = 'abc' assigns the string abc to $a because the string is enclosed with quotes.

- If a number does not contain a point, it is treated as an integer value: $a = 23 means that 23 is assigned to $a. The value 23 is an integer value because there is no point in it.

- If a number contains a point, it will be treated as a floating-point number: $a = 3.14159 makes PHP assign a floating-point value to $a.

Knowing these three rules will make it easy for you to forecast the result of an operation and will make it easier for you to write bug-free applications.

3.3.3 Checking Data Types and Explicit Casting

Sometimes it is necessary to change the data type of a variable explicitly. Although PHP does a lot of type casting internally, it might help in some cases to make sure that a variable is assigned to a certain data type. To perform operations like that, PHP provides the required functions. Before you learn about these functions, you will see how you can find the data type of a variable:

```php
<?php
        $a = 3.14159;
        $b = 12;
        $c = "I am a string";
        $d = array(1, 2, 3);

        echo '$a is a '.gettype($a)." value<br>\n";
        echo '$b is an '.gettype($b)." value<br>\n";
        echo '$c is a '.gettype($c)." value<br>\n";
        echo '$d is an '.gettype($d)." value<br>\n";
?>
```

With the help of a function called gettype, it is possible to retrieve the data type of a variable easily. If you use the rules described in the previous section, it will be easy to predict the result of the script:

```
$a is a double value
$b is an integer value
$c is a string value
$d is an array value
```

The first value is a floating-point value because it contains a comma. The second value is an integer value because it does not contain a comma. The third value is enclosed by quotes and therefore it is treated as a string. The last value is an array because the expression on the right side of the = returns an array of integer values.

Another way to check the data type of a variable is to use a special, data type–specific function as shown following:

```php
<?php
        $a = 3.14159;
        $b = 12;
        $c = "I am a string";
        $d = array(1, 2, 3);

        echo '$a: '.is_double($a)."<br>\n";
        echo '$b: '.is_integer($b)."<br>\n";
        echo '$c: '.is_string($c)."<br>\n";
        echo '$d: '.is_array($d)."<br>\n";
        echo '$d: '.is_object($d)."<br>\n";
?>
```

You use the functions is_double, is_integer, is_string, is_array, and is_object. If the value passed to the function has the appropriate data type, 1 will be returned. The next listing contains the result of the script you have just seen:

```
$a: 1
$b: 1
$c: 1
$d: 1
$d:
```

All values but the last one are true. The last line shows that $d is not an object.

If you perform an explicit cast, it can easily happen that some of the data stored in the variable you want to cast is lost. This is not a weak point of PHP because casting cannot be done differently by the PHP interpreter. Let's have a look at the next example:

```php
<?php
        $a = 3.14159;
        $b = 12;

        $a_cast = (int)$a;
        $b_cast = (double)$b;
```

```
        echo "a_cast: $a_cast<br>";
        echo "b_cast: $b_cast<br>";
?>
```

$a is a floating-point number that is cast to integer and displayed on the screen. $b is cast to double and displayed on the screen as well. If you have a look at the result, you will see that $a_cast is not as precise as $a_cast because an integer value is not allowed to store digits right of the comma. $b_cast and $b are the same because integers can also be represented as double values without losing data:

```
a_cast: 3
b_cast: 12
```

Some general rules and hints should be taken into consideration when performing casts. Table 3.2 contains a compilation of the most important information concerning casts.

TABLE 3.2   Rules in PHP

Data Type of Result	Data Type Before the Cast	Changes
Integer	Double	Data right of the point is silently omitted—the value is not rounded.
Integer	String	If no number is recognized, 0 is returned.
Double	Integer	No changes.
Double	String	If no number is recognized, 0 is returned.
String	Integer	Returns the number as a sequence of characters.
String	Double	Returns the number as a sequence of characters.
Array	Object	Will be transformed directly.
Array	Integer	An array of integer values will be created.
Array	String	An array of string values will be created.
Array	Double	An array of floating-point values will be created.
Object	Array	Will be transformed directly.
Object	Integer	An object with the same properties as an integer value is generated.
Object	String	An object with the same properties as a string value is generated.
Object	Double	An object with the same properties as a double value is generated.

From this table, you can easily see which dangers you might have to face when performing typecast operations.

3.3.4 Functions

Functions are the heart of every programming language. They are used to isolate certain tasks of a program and help the programmer to use the same code in various places without having to copy it. Functions can be called with parameters and perform a fixed set of instructions. If necessary, a function can return values to the function or object that has called it.

You have already worked with functions. One of the functions you have dealt with is called `gettype`, and it returns the data type of a variable. This function is a good example of what the topic is all about. You pass a variable to it and a value will be returned.

In recent years, the word *function* has lost popularity because in the object-oriented programming paradigm, it no longer exists. As you will see in the chapter about object-oriented PHP (see Chapter 4, "Object-Oriented PHP"), functions are called *methods* in object-oriented PHP. This makes no difference in the way things work—it is just a new name for an old and useful invention.

3.3.5 Output Functions and Working with Strings

Like Pascal, a programming language defined by Prof. Niklaus Wirth at the Eidgenössische Technische Hochschule (ETH) Zürich in 1970, PHP supports a data type called `string`. Strings are a sequence of characters and are often used to store text. Unlike in C/C++, handling strings is an easy task in PHP because the programmer does not have to take care of memory management and segmentation faults that occur because of problems with memory allocation. This makes PHP suitable for fast and reliable software development.

The list of functions for working with strings in PHP seems to be endless. We will try to cover the most important ones in this section.

To display ASCII characters on the screen, PHP provides a function called `chr`. Simply pass the ASCII code to the function, and the desired character will be returned. The next example shows how the e-mail address of one of the authors can "easily" be displayed using `chr`.

```php
<?php
        echo chr(104).chr(115).chr(64).chr(99).chr(121).chr(98).
             chr(101).chr(114).chr(116).chr(101),chr(99).chr(46).
             chr(97).chr(116)."<br>\n";
?>
```

And the result is

hs@cybertec.at

I am sure that there are more efficient ways of displaying e-mail addresses; normally chr is used to display characters that cannot be found on the keyboard.

The exact opposite of the chr is the Ord function, which can be used to compute the ASCII value of a character:

```php
<?php
        $a = "a";
        echo Ord($a);
?>
```

Nowadays encrypting data is an extremely important task because security standards are increasing and hackers might threaten your networks. With the arrival of all those viruses spreading themselves over networks, security has become an important topic. In the next example you will see how a string can easily be encrypted using PHP's onboard functions:

```php
<?php
        $a = "I am a string";
        echo crypt($a);
?>
```

Simply pass the string you want to process to the crypt function and the result will be encoded using the DES algorithm.

The result will be a string that you won't be able to read:

i34vSr3Aueg2A

As you have already seen, HTML code is a pool of special characters having a certain meaning. A good example for that is the < character, which is used to define the starting point of an HTML tag. The problem is: what can you do when you want to display a < character on the screen? The problem can easily be solved using a function called htmlspecialchars, which converts all characters having a certain meaning or which are not allowed to be used in the appropriate HTML code. The next piece of code shows how this works:

```php
<?php
        $b = "1 > 0";
        echo htmlspecialchars($b);
?>
```

1 > 0 is displayed on the screen, but the HTML code generated by PHP looks slightly different:

1 > 0

> has been substituted for > and that's what you wanted it to be.

Another important character in the list of special symbols is the & symbol. In HTML code & has to be coded as &. As you can see, in the next example, the htmlspecialchars function takes care of that issue:

```php
<?php
        $b = "Mr. Schönig & Mr. Müller are from Austria";
        echo htmlspecialchars($b)." <br>\n";
?>
```

If you have a look at the HTML code you have generated, you can see that the ampersand has been replaced for &.

Mr. Schönig & Mr. Müller are from Austria

printf is the dinosaur of string and text processing. It allows you to display format-ted text on the screen. The C programmers among you might already be familiar with printf. The PHP version of printf is very similar to the C function. Let's have a look at an example:

```php
<?php
        $a = "Hans";
        printf ("This is the diary of %s.<br>\n", $a);

        $b = 23;
        printf ("He is %d years old.<br>\n", $b);
        printf ("$b can also be written as %b (binary) or %o (octal).<br>",
                $b, $b);
        printf ("Let's print $b again but this time as an integer ".
                "printed as a character: %c.<br>", $b, $b);

        $b += 2/12;
        printf ("To be more precise: %s is $b years and two months old; ".
                "as a floating point number this would be: %5.3f.<br>\n",
?>
```

In the first line you define a variable containing the first name of the author. In the next line you want to display this variable as part of a string on the text. Therefore you use `printf`. `%s` is substituted for `$a`. `$a` is interpreted as a string and will be displayed on the screen as a string. In the next step `$b` is defined as an integer value. After that `$b` is displayed as integer value by using `%d`. In the next line `$b` is displayed as a binary and as an octal value. This is the first time you use `printf` with more than just one parameter. Because two substitutions are performed, it is necessary to pass two parameters to `printf`.

One line later, you try to interpret `$b` as an integer value printed as a character. In other words, you try to display the character having `$b` as its ASCII value on the screen.

Finally, you add 2/12 to `$b` (`$b += 2/12` is equal to `$b = $b + 2/12`) and display `$b` as a floating-point number using `%f`. The floating-point number has a total length of five digits, and three of these digits have to be on the right side of the point.

When executing the script, you will receive the this result:

```
This is the diary of Hans.
He is 23 years old.
23 can also be written as 10111 (binary) or 27 (octal).
Let's print 23 again but this time as an integer printed as a character: #.
To be more precise: Hans is 23.166666666667 years and two months old;
as a floating point number this would be: 23.167.
```

`Printf` supports a lot of formatting instructions. Table 3.3 contains a list of shortcuts supported by `printf`.

TABLE 3.3   Formats Accepted by `printf`

Formatting	Meaning
%b	Interpret value as an integer but print it as a binary value.
%c	Interpret value as an integer but print it as a character.
%d	Interpret value as an integer but print it as a decimal value.
%f	Interpret value as a double and print it as a floating-point number.
%o	Interpret value as an integer but print it as an octal value.
%s	Interpret and print as a string.
%x	Interpret value as an integer but print it as a hexadecimal value using lowercase letters.
%X	Interpret value as an integer but print it as a hexadecimal value using uppercase letters.

`Printf` returns 0 or 1 depending on whether the command has been executed successfully. If you want to retrieve the string generated by `printf`, you have to use `sprintf` instead. In contrast to `printf`, `sprintf` returns the string that has been generated and does not print it on the screen. Here is an example:

```php
<?php
    $a = "Hans";
    $result = sprintf ("This is the diary of %s.", $a);
    echo "Result: $result<br>\n";
?>
```

This time the result is assigned to a variable called `result` and displayed on the screen using `echo`.

If you want a backslash to be put before every ., \\, +, *, ?, [, ^,], (, $, or), you can use the `QuoteMeta` function. Especially when building interfaces to other software products or when working with regular expressions, this function might be of interest for you because it helps you to escape special characters.

Here is an example of how the function can be used:

```php
<?php
    $a = "Is 1+2*3=7?";
    $result = QuoteMeta ($a);
    echo "$result";
?>
```

The result will contain many backslashes:

```
Is 1\+2\*3=7\?
```

If you want to remove the backslashes inserted by QuoteMeta, you can use the `stripslashes` function.

`strcmp` can be used to compare strings and is another function that has been borrowed from C. The usage of `strcmp` in PHP is very similar to that of C, as you can see in the following example:

```php
<?php
    $a = "abc";
    $b = "bcd";

    echo strcmp($a, $b)."<br>";
    echo strcmp($b, $a)."<br>";
    echo strcmp($a, $a)."<br>";
?>
```

In the first two lines variables are defined, which will be compared with each other in the next three lines. The first strcmp command returns -1 because the two variables are passed to the function in alphabetical order. The parameters are passed to the second command in reverse order, so 1 is returned. If both values are equal, strcmp will return 0. In the following lines, you can see the output of the script.

```
-1
1
0
```

The strlen function is widely used and can be taken to compute the length of a string. First, a string called $a is defined. In the next step, the length of this string is computed and displayed on the screen.

```php
<?php
        $a = "This is a string";
        echo strlen($a)."<br>\n";
?>$a
```

In some cases it might be useful to remove whitespace characters from the beginning and the end of a string. Therefore you can use trim:

```php
<?php
        $b = "    I am a string    ";
        echo 'beginning:'.trim($b).':end';
?>
```

$b contains a string with a few blanks at the beginning and the end of it. With the help of trim, these blanks can easily be removed:

```
beginning:I am a string:end
```

The result no longer contains these blanks. If you only want to remove the blanks on the left edge of the string, ltrim can be used. If the blanks on the right side have to be removed, rtrim will be the right function.

You can convert strings to uppercase letters and vice versa by using two easy-to-use PHP functions called strtoupper and strtolower. In the next example you will see how these functions can be used:

```php
<?php
        $a = "i am a string";
        $b = strtoupper($a);

        echo "$b<br>\n";
        echo strtolower($b);
?>
```

First, a string is defined. In the next step it is converted to uppercase letters and assigned to $b. Finally both strings are displayed on the screen.

```
I AM A STRING
i am a string
```

In many cases you don't want to convert all characters to upper- or lowercase letters. With the help of the ucfirst function, it is possible to convert only the first letter to uppercase. Ucwords makes sure that every word in a string starts with an uppercase letter:

```php
<?php
        $a = "i am a string";

        echo ucfirst($a)."<br>";
        echo ucwords($a)."<br>";
?>
```

The output of the script is in no way surprising:

```
I am a string
I Am A String
```

PHP supports a lot of functions related to strings and it is beyond the scope of this book to cover all of these functions in detail. We have to decided to mention only the most important and most widely used functions.

3.3.6 Working with One-Dimensional Arrays

The ability to handle arrays easily and efficiently is one of the features that has made PHP so successful in the past few years. Not only can arrays be handled easily, but many functions related to arrays are also available and you will learn about these functions in this section.

Arrays can either be one-dimensional or multidimensional. A one-dimensional array is a data structure used to store a list of values. You have already learned in the section "Data Types and Functions" earlier in this chapter that arrays are one of PHP'S built-in data types. However, arrays are in a way different than data types like integer or double. An array is not an atomic value, which means that it consists of one or more other values, which can be arrays again.

Let's start with an example where you will see how you can find out whether a variable is an array:

```php
<?php
        $a = 12;
        $b = array(23, "Hans", "Vienna", 1.78);

        echo "a: ".is_array($a)."<br>";
        echo "b: ".is_array($b);
?>
```

You can see that an integer value and an array are defined. The array consists of one integer, two strings, and one floating-point value. As you can see, it makes absolutely no difference which values are inserted into an array because it is just a container for storing all kinds of variables. When executing the script, you can see that is_array returns 1 if the variable passed to it is an array:

```
a:
b: 1
```

Now that you have learned to create arrays and to find out if a variable is an array, you will learn to access the components of an array. The first thing to know is to find out how many values are stored in an array. This can be done by using the count function. As soon as you know the number of components of your array, it is an easy task to display the content of the array on the screen:

```php
<?php
        $a = array(23, "Hans", "Vienna", 1.78);

        $vals = count($a);
        echo "Number of values in the array: $vals<br><br>\n";

        for    ($i = 0; $i < $vals; $i++)
        {
               echo "Value number $i: $a[$i]<br>";
        }
?>
```

The output of the script shows that four records were found in the array. Finally all records are displayed on the screen. The various cells of the array are accessed by using parentheses and the index of the value:

```
Number of values in the array: 4

Value number 0: 23
Value number 1: Hans
Value number 2: Vienna
Value number 3: 1.78
```

Displaying all records on the screen can also be done differently:

```php
<?php
        $a = array(23, "Hans", "Vienna", 1.78);

        foreach ($a as $x)
        {
                echo "$x<br>";
        }
?>
```

After defining the array, a loop is entered that is executed for every value in the array. Every value in $a is assigned to $x, which is displayed on the screen using an echo command:

```
23
Hans
Vienna
1.78
```

An array does not have to be consecutively numbered. In many cases it is helpful to use strings to identify the values in an array:

```php
<?php
        $a = array(age => 23, name => "Hans", residence => "Vienna",
                height => 1.78);

        foreach ($a as $x)
        {
                echo "$x<br>";
        }
?>
```

In the preceding example, an associative array is initialized and the content is displayed on the screen as shown in the next listing:

```
23
Hans
Vienna
1.78
```

Many of you might have dealt with associative arrays already in Perl. In PHP things work pretty much the same way as in Perl. An associative array is just an array indexed with strings. The idea is to be able to store every data type in an array and to index it with anything you like.

Retrieving data from an associative array can be done as you have seen for arrays indexed with numbers:

```php
<?php
        $a = array(age => 23, name => "Hans", residence => "Vienna",
                height => 1.78);

        echo "Age: ".$a["age"]." years <br>";
        echo "Name: ".$a["name"]."<br>";
        echo "Residence: ".$a["residence"]."<br>";
        echo "Height: ".$a["height"]." centimeter<br>";
?>
```

All values are displayed on the screen:

```
Age: 23 years
Name: Hans
Residence: Vienna
Height: 1.78 centimeter
```

In this section we have already mentioned that an array can also contain arrays. The next example shows an array with one element containing an array with two elements:

```php
<?php
        $a = array(name => array("Hans", "Epi"));
        $b = $a["name"];
        echo "$b[0] - $b[1]<br>\n";
?>
```

You can insert an array into an array just like any other record. The only thing you have to take care of is when retrieving the values again—this is slightly more difficult than if it was just an ordinary value.

If you execute the script, the values you have inserted will be retrieved:

```
Hans - Epi
```

With the help of arrays, complex data structures can be built. However, if the data structures become very complex, it is useful to use object-oriented PHP instead of complex arrays and procedures. Object-oriented PHP will be covered extensively in the next chapter of this book.

An important command when working with arrays is the reset command. Unlike what some of you might expect, reset is not used to remove elements from an array but to set the pointer to the first element of an array. If you are working with an array, the pointer might not be on the first element and you will have trouble using commands like next and prev safely. In the next example you will see how to define an array, set the pointer to the first element, and display all records including the keys on the screen:

```php
<?php
        $a = array(23, 16, 8, 99);

        reset($a);

        while (list ($key, $val) = each ($a))
        {
                echo "$key: $val<br>\n";
        }
?>
```

As you can see, every value in the array has a key.

```
0: 23
1: 16
2: 8
3: 99
```

Finding the key of a value is an important task because the data structure can be indexed using any other variable.

Sorting data is another important operation:

```php
<?php
        $a = array(23, 16, 8, 99);
        sort($a);

        foreach ($a as $val)
        {
                echo "val: $val<br>\n";
        }
?>
```

For building efficient data structures, it is important to sort data before working with it. The output of the script you have just seen is displayed sorted because you have used sort to change the order of the elements.

```
val: 8
val: 16
val: 23
val: 99
```

To sort data in a reverse order, use `arsort` instead of `sort`:

```php
<?php
        $a = array(23, 16, 8, 99);
        arsort($a);

        foreach ($a as $val)
        {
                echo "val: $val<br>\n";
        }
?>
```

As you can see, the data is now displayed the other way around:

```
val: 99
val: 23
val: 16
val: 8
```

The opposite of sorting an array is to use `shuffle`—a function for putting values in reverse order:

```php
<?php
        $a = range(1, 7);

        shuffle($a);

        while (list ($key, $val) = each ($a))
        {
                echo "$key: $val<br>\n";
        }
?>
```

First, you create an array that contains values from 1 to 7 using the `range` function. In the next step the array is shuffled and all values are displayed on the screen.

```
0: 3
1: 1
2: 2
3: 4
```

```
4:  5
5:  7
6:  6
```

The values are no longer ordered. Shuffling arrays can be useful for many purposes. Imagine a situation where you want to display records in a random order—shuffle will solve the problem for you.

You have seen how an array can be accessed by using an index or a foreach command. Another way to process all values of an array is to use reset and next. Next sets the pointer to the next value in the array and returns the current value. With the help of a do/while loop, it is an easy task to go through the array:

```php
<?php
        $a = array(23, 16, 8, 99);

        reset($a);

        $val = $a[0];
        do
        {
                echo "val: $val<br>\n";
        }
        while   ($val = next($a));
?>
```

As you can see following, all values are displayed on the screen:

```
val: 23
val: 16
val: 8
val: 99
```

Stacks are a special kind of array. They are a fundamental data structure and are heavily used by many programmers. If you want to process commands using postfix notation, stacks are an essential instrument. Two operations are defined for stacks: Push adds a value to the stack. Pop returns the last value that was added to the array and removes it from the list—in other words stacks use a LIFO algorithm (LIFO = last in first out).

To make clear what you have just learned, we have included an example:

```php
<?php
        $a = array();
        array_push($a, 'the first value');
```

```
array_push($a, 'the second value');
array_push($a, 'the third value');

while (list ($key, $val) = each ($a))
{
        echo "$key: $val<br>\n";
}

echo "<br>removing: ".array_pop($a)."<br>";
echo "removing: ".array_pop($a)."<br><br>";

while (list ($key, $val) = each ($a))
{
        echo "$key: $val<br>\n";
}
?>
```

In the first line, an empty array is defined. In the next three lines, values are added to the stack using array_push, and all values are displayed on the screen. Then two values are removed from the stack and displayed on the screen. As you can see, the return value of array_pop is returned and removed from the array. After adding three values to the array and removing two values from the array, one value is left and displayed on the screen:

```
0: the first value
1: the second value
2: the third value

removing: the third value
removing: the second value

0: the first value
```

Counting the values of an array can be done by using the array_count_values function. The idea of this function is to compute the frequency with which a value occurs in the array.

Sometimes it is necessary to remove duplicated values from an array. Array_unique will do the job for you:

```
<?php
        $a = array(23, 23, 12, 9, 23, 9);
        $counted = array_count_values($a);
```

```
        echo "Return data counted: <br>\n";
        while (list ($key, $val) = each ($counted))
        {
                echo "$key: $val<br>\n";
        }

        echo "<br>Return unique data: <br>\n";
        $a = array_unique($a);
        while (list ($key, $val) = each ($a))
        {
                echo "$key: $val<br>\n";
        }
?>
```

After defining an array containing some value, an array is initialized containing the frequency with which various values in $a occur. In the first column the key is displayed. The second column tells us how often the key was found in the array.

In the next step the array_unique function is used to remove duplicated entries. The key to a value is the position in which a certain value has occurred in the original array. The value 9, for instance, was found on the fourth and the last position of the array. Because this is redundant, the last field in the array has been deleted and only the value in position number 4 remains:

```
Return data counted:
23: 3
12: 1
9: 2

Return unique data:
0: 23
2: 12
3: 9
```

The output of the function shows what comes out when the script is executed.

If you are working with more than just one array, it might happen that you have to compare arrays with each other. Therefore PHP provides some powerful and easy-to-use functions. One of the functions is called array_merge and is used to combine two arrays:

```
<?php
        $a = array(23, 12, 9);
        $b = array(12, 13, 14);
```

```
$res = array_merge($a, $b);

while (list ($key, $val) = each ($res))
{
        echo "$key: $val<br>\n";
}
?>
```

Two arrays are defined, which are merged. If you execute the script, the result will contain all values of both arrays as shown in the following listing:

```
0: 23
1: 12
2: 9
3: 12
4: 13
5: 14
```

The counterpart of array_merge is the array_diff function, which can be used to compute the difference of two arrays as shown following:

```
<?php
$a = array(23, 12, 9);
$b = array(12, 13, 14);

$res = array_diff($a, $b);

while (list ($key, $val) = each ($res))
{
        echo "$key: $val<br>\n";
}
?>
```

Two values can be found in $a that are not in $b:

```
0: 23
2: 9
```

If you want to compute the intersection of two arrays instead of the difference, you can use the array_intersect function. Just like array_diff and array_merge, array_intersect needs to have two arrays passed to it:

```
<?php
$a = array(23, 12, 9);
$b = array(12, 13, 14);
```

```php
        $res = array_intersect($a, $b);

        while (list ($key, $val) = each ($res))
        {
                echo "$key: $val<br>\n";
        }
?>
```

One value is returned:

```
1: 12
Calculating the sum of all values in an array can be done in many ways
but the easiest one is to use array_sum:
<?php
        $a = array(23, 12, 9);
        echo array_sum($a);
?>
```

The resulting value 44 will be displayed on the screen.

Splitting a string and generating an array out of it is an important operation. If you have to process tab-separated files, for instance, splitting strings and generating arrays is an essential procedure. PHP provides a function called explode. Explode has to be called with two parameters. The first one tells PHP where to split the string by defining a pattern. The second parameter contains the variable you want to process.

The counterpart of explode is implode, which does exactly the opposite of explode:

```php
<?php
        $a = "This is a string";
        $b = explode(" ", $a);

        while (list ($key, $val) = each ($b))
        {
                echo "$key: $val<br>\n";
        }

        $c = implode(" ", $b);
        echo "<br>$c<br>";
?>
```

At the beginning of the script, a variable is defined that is used to generate an array in the second line. A space character is selected as separator. In the next step the content of $b is displayed on the screen. Finally all values in $b are combined into a string again. Again a blank is chosen as the separator.

If you execute the script, the output will be displayed on the screen:

```
0: This
1: is
2: a
3: string
```

```
This is a string
```

As you can see in the last line of the result, the array has been combined to the string you have defined in the first line again.

3.3.7 Working with Multidimensional Arrays

Multidimensional arrays are a little bit more difficult to handle than their one-dimensional counterparts. However, with some basic techniques, it is possible to perform complex operations.

Each can be used for processing one-dimensional or multidimensional arrays. Even for more complex data structures, each will play an important role:

```php
<?php
        $a[0][0] = "Rock me Amadeus";
        $a[0][1] = "Jeanny";
        $a[0][2] = "Vienna Calling";
        $a[1][0] = "Satellite to Satellite";

        echo "<b>Falco's masterpieces:</b><br>\n";
        while (list ($key, $val) = each ($a))
        {
                echo "$key: $val<br>\n";
        }
?>
```

In the first four lines, a two-dimensional array is created and four values are assigned to it. The target is to display all records on the screen.

The next listing shows what comes out when you execute the script:

```
Falco's masterpieces:
0: Array
1: Array
```

The listing does not contain the desired result because each extracts a list of arrays instead of a list of single values from the multidimensional array. To display the data, you have to make some minor changes in the code:

```php
<?php
        $a[0][0] = "Rock me Amadeus";
        $a[0][1] = "Jeanny";
        $a[0][2] = "Vienna Calling";
        $a[1][0] = "Satellite to Satellite";

        echo "<b>Falco's masterpieces:</b><br>\n";
        while (list ($key, $val) = each ($a))
        {
                while (list ($subkey, $subval) = each ($val))
                {
                        echo "key:$key - subkey: $subkey - value: $subval<br>\n";
                }
        }
?>
```

A second loop has to be added to extract all fields from the arrays extracted from the multidimensional array. If you execute the script now, the result will contain all values:

```
Falco's masterpieces:
key:0 - subkey: 0 - value: Rock me Amadeus
key:0 - subkey: 1 - value: Jeanny
key:0 - subkey: 2 - value: Vienna Calling
key:1 - subkey: 0 - value: Satellite to Satellite
```

In the next step you want to sort the values in the array. To achieve that target, you can try to add a sort command after assigning the values to the array:

```
        sort($a);
```

This won't lead to the desired result because PHP will sort the keys and not the values:

```
Falco's masterpieces:
key:0 - subkey: 0 - value: Satellite to Satellite
key:1 - subkey: 0 - value: Rock me Amadeus
key:1 - subkey: 1 - value: Jeanny
key:1 - subkey: 2 - value: Vienna Calling
```

If you want to sort the content of the array and not the keys, you have to build a multidimensional array where all axes have the same amount of values. In your case you can build a matrix with four values (2×2 matrix):

```
$a[0][0] = "Rock me Amadeus";
$a[0][1] = "Jeanny";
$a[1][0] = "Vienna Calling";
$a[1][1] = "Satellite to Satellite";
```

This matrix can easily be sorted by using the `array_multisort` command:

```
array_multisort($a[0], SORT_ASC, SORT_STRING,
        $a[1], SORT_ASC, SORT_STRING);
```

Both columns are sorted in ascending order. If you execute the script now, you will receive a sorted list:

```
Falco's masterpieces:
key:0 - subkey: 0 - value: Jeanny
key:0 - subkey: 1 - value: Rock me Amadeus
key:1 - subkey: 0 - value: Satellite to Satellite
key:1 - subkey: 1 - value: Vienna Calling
```

If you hadn't changed the data structure, you'd run into trouble because the size of the arrays would be inconsistent:

```
Warning: Array sizes are inconsistent in /var/www/html/test/hello.php on line 8
```

Array_multisort accepts two flags for influencing the way data is sorted. PHP supports two sorting order flags:

- SORT_ASC—Sort in ascending order

- SORT_DESC—Sort in descending order

In addition, three sorting type flags are provided:

- SORT_REGULAR—Compare items normally

- SORT_NUMERIC—Compare items numerically

- SORT_STRING—Compare items as strings

As you can see, array_multisort is a powerful and flexible function. However, it has to be used with care to make sure that the result of a sort process contains exactly the desired data.

You have already seen that a multidimensional array consists of many arrays that have one dimension less than the parent array. Knowing this will allow you to perform all operations you want to perform. Especially when working with multidimensional stacks, it is important to know what happens inside PHP and how data is stored by the interpreter.

3.4 Building Functions

Functions are the key to reusability. You have already learned to call PHP's built-in functions in this chapter but up to now you have not implemented your own functions. In this section you will learn to build your own PHP functions.

3.4.1 Simple Functions

Let's start with a simple example: Gauss's Formula for the sum of integers.

Johann Carl Friedrich Gauss was born on April 30, 1777, in Brunswick, Germany. At the age of seven, Carl Friedrich Gauss started elementary school, and his potential was noticed almost immediately. His teacher, Büttner, and his assistant, Martin Bartels, were amazed when Gauss summed the integers from 1 to 100 instantly by spotting that the sum was 50 pairs of numbers each pair summing to 101. Gauss's Formula for the sum of integers was born.

```php
<?php
        $result = gauss(4);
        echo "Sum from 1 to 4: $result<br>\n";


# function for calculating the sum from 1 to $upper
function gauss($upper)
{
        if      (is_int($upper) && ($upper > 0))
        {
                return($upper*($upper+1)/2);
        }
}
?>
```

In the first line you can see that the function Gauss is called. One parameter has to be passed to the function. This parameter will define the upper limit for the sum you want to compute.

If the parameter passed to the function is an integer value and if it is higher than zero, the result is computed and returned to the main function. The result is passed to the main function by using the return command.

In this case 10 will be returned and displayed on the screen:

```
Sum from 1 to 4: 10
```

Functions can also be called with more than just one parameter. The next example shows a slightly adapted version of the function you have seen before. With the help of this function it is possible to compute the sum of integer values from a starting value to an upper value (the starting value is not included in the sum):

```php
<?php
        $lower = 4;
        $upper = 10;

        $result = gauss($lower, $upper);
        echo "Result: $result<br>\n";

function gauss($lower, $upper)
        {
                if       ($upper >= $lower && $lower >= 0)
                {
                        return ($upper*($upper+1)/2) - ($lower*($lower+1)/2);
                }
        }
?>
```

If you execute the script, the result will be displayed on the screen:

```
Result: 45
```

3.4.2 Passing Arrays to a Function

Sometimes it is necessary to pass entire arrays to a function. PHP does not support function overloading, but with the help of arrays it is possible to build simple workarounds.

The target of the next example is to compute the geometric mean of an array of values:

```php
<?php
        $values = array(4, 3, 19, 23, 15);

        $result = geomean($values);
        echo "Result: $result<br>\n";
```

```
function geomean($invalues)
{
        foreach ($invalues as $val)
        {
                $sum += $val*$val;
        }
        return sqrt($val);
}
?>
```

First, an array containing various values is created. In the next step the function called geomean is called and the array is passed to it. Geomean computes the sum of all values to a power of 2 in the array. After that the square root is computed and returned to the main function. The result will be displayed on the screen:

```
Result: 3.8729833462074
```

3.4.3 Functions Returning More Than One Value

Up to now, you have dealt with functions returning just one value. However, it is possible for one function to return many values.

Let's have a look at the next example:

```
<?php
        $values = array(4, 3, 19, 23, 15);

        $result = compute($values);
        foreach ($result as $val)
        {
                echo "val: $val<br>\n";
        }

function compute($invalues)
{
        $result = array();
        $sum = 1;
        foreach ($invalues as $val)
        {
                $sum += $val*$sum;
                array_push($result, $sum);
        }
        return $result;
}
?>
```

First, an array is generated and passed to the function called `compute`, which performs some simple operations and returns an array of values.

The output is displayed on the screen:

```
val: 5
val: 20
val: 400
val: 9600
val: 153600
```

As you can see, it makes no difference if you want to return an ordinary variable or an array of values—the syntax is the same.

3.5 Exception Handling

Exception handling is a core feature of almost any programming language. Exception handling is not only necessary to detect errors but also for flow control. PHP provides a powerful exception-handling model that can easily be used by programmers. To show you how exception handling can be done, we have included a simple example:

```php
<?php
        $a = "a string";
        if        (sqrt($a))
        {
                echo "Result: $b";
        }
        else
        {
                echo "The operation cannot be performed";
        }
?>
```

First, a string is defined. Then the script tries to compute the square root of the string, which is not possible. Therefore the condition evaluated by the `if` statement is not true and the `else` branch is entered.

If something happens that is not allowed in the script, it is necessary to quit the execution of a program. This can easily be done with the help of the `die` function:

```php
<?php
        $a = 3;
        if        ($a < 5)
        {
```

```
        echo '$a is lower than 5';
        exit;
    }
    echo "This won't be executed";
?>
```

As you can see, $a is lower than 5, so the `if` condition is true and the script quits:

```
$a is lower than 5
```

The output of the `echo` command at the end of the script won't be displayed any more.

`exit` is not the only function provided by PHP to exit a script. If a message has to be displayed before exiting a script, `die` can be used instead of `exit`.

```
<?php
    $a = 3;
    array_push($a, 4) or
            die ('$a is not an array');

    echo "This won't be executed";
?>
```

A PHP error message is displayed on the screen. In addition, the message that has been passed to `die` is displayed as well:

```
Warning: First argument to array_push() needs to be an array in
/var/www/html/index.php on line 3
$a is not an array
```

For real-world applications the error message generated by PHP is not suitable because it makes the user think that an error in the application has occurred. To make sure that no error is displayed to PHP, you can use @ to suppress the error:

```
<?php
    $a = 3;
    @array_push($a, 4) or
            die ('$a is not an array');

    echo "This won't be executed";
?>
```

If you execute the script, you will see that no PHP error is displayed:

```
$a is not an array
```

As you can see, PHP provides a flexible exception-handling system that can easily be used to catch almost all errors occurring during the execution of a script.

3.6 Working with Files

Workingwith files is easy in PHP. Files need not be located on the local machine to be accessible. It is also possible to work with remote files. In this section you learn to work with local and remote files efficiently.

3.6.1 Performing Basic Operations with Local Files

Working with files is an important issue for every programming language. The same applies to PHP. Functions for accessing the filesystem allow the user to build highly sophisticated applications. With the help of files it is possible to store information about what's going on in your application, or you can access external data sources. Nowadays a lot of information is stored in databases, but files are still a fundamental component of every applications. This section guides you through PHP's functions related to files and filesystems.

The first thing you have to know about files is how to open and close them:

```php
<?php
        $handle = @fopen("data.file", "r") or
                die ("cannot open file");
        echo 'File has successfully been opened<br>';
        fclose($handle);
?>
```

In this example `fopen` and `fclose` are used. These functions are available in many programming languages and have been borrowed from C.

In the script a file called `data.file` is opened for reading. This is done with the `fopen` function. The first parameter defines the name of the file that has to be opened. The second parameter tells PHP in which mode the file has to be opened. The following modes are supported by PHP:

- r—Reading only

- r+—Opens for reading and writing

- w—Opens the file for writing and creates an empty file

- w+—Opens the file for reading and writing

- a—Opens the file for writing only and sets the pointer to the end of the file

- a+—Opens the file for reading and writing and sets the pointer to the end of the file

Closing the file again is done by using `fclose`. Let's have a look at the content of the file the script has processed:

```
Hans::Vienna::Database Developer
Epi::Vienna::Consultant
Kuli::Vienna::Sales Manager
Sunny::Murau::Student
```

The file consists of four lines. Let's see what you can find out about the file using a Unix command:

```
[hs@athlon test]$ ls -l data.file
-rw-r--r--   1 hs        cybertec      107 Oct 21 13:21 data.file
```

The file is 107 bytes long and belongs to user `hs` in group `cybertec`.

Sometimes it is necessary to find out even more about a file. Therefore PHP provides a command called `stat`:

```php
<?php
        $fileinfo = stat("data.file") or
                die ("cannot find information about file");

        echo "device: $fileinfo[0]<br>\n";
        echo "inode: $fileinfo[1]<br>\n";
        echo "inode protection mode: $fileinfo[2]<br>\n";
        echo "number of links: $fileinfo[3]<br>\n";
        echo "user id of owner: $fileinfo[4]<br>\n";
        echo "group id of owner: $fileinfo[5]<br>\n";
        echo "device type if inode device: $fileinfo[6]<br>\n";
        echo "size in bytes: $fileinfo[7]<br>\n";
        echo "time of last access: $fileinfo[8]<br>\n";
        echo "time of last modification: $fileinfo[9]<br>\n";
        echo "time of last change: $fileinfo[10]<br>\n";
        echo "blocksize for filesystem I/O: $fileinfo[11]<br>\n";
        echo "number of block allocated: $fileinfo[12]<br>\n";
?>
```

If you execute the script, a lot of information will be displayed on the screen:

```
device: 773
inode: 470215
inode protection mode: 33188
number of links: 1
user id of owner: 500
group id of owner: 500
device type if inode device: 2817
size in bytes: 107
time of last access: 1003663763
time of last modification: 1003663300
time of last change: 1003663300
blocksize for filesystem I/O: 4096
number of block allocated: 8
```

The output displayed by stat contains the same information that is also returned by the C function PHP's stat function is based on. To show you that PHP's functions for working with filesystems are based on C, we have included the structure returned by C's stat function:

```
struct stat {
        dev_t       st_dev;     /* device */
        ino_t       st_ino;     /* inode */
        mode_t      st_mode;    /* protection */
        nlink_t     st_nlink;   /* number of hard links */
        uid_t       st_uid;     /* user ID of owner */
        gid_t       st_gid;     /* group ID of owner */
        dev_t       st_rdev;    /* device type (if inode device) */
        off_t       st_size;    /* total size, in bytes */
        unsigned long st_blksize; /* blocksize for filesystem I/O */
        unsigned long st_blocks;  /* number of blocks allocated */
        time_t      st_atime;   /* time of last access */
        time_t      st_mtime;   /* time of last modification */
        time_t      st_ctime;   /* time of last change */
};
```

As you can see, the content of the result generated by PHP is nearly equal to the result generated by C. This shows clearly that PHP and C are strongly related. Knowing this will make it easy for you to understand the behavior and the functions of the PHP interpreter.

Up to now, you have learned to open and close files. You have also seen how to find out information about a file, but you haven't read and written data yet. Let's start with an example where you can see how data can be read from a file:

```php
<?php
        $file = "data.file";

        $handle = fopen($file, "r") or
                die ("cannot open file");
        $fileinfo = stat($file);

        $data = fgets($handle, $fileinfo[7]);
        echo "data using fgets: <br>$data<br><br>";

        $data = fread($handle, $fileinfo[7]);
        echo "data using fread: <br>$data<br><br>";

        rewind($handle);
        echo "Pointer is at position: ".ftell($handle)."<br>";

        fseek($handle, 20);
        echo "Pointer is at position: ".ftell($handle);

        fclose($handle);
?>
```

First, a file is opened and information about that file is retrieved by using stat. $fileinfo[7] contains the size of the file. Although you have passed the content of $fileinfo[7] to fgets, only the first line will be read because fgets interprets newline characters. After reading the first line, the pointer is set to the beginning of the second line. Then fread is used. This time the rest of the file will be read and displayed on the screen because fread does not take care of newline characters. After reading all data, the file pointer is at the end of the file. To perform further reads, it is necessary to set it to a different position. Therefore rewind is used to set the pointer to the first position in the file. After that fseek sets the pointer to the 20th position in the file. Fseek and rewind are two essential functions when working with files because you can use them to go to any position within the file you are working with. Let's have a look at the output of the script:

```
data using fgets:
Hans::Vienna::Database Developer
```

```
data using fread:
Epi::Vienna::Consultant Kuli::Vienna::Sales Manager Sunny::Murau::Student

Pointer is at position: 0
Pointer is at position: 20
```

As you can see, the result is displayed on the screen correctly.

The next example shows how data can be written to a file:

```php
<?php
        $file = "data.file2";

        $handle = fopen($file, "w") or
                die ("cannot open file");
        fputs($handle, "Hello World");
        fclose($handle);
?>
```

$handle contains the pointer of the new file created by fopen. Then fputs is calledand a string is written to the file before closing it.

Up to now, you have only used rudimentary I/O functions. In some cases, it is more comfortable to read an entire file into an array:

```php
<?php
        $file = "data.file";

        $data = file($file);

        echo '<table border="1"><tr>';
        echo "<th>name</th><th>location</th><th>profession</th></tr>";

        foreach         ($data as $line)
        {
                $val = explode("::", $line);
                echo "<tr><td>$val[0]</td><td>$val[1]</td><td>
                        $val[2]</td></tr>";
        }
        echo "</table>";
?>
```

Reading a file into an array can be done with a function called `file`. To use `file`, it is not necessary to open the file first with `fopen` becausethis done implicitly by `file`. An array is returned. In the example the array is processed line by line and the string in the line is split after every `::`. That way an array called `$val` is initialized every time the loop is processed and a table can be generated, which you can see in Figure 3.2.

FIGURE 3.2   A simple table.

If you want to display the content of the file on the screen without processing the data beforehand, you can use the `readfile` function instead. `readfile(filename)` opens a file and displays the content on the screen directly. This is very useful when the file already contains HTML code.

3.6.2 Performing Basic Operations with Remote Files

In the previous section you have seen how local files can be treated with PHP. Remote files can be processed in a similar way.

Here is the example you have just seen, but this time the data comes from a remote host:

```php
<?php
        $file = "http://212.186.25.254:/test/data.file";

        $data = file($file);

        echo '<table border="1"><tr>';
        echo "<th>name</th><th>location</th><th>profession</th></tr>";

        foreach         ($data as $line)
        {
```

```
            $val = explode("::", $line);
            echo "<tr><td>$val[0]</td><td>$val[1]</td><td>
                    $val[2]</td></tr>";
    }
    echo "</table>";
?>
```

As you can see, the only change that has to be made is that the position of the file is now defined by an URL. If you have the permissions to read that file, it can be processed like any other file.

Every time the script is processed, however, the Web server will add one line to the logfile:

```
212.186.25.254 - - [21/Oct/2001:16:30:02 +0200] "GET /test/data.file HTTP/1.0"
➥ 200 107 "-" "PHP/4.0.4pl1"
```

As we have already mentioned, working with remote files works just the same way as with local files. However, some important things have to be taken into consideration:

```
<?php
    $file = "http://212.186.25.254:/test/data.file";
    $handle = fopen($file, "a+") or
            die ("cannot open $file");
    fputs($handle, "Pat::Indianapolis::Lawyer") or
            die ("cannot write to file");
    fclose($handle) or
            die ("cannot close file");
    echo "it works";
?>
```

Most people expect that the script will append data to the remote file, but this does not happen:

```
[hs@athlon test]$ cat data.file
Hans::Vienna::Database Developer
Epi::Vienna::Consultant
Kuli::Vienna::Sales Manager
Sunny::Murau::Student
```

Nothing has been appended to the remote file, although the output of the script is "it works" and no error has occurred while executing. This has to be taken into consideration when working with remote files; otherwise, you might wonder why your application returns no errors and produces no output.

3.6.3 Additional Filesystem Functions

As you have already seen, PHP offers functions for working with local and remote files. Up to now, you have seen how to perform all basic operations. In this section you will see that PHP provides a lot more functions than you have already seen:

- `string basename (string path [, string suffix])`—If you pass a filename including the path to `basename`, the filename without path will be returned.

- `int chgrp (string filename, mixed group)`—`chgrp` can be used to change the group a file belongs to.

- `int chmod (string filename, int mode)`—`chmod` can be used to change the mode of a file. This function does not work on Windows servers.

- `int chown (string filename, mixed user)`—`chown` can be used to change the owner of a file.

- `void clearstatcache (void)`—Clears file stat cache. Usually the result of stat is cached because it takes a lot of time to retrieve status information about a file. With the help of `clearstatcache`, you can force PHP to redo the status-checking function.

- `int copy (string source, string dest)`—`copy` can be used to copy files.

- `string dirname (string path)`—`dirname` is the counterpart of `basenames`—it returns the path to a file.

- `float diskfreespace (string directory)`—Can be used to find out how much space is left in the current directory.

- `float disk_total_space (string directory)`—Returns the total amount of storage provided by the partition the directory passed to the function provides.

- `bool fclose (int fp)`—Closes an open file.

- `int feof (int fp)`—Checks whether the pointer is set to EOF (end of file).

- `int fflush (int fp)`—Flushes the buffered output to disk.

- `string fgetc (int fp)`—Reads a single character from the file.

- `array fgetcsv (int fp, int length [, string delimiter])`—Reads a comma-separated values (CSV) file and returns an array of values. The delimiter to split a line can be passed to the function optionally.

- `string fgets (int fp, int length)`—Can be used to read from the file.

- `string fgetss (int fp, int length [, string allowable_tags])`—Is equal to `fgets` but tries to strip HTML tags.

- `array file (string filename [, int use_include_path])`—Returns the content of a file in an array.

- `bool file_exists (string filename)`—Returns true if the file passed to it exists.

- `int fileatime (string filename)`—Retrieves the access time of a file.

- `int filectime (string filename)`—Returns the modification time of the inode number.

- `int filegroup (string filename)`—Returns the group a file belongs to.

- `int fileinode (string filename)`—Retrieves the inode number of file.

- `int filemtime (string filename)`—Returns modification time.

- `int fileowner (string filename)`—Returns owner of file.

- `int fileperms (string filename)`—Returns the permissions of the file.

- `int filesize (string filename)`—Returns the size of the file.

- `string filetype (string filename)`—Returns the type of a file (`fifo`, `char`, `dir`, `block`, `link`, `file`, or `unknown`).

- `bool flock (int fp, int operation [, int wouldblock])`—Can be used to lock files in an advisory way.

- `int fopen (string filename, string mode [, int use_include_path])`—Opens a file or an URL and returns a file handle.

- `int fpassthru (int fp)`—Writes all data from the current position of the file pointer to the end of the file on standard output.

- `int fputs (int fp, string str [, int length])`—Writes data to a file starting at the current position of the file pointer.

- `string fread (int fp, int length)`—Binary-safe file read.

- `mixed fscanf (int handle, string format [, string var1...])`—Interprets the input based on a format.

- `int fseek (int fp, int offset [, int whence])`—Can be used to move the file pointer within a file. `whence` can be—`SEEK_SET` (set position of the file pointer equal to offset bytes), `SEEK_CUR` (set position of file pointer to current location plus offset), or `SEEK_END` (set position of file pointer to end-of-file plus offset).

- `array fstat (int fp)`—Retrieves information about a file.

- `int ftell (int fp)`—Can be used to find out on which position the file pointer can be found.

- `int ftruncate (int fp, int size)`—Can be used to truncate the file to a certain length.

- `int fwrite (int fp, string string, int [length])`—Binary-safe file write.

- `int set_file_buffer (int fp, int buffer)`—Modifies the file buffer to a certain size; by default the size is 8k.

- `bool is_dir (string filename)`—Can be used to find out whether the filename is a directory.

- `bool is_executable (string filename)`—Checks whether the given file is executable.

- `bool is_file (string filename)`—Checks whether `filename` is a file.

- `bool is_link (string filename)`—Checks whether `filename` is a symbolic link.

- `bool is_readable (string filename)`—Checks whether a file is readable.

- `bool is_writable (string filename)` and `bool is_writeable (string filename)`—Checks if a file is writable.

- `bool is_uploaded_file (string filename)`—Returns `true` if file was uploaded using HTTP POST.

- `int link (string target, string link)`—Creates a hard link.

- `int linkinfo (string path)`—Returns information about a link.

- `int mkdir (string pathname, int mode)`—Creates a new directory.

- `bool move_uploaded_file (string filename, string destination)`—Can be used to change the location of an uploaded file.

- `array pathinfo (string path)`—Returns information about a path in an array.

- `int pclose (int fp)`—Closes a pipe opened with `popen`.

- `int popen (string command, string mode)`—Opens a pipe.

- `int readfile (string filename, int [use_include_path])`—Reads the data from a file and prints it on standard output.

- `string readlink (string path)`—Returns the target of a symbolic link.

- `int rename (string oldname, string newname)`—Renames a file.

- int rewind (int fp)—Sets the pointer to the beginning of the file.

- int rmdir (string dirname)—Removes a directory.

- array stat (string filename)—Retrieves detailed information about a file.

- array lstat (string filename)—Returns information about a symbolic link.

- string realpath (string path)—Returns the canonicalized absolute pathname.

- int symlink (string target, string link)—Generates a symbolic link to a file.

- string tempnam (string dir, string prefix)—Creates a unique temporary filename.

- int tmpfile (void)—Creates a temporary file with a unique filename.

- int touch (string filename, int [time])—Sets modification time of the file to the current time.

- int umask (int mask)—Modifies the current umask of a file.

- int unlink (string filename)—Deletes a file.

As you can see, PHP provides an endless list of built-in functions. Most functions work with all common filesystems. Especially on Unix systems, PHP shows its tremendous power because some functions can only be used on Unix.

3.7 Variables and Scope

Variables cannot be "seen" in the entire application. This is a very important issue because otherwise programmers would easily run into trouble. Especially when building huge applications, it is important to know where which variables can be seen and used.

Let's start with a simple example:

```php
<?php
        $a = "Hello World";
        echo "main: $a<br>\n";
        display_data();

function display_data()
{
        echo "display data: $a<br>\n";
}
?>
```

First, $a is initialized and displayed on the screen. Then display_data is called, which tries to display $a again:

```
main: Hello World
display data:
```

As you can see, display_data displays nothing because $a cannot be seen by the function. $a has been initialized in the main function and therefore it is not visible for functions called by the main function.

However, if you have to access $a in display_data, it has to be declared as global:

```php
<?php
        $a = "Hello World";
        echo "main: $a<br>\n";
        display_data();
        echo "main: $a<br>\n";

function display_data()
{
        global $a;
        echo "display data: $a<br>\n";
        $a = "Hello Frank";
}
?>
```

With the help of the keyword global, it is possible to read and modify any global variable:

```
main: Hello World
display data: Hello World
main: Hello Frank
```

As you can see, the content of $a can be modified by display_data.

Another way to access $a is to use an array called $GLOBALS:

```php
<?php
        include("inc/vars.php");

        echo "main: $a<br>\n";
        display_data();

function display_data()
{
```

```
        echo "display data:".$GLOBALS["a"];
}
?>
```

With the help of $GLOBALS, it is possible to access any variable that has been defined globally. When executing the script, the output will be displayed on the screen:

```
main: Hello World
display data:Hello World
```

Another important thing, especially when dealing with huge projects, is to include variables using a command called include. With the help of include, files containing functions and variables can be added to a PHP script and will be visible for the interpreter. In the next example you will see a file called vars.php, which will be included in the script.php. Let's get to vars.php first:

```
<?php
        # Defining a string
        $a = "Hello World";
?>
```

As you can see, the file contains only the definition of $a. In script.php vars.php is included, so $a can be accessed as if it were defined in script.php.

```
<?php
        include("inc/vars.php");

        echo "main: $a<br>\n";
        display_data();

function display_data()
{
        global $a;
        echo "display data: $a<br>\n";
}
?>
```

It is recommended to put files that contain only definitions of variables in a separate directory so that these files cannot be mixed up with files containing other source code.

When executing the script, you will see that the result will be the same as in the previous example:

```
main: Hello World
display data: Hello World
```

Including one file is simple, but what happens when the file included in `script.php` contains included files? Let's have a look at the code of `script.php`.

```php
<?php
        include ("inc/vars.php");

        echo "$a<br>";
        echo "$b";
?>
```

This time `vars.php` does not contain the definition of the variables but includes two files containing the definition of $a and $b.

```php
<?php
        include ("inc/base_a.php");
        include ("inc/base_b.php");
?>
```

$a is defined in `base_a.php`:

```php
<?php
        $a = "Hello World";
?>
```

$b is defined in `base_b.php`:

```php
<?php
        $b = "Greetings from Austria";
?>
```

What happens when `script.php` is executed?

```
Hello World
Greetings from Austria
```

Both variables will be displayed. All variables included in `vars.php` are visible in `script.php` as well.

Static variables, like many other components of PHP, have been borrowed from C/C++. Static variables can be used to build functions that are able to remember values. Especially for recursions, this is an important feature. To show you what you can do with static variables, we have included a brief example:

```php
<?php
        for     ($i=1; $i<=6; $i++)
        {
```

```
                    echo display_data($i)."<br>\n";
        }

function display_data($i)
{
        static $var;
        $var .= "$i";
        return $var;
}
?>
```

A loop makes sure that `display_data` is called six times. `$var` is defined as a static variable, which means that it will remember the value it had the last time `display_data` was called. Every time the function is called, the current value of `$i` is added to `$var`.

If you execute the script, you will see that the length of `$var` grows every time `display_data` is processed:

```
1
12
123
1234
12345
123456
```

Static variables have disadvantages as well as advantages. Bugs caused by static variables are sometimes difficult to find, and it can be very painful to look for errors that can only be found by extensive debugging.

3.8 Building Packages

Even when writing very small applications, it is recommended to block functions used for certain parts of the applications in separate files. When writing an application used for displaying stock charts, for instance, it can be useful to have separate libraries for functions related to retrieving data and functions for displaying the data. This will help you to reuse code for other applications. In addition, your functions are more consistent because not every application has its own implementation of a block of functions.

Writing reusable code is the first step to writing reliable code. The more often a piece of code is used, the more mature it will be because more testing has been done.

Another important issue is that packages must be independent from the programs using them. In other words, don't access global variables of the main program from a library, or your code might not be reusable any more and the programmer using a library has to know what is going on inside your library. A library will be a black box for those people using it. According to the KISS principle (Keep It Small and Simple) of Unix systems, this is an essential point because other things will be far too complicated.

Try to build small, easy-to-understand, and independent modules with a fixed interface and make sure that the user of a library does not have to know what is going on inside your library.

The next code fragment shows a small example. The target is to write a module that swaps the content of two variables. Let's have a look at the main program first:

```php
<?php
        include ("lib/transform_data.php");

        $a = 23;
        $b = 37;

        swapdata_ref($a, $b);
        echo "a: $a<br>";
        echo "b: $b";
?>
```

At the beginning of the script a library is included. In the next step two variables are defined. These are the variables you want to swap. Then swapdata_ref is called and the values are passed to the function. After that the variables are displayed so that you can see that they have really been swapped. Up to now, swapdata_ref is a black box, and it is not necessary to know how variables can be swapped because the interface is the function is clearly defined. However, let's have a look at what the function does internally:

```php
<?php

function swapdata_ref(&$x, &$y)
{
        $c = $x;
        $x = $y;
        $y = $c;
}

?>
```

A reference is passed to the function and the values are swapped using a temporary variable called $c. As you can see, the function has no return values. Because a reference is passed to the swapdata_ref, the function is able to access the variables directly (using the internal addresses of the values) without having to access the variables using global variables. This way of solving the problem is very comfortable because swapdata_ref does not have to know how the variables in the function calling the swap function are called—the addresses of the values that have to be processed are assigned to their new names when the function is called.

When executing the script, you will see that the variables have been swapped:

```
a: 37
b: 23
```

Like many other things, references are borrowed from C and are a powerful feature because it would be far too uncomfortable to work with global variables or passing huge amounts of data to a function.

3.9 Working with Forms

Up to now, you have seen how to write simple PHP applications. However, for building interactive Web sites it is necessary to allow the user to insert data into so-called forms. The content of such forms can be transmitted to the server and a PHP script can react based on the data sent to it. Interacting with a Web server can be done with two methods called GET and POST.

3.9.1 GET and POST

The methods GET and POST are described in RFC2068, which is longer than 160 pages. In this section you learn about the main ideas behind GET and POST, and you learn to use these two methods efficiently.

3.9.1.1 GET

GET is the standard request method for retrieving data from a Web server. When calling a Web site, GET is used to get the document you have selected. Normally calls like that don't have side effects, and that is what GET should be used for. Browsers assume that GET has no side effects and if the page is not in the browser's cache any more, the page will be retrieved again. However, if the original request was via POST, the user would receive a message that the document is no longer in the cache (in section "Building Forms" in this chapter, you will learn to get around this problem).

3.9.1.2 POST

POST is the standard method for submitting data stored in a form to Web server. In the case of POST, the request always contains a body where the information related to the request is stored. This information is coded like a query string. Normally Web developers use POST even when no data on the server is modified.

3.9.2 Building Forms

After you have seen which methods can be used to retrieve data from a Web server, you have a look at a simple form that can be used to send text to a PHP file:

```
<html>
<body>
        A Simple Form
        <br><br>
        <form action="reaction.php" method="POST">
                <input type="text" name="field_1" size="10"><br><br>
                <input type="submit" name="submitbutton">
        </form>
</body>
</html>
```

In line number 5 a form is defined. When the user clicks on the Submit button, the data will be sent to reaction.php. The form consists of two components. The first component is a text field called field_1. The second component is the button to submit the form. The end of the form is marked by </form>.

Let's start the script and see what the browser displays (see Figure 3.3).

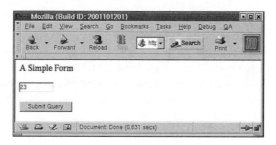

FIGURE 3.3   A simple form.

If you click the button, reaction.php will be started:

```php
<?php
        if      ($field_1)
        {
                echo "field_1: $field_1";
        }
        else
        {
                echo "nothing has been passed to this script";
        }
?>
```

The first thing done by the script is to see if $field_1 is defined. If the user has inserted data into the form, the variable will be defined in PHP automatically. In contrast to Perl, PHP programmers do not have to extract the variables from the query string themselves because everything is done by PHP.

If $field_1 is defined, the content of the variable will be displayed on the screen.

As you can see, retrieving data from a form is an easy task. In the next step you will see how more complex forms can be built with the help of HTML:

```html
<html>
<body>
        A more complex form
        <br><br>
        <form action="reaction.php" method="POST">
                <input type="text" name="field_1" size="10"><br><hr>

                <input type="checkbox" name="box_1">
                        display time<br><hr>

                <input type="radio" name="myradio" value=1>Value 1<br>
                <input type="radio" name="myradio" value=2>Value 2<br>
                <input type="radio" name="myradio" value=2>Value 3<br><hr>

                <input type="password" name="passwd">
                        Enter passwords here<br><hr>

                <input type="file" name="filename">
                        enter the filename<br><hr>
```

```
            <input type="reset" name="resetbutton">
            <input type="submit" name="submitbutton">
      </form>
</body>
</html>
```

The first component defined in the form is a text field again. The length of the field is set to 10. In addition to the size of the field, it would also be possible to define the maximum length of the text the user is allowed to insert. This can be done by using maxlength. After defining the text field, a check box is defined. The name is set to box_1. After that you can see how radio buttons can be added to a HTML document. In the example you can see that myradio consists of three components. Only one of those three components can be activated. Depending on which of the three buttons is checked, the appropriate value is sent to reaction.php. If you need fields for inserting passwords, password will be the right type for you. While typing, the user will only see asterisks, so nobody can grab the user's password.

To select a file on the user's hard disk, the type called file can be used. File will create a text box and a button you can click if you need a window where you can select the file using a graphical interface.

Finally, the Submit button is added to the screen. Figure 3.4 shows what comes out when you execute the script.

FIGURE 3.4   A more complex form.

If you click on the Submit button, the data inserted into the form will be sent to `reaction.php`:

```php
<?php
        echo "field_1: $field_1<br>";
        echo "myradio: $myradio<br>";
        echo "passwd: $passwd<br>";
        echo "filename: $filename<br>";
?>
```

The script displays the values on the screen:

```
field_1: 23
myradio: 2
passwd: a password
filename: /home/hs/boot.img
```

Keep in mind that the values in the listing show what you have inserted into the form. The gist of the example is that the information from every field in the HTML form will be stored in a variable after being submitted to a PHP file.

Sometimes it is necessary to give the user the opportunity to select more than just one value in a list. Therefore HTML offers a simple solution using `select` and `option`:

```html
<html>
<body>
        Select:
        <br><br>
        <form action="reaction.php" method="POST">
                <select name="fruits[]" multiple size=4>
                        <option value="Orange">Orange
                        <option value="Banana">Banana
                        <option value="Apple">Apple
                        <option value="Pineapple">Pineapple
                        <option value="Strawberry">Strawberry
                        <option value="Cherry">Cherry
                        <option value="Coconut">Coconut
                </select><br><br>

                <input type="submit" name="submitbutton">
        </form>
</body>
</html>
```

Now the user can choose some of the fruits presented in the list. Because more than one fruit can be selected, the data structure used by PHP must be an array. In our example this array is called `fruits[]`. After submitting the content of the form, the array will contain all values the user has selected. To display the content of the array, a simple function can be used:

```php
<?php
        foreach ($fruits as $var)
        {
                echo "$var<br>";
        }
?>
```

The fruits will be listed one after the other.

3.9.3 Passing Parameters to a Script

In many cases it is useful to call a script and pass some parameters to it. Techniques like that are often needed for banners because the person who has paid for the banner wants to know where a click comes from. For that purpose, parameters are passed to a script that contains information on whose Web site contained the banner.

Let's have a look at a very simple script that does nothing except display two variables.

```php
<?php
        echo "a: $a<br>\n";
        echo "b: $b\n";
?>
```

The target is to pass parameters to that script via an URL:

```
http://localhost/test/script.php?a=234&b=197
```

The script named `script.php` located in a directory named `test` on the local Web server is called with the parameter a=237 and b=197. The names of the script and the parameters are separated using a question mark (?). The list of parameters is separated using ampersands (&).

When executing `script.php`, the result will be displayed by the browser:

```
a: 234
b: 197
```

You have already seen that question marks and ampersands are used as delimiters. What happens if you want to pass one of these signs to the script? Does the Web server get confused because it has to find out which symbols are used as delimiters of which ones are parts of a string? The answer is yes. All "special" characters have to be escaped so that the Web server can parse the URL easily. Luckily PHP provides a function called urlencode, which takes care of things like that. Let's write a small script that generates a list of URLs:

```php
<?php
        echo "<html><body>\n";

        $messages[0] = "Pat and Shelley";
        $messages[1] = "Pat & Shelley";
        $messages[2] = "Pat & Shelley!";
        $messages[3] = "Are you sure?";
        $messages[4] = "Hans-Jürgen Schönig";

        foreach ($messages as $var)
        {
                echo '<a href="script.php?a='.urlencode($var).
                    '"> '.$var."</a><br>\n";
        }

        echo '</body></html>';
?>
```

After displaying some HTML code, five strings are defined and assigned to an array called $messages. Each of the strings contains certain characters that have to be escaped by PHP.

In the next step, links are generated using urlencode. Let's call PHP from the command line and see what the HTML code generated by the script looks like:

```
[hs@athlon test]$ php genurl.php
X-Powered-By: PHP/4.0.4pl1
Content-type: text/html

<html><body>
<a href="script.php?a=Pat+and+Shelley"> Pat and Shelley</a><br>
<a href="script.php?a=Pat+%26+Shelley"> Pat & Shelley</a><br>
<a href="script.php?a=Pat+%26+Shelley%21"> Pat & Shelley!</a><br>
<a href="script.php?a=Are+you+sure%3F"> Are you sure?</a><br>
<a href="script.php?a=Hans-J%FCrgen+Sch%F6nig"> Hans-Jürgen Schönig</a><br>
</body></html>
```

As you can see, all characters have been escaped. When executing the script using a Web browser, the strings in the array are displayed as links:

```
Pat and Shelley
Pat & Shelley
Pat & Shelley!
Are you sure?
Hans-Jürgen Schönig
```

If you click on the first link, `script.php` will be called:

```
a: Pat and Shelley
b:
```

The text is displayed on the screen. Because no parameters for $b have been passed to the script, the field is empty.

3.9.4 Working with Hidden Fields

Sometimes it is necessary to pass parameters to a script that should not be seen by the user. In HTML it is possible to use hidden fields. The difference between "ordinary" fields and hidden fields is that hidden fields are not displayed by the browser. Therefore parameters can easily be passed from one script to another without giving the user the opportunity to modify the information stored in a hidden field.

Let's assume that you want to write a script that displays the time the previous script has been created:

```php
<?php
        $curtime = localtime();
        $timestr = strftime("%Y %b %d: %T %Z");
        echo "timestr: $timestr<br>\n";

        echo '
                <html>
                <body>
                        Hello World
                        <form action="reaction.php" method="POST">
                        <input type="hidden" value="'.$timestr.
                                '" name="gentime">
                        <input type="submit" name="submitbutton">
                </form>
                </body>
                </html>
        ';
?>
```

The first script generates the current time and stores it in $timestr. Now a form is generated and the value $timestr is used as the default value of the field called gentime. The only two things that are displayed on the screen are the content of $timestr, Hello World, and a button to submit the information. Reaction.php is called when the user hits the button. Let's have a look at reaction.php:

```php
<?php
        echo "gentime: $gentime";
?>
```

The content of $gentime is displayed on the screen:

```
gentime: 2001 Nov 01: 12:31:57 CET
```

The previous script has been generated at the time listed in the output of reaction.php. Sometimes it is useful to pass the time when the first HTML was generated to all files because this way it is possible to find out when a user has entered the page.

3.10 Debugging PHP

After you have learned to write simple PHP applications, it is time to verify that your applications work. Therefore debugging has to be done.

In PHP3 a debugger was included that was able to send data to a TCP port where it can easily be monitored with the help of a listener.

Unfortunately in PHP this debugger can only be used if you buy the ZEND IDE (http://www.zend.com/store/). Some other debuggers are available for PHP, but we do not cover these products in this book. However, in this section you learn to debug PHP programs using PHP onboard tools.

The easiest way to debug PHP code is to write a debugging function. Let's assume that you want to monitor the content of $i:

```php
<?php
        include ("debug.php");

        for     ($i=1; $i <= 5; $i++)
        {
                echo "i: $i<br>\n";
                debug("\$i: $i");
        }
?>
```

Every time the loop is processed, you can call a function called debug, which can be found in debug.php.

Let's see how we implemented this function:

```php
<?php

# Write debugging info to a logfile
function debug($var)
{
        setlocale("LC_TIME","en_US");
        $datum=strftime("[%d/%b/%Y:%T %Z]");
        $log_str="$datum -- $var\n";
        $fp=fopen("/tmp/debug.log","a+");
        if ($fp)
        {
                fwrite($fp,$log_str);
                fclose($fp);
        }
        else
        {
                echo"error";
                exit;
        }
}
?>
```

First, the way time is displayed is set to English style. In the next step the date is compiled and stored in $datum. $log_str will contain the complete string added to the logfile, which will be located in the /tmp directory.

With the help of fwrite, $log_str is added to the file before it is closed again.

After executing the script, you can find the debugging information in the logfile:

```
[27/Oct/2001:09:38:31 CEST] -- $i: 1
[27/Oct/2001:09:38:31 CEST] -- $i: 2
[27/Oct/2001:09:38:31 CEST] -- $i: 3
[27/Oct/2001:09:38:31 CEST] -- $i: 4
[27/Oct/2001:09:38:31 CEST] -- $i: 5
```

As you can see, the logfile is generated using the Apache style of logging. With the help of logfiles, it is an easy task to monitor your application and find out what has happened inside a program.

However, this information might not be enough for you. Especially when monitoring production environments in which many concurrent processes are running on the system, it is necessary to have some information about which process generated what kind of information. To compute this information, PHP offers some easy-to-use functions. `getmypid` retrieves the process ID of the current process and `get_current_user` finds out which user executes the script.

The information can be added to the logfile by modifying the line generating `$log_str`:

```
$log_str="$datum [".getmypid()."] ".get_current_user()." -- $var\n";
```

Now the logfile will contain the process ID and the name of the user executing the script:

```
[27/Oct/2001:10:06:11 CEST] [4661] hs -- $i: 1
[27/Oct/2001:10:06:11 CEST] [4661] hs -- $i: 2
[27/Oct/2001:10:06:11 CEST] [4661] hs -- $i: 3
[27/Oct/2001:10:06:11 CEST] [4661] hs -- $i: 4
[27/Oct/2001:10:06:11 CEST] [4661] hs -- $i: 5
```

With the help of this information, it is an easy task to distinguish the scripts running on the server.

In general it is hard to give rules for how debugging can be done best. In most cases, how to find bugs fast and reliably is a matter of personal preference. One thing can be said for sure: Don't hurry when looking for bugs.

3.11 Summary

PHP is a powerful and easy-to-use language. The main advantages of PHP are its flexibility and simplicity. Web applications can be written easily and fast. This makes PHP a good choice for prototyping and rapid application development.

4

Object-Oriented PHP

The basic concept of object orientation is about three decades old and has been implemented in many programming languages, such as Smalltalk and many others. In recent years, object orientation has become more and more popular.

PHP can be used as a procedural language as well as an object-oriented language. This feature makes PHP flexible and powerful because it offers concepts for almost all programmers.

This chapter focuses entirely on object orientation. You will be guided through the basic concepts of object orientation and PHP's syntax for dealing with objects.

4.1 The Concepts of Object Orientation

In contrast to procedural languages, object-oriented languages treat all pieces of data that functions are working with as objects. When using the strict object-oriented paradigm, functions are no longer called *functions* but are called *methods*. Methods can only be defined for objects. A method for computing the sum of two values that has been defined for the object called a cannot be used for computing the sum of two values belonging to the object called b. At first glance, this seems stupid because you need two methods for performing one simple calculation, but in fact it can be an advantage. All methods belonging to a certain object can be treated as one union. Every object has a predefined programming interface, but the way things are treated by the object internally should not affect the person using that object. The advantage of this concept is that the user only has to be familiar with the interface and does not have to waste his time understanding things he doesn't need to know. If the programming interface of an object stays the same, the way things are done by the object internally can easily be changed without affecting the applications using that object.

Objects are also called *classes*. A class contains the definition of an object as well as all functions related to that object. Every class must have a constructor, which is used to create a new instance of an object. An instance of an object is an object created by a constructor. Imagine a class called *people*, which defines persons. Therefore a specific *person* is an instance of the class people. A class is simply a template, and all instances of an object have the same scheme as the class defining how an instance has to look.

4.1.1 Constructors and Destructors

To generate new instances of an object, a constructor has to be implemented into the object. Every time the constructor is called, an instance of the object is returned.

The constructor assigns all properties of an object to the variables defining an instance.

The counterpart of constructors is destructors. Destructors are used to destroy objects and to free the memory allocated by an object.

4.1.2 Inheritance

Object-oriented languages support inheritance. This means that child classes can inherit functions and attributes from parent classes. Assume a class for storing geometric objects. All geometric objects have attributes, such as color, in common. Circles, however, have additional attributes, such as the radius. Therefore it is possible that the class `circle` inherits all methods and functions from the parent class used to store all attributes that geometric objects have in common.

The ability to inherit methods and functions helps the programmer to keep code short because functions needed by many classes that are related to each other only have to be implemented once. One disadvantage of this feature is that applications that make heavy use of inheritance are difficult to debug because the function executed has to be found in the object tree. In this case, the procedural paradigm is easier to understand: In most cases, it is clear which function has been executed because there is only one with a certain name.

4.1.3 Function Overloading

Function overloading is another feature of object-oriented languages. Function overloading means that one function is implemented more than once. Every implementation of the function accepts different arguments passed to it. Imagine a function called `sum` that is used to compute the sum of two values. An additional function that is called sum as well is used to compute the sum of three values. Both functions have the same name but one function accepts two parameters, whereas the second function accepts three parameters.

PHP does not support explicit function overloading because there is an easy way to get around it by passing arrays to a function.

4.2 Building Classes

Now that you have learned about the theoretical background of object-oriented software development, it is time to return to PHP-specific subject matter.

In this section you will learn to write your own PHP classes and you will see how inheritance and function overloading can be done in PHP.

4.2.1 A Simple Class

Writing classes in PHP is as simple as writing functions. However, some things have to be taken into consideration when working with classes and instances.

The following piece of code shows the class called human, which stores information all human beings have in common:

```php
<?php

# Class human
class human
{
        var $age;
        var $gender;

        # Constructor
        function human()
        {
                # an empty constructor
        }

        # Setting the age of a person
        function setage($age)
        {
                $this->age = $age;
        }

        function setgender($gender)
        {
```

```
                   $this->gender = $gender;
         }
}

?>
```

The keyword `class` defines the name of the class, which can be found in curly brackets. The name of the class is defined as `human`. At the beginning of the class some values are defined using the keyword `var`. These values are the attributes of the class. After that you can see the implementation of a constructor. In this example the constructor has nothing to do.

Let's have a closer look at the script using the class:

```
<?php
         include("human.php");

         # Generating two humans
         $epi = new human();
         $hans  = new human();

         $epi->age = 25;
         $hans->setage(23);

         echo "Epi is $epi->age years old<br>\n";
         echo "Hans is $hans->age years old<br>\n";
?>
```

After including the file containing the class, two instances of the class called `human` are created. In the next step the age of `$epi` is set to 25 by accessing an attribute of `$epi`. All attributes of the class have been defined in the code of the class using the keyword `var`. Another method of defining the age of a human in this example is to call the function called `setage` as was done for the instance `$hans`. `setage` modifies the value of the attribute to 23.

Finally, the values assigned to the instances are displayed on the screen:

```
Epi is 25 years old
Hans is 23 years old
```

4.2.2 Objects and Scope

After you have seen how to implement a simple class, you'll have a closer look at what effect object orientation has on scope. As you have already seen, the idea behind object orientation is to combine functions related to a certain topic in an object. The same applies to the attributes related to an object. All attributes of an object can only be seen inside an object. If one of these variables has to be accessed from outside an object, it can only be done by accessing it via the instance of an object:

```
<?
# Class human
class human
{
        var $age;
        var $gender;

        # Constructor
        function human($age, $in_gender)
        {
                $this->age = $age;
                $gender = $in_gender;
        }
}

$hans = new human(23, 'm');

echo "age: $age<br>\n";
echo "age: $hans->age<br>\n";

echo "gender: $gender<br>\n";
echo "gender: $hans->gender<br>\n";

?>
```

At the beginning of the class, two attributes are defined. This time the constructor is designed to work with two parameters. The first parameter is assigned to $this->age. The second parameter is assigned to the local variable called $gender.

When creating the new instance, $hans, the constructor is called. Four variables are displayed on the screen. First $age is displayed. Then $hans->age is accessed. The same operations are performed for $gender as well.

When executing the script, you will see that only one variable is defined:

```
age:
age: 23
gender:
gender:
```

The first echo command displays an empty variable because $age has not been defined in the main program and $age in $hans cannot be accessed this way. The second echo command displays the desired result because $age is accessed via $hans. This way PHP knows which $age to access.

In the case of $gender, the echo command displays nothing for the same reasons we gave for the first echo command. The last echo command returns nothing as well because $in_gender has not been assigned to an attribute of $hans. $gender is treated as a local variable and is destroyed automatically at the end of the constructor. Many people forget to assign variables to the attributes of an instance; as you can see, this will lead to bugs and trouble.

4.2.3 Simulating Function Overloading

Function overloading is not supported by PHP explicitly. In general, a user can pass as many parameters to a constructor as he wants to. Therefore it is not useful to implement functions accepting a certain number of parameters.

Because PHP is a very flexible language, there is an easy way to get around function overloading by working with arrays:

```
<?
# Class human
class human
{
        var $age;
        var $gender;
        var $income;

        # Constructor
        function human($data)
        {
                $this->age = $data["age"];
                $this->gender = $data["gender"];
                $this->income = $data["income"];
        }
}

$hans_data["age"] = 23;
$hans_data["gender"] = 'm';
$hans_data["income"] = 25000;
$hans = new human($hans_data);

$epi_data["age"] = 25;
$epi = new human($epi_data);
```

```
echo "Hans - age: $hans->age<br>\n";
echo "Hans - gender: $hans->gender<br>\n";
echo "Hans - income: $hans->income<br><br>\n";

echo "Epi - age: $epi->age<br>\n";
echo "Epi - gender: $epi->gender<br>\n";
echo "Epi - income: $epi->income<br>\n";

?>
```

This time the constructor is designed to accept one parameter, which in this case is an array. All appropriate values in this array are assigned to the attributes of the class by the constructor. As you can see, $hans is generated by using an array containing all attributes supported by the class. In the case of $epi, this is different because you pass an array with just one value to the constructor.

When you execute the script using your favorite Web browser, you will see what comes out:

```
Hans - age: 23
Hans - gender: m
Hans - income: 25000

Epi - age: 25
Epi - gender:
Epi - income:
```

The result is no surprise. $epi has been created successfully, but not all of the attributes have been initialized with a useful value.

What happens when a constructor designed for one value is called with two values? Let's have a look at the next example:

```
<?
# Class human
class human
{
        var $age;
        var $gender;
        var $income;

        # Constructor
        function human($age)
        {
```

```
                    $this->age = $age;
        }
}

$hans = new human(23);
$epi = new human(25, 'm');

echo "Hans: $hans->age<br>\n";
echo "Epi: $epi->age<br>\n";

?>
```

In the main program $hans is generated by calling the constructor with just one parameter. $epi, however, is generated by calling the constructor with two parameters. Let's see what comes out when the script is executed:

```
Hans: 23
Epi: 25
```

The second parameter is silently omitted by PHP and the program works as if you had called the constructor with just one parameter.

Let's modify the script and implement an additional constructor designed for accepting two parameters:

```php
<?php
# Class human
class human
{
        var $age;
        var $gender;

        # Constructor
        function human($age, $gender)
        {
                echo "constructor with two parameters<br>\n";
                $this->age = $age;
                $this->gender = $gender;
        }

        function human($age)
        {
```

```
                echo "constructor with one parameter<br>\n";
                $this->age = $age;
        }
}

$hans = new human(23);
$epi = new human(25, 'm');

echo "Hans: $hans->age<br>\n";
echo "Epi: $epi->age<br>\n";

?>
```

As you can see, two constructors have been implemented. C++ programmers might think that PHP finds out which constructor has to be called depending on the number of parameters the constructor has to be called with, but this won't happen:

```
constructor with one parameter
constructor with one parameter
Hans: 23
Epi: 25
```

The second constructor is always called. In this example PHP won't display an error, but for people who are used to programming C++, the behavior of the interpreter seems strange.

4.2.4 Cloning Objects

After you have created an instance of an object, you might want to clone it. In many languages it is necessary to implement a copy-constructor. In the case of PHP, it is not necessary in most situations to implement an additional function because almost all cloning operations can be performed by using the = operator.

In this section you will have a closer look at how to treat more than just one instance of an object and how to clone objects.

Let's start with an example:

```
<?php

# Class human
class creature
{
        var $name;
        var $color;
```

```
            function creature($name, $color)
            {
                    $this->name = $name;
                    $this->color = $color;
                    echo "creature called $name has been created<br>\n";
            }
    }

# creating two creatures
$acreature = new creature('Kertal', 'white');
$ccreature = new creature('Broesl', 'yellow');

# bcreature references a creature
$bcreature = &$acreature;

# cloning acreature
$ccreature = $acreature;
# modifying acreature
$acreature->color = 'black';

# displaying results
echo '<br>';
echo "acreature: $acreature->name; $acreature->color<br>\n";
echo "bcreature: $bcreature->name; $bcreature->color<br>\n";
echo "ccreature: $ccreature->name; $ccreature->color<br>\n";

?>
```

First, a class called creature is implemented. It has two attributes and one construc-tor to create new instances of the object.

In the next step two instances of creature are created. The name of the first creature is $acreature and the name of the second instance is $bcreature. After creating the two instances of creature, $bcreature is assigned to a reference of $acreature. This means that $bcreature is not a separate object any more but is an alias for $acrea-ture. Every modification of $acreature will affect $bcreature.

In the next step $ccreature is created. This time the object is not a reference of $acreature but an individual and independent object. If $acreature is modified, the changes won't affect $ccreature.

Finally, $acreature is modified and the attributes of the various objects are displayed on the screen:

```
creature called Kertal has been created
creature called Broesl has been created

acreature: Kertal; black
bcreature: Kertal; black
ccreature: Kertal; white
```

As you can see, $acreature and $bcreature contain the values while $ccreature is still white because it has been created as an independent object.

4.3 Working with Inheritance

Inheritance is a core component of the object-oriented paradigm. With the help of inheritance, it is possible to build short and efficient code. However, if the hierarchy of objects becomes too complex, your applications will be difficult to debug.

Inheritance means that a class can inherit methods and attributes from a parent class. In PHP, a class can only inherit from the parent class—it is not possible for one class to have more than one parent.

After this theoretical overview, you will see an example of a class that inherits from a parent class:

```php
<?php
# Class human
class human
{
        var $age;
        var $gender;

        # Constructor
        function human($age, $gender)
        {
                $this->age = $age;
                $this->gender = $gender;
        }

        function getage()
        {
```

```
                echo "age: $this->age<br>\n";
                return $this->age;
        }
}

class child extends human
{
        var $mother;
        var $father;

        function child($age, $gender, $mother, $father)
        {
                $this->age = $age;
                $this->gender = $gender;
                $this->mother = $mother;
                $this->father = $father;
        }

        function getfather()
        {
                echo "father: $this->father<br>\n";
                return $this->father;
        }
}
?>
```

The class called human has two attributes and one constructor. In addition, it provides
a function to extract the age of a human being. getage displays the age on the
screen and returns it to the calling function. The next class you can find in the code
is the class called child. child extends human, which means that child inherits all
attributes and functions from human. child has two more attributes than the parent.
$mother and $father can be used to store the names of the parents of a child. These
attributes don't have to be listed at the beginning of the class: It is clear that these
attributes are part of the class because they have been inherited from the parent
class. child has a constructor that assigns all attributes passed to it to the attributes
of the class. The function called getfather can be used to retrieve attribute father.

Let's have a look at a script using the classes human and child:

```
<?php
        include("human.php");
```

```
        # Generating two humans
        $baby  = new child(1, 'f', 'Christina', 'Epi');

        echo "<b>The father's name is ".$baby->getfather()."<br></b>\n";
        echo "<b>The baby is ".$baby->getage()." years old</b><br>\n";
?>
```

First, the file containing the two classes is included. In the next step $baby is created.
$baby is an instance of child. As you can see, the constructor is called with four
parameters and each of these parameters is assigned to the attributes of the instance.
In the next step the father of the baby and the age will be displayed on the screen.
First getfather is called, which retrieves the name of the father and displays it on
the screen. In the next step the age of the baby has to be displayed. Because you
don't want to access $age via $baby, getage is called. As you have seen before, child
does not contain the function getage. Because human is the parent class of child,
child inherits all functions from human. If PHP does not find a function in a class, it
will automatically look for a function with the same name in the parent class:

```
father: Epi
The father's name is Epi
age: 1
The baby is 1 years old
```

As you can see, PHP has found the appropriate function in the parent class, so it can
be used for working with $baby.

In the next example you will see how a hierarchy of classes can be built. The target is
to write three classes. The parent class contains some information that is inherited
by a child class. The child class, however, is the parent class of an additional class:

```
<?php
# Class human
class creature
{
        var $name;

        function creature($name)
        {
                $this->name = $name;
                echo "creature created<br><br>\n";
        }
}
```

```
class human extends creature
{
        var $gender;

        function human($name, $gender)
        {
                $this->name = $name;
                $this->gender = $gender;
                echo "human created<br><br>\n";
        }
}

class worker extends human
{
        var $profession;

        function worker($name, $gender, $profession)
        {
                $this->name = $name;
                $this->gender = $gender;
                $this->profession = $profession;
                echo "worker created<br><br>\n";
        }
}

# Main program
$myworker = new worker('Paul', 'male', 'chief cleaning manager');

echo "name: $myworker->name<br>\n";
echo "gender: $myworker->gender<br>\n";
echo "profession: $myworker->profession<br>\n";

?>
```

The parent class is called creature. In this model, every creature has a name. The table for storing humans can be used to store special attributes of humans. Human inherits everything from creature. Workers are special humans and therefore worker inherits everything from human and adds its own extensions. Let's execute the script:

```
worker created

name: Paul
gender: male
profession: chief cleaning manager
```

As you can see, the constructor of `worker` is called and all values are displayed on the screen.

All classes inherit attributes and methods from a parent class. It is not possible for a parent class to inherit from a child class, as shown in Figure 4.1:

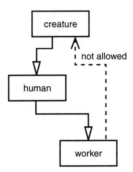

FIGURE 4.1   An object model.

Inheritance is a one-way street—it is not possible for parents to inherit from the children.

With the help of PHP, it is possible to build complex models and to make heavy use of inheritance.

4.4 Summary

PHP has great object-oriented capabilities, although some important features such as private functions and multiple inheritance are still missing. However, object-oriented PHP can help you to make the code of your applications clearer and easier to understand.

PART II

Getting Started with PostgreSQL

IN THIS PART

5

Relational and Object-Relational Database Concepts

The relational model was originally developed by E. F. Codd in the '70s. The relational concept is a simple but strict concept and describes the treatment of two-dimensional data with the help of tables.

PostgreSQL can be used as a relational database. However, PostgreSQL is also capable of handling object and hierarchical data. The object-oriented paradigm differs significantly from the relational concept, and with the help of PostgreSQL, it is possible to utilize both concepts in order to build even more powerful applications. Especially in combination with object-oriented languages, PostgreSQL's concepts can be a significant advantage and will help you to build databases that are easier to understand.

According to the relational concept, two ways of looking at data are defined: The organization of data into relational tables is known as the *logical view* of the database. The counterpart of the logic view is the *internal view* of the data. Depending on the kind of data your database stores, the logical and internal view of the data can differ. When working with SQL, the user is accessing data via a predefined interface, which in the case of PostgreSQL, is SQL. The way data is stored by PostgreSQL internally need not affect the user. The idea is to have a standard interface for interacting with the data—it is not necessary to think about how the data is stored by the database internally.

However, the logic structure of your database is one of the most important things when storing data in a database. To store data in a flexible and efficient way, normalization has to be done.

5.1 Normalization

In relational database theory, five normal forms are defined. Normal forms represent a guideline for record design and are essential when building complex data structures. They can be used to prevent inconsistencies and anomalies in the data and will help you to build clear and efficient data structures. In this book normal forms will only be covered very briefly because normalization can be a complicated subject if you want to build data models that satisfy all demands of the fifth normal form.

5.1.1 The First Normal Form

In the first normal form, all records in the table must have the same number of columns and all columns have to be the same data type. Every name of a field has to be unique within a table. The relational theory does not allow records with a variable number of columns, and the name of a column has to be unambiguous. In addition, a table should be created for every group of related data. Every table must have one unique column, which will be the primary key. One cell must not contain more than one value.

All restrictions of the first normal form have nothing to do with database design, but these restrictions are important for definition purposes.

5.1.2 The Second Form

The second and the third normal form deal with the relations between fields used as keys and fields that are not keys.

The most important condition that has to be fulfilled is that separate tables for sets of values that apply to multiple records have to be created. These tables have to be related to a foreign key.

In addition to the demands of the second form, all demands of the first normal form have to be fulfilled as well.

5.1.3 The Third Normal Form and Beyond

A model in third normal form has to satisfy all demands of the first and second normal forms. In addition, fields that do not depend on a key have to be eliminated.

Normally, people do not build database models that satisfy more than the demands of the third normal form. In addition to the third normal form, three more normal forms are defined. The next normal forms in the list are the Boyce-Codd normal form, the fourth, and the fifth normal form.

5.1.4 An Example

In order to illustrate what you have just learned, here is a practical example of how normalization can be done.

Table 5.1 shows an unnormalized table.

TABLE 5.1   An Unnormalized Table

Student	Advisor	Adv-Room	Class 1	Class 2	Class 3
999	Alan	214	101	341	951
2300	Carl	612	102	112	412

The problem with this table is that more than one column containing the same kind of data is in the table. This is extremely inflexible because in this model there is only space for three classes—every class added to the scenario would need a separate column. To solve this problem, we use Codd's first normal form, as shown in Table 5.2.

TABLE 5.2   First Normal Form

Student	Advisor	Adv-Room	Class
999	Alan	214	101
999	Alan	214	341
999	Alan	214	951
2300	Carl	612	102
2300	Carl	612	112

We have made one column out of three to avoid repeatable columns in first normal form. As you can see, the table is much longer now and a lot of redundancies are in the table because the names of the advisor and the IDs of the students are listed more than just once. This is extremely bad because a lot of space is wasted and UPDATE operations will take far too long. In addition, it is not useful to update a lot of records if only one name changes. The problem can be solved by using Codd's second normal form, as shown in Table 5.3.

TABLE 5.3   The Main Table

Student	Advisor	Adv-Room
999	Alan	214
2300	Carl	612

TABLE 5.3   Continued

Students and Classes

Student	Class
999	101
999	341
999	951
2300	102
2300	122
2300	412

Two tables have been made out of one. This way the redundancies in the table have been reduced. Names are listed only once, so UPDATE operations can be performed more easily. In this example, the column Student in the second table is a foreign key of the first table.

As you can see, modifying a model so that it satisfies the demands of the second normal form is easy. In most cases second, or respectively third, normal form will be enough; otherwise, the number of tables will be far too high and performing simple selections will be more complicated. Having a lot of tables might help you to build more flexible data structures, but on the other hand, it will be more complicated for the database to find the best way through a query because the number of ways through a query will grow exponentially.

5.2 Basic Operations in the Relational Model

According to Codd's theory, several operations on a relational model are defined. These operations are one fundamental of relational databases. Knowing these operations will help you to understand what your database does internally:

- SELECT—This operation is used to extract a list of tuples from a table. These tuples have to fulfill certain conditions in order to be selected.

- PROJECT—To retrieve certain columns from a relation, a PROJECT operation has to be performed.

- PRODUCT—PRODUCT builds the Cartesian product of two tables. Whenever a join is performed, the database will (at least theoretically) compute the Cartesian product of two objects. After that the result will in most cases be reduced to the desired records by using certain conditions.

- UNION—In many cases the result of two queries has to be combined. Therefore an operation called UNION has to be performed.

- INTERSECT—To build the set-theoretical intersection of the result of two queries, the database has to perform a so-called INTERSECT operation.

- DIFFERENCE—The DIFFERENCE operation finds all records that do not belong to both sets being processed.

- JOIN—Joining two tables means to connect two tables using a common attribute that occurs in both tables you want to join.

With the help of these basic operations, the database can perform all basic operations on a relational database model.

5.3 PostgreSQL as an Object Relational Database

In contrast to the purely relational model, PostgreSQL provides object-oriented capabilities as well. However, PostgreSQL is not a pure object database because it can also be used for building relational models that do not use objects and features like inheritance or other object-oriented features.

In this section you will see a brief overview of PostgreSQL's object-oriented features.

5.3.1 Inheritance

Inheritance is a key feature of every object-oriented system. Just as in PHP, objects inherit from each other. However, some significant differences have to be taken into consideration. In general, two kinds of inheritance have to be distinguished.

5.3.1.1 Dynamic Inheritance

Dynamic inheritance means that a class inherits from the parent class every time a new instance of an object is created. In other words: If the parent class changes, all children of a parent class will automatically be affected by it. In the case of PostgreSQL, tables can inherit columns from other tables. If a column in a parent table is renamed, all child tables will automatically inherit the new name. Dynamic inheritance allows the user to build very flexible data structures that can easily be changed.

5.3.1.2 Static Inheritance

The counterpart of dynamic inheritance is *static* inheritance. In contrast to dynamic inheritance, static inheritance means that a child inherits only once. If the parent is changed, the child will never inherit these changes because the child is completely independent from the parent class.

This concept is used for database clusters. In the case of PostgreSQL, a database cluster is a set of databases. Every time a database is created, it inherits things like data types and system tables from a parent database. If a data type is added to a parent database, the child data type cannot use the data type unless somebody adds it to it manually.

The concept of static inheritance can be seen as a help, not a burden. With the help of static inheritance, it is easily possible to remove certain elements from a child. This is not possible in the dynamic concept because a child will always inherit everything every time. Because static inheritance means that things are only inherited once, it is an easy task to remove components of the child object without having to worry that they will be inherited again.

5.4 Modeling Techniques

Defining a model of your data is the first step when building a new application. If the structure of your database is not flexible enough and if it cannot be extended easily, your entire application will suffer. After an application has been built, it is hard to change the structure of the database it is based on. Therefore it is worth the effort to think about the database model extensively. In the past few decades, a lot of people have been thinking about the right ways to build database models. In this section you will find out about the basics of building database models. A topic like modeling data can never be covered sufficiently, but we will try to guide you through the most important models and to show you what can be done to make your databases more flexible and easier to extend.

5.4.1 Entity Relationship Models

One of the most intuitive models for building databases is the Entity Relationship Model (ERM). Today ERM is the state of the art when designing large database projects. The idea behind ERM models is to display the interactions between various entities.

Entities are objects for storing various attributes that are relevant for the system you want to build. Depending on the scope the system has to cover, a certain entity will or will not be part of your model.

An important decision that has to be made is how many details and exceptions will be covered in your model. The more details your system will cover, the more complex it will be.

Entities that cannot be used to store attributes are not entities and have to be omitted because they cannot be transformed into relations. Entities are always objects and are labeled with nouns.

Attributes are always stored in combination with entities. An attribute describing an entity can either be part of a second entity or not. This shows that entities are related to each other.

The way ERMs are displayed is unitary. Almost every book uses a different way to draw ERMs and so it is not possible to include a set of common rules how to draw an ERM best. Some things, however, have all ERM drawings in common: Entities are displayed as boxes containing the name of the entity. Entities related with each other are connected using lines or arrows.

Figure 5.1 shows a simple ER diagram.

FIGURE 5.1   A simple ERM model.

The model consists of two entities. The entity Student has two attributes called first name and surname. The second relation is called Training and has two attributes as well. Every training course has a unique course id and can be done in a certain semester. Of course, students and training courses have a lot of additional attributes, but for an easy model, it is enough to work with two attributes for each entity.

Student and Training Courses are in a 1 : n relation, which means that every student can attend more than just one training course.

Keep in mind that Figure 5.1 shows one way of drawing an Entity Relationship model. Depending on which book you are reading, ERMs might look slightly different.

5.4.2 Transforming ERMs to SQL

The target of ERMs is to have a graphical way of displaying the way various objects in your database can interact with each other. However, what databases really need is plain SQL, not bitmaps. Therefore, ERMs have to be transformed to SQL code that can be used to build up a data structure inside the database. For this operation some rules have been defined, which will be discussed in this section.

5.4.2.1 Rules for Transforming ERMs to SQL

Let's see what has to be done to make SQL out of an ERM:

- **Entities to tables**—Every entity in your model will be a table in your database.

- **Attributes to columns**—Every attribute of an entity will be a column of the table the attribute belongs to.

- **Identifiers to primary keys**—Every unique identifier of an object will be a primary key. Every entity needs exactly one identifier.

- **Relations to foreign keys**—Entities that are related to each other have to be connected using a foreign key. This way the integrity of your data will be guaranteed.

With the help of these simple rules, any ERM can be transformed to SQL.

5.4.2.2 PostgreSQL Specifics

PostgreSQL provides some important add-ons to traditional relational concepts. The problem is that these things can hardly be used when working with ERMs. Just think of things like inheritance or arrays—using the original ERM will not allow you to use these features of PostgreSQL.

5.4.2.3 Automatic Transformations

Today some tools for building data models are available. Some of these tools are able to generate platform-specific SQL commands out of ERMs. This way it is an easy task to build complex models. The problem with tools like that is that at the moment this book was written, no such tool was available for PostgreSQL. Things will change in the near future and PostgreSQL will be supported as are many other databases like DB2 or Oracle.

5.4.3 UML

UML is short for *Unified Modeling Language*. The idea behind UML is to have a tool for creating software more effectively and more reliably. UML is a language for describing the interaction of objects and is very similar to Entity Relationship Models. Because Entity Relationship Models can be drawn in many ways and because there is no unified standard, UML is very often used as the common language everybody can understand easily. Because UML is a language for describing things, it can be used to build models for complex subjects and to visualize the way various components interact with each other. Models built with the help of UML can easily be understood because every UML model is a graphical description of what has to go on inside an application.

UML was developed by Rational Software and its partners. It is the successor to the languages used for modeling found in the Booch, OOSE/Jacobson, OMT, and other methods.

Today UML is widely used as the standard modeling language and helps to reduce the time needed for developing a software product.

5.5 Components of Relational Databases and Technical Terms

A relational database consists of various components. In this section you will be guided through the most important terms that are often used when working with relational databases. Knowing the meaning of the most important words used in the database arena is important in order to understand the next few chapters of this book.

- **Tables and relations**—Every database consists of fundamental components called *relations*. Relations are tables consisting of various lines and a fixed number of columns.

- **Primary keys**—In order to identify a row of data, every table should have a column containing unique values. This column is called the primary key of a table. A column that is the primary key must not contain duplicated entries. Every sophisticated database will take care of that in order to satisfy the demands of the relational database concept. In the case of PostgreSQL, a table need not have a primary key—primary keys are optional.

- **Foreign keys**—Foreign keys are columns that are related to a certain column in a second table. The values in a foreign key column are treated according to the constraints defined for the column.

- **Constraints**—Constraints are attributes defined for a certain object. Constraints can either be restrictions or rules on how to perform certain operations.

- **Data types**—Every column in a table must have a predefined data type. In contrast to some programming languages, PostgreSQL, like most other databases, has strict rules concerning data types. For instance, a column defined as date must not contain values other than dates.

- **Indexes**—To speed up queries, indexes can be used. Internally indexes are a complex tree structure that allows fast access to individual records.

- **Sequences**—Sequences can be used to generate consecutively listed numbers that are unique. Even in case of concurrent accesses to the sequence, PostgreSQL will make sure that every number in the list can only be used once. To guarantee that the value returned by the sequence is unique, accessing the current value of the sequence will automatically increment the value of the sequence.

- **Joins**—In the relational database model, data is stored in tables. If information from more than just one table has to be retrieved from the database, so-called joins have to be performed. Joining means that tables are connected with each other by using a common column.

- **Triggers**—All sophisticated databases support triggers. Triggers are a feature that can be used to start certain functions whenever a predefined event occurs. Triggers are defined on tables and can fire when INSERT, UPDATE, or DELETE operations occur.

- **Views**—Views are virtual tables. This means that users can select data from a view just as they can from a table. However, in reality, a view is not a real table but the result of executing a SQL statement. Performing INSERT and UPDATE operations can only be done by defining rules that tell PostgreSQL what to do in case of INSERT or UPDATE.

- **Aggregate expressions**—Aggregate expressions are used to perform operations with multiple lines returned by a query.

- **Aggregate functions**—Aggregate functions are used to perform data calculations, like maximum, minimum, or average.

5.6 Summary

The original relation model was developed by E. F. Codd three decades ago. The main idea of the model is that all data is stored in tables that are related to each other.

The object-oriented model adds various additional features such as inheritance to the relational concept.

In order to build flexible and easy-to-understand database models, many different approaches can be used. One way is to use normalization as proposed by Codd's theory. Normalization is used to avoid redundancies, to make your model more flexible and easier to understand.

6

Installing PostgreSQL

To work with PostgreSQL, you need to find out whether your operating system is supported. In general, every system on which an ANSI C compiler is available should be able to run PostgreSQL. The list of platforms supported by PostgreSQL is constantly growing. Table 6.1 contains a list of all platforms supported by PostgreSQL 7.2.

TABLE 6.1 Platforms Supported by PostgreSQL 7.2

OS	Processor
AIX 4.3.3	RS6000
BeOS 5.0.4	x86
BSD/OS 4.01	x86
FreeBSD 4.4	x86
HP-UX	PA-RISC
IRIX 6.5.11	MIPS
Linux 2.2.x	Alpha
Linux 2.2.x	armv4l
Linux 2.0.x	MIPS
Linux 2.2.18	PPC74xx
Linux	S/390
Linux 2.2.15	Sparc
Linux	x86
MacOS X	PPC
NetBSD 1.5	Alpha
NetBSD 1.5E	arm32
NetBSD	m68k
NetBSD	PPC
NetBSD	Sparc
NetBSD 1.5	VAX
NetBSD 1.5	x86
OpenBSD 2.8	Sparc
OpenBSD 2.8	x86
SCO UnixWare 7.1.1	x86
Solaris 2.7-8	Sparc

TABLE 6.1   Continued

OS	Processor
Solaris 2.8	x86
SunOS 4.1.4	Sparc
Tru64 Unix	Alpha
Windows NT/2000 with Cygwin	x86

These platforms have been tested with the most recent version of PostgreSQL. However, additional platforms, as shown in Table 6.2, are also capable of running PostgreSQL, but not all of them are officially supported.

TABLE 6.2   Platforms Not Officially Supported by PostgreSQL 7.2

OS	Processor
DGUX 5.4R4.11	m88k
MkLinux DR1	PPC750
NextStep	x86
QNX 4.25	x86
SCO OpenServer 5	x86
System V R4	m88k
System V R4	MIPS
Ultrix	MIPS
Ultrix	VAX
Windows 9x, Me, NT, 2000, OS/2 (native)	x86; native mode only applied to the C-Client library (libpq) and the interactive terminal (psql). There was also a build of libpq and psql for OS/2 Warp in 6.3.x or 6.4.x.

These platforms are not officially supported but will most likely work with PostgreSQL 6.3.x or later.

After you have found out whether your system is capable of running PostgreSQL, you can start installing the database.

6.1 Installing PostgreSQL on Unix

In general two ways of installing PostgreSQL are available. On the one hand, it is possible to install precompiled binaries that are available for the most widespread Unix systems. On the other hand, it is possible to install and compile the source code of PostgreSQL. Both methods are covered extensively in this section.

6.1.1 Installing Binaries

Installing binary packages is in most cases much more comfortable than installing the source code of PostgreSQL because it can be done much faster and it's difficult to do something wrong. Binaries are available for all major Linux distributions such as Red Hat and Mandrake.

In this section you will learn to deal with PostgreSQL binaries on Linux Debian and Linux Red Hat.

6.1.1.1 Installing and Removing RPM Packages

Installing RPM packages is an easy task. Download the latest RPM packages from a PostgreSQL mirror near you and install them with a simple shell command:

```
[root@router postgres]# rpm -Uvh *rpm
Preparing...                ########################################### [100%]
   1:postgresql-docs        ########################################### [  7%]
   2:postgresql-jdbc        ########################################### [ 15%]
   3:postgresql-libs        ########################################### [ 23%]
   4:postgresql             ########################################### [ 30%]
   5:postgresql-contrib     ########################################### [ 38%]
   6:postgresql-devel       ########################################### [ 46%]
   7:postgresql-odbc        ########################################### [ 53%]
   8:postgresql-perl        ########################################### [ 61%]
   9:postgresql-python      ########################################### [ 69%]
  10:postgresql-server      ########################################### [ 76%]
  11:postgresql-tcl         ########################################### [ 84%]
  12:postgresql-test        ########################################### [ 92%]
  13:postgresql-tk          ########################################### [100%]
```

-U makes sure that all packages are updated if an older version of PostgreSQL is already installed. v and h can be used to generate easy-to-read output. On some systems a package called mx might be missing and therefore rpm fails. In this case --nodeps can be added to the RPM command so that no dependencies will be checked. If the mx package is missing, this won't affect PostgreSQL.

Some Linux systems such as SuSE Linux provide tools like Yast to install and remove binary packages. These tools have a graphical user interface and can easily be used. However, on all RPM-based systems, PostgreSQL can also be installed using a fixed set of shell commands.

After packages have been installed, it might be necessary to remove them from the system. Removing packages can also be done using RPM. If you want to find out which PostgreSQL packages are installed on your system, use the following command:

```
[root@router /root]# rpm -qva | grep postgresql | sed -e 's/-7.*//gi'
postgresql-docs
postgresql-devel
postgresql-tk
postgresql-tcl
postgresql-contrib
postgresql-server
postgresql
postgresql-libs
postgresql-jdbc
postgresql-python
postgresql-perl
postgresql-odbc
postgresql-test
```

rpm -qva returns a list of all packages installed on the system. From this list you can easily extract all packages related to PostgreSQL by piping the list to the grep command. Now that you have all PostgreSQL packages, you can easily remove the version number of the packages using good old sed. The remaining list can now be used by PRM to remove the packages. With the help of the following command, all PostgreSQL packages are removed:

```
[root@router /root]# rpm -ev `rpm -qva | grep postgresql |
sed -e 's/-7.*//gi' ` --nodeps
error: cannot remove /var/lib/pgsql/data - directory not empty
error: cannot remove /var/lib/pgsql - directory not empty
error: cannot remove /usr/share/pgsql - directory not empty
error: cannot remove /usr/lib/pgsql - directory not empty
error: cannot remove /usr/share/man/man1 - directory not empty
error: cannot remove /usr/lib/perl5/site_perl/5.6.0/i386-linux/auto/Pg -
directory not empty
```

The command generating the list of PostgreSQL packages installed on the system is added to rpm -ev --nodeps. With the help of command-line substitution, the list of files will be passed to rpm -ev --nodeps. --nodeps makes sure that RPM does not check for dependencies. This can be useful when substituting packages. If you want to install qmail instead of sendmail, for instance, it is useful to uninstall sendmail using the --nodeps flag because otherwise you'd have to uninstall half of the system to fulfill all dependencies before installing qmail.

As you can see, some errors are displayed on the screen. PostgreSQL does not delete the directory where databases are located because this might lead to trouble. Therefore error messages are displayed to tell the user that some components still reside on the system.

6.1.1.2 Installing and Removing Debian Packages

Debian is not based on RPM because it has its own package managing system. Installing and removing Debian packages can easily be done using `dselect`, which has a curses-based user interface.

If you want to install PostgreSQL using a shell command, you can use `dpkg`.

If recent Debian packages are not available, you can generate them with the help of `alien`. Alien is a package for converting Unix packages from one format to another. With `alien`, it is an easy task to generate Debian packages out of RPM packages.

To download `alien`, check out `http://kitenet.net/programs/alien`.

6.1.1.3 Starting PostgreSQL

Now that PostgreSQL has been installed successfully, it is time to start the database daemon so that the server can be accessed.

If you have installed the binary packages, this can easily be done with the help of init scripts, which are included in PostgreSQL's binary distribution. In the case of Red Hat Linux, PostgreSQL can easily be started as follows:

```
[root@router /root]# /etc/rc.d/init.d/postgresql start
Initializing database:                              [  OK  ]
Starting postgresql service:                        [  OK  ]
```

The script checks whether the server has been started the first time and takes appropriate action. Now PostgreSQL can be accessed from the local host.

If you are not using Red Hat Linux, the init scripts might be located in a different directory. In the case of Debian Linux, the init scripts can be found in `/etc/init.d`.

6.1.2 Installing the Source Code

When you want to run the latest version of PostgreSQL, it is useful to install the source code of PostgreSQL instead of the binary distribution. The advantage of installing the source code is that you know perfectly well what you have done and which flags have been set. In addition, it gives you great flexibility and you can add your own extensions to PostgreSQL. If there are no binaries available, you have to install the source code.

Installing the source code is not difficult and can easily be done.

6.1.2.1 Compiling PostgreSQL

The following procedure works for Unix-based operating systems. The first thing to do is to download the latest version of PostgreSQL on your hard disk.

After you've completed the download, extract the tar archive using a simple shell command:

```
[root@athlon postgres]# tar xvfz postgresql-7.2.tar.gz
```

A directory containing the source code will be generated. In the next step, PostgreSQL must be configured. Enter the directory and run configure to see which flags can be set:

```
[root@athlon postgresql-7.2]# ./configure --help
Usage: configure [options] [host]
Options: [defaults in brackets after descriptions]
Configuration:
  --cache-file=FILE      cache test results in FILE
  --help                 print this message
  --no-create            do not create output files
  --quiet, --silent      do not print `checking...' messages
  --version              print the version of autoconf that created configure
Directory and file names:
  --prefix=PREFIX        install architecture-independent files in PREFIX
                         [/usr/local/pgsql]
  --exec-prefix=EPREFIX  install architecture-dependent files in EPREFIX
                         [same as prefix]
  --bindir=DIR           user executables in DIR [EPREFIX/bin]
  --sbindir=DIR          system admin executables in DIR [EPREFIX/sbin]
  --libexecdir=DIR       program executables in DIR [EPREFIX/libexec]
  --datadir=DIR          read-only architecture-independent data in DIR
                         [PREFIX/share]
  --sysconfdir=DIR       read-only single-machine data in DIR [PREFIX/etc]
  --sharedstatedir=DIR   modifiable architecture-independent data in DIR
                         [PREFIX/com]
  --localstatedir=DIR    modifiable single-machine data in DIR [PREFIX/var]
  --libdir=DIR           object code libraries in DIR [EPREFIX/lib]
  --includedir=DIR       C header files in DIR [PREFIX/include]
  --oldincludedir=DIR    C header files for non-gcc in DIR [/usr/include]
  --docdir=DIR           doc documentation in DIR [PREFIX/doc]
  --mandir=DIR           man documentation in DIR [PREFIX/man]
  --srcdir=DIR           find the sources in DIR [configure dir or ..]
  --program-prefix=PREFIX prepend PREFIX to installed program names
  --program-suffix=SUFFIX append SUFFIX to installed program names
  --program-transform-name=PROGRAM
                         run sed PROGRAM on installed program names
```

```
Host type:
  --build=BUILD           configure for building on BUILD [BUILD=HOST]
  --host=HOST             configure for HOST [guessed]
  --target=TARGET         configure for TARGET [TARGET=HOST]
Features and packages:
  --disable-FEATURE       do not include FEATURE (same as --enable-FEATURE=no)
  --enable-FEATURE[=ARG]  include FEATURE [ARG=yes]
  --with-PACKAGE[=ARG]    use PACKAGE [ARG=yes]
  --without-PACKAGE       do not use PACKAGE (same as --with-PACKAGE=no)
  --x-includes=DIR        X include files are in DIR
  --x-libraries=DIR       X library files are in DIR
--enable and --with options recognized:
  --with-includes=DIRS    look for additional header files in DIRS
  --with-libraries=DIRS   look for additional libraries in DIRS
  --with-libs=DIRS        alternative spelling of --with-libraries
  --enable-locale         enable locale support
  --enable-recode         enable character set recode support
  --enable-multibyte      enable multibyte character support
  --enable-nls[=LANGUAGES]    enable Native Language Support
  --with-pgport=PORTNUM   change default port number [5432]
  --with-maxbackends=N    set default maximum number of connections [32]
  --disable-shared        do not build shared libraries
  --disable-rpath         do not embed shared library search path in executables
  --enable-debug          build with debugging symbols (-g)
  --enable-depend         turn on automatic dependency tracking
  --enable-cassert        enable assertion checks (for debugging)
  --with-tcl              build Tcl and Tk interfaces
  --without-tk            do not build Tk interfaces if Tcl is enabled
  --with-tclconfig=DIR    tclConfig.sh and tkConfig.sh are in DIR
  --with-tkconfig=DIR     tkConfig.sh is in DIR
  --with-perl             build Perl interface and PL/Perl
  --with-python           build Python interface module
  --with-java             build JDBC interface and Java tools
  --with-krb4[=DIR]       build with Kerberos 4 support [/usr/athena]
  --with-krb5[=DIR]       build with Kerberos 5 support [/usr/athena]
  --with-krb-srvnam=NAME  name of the service principal in Kerberos [postgres]
  --with-pam[=DIR]        build with PAM support [/usr]
  --with-openssl[=DIR]    build with OpenSSL support [/usr/local/ssl]
  --enable-odbc           build the ODBC driver package
  --with-unixodbc         build ODBC driver for unixODBC
  --with-iodbc            build ODBC driver for iODBC
  --with-odbcinst=DIR     default directory for odbcinst.ini [sysconfdir]
```

```
--with-CXX              build C++ modules (libpq++)
--with-gnu-ld           assume the C compiler uses GNU ld [default=no]
--enable-syslog         enable logging to syslog
```

As you can see, the list of flags seems to be endless and in most cases, you will need only a few of these flags. In many cases you will need additional libraries in order to make PostgreSQL compile properly. Let's have a look at the most important flags you will need to compile PostgreSQL (this is not a complete reference).

- `--prefix=PREFIX`—This flag defines where PostgreSQL's binaries should be installed. Usually this flag is set to define the root directory of PostgreSQL.

- `--datadir=DIR`—This flag defines where the templates of your database will be installed. This is not the directory where your database will be located—this is the directory where the files used to create databases will be stored.

- `--enable-locale`—Local support is very often needed when working with non-English data. This flag will cause a small decrease in performance.

- `--enable-recode`—This flag can be used to recode single-byte characters. For users of the Cyrillic language set, this will be an essential flag, but it can also be used for other character sets.

- `--enable-multibyte`—For users of languages like Japanese, Korean, and Chinese, this flag is required because one character cannot be stored in one byte.

- `--enable-nls[=LANGUAGES]`—Every language has its specific characters and symbols. With the help of this flag, it is possible to use languages other than English.

- `--with-pgport=NUMBER`—Usually port 5432 (TCP) is used as the default port. If you want to use another port as the default value, this flag has to be set.

- `--with-CXX`—If you need the C++ interface to PostgreSQL, this flag has to be enabled.

- `--with-perl`—Builds the Perl modules and installs them in the place where Perl modules are usually installed on your system.

- `--with-python`—To build the Python modules, this flag has to be enabled.

- `--with-tcl`—Builds the TCL/Tk components of PostgreSQL.

- `--without-tk`—This flag will cause PostgreSQL not to build the Tk components of the TCL/Tk modules. If you are working with console applications, this might be useful for you.

- `--enable-odbc`—Builds the ODBC driver.

- `--with-iodbc`—Builds the ODBC driver for the iODBC driver instead of the unixODBC driver.

- `--with-unixodbc`—Builds ODBC for the unixODBC driver.

- `--with-krb5=DIRECTORY`—Builds Kerberos 5 support for PostgreSQL. Only one version of Kerberos can be enabled at a time (either 4 or 5).

- `--with-openssl=DIRECTORY`—To use PostgreSQL with SSL, this flag must be enabled and the path to the OpenSSL installation must be defined.

- `--with-java`—To build Java support, ant must be installed on your system; otherwise, compiling the sources will fail.

- `--enable-syslog`—This flag enables syslog, but it does not mean that syslog has to be used for logging.

In addition, compiler flags can be passed to `configure` using environment variables:

- `CC` and `CXX`—Defines a C or C++ compiler. Using these flags, it is possible to select a C compiler that would not be used by `configure`.

- `CFLAGS` and `CXXFLAGS`—Both variables can be used to pass flags to the C and C++ compiler. In case of Mac OS X, `-flat-namespace` should be used.

After you have seen which flags are accepted by `configure`, it is time to configure PostgreSQL. Therefore it is useful to write a short shell script, which in this example is called `compile.sh`. This is not necessary, but it will help you to remember how the current version of PostgreSQL has been compiled:

```
#!/bin/sh

env CFLAGS=' -march=athlon -O3 ' ./configure --prefix=/usr/local/postgresql \
        --enable-locale --enable-recode --enable-multibyte --with-tcl \
        --with-perl --with-python --with-openssl=/usr/share/ssl \
        --enable-odbc --with-unixodbc --with-CXX

make
make install         .
```

Before you can start `compile.sh`, it is necessary to create the directory where the binaries will be installed:

```
[root@athlon postgresql-7.2]# mkdir /usr/local/postgresql
```

As you can see, the name of the directory created is the same as you have defined in `compile.sh`.

Two flags are passed to `configure` via the environment variable `CFLAGS`. `-march=athlon` tells GCC to optimize the code for Athlon CPUs, and `-O3` tells GCC that functions can be substituted by inline code, which in some cases leads to faster code. If you are not using AMD CPUs as we have in this example, you can optimize the code for any other CPU. For information about other hardware architectures and optimization, check out the `man` pages of the compiler you are planning to use. Keep in mind that these flags passed to `configure` are optional and need not be defined.

In addition to `--prefix`, multibyte support and some flags related to languages are also enabled. Interfaces to Tcl, Perl, Python, and C++ will also be built. To compile SSL, you can see that the directory of the local SSL installation has been defined. The directory in the script works for Red Hat 7.1—if you want to build SSL support for other distributions, check out the documentation of the software you are using. For building ODBC, two flags have been set. First ODBC is enabled. The second flag tells that the interface should be built for `unixODBC`, which is included in Red Hat 7.1. In general two ODBC drivers for Unix are available. In addition to `unixODBC`, `iODBC` can be used. Depending on the Linux distribution you are using, the driver installed on your system may vary.

Now that the server has been configured, `make` is used to compile the code. With the help of `make install`, the binaries are copied to the desired location.

6.1.2.2 Creating a Database Cluster

Before you can start PostgreSQL, it is necessary to create a set of databases, which in PostgreSQL is called a *database cluster*. A database cluster contains a set of database templates plus the database you will define. To create a database cluster, it is first necessary to create a user for running PostgreSQL. Usually this user is called postgres. To create a new user, you can use `useradd`:

```
[root@athlon postgresql-7.2]# useradd postgres
```

If no error is displayed, the user has successfully been added to the system. Now it is time to assign a password to the new user:

```
[root@athlon postgresql-7.2]# passwd postgres
Changing password for user postgres
New Unix password:
Retype new Unix password:
passwd: all authentication tokens updated successfully
```

The password has to be passed to the system twice so that the operating system can make sure that everything is correct.

In the next step you can create a directory where the database cluster should be located. This can easily be done by using mkdir. Make sure that the owner and the group of the directory are changed to the right user after you have created it:

```
[root@athlon postgresql-7.2]# mkdir /var/pgdb
[root@athlon postgresql-7.2]# chown postgres.postgres /var/pgdb/
```

Now the bin directory of PostgreSQL has to be added to the path so that the shell can find the executables. This can be done in /etc/profile by adding the appropriate directory to $PATH.

After you've performed all the steps described in this section, a database cluster can finally be generated using initdb:

```
bash-2.04$ initdb -L /usr/local/postgresql/share/ -D /var/pgdb/
The files belonging to this database system will be owned by user "postgres".
This user must also own the server process.

Fixing permissions on existing directory /var/pgdb/... ok
creating directory /var/pgdb//base... ok
creating directory /var/pgdb//global... ok
creating directory /var/pgdb//pg_xlog... ok
creating directory /var/pgdb//pg_clog... ok
creating template1 database in /var/pgdb//base/1... ok
creating configuration files... ok
initializing pg_shadow... ok
enabling unlimited row size for system tables... ok
creating system views... ok
loading pg_description... ok
vacuuming database template1... ok
copying template1 to template0... ok

Success. You can now start the database server using:

    /usr/local/postgresql/bin/postmaster -D /var/pgdb/
or
    /usr/local/postgresql/bin/pg_ctl -D /var/pgdb/ -l logfile start
```

If no error was displayed on the screen, a new database cluster has been added to the system.

6.1.2.3 Starting and Stopping PostgreSQL

If a database cluster has been created, you can start the database now. Starting the database means that a daemon called postmaster has to be started. This can be done in two ways: The postmaster can be started directly, or the postmaster can be started by pg_ctl.

Let's have a look at the command-line parameters the postmaster accepts:

```
bash-2.04$ postmaster --help
postmaster is the PostgreSQL server.

Usage:
  postmaster [options...]

Options:
  -B NBUFFERS       number of shared buffers (default 64)
  -c NAME=VALUE     set run-time parameter
  -d 1-5            debugging level
  -D DATADIR        database directory
  -F                turn fsync off
  -h HOSTNAME       host name or IP address to listen on
  -i                enable TCP/IP connections
  -k DIRECTORY      Unix-domain socket location
  -l                enable SSL connections
  -N MAX-CONNECT    maximum number of allowed connections (default 32)
  -o OPTIONS        pass 'OPTIONS' to each backend server
  -p PORT           port number to listen on (default 5432)
  -S                silent mode (start in background without logging output)

Developer options:
  -n                do not reinitialize shared memory after abnormal exit
  -s                send SIGSTOP to all backend servers if one dies

Please read the documentation for the complete list of run-time
configuration settings and how to set them on the command line or in
the configuration file.

Report bugs to <pgsql-bugs@postgresql.org>.
```

As you can see, the postmaster accepts many parameters and many things can be defined when starting the daemon. One of the most important flags is the -D flag, which defines the database cluster the postmaster should work on. Another flag you should not forget about is the -i flag. If this flag is not enabled, PostgreSQL will not accept TCP/IP connections. Without -i, PostgreSQL is only capable of accepting local connections. Many people forget about this and have problems connecting PostgreSQL to the Internet.

Normally the postmaster is not started directly. In most cases it is started using pg_ctl. Using pg_ctl has many advantages because it allows you to start and shut down PostgreSQL comfortably and in a secure way. Let's have a look at the syntax overview of pg_ctl:

```
bash-2.04$ pg_ctl --help
pg_ctl is a utility to start, stop, restart, reload configuration files,
or report the status of a PostgreSQL server.

Usage:
  pg_ctl start   [-w] [-D DATADIR] [-s] [-l FILENAME] [-o "OPTIONS"]
  pg_ctl stop    [-W] [-D DATADIR] [-s] [-m SHUTDOWN-MODE]
  pg_ctl restart [-w] [-D DATADIR] [-s] [-m SHUTDOWN-MODE] [-o "OPTIONS"]
  pg_ctl reload  [-D DATADIR] [-s]
  pg_ctl status  [-D DATADIR]


Common options:
  -D DATADIR         Location of the database storage area
  -s                 Only print errors, no informational messages
  -w                 Wait until operation completes
  -W                 Do not wait until operation completes
(The default is to wait for shutdown, but not for start or restart.)


If the -D option is omitted, the environment variable PGDATA is used.


Options for start or restart:
  -l FILENAME        Write (or append) server log to FILENAME.  The
                     use of this option is highly recommended.
  -o OPTIONS         Command line options to pass to the postmaster
                     (PostgreSQL server executable)
  -p PATH-TO-POSTMASTER Normally not necessary


Options for stop or restart:
  -m SHUTDOWN-MODE   May be 'smart', 'fast', or 'immediate'


Shutdown modes are:
  smart              Quit after all clients have disconnected
  fast               Quit directly, with proper shutdown
```

```
immediate                    Quit without complete shutdown; will lead
                             to recovery run on restart
```

Report bugs to <pgsql-bugs@postgresql.org>.

pg_ctl accepts many parameters as well. Keep in mind that pg_ctl does nothing except start the postmaster. Therefore -D must also be defined to tell the postmaster which database cluster should be used. If you want to create a logfile containing all information returned by the database, server -l has to be used. Writing the logging information into a file is highly recommended because it allows you to keep track of what is going on inside your database. In some cases it might also help you to debug your applications. -o can be used to pass parameters to the backend processes, which are responsible for handling connections to the database. This is very important because it allows you to configure the database to your needs while it is running. One parameter that has to be passed to the postmaster is the -i flag. As you can see, pg_ctl does not provide a -i flag itself, so it has to be sent to the postmaster using -o.

Let's start the postmaster with the help of pg_ctl:

```
bash-2.04$ pg_ctl -D /var/pgdb/ -l /tmp/postgresql.log -o "-i" start
postmaster successfully started
```

-D tells PostgreSQL to use the database cluster you have created before. The logging information will be stored in /tmp/postgresql.log. All values defined by -o are passed to the postmaster process. In this example, you want -i to be passed to the back end.

To see if PostgreSQL has been started successfully, you can use ps in combination with grep. ps ax lists all processes running on the system, and grep post makes sure that only those processes belonging to PostgreSQL are displayed:

```
bash-2.04$ ps ax | grep post
29459 pts/2    S       0:00 su - postgres
29546 pts/2    SW      0:00 su postgres
29882 pts/2    S       0:00 /usr/local/postgresql/bin/postmaster -i
29883 pts/2    S       0:00 postgres: stats buffer process
29885 pts/2    S       0:00 postgres: stats collector process
29888 pts/2    S       0:00 grep post
```

As you can see, three processes are running. Those of you who are running PostgreSQL < 7.2 will see that only one process is running.

To stop PostgreSQL again, you can use `pg_ctl` as well:

```
bash-2.04$ pg_ctl -D /var/pgdb/ stop
waiting for postmaster to shut down......done
postmaster successfully shut down
```

Because many `postmaster` processes can run simultaneously, it is necessary to define the location of the database the `postmaster` you want to shut down is operating on.

If you want to run many `postmaster`s at once, every `postmaster` needs its own database cluster to work with—it is not possible to start two `postmaster`s working on just one cluster. You also have to make sure that every `postmaster` has its own TCP port to listen to. Otherwise PostgreSQL is not able to find out which request is related to which `postmaster` process.

As you can see, PostgreSQL provides several methods for shutting down. Depending on how fast the database should quit, the user can decide which method is best to use. With the help of the `-m` flag, you can choose what kind of shutdown you consider to be useful.

6.2 Installing PostgreSQL on Windows

Installing PostgreSQL on Microsoft Windows differs significantly from installing it on Unix. However, PostgreSQL can be run on Windows reliably and many people have chosen Windows as their default platform.

People using PostgreSQL on Windows usually use the binary distribution of PostgreSQL, which is included in Red Hat's Cygwin package. Cygwin is a product that provides a rich set of Unix tools for Windows users. One of these packages is PostgreSQL.

6.2.1 Installing the Cygwin Tools

To install Cygwin, check out `http://sources.redhat.com/cygwin/` and click on Install Cygwin now to download a file called `setup.exe`. Start `setup.exe` and follow the instructions to install Cygwin. PostgreSQL is part of the Cygwin binary distribution and need not be installed manually.

Usually people install the binary distribution and don't install PostgreSQL from source because many platform-dependent questions have to be taken into consideration when compiling PostgreSQL on Windows machines.

6.2.2 Preparing Windows for PostgreSQL

The most important thing when working with Windows is to install the `cygipc` package. Because Windows does not provide a useful shared memory interface, this daemon is necessary; otherwise, there is no way to start the `postmaster` daemon.

After installing the `cygipc` package, the `postmaster` can be started on Windows just as you would start the `postmaster` on a Unix machine by using `pg_ctl`.

To download `cygipc`, check out
`http://www.neuro.gatech.edu/users/cwilson/cygutils/V1.1/cygipc/`.

Do not use versions prior to 1.04; they will not work with PostgreSQL.

To install the shared memory daemon, unpack the source and follow the instructions in the `README` file.

In the next step you have to add the path of Cygwin's `bin` directory to the path on your system. Make sure that this directory is the first one in the list because of the sort command. Cygwin's `sort.exe` must be found before the `sort.exe` command provided by Windows.

On Windows versions based on NT technology (Windows NT, Windows 2000, Windows XP), the ipc daemon can be installed as a service. To start the service you can use:

```
net start ipc-daemon
```

On systems based on DOS technology such as Windows 95, Windows 98, or Windows Me, the following command must be used:

```
ipc-daemon &
```

6.2.3 Running PostgreSQL on Windows

After starting the `cygipc` daemon, PostgreSQL can be used just as on Unix machines.

The first thing you have to do is to create a database cluster. This can be done with the help of the `createdb` command. If no error has occurred, the `postmaster` daemon can be started using `pg_ctl`.

6.3 Creating and Removing Databases

After creating the database cluster and starting PostgreSQL, it is time to create a database. Before you see how to do this, you will learn to find out which databases are already installed on the system:

```
bash-2.04$ psql -l
        List of databases
  Name    |  Owner   | Encoding
----------+----------+-----------
 template0 | postgres | SQL_ASCII
 template1 | postgres | SQL_ASCII
(2 rows)
```

psql -l displays a list of all databases available on the system. As you can see, two databases are installed. These two databases are essential for PostgreSQL. template1 contains all data types and system tables a database usually has. Every database created will inherit all these data types and system tables from template1. This is a very comfortable feature because if you want to change the layout of all databases, you can simply modify template1 to your needs and all databases created after template1 will automatically contain these changes.

Creating databases can be done using a command called createdb:

```
bash-2.04$ createdb --help
createdb creates a PostgreSQL database.

Usage:
  createdb [options] dbname [description]

Options:
  -D, --location=PATH         Alternative place to store the database
  -T, --template=TEMPLATE     Template database to copy
  -E, --encoding=ENCODING     Multibyte encoding for the database
  -h, --host=HOSTNAME         Database server host
  -p, --port=PORT             Database server port
  -U, --username=USERNAME     Username to connect as
  -W, --password              Prompt for password
  -e, --echo                  Show the query being sent to the backend
  -q, --quiet                 Don't write any messages

By default, a database with the same name as the current user is created.

Report bugs to <pgsql-bugs@postgresql.org>.
```

createdb is a very powerful and easy-to-use tool. It allows you to create databases on local and remote hosts. You can also define which character set should be used by the database. Although createdb provides many options, it is just a very small shell script. This shows how efficiently PostgreSQL works and how well the server has been implemented by the PostgreSQL development team.

Let's create a database:

```
bash-2.04$ createdb phpbook -e
CREATE DATABASE "phpbook"
CREATE DATABASE
```

You have created a database called phpbook. No character set has been defined, so PostgreSQL will take the default character set, which in this case is SQL_ASCII. In most cases SQL_ASCII will be enough and the character set does not have to be changed. When working with languages like Chinese, however, the character set has to be defined and set to the correct language. Because Chinese is beyond the scope of this book, we have decided to stick with English.

-e tells createdb to display the SQL command used to generate the database on the screen. As you can see, the SQL code is not complicated.

After creating the database, you can see it in the list generated by psql -l.

```
bash-2.04$ psql -l
        List of databases
   Name    |  Owner   | Encoding
-----------+----------+-----------
 phpbook   | postgres | SQL_ASCII
 template0 | postgres | SQL_ASCII
 template1 | postgres | SQL_ASCII
(3 rows)
```

If not defined differently, the database is owned by postgres, which is the superuser on the system.

To remove a database from the system, dropdb can be used. The syntax of dropdb can easily be listed by using dropdb -help:

```
bash-2.04$ dropdb --help
dropdb removes a PostgreSQL database.

Usage:
  dropdb [options] dbname

Options:
  -h, --host=HOSTNAME        Database server host
  -p, --port=PORT            Database server port
  -U, --username=USERNAME    Username to connect as
  -W, --password             Prompt for password
  -i, --interactive          Prompt before deleting anything
```

```
-e, --echo                    Show the query being sent to the backend
-q, --quiet                   Don't write any messages
```

Report bugs to <pgsql-bugs@postgresql.org>.

To drop the database you have just created, you can use the following:

```
bash-2.04$ dropdb phpbook
DROP DATABASE
```

Now the database has successfully been removed from the system again.

As you can see, creating and removing databases is an easy task. Simply use `createdb` and `dropdb` to create and remove databases. These two commands can also be used to work on a remote host. However, you need the rights to access PostgreSQL on the remote machine.

6.4 The User Interface

You have seen how to create a database cluster and how to create and remove databases, and it is time to learn about PostgreSQL's user interface. The standard front end that is included in the core distribution of PostgreSQL is called `psql`. `psql` is an interactive tool for communicating with a PostgreSQL database. A database accessed by `psql` need not be situated on the local machine because `psql` can even communicate with remote machines.

```
bash-2.04$ createdb phpbook -e
CREATE DATABASE "phpbook"
CREATE DATABASE
```

After creating the database, you can start `psql` to work with the database interactively. Therefore you simply have to pass the name of the database to `psql`:

```
bash-2.04$ psql phpbook
Welcome to psql, the PostgreSQL interactive terminal.

Type:  \copyright for distribution terms
       \h for help with SQL commands
       \? for help on internal slash commands
       \g or terminate with semicolon to execute query
       \q to quit


phpbook=#
```

If no error has occurred, you will be in an interactive shell where you can send
queries to the server. To see if PostgreSQL works correctly, you can write a query that
does nothing but compute the sum of 1+1:

```
phpbook=# SELECT 1+1;
 ?column?
----------
        2
(1 row)
```

Not surprisingly, the result returned by the database is 2.

Sometimes queries are longer than just one line. PostgreSQL will execute the string
until the first semicolon is found. If you are in the middle of a command, the
command prompt will look slightly different, as you can see in the following
example:

```
phpbook=# SELECT 1+
phpbook-# 1
phpbook-# ;
 ?column?
----------
        2
(1 row)
```

After you have performed your first steps with the PostgreSQL interactive terminal,
you will be guided through some features of psql that make this tool powerful and
comfortable.

To find out more about psql, you can use \? to get a list of all commands provided
by the shell:

```
phpbook=# \?
 \a              toggle between unaligned and aligned output mode
 \c[onnect] [DBNAME|- [USER]]
                 connect to new database (currently "phpbook")
 \C TITLE        set table title
 \cd [DIRNAME]   change the current working directory
 \copy ...       perform SQL COPY with data stream to the client host
 \copyright      show PostgreSQL usage and distribution terms
 \d TABLE        describe table (or view, index, sequence)
 \d{t|i|s|v}... list tables/indexes/sequences/views
 \d{p|S|l}       list access privileges, system tables, or large objects
 \da             list aggregate functions
```

```
\dd NAME        show comment for table, type, function, or operator
\df             list functions
\do             list operators
\dT             list data types
\e FILENAME     edit the current query buffer or file with external editor
\echo TEXT      write text to standard output
\encoding ENCODING  set client encoding
\f STRING       set field separator
\g FILENAME     send SQL command to server (and write results to file or |pipe)
\h NAME         help on syntax of SQL commands, * for all commands
\H              toggle HTML output mode (currently off)
\i FILENAME     execute commands from file
\l              list all databases
\lo_export, \lo_import, \lo_list, \lo_unlink
                large object operations
\o FILENAME     send all query results to file or |pipe
\p              show the content of the current query buffer
\pset VAR       set table output option (VAR := {format|border|expanded|
                fieldsep|null|recordsep|tuples_only|title|tableattr|pager})
\q              quit psql
\qecho TEXT     write text to query output stream (see \o)
\r              reset (clear) the query buffer
\s FILENAME     print history or save it to file
\set NAME VALUE set internal variable
\t              show only rows (currently off)
\T TEXT         set HTML table tag attributes
\unset NAME     unset (delete) internal variable
\w FILENAME     write current query buffer to file
\x              toggle expanded output (currently off)
\z              list table access privileges
\! [COMMAND]    execute command in shell or start interactive shell
```

The list seems endless, but let's have a look at the most widely used commands.

Usually all commands executed by psql start with a backslash. This makes it easy to distinguish a built-in feature of psql from a command that has to be sent to the backend process, which is responsible for executing SQL code.

psql provides many useful commands for making daily life with the database easier. With the help of \d, for example, it is possible to list all relations a database contains:

```
phpbook=# \d
No relations found.
```

In this case no relations can be found because no tables have been defined yet. If \d is called with a table, a view, or any other object as the first parameter, the data structure of the table or view will be listed:

```
phpbook=# \d pg_rules
         View "pg_rules"
   Column    | Type | Modifiers
-------------+------+-----------
 tablename | name |
 rulename  | name |
 definition | text |
View definition: SELECT c.relname AS tablename, r.rulename, pg_get_ruledef
(r.rulename) AS definition FROM pg_rewrite r, pg_class c WHERE ((r.rulename
!~ '^_RET'::text) AND (c.oid = r.ev_class));
```

pg_rules is a view consisting of three columns and is defined by the SQL command listed in the definition of the view. As you can see, finding the definition of a table or a view is an easy task when using PostgreSQL's onboard tools.

In addition, it is also possible to get a list of all data types, functions, or operators available in the current database.

Another command that is widely used is \h. With the help of \h, it is possible to retrieve information about the syntax of a SQL command. If you are using \h only, you will get a list of all commands available:

```
phpbook=# \h
Available help:
  ABORT                         CREATE TABLE AS         FETCH
  ALTER GROUP                   CREATE TRIGGER          GRANT
  ALTER TABLE                   CREATE TYPE             INSERT
  ALTER USER                    CREATE USER             LISTEN
  ANALYZE                       CREATE VIEW             LOAD
  BEGIN                         DECLARE                 LOCK
  CHECKPOINT                    DELETE                  MOVE
  CLOSE                         DROP AGGREGATE          NOTIFY
  CLUSTER                       DROP DATABASE           REINDEX
  COMMENT                       DROP FUNCTION           RESET
  COMMIT                        DROP GROUP              REVOKE
  COPY                          DROP INDEX              ROLLBACK
  CREATE AGGREGATE              DROP LANGUAGE           SELECT
  CREATE CONSTRAINT TRIGGER DROP OPERATOR               SELECT INTO
  CREATE DATABASE               DROP RULE               SET
  CREATE FUNCTION               DROP SEQUENCE           SET CONSTRAINTS
```

```
CREATE GROUP          DROP TABLE          SET SESSION AUTHORIZATION
CREATE INDEX          DROP TRIGGER        SET TRANSACTION
CREATE LANGUAGE       DROP TYPE           SHOW
CREATE OPERATOR       DROP USER           TRUNCATE
CREATE RULE           DROP VIEW           UNLISTEN
CREATE SEQUENCE       END                 UPDATE
CREATE TABLE          EXPLAIN             VACUUM
```

If you need information about a specific SQL command, you can call \h and add the name of the command to it:

```
phpbook=# \h UPDATE
Command:     UPDATE
Description: update rows of a table
Syntax:
UPDATE [ ONLY ] table SET col = expression [, ...]
    [ FROM fromlist ]
    [ WHERE condition ]
```

In this example you see an overview of the UPDATE commands syntax. The description shows what parts of the command are optional and which tokens are required by PostgreSQL. All words in brackets are optional and do not have to be passed to the server.

If you want PostgreSQL to return HTML code instead of ordinary ASCII code, you can use \H to turn HTML output on:

```
phpbook=# \H
Output format is html.
phpbook=# SELECT 1+1;
<table border=1>
  <tr>
    <th align=center>?column?</th>
  </tr>
  <tr valign=top>
    <td align=right>2</td>
  </tr>
</table>
(1 row)<br>
```

This time the result of SELECT 1+1; is returned as an HTML document. To turn off HTML again, you have to use \H again:

```
phpbook=# \H
Output format is aligned.
```

To generate a list of all databases located in the database cluster you are working on, you can use \l:

```
phpbook=# \l
        List of databases
   Name     |  Owner   | Encoding
-----------+----------+-----------
 phpbook   | postgres | SQL_ASCII
 template0 | postgres | SQL_ASCII
 template1 | postgres | SQL_ASCII
(3 rows)
```

You have already seen this output in the section called "Creating and Removing Databases"—it is the same output you can also generate with the help of psql -l.

If you want to redirect the output generated by PostgreSQL to a file, \o will do the job for you. Just define a file and the output of all SQL commands sent to the server will be stored in the file:

```
phpbook=# \o /tmp/result.txt
phpbook=# SELECT 1+1;
```

The result of SELECT 1+1; will be stored in /tmp/result.txt. To make sure that this has happened, you can quit psql:

```
phpbook=# \q
```

cat will list the content of the file on the screen:

```
bash-2.04$ cat /tmp/result.txt
 ?column?
----------
        2
(1 row)
```

psql is a powerful tool. In addition to the functions you have just seen, psql provides a variety of command-line parameters you can use to access PostgreSQL.

Let's have a look at the command-line parameters accepted by psql:

```
bash-2.04$ psql --help
This is psql, the PostgreSQL interactive terminal.

Usage:
  psql [options] [dbname [username]]
```

```
Options:
  -a              Echo all input from script
  -A              Unaligned table output mode (-P format=unaligned)
  -c COMMAND      Run only single command (SQL or internal) and exit
  -d DBNAME       Specify database name to connect to (default: postgres)
  -e              Echo commands sent to server
  -E              Display queries that internal commands generate
  -f FILENAME     Execute commands from file, then exit
  -F STRING       Set field separator (default: "|") (-P fieldsep=)
  -h HOSTNAME     Specify database server host (default: local socket)
  -H              HTML table output mode (-P format=html)
  -l              List available databases, then exit
  -n              Disable enhanced command line editing (readline)
  -o FILENAME     Send query results to file (or |pipe)
  -p PORT         Specify database server port (default: 5432)
  -P VAR[=ARG]    Set printing option 'VAR' to 'ARG' (see \pset command)
  -q              Run quietly (no messages, only query output)
  -R STRING       Set record separator (default: newline) (-P recordsep=)
  -s              Single step mode (confirm each query)
  -S              Single line mode (end of line terminates SQL command)
  -t              Print rows only (-P tuples_only)
  -T TEXT         Set HTML table tag attributes (width, border) (-P tableattr=)
  -U NAME         Specify database user name (default: postgres)
  -v NAME=VALUE   Set psql variable 'NAME' to 'VALUE'
  -V              Show version information and exit
  -W              Prompt for password (should happen automatically)
  -x              Turn on expanded table output (-P expanded)
  -X              Do not read startup file (~/.psqlrc)

For more information, type "\?" (for internal commands) or "\help"
(for SQL commands) from within psql, or consult the psql section in
the PostgreSQL documentation.

Report bugs to <pgsql-bugs@postgresql.org>.
```

With the help of -c, it is possible to send a single command to the server. This is very useful when you are running PostgreSQL on a remote host or in batch mode. This way it is an easy task to use PostgreSQL's output in a shell script.

To tell psql which database has to be used, -d is provided. Depending on whether the database is located on the local machine or a remote host, you might have to use -h. With the help of -h, you can define a host psql should connect to.

If you want to connect to PostgreSQL with a different user, the default flag, `-U`, has to be used. Using this flag, you can connect to the database as any user known by the database. By default this is only the user called `postgres`.

6.5 The Architecture of PostgreSQL

In this section you will learn about the basic concepts of PostgreSQL's architecture. With this knowledge, it will be easier for you to understand the behavior of the server and to build sophisticated applications. Knowing about PostgreSQL's internals will also help you to write your own server-side extensions you can use to solve problems and challenges more efficiently and more reliably.

6.5.1 Postmasters and Children

PostgreSQL is based on a clear and easy-to-understand architecture. The key to PostgreSQL's power and stability lies in its flexibility. The entire project is built on the KISS principle (Keep It Small and Simple), which means that the server consists of easy-to-understand modules.

When you start PostgreSQL, a daemon called `postmaster` is started. This daemon starts a process for every connection established to the server. These processes started by the `postmaster` are called *backend* processes. The `postmaster` is also responsible for managing the memory usage of the system as well as things like caching and security. One backend process can only handle one connection at a time, and one `postmaster` daemon can only operate on one database cluster.

All parameters that a backend needs are passed to it by the `postmaster`, which allows dynamic reconfiguration of your server because the parameters are passed to a backend every time a connection to the server is established.

6.5.2 The Database Cluster

Every postmaster running is working on one database cluster. (In the case of PostgreSQL, a database cluster is not a set of machines but a set of databases located on one machine.) Every database cluster contains at least two databases. The database `template0` is the parent database. `template1` inherits everything from `template0`. `template1` contains everything a new PostgreSQL database normally consists of, such as system tables and a set of data types.

Every database created on the system will inherit all components of `template1` if not defined otherwise. Every new database is an exact copy of `template1`, which means that it contains all data types and all system tables that `template1` contains as well. However, if `template1` is modified after a database has been created, these modifications will not be inherited by the new databases. PostgreSQL does not support dynamic inheritance. This has some significant advantages because every database in the database cluster is an independent island of data that cannot be influenced by other databases. However, if, for instance, a new data type is introduced, all new databases will automatically contain this data type if it has been inserted into template1. All databases that will need this data type as well have to be modified separately.

PostgreSQL's way of treating databases within a cluster makes PostgreSQL extremely flexible. It allows you to define groups of databases that have their own sets of functions and data types. Especially when working with extensions to PostgreSQL, this is extremely comfortable because you can work with many different versions of one data type by simply using it in various databases. This allows you to separate your development environment from the production system (if it is located on the same machine).

6.6 License

PostgreSQL is freely available under the terms of the BSD license. This license allows the user to modify and use the source code without restrictions. We have included the full text of PostgreSQL's copyright agreement:

```
PostgreSQL Data Base Management System

Portions Copyright (c) 1996-2001, PostgreSQL Global Development Group

This software is based on Postgres95, formerly known as Postgres, which
contains the following notice:

Portions Copyright(c) 1994 - 7 Regents of the University of California

Permission to use, copy, modify, and distribute this software and its
documentation for any purpose, without fee, and without a written agreement
is hereby granted, provided that the above copyright notice and this paragraph
and the following two paragraphs appear in all copies.

IN NO EVENT SHALL THE UNIVERSITY OF CALIFORNIA BE LIABLE TO ANY PARTY FOR
DIRECT, INDIRECT, SPECIAL, INCIDENTAL, OR CONSEQUENTIAL DAMAGES, INCLUDING LOST
PROFITS, ARISING OUT OF THE USE OF THIS SOFTWARE AND ITS DOCUMENTATION, EVEN IF
THE UNIVERSITY OF CALIFORNIA HAS BEEN ADVISED OF THE POSSIBILITY OF SUCH
DAMAGE.

THE UNIVERSITY OF CALIFORNIA SPECIFICALLY DISCLAIMS ANY WARRANTIES, INCLUDING,
BUT NOT LIMITED TO, THE IMPLIED WARRANTIES OF MERCHANTABILITY AND FITNESS FOR A
PARTICULAR PURPOSE.THE SOFTWARE PROVIDED HEREUNDER IS ON AN "AS IS" BASIS,
AND THE UNIVERSITY OF CALIFORNIA HAS NO OBLIGATIONS TO PROVIDE MAINTENANCE,
SUPPORT, UPDATES, ENHANCEMENTS, OR MODIFICATIONS.
```

6.7 Summary

PostgreSQL can be run on almost all platforms where an ANSI C compiler is available. Installing PostgreSQL on Unix systems is in general an easy task. Running PostgreSQL on Microsoft Windows is slightly more complicated and is normally only done by using Cygwin, a software package providing many Unix tools for Windows. In addition to Cygwin, a daemon for using shared memory has to be installed.

7

Basic SQL

Back in the '70s the father of the relational database concept, E. F. Codd, invented the first version of Structured Query Language (SQL) at IBM. The model described by Codd was based on tables that could be linked with each other. These tables are called relations.

IBM spent a lot of money to implement software based on Codd's ideas, and in 1978 a product called System/R was introduced. However, other companies have implemented relational databases faster than IBM. The first company to offer a relational database was Oracle, and shortly after Oracle, Ingres was available. In 1982 IBM released improved products called SQL/DS and DB2, which is still a major player in the database arena.

The language relational databases are based on is SQL. SQL is an open standard that does not belong to a company, and this may be one reason why SQL has become so successful in the database arena. The commercial success of SQL was precipitated by the formation of the SQL Standard committees by the American National Standards Institute (ANSI) and the International Standards Organization (ISO) in 1986 and 1987. In 1989 the specification of SQL-89, also known as SQL-1, was published. In 1992 SQL-2, which is also known as SQL-92, was introduced. SQL-92 added some extensions to SQL-89—the entire standard was already some 600 pages long. The most recent version of SQL is SQL-99, which is also known as SQL-3.

Although there is a unitary SQL standard, many flavors and accents of SQL are available. Every database system provides a slightly different implementation of the standard, and so does PostgreSQL. Although the goal of PostgreSQL is to be 100% standard-compliant, there are some minor differences.

In this chapter you will be guided through SQL and you will learn to work with tables as well as other components of relational databases.

7.1 Data Types

Every relational database is built of tables, which consist of various columns. Each column is designed to contain a special, predefined piece of data. Depending on the kind of data you want to store, an appropriate data type must be chosen. A column based on a certain data type can only store information fitting the demands of the data type of the column. For example, a column that has been defined as integer value must not be used to store text.

PostgreSQL provides a powerful set of data types, which can be retrieved by using the \dT command in psql:

```
phpbook=# \dT
                           List of data types
            Name            |                 Description
----------------------------+-------------------------------------------------
------------------
 abstime                    | absolute, limited-range date and time (Unix
system time)
 aclitem                    | access control list
 bigint                     | ~18 digit integer, 8-byte storage
 bit                        | fixed-length bit string
 bit varying                | variable-length bit string
 boolean                    | boolean, 'true'/'false'
 box                        | geometric box '(lower left,upper right)'
 bytea                      | variable-length string, binary values escaped
 "char"                     | single character
 character                  | char(length), blank-padded string, fixed storage
 length
 character varying          | varchar(length), non-blank-padded string,
variable storage length
 cid                        | command identifier type, sequence in transaction
 id
 cidr                       | network IP address/netmask, network address
 circle                     | geometric circle '(center,radius)'
 date                       | ANSI SQL date
 double precision           | double-precision floating point number, 8-byte
storage
 inet                       | IP address/netmask, host address, netmask
optional
```

```
int2vector                   | array of 16 int2 integers, used in system tables
integer                      | -2 billion to 2 billion integer, 4-byte storage
interval                     | @ <number> <units>, time interval
line                         | geometric line '(pt1,pt2)'
lseg                         | geometric line segment '(pt1,pt2)'
macaddr                      | XX:XX:XX:XX:XX:XX, MAC address
money                        | $d,ddd.cc, money
name                         | 31-character type for storing system identifiers
numeric                      | numeric(precision, decimal), arbitrary precision
number
oid                          | object identifier(oid), maximum 4 billion
oidvector                    | array of 16 oids, used in system tables
path                         | geometric path '(pt1,...)'
point                        | geometric point '(x, y)'
polygon                      | geometric polygon '(pt1,...)'
real                         | single-precision floating point number, 4-byte
storage
refcursor                    | reference cursor (portal name)
regproc                      | registered procedure
reltime                      | relative, limited-range time interval (Unix
delta time)
"SET"                        | set of tuples
smallint                     | -32 thousand to 32 thousand, 2-byte storage
smgr                         | storage manager
text                         | variable-length string, no limit specified
tid                          | (Block, offset), physical location of tuple
timestamp without time zone  | date and time
timestamp with time zone     | date and time with time zone
time without time zone       | hh:mm:ss, ANSI SQL time
time with time zone          | hh:mm:ss, ANSI SQL time
tinterval                    | (abstime,abstime), time interval
unknown                      |
xid                          | transaction id
(47 rows)
```

By default PostgreSQL provides the incredible number of 47 data types. Some of these types are used only for internal purposes, but the majority of the data types are ready for use in real-world applications.

7.2 Building Tables

The core components of all relational databases are tables. A table consists of columns, which have certain data types. In this section you will learn how to create simple tables.

To create tables, the CREATE TABLE command must be used. CREATE TABLE is one of the most flexible and most powerful commands available. If you take a look at the syntax overview of the command, you will see that it provides many settings and attributes that can be assigned to a table:

```
phpbook=# \h CREATE TABLE
Command:     CREATE TABLE
Description: define a new table
Syntax:
CREATE [ [ LOCAL ] { TEMPORARY | TEMP } ] TABLE table_name (
    { column_name data_type [ DEFAULT default_expr ] [ column_constraint
[, ... ] ]
    | table_constraint }  [, ... ]
)
[ INHERITS ( parent_table [, ... ] ) ]
[ WITH OIDS | WITHOUT OIDS ]

where column_constraint is:

[ CONSTRAINT constraint_name ]
{ NOT NULL | NULL | UNIQUE | PRIMARY KEY |
  CHECK (expression) |
  REFERENCES reftable [ ( refcolumn ) ] [ MATCH FULL | MATCH PARTIAL ]
    [ ON DELETE action ] [ ON UPDATE action ] }
[ DEFERRABLE | NOT DEFERRABLE ] [ INITIALLY DEFERRED | INITIALLY IMMEDIATE ]

and table_constraint is:

[ CONSTRAINT constraint_name ]
{ UNIQUE ( column_name [, ... ] ) |
  PRIMARY KEY ( column_name [, ... ] ) |
  CHECK ( expression ) |
  FOREIGN KEY ( column_name [, ... ] ) REFERENCES reftable [ ( refcolumn
[, ... ] ) ]
    [ MATCH FULL | MATCH PARTIAL ] [ ON DELETE action ] [ ON UPDATE action ] }
[ DEFERRABLE | NOT DEFERRABLE ] [ INITIALLY DEFERRED | INITIALLY IMMEDIATE ]
```

As you can see, `CREATE TABLE` provides many constraints that you will need to build sophisticated data structures. Detailed coverage of constraints will be provided in Chapter 8, "Advanced SQL."

Let's create a table now:

```
phpbook=# CREATE TABLE t_person(id int4, name varchar(10));
CREATE
```

The preceding code generates a table containing two columns. The first column is called `id` and can contain 4-byte integers. The second column is called `name` and can contain strings of variable length that can be up to 10 characters long. Take a look at the data structure:

```
phpbook=# \d t_person
            Table "t_person"
 Column |         Type         | Modifiers
--------+----------------------+-----------
 id     | integer              |
 name   | character varying(10) |
```

With the help of \d, it is easy to find out about the data structure of the table you have just created.

To remove the table from the system, SQL provides a command called `DROP TABLE`:

```
phpbook=# \h DROP TABLE
Command:     DROP TABLE
Description: remove a table
Syntax:
DROP TABLE name [, ...]
```

As you can see, the syntax of the command is easy. Simply pass the name of the table you want to drop to the command and press Enter:

```
phpbook=# DROP TABLE t_person;
DROP
```

If no error occurred, the table has now been successfully removed from the database.

If more than one table has to be created, it can also be uncomfortable to use the interactive shell. Therefore PostgreSQL provides an additional way of communicating with the user.

Let's write an ASCII file containing the code you want PostgreSQL to execute:

```
CREATE TABLE t_person (id serial,
                name text,
                zip_code int4,
                city text,
                        PRIMARY KEY (id));


CREATE TABLE t_children (id serial,
                pers_id int4,
                name text,
                        PRIMARY KEY(id));
```

This code can easily be executed by sending it to psql using the < symbol in your favorite Unix shell:

```
[postgres@athlon postgres]$ psql phpbook < code.sql
NOTICE:  CREATE TABLE will create implicit sequence 't_person_id_seq' for
SERIAL column 't_person.id'
NOTICE:  CREATE TABLE/PRIMARY KEY will create implicit index 't_person_pkey'
for table 't_person'
CREATE
NOTICE:  CREATE TABLE will create implicit sequence 't_children_id_seq' for
SERIAL column 't_children.id'
NOTICE:  CREATE TABLE/PRIMARY KEY will create implicit index 't_children_pkey'
for table 't_children'
CREATE
```

Two tables have been created. The first columns of the two tables are defined as serial. Serials are a data type for generating a consecutively numbered list. In this case, the first column will contain a unique number that can be used to identify every record in the table. Because the first column of both tables is unique, it can be used as primary key. A column defined as a primary key must always have a unique value—duplicated entries are not allowed. As you can see, serial causes PostgreSQL to generate an implicit sequence that makes sure that every value can only occur once.

Documentation is the key to success. When creating more than just one table on the system, it is useful to add comments to the data structure so that other people can easily understand what the various fields are good for. PostgreSQL provides an easy way to add comments to a data structure. In the case of the CREATE TABLE command, comments can easily be added as shown in the next listing:

```
CREATE TABLE t_person (id serial,              -- serial number
                name text,                     -- name of the person
                zip_code int4,                 -- postcode
                city text,                     -- name of the city where the
                                               -- person lives
                    PRIMARY KEY (id));

CREATE TABLE t_children (id serial,            -- serial number
                pers_id int4,                  -- id of one parent
                name text,                     -- name of the child
                    PRIMARY KEY(id));
```

If you want to comment one of your objects after you have created it, PostgreSQL provides a command called COMMENT. COMMENT is a powerful command and can be used to add comments to any object in your database. We recommend adding at least a description of the content of the columns in your tables. This way it is easy for other people to understand what you have done and how your data structure works.

Take a look at the syntax overview of COMMENT:

```
phpbook=# \h COMMENT
Command:    COMMENT
Description: define or change the comment of an object
Syntax:
COMMENT ON
[
  [ DATABASE | INDEX | RULE | SEQUENCE | TABLE | TYPE | VIEW ] object_name |
  COLUMN table_name.column_name |
  AGGREGATE agg_name (agg_type) |
  FUNCTION func_name (arg1, arg2, ...) |
  OPERATOR op (leftoperand_type rightoperand_type) |
  TRIGGER trigger_name ON table_name
] IS 'text'
```

As you can see, comments can be defined for all kinds of objects in your database, including tables, triggers, and views. In the next example you will see how a comment can be added to a table:

```
phpbook=# COMMENT ON TABLE t_person IS 'this is a comment on the table';
COMMENT
```

The only thing you have to tell PostgreSQL is on which table the comment should be added and what string will be used as the comment. After adding the comment, you can retrieve it from the database by using a `psql` built-in command:

```
phpbook=# \dd t_person
                Object descriptions
   Name   | Object |          Description
----------+--------+---------------------------------
 t_person | table  | this is a comment on the table
(1 row)
```

As you can see, \dd will cause `psql` to display the comments defined on the table.

Comments on columns can be added to a table pretty much the same way as comments on tables:

```
phpbook=# COMMENT ON COLUMN t_person.zip_code IS 'this is a comment on a
column';
COMMENT
```

The syntax of the command does not differ.

7.3 Building Simple SQL Statements

Now that you have seen how tables can be added to a database, it is time to perform some simple SQL statements.

One of the most important commands when working with SQL is the INSERT command. INSERT is one way to add data to a table. Since the first days of SQL, the INSERT command has been part of the ANSI SQL specification, and it is a core component of every relational and object relational database built in SQL. The syntax overview of the INSERT command is not too complicated:

```
phpbook=# \h INSERT
Command:    INSERT
Description: create new rows in a table
Syntax:
INSERT INTO table [ ( column [, ...] ) ]
    { DEFAULT VALUES | VALUES ( expression [, ...] ) | SELECT query }
```

The first thing you have to define is into which table the data passed to the database by the command has to be inserted. In the next step it is possible to define a list of columns into which you want to insert data. If no list is provided, PostgreSQL assumes that data has to be added to all columns of a record.

Take a look at an example of a simple INSERT command:

```
phpbook=# INSERT INTO t_person (name, zip_code, city) VALUES ('Hans', 1150,
'Vienna');
INSERT 21709 1
```

If no error occurred, the record has successfully been added to the table. Three columns in the record have been defined in the SQL statement. In this example no value has been assigned to the column called id. The list defining the list of columns comes directly after the name of the data the data has been added to. After the keyword VALUES, the table is passed to the database. In the next step, only two columns should be inserted into the table. You can try to remove one column from the list:

```
phpbook=# INSERT INTO t_person (name, zip_code) VALUES ('Epi', 1060, 'Vienna');
ERROR:  INSERT has more expressions than target columns
```

In this case PostgreSQL will fail because only two columns should be added to the database, but three values are passed to the database by the SQL statement. To make sure that PostgreSQL can accept the command, one value has to be removed from the list:

```
phpbook=# INSERT INTO t_person (name, zip_code) VALUES ('Epi', 1060);
INSERT 21710 1
```

In the next step you will see how the data you have just added to the database can easily be retrieved. For selecting data stored in one or more than just one table, you can use the SELECT command. The syntax overview of the SELECT command is impressive, and SELECT is one of the most powerful commands provided by PostgreSQL. To retrieve the syntax overview of SELECT, you can use \h:

```
phpbook=# \h SELECT
Command:    SELECT
Description: retrieve rows from a table or view
Syntax:
SELECT [ ALL | DISTINCT [ ON ( expression [, ...] ) ] ]
    * | expression [ AS output_name ] [, ...]
    [ FROM from_item [, ...] ]
    [ WHERE condition ]
    [ GROUP BY expression [, ...] ]
    [ HAVING condition [, ...] ]
    [ { UNION | INTERSECT | EXCEPT } [ ALL ] select ]
    [ ORDER BY expression [ ASC | DESC | USING operator ] [, ...] ]
    [ FOR UPDATE [ OF tablename [, ...] ] ]
```

```
    [ LIMIT { count | ALL } ]
    [ OFFSET start ]

where from_item can be:

[ ONLY ] table_name [ * ]
    [ [ AS ] alias [ ( column_alias_list ) ] ]
|
( select )
    [ AS ] alias [ ( column_alias_list ) ]
|
from_item [ NATURAL ] join_type from_item
    [ ON join_condition | USING ( join_column_list ) ]
```

In this section you will not learn about all the details of the SELECT command, but you will see how to write simple SELECT statements and how to retrieve data from a table efficiently. In Chapter 8 SELECT and many other commands will be covered in a more detailed way.

Now that you have seen the syntax overview of the SELECT command, take a look at a simple SQL statement you can use to retrieve all records from a table.

```
phpbook=# SELECT * FROM t_person;
 id | name | zip_code |  city
----+------+----------+--------
  1 | Hans |     1150 | Vienna
  2 | Epi  |     1060 |
(2 rows)
```

The asterisk tells PostgreSQL to retrieve all columns from t_person. The result of the query is a list of two records. These are the two records you have just inserted into the table, but why is there already a value in the first column? As you have seen, the id of a record has never been added to the table. However, the id is obviously in the table. If you take a look at the SQL commands for creating the tables, you will find out that the first column has been defined as serial. This means that PostgreSQL will create a sequence used for consecutively numbering every record inserted into the table automatically. This makes it easy to generate an index consisting of a list of unique values. The column containing the serial will automatically be the primary key of the table.

In the preceding example you saw that you can use an asterisk to retrieve all columns from a table. In some cases it is not necessary to retrieve all columns, so it is also possible to list only those columns needed in the result:

```
phpbook=# SELECT id, name, zip_code, city FROM t_person;
 id | name | zip_code |  city
----+------+----------+--------
  1 | Hans |     1150 | Vienna
  2 | Epi  |     1060 |
(2 rows)
```

The order of the columns is flexible as well. If city has to be listed before id, it has to be changed in the list of columns:

```
phpbook=# SELECT city, id, name, zip_code FROM t_person;
  city   | id | name | zip_code
---------+----+------+----------
 Vienna  |  1 | Hans |     1150
         |  2 | Epi  |     1060
(2 rows)
```

Another way to retrieve data is to tell PostgreSQL explicitly where to take the columns from. In the next example you tell PostgreSQL that all columns in table t_person must be listed. This syntax is important when working with more than just one table:

```
phpbook=# SELECT t_person.* FROM t_person;
 id | name | zip_code |  city
----+------+----------+--------
  1 | Hans |     1150 | Vienna
  2 | Epi  |     1060 |
(2 rows)
```

One thing you have to take care of when retrieving data is that you must not list columns that are not in the table because PostgreSQL will not accept such queries.

```
phpbook=# SELECT t_person.Hans FROM t_person;
ERROR:  No such attribute or function 'hans'
```

7.3.1 Using WHERE Clauses

In most cases, you don't want to retrieve all values from a table but only data satisfying certain conditions. This is the typical task for a database. Just like any other database, PostgreSQL has been optimized for this kind of operation. To restrict the data returned, a WHERE clause has to be added to the query. In the next example you can see how you can find all records where the id is exactly 1:

```
phpbook=# SELECT id, name, zip_code FROM t_person WHERE id=1;
 id | name | zip_code
----+------+----------
  1 | Hans |     1150
(1 row)
```

One record is returned because there is no other record having the same id. The desired value has to be passed to the server without single quotes. With integer values this will work, but how can you pass strings to the database?

```
phpbook=# SELECT * FROM t_person WHERE name='Hans';
 id | name | zip_code |  city
----+------+----------+--------
  1 | Hans |     1150 | Vienna
(1 row)
```

In this example you want to find all records where the name is Hans. As you can see, the values have to be defined using single quotes.

7.3.1.1 Escaping Special Characters
Let's insert an additional record into the table:

```
phpbook=# INSERT INTO t_person (name) VALUES ('o'Connor');
phpbook'#
```

You want to insert the name o'Connor into the table but somehow it does not seem to work. PostgreSQL is still prompting for input because the SQL statement is not complete. The problem is that the database cannot distinguish single quotes in the string you want to insert, and single quotes are needed for telling SQL where a string starts and ends. To get around the problem, single quotes must be escaped. You can do this in two ways:

```
phpbook=# INSERT INTO t_person (name) VALUES ('o''Connor');
INSERT 21712 1
```

The first thing you can do is to use two single quotes instead of one. This way PostgreSQL will know that a single quote has to be sent to the database. The second possibility is to use a backslash instead:

```
phpbook=# INSERT INTO t_person (name) VALUES ('o\'Connor');
INSERT 21713 1
```

Let's see if both values have successfully been inserted into the table:

```
phpbook=# SELECT * FROM t_person;
 id |   name   | zip_code |  city
----+----------+----------+--------
  1 | Hans     |     1150 | Vienna
  2 | Epi      |     1060 |
  3 | o'Connor |          |
  4 | o'Connor |          |
(4 rows)
```

Both records are in the table and are the same. In the next step you can try to retrieve all values where the name is o'Connor:

```
phpbook=# SELECT * FROM t_person WHERE name='o''Connor';
 id |   name   | zip_code | city
----+----------+----------+------
  3 | o'Connor |          |
  4 | o'Connor |          |
(2 rows)
```

The single quotes have to be escaped as you saw when writing the INSERT statements.

7.3.1.2 Handling NULL Values

All columns that have not been defined in the INSERT operation are set to NULL. NULL does not mean zero and NULL does not mean blank. NULL is a special value and means that the column does not contain a value.

To retrieve all records where no value has been inserted into city, you can write a query that checks for NULL values:

```
phpbook=# SELECT * FROM t_person WHERE city IS NULL;
 id |   name   | zip_code | city
----+----------+----------+------
  2 | Epi      |     1060 |
  3 | o'Connor |          |
  4 | o'Connor |          |
(3 rows)
```

As you can see, IS NULL can be used to retrieve NULL values from the column. Let's try something else:

```
phpbook=# SELECT * FROM t_person WHERE city='';
 id | name | zip_code | city
----+------+----------+------
(0 rows)
```

In this scenario you are looking for an empty string, but because NULL is not an empty string no records will be returned. This is an important point.

In PostgreSQL 7.2, there is another thing you should take care of:

```
phpbook=# SELECT * FROM t_person WHERE city=NULL;
 id | name | zip_code | city
----+------+----------+------
(0 rows)
```

Don't check for NULL the way it is shown in the listing—it won't work.

7.3.1.3 Multiple Conditions

In most cases it is not enough to have just one condition. The more complex your application is, the more likely it will be that you have to write more complex WHERE clauses.

Let's start with a simple query:

```
phpbook=# SELECT * FROM t_person WHERE zip_code=1150 AND city='Vienna';
 id | name | zip_code |  city
----+------+----------+--------
  1 | Hans |     1150 | Vienna
(1 row)
```

The query can be used to retrieve all records from the table where the postal code is 1150 and the city is Vienna. Both conditions have to be fulfilled if a record should be displayed in the result.

Sometimes it is necessary to see if a certain value in a column is higher than a predefined value. In this case, use the > operator:

```
phpbook=# SELECT * FROM t_person WHERE zip_code=1150 AND id>1;
 id | name | zip_code | city
----+------+----------+------
(0 rows)
```

No record is retrieved because the only record satisfying the first condition has an id that is exactly 1. If you want to find all records where the id is higher or equal than 1, use the >= operator:

```
phpbook=# SELECT * FROM t_person WHERE zip_code=1150 AND id>=1;
 id | name | zip_code |  city
----+------+----------+--------
  1 | Hans |     1150 | Vienna
(1 row)
```

The counterpart of the = operator is the <> operator:

```
phpbook=# SELECT * FROM t_person WHERE zip_code=1150 AND id <> 1;
 id | name | zip_code | city
----+------+----------+------
(0 rows)
```

As you can see, no record matches the conditions in the WHERE clause. Now that you've used the AND operator, you will learn to use the OR operator:

```
phpbook=# SELECT * FROM t_person WHERE name='Hans' OR name='Epi';
 id | name | zip_code |  city
----+------+----------+--------
  1 | Hans |     1150 | Vienna
  2 | Epi  |     1060 |
(2 rows)
```

In this scenario, name can be Hans or Epi. If one of the two conditions matches, the record will be returned.

In the next example you see a slightly more complex query:

```
phpbook=# SELECT * FROM t_person WHERE (name='Hans' OR name='Epi') AND city=
'Vienna';
 id | name | zip_code |  city
----+------+----------+--------
  1 | Hans |     1150 | Vienna
(1 row)
```

This query has selected every record where the name is Hans or Epi. city has to be Vienna but two names are considered to be valid.

The next query will lead to the same result:

```
phpbook=# SELECT * FROM t_person WHERE name='Hans' OR (name='Epi' AND city=
'Vienna');
 id | name | zip_code |  city
----+------+----------+--------
  1 | Hans |     1150 | Vienna
(1 row)
```

PostgreSQL does not take the parentheses into consideration when executing the query.

7.3.2 Formatting the Output

In some cases it is necessary to format the output of a query. Today this is not as important as it used to be, but it is still something worth mentioning. Back in the early days of SQL, people used to build entire reports with the help of command-line tools, so operations like concatenating the content of columns were essential. Nowadays most of the formatting is done on the application level.

Before you learn how to concatenate columns, you will see how Hello World can be implemented using SQL:

```
phpbook=# SELECT 'Hello World';
  ?column?
-------------
 Hello World
(1 row)
```

Simply select the string Hello World and it will be displayed by the database. In this case you don't need a table to select the data from because it is not stored in the database. In some databases, such as Oracle, having a FROM clause is necessary, but in PostgreSQL this is redundant.

Now that you have seen how to select a string, you will see how to connect various columns with each other:

```
phpbook=# SELECT name || ' lives in ' || city FROM t_person WHERE id=1;
       ?column?
---------------------
 Hans lives in Vienna
(1 row)
```

In this example the column labeled name is selected from the database. With the help of the || operator, the column is combined with the string lives in and the column called city. The column generated by concatenating the various values is called ?column?. This name might not be what you need. You can change the caption of the column:

```
phpbook=# SELECT name || ' lives in ' || city AS "the caption" FROM t_person
WHERE id=1;
     the caption
----------------------
 Hans lives in Vienna
(1 row)
```

As you can see, it is an easy task to combine various columns to one string, but let's see how you can use WHERE clauses:

```
phpbook=# SELECT name || ' lives in ' || city AS caption FROM t_person WHERE
name || ' lives in ' || city = 'Hans lives in Vienna';
       caption
----------------------
 Hans lives in Vienna
(1 row)
```

The entire command for concatenating the various fields has to be added to the WHERE clause. As the next listing shows you cannot use the name specified by using AS:

```
phpbook=# SELECT name || ' lives in ' || city AS caption FROM t_person WHERE
caption = 'Hans lives
in Vienna';
ERROR:  Attribute 'caption' not found
ERROR:  Attribute 'caption' not found
```

Caption is not an attribute of a table in the FROM clause, so an error occurs.

7.3.3 LIMIT and OFFSET

LIMIT and OFFSET are two commands for restricting the rows returned by the database. With the help of LIMIT it is possible to tell PostgreSQL that only some records at the beginning of the result should be displayed. The number of records you want to be displayed has to be added to the LIMIT command. In the next listing you can see how two values can be displayed:

```
phpbook=# SELECT * FROM t_person LIMIT 2;
 id | name | zip_code |  city
----+------+----------+--------
  1 | Hans |     1150 | Vienna
  2 | Epi  |     1060 |
(2 rows)
```

The first two records of the result have been displayed on the screen. If you want to omit a fixed number of records at the beginning of the result, you can use the query in the next listing:

```
phpbook=# SELECT * FROM t_person LIMIT 2,1;
 id |   name   | zip_code | city
----+----------+----------+------
  2 | Epi      |     1060 |
  3 | o'Connor |          |
(2 rows)
```

This syntax was supported by PostgreSQL databases prior to 7.3. If you are currently building new applications, don't use this syntax because it will be removed in version 7.3. To get around the problem, use OFFSET:

```
phpbook=# SELECT * FROM t_person LIMIT 2 OFFSET 1;
 id |   name   | zip_code | city
----+----------+----------+------
  2 | Epi      |     1060 |
  3 | o'Connor |          |
(2 rows)
```

The previous two queries are equal and will lead to the same result.

7.3.4 Temporary Tables

Temporary tables are a very comfortable feature of PostgreSQL and they can be used to store information in tables that are only needed in the current session. Temporary tables can only be seen by the person who has created them and as soon as the connection terminates, temporary tables are deleted automatically.

Let's connect to the database called phpbook:

```
[postgres@athlon postgres]$ psql phpbook
```

If no error occurred, psql has been started successfully. Now you can create a temporary table:

```
phpbook=# CREATE TEMPORARY TABLE tmp_data(id int4, data text);
CREATE
```

Let's see if the definition of the table can be retrieved by using \d:

```
phpbook=# \d tmp_data
Did not find any relation named "tmp_data".
```

The table cannot be found in the list of tables because it is only a temporary table.

The next piece of code shows how to add data to the table:

```
phpbook=# INSERT INTO tmp_data VALUES (1, 'one');
INSERT 24755 1
```

As you can see, you can add data to a temporary table just as you would if it were not a temporary table. Selecting data also works the same way:

```
phpbook=# SELECT * FROM tmp_data;
 id | data
----+------
  1 | one
(1 row)
```

If you leave psql and connect to the database again, you will find out that the table is not in the database any more:

```
phpbook=# SELECT * FROM tmp_data;
ERROR:  Relation 'tmp_data' does not exist
ERROR:  Relation 'tmp_data' does not exist
```

Another important thing is that a user can only see his personal set of temporary tables. Therefore it is possible that many users can create temporary tables having the same name. Table 7.1 gives some examples.

TABLE 7.1 Temporary Tables and Scope

User 1	User 2	Comment
psql phpbook		User 1 connects to the database
	psql phpbook	User 2 connects to the database
CREATE TEMPORARY TABLE tmp_data (id int4, data text);		User 1 creates a table
	CREATE TEMPORARY TABLE tmp_data (id int4);	User 2 creates a table

TABLE 7.1   Continued

User 1	User 2	Comment
`INSERT INTO tmp_data` `VALUES(1, 'a');`		User 1 inserts a record
	`INSERT INTO tmp_` `data VALUES(2);`	User 2 inserts a record
`SELECT * FROM tmp_data;`		User 1 retrieves one record from the database
`\q`		User 1 disconnects
	`SELECT * FROM tmp_data;`	User 2 retrieves one record from the database
	`\q`	User 2 disconnects

As you can see, user 1 and user 2 have their own temporary tables with the same name but PostgreSQL is not confused by this.

7.3.4.1 Temporary Tables and Serials

When working with temporary tables, there is one topic worth looking at. When creating a table containing a serial, PostgreSQL will implicitly create a sequence. Because the serial is not part of the table itself, it is important to find out if the sequence and the table are removed or if the sequence remains. Let's create a table:

```
phpbook=# CREATE TEMPORARY TABLE tmp_data(id serial, data text);
NOTICE:  CREATE TABLE will create implicit sequence 'tmp_data_id_seq' for
SERIAL column 'tmp_data.id'
NOTICE:  CREATE TABLE/UNIQUE will create implicit index 'tmp_data_id_key' for
table 'tmp_data'
CREATE
```

A sequence has been created. After you disconnect from the database and connect again, the sequence cannot be found in the database:

```
phpbook=# \d tmp_data_id_seq
Did not find any relation named "tmp_data_id_seq".
```

To make sure that it has really been removed, you can try to select the next value in the sequence.

```
phpbook=# SELECT nextval("tmp_data_id_seq");
ERROR:  Attribute 'tmp_data_id_seq' not found
```

It seems as if the sequence has already been removed, which is true.

To see how this can easily be handled, it is worth looking at the syntax overview of
the CREATE SEQUENCE command:

```
phpbook=# \h CREATE SEQUENCE
Command:     CREATE SEQUENCE
Description: define a new sequence
Syntax:
CREATE [ TEMPORARY | TEMP ] SEQUENCE seqname [ INCREMENT increment ]
    [ MINVALUE minvalue ] [ MAXVALUE maxvalue ]
    [ START start ] [ CACHE cache ] [ CYCLE ]
```

As you can see, PostgreSQL is capable of handling temporary sequences. Therefore
PostgreSQL automatically generates a temporary sequence when a table is created, so
no problems occur when working with serials.

7.3.5 SELECT INTO

From time to time it is necessary to store the result of a query in a table. This can be
done by using the SELECT INTO command. In contrast to using views, SELECT INTO
generates a physical copy of the query and stores it in a table.

Take a look at the syntax overview of the SELECT INTO command:

```
phpbook=# \h SELECT INTO
Command:     SELECT INTO
Description: create a new table from the results of a query
Syntax:
SELECT [ ALL | DISTINCT [ ON ( expression [, ...] ) ] ]
    * | expression [ AS output_name ] [, ...]
    INTO [ TEMPORARY | TEMP ] [ TABLE ] new_table
    [ FROM from_item [, ...] ]
    [ WHERE condition ]
    [ GROUP BY expression [, ...] ]
    [ HAVING condition [, ...] ]
    [ { UNION | INTERSECT | EXCEPT } [ ALL ] select ]
    [ ORDER BY expression [ ASC | DESC | USING operator ] [, ...] ]
    [ FOR UPDATE [ OF tablename [, ...] ] ]
    [ LIMIT [ start , ] { count | ALL } ]
    [ OFFSET start ]

where from_item can be:

[ ONLY ] table_name [ * ]
    [ [ AS ] alias [ ( column_alias_list ) ] ]
```

```
|
( select )
    [ AS ] alias [ ( column_alias_list ) ]
|
from_item [ NATURAL ] join_type from_item
    [ ON join_condition | USING ( join_column_list ) ]
```

As you can see, SELECT INTO is nothing more than a special sort of SELECT statement that generates a table based on the result of a query. Recall the content of t_person:

```
phpbook=# SELECT * FROM t_person;
 id |   name    | zip_code |  city
----+-----------+----------+--------
  1 | Hans      |     1150 | Vienna
  2 | Epi       |     1060 |
  3 | o'Connor  |          |
  4 | o'Connor  |          |
(4 rows)
```

The target of the next example is to use SELECT INTO to generate a copy of t_person:

```
phpbook=# SELECT * INTO TEMPORARY TABLE tmp_person FROM t_person;
SELECT
```

tmp_person is a temporary table containing the same data as the original table:

```
phpbook=# SELECT * FROM tmp_person;
 id |   name    | zip_code |  city
----+-----------+----------+--------
  1 | Hans      |     1150 | Vienna
  2 | Epi       |     1060 |
  3 | o'Connor  |          |
  4 | o'Connor  |          |
(4 rows)
```

Because tmp_person is a temporary table, it will be deleted automatically as soon as the user terminates the connection to the database.

7.3.5.1 Views versus SELECT INTO

Using views and SELECT INTO makes a significant difference. SELECT INTO stores the result of a query in a table, but if the data in the original tables changes, the new tables will not be updated. In contrast, a view always contains the most recent result because it is generated every time the view is accessed.

The problem with views is that if several computations that take a lot of time have to be performed using the same snapshot of data, it might take far too long to use views. In this case temporary tables generated by SELECT INTO might be a good choice because this way it is easy to reduce the amount of data involved in the query. The new table will only contain a brief excerpt of the data, and this is much faster than accessing the original tables every time.

7.4 Updates and Deletes

Up to now you have seen how to create tables, how to insert records, and how to select data. In this section you will learn to modify data and to remove records from a table.

To modify data, SQL provides a command called UPDATE. The next listing shows the syntax overview of the UPDATE command:

```
phpbook=# \h UPDATE
Command:     UPDATE
Description: update rows of a table
Syntax:
UPDATE [ ONLY ] table SET col = expression [, ...]
    [ FROM fromlist ]
    [ WHERE condition ]
```

UPDATE can be used to modify a list of columns. Just like SELECT statements, UPDATE statements can contain WHERE clauses for restricting the data modified by the UPDATE query.

Take a look at a simple UPDATE operation:

```
phpbook=# UPDATE t_person SET city='Mauerbach' WHERE id=2;
UPDATE 1
```

In every record where the id is equal to 2, city is set to Mauerbach. PostgreSQL displays two parameters returned by the query. The first word defines the operation performed by the query. The second value tells us that one record has been affected by the operation. This value is important because this way it is possible to see what has been caused by the SQL statement.

Let's see if the operation has been performed correctly:

```
phpbook=# SELECT * FROM t_person WHERE id=2;
 id | name | zip_code |   city
----+------+----------+----------
  2 | Epi  |     1060 | Mauerbach
(1 row)
```

The value of city is Mauerbach instead of NULL now.

If you want to update more than just one column, it can be done with one UPDATE command as well:

```
phpbook=# UPDATE t_person SET name='Ewald Geschwinde', zip_code=2300 WHERE id=2;
UPDATE 1
```

In this example name and zip_code are modified. Just pass a list of columns, including the new values, to the database and PostgreSQL will change the required values:

```
phpbook=# SELECT * FROM t_person WHERE id=2;
 id |       name        | zip_code |   city
----+-------------------+----------+-----------
  2 | Ewald Geschwinde  |     2300 | Mauerbach
(1 row)
```

Both values have been changed.

To remove values from a table, SQL provides the DELETE command. The syntax overview of DELETE is simple:

```
phpbook=# \h DELETE
Command:    DELETE
Description: delete rows of a table
Syntax:
DELETE FROM [ ONLY ] table [ WHERE condition ]
```

Here is an example of a simple DELETE command:

```
phpbook=# DELETE FROM t_person WHERE id>3;
DELETE 1
```

One record has been removed from the table because only one record satisfies the condition passed to the DELETE statement.

If you want to remove all records from a table, you can use TRUNCATE instead of DELETE. Because no condition has to be checked, TRUNCATE can be faster than DELETE. Take a look at the syntax of the command:

```
phpbook=# \h TRUNCATE
Command:    TRUNCATE
Description: empty a table
Syntax:
TRUNCATE [ TABLE ] name
```

7.5 Writing Joins

According to the relational concept, data is stored in various tables. To combine this data, so-called joins have to be performed. Joining means that tables are combined using common attributes.

The next scenario shows a relation between students and training courses. Every student can attend multiple training courses, so you need two tables. One table stores information about students and the second table contains the list of training courses a student attends. Here is the SQL code needed for generating the two tables:

```
phpbook=# CREATE TABLE student (id int4, name text);
CREATE
phpbook=# CREATE TABLE course(student_id int4, course text);
CREATE
```

Let's insert some data into the tables:

```
phpbook=# INSERT INTO student VALUES (1, 'Epi');
INSERT 24792 1
phpbook=# INSERT INTO student VALUES (2, 'Hans');
INSERT 24793 1
phpbook=# INSERT INTO student VALUES (3, 'Heinz');
INSERT 24794 1
```

Table student contains three records now:

```
phpbook=# SELECT * FROM student;
 id | name
----+-------
  1 | Epi
  2 | Hans
  3 | Heinz
(3 rows)
```

Three students can be found in the table. Let's add a list of training courses these students attend to table course:

```
phpbook=# INSERT INTO course VALUES (1, 'PostgreSQL for Beginners');
INSERT 24795 1
phpbook=# INSERT INTO course VALUES (1, 'PostgreSQL for C Programmers');
INSERT 24796 1
phpbook=# INSERT INTO course VALUES (1, 'PostgreSQL for Tcl Programmers');
INSERT 24797 1
phpbook=# INSERT INTO course VALUES (2, 'PostgreSQL for Tcl Programmers');
INSERT 24798 1
```

If no error occurred, four records will be in the table:

```
phpbook=# SELECT * FROM course;
 student_id |          course
------------+--------------------------------
          1 | PostgreSQL for Beginners
          1 | PostgreSQL for C Programmers
          1 | PostgreSQL for Tcl Programmers
          2 | PostgreSQL for Tcl Programmers
(4 rows)
```

Let's try to find all students who attend training courses. The student id and the name should be displayed:

```
phpbook=# SELECT student.* FROM student, course WHERE student.id=course.student
_id;
 id | name
----+------
  1 | Epi
  1 | Epi
  1 | Epi
  2 | Hans
(4 rows)
```

Epi and Hans attend training courses, but the lazy student called Heinz does not attend a single training course. The problem with the query shown in the previous listing is that every name is listed more than once. Epi attends three training courses and therefore Epi is listed three times. Let's have a closer look at the query: All columns in student will be displayed. Two tables are selected from the database. In the WHERE clause you can see how a join is performed. The id in table student has to be the same as the student_id in the table course. This way two tables are connected using a common attribute.

To solve the problem concerning multiple entries, use DISTINCT:

```
phpbook=# SELECT DISTINCT student.* FROM student, course WHERE
student.id=course.student_id;
 id | name
----+------
  1 | Epi
  2 | Hans
(2 rows)
```

The result is now what it is supposed to be. Every record is only displayed once. DISTINCT makes sure that no duplicated entries can be in the result.

In the next example you will see how to retrieve a list of people and the training courses attended by them:

```
SELECT student.name, course.course
       FROM student, course
       WHERE student.id=course.student_id;
```

In this case you have to select the name of the student from table student and the name of the training course from table course. In this case you don't need DISTINCT because a student cannot attend the same training course twice (in this model this has to be checked on the application level):

The result will contain information from both tables:

```
name |            course
------+----------------------------------
Epi  | PostgreSQL for Beginners
Epi  | PostgreSQL for C Programmers
Epi  | PostgreSQL for Tcl Programmers
Hans | PostgreSQL for Tcl Programmers
(4 rows)
```

Let's try to query for all people attending the Tcl programming course:

```
phpbook=# SELECT student.id, course.course WHERE course.course='PostgreSQL for
Tcl Programmers';
 id |            course
----+----------------------------------
  1 | PostgreSQL for Tcl Programmers
  2 | PostgreSQL for Tcl Programmers
  3 | PostgreSQL for Tcl Programmers
  1 | PostgreSQL for Tcl Programmers
  2 | PostgreSQL for Tcl Programmers
  3 | PostgreSQL for Tcl Programmers
(6 rows)
```

Somehow the query seems to be wrong. Heinz does not attend a single training course, but student number 3 is still in the list.

To understand what went wrong, you can omit the WHERE clause restricting the name of the training course:

```
phpbook=# SELECT * FROM student, course;
 id | name  | student_id |            course
----+-------+------------+------------------------------
  1 | Epi   |          1 | PostgreSQL for Beginners
  1 | Epi   |          1 | PostgreSQL for C Programmers
  1 | Epi   |          1 | PostgreSQL for Tcl Programmers
  1 | Epi   |          2 | PostgreSQL for Tcl Programmers
  2 | Hans  |          1 | PostgreSQL for Beginners
  2 | Hans  |          1 | PostgreSQL for C Programmers
  2 | Hans  |          1 | PostgreSQL for Tcl Programmers
  2 | Hans  |          2 | PostgreSQL for Tcl Programmers
  3 | Heinz |          1 | PostgreSQL for Beginners
  3 | Heinz |          1 | PostgreSQL for C Programmers
  3 | Heinz |          1 | PostgreSQL for Tcl Programmers
  3 | Heinz |          2 | PostgreSQL for Tcl Programmers
(12 rows)
```

PostgreSQL has computed the Cartesian product of the two tables. Building the Cartesian product of a list of tables is one of the core operations defined in the relational concept. In the previous example the Cartesian product has also been generated, but you have only selected those records containing the string PostgreSQL for Tcl Programmers. The problem with the query was that you did not add a join condition to the WHERE clause. A join condition is a condition that tells PostgreSQL that one column in the first table has to be equal to one column in the second table. This way tables can be connected with each other. Always keep in mind that if you don't add join conditions to a query, the database will return the Cartesian product.

Let's rewrite the query returning a list of all people attending the Tcl training course:

```
SELECT *
        FROM student, course
        WHERE student.id=course.student_id
                AND course.course='PostgreSQL for Tcl Programmers';
```

As you can see a join condition is in the query and the result will be correct.

```
 id | name | student_id |            course
----+------+------------+------------------------------
  1 | Epi  |          1 | PostgreSQL for Tcl Programmers
  2 | Hans |          2 | PostgreSQL for Tcl Programmers
(2 rows)
```

Of course, you won't need columns in both tables, but the desired set of data is returned by the query.

After dealing with joins with two tables, you will learn how to write joins with more than just two tables involved. Therefore you have to create an additional table:

```
CREATE TABLE course_desc (
        course_name text,      -- name of the training course
        desc_type text,        -- type of description (short, medium, long)
        desctext text          -- text of description
);

INSERT INTO course_desc VALUES ('PostgreSQL for Tcl Programmers',
        'short', 'a training course about Tcl');
INSERT INTO course_desc VALUES ('PostgreSQL for Tcl Programmers',
        'long', 'a training course about Tcl and PostgreSQL');
```

This table is used to store descriptions about training courses. Two records have been added to the table. One record contains a short description of the Tcl course and the second one contains a longer description of the course.

The target of the next query is to get a list of people attending the training course about Tcl plus the short description of the training course. Therefore three tables have to be joined:

```
SELECT student.name, course.course, course_desc.desctext
       FROM student, course, course_desc
       WHERE student.id=course.student_id
             AND course.course=course_desc.course_name
             AND course_desc.desc_type='short';
```

For every table added to the query you will need additional join conditions; otherwise, PostgreSQL will generate the Cartesian product. Take a look at the result of the query:

```
name |             course              |          desctext
------+--------------------------------+----------------------------
 Epi  | PostgreSQL for Tcl Programmers | a training course about Tcl
 Hans | PostgreSQL for Tcl Programmers | a training course about Tcl
(2 rows)
```

The desired result is returned by the database.

Writing queries with many tables involved can sometimes be difficult. In such cases, it can be useful to work with views. You will learn more about views in Chapter 8.

7.6 Aggregating Data

You have seen how individual records can be inserted, updated, and selected. In many cases, it is necessary to perform computations with more than just one record involved.

Aggregation functions can be used. PostgreSQL provides the standard set of aggregation functions that are also provided by most other relational databases. In this section you will learn to use aggregation functions efficiently and you will see how multiple records can be treated.

7.6.1 COUNT

For counting the records in a set of data, SQL provides a function called COUNT. With the help of COUNT, it is an easy task to find out how many records are in a table or how many records satisfy certain conditions.

Take a look at an example:

```
phpbook=# SELECT COUNT(*) FROM course;
 count
-------
     4
(1 row)
```

The table called course contains four records. If you want to retrieve only those where the name of the training course is PostgreSQL for Tcl Programmers, you have to add a WHERE clause as shown in the next listing:

```
phpbook=# SELECT COUNT(*) FROM course WHERE course='PostgreSQL for Tcl
Programmers';
 count
-------
     2
(1 row)
```

Two records are returned, which is correct.

7.6.2 AVG

The AVG (or average) function can be used to compute the arithmetic mean of a list of values. To show you how the function works, you can create a table and insert some records into it:

```
phpbook=# CREATE TABLE mydata(data int4);
CREATE
phpbook=# INSERT INTO mydata VALUES(23);
INSERT 24808 1
phpbook=# INSERT INTO mydata VALUES(54);
INSERT 24809 1
```

In the next step, you try to compute the arithmetic mean of the records in the table:

```
phpbook=# SELECT AVG(data) FROM mydata;
      avg
--------------
 38.5000000000
(1 row)
```

PostgreSQL will display the result on the screen.

7.6.3 MAX and MIN

MAX and MIN can be used just like all other aggregation functions because the syntax is the same as you have seen when dealing with AVG and COUNT.

Let's look at an example:

```
phpbook=# SELECT MAX(data) FROM mydata;
 max
-----
  54
(1 row)
```

The maximum value in the column has been returned. The MIN function works the same way as the MAX function:

```
phpbook=# SELECT MIN(data) FROM mydata;
 min
-----
  23
(1 row)
```

7.6.4 SUM

To compute the sum of a list of values, use the SUM function. Just like all other aggregation functions, SUM processes the list of values or the column passed to it record by record. With the SUM function, PostgreSQL will add all values and return the result:

```
phpbook=# SELECT SUM(data) FROM mydata;
 sum
-----
  77
(1 row)
```

The sum of all values in the example is 77.

7.6.5 GROUP BY

Recall the content of table course:

```
phpbook=# SELECT * FROM course;
 student_id |            course
------------+------------------------------
          1 | PostgreSQL for Beginners
          1 | PostgreSQL for C Programmers
          1 | PostgreSQL for Tcl Programmers
          2 | PostgreSQL for Tcl Programmers
(4 rows)
```

Four records are in the table. In this example, the number of student_ids is computed:

```
phpbook=# SELECT COUNT(student_id) FROM course;
 count
-------
     4
(1 row)
```

Let's try an additional query. In the next example you want to display the name of the training course as well:

```
phpbook=# SELECT COUNT(student_id), course FROM course;
ERROR:  Attribute course.course must be GROUPed or used in an aggregate function
```

This does not work because PostgreSQL does not know which name to display. To count the number of people attending a certain training course, it is necessary to add a GROUP BY statement to the query:

```
phpbook=# SELECT COUNT(student_id), course FROM course GROUP BY course;
 count |            course
-------+------------------------------
     1 | PostgreSQL for Beginners
     1 | PostgreSQL for C Programmers
     2 | PostgreSQL for Tcl Programmers
(3 rows)
```

As you can see, one person is attending the beginners' course, one person attends the C training course, and two people are in favor of the Tcl training course. Every column you want to display has to be added to the GROUP BY statement because otherwise PostgreSQL will not know which data should be displayed on the screen. The same applies to all other aggregation functions.

7.6.6 HAVING

In the previous section about GROUP BY, you have seen how to perform simple aggregations. In many cases it is necessary to process the result of an aggregation and to perform additional operations. HAVING clauses can be used. A HAVING clause is like an ordinary WHERE clause except that it does not operate on the original data but on the result of an aggregation function. This way, it is possible to perform many operations with just one SQL statement.

Here's an example. Imagine that you want to retrieve all training courses where exactly one student is going to participate:

```
SELECT COUNT(student_id), course
        FROM course
        GROUP by course
        HAVING COUNT(student_id)=1;
```

You can perform the same query you have already seen when counting the people attending a certain training course, but this time you have to add a HAVING clause that tells PostgreSQL to select only these values. The result will contain two records:

```
 count |           course
-------+----------------------------------
     1 | PostgreSQL for Beginners
     1 | PostgreSQL for C Programmers
(2 rows)
```

As you can see, the entry for the Tcl training course is missing because two people will attend the training course. If you need more than just one condition in the HAVING clause, it can be added just as you would do in a WHERE clause. In the next example you can see that a second condition has been added to the HAVING clause:

```
SELECT COUNT(student_id), course
        FROM course
        GROUP by course
        HAVING COUNT(student_id)=1
                AND COUNT(student_id) > 0;
```

The result is still the same because no record in the table is lower or equal than zero:

```
count |             course
------+-------------------------------
    1 | PostgreSQL for Beginners
    1 | PostgreSQL for C Programmers
(2 rows)
```

HAVING clauses are a comfortable way to solve many common problems. However, if you have to perform more than one operation on the result of an aggregation function, it might be more useful to work with temporary tables:

```
SELECT COUNT(student_id), course INTO TEMP TABLE tmp_tab
        FROM course
        GROUP by course;
```

After creating the temporary table, it is an easy task to retrieve values:

```
phpbook=# SELECT * FROM tmp_tab;
count |             course
------+-------------------------------
    1 | PostgreSQL for Beginners
    1 | PostgreSQL for C Programmers
    2 | PostgreSQL for Tcl Programmers
(3 rows)
```

Let's select all records where the number of people attending the training course is equal to 1:

```
phpbook=# SELECT * FROM tmp_tab WHERE count=1;
count |             course
------+-------------------------------
    1 | PostgreSQL for Beginners
    1 | PostgreSQL for C Programmers
(2 rows)
```

The result of the query is equal to the one you have achieved when using the HAVING clause.

7.7 Inserting Huge Amounts of Data

Until now you have only dealt with small amounts of data. Inserting only a few records can easily be done by using INSERT statements. With huge amounts of data, using INSERT would be far too slow due to a lot of parsing and transaction overhead.

To insert data more efficiently, PostgreSQL provides a command called COPY, which can also be used to store tables in external files. Let's look at the syntax overview of the COPY command:

```
phpbook=# \h COPY
Command:    COPY
Description: copy data between files and tables
Syntax:
COPY [ BINARY ] table [ WITH OIDS ]
    FROM { 'filename' | stdin }
    [ [USING] DELIMITERS 'delimiter' ]
    [ WITH NULL AS 'null string' ]
COPY [ BINARY ] table [ WITH OIDS ]
    TO { 'filename' | stdout }
    [ [USING] DELIMITERS 'delimiter' ]
    [ WITH NULL AS 'null string' ]
```

As you can see, the COPY command is a powerful feature of PostgreSQL. To insert some data into the table called student, you can use PostgreSQL's interactive shell:

```
phpbook=# COPY student FROM stdin;
Enter data to be copied followed by a newline.
End with a backslash and a period on a line by itself.
>> 4    Paul
>> 5    Henry
>> 6    Sheila
>> 7    Shelley
>> 8    Pat
>> 9    Pauline
>> \.
```

After starting the COPY command, the data has to be passed to the database using tabs as separators. To tell PostgreSQL that no more data will be inserted, \. has to be used. If no error occurred, the data has successfully been inserted into the table:

```
phpbook=# SELECT * FROM student;
 id | name
----+---------
  1 | Epi
  2 | Hans
  3 | Heinz
  4 | Paul
  5 | Henry
  6 | Sheila
```

```
 7 | Shelley
 8 | Pat
 9 | Pauline
(9 rows)
```

In many cases the data that has to be imported does not contain tabs for separating the various fields. In this case it is necessary to tell COPY which symbol has to be used as delimiter. In addition, it is possible to import the data from files as shown in the next example:

The file called data.sql contains two lines of data:

```
COPY student FROM stdin USING DELIMITERS ';';
10;Olaf
11;Andrea
\.
```

To import the data you can send the data in data.sql to psql:

psql phpbook < data.sql

The table contains two additional values now:

```
phpbook=# SELECT * FROM student WHERE id > 9;
 id |   name
----+---------
 10 | Olaf
 11 | Andrea
(2 rows)
```

Another important thing is to tell PostgreSQL what to treat as NULL values. If NULL is passed to the COPY command, PostgreSQL will treat it just like a string, which is not the desired behavior. If a blank value is passed to COPY, it will be treated as an empty string but not as blank.

Take a look at an example where the string null should be treated as NULL:

```
phpbook=# COPY student FROM stdin WITH NULL AS 'null';
Enter data to be copied followed by a newline.
End with a backslash and a period on a line by itself.
>> 12    Carlos
>> 13    null
>> null James
>> \.
```

Two records contain NULL values. The next query returns a record if either id or name contains a NULL value.

```
phpbook=# SELECT * FROM student WHERE id is NULL OR name IS NULL;
 id | name
----+-------
 13 |
    | James
(2 rows)
```

In this example two records contain NULL values.

PostgreSQL is capable of handling extremely huge amounts of data, and with the help of the COPY command it is possible to insert data fast and reliably.

As you have seen in the syntax overview, it is also possible to work with binary data. However, we recommend using binary data only when you have exported the data in binary format and you want to import it into the database again. When you are only importing the data, it is easier to use ASCII files because using ASCII will make your applications easier to understand.

7.8 Indexes

The more records you want to store in a table, the longer it will take to find the appropriate values because the database has to check every record in the table at least once to generate the result. If you are working with millions of records, this will take far too long and the performance of your application will suffer if the number of records in the database increases.

Trees are a fundamental data structure and can be used to speed up the access to huge amounts of data. Indexes (non-American readers will spell the plural of the word *index* as *indices*, which is the correct Latin plural of the word) are based on trees, and in this section you will learn how to create and drop indexes. You will also have a brief look at PostgreSQL internals.

7.8.1 Creating and Removing Indexes

Creating indexes is as simple as creating any other object in PostgreSQL. To define an index, use the CREATE INDEX command. Let's look at the syntax overview of the command:

```
phpbook=# \h CREATE INDEX
Command:     CREATE INDEX
Description: define a new index
```

Syntax:
```
CREATE [ UNIQUE ] INDEX index_name ON table
    [ USING acc_method ] ( column [ ops_name ] [, ...] )
    [ WHERE predicate ]
CREATE [ UNIQUE ] INDEX index_name ON table
    [ USING acc_method ] ( func_name( column [, ... ]) [ ops_name ] )
    [ WHERE predicate ]
```

As you can see, the syntax is easy to understand. Let's create an index:

```
phpbook=# CREATE INDEX idx_student_id ON student(id);
CREATE
```

The name of the index is idx_student_id and it has been defined on the column called id in table student. When looking for data in the specific column, PostgreSQL might use the index in order to retrieve the data faster. PostgreSQL *might* use the index—PostgreSQL is not forced to use the index. Depending on the decision of the optimizer, which is responsible for finding the best way through a query, PostgreSQL might neglect the index if it thinks that it is faster to perform a sequential scan. Performing a sequential scan means that the table is read from the beginning to the end without using an index. Query optimization is covered in detail in Chapter 18, "Tuning."

When creating the index, PostgreSQL will sort the data internally and a tree structure will be built. If a table is huge, the operation will take some time.

Indexes can also defined for more than just one column. This does not mean that both columns can be accessed fast when looking for values in one column. Defining an index on more than just one column means that PostgreSQL will retrieve values fast when you are looking for a pair of values that is in the column you have defined an index on. To generate an index on more than just one column, a list of columns has to be passed to the CREATE INDEX command:

```
phpbook=# CREATE INDEX idx_student_id_name ON student(id, name);
CREATE
```

So far, two indexes have been generated. To see which indexes have been defined on one table, you can use \d:

```
phpbook=# \d student
       Table "student"
 Column |  Type   | Modifiers
--------+---------+-----------
 id     | integer |
 name   | text    |
```

```
Indexes: idx_student_id,
         idx_student_id_name
```

As you can see, two indexes have been generated. The indexes are listed when retrieving information about the tables, but the columns they have been defined on will not be listed. Therefore we recommend assigning useful names to indexes that contain the names of the column the indexes have been defined for. Of course, it is possible to ask PostgreSQL about the index, but it is better to store this information in the name as well.

Let's retrieve some information about an index:

```
phpbook=# \d idx_student_id
Index "idx_student_id"
 Column |  Type
--------+---------
 id     | integer
btree
```

PostgreSQL returns the name of the column the index has been defined for, but this time you will not find the table the index has been defined for. In addition, the data type of the values in the index is returned. In this example the index is based on B-trees.

To remove an index from a column, use DROP INDEX:

```
phpbook=# \h DROP INDEX
Command:     DROP INDEX
Description: remove an index
Syntax:
DROP INDEX index_name [, ...]
```

Let's remove an index:

```
phpbook=# DROP INDEX idx_student_id_name;
DROP
```

If no error occurred, the index has been removed successfully.

7.8.2 Repairing a Corrupt System Index

This section deals with an extremely unlikely situation. We have been working with PostgreSQL for years, but we have never seen PostgreSQL collapse because it is an extremely reliable piece of software. However, let's look at a command called REINDEX, which can be used to recover corrupted system indexes.

```
phpbook=# \h REINDEX
Command:     REINDEX
Description: recover a corrupted system index
Syntax:
REINDEX { TABLE | DATABASE | INDEX } name [ FORCE ]
```

As you can see, REINDEX can be used not only for restoring indexes, but corrupted indexes are the most likely scenario. Let's try the command:

```
phpbook=# REINDEX INDEX idx_student_id;
REINDEX
```

As you can see, everything works just the way it should. You will have a closer look at REINDEX in Chapter 10, "PostgreSQL Administration."

7.8.3 PostgreSQL Internals

PostgreSQL provides three types of indexes:

- **B-trees**—B-tree indexes are an implementation of Lehman-Yao high-concurrency B-trees and are the standard index structure of PostgreSQL. If you are not working with geometric data types, PostgreSQL will automatically use B-trees.

- **R-trees**—R-trees are used for spatial searching and are based on Guttman's quadratic split algorithm. Spatial searching means that it is possible to perform a basic set of geometric operations using indexes. Therefore PostgreSQL is an excellent database for systems storing geographic data.

- **Hashes**—PostgreSQL's hashes are based on Litwin's linear hashing. Hashes are not used very often.

You have already heard about trees and indexes, but what do trees look like and how do they work? Take a look at Figure 7.1.

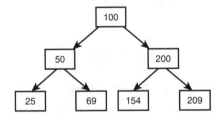

FIGURE 7.1   A B-tree.

The root node contains the value 100. Every value lower than the root node is on the left side—all values higher than the root node are stored on the right side. In this scenario every node has two children. Those nodes that don't have children are called *leaves*. If you are reading the values from left to right, you will find that the tree contains a sorted list of the data. The advantage of a sorted list is that a record can be found fast. Assume that you are looking for the value 154. It will take 2 steps to find the correct value out of 7 records. In a sequential scan, the average would be 3.5 steps (7 divided by 2). If the number of records in the table doubles, PostgreSQL will need just one more step to find the correct value—in an unsorted list it would take twice the time. To retrieve one record out of 1,000,000 records, it takes about 20 steps when using an index—if no index is used it would take about 500,000 steps. This example shows how much faster it can be to use an index instead of a sequential scan.

Figure 7.1 shows the idea of working with trees. The real implementation of PostgreSQL is far more complex because things like transactions and overhead due to hardware-related questions have to be taken into consideration, but the most important thing is to understand why things can be much faster when working with indexes.

7.9 Modifying Objects

After objects like tables have been created, it might be necessary to modify those objects. Therefore PostgreSQL provides some simple commands, which you will learn about in this section.

7.9.1 Modifying Tables

Most modifications can be done with the command UPDATE and ALTER. You have already learned about UPDATE in this chapter, and now it is time to have a closer look at the ALTER command. Many activities, such as modifying users, groups, and tables, can be done with ALTER. In this section you will focus on ALTER TABLE. Let's look at the syntax overview of the command:

```
phpbook=# \h ALTER TABLE
Command:     ALTER TABLE
Description: change the definition of a table
Syntax:
ALTER TABLE [ ONLY ] table [ * ]
    ADD [ COLUMN ] column type [ column_constraint [ ... ] ]
ALTER TABLE [ ONLY ] table [ * ]
    ALTER [ COLUMN ] column { SET DEFAULT value | DROP DEFAULT }
ALTER TABLE [ ONLY ] table [ * ]
    ALTER [ COLUMN ] column SET STATISTICS integer
```

```
ALTER TABLE [ ONLY ] table [ * ]
    RENAME [ COLUMN ] column TO newcolumn
ALTER TABLE table
    RENAME TO newtable
ALTER TABLE table
    ADD table constraint definition
ALTER TABLE [ ONLY ] table
        DROP CONSTRAINT constraint { RESTRICT | CASCADE }
ALTER TABLE table
        OWNER TO new owner
```

As you can see, the command is powerful and provides a lot of features.

One of the most important things you can do with the help of ALTER TABLE is to add columns to a table. Let's look at the table called student:

```
phpbook=# \d student
        Table "student"
 Column |  Type   | Modifiers
--------+---------+-----------
 id     | integer |
 name   | text    |
Indexes: idx_student_id
```

The table contains two columns. To add a third column for storing the birthday, use ALTER TABLE:

```
phpbook=# ALTER TABLE student ADD COLUMN birthday timestamp;
ALTER
```

If no error occurred, the column has successfully been added to the table:

```
phpbook=# \d student
                Table "student"
  Column  |             Type             | Modifiers
----------+------------------------------+-----------
 id       | integer                      |
 name     | text                         |
 birthday | timestamp(6) with time zone  |
Indexes: idx_student_id
```

The table contains three columns now. To modify the name of the column you have just added, ALTER TABLE can be used again:

```
phpbook=# ALTER TABLE student RENAME COLUMN birthday TO day_of_birth;
ALTER
```

day_of_birth will be the new name of the column:

```
phpbook=# \d student
                    Table "student"
     Column    |             Type            | Modifiers
---------------+-----------------------------+-----------
 id            | integer                     |
 name          | text                        |
 day_of_birth  | timestamp(6) with time zone |
Indexes: idx_student_id
```

Sometimes it is necessary to change the name of a table. In general, changing the name of a table should be avoided because this will affect your entire application. However, it is necessary to know how the name of a table can be changed. Let's look at the table whose name you want to change:

```
phpbook=# \d course
          Table "course"
   Column    | Type  | Modifiers
------------+-------+-----------
 student_id | integer |
 course     | text    |
```

The name has to be training_course instead of course. Using a simple command will change the name to the desired string.

```
phpbook=# ALTER TABLE course RENAME TO training_course;
ALTER
```

The old relation does not exist any more and a new name has been assigned to the table:

```
phpbook=# \d course
Did not find any relation named "course".
phpbook=# \d training_course
     Table "training_course"
   Column    | Type  | Modifiers
------------+-------+-----------
 student_id | integer |
 course     | text    |
```

7.9.2 Modifying Sequences

Sequences are an essential feature of every sophisticated database. Sequences can be used to generate consecutively numbered lists and many other things. Normally, sequences are used to generate a list of unique numbers. In some cases, however, it is necessary to modify the current value of a sequence.

Let's create a sequence and see how this can be done:

```
phpbook=# CREATE SEQUENCE seq_showseq INCREMENT 1 START 1;
CREATE
```

The start of the sequence has been set to 1. To retrieve information about a sequence, it can be accessed just like a table by using SELECT:

```
phpbook=# SELECT * FROM seq_showseq;
 sequence_name | last_value | increment_by |      max_value      | min_value |
cache_value | log_cnt | is_cycled | is_called
---------------+------------+--------------+---------------------+-----------+-
------------+---------+-----------+-----------
 seq_showseq   |          1 |            1 | 9223372036854775807 |         1 |
          1 |
1 | f         | f
(1 row)
```

Let's look at the data structure the SELECT statement is accessing:

```
phpbook=# \d seq_showseq
 Sequence "seq_showseq"
    Column     |  Type
---------------+---------
 sequence_name | name
 last_value    | bigint
 increment_by  | bigint
 max_value     | bigint
 min_value     | bigint
 cache_value   | bigint
 log_cnt       | bigint
 is_cycled     | boolean
 is_called     | boolean
```

As you can see, PostgreSQL has to store quite a lot of information about the sequence.

To select the next value in the sequence, use the function called `nextval`:

```
phpbook=# SELECT nextval('seq_showseq');
 nextval
---------
       1
(1 row)
```

The first value in the sequence is 1. If the sequence is accessed again, the value will be two:

```
phpbook=# SELECT nextval('seq_showseq');
 nextval
---------
       2
(1 row)
```

In some cases it is necessary to modify this value. Especially when something has gone wrong in your application, it might be necessary to change to the next value. This can easily be done with the help of the `setval` function:

```
phpbook=# SELECT setval('seq_showseq', 400);
 setval
--------
    400
(1 row)
```

The value of the sequence has been set to 400. If the sequence is accessed the next time, the value will be 401:

```
phpbook=# SELECT nextval('seq_showseq');
 nextval
---------
     401
(1 row)
```

As you have seen in the first example of this section, the sequence can be accessed just like a table. But is it possible to work with UPDATE instead of `setval`?

```
phpbook=# UPDATE seq_showseq SET last_value=999;
ERROR:  You can't change sequence relation seq_showseq
```

PostgreSQL does not accept the UPDATE command when working with sequences, so `setval` has to be used.

7.10 Mathematical Functions and Operators

Functions and operators are essential for every application. You have already used some operators in this book but in this section you will find a complete list of mathematical functions. Operators related to geometric data types will not be discussed in this chapter.

Let's look at the mathematical operators first in Table 7.2.

TABLE 7.2   Mathematical Operators

Operator	Description	Example	Result
+	Addition	SELECT 1+1;	2
-	Subtraction	SELECT 14-3;	11
*	Multiplication	SELECT 3*4;	12
/	Division	SELECT 18/3;	6
%	Modulo	SELECT 14%3;	2
^	Exponentiation	SELECT 2^10;	1024
|/	Square root	SELECT |/ 361;	19
||/	Cube root	SELECT 5832;	18
!	Factorial	SELECT 23!;	862453760
!!	Factorial (prefix operator)	SELECT !! 23;	862453760
@	Absolute value	SELECT @ -23;	23
&	Binary AND	SELECT 12 & 24;	8
|	Binary OR	SELECT 12 | 24;	28
#	Binary XOR	SELECT 12 # 24;	20
~	Binary NOR	SELECT 12 ~ 24;	f
<<	Binary shift left	SELECT 2 << 4;	32
>>	Binary shift right	SELECT 5 >> 2;	1

The mathematical functions are shown in Table 7.3.

TABLE 7.3   Mathematical Functions

Function	Description
abs(x)	Absolute value
cbrt(double precision)	Cube root
ceil(numeric)	Next integer higher than the argument of the function
degrees(double precision)	Convert radians to degrees
exp(double precision)	Exponential function
floor(numeric)	Next integer lower than the argument of the function
ln(double precision)	Natural logarithm
log(double precision)	Base 10 logarithm

TABLE 7.3   Continued

Function	Description
log(base numeric, x numeric)	Logarithm to specified base
mod(*y*, *x*)	Remainder (modulo) of the division y/x
pi()	The value of Pi
pow(double precision, double precision)	Raise a number to the specified exponent
radians(double precision)	Convert degrees to radians
random()	Generates a random number between 0 and 1
round(double precision)	Rounds to the nearest integer value
round(*value* numeric, *scale* integer)	Rounds to a certain precision
sqrt(double precision)	Square root
trunc(double precision)	Truncate (toward zero)
trunc(*value* numeric, *scale* integer)	Truncate to specified number of decimal places

Finally, take a look at PostgreSQL's trigonometric functions in Table 7.4.

TABLE 7.4   Trigonometric Functions

Function	Description
acos(*x*)	inverse cosine
asin(*x*)	inverse sine
atan(*x*)	inverse tangent
atan2(*x*, *y*)	inverse tangent of *y*/*x*
cos(*x*)	cosine
cot(*x*)	cotangent
sin(*x*)	sine
tan(*x*)	tangent

7.11 Summary

SQL is a powerful language and can be used to solve almost all problems because the language has been designed as a database language.

The goal of PostgreSQL is to be 100% ANSI-compliant, and the major part of the ANSI SQL specification as well as some PostgreSQL specific add-ons has been implemented.

8

Advanced SQL

SQL is a language that has been designed to perform complex queries. No matter what kind of query you have to write, in most cases you can easily do it with SQL.

PostgreSQL provides a rich set of SQL commands, and it is the perfect database for nearly all kinds of complex operations. Even if you want to work with complex integrity constraints such as inheritance, PostgreSQL will provide the right solution for you.

In this chapter, you will be guided through PostgreSQL's advanced SQL capabilities and you will learn to develop complex and powerful data structures. You will need this information when building sophisticated PHP applications with the help of PostgreSQL.

8.1 Advanced Data Types

So far you have dealt with the basic set of PostgreSQL's data types such as int4, numeric, and text. These basic data types are provided by almost all common databases. In PostgreSQL an impressive list of additional data types is provided. These data types can be used to store specific pieces of information more efficiently than could be done using commonly known data types.

In addition to a broad range of data types, PostgreSQL provides an easy C interface for defining your own data types. Only a few functions need to be implemented in order to create new data types. When working with your own data types, you need not worry about accessing your data using PHP because data is always returned as text, so new data types do not affect your PHP application.

In this section, you will be guided through some data types provided by PostgreSQL and you will learn to work with these data types.

8.1.1 Working with Geometric Data Types

Geometric data types are a core feature of PostgreSQL and they are often used for building highly reliable and sophisticated systems that use Geographic Information Systems (GIS). GIS systems are software products used for analyzing and storing geographic data with the help of databases. For these purposes, PostgreSQL is a good choice because it provides an efficient index structure for accessing geometric data extremely fast. This index structure is called R-tree and it allows spatial searching as well as numerous other operations.

Table 8.1 lists the geometric data types provided by PostgreSQL.

TABLE 8.1   PostgreSQL's Geometric Data Types

Data Type	Description
box	A geometric box, rectangle
circle	A circle defined by a point and a radius
line	A line defined by a starting point and an end point
lseg	A geometric line segment
path	A sequence of lines defined by points
point	A point defined by two coordinates
polygon	A polygon defined by a list of points

As you can see, PostgreSQL provides data types for storing all kinds of geometric information. Of course, it is possible to store geometric data differently, but using PostgreSQL's built-in data types has some significant advantages because of efficiency.

8.1.1.1 Points

Points are the key data structure of PostgreSQL's implementation of geometric data types. Most other geometric data types are built on points, so knowing how to deal with points is an extremely important task.

Let's create a table containing one column for storing points:

```
phpbook=# CREATE TABLE store_point(mypoint point);
CREATE
```

Creating the table is an easy task, but let's try to insert some data into it:

```
phpbook=# INSERT INTO store_point VALUES ('23, 17');
INSERT 24836 1
```

A point consists of two values, or coordinates. The first coordinate defines the x-coordinate and the second value contains the y-coordinate of the point. Currently PostgreSQL supports only two-dimensional points. At the moment it is not possible to work with multidimensional points without implementing a separate data type.

In the next step you can retrieve the point you just added to the table:

```
phpbook=# SELECT * FROM store_point;
 mypoint
----------
 (23,17)
(1 row)
```

8.1.1.2 Boxes

The data type box is used to store rectangles. A rectangle can be defined by two opposite points, and that's the way rectangles are stored internally.

Let's create a table:

```
phpbook=# CREATE TABLE store_box(data box);
CREATE
```

After creating the table, you can try to insert some values into it. The next examples all lead to the same result:

```
phpbook=# INSERT INTO store_box VALUES ('(1,1), (3,3)');
INSERT 24839 1
phpbook=# INSERT INTO store_box VALUES ('1,1, 3,3');
INSERT 24840 1
phpbook=# INSERT INTO store_box VALUES ('(1,1, 3,3)');
INSERT 24841 1
phpbook=# INSERT INTO store_box VALUES ('((1,1), (3,3))');
INSERT 24842 1
```

The way parentheses are used does not affect the way PostgreSQL treats the data. The first two values are used to define one edge of the rectangle, and the third and fourth value contain information about the second point defining the rectangle. Take a look at the content of the table:

```
phpbook=# SELECT * FROM store_box;
    data
-------------
 (3,3),(1,1)
 (3,3),(1,1)
 (3,3),(1,1)
 (3,3),(1,1)
(4 rows)
```

You can easily look for a specific box in the table by using the = operator:

```
phpbook=# SELECT * FROM store_box WHERE data = '(3,3),(1,1)' LIMIT 1;
    data
- - - - - - - - - - - - -
 (3,3),(1,1)
(1 row)
```

8.1.1.3 Lines

Lines consist of two points as well. One point defines the beginning and one point defines the end of the line. At the time this book was written, lines have not yet been fully implemented in PostgreSQL.

However, tables containing lines can be created:

```
phpbook=# CREATE TABLE store_line(data line);
CREATE
```

Creating a table containing lines is already possible, but it is not yet possible to insert and select records:

```
phpbook=# SELECT '(1,1), (2,2)'::line;
ERROR:  line not yet implemented
```

We hope that full support for lines will be implemented in future versions.

8.1.1.4 Line Segments

Line segments are represented by a pair of points. You can create a table that contains line segments just as you have seen for the other data types:

```
phpbook=# CREATE TABLE store_line (data line);
CREATE
```

PostgreSQL provides a sophisticated parsing function for line segments, so the input format is flexible:

```
phpbook=# INSERT INTO store_lseg VALUES ('(1,1), (2,2)');
INSERT 24848 1
phpbook=# INSERT INTO store_lseg VALUES ('(1,1, 2,2)');
INSERT 24849 1
phpbook=# INSERT INTO store_lseg VALUES ('1,1, 2,2');
INSERT 24850 1
```

All INSERT statements are equal and will lead to the same result, as you can see in the table:

```
phpbook=# SELECT * FROM store_lseg;
     data
----------------
 [(1,1),(2,2)]
 [(1,1),(2,2)]
 [(1,1),(2,2)]
(3 rows)
```

The definition of a line segment looks similar to boxes, but internally things are treated differently. Different data types are defined, so things are only similar but not equal.

8.1.1.5 Paths

Paths consist of a set of points. In general two kinds of paths are available. Open paths are paths where the first and the last point do not match. In closed paths the beginning of a path is defined by the same point as the end of the path. PostgreSQL provides easy methods to find out whether a path is closed or not.

To show you how you can work with paths, we create a table called store_path:

```
phpbook=# CREATE TABLE store_path(data path);
CREATE
```

Let's insert an open path into the table:

```
phpbook=# INSERT INTO store_path VALUES ('[(1,1), (2,2), (-3,2)]');
INSERT 24856 1
```

The square brackets at the beginning of the string tell PostgreSQL that the path has to be treated as a closed path. To insert a closed path into the table, parentheses must be used:

```
phpbook=# INSERT INTO store_path VALUES ('((1,1), (2,2), (-3,2))');
INSERT 24857 1
```

You used the same values inside the path. However, because one path is closed and one is open, the two values you have just inserted into the database differ:

```
phpbook=# SELECT '((1,1), (2,2), (-3,2))' = '[(1,1), (2,2), (-3,2)]';
 ?column?
----------
 f
(1 row)
```

`False` is returned, which means that the two records are not the same.

Let's see what is in the table:

```
phpbook=# SELECT * FROM store_path;
          data
-----------------------
 [(1,1),(2,2),(-3,2)]
 ((1,1),(2,2),(-3,2))
(2 rows)
```

As you can see, PostgreSQL displays the correct brackets for every record. This way it is easy to find out if a path is open or not. However, when building applications, it won't be useful to see things on first sight because things must be checked by the database. Therefore PostgreSQL provides two functions called `isopen` and `isclosed`. As you can easily imagine, `isopen` returns `true` if a path is open:

```
phpbook=# SELECT data, isopen(data) FROM store_path;
          data        | isopen
----------------------+--------
 [(1,1),(2,2),(-3,2)] | t
 ((1,1),(2,2),(-3,2)) | f
(2 rows)
```

The first path is open and the second path in the table is closed. The `isclosed` function is the exact opposite of the `isopen` function:

```
phpbook=# SELECT data, isclosed(data) FROM store_path;
          data        | isclosed
----------------------+----------
 [(1,1),(2,2),(-3,2)] | f
 ((1,1),(2,2),(-3,2)) | t
(2 rows)
```

8.1.1.6 Polygons
Polygons are similar to closed paths. However, internally PostgreSQL has a separate set of functions and operators in order to handle polygons efficiently.

The syntax and the way polygons are treated are equal to what you have just seen in the section called "Paths." Tables with polygons can be created in the same way as tables with paths:

```
phpbook=# CREATE TABLE store_polygon(data polygon);
CREATE
```

8.1.1.7 Circles

Circles consist of a point that marks the center of the circle and a radius. Let's see how circles can be inserted into the database:

```
phpbook=# CREATE TABLE store_circle(data circle);
CREATE
```

The table has been created successfully. Here is a list of the most important ways circles can be inserted into a table:

```
phpbook=# INSERT INTO store_circle VALUES ('1,0, 12');
INSERT 24860 1
phpbook=# INSERT INTO store_circle VALUES ('((1,0), 12)');
INSERT 24861 1
phpbook=# INSERT INTO store_circle VALUES ('<(1,0), 12>');
INSERT 24862 1
```

The table will contain three values that are all the same:

```
phpbook=# SELECT * FROM store_circle;
    data
-----------
 <(1,0),12>
 <(1,0),12>
 <(1,0),12>
(3 rows)
```

To retrieve records from the table, every syntax shown in the previous examples can be used. PostgreSQL will parse the data internally, so it does not matter in which format the data is actually passed to the database:

```
phpbook=# SELECT * FROM store_circle WHERE data = '1,0,12' LIMIT 1;
    data
-----------
 <(1,0),12>
(1 row)
```

No matter what the WHERE clause looks like, PostgreSQL will always display the data in the same way.

8.1.1.8 Geometric Data Types and Operators

As we promised, PostgreSQL provides a rich set of operators and functions that can easily be used in combination with geometric data types. Together with R-trees, which are the standard index structure for indexing geometric data types, these operators are a strong team for a broad range of applications.

In this section, you will learn about the most important and most useful operators defined for geometric data types. Because the list of operators provided by the database is nearly endless, only the most important and most frequently used operators will be covered and discussed in detail.

Take a look at the list of geometric operators in Table 8.2. Keep in mind that not all of these operators are defined for every data type.

TABLE 8.2   Geometric Operators

Operator	Description
+	Translation
-	Translation
*	Scaling/rotation
/	Scaling/rotation
#	Intersection or number of points in a polygon
##	Point of closest proximity
&&	Overlaps?
&<	Overlaps to left?
&>	Overlaps to right?
<->	Distance between
<<	Left of?
<^	Is below?
>>	Is right of?
>^	Is above?
?#	Intersects or overlaps
?-	Is horizontal?
?-|	Is perpendicular?
@-@	Length or circumference
?|	Is vertical?
?||	Is parallel?
@	Contained or on
@@	Center of
~=	Same as

After taking a look at the list of operators, it is time to do some practical examples.

To add the coordinates of two objects, use the + operator. In the next example you will use it for adding two points:

```
phpbook=# SELECT '1,1'::point + '3,4'::point;
 ?column?
----------
 (4,5)
(1 row)
```

It is also possible to add a point and a box. To cast the string to the right data type, use the :: operator. The string '1,1' is cast to point in order to tell PostgreSQL what to do with it. In this example every point defining the box will be increased, as shown in the next code segment:

```
phpbook=# SELECT '(1,1), (2,2)'::box + '3,4'::point;
  ?column?
-------------
 (5,6),(4,5)
(1 row)
```

As you can see, this way it is easily possible to work with vector operations on a database level. This makes building applications simple because you don't have to implement these things on the application level.

It is also possible to add circles to each other:

```
phpbook=# SELECT '1,1, 2'::circle + '1,1, 1'::circle;
  ?column?
-----------
 <(2,2),2>
(1 row)
```

The radius of the first circle is not modified—the two radiuses have not been added. Let's swap the order of the circles passed to the database:

```
phpbook=# SELECT '1,1, 1'::circle + '1,1, 2'::circle;
  ?column?
-----------
 <(2,2),1>
(1 row)
```

The result is not the same as you saw in the previous example. In circles, the + operator is not commutative, which means that it makes a difference if you use A+B or B+A. This is extremely dangerous because you have to know exactly what you are doing and how certain operations are defined. I want to point out that this is not a weak spot of PostgreSQL—it is a matter of how things are defined internally. We strongly recommend trying out a few examples before making heavy use of PostgreSQL's operators.

The operators -, *, and / work pretty much the same way as the + operator does.

To compute the intersection of two geometric objects, PostgreSQL provides the # operator. In the next example you see how the intersection of two boxes can be computed:

```
phpbook=# SELECT '(4,4), (6,6)'::box # '(6,6), (7,7)'::box;
  ?column?
-------------
 (6,6),(6,6)
(1 row)
```

The result seems obvious because the two boxes have only one point in common. Here's an additional example:

```
phpbook=# SELECT '(4,4), (6,6)'::box # '6,6, 7'::circle;
  ?column?
-------------
 (6,6),(4,4)
(1 row)
```

In this example the intersection of the two objects is the entire first object. As you can see, it is also possible to compute the intersection of objects that do not have the same data type.

Recall the structure of store_polygon:

```
phpbook=# \d store_polygon
    Table "store_polygon"
 Column |  Type   | Modifiers
--------+---------+-----------
 data   | polygon |
```

The table contains one column for storing polygons. Let's insert one value into the table:

```
phpbook=# INSERT INTO store_polygon VALUES('(4,4), (6,6), (-3,1), (2,9)');
INSERT 24868 1
```

The # operator can also be used to compute the number of points a polygon contains:

```
phpbook=# SELECT data, #data FROM store_polygon;
           data            | ?column?
---------------------------+----------
 ((4,4),(6,6),(-3,1),(2,9)) |        4
(1 row)
```

The polygon you have inserted into the table consists of four points.

To find the point of closest proximity, the ## has been implemented:

```
phpbook=# SELECT '<(0,0), 4>'::circle ## '<(7,8), 3>'::circle;
            ?column?
- - - - - - - - - - - - - - - - - - - - - - - - - - - - - - - - - - - -
 (4.87867965644036,5.87867965644036)
(1 row)
```

Sometimes it is necessary to find out if two objects overlap. You can use the && operator:

```
phpbook=# SELECT '(1,1), (2,2)'::box && '(1,1) ,(3,3)'::box;
 ?column?
- - - - - - - - - -
 t
(1 row)
```

Take a look at three additional examples:

```
phpbook=# SELECT '(1,1), (2,2)'::box && '(-1,-1) ,(0,0)'::box;
 ?column?
- - - - - - - - - -
 f
(1 row)
phpbook=# SELECT '(1,1), (2,2)'::box &< '(-1,-1) ,(0,0)'::box;
 ?column?
- - - - - - - - - -
 f
(1 row)
phpbook=# SELECT '(1,1), (2,2)'::box &> '(-1,-1) ,(0,0)'::box;
 ?column?
- - - - - - - - - -
 t
(1 row)
```

As you can see, in the first example, the two boxes do not overlap. In the second example, you want to find out if the left box overlaps to the left, whereas the third example computes whether they overlap to the right. In the third example true is returned.

One of the most commonly used operators when working with geometric data types is the <-> operator:

```
phpbook=# SELECT '1,1'::point <-> '2,2'::point;
    ?column?
------------------
 1.4142135623731
(1 row)
```

The distance between the two points is about 1.41, which is the square root of 2.

To find out if an object contains a second object, PostgreSQL provides the @ operator:

```
phpbook=# SELECT '(-3,-3), (4,5)'::box @ '(2,2), (3,3)'::box;
 ?column?
----------
 f
(1 row)
```

In this example the first object does not contain the second one. Just like the + operator, the @ operator is not commutative. If the order of the two objects in the query is changed, the result will be true:

```
phpbook=# SELECT '(2,2), (3,3)'::box @ '(-3,-3), (4,5)'::box;
 ?column?
----------
 t
(1 row)
```

The next example shows how to compute the center of an object:

```
phpbook=# SELECT @@ '(2,2), (3,3)'::box;
 ?column?
----------
 (2.5,2.5)
(1 row)
```

With boxes, the center of the object is the average of the two points. The same operation also works for polygons:

```
phpbook=# SELECT @@ '(2,2), (3,3), (-3,2), (0,3)'::polygon;
 ?column?
----------
 (0.5,2.5)
(1 row)
```

As you can see, PostgreSQL provides a rich set of operators for working with geometric data types. It is not possible to cover all operators in detail because this would be beyond the scope of this book.

8.1.1.9 Functions for Geometric Data Types

PostgreSQL supports not only a rich set of operators, but a number of functions that you can use to perform all basic operations concerning geometric data types. In this section, you will find out about the most important of these functions and see how these functions can be used.

One of these functions is called area and can be used to compute the area of an object:

```
phpbook=# SELECT area('<(1,1), 5>'::circle);
    area
------------
 78.53981634
(1 row)
```

The area of a circle can be computed by calculating the square of the radius and multiplying it by Pi as shown in the next example:

```
phpbook=# SELECT (5^2)*pi();
     ?column?
------------------
 78.5398163397448
(1 row)
```

The calculation shown in the SQL statement is performed by PostgreSQL internally. The function called pi returned the value of Pi:

```
phpbook=# SELECT pi();
        pi
-----------------
 3.14159265358979
(1 row)
```

Center retrieves the center of an object. You have already seen the @@ operator, which is equal to the center function. Let's use the center function to find the center of a circle:

```
phpbook=# SELECT center('<(1,1), 5>'::circle);
 center
--------
 (1,1)
(1 row)
```

The result is not surprising because the center of the circle is already in the string, but what is this function good for when working with circles? The advantage of the function is that you don't have to write a function for parsing the string provided by PostgreSQL.

For computing the diameter, PostgreSQL provides a function called `diameter`:

```
phpbook=# SELECT diameter('<(1,1), 5>'::circle);
 diameter
----------
       10
(1 row)
```

In circles, the `diameter` is twice the value of the radius.

The height of an object can be computed as shown in the next example:

```
phpbook=# SELECT height('(1,1), (3,3)'::box);
 height
--------
      2
(1 row)
```

The result is not surprising because all PostgreSQL does is to compute the difference between the two y-coordinates.

The counterpart of the `height` function is the `width` function:

```
phpbook=# SELECT width('(1,1), (3,4)'::box);
 width
-------
     2
(1 row)
```

Internally PostgreSQL computes the difference of the x-coordinates of the box.

Another important attribute of an object is its length:

```
phpbook=# SELECT length('(2,2), (3,3), (-3,2), (0,3)'::polygon);
       length
-----------------
 12.8953217303395
(1 row)
```

The `length` function can be used to retrieve the length of an object. In this example you have computed the length of a polygon.

8.1.2 Working with Network Data Types

Now that you have dealt with geometric data types in detail, it is time to have a closer look at the data types related to network data types. PostgreSQL provides three data types for storing network information, as shown in Table 8.3.

TABLE 8.3   Network Data Types in PostgreSQL

Data Type	Internal Size	Description
cidr	12 bytes	Stores valid Ipv4 network addresses
inet	12 bytes	Stores IP addresses or network addresses
macaddr	6 bytes	Stores MAC addresses

The advantage of these data types is that data can be stored much more efficiently than when working with data types such as text. Just think of a MAC address that is usually 12 characters long. With the help of the data type macaddr, it will only take 6 bytes to store one record. Another advantage of network data types is that PostgreSQL does not allow invalid data to be inserted into the database. The parser makes sure that no IP address contains values lower than 0 or higher than 255. Things like that will save a lot of overhead and protect your data because no syntactically incorrect IP addresses can be stored in the database.

Let's take a detailed look at the various data types.

8.1.2.1 inet
Fields defined as inet can hold an IP host address and optionally the identity of the subnet it is in. The IP address and the subnet are stored in one field, which guarantees that the subnet and the IP are stored as one item of information.

Let's look at an example:

```
phpbook=# CREATE TABLE store_inet(data inet);
CREATE
```

After creating the table, you can try to insert some data. The next SQL statement shows how to insert an IP address into the table:

```
phpbook=# INSERT INTO store_inet VALUES ('192.168.1.1');
INSERT 24870 1
```

Sometimes you might want to add a netmask to the IP address. You can do this by adding a slash and the number of bit sets in the netmask to the string. In the next example you want the column to contain a 24-bit netmask (255.255.255.0):

```
phpbook=# INSERT INTO store_inet VALUES ('192.168.1.1/24');
INSERT 24871 1
```

If the IP address should be in a net consisting of only one machine, you have to use 32 bits instead of 24 bits:

```
phpbook=# INSERT INTO store_inet VALUES ('192.168.1.1/32');
INSERT 24872 1
```

What happens when an incorrect netmask is passed to the database?

```
phpbook=# INSERT INTO store_inet VALUES ('192.168.1.1/33');
ERROR:  invalid INET value '192.168.1.1/33'
```

Because the netmask is not valid, PostgreSQL will display an error as shown in the listing. Let's see what is in the table:

```
phpbook=# SELECT * FROM store_inet;
      data
----------------
 192.168.1.1/24
 192.168.1.1
 192.168.1.1
(3 rows)
```

Three records have been inserted into the table successfully. The first record contains an IP address and the netmask and the remaining two records contain only the IP address. In the case of a 32-bit netmask, the netmask will be omitted because it is redundant to mention it.

8.1.2.2 `cidr`

`cidr` is used to store IPv4 network addresses. Here's an example:

```
phpbook=# CREATE TABLE store_cidr(data cidr);
CREATE
```

Let's insert a new record into the table. The next example shows how a netmask can be inserted into the table:

```
phpbook=# INSERT INTO store_cidr VALUES('192/8');
INSERT 24876 1
```

The zeros in the netmask don't have to be displayed—192 is equal to 192.0.0.0, which is an entire subnet.

The next three examples show how smaller nets can be added to the table:

```
phpbook=# INSERT INTO store_cidr VALUES('192.168/16');
INSERT 24877 1
phpbook=# INSERT INTO store_cidr VALUES('192.168.1/24');
INSERT 24878 1
phpbook=# INSERT INTO store_cidr VALUES('192.168.1.1/32');
INSERT 24879 1
```

Four records have been inserted into the table:

```
phpbook=# SELECT * FROM store_cidr;
      data
----------------
 192.0.0.0/8
 192.168.0.0/16
 192.168.1.0/24
 192.168.1.1
(4 rows)
```

As you can see, the IP addresses are displayed, including the zeros at the end.

8.1.2.3 macaddr

Every piece of hardware in a network, such as network cards, print servers, switches, routers, and so forth have a so-called MAC address. A MAC address is a unique identification number for a network device and it is essential for keeping a network up and running. PostgreSQL provides a separate data type called macaddr for storing MAC addresses in a column.

To show you how this works, we have included an example:

```
phpbook=# CREATE TABLE store_macaddr (data macaddr);
CREATE
```

In the next step a MAC address will be added to the table in four different ways:

```
phpbook=# INSERT INTO store_macaddr VALUES ('123456-7890ab');
INSERT 24882 1
phpbook=# INSERT INTO store_macaddr VALUES ('12:34:56:78:90:ab');
INSERT 24883 1
phpbook=# INSERT INTO store_macaddr VALUES ('1234.5678.90ab');
INSERT 24884 1
phpbook=# INSERT INTO store_macaddr VALUES ('12-34-56-78-90-ab');
INSERT 24885 1
```

All values are the same and will be displayed using the format shown in the next example:

```
phpbook=# SELECT * FROM store_macaddr LIMIT 1;
      data
------------------
 12:34:56:78:90:ab
(1 row)
```

8.2 Working with Views

The way you look at your data affects the way you can process the data in your database. Looking at your data starts with building a model of a piece of reality and does not end with writing queries.

Certain database models allow certain ways of accessing the data. If the model of your data is a good one, you will be able to retrieve the information you need in most cases. However, in some situations it is necessary to change the way you look at your data. In that case, you should consider working with views.

Views are virtual tables that can be used to select data just as you would with ordinary tables. For the user a view is a table that contains the result of a SELECT statement. This way SELECT statements can be used on top of SELECT statements that appear as views. In this section you will learn to work with views efficiently and you will see how you can query a database efficiently using views.

8.2.1 Creating and Removing Views

To create a view, PostgreSQL provides a command called CREATE VIEW. The syntax of this command is displayed in the next listing:

```
phpbook=# \h CREATE VIEW
Command:    CREATE VIEW
Description: define a new view
Syntax:
CREATE VIEW view [ ( column name list ) ] AS SELECT query
```

As you can see, the view is defined as the result of a SELECT statement. Let's try an example:

```
phpbook=# CREATE TABLE product (id int4, name text, stored int4);
CREATE
```

The table consists of three columns. The first column contains a product id, the second column is used to store the name of a product, and the third column contains the number of products that are still in the store.

Let's insert some records into the table:

```
phpbook=# INSERT INTO product VALUES (1, 'umbrella', 23);
INSERT 24891 1
phpbook=# INSERT INTO product VALUES (2, 'carpet', 0);
INSERT 24892 1
phpbook=# INSERT INTO product VALUES (3, 'flowerpot', 3);
INSERT 24893 1
```

Three products have been inserted into the table:

```
phpbook=# SELECT * FROM product;
 id |   name    | stored
----+-----------+--------
  1 | umbrella  |     23
  2 | carpet    |      0
  3 | flowerpot |      3
(3 rows)
```

One of the products is already sold out and can no longer be bought. To retrieve only those records that can still be bought, you have to add a WHERE clause to the query:

```
phpbook=# SELECT * FROM product WHERE stored > 0;
 id |   name    | stored
----+-----------+--------
  1 | umbrella  |     23
  3 | flowerpot |      3
(2 rows)
```

In more complex operations, it might be tedious to add a WHERE clause every time you want to retrieve all products that can still be bought. Therefore it is possible to define a view:

```
phpbook=# CREATE VIEW product_instock AS SELECT * FROM product WHERE stored > 0;
CREATE
```

The view is called product_instock and contains all records where the number of products in the store is higher than 0. Take a look at the definition of the view:

```
phpbook=# \d product_instock
    View "product_instock"
 Column |   Type   | Modifiers
--------+----------+-----------
 id     | integer  |
 name   | text     |
 stored | integer  |
View definition: SELECT product.id, product.name,
product.stored FROM product WHERE (product.stored > 0);
```

As you can see, the columns of the view have the same structure as the original table. After you've defined the view, it can be accessed just like any real table:

```
phpbook=# SELECT * FROM product_instock;
 id |   name    | stored
----+-----------+--------
  1 | umbrella  |     23
  3 | flowerpot |      3
(2 rows)
```

If all records are selected from the view, there won't be products that can no longer be bought in the result.

When you're working with join operations, views can be used just like any other table. In the next step you will see how to retrieve all values that can be found in product and product_instock:

```
SELECT product_instock.*
       FROM product_instock, product
       WHERE product_instock.id=product.id;
```

The result is not surprising:

```
 id |   name    | stored
----+-----------+--------
  1 | umbrella  |     23
  3 | flowerpot |      3
(2 rows)
```

The most interesting thing about this example is that views can be joined with tables—even if the table and the view access the same piece of data.

To remove a view, you can use the DROP VIEW command:

```
phpbook=# \h DROP VIEW
Command:     DROP VIEW
Description: remove a view
Syntax:
DROP VIEW name [, ...]
```

8.2.2 Defining Rules

So far you have seen how to define views and retrieve data from a view. These are the basic operations that can be performed. In addition, PostgreSQL provides more useful and more sophisticated ways of dealing with views.

Take a look at the next example:

```
phpbook=# UPDATE product SET stored=22 WHERE id=1;
UPDATE 1
```

It is an easy task to update a record, but what happens if you want to update a record in the view?

```
phpbook=# UPDATE product_instock SET stored=21 WHERE id=1;
ERROR:  Cannot update a view without an appropriate rule
```

PostgreSQL complains that a rule is missing. It is not possible for the database to find out what to do if a record should be updated in the view. This behavior of PostgreSQL seems obvious because it is not possible for the database to find out what to do in case of multiple tables. The same applies to INSERT statements—rules must be defined in order to tell PostgreSQL what to do in case of an INSERT statement.

To create rules, use the CREATE RULE command:

```
phpbook=# \h CREATE RULE
Command:     CREATE RULE
Description: define a new rewrite rule
Syntax:
CREATE RULE name AS ON event
    TO object [ WHERE condition ]
    DO [ INSTEAD ] action

where action can be:

NOTHING
|
```

```
query
|
( query ; query ... )
|
[ query ; query ... ]
```

As the syntax overview of the CREATE RULE command shows, rules are defined on a certain event. In this case the event is either an INSERT or an UPDATE operation on a view. In the next example you will see how a rule for INSERT statements can be defined:

```
CREATE RULE rule_insert_product_instock AS ON INSERT
        TO product_instock
        DO INSTEAD INSERT INTO product VALUES (
                NEW.id,
                NEW.name,
                NEW.stored);
```

The rule called rule_insert_product_instock will be applied if somebody tries to insert data into product_instock. Instead of inserting data into the view, PostgreSQL has to insert the data into product. The values inserted into the table will be taken from a virtual relation called NEW. Just as when working with triggers written in PL/pgSQL, NEW contains the data passed to the INSERT or UPDATE statement. In this example all three values should be inserted into product. This is just a simple example because there is only a view built on one table involved. In more complex views, the rules will be far more complex as well.

Let's insert the rule into the database:

```
[postgres@athlon rules]$ psql phpbook < rule.sql
CREATE
```

If no syntax error occurred, the rule has been added to the database successfully. Let's try to insert a record into the view:

```
phpbook=# INSERT INTO product_instock VALUES(4, 'dictionary', 49);
INSERT 24899 1
```

Everything worked just fine and no errors occurred. Now the new value can be found in the view and the underlying table:

```
phpbook=# SELECT * FROM product WHERE id=4;
 id |    name    | stored
----+------------+--------
  4 | dictionary |     49
(1 row)
```

```
phpbook=# SELECT * FROM product_instock WHERE id=4;
 id |   name     | stored
----+------------+--------
  4 | dictionary |    49
(1 row)
```

To perform UPDATE operations, an additional rule must be defined:

```
CREATE RULE rule_update_product_instock AS ON UPDATE
        TO product_instock
        DO INSTEAD UPDATE product
            SET
                    id=NEW.id,
                    name=NEW.name,
                    stored=NEW.stored
            WHERE
                    id=OLD.id
                    AND name=OLD.name
                    AND stored=OLD.stored;
```

The rule is already slightly more complex because the WHERE clause of the UPDATE operation must have the appropriate values to perform the operation correctly. To tell PostgreSQL which values to use in the WHERE clause, a virtual relation called OLD is used. In contrast to NEW, OLD contains the values that were valid before the operation. In this example OLD will contain the values you have used in the WHERE clause of the UPDATE operation the rule is used for.

Recall the content of the view:

```
phpbook=# SELECT * FROM product_instock;
 id |   name     | stored
----+------------+--------
  3 | flowerpot  |     3
  1 | umbrella   |    22
  4 | dictionary |    49
(3 rows)
```

In the next step you can use an UPDATE operation to modify one of the values:

```
phpbook=# UPDATE product_instock SET stored=2 WHERE id=3;
UPDATE 1
```

The operation has been executed successfully. Let's see if the values have been changed correctly:

```
phpbook=# SELECT * FROM product_instock;
 id |    name     | stored
----+-------------+--------
  1 | umbrella    |     22
  4 | dictionary  |     49
  3 | flowerpot   |      2
(3 rows)
```

The third column of the table has been set to the new value and only one row was affected by the query.

To remove the rules from the database, use the DROP RULE command:

```
DROP RULE rule_insert_product_instock;
DROP RULE rule_update_product_instock;
```

Simply pass the name of the rule to the command and PostgreSQL will take care of the rest. DROP RULE is an important command because in contrast to PL/pgSQL functions, DROP RULE does not support the CREATE OR REPLACE command, so DROP RULE must be used before creating a rule with a name that is already in use.

In some cases it can be useful to define rules that do nothing. If you are building prototype applications or if you just want to turn off certain operations without affecting the applications built on top of your database, rules can be useful. In the next example you can see a rule that neglects an INSERT statement:

```
CREATE RULE rule_insert_product_instock AS ON INSERT
        TO product_instock
        DO INSTEAD NOTHING;
```

The advantage of this rule is that PostgreSQL does not complain that a rule is missing and silently omits the INSERT operation, as you can see in the next listing:

```
phpbook=# INSERT INTO product_instock VALUES(5, 'orange juice', 8);
phpbook=#
```

No SQL statement has been performed:

```
phpbook=# SELECT * FROM product_instock;
 id |    name     | stored
----+-------------+--------
  1 | umbrella    |     22
  4 | dictionary  |     49
  3 | flowerpot   |      2
(3 rows)
```

The content of the table is still the same as it was before the INSERT statement.

Rules also make it possible to execute more than one statement at once. This is necessary when a view is based on a complex join or when other important operations must be performed. The following example shows what rules with multiple SQL statements can be good for:

```
phpbook=# ALTER TABLE product ADD COLUMN valid bool;
ALTER
```

First, a column called valid is added to the table. This column defines whether the record stored for a product is still valid. Take a look at the data structure of the table:

```
phpbook=# \d product
        Table "product"
 Column |   Type   | Modifiers
--------+----------+-----------
 id     | integer  |
 name   | text     |
 stored | integer  |
 valid  | boolean  |
```

The table contains four columns. After that you can create a second table for storing logging information:

```
phpbook=# CREATE TABLE logtab(tstamp timestamp, action text);
CREATE
```

This table contains the time when a change has taken place and text describing the action. In the next step you can write a rule that will be used with DELETE statements:

```
CREATE RULE rule_delete_product AS ON DELETE
        TO product
        DO INSTEAD
                ( INSERT INTO logtab VALUES (now(), 'deleting from product');
                UPDATE product SET valid='f'
                        WHERE id=OLD.id; );
```

Every time a record in product should be deleted, PostgreSQL will execute two SQL statements. The first one inserts a record into the logging table. The second one updates the record in product and sets it to invalid. This way it is possible to change the behavior of certain operations without changing the code on the application level. However, we recommend that you use this feature carefully; otherwise, your applications will become increasingly complicated and difficult to understand.

Let's test the rule:

```
phpbook=# DELETE FROM product WHERE id=3;
UPDATE 1
```

One record will be changed, as you can see in the next listing.

```
phpbook=# SELECT * FROM product;
 id |   name     | stored | valid
----+------------+--------+-------
  2 | carpet     |      0 |
  1 | umbrella   |     22 |
  4 | dictionary |     49 |
  3 | flowerpot  |      2 | f
(4 rows)
```

In addition, one record has been added to logtab:

```
phpbook=# SELECT * FROM logtab;
           tstamp            |       action
-----------------------------+---------------------
 2001-11-27 17:09:31.498421+01 | deleting from product
(1 row)
```

To understand the next example, it is necessary to have a closer look at the rule: In the rule it says id=OLD.id. This means that the UPDATE operation is performed when the id is equal to the id in the virtual relation called OLD. What happens if a different operator than the = operator is used in the DELETE statement?

```
phpbook=# DELETE FROM product WHERE id<3;
UPDATE 2
```

Two UPDATE operations are performed because the rule is executed for every record being processed. logtab will contain two additional records now:

```
phpbook=# SELECT * FROM logtab;
           tstamp            |       action
-----------------------------+---------------------
 2001-11-27 17:09:31.498421+01 | deleting from product
 2001-11-27 17:10:30.809778+01 | deleting from product
 2001-11-27 17:10:30.809778+01 | deleting from product
(3 rows)
```

Two records have been updated in table product:

```
phpbook=# SELECT * FROM product;
 id |    name    | stored | valid
----+------------+--------+-------
  4 | dictionary |     49 |
  3 | flowerpot  |      2 | f
  1 | umbrella   |     22 | f
  2 | carpet     |      0 | f
(4 rows)
```

So far, you have seen how to define rules on views and tables. You have also seen how to perform certain operations instead of other operations. However, sometimes it is not necessary to perform an operation instead of another operation because an additional SQL statement must be executed. In the next example you will learn to define a rule that performs an additional SQL statement:

```
CREATE RULE rule_insert_product AS ON INSERT
        TO product
        DO
                INSERT INTO logtab VALUES (now(), 'inserting into product');
```

The only thing you have to do is to omit the keyword INSTEAD and PostgreSQL will automatically perform the original operation without modifications.

To find out if rules have been defined, you can use \d:

```
phpbook=# \d product
        Table "product"
 Column |  Type   | Modifiers
--------+---------+-----------
 id     | integer |
 name   | text    |
 stored | integer |
 valid  | boolean |
Rules: rule_delete_product,
       rule_insert_product
```

Because rules are defined on tables and events, a list of rules is displayed at the end of the listing generated by \d.

8.3 Working with Subselects

Subqueries can be used to obtain search criteria within a SELECT statement. Normally the WHERE clause contains fixed parameters that cannot be modified. In subqueries, the parameters of a WHERE clause can be generated at runtime, which means that the query can stay the same even if the data in your tables changes. In addition, it will help you to reduce the number of queries needed to achieve a certain result.

8.3.1 Why Should You Use Subselects?

To see what you have just learned, we have included a simple example:

```
phpbook=# CREATE TABLE stock (name text, pday date, price numeric(9,2));
CREATE
```

You have just created a table containing information about the stock market. Now that the table has been created, it is time to insert some data. To save some overhead, you can use a COPY command instead of multiple INSERT commands:

```
phpbook=# COPY stock FROM stdin;
Enter data to be copied followed by a newline.
End with a backslash and a period on a line by itself.
>> Cybertec      2002/06/12      23.4
>> Cybertec      2002/06/13      27.8
>> Cybertec      2002/06/14      27.5
>> Cybertec      2002/06/15      29.0
>> Cybertec      2002/06/16      32.1
>> \.
```

The target is to retrieve all records where the price of the stock is higher than the average price in the table. This can be done by using two SELECT statements:

```
phpbook=# SELECT AVG(price) FROM stock;
      avg
--------------
 27.9600000000
(1 row)
```

The first SELECT statement retrieves the average price and this price can be used in the second query:

```
phpbook=# SELECT * FROM stock WHERE price>'27.96';
   name   |    pday    | price
----------+------------+-------
 Cybertec | 2002-06-16 | 32.10
 Cybertec | 2002-06-15 | 29.00
(2 rows)
```

The result is correct. However, that's not the way things should be done for various reasons. The next example shows what happens when the database has to face concurrent operations on the data:

Concurrent Operations

User 1	User 2
```phpbook=# SELECT AVG(price) FROM stock;``` avg --------------- 27.9600000000 (1 row)	
	```INSERT INTO stock VALUES``` ```('Cybertec', '2002/06/17',``` ```'50');```
```phpbook=# SELECT * FROM stock WHERE price>'27.96';``` name | pday | price ----------+------------+------- Cybertec | 2002-06-16 | 32.10 Cybertec | 2002-06-15 | 29.00 Cybertec | 2002-06-17 | 50.00 (3 rows)	

First User 1 computes the average of the values in the database. While User 1 is preparing a second SELECT statement, User 2 inserts a value into the database. After that User 1 queries the table again, and all of a sudden three values instead of two values are returned. The problem with this result is that the average value has changed after the record has been inserted, so the second query of User 2 does not return the records where the price is higher than the average price because the value of June 15th is still in the result. The new average price is found as follows:

```
phpbook=# SELECT AVG(price) FROM stock;
     avg
---------------
 31.6333333333
(1 row)
```

To get around the problem, you must use a subquery. One query is always looking at a consistent snapshot of data, so the result will always be correct—changes during one query no longer affect running queries.

Take a look at a subquery:

```
phpbook=# SELECT * FROM stock WHERE price > (SELECT AVG(price) FROM stock);
   name    |    pday    | price
-----------+------------+-------
 Cybertec  | 2002-06-16 | 32.10
 Cybertec  | 2002-06-17 | 50.00
(2 rows)
```

As you can see, the price is computed using a subquery and the result is added to the WHERE clause afterward. The concept of subqueries is easy, but there is one thing you have to take care of. Take a look at a slightly modified version of the query:

```
phpbook=# SELECT * FROM stock WHERE price > (SELECT * FROM stock);
ERROR:  Subselect must have only one field
```

PostgreSQL complains that the query returns more than just one cell, so the WHERE clause is wrong. This seems logical because PostgreSQL needs exactly one cell as price.

PostgreSQL provides a flexible system for handling subqueries. Every subquery can contain additional subqueries, so it is possible to perform even extremely complex queries with many subqueries involved.

8.3.2 Alternatives to Subselects

If you don't like complex subselects, it is possible to build simple workarounds by using views. The values generated by the subselect can be computed by the view and used by a query. Let's see how this can be done:

```
phpbook=# CREATE VIEW view_stock_avgprice AS SELECT AVG(price) FROM stock;
CREATE
```

First a view is defined that is used to compute the average price of the stock. In the next step you can write a query to find the records:

```
SELECT stock.*
        FROM stock, view_stock_avgprice
        WHERE price > view_stock_avgprice.avg;
```

The correct result is returned:

```
   name    |    pday    | price
-----------+------------+-------
 Cybertec  | 2002-06-16 | 32.10
 Cybertec  | 2002-06-17 | 50.00
(2 rows)
```

In this case PostgreSQL will also make sure that the result is based on a consistent snapshot of data. Because the view does not contain the data, it will always return the most recent average value, so the query will return the right result.

8.4 Working with Aliases and Self-Joins

Aliases are supported by almost every sophisticated database. Aliases are not only comfortable for writing shorter queries; they can also be used to build more complex queries where one table is treated as a set of tables.

8.4.1 Using Aliases

Before you learn about self-joins, it is time to have a closer look at aliases. An alias is an alternative name for an object.

Take a look at an example:

```
phpbook=# SELECT a.* FROM stock AS a LIMIT 1;
  name    |    pday     | price
----------+-------------+-------
 Cybertec | 2002-06-12  | 23.40
(1 row)
```

a is an alias for stock and can be used just like the original name. To define an alias, the keyword AS and the name of the alias must be added to the FROM clause. In this example you have seen how to define an alias for a table. If you want to define an alias for a column, you will find out that it is not possible:

```
phpbook=# SELECT pday AS date_of_price FROM stock WHERE
date_of_price='2002/06/12';
ERROR:  Attribute 'date_of_price' not found
```

In some cases it can be uncomfortable that aliases cannot be used in WHERE clauses—especially when working with aggregated information:

```
phpbook=# SELECT COUNT(*) FROM stock HAVING COUNT(*) > 2;
 count
-------
     6
(1 row)
```

As you can see, we have added the COUNT function to the HAVING clause as well. Let's add an alias for the column:

```
phpbook=# SELECT COUNT(*) AS a FROM stock HAVING COUNT(*) > 2;
 a
---
 6
(1 row)
```

The new headline of the column is a instead of count now. Let's try to use the alias in the HAVING clause:

```
phpbook=# SELECT COUNT(*) AS a FROM stock HAVING a > 2;
ERROR:  Attribute 'a' not found
```

PostgreSQL 7.2 will display an error because the alias is not a valid attribute in the HAVING clause. We strongly recommend that you keep this syntax in mind because otherwise you might have trouble writing complex queries that use HAVING clauses.

8.4.2 Self-Joins Built on Aliases

One of the most important situations when you need to work with aliases is when performing a self-join. Performing a self-join means that a table is being joined with itself. To show you in a practical way what this means, you can take a look at the next example.

Imagine a table storing a list of products and the category these products belong to:

```
phpbook=# CREATE TABLE product_cat(name text, category text);
CREATE
```

The table consists of two columns. The first column contains the name of the product and the second column contains the category of the product. Let's insert some values into the table:

```
phpbook=# INSERT INTO product_cat VALUES('PostgreSQL Developer''s Handbook',
'literature');
INSERT 25362 1
phpbook=# INSERT INTO product_cat VALUES('PostgreSQL Developer''s Handbook',
'book');
INSERT 25363 1
phpbook=# INSERT INTO product_cat VALUES('PostgreSQL Developer''s Handbook',
'computer');
INSERT 25364 1
phpbook=# INSERT INTO product_cat VALUES('Sendmail for Linux', 'book');
```

```
INSERT 25365 1
phpbook=# INSERT INTO product_cat VALUES('1984', 'book');
INSERT 25366 1
phpbook=# INSERT INTO product_cat VALUES('1984', 'literature');
INSERT 25367 1
```

Six records have been added to the table. In the *PostgreSQL Developer's Handbook*, the single quote had to be escaped:

```
phpbook=# SELECT * FROM product_cat;
              name              |  category
--------------------------------+------------
 PostgreSQL Developer's Handbook | literature
 PostgreSQL Developer's Handbook | book
 PostgreSQL Developer's Handbook | computer
 Sendmail for Linux             | book
 1984                           | book
 1984                           | literature
(6 rows)
```

The goal of the next example is to write a query that retrieves all products that belong to the categories literature and book. The problem is that this information cannot be retrieved with things you have learned so far because attributes in different records must be combined. Things would be much easier if the list of categories a product belongs to could be listed as separate columns, but this would be far too inflexible.

To get around the problem, you can use aliases. One table will be assigned to two aliases, so this table will appear as two independent tables that can be joined. Take a look at a piece of code:

```
SELECT a.*
    FROM product_cat AS a, product_cat AS b
    WHERE a.name=b.name
        AND a.category='literature'
        AND b.category='book';
```

The query will retrieve all records that belong to the categories literature and book. If you take a closer look at the query, you can see how things work: Two aliases are being created, so the tables appear just as if they were two independent copies of the same table. These two tables can easily be joined and the category of the first table is set to literature, whereas the category selected from the second table is set to book. This way it is an easy task to retrieve records that belong to exactly two categories.

In this example two records will be returned:

```
          name              | category
----------------------------+-----------
PostgreSQL Developer's Handbook | literature
1984                        | literature
(2 rows)
```

The same result can also be included by using just one alias. In this book we have included both versions so that you can see better how to do this. Some books about SQL use the version with two aliases and others show examples like that with only one alias:

```
SELECT a.*
        FROM product_cat AS a, product_cat
        WHERE a.name=product_cat.name
                AND a.category='literature'
                AND product_cat.category='book';
```

Self-joins can also be performed to retrieve records that belong to three or more categories. In this case the SQL statement will be more complex because three tables must be joined, as shown in the next listing:

```
SELECT a.name
        FROM product_cat AS a,
                product_cat AS b,
                product_cat AS c
        WHERE a.name=b.name
                AND b.name=c.name
                AND a.category='literature'
                AND b.category='book'
                AND c.category='computer';
```

There is only one record in the table belonging to all three categories listed in the query:

```
          name
----------------------------------
PostgreSQL Developer's Handbook
(1 row)
```

As you can see, self-joins are a powerful method for performing complex queries where conditions affect more than just one line.

8.5 Object-Oriented SQL

Modern object-oriented features are not just a trendy thing; object orientation can be an important help when implementing huge and sophisticated applications. With the help of object orientation, it is possible to use the same functions and attributes in more than just one object by using inheritance. Inheritance means that a child class can inherit attributes from a parent class. Just like PHP, PostgreSQL supports inheritance and that's what this section covers.

8.5.1 Inheritance and Tables

Tables can easily inherit attributes from each other. In tables, attributes are columns. Take a look at an example:

```
phpbook=# CREATE TABLE person (name text, birthday date);
CREATE
```

The table called person contains two columns. In the next step you can define a table for storing information about students. A student has additional information such as the university the student is attending and the subject matter he is studying. To model these circumstances, inheritance can be used:

```
phpbook=# CREATE TABLE student (university text, subject text) INHERITS
(person);
CREATE
```

By adding the keyword INHERITS, you can tell PostgreSQL which parent tables must be used. It is important to point out that a table can inherit from more than just one parent. This differs significantly from PHP where a child can only have one parent. Take a look at the columns of student:

```
phpbook=# \d student
        Table "student"
  Column     | Type | Modifiers
------------+------+-----------
 name       | text |
 birthday   | date |
 university | text |
 subject    | text |
```

The first two columns are taken from the parent table. Let's see what happens when a column is added to the parent table:

```
phpbook=# ALTER TABLE person ADD COLUMN gender char(1);
ALTER
```

The column has been added to the table successfully:

```
phpbook=# \d person
          Table "person"
 Column  |     Type     | Modifiers
---------+--------------+----------
 name    | text         |
 birthday| date         |
 gender  | character(1) |
```

Because student is a child of person, the column can be found in student as well:

```
phpbook=# \d student
          Table "student"
  Column   |     Type     | Modifiers
-----------+--------------+----------
 name      | text         |
 birthday  | date         |
 university| text         |
 subject   | text         |
 gender    | character(1) |
```

Now that you have seen how to create tables, it is time to see how tables can be removed. Let's try to remove the parent table:

```
phpbook=# DROP TABLE person;
ERROR:  Relation "student" inherits from "person"
```

It is not possible to remove a table that still has children. This seems obvious because otherwise all children of the parent table would lose the entire set of columns that can be found in the parent table. To remove a table, it is necessary to remove the children first.

8.5.2 Inserting and Selecting Data

In this section you will see how to insert and retrieve data from tables that are built on inherited columns. The first thing is to insert some data. The first record will be added to the parent table:

```
phpbook=# INSERT INTO person VALUES ('Shelley', '1980/03/14', 'f');
INSERT 25428 1
```

The second record will be added to the child table:

```
phpbook=# INSERT INTO student VALUES ('Carlos', '1972/12/30', 'Technical
University of Vienna', 'French', 'm');
INSERT 25429 1
```

To see how inheritance works, you can query the parent table:

```
phpbook=# SELECT * FROM person;
  name   |  birthday  | gender
---------+------------+--------
 Shelley | 1980-03-14 | f
 Carlos  | 1972-12-30 | m
(2 rows)
```

Both records you have inserted have been retrieved. When retrieving data from a parent table, PostgreSQL will display all data stored in the child tables as well. However, the result will only contain the columns of the parent table—in this case the columns university and subject won't be returned because they can only be found in the child table. Let's query the child:

```
phpbook=# SELECT * FROM student;
  name   |  birthday  |          university          | subject | gender
---------+------------+------------------------------+---------+--------
 Carlos  | 12-30-1972 | Technical University of Vienna | French  | m
(1 row)
```

Only the record that has been added to the child table has been returned. As you can see, the records in the parent table won't be returned.

Tables that inherit columns from other tables can be treated just like "normal" tables. Just as with any other table, it is possible to perform simple join operations. In the next example you can see how to join the parent table with the child table:

```
phpbook=# SELECT person.name FROM student, person WHERE
student.name=person.name;
  name
--------
 Carlos
(1 row)
```

In many cases this is not a useful operation, but this example shows the tremendous power of PostgreSQL and what kind of operations can be done with the database.

8.5.3 Rules and Inheritance

Rules and inheritance are two important features of PostgreSQL. In this section, you will find out what happens when both features are used simultaneously and what you have to take care of.

The goal of the next example is to write a rule that inserts logging information into a table. Let's start and create a table called logtab that consists of two columns (if there is already a table in the database that is called logtab, just delete it):

```
phpbook=# CREATE TABLE logtab (tstamp timestamp, action text);
CREATE
```

```
phpbook=# \d logtab
                  Table "logtab"
 Column |            Type            | Modifiers
--------+----------------------------+-----------
 tstamp | timestamp(6) with time zone |
 action | text                       |
```

In the next step a rule can be defined. The rule is executed every time somebody inserts a record into the table called person:

```
CREATE RULE rule_insert_person AS ON INSERT
        TO person
        DO
                INSERT INTO logtab VALUES (now(), 'inserting ...');
```

person is the parent table of student. What happens if a record is inserted into student? Will the rule be inherited by the child table?

```
phpbook=# INSERT INTO student VALUES ('Sheila', '1974/12/12',
'PostgreSQL Academy Vienna', 'PostgreSQL', 'f');
INSERT 25437 1
```

Let's query the logging table to see if a record has been added to it:

```
phpbook=# SELECT * FROM logtab;
 tstamp | action
--------+--------
(0 rows)
```

The table is still empty, so the rule has not been executed. To insert data into logtab when a record is being added to student, a second rule must be defined:

```
CREATE RULE rule_insert_student AS ON INSERT
        TO student
        DO
                INSERT INTO logtab VALUES (now(), 'inserting into student');
```

With the help of this rule, a record in the logging table will be added automatically every time data is added to student:

```
phpbook=# INSERT INTO student VALUES ('John', '1982/1/9',
'PostgreSQL Academy Vienna', 'PostgreSQL', 'm');
INSERT 25442 1
```

Take a look at the content of the logging table:

```
phpbook=# SELECT * FROM logtab;
            tstamp              |          action
-------------------------------+------------------------
 2001-11-29 14:39:40.784463+01 | inserting into student
(1 row)
```

PostgreSQL does not provide the opportunity for a child class to inherit triggers. A rule can only be defined on one table and will not be valid for child tables. This is an extremely important subject because you have to take it into consideration when designing applications.

In future versions of PostgreSQL, inheriting rules might be possible.

8.5.4 Changing PostgreSQL's Behavior

In this chapter you have already learned that a query automatically returns all values from the current table as well as from all child tables of the table you want to retrieve data from. Sometimes this behavior won't be what you are looking for. In these cases it is necessary to change the way PostgreSQL deals with inheritance.

To influence the behavior, PostgreSQL provides a variable named sql_inheritance, which can be changed at runtime. To retrieve the current value of sql_inheritance, use the SHOW command:

```
phpbook=# SHOW sql_inheritance;
NOTICE:  sql_inheritance is on
SHOW VARIABLE
```

By default inheritance is turned on. To change the value temporarily, use the SET command:

```
phpbook=# \h SET
Command:     SET
Description: change a run-time parameter
Syntax:
SET variable { TO | = } { value | 'value' | DEFAULT }
SET TIME ZONE { 'timezone' | LOCAL | DEFAULT }
```

Let's change the way inheritance is treated:

```
phpbook=# SET sql_inheritance TO off;
SET VARIABLE
```

In this example the value is set to off and PostgreSQL will now treat all tables as separate and independent tables. If you query student, only three records will be retrieved:

```
phpbook=# SELECT * FROM student;
  name  |  birthday  |            university            |  subject   | gender
--------+------------+---------------------------------+------------+--------
 Carlos | 1972-12-30 | Technical University of Vienna  | French     | m
 Sheila | 1974-12-12 | PostgreSQL Academy Vienna       | PostgreSQL | f
 John   | 1982-01-09 | PostgreSQL Academy Vienna       | PostgreSQL | m
(3 rows)
```

The behavior of PostgreSQL has not changed when querying the child table, but when data from the parent table is selected, it won't contain information taken from child tables any more:

```
phpbook=# SELECT * FROM person;
  name   |  birthday  | gender
---------+------------+--------
 Shelley | 1980-03-14 | f
(1 row)
```

Only one record has been retrieved.

To change sql_inheritance back to the default value, you can use SET:

```
phpbook=# SET sql_inheritance TO DEFAULT;
SET VARIABLE
```

8.5.5 Serials and Inheritance

For generating primary keys, many people rely on serials. When dealing with inheritance, serials are dangerous in a way because you have to know perfectly well what PostgreSQL does internally—otherwise you will have trouble with the primary key because of duplicated entries.

To show you how things work, we have included an example. Let's create a table for storing the ids and the names of plants:

```
phpbook=# CREATE TABLE plant (id serial, name text);
NOTICE:  CREATE TABLE will create implicit sequence 'plant_id_seq' for SERIAL
column 'plant.id'
NOTICE:  CREATE TABLE/UNIQUE will create implicit index 'plant_id_key' for
table 'plant'
CREATE
```

The first column has been defined as a serial number, so PostgreSQL has automatically generated a sequence. In the next step a second table can be defined that contains a column called id as well:

```
phpbook=# CREATE TABLE flower (id serial, color text) INHERITS (plant);
NOTICE:  CREATE TABLE will create implicit sequence 'flower_id_seq' for
SERIAL column 'flower.id'
NOTICE:  CREATE TABLE/UNIQUE will create implicit index 'flower_id_key' for
table 'flower'
NOTICE:  CREATE TABLE: merging attribute "id" with inherited definition
CREATE
```

An additional sequence will be generated, and PostgreSQL mentions that the two columns having the same name will be merged into one column. This way PostgreSQL will use the sequence called flower_id_seq instead of the one called plant_id_seq to generate the values inserted into the column. To see what this means, insert one record into every table and see what happens:

```
phpbook=# INSERT INTO plant (name) VALUES ('birch');
INSERT 25463 1
phpbook=# INSERT INTO flower (name, color) VALUES ('rose', 'red');
INSERT 25464 1
```

After inserting the records, you can retrieve them from the table:

```
phpbook=# SELECT * FROM plant;
 id | name
----+-------
  1 | birch
  1 | rose
(2 rows)
```

As you can see, both records have the same id because every sequence defined by the serials has been accessed exactly once. If you add an additional record to table flower, the id of the new record will be 2:

```
phpbook=# INSERT INTO flower (name, color) VALUES ('cactus', 'green');
INSERT 25465 1
phpbook=# SELECT * FROM plant;
 id |  name
----+--------
  1 | birch
  1 | rose
  2 | cactus
(3 rows)
```

Because the ids in the column are not unique, the first column cannot be used as the primary key of the table. To get around the problem, you can define triggers. You'll find more information on triggers in Chapter 9, "Embedded Languages."

In the next example you can see how serials can affect child tables. Two tables will be created, but this time the name of the columns containing the sequence won't be the same:

```
phpbook=# CREATE TABLE building (bid serial, owner text);
NOTICE:  CREATE TABLE will create implicit sequence 'building_bid_seq'
for SERIAL
column 'building.bid'
NOTICE:  CREATE TABLE/UNIQUE will create implicit index 'building_bid_key' for
table 'building'
CREATE
```

The column containing the serial is called bid. In the next step an additional table will be created, which contains a sequence as well. This time the column will be called rid:

```
phpbook=# CREATE TABLE residential (rid serial, people int) INHERITS (building);
NOTICE:  CREATE TABLE will create implicit sequence 'residential_rid_seq'
for SERIAL column 'residential.rid'
NOTICE:  CREATE TABLE/UNIQUE will create implicit index 'residential_rid_
key' for table 'residential'
CREATE
```

If you look at the data structure of residential, you will see that the default value of two columns is defined as a sequence. This time the two sequences are independent and the sequence of the parent table will also be used by the child table:

```
phpbook=# \d residential
                        Table "residential"
 Column |  Type   |                    Modifiers
--------+---------+------------------------------------------------------------
 bid    | integer | not null default nextval('"building_bid_seq"'::text)
 owner  | text    |
 rid    | integer | not null default nextval('"residential_rid_seq"'::text)
 people | integer |
Unique keys: residential_rid_key
```

Let's insert some values into the child table and see what happens:

```
phpbook=# INSERT INTO residential (owner, people) VALUES ('Epi', 3);
INSERT 25482 1
phpbook=# INSERT INTO residential (owner, people) VALUES ('Edward', 1);
INSERT 25483 1
```

After inserting the data, you can retrieve all values from `residential`:

```
phpbook=# SELECT * FROM residential;
 bid | owner  | rid | people
-----+--------+-----+--------
   1 | Epi    |   1 |      3
   2 | Edward |   2 |      1
(2 rows)
```

As you see, the sequences have been incremented independently.

8.6 Transactions and Locking

In contrast to some other open source databases, PostgreSQL provides a highly developed system for handling transactions. This is one of the features that makes PostgreSQL such a good choice for almost all purposes.

In this section you will learn about PostgreSQL's transaction-handling capabilities, and you will see how transactions can be used efficiently to build even more sophisticated applications and to protect your data.

8.6.1 The Main Idea of Transactions

Imagine a simple example: Your database contains a table with 200 million records in it. One user starts a query that goes through all records and computes the average of a column. Because the table is very large, this will take some time. While the query of this user is running, a second user starts to delete records at the beginning of the table. What will happen to the first user's query? Logically you don't want the second user's changes to affect the first user's query. One way to solve the problem would be to make the second user wait until the first user is ready. This would be a problem because if the query to compute the average takes very long, your system would be down for the time needed to execute the query. This is obviously not the best solution, although some other databases have solved the problem this way.

However, in the case of PostgreSQL, every query sees a consistent snapshot of the data no matter what other users do meanwhile. In PostgreSQL the changes of User 2 will not affect User 1 until the query has been processed successfully. This way the result of the query will always be consistent because it is built on a consistent snapshot of data. Internally things are very complicated because PostgreSQL has to make sure that every user sees the correct set of data.

Another important point when talking about transactions is that various queries can be combined into one block. The advantage of blocking queries is that if one query in the list fails, the changes made by the queries in the list won't be performed. Just think of a program used to import data into the database. If the entire import is performed using just one transaction, PostgreSQL adds the data to the table at the end of the transaction—if the import stops after half the records, these records won't be in the database. The advantage of this behavior is that changes are made only if the entire block is successful. This is comfortable when importing data because you don't have to delete those records from the table that have been imported successfully. Things like that can save you a lot of work and help you to build more secure applications because your data is protected by PostgreSQL's behavior.

8.6.2 Starting and Committing Transactions; Rollback

Normally every SQL statement processed by the server is executed as one transaction. To block various SQL statements, transactions must be started and committed manually.

Let's create a table first:

```
phpbook=# CREATE TABLE city (name text, country text);
CREATE
```

To start a transaction, use the BEGIN command. In the next listing you can see the syntax overview of the command:

```
phpbook=# \h BEGIN
Command:     BEGIN
Description: start a transaction block
Syntax:
BEGIN [ WORK | TRANSACTION ]
```

As you can see, the syntax of the command is easy. Now that you have seen how the COMMIT command works, you can start to insert some data into the table:

```
phpbook=# BEGIN;
BEGIN
phpbook=# INSERT INTO city VALUES ('New York', 'USA');
INSERT 25560 1
phpbook=# INSERT INTO city VALUES ('Paris', 'France');
INSERT 25561 1
```

To end a transaction, use COMMIT:

```
phpbook=# \h COMMIT
Command:     COMMIT
Description: commit the current transaction
Syntax:
COMMIT [ WORK | TRANSACTION ]
```

Let's commit the transaction:

```
phpbook=# COMMIT;
COMMIT
```

If no error occurred, the transaction has been terminated successfully. Two records can be found in table city:

```
phpbook=# SELECT * FROM city;
   name   | country
----------+---------
 New York | USA
 Paris    | France
(2 rows)
```

In the next step you can write a SQL file containing some data, including the commands for transaction control:

```
BEGIN;
INSERT INTO city VALUES ('Vienna', 'Austria');
INSERT INTO city VALUES ('Geneve', Switzerland);
COMMIT;
```

If the data is sent to PostgreSQL using the front end, an error will occur:

```
[postgres@athlon postgres]$ psql phpbook < data.sql
BEGIN
INSERT 25563 1
ERROR:  Attribute 'switzerland' not found
COMMIT
```

You have forgotten to add single quotes around Switzerland, so PostgreSQL is not able to parse the INSERT command. If you look at the content of city, you will see that no record has been added to the table:

```
phpbook=# SELECT * FROM city;
   name    | country
-----------+---------
 New York  | USA
 Paris     | France
(2 rows)
```

This is efficient because this way, nothing has happened to the data in the database. If the explicit transaction handling is omitted, things will be treated differently:

```
INSERT INTO city VALUES ('Vienna', 'Austria');
INSERT INTO city VALUES ('Geneve', Switzerland);
```

If the data is added to the table, the same problem will still occur:

```
[postgres@athlon postgres]$ psql phpbook < data.sql
INSERT 25564 1
ERROR:  Attribute 'switzerland' not found
```

However, this time one record has been added to the table, so it has to be removed before importing the data again:

```
phpbook=# SELECT * FROM city;
   name    | country
-----------+---------
 New York  | USA
 Paris     | France
 Vienna    | Austria
(3 rows)
```

When you are importing data, make sure that the entire data is always imported in just one transaction. This way failures will be corrected by the database automatically and you don't have to do these corrections yourself.

Another important command when dealing with transactions is ROLLBACK. In order to undo a transaction, ROLLBACK is essential. Take a look at an example:

```
phpbook=# BEGIN;
BEGIN
```

After starting a transaction, you can add a record to the table:

```
phpbook=# INSERT INTO city VALUES ('London', 'UK');
INSERT 25565 1
```

The record can be found in the table:

```
phpbook=# SELECT * FROM city;
   name    | country
----------+---------
 New York | USA
 Paris    | France
 Vienna   | Austria
 London   | UK
(4 rows)
```

In the next step you want to abort the transaction and cancel all operations. This can be done by using ROLLBACK:

```
phpbook=# ROLLBACK;
ROLLBACK
```

If you look at the table now, London has been removed from the table:

```
phpbook=# SELECT * FROM city;
   name    | country
----------+---------
 New York | USA
 Paris    | France
 Vienna   | Austria
(3 rows)
```

The transaction has been interrupted by ROLLBACK, so all operations that have been performed were canceled as well because all commands in the transaction can be seen as one big command.

If you try to commit the transaction, you will find out that the connection has already been terminated by ROLLBACK:

```
phpbook=# COMMIT;
NOTICE:  COMMIT: no transaction in progress
COMMIT
```

PostgreSQL does not support nested transactions, which means that it is not possible to run a transaction inside a transaction:

```
phpbook=# BEGIN;
BEGIN
phpbook=# BEGIN;
NOTICE:  BEGIN: already a transaction in progress
BEGIN
```

Maybe we will see this feature in future versions of PostgreSQL.

8.6.3 Transaction Isolation

Transaction isolation is important for concurrent transactions. Data can never be seen by a transaction before it has been committed. Therefore some types of reads must not happen:

- **Dirty reads**—Data from an uncommitted concurrent transaction must not be read by a transaction.

- **Non-repeatable reads**—If a transaction has to read the same piece of data more than once (this can happen in case of complex queries), the data read by the query must not have changed.

- **Phantom read**—The changes made by a concurrent connection that is committed must not affect other transactions that are already running.

According to the ANSI SQL specification, four transaction isolation levels have been defined: read uncommitted, read committed, repeatable read, and serializable.

Two of these transaction isolation levels are supported by PostgreSQL: read committed and serializable. The default transaction isolation level is read committed.

Table 8.3 shows the difference between these various levels.

TABLE 8.3   Transaction Isolation Levels

	Dirty Read	Non-Repeatable	Phantom Read
Read uncommitted	Possible	Possible	Possible
Read committed	Not possible	Possible	Possible
Repeatable read	Not possible	Not possible	Possible
Serializable	Not possible	Not possible	Not possible

As you can see, various transaction isolation levels provide certain levels of security. Usually the default transaction isolation level will satisfy your demands.

Let's see how the transaction isolation level can be changed.

To see which level is currently used, use the SHOW command:

```
phpbook=# SHOW TRANSACTION ISOLATION LEVEL;
NOTICE:  TRANSACTION ISOLATION LEVEL is READ COMMITTED
SHOW VARIABLE
```

To use SERIALIZABLE as the current transaction isolation level, use the SET command:

```
phpbook=# SET TRANSACTION ISOLATION LEVEL SERIALIZABLE;
SET VARIABLE
```

To change the transaction isolation to the default value, use SET as well.

8.6.4 PostgreSQL's Locking System

Locking is an essential part of the internals of every database. Depending on the quality of your database, the way locking is performed varies significantly. In general two basic ways of locking can be distinguished:

- **Table locking**—Entire tables are locked in order not to conflict with other operations.

- **Row-level locking**—Individual rows are locked instead of tables.

In the case of more than just one concurrent operation, row-level locking has significant advantages over table locking. Because PostgreSQL is a highly developed and high-quality database, the server rarely uses table locks. Especially when many users are performing concurrent operations including long and complex queries, this is much better and will lead to fewer conflicts.

To lock an object, use a command called LOCK. Take a look at the syntax overview of the command:

```
phpbook=# \h LOCK
Command:    LOCK
Description: explicitly lock a table
Syntax:
LOCK [ TABLE ] name [, ...]
LOCK [ TABLE ] name [, ...] IN lockmode MODE

where lockmode is one of:

        ACCESS SHARE | ROW SHARE | ROW EXCLUSIVE | SHARE UPDATE EXCLUSIVE |
        SHARE | SHARE ROW EXCLUSIVE | EXCLUSIVE | ACCESS EXCLUSIVE
```

In this book the way locking is performed by the database internally will not be covered because this topic is beyond the scope of this book. For further information, we recommend that you read the *PostgreSQL Developer's Handbook*.

8.6.5 Examples Using Transactions

This section presents some practical examples to show how transactions affect your everyday life with the database. It is necessary to understand what happens in case of concurrent transactions. To reduce the data involved in the process, you can delete the records stored in `city`:

```
phpbook=# DELETE FROM city;
DELETE 3
```

Take a look at some more examples.

Example One

User 1	User 2	Description
BEGIN;		User 1 starts a transaction.
INSERT INTO city		User 1 inserts a record.
VALUES ('London', 'UK');		
	SELECT * FROM city;	User 2 sees an empty table.
SELECT * FROM city;		User 1 can see his record.
COMMIT;		
	SELECT * FROM city;	User 2 can see one record.

First User 1 starts a transaction and inserts one record into the table. While the transaction of User 1 is still in progress, User 2 queries the table. No records will be retrieved because User 2 cannot see uncommitted data. User 1 can see the data he has inserted because he is inside his personal transaction. After the transaction has been committed, User 2 can see the data as well.

Take a look at a slightly more complex example. Remember, one record is already in the table:

Example Two

User 1	User 2	Description
BEGIN;		User 1 starts a transaction.
	BEGIN;	User 2 starts a transaction.
INSERT INTO city		User 1 inserts a record into
VALUES ('Salzburg',		the table.
'Austria');		
	DELETE FROM city;	User 2 deletes all records in
		the table.

User 1	User 2	Description
COMMIT;		User 1 commits his transaction.
	COMMIT;	User 2 commits his transaction.
SELECT * FROM city;		User 1 retrieves all records.
	SELECT * FROM city;	User 2 retrieves all records.

At the beginning the two users start two transactions and User 1 inserts one record into the table. In the next step User 2 deletes all records in the table. Because User 2 can only see the data that is already in the table, only one record will be deleted (the one containing London). Finally User 1 and User 2 commit the transactions. The question now is: Will Salzburg still be in the database? The first transaction has been committed before the second one, so the record is already in the table when the second transaction is committed. However, Salzburg can be found in the table:

```
phpbook=# SELECT * FROM city;
   name   | country
----------+----------
 Salzburg | Austria
(1 row)
```

As you can see, the way transactions are processed is not always obvious, but it is necessary to understand the basics of how transactions are processed and how your work is affected by them.

A crucial point when dealing with transactions is the way PostgreSQL deals with sequences. Take a look at an example:

Example Three

User 1	User 2	Description
BEGIN;		User 1 starts a transaction.
	BEGIN;	User 2 starts a transaction.
CREATE SEQUENCE seq_test INCREMENT 1 START 1;		User 1 creates a sequence.
SELECT nextval('seq_test');		The sequence returns 1.
	SELECT nextval('seq_test');	User 2 cannot see the relation.
COMMIT;		
	COMMIT;	

Two transactions are started. In the next step User 1 creates a sequence and retrieves a value from the sequence. User 2 cannot see the sequence yet. So far you haven't seen anything unusual, but let's get to the next example:

Example Four

User 1	User 2	Description
BEGIN;		User 1 starts a transaction.
	BEGIN;	User 2 starts a transaction.
SELECT nextval('seq_test');		The sequence returns 2.
	SELECT nextval('seq_test');	The sequence returns 3.
	ROLLBACK;	User 2 performs a
ROLLBACK.		
	SELECT nextval('seq_test');	The sequence returns 4.
COMMIT;		User 1 commits the transaction.
	COMMIT;	User 2 commits the transaction.

First, two transactions are started and both users select a value from the sequence. As you can see, the value is incremented. Although both users access the same consistent snapshot of data, the sequence increases. Even in the case of ROLLBACK, the sequence is not set to the old value. This behavior of PostgreSQL is necessary because otherwise it would not be possible to retrieve unique values from the sequence in the case of concurrent transactions. Another important point is that there is no need to wonder if a list of numbers generated by a sequence is not complete—things like that can easily happen if you make heavy use of PostgreSQL's transaction code. To point it out more clearly—PostgreSQL must behave the way we have shown in order to generate unique values.

8.6.6 Limitations of PostgreSQL's Transaction System

Although PostgreSQL's way of handling transactions is a good one, several restrictions must be taken into consideration when using transactions. In this section we will provide a brief overview of these restrictions.

PostgreSQL currently supports two of four transaction isolation levels defined by the ANSI standard. In most cases, this will be enough.

Oracle users might miss being able to add savepoints to a transaction. Currently savepoints are not yet supported. In addition, PostgreSQL does not supported nested transactions, which means that you cannot start a transaction within a transaction.

8.7 Constraints

Constraints are attributes of an object that are used to restrict certain events from happening. Using constraints will help you to prevent things from happening. Especially when you want to protect the integrity of your data, constraints will be essential. The constraints provided by PostgreSQL have to a large extent been defined in the ANSI standard, so using constraints should not affect the portability of your data structures significantly as long as the database you are porting your data structures to supports ANSI SQL-92 as well.

8.7.1 The CREATE TABLE Command and Constraints

In most cases, constraints are defined when creating tables. Therefore the CREATE TABLE command provides many options to define the right set of constraints. Recall the syntax overview of the CREATE TABLE command. We have included it here again to avoid some unnecessary page turning:

```
phpbook=# \h CREATE TABLE
Command:     CREATE TABLE
Description: define a new table
Syntax:
CREATE [ [ LOCAL ] { TEMPORARY | TEMP } ] TABLE table_name (
    { column_name data_type [ DEFAULT default_expr ] [ column_constraint
[, ... ] ]
    | table_constraint }  [, ... ]
)
[ INHERITS ( parent_table [, ... ] ) ]
[ WITH OIDS | WITHOUT OIDS ]

where column_constraint is:

[ CONSTRAINT constraint_name ]
{ NOT NULL | NULL | UNIQUE | PRIMARY KEY |
  CHECK (expression) |
  REFERENCES reftable [ ( refcolumn ) ] [ MATCH FULL | MATCH PARTIAL ]
    [ ON DELETE action ] [ ON UPDATE action ] }
[ DEFERRABLE | NOT DEFERRABLE ] [ INITIALLY DEFERRED | INITIALLY IMMEDIATE ]

and table_constraint is:

[ CONSTRAINT constraint_name ]
{ UNIQUE ( column_name [, ... ] ) |
```

```
  PRIMARY KEY ( column_name [, ... ] ) |
  CHECK ( expression ) |
  FOREIGN KEY ( column_name [, ... ] ) REFERENCES reftable [ ( refcolumn
[, ... ] ) ]
     [ MATCH FULL | MATCH PARTIAL ] [ ON DELETE action ] [ ON UPDATE action ] }
[ DEFERRABLE | NOT DEFERRABLE ] [ INITIALLY DEFERRED | INITIALLY IMMEDIATE ]
```

In this section you will take a closer look at most of the features of the CREATE TABLE command and you will learn about the power of this command.

8.7.1.1 CHECK **Constraints**

One of the most widespread constraints is the CHECK constraint. It can be used to check whether the input satisfies certain conditions and helps you to protect your data by omitting data that is obviously wrong. With the help of CHECK constraints, a lot of work that is often done on the application level is passed to the database, and in many cases the database can deal with things like that much more efficiently.

Imagine a situation where you want to implement a table for storing a list of products you have sold. Some columns in the table must not have invalid data, so CHECK constraints can be used:

```
CREATE TABLE sales (
        id int4,
        tstamp timestamp      CHECK (tstamp < now()),
        product_id int4       CHECK (product_id > 0),
        product_name text     CHECK (length(product_name) > 3),
        units int4            CHECK (units > 0 AND units < 1000),
        price numeric(9,2)    CHECK (price > 0)
);
```

The data in id is not restricted by a constraint. The second column may only contain values where the date the sale took place was before the time the record is inserted into sales. This will help you to find bugs in your application because future sales cannot be inserted into the database, so one source of trouble can be avoided. In column number 3 you make sure that the product id must not be a negative value. In the next line of code you can see that the name of a product must be at least three characters long. The column called units has to satisfy two conditions: The first condition is that a product must be sold more than zero times. In addition, a product cannot be sold more than one thousand times. Take a look at the definition of the table:

```
phpbook=# \d sales
                    Table "sales"
    Column    |             Type              | Modifiers
--------------+-------------------------------+-----------
 id           | integer                       |
 tstamp       | timestamp(6) with time zone   |
 product_id   | integer                       |
 product_name | text                          |
 units        | integer                       |
 price        | numeric(9,2)                  |
Check constraints: "sales_tstamp" (tstamp < now())
                   "sales_product_id" (product_id > 0)
                   "sales_product_name" (length(product_name) > 3)
                   "sales_units" ((units > 0) AND (units < 1000))
                   "sales_price" (price > '0'::"numeric")
```

As you can see, the definition of the table contains information about CHECK constraints you have added to the table. This is comfortable because you don't have to look this information up in one of the system tables manually—\d does the job for you.

After you have defined the table, it is time to insert some data into it:

```
phpbook=# INSERT INTO sales VALUES (1, '2001/1/1', 3243243, 'cheeseburger', 2,
'3.16');
INSERT 25494 1
phpbook=# INSERT INTO sales VALUES (2, '2001/1/1', 3243242, 'hamburger', -200,
'3.16');
ERROR:  ExecAppend: rejected due to CHECK constraint sales_units
phpbook=# INSERT INTO sales VALUES (3, '2001/1/1', 3243244, 'do', 1, '4.95');
ERROR:  ExecAppend: rejected due to CHECK constraint sales_product_name
```

The first record can be added to the table without any problems because none of the columns violates the condition of a CHECK constraint. In case of the second record the amount of products bought by the customer is negative. In this example this is not allowed because you do not allow orders to be canceled. The third INSERT statement tries to insert a product into the table where the name is too short, so the INSERT statement is not performed.

As you can see, a lot of things can be prevented from happening when working with CHECK constraints and this way your data can be protected.

8.7.1.2 DEFAULT Values

In order to tell PostgreSQL which data to insert into a column if an INSERT statement does not pass the value to the database, you can use default values. Before you can re-create sales, you have to drop the old sales table by using DROP TABLE:

```
phpbook=# DROP TABLE sales;
DROP
```

In the next step the table can be generated and DEFAULT constraints can be used:

```
CREATE TABLE sales (
        id int4,
        tstamp timestamp        DEFAULT now(),
        product_id int4 ,
        units int4              DEFAULT 1 CHECK (units > 0 AND units < 1000),
        price numeric(9,2)
);
```

In this example the timestamp is set to the current time. If no value for this column is specified, PostgreSQL will use the current transaction time as the default value. More than just one constraint is assigned to the units column. First a DEFAULT constraint is defined and in addition, CHECK constraints have been defined. As you can see, a list of constraints can be defined on one column, which makes the entire process very flexible.

Take a look at the data structure of the table:

```
phpbook=# \d sales
                     Table "sales"
    Column    |             Type             |   Modifiers
--------------+------------------------------+---------------
 id           | integer                      |
 tstamp       | timestamp(6) with time zone  | default now()
 product_id   | integer                      |
 units        | integer                      | default 1
 price        | numeric(9,2)                 |
Check constraints: "sales_units" ((units > 0) AND (units < 1000))
```

The DEFAULT values as well as the CHECK constraints are listed in the output. Now it is time to insert some data into the table:

```
phpbook=# INSERT INTO sales (id, product_id, price) VALUES ('1', '2343240',
'12.9');
INSERT 25497 1
```

```
phpbook=# INSERT INTO sales (id, product_id, units, price) VALUES ('2',
'2343240', -1, '12.9');
ERROR:  ExecAppend: rejected due to CHECK constraint sales_units
```

The first record can be added to the table without any problems. However, the second INSERT statement violates the CHECK constraint and won't be performed successfully. Therefore the table contains exactly one record:

```
phpbook=# SELECT * FROM sales;
 id |           tstamp          | product_id | units | price
----+---------------------------+------------+-------+-------
  1 | 2001-11-30 11:16:29.199441+01 |   2343240 |     1 | 12.90
(1 row)
```

The values of columns that have not been in the INSERT statement have been assigned to the DEFAULT value.

8.7.1.3 Column Constraints

Some additional constraints can be defined that add certain attributes to a column. The UNIQUE constraint guarantees that no duplicated values can be inserted into a column. NOT NULL makes sure that a column can never contain a NULL value, and the NULL constraint sets the default value to NULL. Let's drop and create the table sales again and use these constraints:

```
CREATE TABLE sales (
        id int4              UNIQUE,
        tstamp timestamp     NOT NULL,
        product_id int4 ,
        units int4           NULL,
        price numeric(9,2)
);
```

To insert the data structure into the table, we suggest that you use psql:

```
[postgres@athlon const]$ psql phpbook < constraint.sql
NOTICE:  CREATE TABLE/UNIQUE will create implicit index 'sales_id_key' for
table 'sales'
CREATE
```

If no errors occurred, PostgreSQL has created a table and an index has been defined automatically. This index has been defined as a unique index; this way, PostgreSQL makes sure that no duplicated values can be added to the column. It seems obvious that an index is created automatically because otherwise PostgreSQL would have to read the entire table every time a record is added to the table in order to find out if a certain value already exists.

```
phpbook=# \d sales
                 Table "sales"
   Column   |            Type            | Modifiers
------------+---------------------------+-----------
 id         | integer                   |
 tstamp     | timestamp(6) with time zone | not null
 product_id | integer                   |
 units      | integer                   |
 price      | numeric(9,2)              |
Unique keys: sales_id_key
```

Let's insert some data into the relation:

```
phpbook=# INSERT INTO sales VALUES (1, now(), 2323411, 4, '23.1');
INSERT 25501 1
```

No errors occurred. In the next example you will see what happens when you try to insert a NULL value in the second column:

```
phpbook=# INSERT INTO sales VALUES (2, NULL, 2323411, 4, '23.1');
ERROR:  ExecAppend: Fail to add null value in not null attribute tstamp
```

The INSERT statement will not succeed because the column is not allowed to contain NULL values because of the NOT NULL constraint.

In the next step two records with the same id will be added to the table:

```
phpbook=# INSERT INTO sales VALUES (2, now(), 2323412, 3, '29.4');
INSERT 25502 1
phpbook=# INSERT INTO sales VALUES (2, now(), 2323412, 3, '29.4');
ERROR:  Cannot insert a duplicate key into unique index sales_id_key
```

The second INSERT statement has failed because the first column is defined to be unique. Therefore duplicated values are not allowed.

8.7.1.4 Primary Keys and Object Ids

Primary keys are a fundamental component of the relation database model. A primary key of a table is a unique identifier of a row in a table. Therefore a column defined as a primary key must not contain duplicated values.

Let's try an example:

```
phpbook=# CREATE TABLE book (isbn text PRIMARY KEY, title text, author text);
NOTICE:  CREATE TABLE/PRIMARY KEY will create implicit index 'book_pkey' for
table 'book'
CREATE
```

A table for storing books has been created and the first column has been defined as a primary key. Using the ISBN number of a book as the primary key is a good choice because this number is unique.

After creating the table, you can take a look at the definition of the table:

```
phpbook=# \d book
         Table "book"
 Column | Type | Modifiers
--------+------+-----------
 isbn   | text | not null
 title  | text |
 author | text |
Primary key: book_pkey
```

PostgreSQL mentions in the listing that the primary key is book_pkey.

8.7.1.5 Integrity Constraints

Up to now you have dealt with a set of independent tables. In real-world applications this is more often an exception than the normal status. Data stored in various tables is in many cases not independent. Imagine a situation where one table stores the salary of a person and the second table stores the attributes of the person. If a person is deleted from the table storing the attributes, it might be useful to remove the person from the table storing the salaries as well. For this purpose, you can use integrity constraints. PostgreSQL provides a rich set of integrity constraints, and you will learn about these in this section.

Foreign key constraints are fundamental when working with data integrity on the database level. A column defined as a foreign key must always be related to a column in another table. In many cases, a foreign key column is related to a primary key of another table as shown in the next listing:

```
CREATE TABLE company (id int4 PRIMARY KEY,
            name    text    NOT NULL,
            city    text    NOT NULL
);


CREATE TABLE employee (company_id int4 REFERENCES company,
            name    text    NOT NULL,
            salary  numeric(9,2)
);
```

The table called company stores information about companies and employee stores information about the workers employed at the company. The column called company_id is a foreign key and it is related to the primary key of the table called company. To create the table we recommend using an ASCII file containing the SQL code:

```
[postgres@athlon postgres]$ psql phpbook < comp.sql
NOTICE:  CREATE TABLE/PRIMARY KEY will create implicit index 'company_pkey'
for table 'company'
CREATE
NOTICE:  CREATE TABLE will create implicit trigger(s) for FOREIGN KEY check(s)
CREATE
```

When creating the tables, PostgreSQL will automatically create triggers to guarantee data integrity. Triggers are used to call functions automatically and that's exactly what has to be done. Every time a record is changed, PostgreSQL will fire a trigger to see if data integrity is violated.

Take a look at the definition of the tables you have just created:

```
phpbook=# \d company
        Table "company"
 Column |  Type   | Modifiers
--------+---------+-----------
 id     | integer | not null
 name   | text    | not null
 city   | text    | not null
Primary key: company_pkey
Triggers: RI_ConstraintTrigger_25546,
          RI_ConstraintTrigger_25548


phpbook=# \d employee
           Table "employee"
   Column   |     Type     | Modifiers
------------+--------------+-----------
 company_id | integer      |
 name       | text         | not null
 salary     | numeric(9,2) |
Triggers: RI_ConstraintTrigger_25544
```

As you can see, the triggers used by PostgreSQL are listed in the description.

After creating the tables, it is time to insert some values. First a record is added to the table used to store the companies:

```
phpbook=# INSERT INTO company VALUES (1, 'Cybertec', 'Vienna');
INSERT 25575 1
```

Cybertec has been assigned to the id 1. In the next step two employees are added. Both persons are employees of Cybertec, so the id of company is used as a foreign key:

```
phpbook=# INSERT INTO employee VALUES (1, 'Susi', '40000');
INSERT 25576 1
phpbook=# INSERT INTO employee VALUES (1, 'Horst', '38000');
INSERT 25577 1
```

The records have been added successfully, but what happens if the first column is defined as NULL?

```
phpbook=# INSERT INTO employee VALUES(NULL, 'Epi', 52000);
INSERT 25578 1
```

No problem occurred because columns that have been defined as foreign key may contain NULL values. In the next step you can try to insert a person who is employed at a company having the id 2:

```
phpbook=# INSERT INTO employee VALUES (2, 'Pauline', '39500');
ERROR:  <unnamed> referential integrity violation - key referenced from
employee not found in company
```

No data can be added to the table because there is no appropriate company to add the person to. The foreign key makes sure that no invalid persons can be added to the table.

If a company has employees, it cannot be deleted:

```
phpbook=# DELETE FROM company;
ERROR:  <unnamed> referential integrity violation - key in company still
referenced from employee
```

To remove Cybertec, all employees must be removed, and if the id of Cybertec is no longer needed as a foreign key, the company can be removed.

In this example you have seen that the id is used as a foreign key. Because the id is the primary key of company, no problems have occurred, but things can also be done differently. Before you get to the next example, the two tables you have created must be removed by using DROP TABLE:

```
phpbook=# DROP TABLE employee;
NOTICE:  DROP TABLE implicitly drops referential integrity trigger from table
"company"
NOTICE:  DROP TABLE implicitly drops referential integrity trigger from table
"company"
```

```
DROP
phpbook=# DROP TABLE company;
DROP
```

When deleting the first table, PostgreSQL mentions that the integrity constraints have been removed from the table as well:

```
CREATE TABLE company (id int4 PRIMARY KEY,
             name    text    NOT NULL UNIQUE,
             city    text    NOT NULL
);

CREATE TABLE employee (company_name text REFERENCES company(name),
             name    text    NOT NULL,
             salary  numeric(9,2)
);
```

In this example the column called name is referenced and taken as the primary key.

Let's insert one record into each table:

```
phpbook=# INSERT INTO company VALUES (1, 'Cybertec', 'Vienna');
INSERT 25784 1
phpbook=# INSERT INTO employee VALUES('Cybertec', 'Epi', 52000);
INSERT 25786 1
```

The target of the next example is to see what happens when the primary key has to be updated. Imagine that the name of the company changes:

```
phpbook=# UPDATE company SET name='Cybertec Geschwinde and Schoenig OEG';
ERROR:  <unnamed> referential integrity violation - key in company still
referenced from employee
```

The UPDATE operation cannot be performed because referential integrity would be violated.

This behavior is not a good one because you cannot change the data used as foreign key. To get around the problem, PostgreSQL offers additional constraints. Therefore the SQL commands for generating the tables have to be changed. Before inserting the SQL commands in the next listing, don't forget to delete the old tables using DROP TABLE:

```
CREATE TABLE company (id int4 PRIMARY KEY,
             name    text    NOT NULL UNIQUE,
             city    text    NOT NULL
);
```

```
CREATE TABLE employee (company_name text
                       REFERENCES company(name)
                       INITIALLY DEFERRED,
               name    text    NOT NULL,
               salary  numeric(9,2)
);
```

As you can see, an additional constraint has been added to employee. This command makes sure that the integrity is only changed at the end of a transaction and not after every statement. The advantage of this is that the name of the company can be changed in both tables before committing the transaction. This way data can easily be changed. The next listing shows how this can be done:

```
INSERT INTO company VALUES (1, 'Cybertec', 'Vienna');
INSERT INTO employee VALUES('Cybertec', 'Epi', 52000);

BEGIN;
UPDATE company SET name='Cybertec Geschwinde and Schoenig OEG' WHERE
name='Cybertec';
UPDATE employee SET company_name='Cybertec Geschwinde and Schoenig OEG'
       WHERE company_name='Cybertec';
COMMIT;
```

First, two records have been added. In the next step a transaction is started and the name is changed in both tables. During the transaction PostgreSQL will not check data integrity and therefore both operations can easily be performed.

The opposite of the INITIALLY DEFERRED constraint is the INITIALLY IMMEDIATE constraint, which checks data integrity after every SQL statement.

Working with INITIALLY DEFERRED will in some cases help you to solve problems concerning data integrity, but sometimes other constraints are more comfortable. Take a look at the next example:

```
CREATE TABLE company (id int4 PRIMARY KEY,
            name    text    NOT NULL UNIQUE,
            city    text    NOT NULL
);

CREATE TABLE employee (company_id int4 REFERENCES company(id)
                       ON UPDATE CASCADE,
            name    text    NOT NULL,
            salary  numeric(9,2)
);
```

In the second table the column called company_id has been set to ON UPDATE CASCADE. This means that every time the primary key of the first table is changed, PostgreSQL will automatically change all columns referring to it. Let's see how this works:

```
phpbook=# INSERT INTO company VALUES (1, 'Cybertec', 'Vienna');
INSERT 25757 1
phpbook=# INSERT INTO employee VALUES(1, 'Epi', 52000);
INSERT 25758 1
```

First, two records have been added to the database. In the next step an UPDATE operation is performed to change the id of the company stored in the first table:

```
phpbook=# UPDATE company SET id=2 WHERE id=1;
UPDATE 1
```

PostgreSQL does not complain that something has gone wrong and has changed the value in company:

```
phpbook=# SELECT * FROM company;
 id |   name   |  city
----+----------+--------
  2 | Cybertec | Vienna
(1 row)
```

In addition, the column company_id has been changed:

```
phpbook=# SELECT * FROM employee;
 company_id | name |  salary
------------+------+----------
          2 | Epi  | 52000.00
(1 row)
```

This wayonly one operation has to be performed to change all values referring to company. This is comfortable and will save a lot of time as well as a lot of overhead.

In general ON can be used in combination with two SQL commands: UPDATE and DELETE. Both commands support a list of possible settings. Let's go through the DELETE command's settings:

- NO ACTION and RESTRICT—An error is displayed if the foreign key is violated; this is the default setting.

- CASCADE—All rows referenced by the deleted row are deleted as well.

- SET NULL—sets the referencing columns to NULL.

- SET DEFAULT—Sets the referencing column to the default value.

Here is a list of what can be done with the options provided by UPDATE:

- NO ACTION and RESTRICT—An error is displayed if the foreign key is violated; this is the default setting.

- CASCADE—Update the values in the columns referencing a key.

- SET NULL—Sets the referencing columns to NULL.

- SET DEFAULT—Sets the referencing column to the default value.

- [NOT] DEFERRABLE—DEFERRABLE makes sure that data integrity is checked at the end of the transaction. NOT DEFERRABLE is the default setting and makes PostgreSQL check data integrity after every operation.

As you can see, PostgreSQL provides many ways to make sure that data integrity is not violated. Because PostgreSQL is able to take care of data integrity, it is not necessary to do it on the application level.

8.8 Basic Optimizations Using EXPLAIN

After you have written the queries needed by your application, you will soon find out that some sort of tuning might be necessary. The more complex your queries are, the more likely it is that a lot of performance can be gained by changing some simple parameters.

8.8.1 Using EXPLAIN

To find out what the database does internally, PostgreSQL provides a command called EXPLAIN:

```
phpbook=# \h EXPLAIN
Command:     EXPLAIN
Description: show the execution plan of a statement
Syntax:
EXPLAIN [ ANALYZE ] [ VERBOSE ] query
```

As you can see, the syntax of the command is easy.

With the help of EXPLAIN it is possible to find out how PostgreSQL processes a query internally. EXPLAIN displays the so-called execution plan on the screen. In this execution plan you can see every step performed by PostgreSQL.

Take a look at a simple join operation:

```
SELECT company.*, employee.name, employee.salary
     FROM company, employee
     WHERE company.name=employee.company_name;
```

The query returns exactly one record:

```
id |                      name                      |  city  | name |  salary
---+------------------------------------------------+--------+------+----------
 1 | Cybertec Geschwinde and Schoenig OEG           | Vienna | Epi  | 52000.00
(1 row)
```

In the next step EXPLAIN can be used to display the internal execution plan of the query:

```
phpbook=# EXPLAIN SELECT company.*, employee.name, employee.salary FROM
company, employee WHERE company.name=employee.company_name;

NOTICE:  QUERY PLAN:

Merge Join  (cost=69.83..139.33 rows=1000 width=147)
  -> Index Scan using company_name_key on company  (cost=0.00..52.00
rows=1000 width=68)
    -> Sort  (cost=69.83..69.83 rows=1000 width=79)
        -> Seq Scan on employee  (cost=0.00..20.00 rows=1000 width=79)


EXPLAIN
```

You have to read the execution plan from right to left. In this example this means that PostgreSQL starts with scanning employee and continues with sorting and scanning the primary key of company. After that the results of the sort operation and the index scan are merged.

When using EXPLAIN, PostgreSQL does not execute the query—only the execution plan is displayed. This is an important point because you don't have to take care of what the query you are analyzing is doing.

To get a little bit more information about the execution plan, you can also use EXPLAIN ANALYSE. This feature has been introduced with PostgreSQL 7.2 and is a significant improvement over previous versions of PostgreSQL:

```
phpbook=# EXPLAIN ANALYZE SELECT company.*, employee.name, employee.salary
FROM company, employee WHERE company.name=employee.company_name;

NOTICE:  QUERY PLAN:

Merge Join  (cost=69.83..139.33 rows=1000 width=147) (actual time=0.24..0.26
rows=1 loops=1)
  -> Index Scan using company_name_key on company  (cost=0.00..52.00
rows=1000 width=68) (actual time=0.05..0.06 rows=1 loops=1)
    -> Sort  (cost=69.83..69.83 rows=1000 width=79) (actual time=0.12..0.12
```

```
rows=1 loops=1)           -> Seq Scan on employee  (cost=0.00..20.00 rows=1000
width=79)
(actual time=0.02..0.02 rows=1 loops=1)
Total runtime: 0.47 msec
```

As you can see, PostgreSQL also displays information about the time it might take to perform the query. This is extremely helpful when working with more complex queries because you get an idea of how long things will take to be executed.

An additional feature provided by EXPLAIN is the keyword VERBOSE. VERBOSE displays detailed information about what is going on inside the database when executing a query. The next listing shows the detailed execution plans of a simple query. (We have decided not to use a more complex query here because the result would be far too long.)

```
phpbook=# EXPLAIN VERBOSE SELECT 1+1;
NOTICE:  QUERY DUMP:

{ RESULT :startup_cost 0.00 :total_cost 0.01 :rows 1 :width 0 :qptargetlist ({
TARGETENTRY :resdom
{ RESDOM :resno 1 :restype 23 :restypmod -1 :resname ?column? :reskey
0 :reskeyop 0 :ressortgroupref 0 :resjunk false } :expr { CONST
:consttype 23 :constlen 4 :constbyval true :constisnull false :
constvalue  4 [ 2 0 0 0 ] }}) :qpqual <> :lefttree <> :righttree
<> :extprm () :locprm () :initplan
<> :nprm 0   :resconstantqual <>}
NOTICE:  QUERY PLAN:

Result  (cost=0.00..0.01 rows=1 width=0)

EXPLAIN
```

Even a simple operation such as 1+1 has a complex-looking execution plan. However, if you take a closer look at the listing, you will discover that most of the data returned by PostgreSQL consists of attributes (for example, ?column?, which defines the name of the column displayed in the result).

8.8.2 Optimizing a Query

After analyzing a query using EXPLAIN, you can try to optimize the execution time of a query by giving PostgreSQL's planner some hints what to do best. The planner is responsible for generating the execution plan of a query. This execution plan needs to be analyzed and bottlenecks have to be found in order to speed up your applications.

To see what can be done to gain speed, you can generate some records. We always recommend that you test your data structures with many records because this is the only way to detect bottlenecks. If you have only a few records, it is not possible to tune your database efficiently because it is difficult to measure the time gained by a certain change. Therefore it is useful to generate some dummy records and to test your data structures with these records. In many cases this will help you to test your system under real-world load. To generate some data you can build a small PHP script:

```php
<?php
        $fp = fopen("/tmp/data.sql", "w+");
        if      (!$fp)
        {
                echo "cannot open file\n";
                exit;
        }

        fwrite($fp,"COPY data FROM stdin;\n");

        for     ($i = 1; $i < 250000; $i++)
        {
                $string = "$i    ".($i*2)."        ".cos($i)."\n";
                $status = fwrite($fp, $string);
        }

        fwrite($fp,"\.\n");
        fclose($fp);
?>
```

First a file is opened for writing. If the file has been opened successfully, you can continue with a COPY command. In this case data will be inserted into a table called data—this table can be created after generating the data.

After generating the header of the COPY command, many records are generated. Every record consists of three columns storing numbers and is written into the file using fwrite.

Finally, the file is closed.

To execute the file, you can use PHP from the command line as shown in the next listing:

```
bash-2.04$ php makedata.php
X-Powered-By: PHP/4.0.4pl1
Content-type: text/html
```

In most default installations, the maximum time the PHP script is allowed to run is set to 30 seconds—if no data is displayed on the screen, this has to be taken into consideration.

After generating the data, you can create the table for storing the records:

```
CREATE TABLE data (id int4, two int4, three numeric(10, 9));
```

As you can see, the table contains three records:

```
phpbook=# \d data
            Table "data"
 Attribute |     Type      | Modifier
-----------+---------------+----------
 id        | integer       |
 two       | integer       |
 three     | numeric(10,9) |
```

Your PHP script has generated a COPY command and the data has been added to the table by the command. With the help of the Unix command head, you can list the first records in the file you have just created:

```
bash-2.04$ head data.sql
COPY data FROM stdin;
1       2       0.54030230586814
2       4       -0.41614683654714
3       6       -0.98999249660045
4       8       -0.65364362086361
5       10      0.28366218546323
6       12      0.96017028665037
7       14      0.7539022543433
8       16      -0.14550003380861
9       18      -0.91113026188468
```

The data has been generated successfully. To retrieve the last few lines from the file, you can use tail:

```
bash-2.04$ tail data.sql -n3
249998  499996  -0.8685165807682
249999  499998  -0.88634511580316
\.
```

The last line of the COPY command has to be \.—this way PostgreSQL will know that no more data is going to come.

To insert the data into the database, use the following command:

```
psql phpbook < data.sql
```

Now that the data is in the table, you can try to send a simple query to the server. In this example the query is sent to the server using a shell command. This is necessary to measure the time the query takes:

```
bash-2.04$ time psql -d phpbook -c "SELECT * FROM data WHERE id=200000"
   id   |  two   |   three
--------+--------+------------
 200000 | 400000 | 0.997444047
(1 row)


real    0m1.601s
user    0m0.020s
sys     0m0.010s
```

The query takes more than one and a half seconds, which is far too long. If you use EXPLAIN to analyze the execution plan, you will soon find the reason for the disaster: PostgreSQL has to perform a sequential scan, which means that the entire table has to be read from the beginning to the end—which takes a long time. To get around the problem, you can define an index:

```
phpbook=# CREATE INDEX idx_data_id ON data (id);
CREATE
```

Now the query should run significantly faster:

```
bash-2.04$ time psql -d phpbook -c "SELECT * FROM data WHERE id=200000"
   id   |  two   |   three
--------+--------+------------
 200000 | 400000 | 0.997444047
(1 row)


real    0m0.087s
user    0m0.040s
sys     0m0.000s
```

The performance gain is impressive because PostgreSQL can use an index now. Take a look at the execution plan of the query:

```
phpbook=# EXPLAIN SELECT * FROM data;
NOTICE:  QUERY PLAN:

Index Scan using idx_data_id on data  (cost=0.00..4.68 rows=1 width=32)

EXPLAIN

phpbook=# EXPLAIN SELECT * FROM data where id = 200000;
NOTICE:  QUERY PLAN:
Index Scan using idx_data_id on data  (cost=0.00..4638.01 rows=2500 width=20)
EXPLAIN
```

If the numbers in parentheses do not match the numbers you have, don't worry—these values are taken from internal statistics and might vary.

8.9 Sophisticated Joins

Joins are the heart of every complex query. Whenever more than just one table is involved in a query, joins must be performed. So far you have dealt with normal joins, but in this section you will take a closer look at some more helpful and useful features.

8.9.1 Left, Right, and Co.

In general performing simple joins is easy—in some cases, however, it is necessary to perform some more complex operations. In this section you will start to deal with a set of different join operations such as left and right joins.

Let's start with an example. Two tables must be created:

```
phpbook=# CREATE TABLE event (id int4, name text);
CREATE
phpbook=# CREATE TABLE comment (event_id int4, comment text);
CREATE
```

The first table stores the id and the name of an event. The second table contains the id of the event stored in the first table and a comment. No integrity constraints have been defined.

In the next step three records can be inserted into event:

```
phpbook=# INSERT INTO event VALUES (1, 'concert of Manifold');
INSERT 26009 1
phpbook=# INSERT INTO event VALUES (2, 'concert of Scentless Work');
INSERT 26010 1
phpbook=# INSERT INTO event VALUES (3, 'concert of Le Craval');
INSERT 26011 1
```

Then some records can be added to the second table:

```
phpbook=# INSERT INTO comment VALUES (1, 'great concert on La Palma (Spain)');
INSERT 26012
phpbook=# INSERT INTO comment VALUES (1, 'I liked the Rolling Stones songs
most');
INSERT 26013 1
phpbook=# INSERT INTO comment VALUES (2, 'they played Falco''s "Rock me
Amadeus"');
INSERT 26014 1
phpbook=# INSERT INTO comment VALUES (4, 'nice workshop and nice food');
INSERT 26015 1
```

As you can see, the id 3 can only be found in the first table and the id 4 can only be found in the second table. The target of the first example is to perform a simple join used to retrieve all records that have an id in common:

```
SELECT event.name, comment.comment
        FROM event, comment
        WHERE event.id=comment.event_id;
```

This join is nothing new for you, so the result is not surprising:

```
            name            |                  comment
----------------------------+--------------------------------------------
 concert of Manifold        | great concert on La Palma (Spain)
 concert of Manifold        | I liked the Rolling Stones songs most
 concert of Scentless Work  | they played Falco's "Rock me Amadeus"
(3 rows)
```

You have displayed the name of the event as well as the comment on the event. The same result can be achieved by using an INNER JOIN:

```
SELECT event.name, comment.comment
        FROM event INNER JOIN comment
                ON event.id=comment.event_id;
```

In the previous result you have seen that every record having a counterpart in comment has been listed. The target of the next example is to display all events even if there is no comment:

```
SELECT event.name, comment.comment
       FROM event LEFT JOIN comment ON
               event.id=comment.event_id;
```

The result contains one additional record:

```
          name             |               comment
---------------------------+----------------------------------------
 concert of Manifold       | great concert on La Palma (Spain)
 concert of Manifold       | I liked the Rolling Stones songs most
 concert of Scentless Work | they played Falco's "Rock me Amadeus"
 concert of Le Craval      |
(4 rows)
```

No comment has been added for the concert of the band called Le Craval, but you have performed a left join. If you want to have all records that have a comment but no event, you can use a right join:

```
SELECT event.name, comment.comment
       FROM event RIGHT JOIN comment
               ON event.id=comment.event_id;
```

Again, four records are displayed, but this time the column containing the name is displayed completely:

```
          name             |               comment
---------------------------+----------------------------------------
 concert of Manifold       | great concert on La Palma (Spain)
 concert of Manifold       | I liked the Rolling Stones songs most
 concert of Scentless Work | they played Falco's "Rock me Amadeus"
                           | nice workshop and nice food
(4 rows)
```

Let's see what happens if the list of tables in the FROM clause is changed:

```
SELECT event.name, comment.comment
       FROM comment RIGHT JOIN event
               ON event.id=comment.event_id;
```

The result of the query is equal to the left join you have seen before. As you can see, there is more than one way to solve the problem:

```
          name             |                 comment
---------------------------+-----------------------------------------
 concert of Manifold       | great concert on La Palma (Spain)
 concert of Manifold       | I liked the Rolling Stones songs most
 concert of Scentless Work | they played Falco's "Rock me Amadeus"
 concert of Le Craval      |
(4 rows)
```

Left and right joins are a powerful feature of SQL and especially of PostgreSQL. With the help of these joins, it is possible to compute complex results with little effort and in an efficient way.

8.10 Working with Arrays

Arrays are a core feature of PostgreSQL. Many people admire PostgreSQL because of this feature because it is a comfortable way to reduce the number of relations in your data structure as well as to store multiple values in just one cell.

8.10.1 One-Dimensional Arrays

To define a column as an array, brackets have to be added to the data type:

```
phpbook=# CREATE TABLE parent (name_mother text, name_children text[]);
CREATE
```

If you have a look at the data structure, you will see that the second column has been defined as an array:

```
phpbook=# \d parent
         Table "parent"
    Column     | Type   | Modifiers
---------------+--------+-----------
 name_mother   | text   |
 name_children | text[] |
```

To insert a record into the table, you can use a special syntax:

```
phpbook=# INSERT INTO parent VALUES ('Andrea', '{"Paul", "Lisa"}');
INSERT 26021 1
```

Curly brackets tell PostgreSQL that an array is being passed to the database. The string values in the array must be surrounded by double quotes. Let's query the table:

```
phpbook=# SELECT * FROM parent;
 name_mother | name_children
-------------+----------------
 Andrea      | {"Paul","Lisa"}
(1 row)
```

Just as in any other programming language, values can be accessed by using an index:

```
phpbook=# SELECT name_mother, name_children[0] FROM parent;
 name_mother | name_children
-------------+----------------
 Andrea      |
(1 row)
```

As you can see, the element number zero is empty because PostgreSQL starts to count the values at index number one:

```
phpbook=# SELECT name_mother, name_children[1] FROM parent;
 name_mother | name_children
-------------+----------------
 Andrea      | Paul
(1 row)
```

Various fields of an array can be displayed in just one column:

```
phpbook=# SELECT name_mother, name_children[1], name_children[2] FROM parent;
 name_mother | name_children | name_children
-------------+---------------+----------------
 Andrea      | Paul          | Lisa
```

This is comfortable because you don't have to perform join operations—everything can be found in just one table. Some of you might think that arrays violate Codd's Normal Forms—that's correct, but arrays are just an extra feature and need not be used. It is up to you to decide whether arrays are useful for you.

8.10.2 Limited Arrays

The table you have just dealt with contains an unlimited array, which means that many values can be inserted into it. If you want to limit an array, that can also be done. Let's drop the table you have just created and generate a new one:

```
phpbook=# DROP TABLE parent;
DROP
phpbook=# CREATE TABLE parent (name_mother text, name_children text[2]);
CREATE
```

The description of the table is exactly the same as you have seen before:

```
phpbook=# \d parent
          Table "parent"
    Column     |  Type  | Modifiers
---------------+--------+-----------
 name_mother   | text   |
 name_children | text[] |
```

Although the size of the column is limited to two records, you can add as many values to the columns as you want because PostgreSQL 7.2 treats limited and unlimited columns the same way:

```
phpbook=# INSERT INTO parent VALUES ('Andrea', '{"Paul", "Lisa"}');
INSERT 26027 1
phpbook=# INSERT INTO parent VALUES ('Pauline', '{"Charles", "Pat", "Jim"}');
INSERT 26028 1
```

Pauline's three children are listed in the result:

```
phpbook=# SELECT * FROM parent;
 name_mother |      name_children
-------------+-------------------------
 Andrea      | {"Paul","Lisa"}
 Pauline     | {"Charles","Pat","Jim"}
(2 rows)
```

8.10.3 Multidimensional Arrays

PostgreSQL is capable of handling multidimensional arrays. Take a look at an example:

```
phpbook=# DROP TABLE parent;
DROP
phpbook=# CREATE TABLE parent (name_mother text, name_gender_children text[][]);
CREATE
```

A two-dimensional array has been generated:

```
phpbook=# \d parent
           Table "parent"
      Column          | Type  | Modifiers
----------------------+-------+-----------
 name_mother          | text  |
 name_gender_children | text[]|
```

In the next step values can be added to the array. The syntax for multidimensional arrays does not differ from the one you have just dealt with significantly:

```
phpbook=# INSERT INTO parent VALUES ('Andrea', '{{"Paul", "Lisa"}, {"male",
"female"}}');
INSERT 26034 1
```

The values are displayed in the table the same way:

```
phpbook=# SELECT * FROM parent;
 name_mother |        name_gender_children
-------------+-------------------------------------
 Andrea      | {{"Paul","Lisa"},{"male","female"}}
(1 row)
```

To retrieve the data, both dimensions have to be defined:

```
phpbook=# SELECT name_gender_children[1][1], name_gender_children[2][1] FROM
parent;
 name_gender_children | name_gender_children
----------------------+----------------------
 Paul                 | male
(1 row)
```

In some cases it is necessary to find the size of an array. Therefore PostgreSQL provides a function called array_dims:

```
phpbook=# SELECT array_dims(name_gender_children) FROM parent;
 array_dims
------------
 [1:2][1:2]
(1 row)
```

In this scenario each dimension contains two elements. The information retrieved from the database can be used to select entire ranges from an array, as shown in the next listing:

```
phpbook=# SELECT name_mother, name_gender_children[1][1:2] FROM parent;
 name_mother | name_gender_children
-------------+----------------------
 Andrea      | {{"Paul","Lisa"}}
(1 row)
```

Both elements of the second axis are displayed because a range has been defined.

In the next step you will try to remove elements from an array. Let's try to set a cell to NULL:

```
phpbook=# UPDATE parent SET name_gender_children[1][1] = NULL;
UPDATE 1
```

Although one row has been updated, no changes have been made—the array is still the same:

```
phpbook=# SELECT name_mother, name_gender_children[1][1:2] FROM parent;
 name_mother | name_gender_children
-------------+----------------------
 Andrea      | {{"Paul","Lisa"}}
(1 row)
```

One way to get rid of an element is to assign an empty string to the cell. This is not a good solution, but in some cases it will help you:

```
phpbook=# UPDATE parent SET name_gender_children[1][1] = '';
UPDATE 1
```

The element is still in the array but it is empty:

```
phpbook=# SELECT name_mother, name_gender_children FROM parent;
 name_mother |        name_gender_children
-------------+------------------------------------
 Andrea      | {{"","Lisa"},{"male","female"}}
(1 row)
```

A better solution would be to write a PL/pgSQL or PL/Perl function that parses cells containing the array and updates the entire cell. We have decided not to include a function like that because it would be far beyond the scope of this book.

8.11 Combining Queries and Ranges of Values

In some cases the queries you have already seen will not be enough to satisfy your demands. The ANSI SQL standard defines several ways to combine queries, which are covered in this section.

Let's define two tables: The first one stores a list of registered users. The second table contains the postings of the various users:

```
phpbook=# CREATE TABLE reg_user (name text, regdate date);
CREATE
phpbook=# CREATE TABLE user_post (name text, postdate date, message text);
CREATE
```

For this scenario three users are added to the table:

```
phpbook=# INSERT INTO reg_user VALUES ('Paul', '2001/03/12');
INSERT 26059 1
phpbook=# INSERT INTO reg_user VALUES ('Shelley', '2001/02/22');
INSERT 26060 1
phpbook=# INSERT INTO reg_user VALUES ('Alan', '1999/12/01');
INSERT 26061 1
```

In addition, the postings of the various users are added to the second table:

```
phpbook=# INSERT INTO user_post VALUES ('Paul', '2001/03/13','do you think
this is true?');
INSERT 26062 1
phpbook=# INSERT INTO user_post VALUES ('Paul', '2001/03/14','i would use a
trigger instead');
INSERT 26063 1
phpbook=# INSERT INTO user_post VALUES ('Shelley', '2001/03/15','rules are
much better');
INSERT 26064 1
```

Three keywords for combining queries are defined: EXCEPT is used to subtract one result from the other. INTERSECT computes those records that can be found in both queries and UNION adds the results of two queries. Take a look at a query using EXCEPT:

```
phpbook=# SELECT name FROM reg_user EXCEPT SELECT name FROM user_post;
 name
------
 Alan
(1 row)
```

This query returns all records that cannot be found in the second table. In other words all users who have not posted yet will be returned.

The next example shows a query containing two EXCEPT statements:

```
phpbook=# SELECT name FROM reg_user EXCEPT SELECT name FROM user_post EXCEPT
SELECT 'Alan';
 name
 ------
(0 rows)
```

All people who haven't posted yet except Alan are returned.

If you want to retrieve all names that can be found in both tables, you can use INTERSECT:

```
phpbook=# SELECT name FROM reg_user INTERSECT SELECT name FROM user_post;
  name
 ---------
 Paul
 Shelley
(2 rows)
```

Two people are registered and have posted messages. The same result can be achieved by performing a simple join operation. However, some details must be taken into consideration:

```
phpbook=# SELECT reg_user.name FROM reg_user, user_post WHERE
reg_user.name=user_post.name;
  name
 ---------
 Paul
 Paul
 Shelley
(3 rows)
```

DISTINCT has to be added to the query in order to retrieve every record only once:

```
phpbook=# SELECT DISTINCT reg_user.name FROM reg_user, user_post WHERE
reg_user.name=user_post.name;
  name
 ---------
 Paul
 Shelley
(2 rows)
```

To combine the result of two queries, you can use UNION:

```
phpbook=# SELECT name FROM reg_user UNION SELECT name FROM user_post;
  name
----------
 Alan
 Hugo
 Paul
 Shelley
(4 rows)
```

All names that can be found in req_user and user_post are retrieved. Let's try to retrieve two columns:

```
phpbook=# SELECT name FROM reg_user UNION SELECT name, postdate FROM user_post;
ERROR:  Each UNION query must have the same number of columns
```

As you can see, PostgreSQL does not accept queries connected with either EXCEPT, INTERSECT, or UNION when the number of columns in the queries do not match. This is an important point that has to be taken into consideration when combining queries.

The queries combined are flexible, as you can see in the next example:

```
SELECT name
        FROM reg_user
UNION SELECT name
        FROM user_post
        WHERE postdate BETWEEN '2000/1/1' AND '2002/1/1';
```

BETWEEN can be used to define ranges of values. In this case postings between January 1, 2000 and January 1, 2002 are retrieved:

```
  name
----------
 Alan
 Paul
 Shelley
(3 rows)
```

8.12 Summary

PostgreSQL is a highly developed database that is mainly based on ANSI SQL. Up to now a major part of the ANSI specification has been implemented in the server and the developers are working hard to continue this project.

Constraints are used to define certain attributes and restrictions as well as to guarantee data integrity. PostgreSQL provides a pool of constraints used to work with data integrity.

To speed up your database, you can tune PostgreSQL, making heavy use of optimizer settings.

Queries can be combined with each other in order to build more complex operations. For this purpose, ANSI SQL defines many keywords.

9

Embedded Languages

Almost all sophisticated database systems support at least one embedded language. PL/SQL, for instance, is a block-oriented language supported by Oracle databases. In PostgreSQL a set of languages can be used for writing functions you can use in SQL:

- **SQL**—Pure SQL code can be used to write functions.

- **C**—Shared objects can be written and every function in the shared object can be added to PostgreSQL as long as some basic rules are fulfilled.

- **PL/pgSQL**—PL/pgSQL is similar to PL/SQL and it is the standard way of writing functions.

- **PL/Perl**—Perl can be used as an embedded language. In PostgreSQL 7.2, PL/Perl has been improved significantly.

- **PL/Tcl**—Tcl has been designed to be an embedded language and can easily be used in combination with PostgreSQL. Especially for writing triggers, PL/Tcl is a good choice.

PostgreSQL provides an easy interface for adding your own languages. Just a few interfaces have to be implemented and you can use almost any programming language inside PostgreSQL. However, it is only recommended for languages based on C because interacting with libraries or languages that are not written in C is very difficult.

In this chapter we will focus on PL/pgSQL because other languages are beyond the scope of this book.

To implement additional functions for your database, embedded languages are essential, and in most cases it is easy to write extensions for the database. Depending on the kind of functions you want to write, you must choose the best language for your purpose.

When working with PostgreSQL, many people rely on PL/pgSQL. PL/pgSQL is a powerful language that is similar to PL/SQL. It is block-oriented and can only be used from inside PostgreSQL. In this section you will take a closer look at this powerful component of PostgreSQL and you will see how to use PL/pgSQL efficiently.

9.1 Writing SQL Functions

Writing functions with the help of SQL is just as easy as writing SQL statements. The idea behind SQL functions is to have an easy way to add new features to a database. In addition, it is not necessary to use embedded languages such as PL/pgSQL or PL/Perl for implementing minor extensions. This is an important point because it increases the portability and flexibility of your database significantly.

9.1.1 An Example

Let's start by writing a simple function based on pure SQL code. For adding new functions to the database, you must use CREATE FUNCTION. The syntax of CREATE FUNCTION can easily be retrieved from the database by using the \h command:

```
phpbook=# \h CREATE FUNCTION
Command:    CREATE FUNCTION
Description: define a new function
Syntax:
CREATE [ OR REPLACE ] FUNCTION name ( [ argtype [, ...] ] )
    RETURNS rettype
    AS 'definition'
    LANGUAGE langname
    [ WITH ( attribute [, ...] ) ]
CREATE [ OR REPLACE ] FUNCTION name ( [ argtype [, ...] ] )
    RETURNS rettype
    AS 'obj_file', 'link_symbol'
    LANGUAGE langname
    [ WITH ( attribute [, ...] ) ]
```

As you can see, the command is very powerful and allows you to add functions easily. Let's take a look at a practical example:

```
CREATE FUNCTION pythagoras (numeric, numeric) RETURNS numeric AS '
        SELECT sqrt($1 * $1 + $2 * $2)
' LANGUAGE 'sql';
```

The function is called pythagoras and accepts two numeric values. It can be used to compute the length of the longest component in a triangle containing a 90-degree angle. In Figure 9.1, it is the line labeled as c.

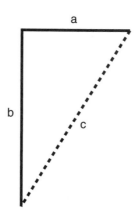

FIGURE 9.1 A triangle.

The data type returned by the function is numeric and the result will be of high precision. To insert the function into a database, you can either use PostgreSQL's interactive shell or use a file containing the code, as shown in the next example:

```
bash-2.04$ psql phpbook < function.sql
CREATE
```

The file called function.sql contains the code of the function and is sent to psql. If no error is returned, the function has been added to the database successfully. Keep in mind that this does not mean that the function is correct—it just means that a function with the desired name and desired number of parameters has been added.

To test the function, you can execute it using a simple SELECT statement:

```
phpbook=# SELECT pythagoras(3, 4);
  pythagoras
-------------
 5.0000000000
(1 row)
```

The result is exactly five, which is the correct mathematical result. If you try to add the same function to the server again, it will fail because there is already a function with the same name and number of parameters in the database:

```
bash-2.04$ psql phpbook < function.sql
ERROR:  function pythagoras already exists with same argument types
ERROR:  function pythagoras already exists with same argument types
```

If you want the old function that is already in the database to be replaced, use CREATE OR REPLACE instead of CREATE. This will drop the function implicitly and add the new version of the function to the database:

```
CREATE OR REPLACE FUNCTION pythagoras (numeric, numeric) RETURNS numeric AS '
        SELECT sqrt($1 * $1 + $2 * $2)
' LANGUAGE 'sql';
```

When the function is added to the database, no errors will be displayed.

9.1.2 Removing Functions

If you want to remove a function from the database, you must use DROP FUNCTION. Let's take a look at the syntax specification of DROP FUNCTION:

```
phpbook=# \h DROP FUNCTION
Command:     DROP FUNCTION
Description: remove a user-defined function
Syntax:
DROP FUNCTION name ( [ type [, ...] ] )
```

To remove the function you have just dealt with, use the following command:

```
phpbook=# DROP FUNCTION pythagoras(numeric, numeric);
DROP
```

9.1.3 Caching

When you're working with complex functions, caching is an important thing. The longer a function is and the more time it takes to compute the result, the more important it will be to cache the result of it in order to speed up your applications.

To perform caching, an attribute must be added to the function. This can be done with the help of WITH (iscachable):

```
CREATE OR REPLACE FUNCTION pythagoras (numeric, numeric) RETURNS numeric AS '
        SELECT sqrt($1 * $1 + $2 * $2)
' LANGUAGE 'sql' WITH (iscachable);
```

After reinserting the function into the database, we execute the same SQL statement twice:

```
bash-2.04$ time psql -d phpbook -c "SELECT pythagoras(30000, 400000000000)"
        pythagoras
-------------------------
 400000000000.0011250000
(1 row)
```

```
real    0m0.146s
user    0m0.030s
sys     0m0.000s
bash-2.04$ time psql -d phpbook -c "SELECT pythagoras(30000, 400000000000)"
        pythagoras
----------------------------
 400000000000.0011250000
(1 row)


real    0m0.068s
user    0m0.020s
sys     0m0.000s
```

As you can see, the second time the function is executed, it is significantly faster because of caching effects. The amount of time saved by caching need not always be as huge as shown in the preceding example, but the longer the cached function is, the higher the gain in speed will be.

Take a look at the next example:

```
CREATE OR REPLACE FUNCTION givetime () RETURNS timestamp AS '
        SELECT now()
' LANGUAGE 'sql' WITH (iscachable);
```

This time you have written a function returning the result of the now() function. Although the function is defined as iscachable, the result will not always be the same:

```
phpbook=# SELECT givetime();
          givetime
-------------------------------
 2001-11-10 14:17:32.350287+01
(1 row)


phpbook=# SELECT givetime();
          givetime
-------------------------------
 2001-11-10 14:17:38.25615+01
(1 row)
```

In this example PostgreSQL makes sure that the result of the function is computed again.

9.1.4 Handling NULL Values in SQL Functions

When NULL values are passed to a function, it might not be useful to compute a result because it is NULL anyway. In this case, WITH (isstrict) can be used to tell PostgreSQL that if a NULL value is passed to the function it has not been executed, but NULL must be returned:

```
CREATE OR REPLACE FUNCTION pythagoras (numeric, numeric) RETURNS numeric AS '
        SELECT sqrt($1 * $1 + $2 * $2)
' LANGUAGE 'sql' WITH (isstrict);
```

Let's run the function:

```
bash-2.04$ time psql -d phpbook -c "SELECT pythagoras(3, NULL)"
 pythagoras
-----------


(1 row)


real    0m0.062s
user    0m0.030s
sys     0m0.010s
```

NULL is being returned without executing the function. When you're dealing with huge and complex examples, this can lead to faster execution.

9.1.5 Function Overloading

Because PostgreSQL has strong object-oriented capabilities, it is possible to work with function overloading. Function overloading means that functions with the same name can exist and each of these functions accepts a different list of parameters.

Let's take a look at an example. The goal is to write two functions for generating the arithmetic mean of two or three values. Therefore two functions will be implemented. The first function accepts just one parameter, and the second function is capable of working with three parameters:

```
CREATE OR REPLACE FUNCTION average (numeric, numeric)
        RETURNS numeric AS '
        SELECT ($1 + $2) / 2;
' LANGUAGE 'sql';

CREATE OR REPLACE FUNCTION average (numeric, numeric, numeric)
        RETURNS numeric AS '
        SELECT ($1 + $2 + $3) / 3;
' LANGUAGE 'sql';
```

Although both functions have the same name, they will be treated as independent functions because the list of parameters accepted by the functions differs. Let's execute both functions to see that the correct result is generated:

```
phpbook=# SELECT average(1, 3);
   average
- - - - - - - - - - - - -
 2.0000000000
(1 row)


phpbook=# SELECT average(1, 3, 4);
   average
- - - - - - - - - - - - -
 2.6666666667
(1 row)
```

In the first example, the function accepting two parameters is called. In the second example, the function accepting three parameters will be executed.

9.1.6 CASE Statements within SQL

Sometimes it is necessary to perform simple, implicit decisions within a SQL statement. Therefore PostgreSQL provides CASE statements, which you can use to build decision functions.

Take a look at a simple example. First a table is created:

```
phpbook=# CREATE TABLE test (name text);
CREATE
```

After that some data can be inserted into the database by using the COPY command:

```
phpbook=# COPY test FROM stdin;
Enter data to be copied followed by a newline.
End with a backslash and a period on a line by itself.
>> 1
>> 3
>> 1
>> \.
```

Let's see what is in the table:

```
phpbook=# SELECT * FROM test;
 name
------
 1
 3
 1
(3 rows)
```

In the next step you can build a function that is similar to Oracle's decode function. The purpose of this function is to perform simple substitutions:

```
CREATE OR REPLACE FUNCTION mydecode (text, text, text)
       RETURNS text AS '
       SELECT CASE $1 WHEN $2 THEN $3 ELSE $1 END;
' LANGUAGE 'sql';
```

The first parameter passed to the function is the value that must be checked. If it is equal to the second parameter, it is substituted for the third parameter. In this example the code of the function is stored in if.sql and can easily be inserted into the database:

```
bash-2.04$ psql phpbook < if.sql
CREATE
```

After inserting the function, it can easily be tested by writing a simple SQL statement:

```
phpbook=# SELECT mydecode(name, 1, 999) FROM test;
 mydecode
----------
 999
 3
 999
(3 rows)
```

As you can see, every time 1 is found in the table it is substituted for 999, which is the third parameter passed to the function.

If additional conditions have to be checked, an additional function must be written. In the next example you can see how two values can be checked.

```
CREATE OR REPLACE FUNCTION mydecode (text, text, text, text, text)
       RETURNS text AS '
```

```
        SELECT CASE $1 WHEN $2 THEN $3
                   WHEN $4 THEN $5 ELSE $1 END;
' LANGUAGE 'sql';
```

This function can be used to check two conditions. If the value passed to the function as the fourth parameter is found, it is substituted for the fifth parameter:

```
phpbook=# SELECT mydecode(name, 1, 999, 3, 23) FROM test;
 mydecode
- - - - - - - - - -
 999
 23
 999
(3 rows)
```

As you can see, 3 has been substituted for 23. However, the problem can also be solved differently by calling mydecode recursively:

```
phpbook=# SELECT mydecode(mydecode(name, 1, 999), 3, 23) FROM test;
 mydecode
- - - - - - - - - -
 999
 23
 999
(3 rows)
```

mydecode is called two times. The result of the first function is returned to and used by the second function.

With the help of recursive function calls, it is possible to build complex applications.

9.2 PL/pgSQL

In this section you will learn to implement simple functions based on PL/pgSQL. PL/pgSQL is an embedded language provided by PostgreSQL for writing extensions to PostgreSQL. Before you can start working with PL/pgSQL and PostgreSQL, you must add the language to the database explicitly by using a command-line tool:

```
bash-2.04$ createlang plpgsql phpbook
```

If no error occurred, the database called phpbook now supports PL/pgSQL.

9.2.1 The Structure of PL/pgSQL Functions

Usually a PL/pgSQL function consists of three components as shown in the next listing:

```
[<<label>>]
[DECLARE
    declarations]
BEGIN
    statements
END;
```

First, a label is defined and after that a section for declaring variables can be added. Finally, the block containing the instructions of the function must be added. This block starts with BEGIN and stops with END;. The label and the DECLARE block of the function are optional.

9.2.2 A Simple Example

After this theoretical overview about PL/pgSQL, let's take a look at an example. The goal is to write a simple function for computing the average of two numeric values:

```
CREATE OR REPLACE FUNCTION average (numeric, numeric) RETURNS numeric AS '
        DECLARE
                result numeric;
        BEGIN
                result := ($1 + $2) / 2;
                RETURN result;
        END;
' LANGUAGE 'plpgsql';
```

After the function has been added to the database, it can be executed:

```
phpbook=# SELECT average(1, 2);
   average
--------------
 1.5000000000
(1 row)
```

Let's take a closer look at the code of the function. First, a variable is defined within a DECLARE block. In the next step the two values passed to the function are averaged. The result is returned to the calling function by using a RETURN statement.

9.2.3 Loops and Conditions

In many cases a block of code has to be executed more than once. In this situation, you can use loops. Loops are strongly related to condition. The code within a loop is executed as long as certain conditions are fulfilled; otherwise, it will be terminated.

One type of loop that is commonly used in many programming languages is called a FOR loop. Almost all programming languages support some kind of FOR loops, and so does PL/pgSQL. A FOR loop is executed as long as a variable is within a certain range of values.

The next example shows a function for generating the geometric mean of a range of values:

```
CREATE OR REPLACE FUNCTION geomean (numeric, numeric) RETURNS numeric AS '
        DECLARE
                i       int4;
                result  numeric;
        BEGIN
                result := 0;
                FOR i IN $1..$2 LOOP
                        result := i * i + result;
                END LOOP;
                RETURN sqrt(result);
        END;
' LANGUAGE 'plpgsql';
```

First, two variables are defined in the DECLARE section. In the next step result is set to zero. The FOR loop is executed as long as i is within the range defined by the first and second parameter passed to the function.

After you have inserted the function into the database, it can be accessed by any SQL statement:

```
phpbook=# SELECT geomean(2, 5);
   geomean
--------------
 7.3484692283
(1 row)
```

The geometric mean of the numbers from 2 to 5 will be the result of the function. To check whether the result is correct, you can send a SQL statement to the server:

```
phpbook=# SELECT sqrt(4+9+16+25::numeric);
      sqrt
--------------
 7.3484692283
(1 row)
```

As you can see, the result is equal to the one generated by the geomean function.

What happens if the parameters are passed to the function in a different order? In the next example you can see what comes out in this case:

```
phpbook=# SELECT geomean(5, 2);
   geomean
--------------
 0.0000000000
(1 row)
```

The result is zero because the loop is never entered by PL/pgSQL. To get around this problem, it is necessary to add a check to the function that swaps the values if the second parameter is lower than the first parameter passed to the function.

Let's try to swap the content of $1 and $2:

```
CREATE OR REPLACE FUNCTION geomean (numeric, numeric) RETURNS numeric AS '
        DECLARE
                i       int4;
                result  numeric;
                tmp     numeric;
        BEGIN
                IF      $1 > $2 THEN
                        tmp := $1;
                        $1 := $2;
                        tmp := $2;
                END IF;

                result := 0;
                FOR i IN $1..$2 LOOP
                        result := i * i + result;
                END LOOP;
                RETURN sqrt(result);
        END;
' LANGUAGE 'plpgsql';
```

The function cannot be executed successfully because $1 and $2 are constant values.

Unlike many other languages, there is no way to modify the input parameters of a PL/pgSQL function, as you can see in the next listing:

```
phpbook=# SELECT geomean(5, 2);
ERROR:  $1 is declared CONSTANT
NOTICE:  plpgsql: ERROR during compile of geomean near line 8
NOTICE:  plpgsql: ERROR during compile of geomean near line 8
ERROR:  $1 is declared CONSTANT
```

To make the function work properly, it is necessary to assign the content of $1 and $2 to temporary variables. This will lead to a minor slowdown but it is the only way to make the function work correctly:

```
CREATE OR REPLACE FUNCTION geomean (numeric, numeric) RETURNS numeric AS '
        DECLARE
                    i       int4;
                    result  numeric;
                    first   numeric;
                    second  numeric;
                    tmp     numeric;
        BEGIN
                    first := $1;
                    second := $2;

                    IF      first > second THEN
                            tmp := first;
                            first := second;
                            second := tmp;
                    END IF;

                    result := 0;
                    FOR i IN first..second LOOP
                            result := i * i + result;
                    END LOOP;
                    RETURN sqrt(result);
        END;
' LANGUAGE 'plpgsql';
```

After inserting the function again, the result will be computed correctly:

```
phpbook=# SELECT geomean(5, 2);
   geomean
--------------
 7.3484692283
(1 row)
```

As you have seen in the function, it is necessary to add an IF statement to the function. In PL/pgSQL, IF works pretty much the same way as it does in PHP. A condition is checked and if it is fulfilled, the IF block will be entered. The main difference between PHP's and PL/pgSQL's IF function is that in PL/pgSQL, no parentheses are needed because PL/pgSQL is a block-oriented language. This is also similar to Python, which also does not force the user to use parentheses.

WHILE loops are another type of loops provided by PL/pgSQL. Let's try to implement the same function with the help of a WHILE loop:

```
CREATE OR REPLACE FUNCTION geomean (numeric, numeric) RETURNS numeric AS '
        DECLARE
                result  numeric;
                i       numeric;
        BEGIN
                i := $1;
                result := 0;
                WHILE   i <= $2 LOOP
                        result := i * i + result;
                        i := i + 1;
                END LOOP;
                RETURN sqrt(result);
        END;
' LANGUAGE 'plpgsql';
```

This time the value of the first parameter is assigned to i. In the next step a WHILE loop is processed until i is equal to $2. The most important part in the code of the function is the line where i is incremented. Without this line the loop would never stop processing because the condition used to stop the loop would always be true. Endless loops are a danger for your programs, so make sure that there is always a way out of the loops in your applications.

Let's test the function you have just seen:

```
phpbook=# SELECT geomean(2, 5);
   geomean
--------------
 7.3484692283
(1 row)
```

The result is correct.

In some cases it might be necessary to quit the execution of a block within a function. Therefore you can use EXIT. If the condition passed to the EXIT function is fulfilled, the loop is terminated. Let's take a look at an example:

```
CREATE OR REPLACE FUNCTION myexit (numeric, numeric) RETURNS numeric AS '
        DECLARE
                i         int4;
        BEGIN
                FOR i IN $1..$2 LOOP
                        EXIT WHEN i = 2;
                        RETURN i;
                END LOOP;
                RETURN 99;
        END;
' LANGUAGE 'plpgsql';
```

If i equals 2, the loop will be terminated and PL/pgSQL will continue executing the code after the loop, which is in this case a simple RETURN statement:

```
phpbook=# SELECT myexit(2, 5);
 myexit
--------
     99
(1 row)
```

9.2.4 Comments

Comments can be used to make your source code clearer. The more documentation you add to your programs, the easier it will be for a programmer to understand your code. In addition, you can use comments to turn off parts of your applications for debugging purposes.

In PL/pgSQL two kinds of comments can be used. Two dashes tell PostgreSQL to ignore the current line. In addition, C-style comments can be used:

```
CREATE OR REPLACE FUNCTION mycomment () RETURNS numeric AS '
        BEGIN
                /* RETURN 0; */
                -- RETURN 1;
                RETURN 2;
        END;
' LANGUAGE 'plpgsql';
```

Just execute the function to see which lines are ignored by PostgreSQL:

```
phpbook=# SELECT mycomment();
 mycomment
-----------
         2
(1 row)
```

Two is returned, which means that only the last line will be executed.

9.2.5 Exception Handling

Let's get back to the function for generating the geometric mean of a range of values. So far, you have seen how to get around the problem concerning the loop and how to compute the right result even if the first parameter is higher than the second one. This time a message should be displayed if the first value passed to the function is higher than the second one. Therefore PostgreSQL provides a function called RAISE NOTICE:

```
CREATE OR REPLACE FUNCTION geomean (numeric, numeric) RETURNS numeric AS '
        DECLARE
                        i       int4;
                        result  numeric;
                        first   numeric;
                        second  numeric;
        BEGIN
                        first := $1;
                        second := $2;

                        IF      first > second THEN
                                RAISE NOTICE ''wrong order of parameters'';
                        END IF;

                        result := 0;
                        FOR i IN first..second LOOP
                                result := i * i + result;
                        END LOOP;
                        RETURN sqrt(result);
        END;
' LANGUAGE 'plpgsql';
```

If the first value passed to the function is higher than the second parameter, a warning is displayed:

```
phpbook=# SELECT geomean(20, 2);
NOTICE:  wrong order of parameters
   geomean
--------------
 0.0000000000
(1 row)
```

Warnings are an important component of the programming language and can be used as an onboard debugger for PL/pgSQL. Because no other way of debugging is available, using RAISE NOTICE is the most comfortable way to find tricky bugs in your application.

If you want your application to terminate in case of an error, RAISE EXCEPTION must be used:

```
RAISE EXCEPTION ''wrong order of parameters'';
```

When using RAISE EXCEPTION instead of RAISE NOTICE, the function will be terminated:

```
phpbook=# SELECT geomean(20, 2);
ERROR:  wrong order of parameters
```

Let's have a closer look at the two ways of making PL/pgSQL complain about some-thing: The string you want to display on the screen has to be passed to PostgreSQL using two single quotes. This is very important for one particular reason: The entire code of the function is defined under single quotes and if a string has to be processed, one pair of single quotes must be escaped by using two single quotes. If you don't escape the single quotes needed by RAISE NOTICE and RAISE EXCEPTION, PL/pgSQL will report an error because it is no longer possible to find the end of the function passed to the database.

9.2.6 Aliases

Aliases are a core feature of PL/pgSQL. With the help of aliases it is possible to assign more than just one name to a variable. In some cases this will make your code more flexible and easier to understand. Let's take a look at a function for computing the sum of two numeric values:

```
CREATE OR REPLACE FUNCTION mysum (numeric, numeric) RETURNS numeric AS '
        DECLARE
                first   ALIAS FOR $1;
                second  ALIAS FOR $2;
```

```
      BEGIN
                  RETURN (first + second);
      END;
' LANGUAGE 'plpgsql';
```

first and second are aliases for $1 and $2, so these names can be used just like the two original values passed to the function.

When executing the function, you will see that the result will be computed as if you had not used aliases:

```
phpbook=# SELECT mysum(23, 45);
 mysum
-------
    68
(1 row)
```

Aliases are just additional names of a certain variable—they cannot be used to modify constant variables:

```
CREATE OR REPLACE FUNCTION mysum (numeric, numeric) RETURNS numeric AS '
      DECLARE
                  first   ALIAS FOR $1;
                  second  ALIAS FOR $2;
      BEGIN
                  first = first + 1;
                  RETURN (first + second);
      END;
' LANGUAGE 'plpgsql';
```

Recall that values passed to a function are constant values, so it is not possible to modify the content of those variables—not even when using aliases:

```
phpbook=# SELECT mysum(23, 45);
ERROR:  $1 is declared CONSTANT
NOTICE:  plpgsql: ERROR during compile of mysum near line 5
NOTICE:  plpgsql: ERROR during compile of mysum near line 5
ERROR:  $1 is declared CONSTANT
```

9.2.7 SQL and Executing Functions

Executing SQL codeinside a PL/pgSQL function is as easy as executing a SQL command using the interactive shell. The target of the next example is to write a simple, database-driven logging function. Therefore you have to create a table for storing the logging information:

```
phpbook=# CREATE TABLE logtable(id serial, tstamp timestamp, message text,
mestype int4);
NOTICE:  CREATE TABLE will create implicit sequence 'logtable_id_seq' for
SERIAL column 'logtable.id'
NOTICE:  CREATE TABLE/UNIQUE will create implicit index 'logtable_id_key' for
table 'logtable'
NOTICE:  CREATE TABLE will create implicit sequence 'logtable_id_seq' for
SERIAL column 'logtable.id'
NOTICE:  CREATE TABLE/UNIQUE will create implicit index 'logtable_id_key' for
table 'logtable'
CREATE
```

In this example the table consists of a column storing a serial, a time stamp, the logging message, and the type of the message. Therefore a PL/pgSQL function can be implemented. In this example the function returns a Boolean value:

```
CREATE OR REPLACE FUNCTION dblog (text, int4) RETURNS bool AS '
        BEGIN
                INSERT INTO logtable(tstamp, message, mestype)
                        VALUES (now(), $1, $2);
                RETURN ''t'';
        END;
' LANGUAGE 'plpgsql';
```

As you can see the SQL statement can be used just like any other PL/pgSQL command. Let's execute the function:

```
phpbook=# SELECT dblog('an error message', 0);
 dblog
-------
 t
(1 row)
```

true has been returned and one record can be found in the table:

```
phpbook=# SELECT * FROM logtable;
 id |             tstamp             |      message      | mestype
----+-------------------------------+-------------------+---------
  1 | 2001-11-12 13:38:19.875317+01 | an error message  |       0
(1 row)
```

In some cases you might want to execute a SQL command without bothering about the result. Therefore you can use a function called EXECUTE.

```
CREATE OR REPLACE FUNCTION checkcontent () RETURNS bool AS '
        BEGIN
                EXECUTE ''CREATE TABLE tmptab (id int4, data text)'';
                RETURN ''t'';
        END;
' LANGUAGE 'plpgsql';
```

The function creates a new table and returns true:

```
phpbook=# SELECT checkcontent();
 checkcontent
--------------
 t
(1 row)
```

If the function has been executed successfully, a table called tmptab can be found in the database now:

```
phpbook=# \d tmptab
        Table "tmptab"
 Attribute |  Type  | Modifier
-----------+--------+----------
 id        | integer |
 data      | text    |
```

The return value of the CREATE TABLE statement has not been checked, but it has been silently omitted.

Another important issue is that PL/pgSQL is often used for is dynamic SQL. In many applications the SQL code that must be executed by the server is not predefined, so the correct parameters of the command have to be computed at runtime. With the help of PL/pgSQL, it is an easy task to build dynamic SQL code and to execute it using a function. The next example shows a function for changing the error level of a logging entry:

```
CREATE OR REPLACE FUNCTION changecontent (int4, int4) RETURNS bool AS '
        BEGIN
                EXECUTE ''UPDATE logtable SET mestype=''|| $1 || '' WHERE ''
                        || ''id='' || $2;
                RETURN ''t'';
        END;
' LANGUAGE 'plpgsql';
```

The SQL command is sent to the server by using the EXECUTE function. The parameters of the SQL command are extracted from the input parameters of the function and may vary. If the function is executed by the user, true will be returned and the values in the table will be updated:

```
phpbook=# SELECT changecontent(1, 1);
 changecontent
---------------
 t
(1 row)
```

As you can see, the record in the table has been updated to the desired value:

```
phpbook=# SELECT * FROM logtable;
 id |            tstamp            |     message     | mestype
----+-----------------------------+-----------------+---------
  1 | 2001-11-12 13:38:19.875317+01 | an error message |       1
(1 row)
```

Depending on the kind of application you are working on, the complexity of your PL/pgSQL function can differ significantly. However, if the computations you have to perform become more complex, you should consider using other embedded languages such as PL/Perl or PL/Tcl.

9.2.8 Working with Queries

In many PL/pgSQL functions, the result of a query must be processed by the function. Therefore it is necessary to retrieve the result of the query inside a PL/pgSQL function. In the next example you will see how easily this can be done by using a loop and a data type called RECORD:

```
CREATE OR REPLACE FUNCTION makebool () RETURNS bool AS '
        DECLARE
                row     RECORD;
        BEGIN
                FOR row IN SELECT * FROM logtable LOOP
                        RAISE NOTICE ''notice: %, %'', row.tstamp, row.message;
                END LOOP;
                RETURN ''t'';
        END;
' LANGUAGE 'plpgsql';
```

First, a variable is defined. This variable is a so-called record, which means that it can be used to store exactly one line of data. One line of data consists of all fields stored in the table, and each field can easily be accessed inside the record. In this example you can see how some fields in the table are displayed on the screen using the NOTICE function. You can see that a field can easily be accessed by a point and the name of the field you want to access.

Before executing the function, recall the content of logtable:

```
phpbook=# SELECT * FROM logtable;
 id |            tstamp            |     message      | mestype
----+-----------------------------+------------------+---------
  1 | 2001-11-12 13:38:19.875317+01 | an error message |    1
(1 row)
```

Let's execute the function and see how the data is displayed:

```
phpbook=# SELECT makebool();
NOTICE:  notice: 2001-11-12 13:38:19.875317+01, an error message
 makebool
----------
 t
(1 row)
```

The result is no surprise. The various fields displayed are listed one after the other and the content is displayed in the same format as would be done by using a SQL statement.

The goal of the next example is to reuse the data retrieved by the query. To make the example a little bit more spectacular, a second record can be added to the table called logtable by using an INSERT statement:

```
phpbook=# INSERT INTO logtable(tstamp, message, mestype) VALUES (now(), 'the
second error', 2);
INSERT 16625 1
```

Let's modify the function and add an UPDATE statement to it that uses the data generated by the SELECT statement:

```
CREATE OR REPLACE FUNCTION makebool () RETURNS bool AS '
        DECLARE
                row     RECORD;
        BEGIN
                FOR row IN SELECT * FROM logtable LOOP
                        UPDATE logtable SET tstamp=now(), mestype=3
                                WHERE id=row.id;
```

```
            END LOOP;
            RETURN ''t'';
        END;
' LANGUAGE 'plpgsql';
```

This might not be the most efficient way of updating the data in a table, but it shows how data can be processed inside a PL/pgSQL function.

When the function executes, `true` will be returned:

```
phpbook=# SELECT makebool();
 makebool
----------
 t
(1 row)
```

After the function is called, the data in the table contains some new values:

```
phpbook=# SELECT * FROM logtable;
 id |            tstamp             |      message      | mestype
----+------------------------------+-------------------+---------
  1 | 2001-11-12 19:08:19.431142+01 | an error message  |    3
  2 | 2001-11-12 19:08:19.431142+01 | the second error  |    3
(2 rows)
```

9.2.9 PL/pgSQL and Transactions

As you can see in table `logtable`, all records contain the same timestamp. Although it takes some time to process the data, the timestamp is the same. This behavior of PostgreSQL has to do with transactions. Every PL/pgSQL function is executed just as a standalone SQL statement. This means that the components of a function are all executed within the same transaction. Because `now()` returns the current transaction time and not the time the function was called, all records contain the same result.

To show PostgreSQL's behavior in combination with PL/pgSQL, we have included an example where transactions are started and committed explicitly.

First, a transaction is started using the `BEGIN` command:

```
phpbook=# BEGIN;
BEGIN
```

Inside the transaction, `makebool` is started and `true` is returned by the function:

```
phpbook=# SELECT makebool();
 makebool
----------
 t
(1 row)
```

To check the content of the table, you can write a SQL statement that selects all data from the table, as shown in the next listing:

```
phpbook=# SELECT * FROM logtable;
 id |             tstamp            |     message      | mestype
----+------------------------------+------------------+---------
  1 | 2001-11-12 19:20:55.652559+01 | an error message |    3
  2 | 2001-11-12 19:20:55.652559+01 | the second error |    3
(2 rows)
```

After that a `ROLLBACK` is performed to see what can be found in the table after undoing all operations:

```
phpbook=# ROLLBACK;
ROLLBACK
```

The table contains the same data as before the `makebool` function was called. This shows that PL/pgSQL does not commit transactions implicitly:

```
phpbook=# SELECT * FROM logtable;
 id |             tstamp            |     message      | mestype
----+------------------------------+------------------+---------
  1 | 2001-11-12 19:08:19.431142+01 | an error message |    3
  2 | 2001-11-12 19:08:19.431142+01 | the second error |    3
(2 rows)
```

Both records still have the same value that they had before starting the transaction.

Another important thing is that transactions cannot be started and committed inside a PL/pgSQL function:

```
CREATE OR REPLACE FUNCTION transtest () RETURNS bool AS '
        BEGIN
                BEGIN TRANSACTION;
                DELETE FROM logtable;
                COMMIT WORK;
                RETURN ''t'';
        END;
' LANGUAGE 'plpgsql';
```

Adding transaction code to a function will lead to syntax errors as well as to execution errors, as shown in the next listing:

```
phpbook=# SELECT transtest();
NOTICE:  plpgsql: ERROR during compile of transtest near line 7
ERROR:  parse error at or near ""
```

9.2.10 Writing Data Type Independent Functions

So far, you have learned to write functions that can only operate with a fixed data type. In many cases this will not be flexible enough because if a data type in a certain column changes, you have to change your function as well. Therefore PostgreSQL supports two keywords: %TYPE and %ROWTYPE.

With the help of %TYPE it is possible to declare a variable using the data type of a certain column. To make this clearer, we have included an example.

First, a table for storing incomes is created. The goal of the example is to write a function for changing the income of a person:

```
phpbook=# CREATE TABLE income(name text, salary int4);
CREATE
```

In the next step, one record is added to the table:

```
phpbook=# INSERT INTO income VALUES ('John', 3400);
INSERT 21635 1
```

If no error occurred, the table will contain one record now:

```
INSERT 21635 1
phpbook=# SELECT * FROM income;
 name | salary
------+--------
 John |   3400
(1 row)
```

After creating a table and adding some data to it, you can start writing the function:

```
CREATE OR REPLACE FUNCTION changesal (text, int4, int4) RETURNS int4 AS '
        DECLARE
                sal income.salary%TYPE;
                inc_table income%ROWTYPE;
                pname ALIAS FOR $1;
                inc ALIAS FOR $2;
                increase ALIAS FOR $3;
```

```
    BEGIN
            SELECT DISTINCT INTO inc_table * FROM income
                    WHERE salary=inc AND name=pname;

            RAISE NOTICE ''inc_table.name: %'', inc_table.name;
            RAISE NOTICE ''inc_table.salary: %'', inc_table.salary;
            RAISE NOTICE ''increase: %'', increase;

            sal := sal + increase;
            RAISE NOTICE ''sal: %'', sal;
            UPDATE income SET salary = sal
                    WHERE salary = inc AND name=pname;

            RETURN 0;
    END;
' LANGUAGE 'plpgsql';
```

In the DECLARE section, three aliases for the parameters passed to the function are defined. In addition, two other variables are defined and it is worthwhile to take a closer look at them: The data type of sal is the same as the data type of the column salary in table income. This way the function does not have to be changed when the data type of salary is changed. inc_table is defined as ROWTYPE. Using ROWTYPE makes accessing various components of the record easy and modifications can easily be done. After the DECLARE section a query is performed and the result of the query, which is exactly one record, is assigned to inc_table. There are no problems with the data type when assigning the value because PostgreSQL will automatically choose the correct data type for every column because ROWTYPE has been used in the DECLARE section. After displaying the content of the record, the salary of a person is increased and an UPDATE query is performed to set the salary to the new value.

Let's execute the function and see what is displayed on the screen:

```
phpbook=# SELECT changesal('John', 3400, 10);
NOTICE:  inc_table.name: John
NOTICE:  inc_table.salary: 3400
NOTICE:  increase: 10
NOTICE:  sal: 3410
 changesal
-----------
         0
(1 row)
```

After the function executes, the value in the table has changed:

```
phpbook=# SELECT * FROM income;
 name | salary
------+--------
 John |   3410
(1 row)
```

As you can see, it is an easy task to work with TYPE and ROWTYPE. If you want to implement flexible functions, these two keywords will be essential for you.

9.3 Writing Triggers

Almost all sophisticated databases support triggers and so does PostgreSQL. Triggers are a method to execute functions automatically whenever a certain event happens. For instance, you can define a trigger that deletes a record from table A every time a record is inserted into table B. In this scenario, you would have to define a trigger on table B, which is waiting for records to be inserted.

A trigger can start almost all kinds of functions, but in many cases PL/pgSQL is used to implement triggers because it has been optimized for being integrated into the database. If you don't like writing PL/pgSQL functions, you can also use PL/Tcl or PL/Perl. However, in this section we will focus entirely on writing triggers with the help of PL/pgSQL and pure SQL.

9.3.1 Creating and Dropping Triggers

The most important command when working with triggers is the CREATE TRIGGER command. Let's take a look at the syntax overview of the CREATE TRIGGER command:

```
phpbook=# \h CREATE TRIGGER
Command:     CREATE TRIGGER
Description: Creates a new trigger
Syntax:
CREATE TRIGGER name { BEFORE | AFTER } { event [OR ...] }
    ON table FOR EACH { ROW | STATEMENT }
    EXECUTE PROCEDURE func ( arguments )
```

As you can see, triggers can be defined to execute a function before or after a certain event. If a trigger is executed before a certain event, it is possible to modify the parameters of the command the trigger was fired for—you will have a closer look at that in this section.

A trigger can either be executed for a certain row or a certain statement. If you are working with COPY commands affecting more than just one line of data, it can make a significant difference whether FOR EACH ROW or FOR EACH STATEMENT is used. In the case of FOR EACH ROW, the trigger will be executed for every row changed in the data. If a lot of data is inserted into the database, this might have a significant impact on performance because at least one function is called for every line processed by PL/pgSQL.

In version 7.2, FOR EACH STATEMENT has not been implemented yet.

With the help of CREATE TRIGGER, it is possible to tell PostgreSQL to pass a list of parameters to the function called by the trigger.

To remove a trigger from the database again, the DROP TRIGGER has to be called:

```
phpbook=# \h DROP TRIGGER
Command:    DROP TRIGGER
Description: Removes the definition of a trigger
Syntax:
DROP TRIGGER name ON table
```

9.3.2 pg_trigger

To understand what CREATE TRIGGER and DROP TRIGGER do internally, it is necessary to have a closer look at the system table called pg_trigger:

```
phpbook=# \d pg_trigger
          Table "pg_trigger"
    Attribute     |    Type    | Modifier
------------------+------------+----------
 tgrelid          | oid        |
 tgname           | name       |
 tgfoid           | oid        |
 tgtype           | smallint   |
 tgenabled        | boolean    |
 tgisconstraint   | boolean    |
 tgconstrname     | name       |
 tgconstrrelid    | oid        |
 tgdeferrable     | boolean    |
 tginitdeferred   | boolean    |
 tgnargs          | smallint   |
 tgattr           | int2vector |
 tgargs           | bytea      |
Indices: pg_trigger_oid_index,
```

```
pg_trigger_tgconstrname_index,
pg_trigger_tgconstrrelid_index,
pg_trigger_tgrelid_index
```

A trigger is nothing more than an entry in PostgreSQL's system table for storing information about triggers. In this system table the identification number of the function the trigger is calling, the name of the trigger, the event it is fired for, the arguments passed to the trigger, and many more attributes defining the trigger are stored. If you want to modify a trigger, you just have to update the content of pg_trigger and the behavior of your trigger will change immediately.

9.3.3 Simple Triggers

After this theoretical overview, it is time to take a look at some real-world examples, so that you can see how triggers can be written and how triggers work.

The goal of the first example is to create a trigger that logs every INSERT operation on a table called data. To create this table, you can use a simple SQL command:

```
phpbook=# CREATE TABLE data(somedata text);
CREATE
```

The function for reporting every INSERT operation into data is called logfunc. It does nothing other than display a warning and perform and insert a record into table logtable:

```
CREATE OR REPLACE FUNCTION logfunc() RETURNS opaque AS '
        BEGIN
                RAISE NOTICE ''trigger logfunc has been fired'';
                INSERT INTO logtable(tstamp, message, mestype)
                        VALUES(now(), ''data has been inserted'', 0);
                RETURN NEW;
        END;
' LANGUAGE 'plpgsql';
```

As you can see, the function returns opaque. This data type can only be used in combination with triggers and can be compared with void in C and C++.

In this example the function does not contain a DECLARE block because no variables are needed by the main function. At the end of the function, NEW is returned. Take a look at the code of the trigger itself:

```
CREATE TRIGGER trig_data AFTER INSERT
        ON data FOR EACH ROW
        EXECUTE PROCEDURE logfunc();
```

The trigger is fired after every `INSERT` operation on `data`. For every line added to the table, `logfunc` is executed exactly once. Before executing the function, take a look at the content of `logtable`:

```
phpbook=# SELECT * FROM logtable;
 id |            tstamp            |     message      | mestype
----+-----------------------------+------------------+---------
  1 | 2001-11-12 19:20:41.270717+01 | an error message |    3
  2 | 2001-11-12 19:20:41.270717+01 | the second error |    3
(2 rows)fs
```

Two records are in the table before performing an `INSERT` operation:

```
phpbook=# INSERT INTO data VALUES ('a piece of text');
NOTICE:  trigger logfunc has been fired
INSERT 16642 1
```

When inserting the data, the message printed by the trigger can be seen on the screen. In addition, one record has been added to `data`.

Let's query `logtable` again:

```
phpbook=# SELECT * FROM logtable;
 id |            tstamp            |       message        | mestype
----+-----------------------------+----------------------+---------
  1 | 2001-11-12 19:20:41.270717+01 | an error message     |    3
  2 | 2001-11-12 19:20:41.270717+01 | the second error     |    3
  3 | 2001-11-13 08:08:12.244384+01 | data has been inserted |    0
(3 rows)
```

One record has been added to the table by the trigger.

Now it is time to write a slightly more sophisticated trigger that handles `INSERT`, `UPDATE`, and `DELETE` statements by using just one function.

9.3.4 Predefined Variables

When a function is called by a trigger, some variables you can access in the function are already predefined and already contain useful values you might need inside your trigger. In this section you will get an overview of these variables and what you can do with them.

Let's take a look at the list of predefined variables:

- `NEW`—In triggers fired for one row of data, `NEW` will contain the new value of the record the trigger has been started for. The data type of `NEW` is `RECORD`. `NEW` can only be used for triggers fired for `INSERT` and `UPDATE` operations.

- OLD—In triggers fired for one row of data, OLD will contain the value of the record before executing the trigger. The data type of OLD is RECORD and the variable is defined for triggers fired for UPDATE and DELETE statements.

- TG_NAME—TG_NAME contains the name of the trigger that is currently fired. The data type of TG_NAME is name.

- TG_WHEN—TG_WHEN contains information about when the trigger has been fired. TG_WHEN can either be AFTER or BEFORE. The data type of the variable is text.

- TG_LEVEL—To find out about the definition of the trigger, TG_LEVEL can be used. The variable can contain either ROW or STATEMENT depending on the trigger's definition. In PostgreSQL 7.2 or below, the content is always ROW because triggers defined on statements are not yet implemented. The data type of TG_LEVEL is text.

- TG_OP—Every trigger is fired for a specified event. TG_OP contains either INSERT, UPDATE, or DELETE depending on the event the trigger has been fired for. The data type is text.

- TG_RELID—All objects in PostgreSQL, such as tables, have an object id that is used to identify an object in the database. The object id of a table a trigger is fired for can be found in TG_RELID. The data type is oid.

- TG_RELNAME—TG_RELNAME contains the name of a table the trigger is fired for. The data type is name.

- TG_NARGS—As you have seen in this section, a number of parameters can be passed to a trigger. TG_NARGS contains the number of arguments passed to the function called by the current trigger. The data type is integer.

- TG_ARGV[ ]—The parameters passed to a function are stored in an array of text variables. The indexes run from 0 to TG_NARGS minus one.

If you are not using PL/pgSQL but a different embedded language, some predefined variables will also be available. PL/Tcl is a particularly comfortable language for implementing functions used for building triggers. This section does not cover PL/Tcl because it is beyond the scope of this book. If you want to find out more about PL/Tcl and other embedded languages, we recommend reading the *PostgreSQL Developer's Handbook* from Sams Publishing.

Before you learn about the scope of predefined variables, you will take a look at a simple trigger that displays a set of variables on the screen using RAISE NOTICE. Recall the content of data:

```
phpbook=# SELECT * FROM data;
    somedata
-----------------
 a piece of text
(1 row)
```

The table contains exactly one record. The function updatemessage will be used to display a list of all predefined variables:

```
CREATE OR REPLACE FUNCTION updatemessage () RETURNS opaque AS '
        BEGIN
                RAISE NOTICE ''NEW: %'', NEW.somedata;
                RAISE NOTICE ''OLD: %'', OLD.somedata;
                RAISE NOTICE ''TG_WHEN: %'', TG_WHEN;
                RAISE NOTICE ''TG_LEVEL: %'', TG_LEVEL;
                RAISE NOTICE ''TG_OP: %'', TG_OP;
                RAISE NOTICE ''TG_RELID: %'', TG_RELID;
                RAISE NOTICE ''TG_RELNAME: %'', TG_RELNAME;
                RAISE NOTICE ''TG_NARGS: %'', TG_NARGS;
                RAISE NOTICE ''TG_ARGV: %'', TG_ARGV[0];
                RETURN NEW;
        END;
' LANGUAGE 'plpgsql';
```

To call the function in case of an UPDATE operation, you have to define a trigger:

```
CREATE TRIGGER trig_updatemessage AFTER UPDATE
        ON data FOR EACH ROW
        EXECUTE PROCEDURE updatemessage();
```

If no error has occurred while inserting the function and the trigger into the database, the trigger will now cause updatemessage to be executed in case of UPDATE:

```
phpbook=# UPDATE data SET somedata='Hello World';
NOTICE:   NEW: Hello World
NOTICE:   OLD: Hello World
NOTICE:   TG_WHEN: AFTER
NOTICE:   TG_LEVEL: ROW
NOTICE:   TG_OP: UPDATE
NOTICE:   TG_RELID: 16647
NOTICE:   TG_RELNAME: data
NOTICE:   TG_NARGS: 0
NOTICE:   TG_ARGV: <OUT_OF_RANGE>
UPDATE 1
```

Every value but `TG_ARGV[0]` contains a useful value. `TG_ARGV` is empty because no parameters have been passed to the function. Therefore index number zero is out of range.

Let's see if the `UPDATE` operation has been executed successfully:

```
phpbook=# SELECT * FROM data;
  somedata
------------
 Hello World
(1 row)
```

The trigger did not affect the `UPDATE` operation at all.

9.3.5 Modifying Data Using Triggers

Sometimes it is necessary to modify the parameters passed to the function for some reason. Many problems concerning the data inserted into a table can be solved by using `CHECK` constraints, but in some cases things are more complicated and cannot or should not be solved by restricting the data a user can insert into a table.

Let's take a look at a table storing delays of airplane flights. Assume that flights can never start too early. Sometimes users might want to insert delays using a negative value instead of a positive integer value. In this case you might not want to restrict the input to positive values, so you can define a trigger that substitutes the values passed to a function for a positive value. Before you see the trigger, you can take a look at the SQL code for creating the table for storing the delays:

```
phpbook=# CREATE TABLE delay(number_of_flight text, minutes_delay int4);
CREATE
```

If the table has been generated successfully, it is time to write the function that is called by the trigger:

```
CREATE OR REPLACE FUNCTION moddata () RETURNS opaque AS '
      BEGIN
              IF      NEW.minutes_delay < 0 THEN
                      NEW.minutes_delay = NEW.minutes_delay * (-1);
                      RAISE NOTICE ''delay modified'';
              END IF;
              RETURN NEW;
      END;
' LANGUAGE 'plpgsql';
```

If the content of `minutes_delay` is lower than zero, the absolute value of the data passed to the function is generated and assigned to the `NEW.minutes_delay` field.

In the next step you can write the code of the trigger used for executing the function:

```
CREATE TRIGGER trig_moddata BEFORE INSERT OR UPDATE
        ON delay FOR EACH ROW
        EXECUTE PROCEDURE moddata();
```

This time the trigger must be fired before performing an INSERT or an UPDATE operation because otherwise the operations would already be over when moddata is called. In this scenario the trigger must be fired for every INSERT and UPDATE operation. If UPDATE was not the reason for calling the trigger, negative values could easily be inserted by modifying the data in the table.

After inserting the trigger and the function into the database, you can perform an INSERT operation to see what is going to happen:

```
phpbook=# INSERT INTO delay VALUES ('IB 0979', -34);
NOTICE:  delay modified
INSERT 19617 1
```

A message is displayed by the RAISE NOTICE command and a record has been added to the table. The table contains exactly one record now:

```
phpbook=# SELECT * FROM delay;
 number_of_flight | minutes_delay
------------------+---------------
 IB 0979          |            34
(1 row)
```

As you can see, the value in the second column is not negative because it has been modified by the function called by the trigger.

9.3.6 Predefined Variables and Functions Called by a Function

In the section called "Predefined Variables" earlier in this chapter, you have already learned about predefined variables in PL/pgSQL. In this section it is worth taking a very brief look at the scope of these variables. In the next example you will see a function started by a trigger that calls an additional function:

```
CREATE OR REPLACE FUNCTION insertmessage () RETURNS opaque AS '
        BEGIN
                RAISE NOTICE ''TG_WHEN: %'', TG_WHEN;
                EXECUTE ''SELECT dismessage()'';
                RETURN NEW;
        END;
' LANGUAGE 'plpgsql';
```

```
CREATE OR REPLACE FUNCTION dismessage () RETURNS int4 AS '
      BEGIN
                RAISE NOTICE ''TG_WHEN: %'', TG_WHEN;
                RETURN 0;
      END;
' LANGUAGE 'plpgsql';
```

Here is the code defining the trigger. Before inserting this trigger into the database, make sure that no triggers are defined on INSERT operations on data.

```
CREATE TRIGGER trig_insertmessage AFTER INSERT
      ON data FOR EACH ROW
      EXECUTE PROCEDURE insertmessage();
```

The function called by the trigger displays the content of TG_WHEN and calls a function called dismessage. The target of the example is to see if dismessage can still see TG_WHEN:

```
phpbook=# INSERT INTO data VALUES('a message');
NOTICE:   TG_WHEN: AFTER
NOTICE:   plpgsql: ERROR during compile of dismessage near line 2
NOTICE:   Error occurred while executing PL/pgSQL function insertmessage
NOTICE:   line 3 at execute statement
ERROR:   parse error at or near "TG_WHEN"
```

As you can see, functions called by functions cannot see predefined variables. This is important because you have to pass the values you will need in dismessage to the function manually.

9.3.7 Endless Loops

This section presents some more examples on triggers. In these examples, we present some PostgreSQL specifics and see what can be done to avoid errors.

Loops are one of the most important things you have to take care of. Recall the content of the table called logtable. As you have seen, a trigger has been defined on data, but what happens when a trigger is defined on logtable?

Let's take a look at the code of logfunc again:

```
CREATE OR REPLACE FUNCTION logfunc () RETURNS opaque AS '
      BEGIN
                RAISE NOTICE ''trigger logfunc has been fired'';
                INSERT INTO logtable(tstamp, message, mestype)
                      VALUES(now(), ''data has been inserted'', 0);
```

```
            RETURN NEW;
      END;
' LANGUAGE 'plpgsql';
```

The definition of the trigger is shown in the next listing.

```
CREATE TRIGGER trig_logfunc AFTER INSERT
        ON logtable FOR EACH ROW
        EXECUTE PROCEDURE logfunc();
```

The trigger will call logtable every time a value is inserted into the database. Because logfunc will also insert a record into the table, a trigger will be fired again. PostgreSQL will run into an endless loop:

```
phpbook=# INSERT INTO logtable (tstamp, message, mestype) VALUES(now(), 'hello
world', 3);
NOTICE:   trigger logfunc has been fired
NOTICE:   trigger logfunc has been fired
NOTICE:   trigger logfunc has been fired
```

The execution has to be stopped manually by using Ctrl+C; otherwise, PostgreSQL will be caught in an endless loop. But if the loop is stopped manually, what will happen to the data in the table?

```
phpbook=# SELECT * FROM logtable;
 id |             tstamp              |       message        | mestype
----+--------------------------------+----------------------+---------
  1 | 2001-11-12 19:20:41.270717+01  | an error message     |       3
  2 | 2001-11-12 19:20:41.270717+01  | the second error     |       3
  3 | 2001-11-13 08:08:12.244384+01  | data has been inserted |     0
(3 rows)
```

Nothing has happened to the table because the entire loop is processed in one transaction and a rollback has been performed when stopping the loop. This way nothing will happen to the data in the table. However, programmers must take care of endless loops because otherwise problems can easily occur, as you have seen in this example.

9.3.8 Triggers and Inheritance

One thing many people are not sure of is what happens when triggers are used in combination with inheritance. Therefore we have decided to include a special section about inheritance and triggers.

Let's create three tables that inherit from each other and store the SQL code in a file called `creature.sql`:

```
CREATE TABLE creature (id int4, name text);
CREATE TABLE human (gender char(1)) INHERITS (creature);
CREATE TABLE worker (income int4) INHERITS (human);
```

The target is to store information about creatures. Creatures usually have a name and a unique identifier. Human beings are special creatures who can also have a gender—the rest of the attributes of a human can be inherited from creature. Workers are special humans who have an additional attribute called income.

```
[postgres@athlon postgres]$ psql phpbook < creature.sql
CREATE
CREATE
CREATE
```

Let's take a look at the table called worker and see which fields are in the table:

```
phpbook=# \d worker
          Table "worker"
 Column |     Type     | Modifiers
--------+--------------+-----------
 id     | integer      |
 name   | text         |
 gender | character(1) |
 income | integer      |
```

As you can see, worker has all fields of creature and human plus one additional field for storing the income.

In the next step you can start inserting some data into the tables by using simple INSERT commands.

```
phpbook=# INSERT INTO creature VALUES(1, 'Kika');
INSERT 21663 1
phpbook=# INSERT INTO worker VALUES(2, 'Paul', 'm', 290000);
INSERT 21684 1
```

If creature is queried, all common columns of all three tables will be displayed. The content of the result consists of all records in all three tables because creature is the parent table.

```
phpbook=# SELECT * FROM creature;
 id | name
----+--------
  1 | Kinka
  2 | Paul
(2 rows)
```

If worker is queried, only one record will be retrieved:

```
phpbook=# SELECT * FROM worker;
 id | name | gender | income
----+------+--------+--------
  2 | Paul | m      | 290000
(1 row)
```

The behavior of PostgreSQL databases has changed in version 7.1. In versions prior to 7.1, the way inheritance has been treated was changed significantly.

Let's create a table where the triggers you are going to build store some logging information:

```
phpbook=# CREATE TABLE triglog(tstamp timestamp, tgname name, tgrelname name);
CREATE
```

The table consists of three columns. The first column stores a timestamp. The second column contains the name of the trigger that causes PostgreSQL to insert the record into the table. The third column contains the name of the table the trigger has been fired for.

Let's write a function that will be executed by the triggers:

```
CREATE OR REPLACE FUNCTION triglogfunc () RETURNS opaque AS '
      BEGIN
              RAISE NOTICE ''TG_NAME: %'', TG_NAME;
              RAISE NOTICE ''TG_RELNAME: %'', TG_RELNAME;
              INSERT INTO triglog VALUES (now(), tg_name, tg_relname);
              RETURN NEW;
      END;
' LANGUAGE 'plpgsql';
```

The function displays some debugging information on the screen and inserts the data into the table called triglog. This way it is an easy task to find out which trigger was fired when and for what reason.

Let's take a look at the code of the trigger:

```
CREATE TRIGGER trig_logtrig AFTER INSERT
        ON creature FOR EACH ROW
        EXECUTE PROCEDURE triglogfunc();
```

The trigger is executed after every `INSERT` statement performed on table `creature`. Both the function and the trigger can easily be inserted into the database by storing the code in a file and sending it to the `psql` as shown in the next listing:

```
[postgres@athlon postgres]$ psql phpbook < trigger.sql
CREATE
CREATE
```

If no error occurred, you can see if the trigger works by inserting one record into the table the trigger has been defined for:

```
phpbook=# INSERT INTO creature VALUES(3, 'Daisy');
NOTICE:  TG_NAME: trig_logtrig
NOTICE:  TG_RELNAME: creature
INSERT 21689 1
```

No surprises—the function has been executed by the trigger and the desired information has been displayed on the screen. What happens if data is inserted into `worker`? As you have seen in the code, `worker` is the child of `human`, which is the child of `creature`:

```
phpbook=# INSERT INTO worker VALUES(4, 'Anna', 'f', 500000);
INSERT 21691 1
```

No trigger has been fired because the trigger has not been inherited by the table: Child tables inherit only columns, not functions. Knowing this is important because it helps you to design your applications and you will need it in order not to forget to define triggers on inherited tables. However, the data has successfully been inserted into `worker`:

```
phpbook=# SELECT * FROM worker;
 id | name | gender | income
----+------+--------+--------
  2 | Paul | m      | 290000
  4 | Anna | f      | 500000
(2 rows)
```

Let's create a second trigger. This time the trigger is defined on human and executes the same function as the previous trigger. To avoid confusion, the trigger is fired when an UPDATE operation is performed:

```
CREATE TRIGGER trig_logtrig2 AFTER UPDATE
        ON human FOR EACH ROW
        EXECUTE PROCEDURE triglogfunc();
```

Let's perform an UPDATE operation on worker and see if the trigger is fired. Worker is a child of human, but the trigger is not executed:

```
phpbook=# UPDATE worker SET income=280000 WHERE id=2;
UPDATE 1
```

Let's see if the trigger is fired when data is inserted into the parent table of human:

```
phpbook=# UPDATE creature SET name='Alan' WHERE id=2;
UPDATE 1
```

Still no trigger fired. As you can see, triggers are not fired when the parent table is modified. As we have already mentioned, triggers cannot be inherited by other functions and don't affect parents.

Finally, let's take a look at the content of triglog:

```
phpbook=# SELECT * FROM triglog;
             tstamp             |    tgname    | tgrelname
--------------------------------+--------------+-----------
 2001-11-16 10:20:56.934013+01 | trig_logtrig | creature
(1 row)
```

One record has been added to the table because PostgreSQL fired the trigger only when the table the trigger was defined for was modified.

9.4 Embedded Languages Versus PHP Functions

Many people are looking for the ultimate answer whether it is better to compute certain results on the application level or to implement additional functions in the database. The discussion is as old as the problem itself.

This section is not designed to present our ultimate view of the problem, but we will try to present an objective overview of the arguments presented by both sides.

Especially when huge amounts of data have to be processed, it might be useful to add functions to the database and not to write a PHP function, but respectively a PHP class. The reason for that is simple. Imagine a function used for computing the average of a list of columns. In the case of only a few records, you won't be able to see a significant difference whether things are done by the database or by the application, but if the amount of data grows, things will change because all the data must be sent to the PHP interpreter. Especially when performing aggregations, this will lead to a significant slowdown.

An additional argument for adding functions directly to the database is that it can be accessed by all programming languages. This is a very important point because features have to be implemented once but can be used by every programming language.

One reason for implementing functions on the application level is that this way it is possible to introduce database abstraction layers for making your application more independent from the database you are using. The question remains: Is there a useful reason to use a different database than PostgreSQL? In world situations the answer could be yes, but the answer to this question has to be found.

The idea of database abstraction layers is old and the concept is used by many protocols and by a lot of software. Just think of Perl's DBI module. The DBI is an abstract layer that was originally developed for Oracle databases, but meanwhile many drivers for almost all databases are available. Thanks to the abstraction layer, writing a new driver is an easy task. The same sort of attempts are made by many PHP developers. However, one problem remains: Not all databases have the same features and the same SQL syntax, so database abstraction layers can only be used to a certain extent and applications cannot be 100% compatible because ANSI SQL-92 compatibility has not been achieved.

If functions are implemented on the application level, they can easily be used by other parts of your application that are not directly interacting with PostgreSQL. This is a significant advantage—especially if basic functions are affected.

As with every question related to the design of your software, you are the one who has to decide. In most cases the answer to the question will be based on your personal philosophy and on technical reasons, but it is still you who has to decide.

9.5 Summary

PostgreSQL provides a set of powerful, embedded languages. Because PostgreSQL can easily be extended, it is an easy task to add new languages to the server.

PL/pgSQL is a block-oriented language you can use to write your own extensions to PostgreSQL. In many aspects PL/pgSQL is similar to Oracle's PL/SQL, but there are also some major differences.

Writing triggers is an easy task when using PL/pgSQL. Triggers can be used to perform certain tasks in your database automatically and are supported by almost all sophisticated databases.

10
PostgreSQL Administration

Administering PostgreSQL is an easy task. However, some important things have to be taken into consideration to make the database run fast. In contrast to other open source databases, PostgreSQL provides a rich set of configuration options. In this section you will learn about the most important settings as well as about user administration.

10.1 User Administration and User Rights

Like all other sophisticated databases, PostgreSQL allows the administrator to define users as well as user rights. This is important for many reasons: On the one hand, it helps you to protect your data from unauthorized access. On the other hand, it helps you to protect yourself. Just imagine various different tables—user rights can help you make sure that you do not accidentally delete important data from one of the tables.

10.1.1 Managing Users and Groups

To create new users, use the CREATE USER command. The next listing shows the syntax overview of the command:

```
phpbook=# \h CREATE USER
Command:     CREATE USER
Description: define a new database user account
Syntax:
CREATE USER username [ [ WITH ] option [ ... ] ]
```

where option can be:

```
SYSID uid
| [ ENCRYPTED | UNENCRYPTED ] PASSWORD 'password'
| CREATEDB | NOCREATEDB
| CREATEUSER | NOCREATEUSER
| IN GROUP groupname [, ...]
| VALID UNTIL 'abstime'
```

The CREATE USER command provides many settings and options to configure a user to your needs. With the help of SYSID, you can assign a user to a specific id. This can be useful in case of changes and modifications after adding or removing existing users. In the next step a password has to be provided. The password can be stored in either an encrypted or an unencrypted way.

A user can be allowed to create new users as well as databases. We strongly recommend not allowing new users to do that unless you like security holes in your user system.

Just as on Unix, a user can be assigned to a list of groups. In general, PostgreSQL's way of handling users and groups is very similar to the one used by Unix.

Let's create a new user called hs:

```
phpbook=# CREATE USER hs ENCRYPTED PASSWORD 'mypasswd' NOCREATEDB NOCREATEUSER;
CREATE USER
```

If no error occurred, the user has been created successfully and you can connect to the database as hs now. The information about the user is stored in so-called system tables. System tables are hidden tables that store internal information about various aspects, such as users, functions, operators, or optimizer statistics. The system table called pg_shadow contains all information about the user:

```
phpbook=# SELECT usename, usesysid, usecreatedb, usetrace, usesuper, usecatupd
  FROM pg_shadow;
 usename  | usesysid | usecreatedb | usetrace | usesuper | usecatupd
----------+----------+-------------+----------+----------+-----------
 postgres |        1 | t           | t        | t        | t
 hs       |      100 | f           | f        | f        | f
(2 rows)
```

As you can see in the third column, hs is not allowed to create new databases and in the fifth column, hs is not a superuser. In this scenario, the password is stored in an encrypted way:

```
phpbook=# SELECT usename, passwd  FROM pg_shadow;
 usename  |                 passwd
----------+------------------------------------
 postgres |
 hs       | md51eafef644f38fe6ce05fbb985bd72fdc
(2 rows)
```

The default superuser called postgres does not have a password—we recommend that you change this when setting up PostgreSQL.

To remove a user from the database, you can use DROP USER. DROP USER removes the user from the system table:

```
phpbook=# \h DROP USER
Command:     DROP USER
Description: remove a database user account
Syntax:
DROP USER name
```

Simply pass the name of the user you want to delete to the function.

Just as on Unix machines, a user can be assigned to a group. Groups can be used to build packages of user rights that can be assigned to more than just one user at once. This will save a lot of administration overhead and help to avoid errors in your user configuration. Let's take a look at the syntax overview of the CREATE GROUP command.

```
phpbook=# \h CREATE GROUP
Command:     CREATE GROUP
Description: define a new user group
Syntax:
CREATE GROUP name [ [ WITH ] option [ ... ] ]

where option can be:

    SYSID gid
  | USER  username [, ...]
```

The command can be used easily:

```
phpbook=# CREATE GROUP cybertec USER hs, postgres;
CREATE GROUP
```

In this example two users have been added to the group called cybertec.

To remove a group, the DROP GROUP command is provided:

```
phpbook=# \h DROP GROUP
Command:     DROP GROUP
Description: remove a user group
Syntax:
DROP GROUP name
```

After groups and users have been created, you might want to change the configuration of a user or a group. Therefore the ALTER command is provided. In SQL you can use the ALTER command to modify almost all objects in a database. Tables, users, groups—all kinds of objects can be modified by using just one single command. To modify users, ALTER USER is the command you need:

```
phpbook=# \h ALTER USER
Command:     ALTER USER
Description: change a database user account
Syntax:
ALTER USER username [ [ WITH ] option [ ... ] ]

where option can be:

        [ ENCRYPTED | UNENCRYPTED ] PASSWORD 'password'
      | CREATEDB | NOCREATEDB
      | CREATEUSER | NOCREATEUSER
      | VALID UNTIL 'abstime'
```

All parameters you have defined when creating the user can be changed using ALTER. Let's look at an example:

```
phpbook=# ALTER USER hs VALID UNTIL '2004/12/31';
ALTER USER
```

In this example you can see that hs is only allowed to access the database until December 31, 2004. The information has been added to the system table:

```
phpbook=# SELECT usename, valuntil  FROM pg_shadow;
 usename  |        valuntil
----------+------------------------
 postgres |
 hs       | 2004-12-31 00:00:00+01
(2 rows)
```

ALTER GROUP is a command used for modifying groups. With the help of this command, it is possible to add or remove users from a group. Take a look at the syntax of the command:

```
phpbook=# \h ALTER GROUP
Command:    ALTER GROUP
Description: add users to a group or remove users from a group
Syntax:
ALTER GROUP name ADD USER username [, ... ]
ALTER GROUP name DROP USER username [, ... ]
```

The syntax is easy—you only have to define the group and the user you want to add or remove from a group. In the next example, the user postgres is removed from the group called cybertec. First, you can take a look at the content of pg_group:

```
phpbook=# SELECT * FROM pg_group;
 groname  | grosysid | grolist
----------+----------+---------
 cybertec |      100 | {100,1}
(1 row)
```

As you can see in the third column, two users are in the group. The list of users is represented by an array and contains the ids of the users. In the next step, the ALTER command can be used:

```
phpbook=# ALTER GROUP cybertec DROP USER postgres;
ALTER GROUP
```

After executing the ALTER command, there is only one user left in the group:

```
phpbook=# SELECT * FROM pg_group;
 groname  | grosysid | grolist
----------+----------+---------
 cybertec |      100 | {100}
(1 row)
```

Creating users and groups is an easy task because PostgreSQL has a simple and easy-to-understand model for managing users.

10.1.2 Managing User Rights

After users have been created, it is time to define the rights of these users. Like almost all other databases, PostgreSQL provides two commands that are essential for managing user rights: GRANT and REVOKE.

10.1.2.1 GRANT

GRANT is used to give a user certain rights. A set of permissions can be granted to a user: SELECT, INSERT, UPDATE, DELETE, RULE, REFERENCES, and TRIGGER.

Rights are usually granted on objects in the database such as tables and sequences. A right can be assigned to a user, a group, or to the public.

Let's look at the syntax of GRANT:

```
phpbook=# \h GRANT
Command:    GRANT
Description: define access privileges
Syntax:
GRANT { { SELECT | INSERT | UPDATE | DELETE | RULE | REFERENCES | TRIGGER }
  [,...] | ALL [ PRIVILEGES ] }
    ON [ TABLE ] objectname [, ...]
    TO { username | GROUP groupname | PUBLIC } [, ...]
```

As you can see, the syntax of the command is easy. After this theoretical overview, it is time to take a look at a practical example.

The first thing to do is to create a new table. This time a table for storing products will be created:

```
phpbook=# CREATE TABLE product (id int4, name text, price numeric(9,2));
CREATE
```

The table has been created as user postgres, which is the default user. With the help of the \c command, it is possible to switch to user hs:

```
phpbook=# \c phpbook hs
You are now connected to database phpbook as user hs.
```

Because hs is not the owner of the table, he is not allowed to select data from the table:

```
phpbook=> SELECT * FROM product;
ERROR:  product: Permission denied.
```

To solve the problem, the owner of the table has to grant some rights to hs. Therefore you can switch to user postgres:

```
phpbook=> \c phpbook postgres
You are now connected to database phpbook as user postgres.
```

To give user hs some rights, you can use the GRANT command:

```
phpbook=# GRANT SELECT, INSERT, UPDATE, DELETE ON product TO hs;
GRANT
```

With the help of the \z command, you can find out which rights have been defined
for which user:

```
phpbook=# \z product
   Access privileges for database "phpbook"
  Table  |           Access privileges
---------+-----------------------------------
 product | {"=","postgres=arwdRxt","hs=arwd"}
(1 row)
```

In this scenario postgres is allowed to do everything and hs is allowed to SELECT,
INSERT, UPDATE, and DELETE records. Now that hs has enough rights to select data
from the table, you can switch back to user hs and select all data from the table:

```
phpbook=# \c phpbook hs
You are now connected to database phpbook as user hs.
phpbook=> SELECT * FROM product;
 id | name | price
----+------+-------
(0 rows)
```

As you can see, hs is allowed to retrieve data now. postgres has given hs a set of
rules but hs wants more:

```
phpbook=> GRANT ALL ON product TO hs;
ERROR:  permission denied
```

The error occurring seems logical because hs is not allowed to grant rights to himself.

10.1.2.2 REVOKE
REVOKE is the counterpart of GRANT and can be used to take rights from a user. The
syntax of the command is almost identical to that of GRANT:

```
phpbook=# \h REVOKE
Command:    REVOKE
Description: remove access privileges
Syntax:
REVOKE { { SELECT | INSERT | UPDATE | DELETE | RULE | REFERENCES | TRIGGER }
[,...] | ALL [ PRIVILEGES ] }
    ON [ TABLE ] object [, ...]
    FROM { username | GROUP groupname | PUBLIC } [, ...]
```

In the previous section (GRANT), you have seen that a user is not allowed to grant himself rights. The next example shows that a user is not allowed to take rights away from himself:

```
phpbook=> REVOKE ALL ON product FROM hs;
ERROR:  permission denied
```

To take some rights from hs, you have to switch to user postgres:

```
phpbook=> \c phpbook postgres
You are now connected to database phpbook as user postgres.
```

Because postgres is the superuser, he is allowed to modify all rights:

```
phpbook=# REVOKE ALL ON product FROM hs;
REVOKE
```

If you have a closer look at the overview of rights defined on product, you can see that hs is not mentioned and he no longer has rights:

```
phpbook=# \z product
Access privileges for database "phpbook"
  Table  |     Access privileges
---------+---------------------------
 product | {"=","postgres=arwdRxt"}
(1 row)
```

After changing the rights, you can switch back to hs:

```
phpbook=# \c phpbook hs
You are now connected to database phpbook as user hs.
```

Because all rights have been revoked from hs, he is no longer allowed to query the table:

```
phpbook=> SELECT * FROM product;
ERROR:  product: Permission denied.
```

10.1.2.3 About Superusers
When working with superusers, some basic points must be taken into consideration. As you have already seen, the default superuser is called postgres. This user has all rights and is allowed to create new users as well as new databases. There is no operation that cannot be performed by the superuser. The difference between a new superuser and a new user is that it is not possible to revoke rights from a superuser using REVOKE. This is an important point when working with PostgreSQL.

To create a new user in our scenario, you have to be a superuser:

```
phpbook=# \c phpbook postgres
You are now connected to database phpbook as user postgres.
```

A new superuser can be created by using CREATE USER in combination with the flag CREATEUSER. If a user is allowed to create new users, he is a superuser. Take a look at an example:

```
phpbook=# CREATE USER superhs ENCRYPTED PASSWORD 'mypasswd' CREATEUSER;
CREATE USER
```

In the next step a table is created:

```
phpbook=# CREATE TABLE pet (name text, birthday date);
CREATE
```

To connect as the new user, you can use \c again:

```
phpbook=# \c phpbook superhs
You are now connected to database phpbook as user superhs.
```

Because superhs is superuser, he is allowed to query the table—even if postgres has not granted rights to him:

```
phpbook=# SELECT * FROM pet;
 name | birthday
------+----------
(0 rows)
```

If you switch back to postgres and ask PostgreSQL which rights have been defined on the table, you will receive an empty list:

```
phpbook=# \c phpbook postgres
You are now connected to database phpbook as user postgres.
phpbook=# \z pet
Access privileges for database "phpbook"
 Table | Access privileges
-------+-------------------
 pet   |
(1 row)
```

If rights are revoked from the superuser, PostgreSQL will list these changes in the list of access privileges:

```
phpbook=# REVOKE ALL ON pet FROM superhs;
REVOKE
phpbook=# \z pet
Access privileges for database "phpbook"
 Table |    Access privileges
-------+--------------------------
 pet   | {"=","postgres=arwdRxt"}
(1 row)
```

Even if superhs has no rights, he is able to query the table:

```
phpbook=# \c phpbook superhs
You are now connected to database phpbook as user superhs.
phpbook=# SELECT * FROM pet;
 name | birthday
------+----------
(0 rows)
```

Why does PostgreSQL change the list of rights if it doesn't affect the behavior of the user? Well, the answer is simple. In pg_shadow you can see if a user is a superuser or not. If you revoke rights from a user and update the usesuper column, the user will have to face all restrictions:

```
phpbook=# SELECT usename, usesuper FROM pg_shadow;
 usename  | usesuper
----------+----------
 postgres | t
 hs       | f
 superhs  | t
(3 rows)
```

10.2 Maintenance and Database Internals

After a database has been set up, the work of an administrator is not over because some things have to be done to keep the system up and running. In contrast to other databases, it takes very little effort to administer a PostgreSQL database because the entire system has been implemented flexibly and reliably. In addition, PostgreSQL is capable of handling huge amounts of data.

However, some basic administration tasks have to be done and you will learn about these in this section. In addition, it is necessary to understand some basic internals of the database. You will need this knowledge for configuring PostgreSQL to your needs.

10.2.1 VACUUM and ANALYZE

VACUUM is the most important command when working with PostgreSQL. It is used for many purposes and should be run periodically. Here is a list of what VACUUM is used for:

- **Regaining disk space**—Running operations like UPDATE will raise the amount of disk space located internally. Because PostgreSQL supports concurrent transactions, it might be necessary to store various versions of the data in the file depending on who is reading what. This will cause the files on disk to grow depending on the operations you are running. Using VACUUM will reduce the size of the files on disk.

- **Updating optimizer statistics**—PostgreSQL's optimizer depends on statistics. VACUUM and ANALYZE will update the statistics stored in the system tables.

- **Avoiding problems occurring because of transaction ID wraparound**—PostgreSQL's transaction code depends on the comparison of transaction ids (XID). The problem now is that a transaction id is a 4-byte integer, which limits the number of transaction ids to about 4 billion transactions. PostgreSQL databases prior to version 7.2 had to be rebuilt using initdb after every 4 billion transactions in order not to run into trouble. Since PostgreSQL 7.2, this limitation no longer exists, but the database must be vacuumed at least once after every billion transactions. On sites with high load, this has to be taken into consideration.

Now that you have seen what VACUUM can be used for, let's take a look at a practical example.

Create an empty table called data:

```
phpbook=# CREATE TABLE data (data int4);
CREATE
```

Currently the database cluster we are working on is about 41.7MB in size. Just go to the directory where your database cluster can be found and run du:

```
[postgres@athlon pgdb]$ du
1716    ./base/1
1716    ./base/16555
3576    ./base/25110
```

```
1716    ./base/26076
8728    ./base
140     ./global
32812   ./pg_xlog
12      ./pg_clog
41732   .
```

In the next step you can write a PHP script for generating a file containing some UPDATE and DELETE operations:

```
<?php
        $fp = fopen("/tmp/data.sql", "w+");
        if      (!$fp)
        {
                echo "cannot open file\n";
                exit;
        }

        for     ($i = 0; $i < 10000; $i++)
        {
                $sql = "INSERT INTO data VALUES ($i);\n";
                $sql.="DELETE FROM data;\n";
                fwrite ($fp, $sql);
        }
        fclose($fp);
?>
```

To generate the file called data.sql, use the PHP command-line interpreter:

```
[postgres@athlon php]$ php makedata.php
X-Powered-By: PHP/4.0.6
Content-type: text/html
```

If no error occurred, the file has been generated successfully and contains a set of UPDATE and DELETE operations as shown in the next listing:

```
[postgres@athlon tmp]$ head data.sql
INSERT INTO data VALUES (0);
DELETE FROM data;
INSERT INTO data VALUES (1);
DELETE FROM data;
INSERT INTO data VALUES (2);
DELETE FROM data;
INSERT INTO data VALUES (3);
```

```
DELETE FROM data;
INSERT INTO data VALUES (4);
DELETE FROM data;
```

This SQL code can be sent to the database easily:

```
[postgres@athlon pgdb]$ psql phpbook < /tmp/data.sql
```

Although not a single additional record is in the database, the amount of disk space needed has grown:

```
[postgres@athlon pgdb]$ du
1716    ./base/1
1716    ./base/16555
3984    ./base/25110
1716    ./base/26076
9136    ./base
140     ./global
32812   ./pg_xlog
12      ./pg_clog
42140   .
```

To solve the problem and to reduce the space allocated on disk, VACUUM can be run. As you have already seen, VACUUM can be run from PostgreSQL's interactive shell, but in some cases it is more comfortable to use a shell program called vacuumdb to perform the job:

```
[postgres@athlon pgdb]$ vacuumdb --help
vacuumdb cleans and analyzes a PostgreSQL database.

Usage:
  vacuumdb [options] [dbname]

Options:
  -h, --host=HOSTNAME           Database server host
  -p, --port=PORT               Database server port
  -U, --username=USERNAME       Username to connect as
  -W, --password                Prompt for password
  -d, --dbname=DBNAME           Database to vacuum
  -a, --all                     Vacuum all databases
  -t, --table='TABLE[(columns)]'  Vacuum specific table only
  -f, --full                    Do full vacuuming
  -v, --verbose                 Write a lot of output
  -z, --analyze                 Update optimizer hints
```

```
   -e, --echo                    Show the command being sent to the backend
   -q, --quiet                   Don't write any output
```

```
Read the description of the SQL command VACUUM for details.
```

```
Report bugs to <pgsql-bugs@postgresql.org>.
```

As you can see, it is possible to define quite a few parameters that are mostly needed for vacuuming a remote database. To vacuum all your databases, you can use the following command:

```
[postgres@athlon pgdb]$ vacuumdb -e -z -a
Vacuuming template1
VACUUM    ANALYZE
VACUUM
Vacuuming phpbook
VACUUM    ANALYZE
VACUUM
```

Because the -e flag has been used, PostgreSQL lists the SQL commands sent to the back end on the screen. After that you can see how much disk space is still allocated:

```
[postgres@athlon pgdb]$ du
1744     ./base/1
1716     ./base/16555
3576     ./base/25110
1744     ./base/26076
8784     ./base
140      ./global
32812    ./pg_xlog
12       ./pg_clog
41788    .
```

The amount of space needed has decreased. If you are running many UPDATE and DELETE operations, it is recommended that you run VACUUM using a cron job when the load on your database is low.

To rebuild the statistics needed by the optimizer, ANALYZE has to be used. Whenever the data in your table changes significantly, you should run ANALYZE to provide the optimizer with correct and reliable information.

10.2.2 WAL

Write Ahead Logs (WAL) are a sophisticated feature of PostgreSQL. The main idea of WAL is to write files to disk after the changes have been logged. This has significant advantages because the number of accesses to the disk is reduced, so a lot of speed can be gained. In case of disaster, it is easy to restore the data because the changes have already been logged. With the help of the log, it is an easy task to repair the data after the crash safely. The concept is in a way similar to the journaling used by some filesystems.

In addition to speed, PostgreSQL can guarantee that the data in the database is consistent and ready for action after a crash.

UNDO operations are not yet implemented, but they will be implemented in future releases of PostgreSQL. With the help of UNDOs, it will be possible to implement savepoints, which will be another important step in history of PostgreSQL.

10.2.3 Maintaining Log Files

PostgreSQL can be configured to produce a lot of logging information. If the database is running for a long time, the logfile will grow and will allocate a lot of disk space. Therefore old information should be removed from time to time.

PostgreSQL does not remove old logging information by itself, so it is necessary to use external software such as Apache's `logrotate`.

10.3 Configuring PostgreSQL

Because PostgreSQL is a flexible and powerful database server, many parameters can be configured and modified to achieve a maximum amount of performance and to make PostgreSQL behave the way you want it to.

In general, two files are important for configuring your database. `pg_hba.conf` contains the network settings and `postgresql.conf` contains almost all other parameters.

In this section you will find out how PostgreSQL can be configured and what settings you can make to achieve your target.

10.3.1 Runtime Parameters

PostgreSQL's runtime parameters can be found in `postgresql.conf`, which is located in your database cluster. The syntax of the file is easy and you will learn about the most important entries in this section. The entries will be discussed in the same order they occur in the default configuration file of PostgreSQL. This way it should be an easy task to find information about a certain setting quickly:

- tcpip_socket—In the default configuration PostgreSQL only accepts Unix sockets. If this flag is set to true, PostgreSQL will also accept connections via TCP/IP.

- ssl—To turn SSL (Secure Socket Layer) on, this flag has to be set to true.

- max_connections—This setting defines how many simultaneous connections PostgreSQL will accept. The default value is 32. The compiled-in upper limit is 1024. If the number of connections is increased, it is also necessary to change the memory settings of PostgreSQL such as the number of shared buffers; otherwise, PostgreSQL will not start up.

- port—In the default configuration PostgreSQL listens to port 5432 TCP. If you want to define another port, you can do it using the port flag.

- hostname_lookup—Normally only IP addresses are listed in the log file. To resolve this hostname_lookup must be set to true.

- show_source_port—This flag shows the outgoing port number of the host trying to establish a connection to PostgreSQL in the connection log messages. You could trace back the port number to find out what user initiated the connection.

- unix_socket_directory—This flag defines the directory the postmaster is listening to. The flag can be changed at compile time. The default directory is /tmp.

- unix_socket_group—A socket can be assigned to a group. Using an empty string means that the default group of the user is used.

- unix_socket_permissions—Unix sockets use the same permissions as any other file on a Unix system. The default setting is 0777, which means that everybody can connect to the database.

- virtual_host—By default PostgreSQL listens to all names assigned to a server. Using virtual_host allows you to tell PostgreSQL to listen to only one hostname.

- krb_server_keyfile—Sets the location of the Kerberos server key file.

- shared_buffers—Defines the number of shared buffers used by PostgreSQL. By default the size of one buffer is exactly the size of one page, which means 8192 bytes. You have to use at least twice the number of shared buffers as the maximum number of connections; otherwise, the postmaster will not start up.

- max_fsm_relations—Sets the maximum number of tables for which free space will be tracked in the shared free-space map. The default value is 100.

- `max_fsm_pages`—Sets the maximum number of disk pages for which free space will be tracked in the shared free-space map.

- `max_locks_per_transaction`—Defines the maximum number of objects that can be locked at a time.

- `wal_buffers`—Defines the number of pages buffers in shared memory for Write Ahead Logs (WAL).

- `sort_mem`—This flag defines how much data can be sorted in memory before moving to temporary files. `sort_mem` does not define the total amount of memory used for sorting, but it defines the amount of memory used per sort process. If you have more than just one concurrent sort process, you might need the amount of memory more than just once.

- `vacuum_mem`—With `VACUUM`, memory is allocated to keep track of the tuples reordered by the command. `vacuum_mem` defines the amount of memory `VACUUM` is allowed to allocate.

- `wal_files`—Defines the number of log files created in advance.

- `wal_fsync_method`—`wal_fsync_method` can have different values depending on the desired behavior of the database. `FSYNC` makes sure that the data is flushed to disk after every commit operation. `FDATASYNC` calls the `fdatasync` function after every commit. `OPEN_SYNC` writes WAL files with `open()` option `O_SYNC`. `OPEN_DATASYNC` writes WAL files with `open()` option `O_DSYNC`. All options are available on every operating system and should be defined in `postgresql.conf`.

- `wal_debug`—Defines the debug level for Write Ahead Log (WAL).

- `commit_delay`—This delay tells PostgreSQL to wait before using `fsync` to flush the WAL buffers to disk. In case of delay it is possible to flush buffers and WAL buffers with just one `fsync`, which is faster. The delay is defined in microseconds.

- `commit_siblings`—Sets the minimum number of concurrent transactions before using `commit_delay`.

- `checkpoint_segments`—Defines the maximum distance between two WAL checkpoints in the log segment. By default one log segment is 16MB.

- `checkpoint_timeout`—Sets the maximum time (in seconds) between two WAL checkpoints.

- `fsync`—To gain speed, the operating system buffers and caches data in memory before writing it to disk. In other words, if PostgreSQL writes data, this does not mean that it is written to disk immediately. In case of disaster, this can be a problem because the image of data the database is working on is not identical to the data on disk. Therefore the `fsync` flag can be used to tell the operating system to write the data to disk immediately. This will lead to a lower performance of the system, but it will help you to protect your data in case of disaster.

- `enable_seqscan`—By default this flag is set to off. If you want to force PostgreSQL to use an index, and if an index exists on a column, this flag has to be set to off. If no index on a column has been defined, PostgreSQL will perform a sequential scan, so you don't have to worry that you cannot look for columns on which no index has been defined.

- `enable_indexscan`—Just like sequential scans, index scans can be turned off.

- `enable_tidscan`—Tells PostgreSQL whether or not it is allowed to use TID scan plan types. Normally this is used for debugging purposes.

- `enable_sort`—To avoid as many sort operations as possible, this flag can be set to off. In some cases sorts can be avoided by using workarounds. Turning sorts off does not mean that absolutely no sorts are performed.

- `enable_nestloop`—Nested loops are loops within loops. Usually nested loops occur when two tables are joined without using an index. Nested loops are often a hint that a query has not been optimized properly.

- `enable_mergejoin` and `enable_hashjoin`—PostgreSQL provides various ways of joining tables. This flag is used to turn hash-joins and merge-joins on and off.

- `ksqo`—The Key Set Query Optimizer is often used in combination with products like Microsoft Access. The idea is that queries containing complex OR and AND conjunctions are substituted for queries using UNION. This will not always return the same result as if `ksqo` was turned off.

- `geqo`—In complex queries, it is possible in most cases to achieve faster results by using a genetic algorithm instead of exhaustive searching.

- `effective_cache_size`—Sets an estimation of the disk cache that will be used by the kernel. The value is defined in 8k blocks.

- `random_page_cost`—Sets the estimation made for loading one block from the disk.

- `cpu_tuple_cost`—Sets the costs of processing one tuple.

- `cpu_index_tuple_cost`—Sets the costs for processing one tuple using an index.

- `cpu_operator_cost`—Sets the costs for processing one tuple in the WHERE clause.

- `geqo_effort, geqo_generations, geqo_pool_size, geqo_random_seed, geqo_selection_bias`—These flags are tuning parameters for geqo. With the help of these settings, it is possible to define how the genetic algorithm works. These parameters should only be changed if you know perfectly well how things work internally; otherwise, the optimizer might produce bad results.

- `silent_mode`—Makes the postmaster run silently, which means that no messages are sent to `stdout` and `stderr`.

- `log_connections`—Displays information about every connection that is established to the server successfully.

- `log_timestamp`—To make PostgreSQL add a timestamp to the logfile, this flag has to be enabled. Setting this flag to `true` is important because this way it is possible to debug your applications easily.

- `log_pid`—In addition to the timestamp it is possible to log the process id of the back end generating the logging entry.

- `debug_level`—The standard debugging level can be set to values ranging from 0 to 16. The higher the debugging level is, the more information will be generated. In real-world applications, it is not useful to use a higher debugging level than 3 or 4.

- `DEBUG_PRINT_PARSE, DEBUG_PRINT_PLAN, DEBUG_PRINT_REWRITTEN, DEBUG_PRINT_QUERY, DEBUG_PRETTY_PRINT`—With the help of these parameters, it is possible to send a variety of values to the logfile.

- `debug_assertions`—If you are facing strange problems, assertion checks can be turned on to analyze strange behavior. This flag can only be used if `--enable-cassert` has been enabled at compile time.

- `syslog`—PostgreSQL supports syslog as a logging mechanism. To use syslog, `--enable-syslog` must be enabled at compile time.

- `syslog_facility`—With the help of this flag you can define the syslog facility you want to use.

- `syslog_ident`—If `syslog` is turned on, this option determines the program name used to identify PostgreSQL messages in `syslog` log messages.

- `show_query_stats, show_parser_stats, show_planner_stats, show_executor_stats, show_btree_build_stats`—To log information about the various components of the database such as the parser or the planner, these flags can be set to on.

- `stats_start_collector`—PostgreSQL provides a subprocess for generating statistics. By default this feature is turned on, but it can be turned off by setting `stats_start_collector` to off.

- `stats_reset_on_server_start`—If this flag is turned on, the statistics are dropped every time the server is started.

- `trace_notify`—Generates a lot of debugging output for the LISTEN and NOTIFY command.

- `dynamic_library_path`—To tell PostgreSQL where dynamically loaded objects can be found, you can define a path using `dynamic_library_path`.

- `australian_timezones`—If this parameter is set to true, CST, EST, and SAT are interpreted as Australian time zones rather than as North American Central/Eastern time zones.

- `authentication_timeout`—An authentication process has to be ready after a certain time. If the time is exceeded, PostgreSQL breaks the connection to avoid hangups.

- `default_transaction_isolation`—PostgreSQL 7.2 supports two of four transaction isolation levels proposed by the ANSI SQL standard. With the help of `default_transaction_isolation`, it is possible to tell PostgreSQL which transaction isolation level is the default one.

- `max_expr_depth`—Sets the maximum depth of an expression accepted by the parser. This way "endless" expressions can be avoided.

- `max_files_per_process`—Sets the maximum number of files a process is allowed to open.

- `password_encryption`—Passwords can be stored in an encrypted or an unencrypted way. This flag sets the default value if neither ENCRYPTED nor UNEN-CRYPTED is passed to the CREATE USER command.

- `sql_inheritance`—To turn inheritance on or off, this flag can be used. If inheritance is turned off, every table will be treated as an independent table.

- `transform_null_equals`—By default expr = NULL is not treated as expr IS NULL. To change the behavior, this flag can be set to on.

If you are running a small database system, most of the default settings will satisfy your demands. In huge installations or complex operations that have to be performed by the database, we recommend that you take a closer look at these settings to get the maximum performance out of your system.

10.3.2 Network Security

So far, you have learned about the runtime parameters of PostgreSQL. In this section you will learn to configure PostgreSQL for use in network environments.

The most important configuration file for running PostgreSQL in a network is called pg_hba.conf. This file is used to restrict or allow access to the database via a TCP/IP network. In addition to allowing and restricting, you can define which computers on the network have to use which kind of user authentication (if any).

The format of the pg_hba.conf file is easy—take a look at the syntax overview:

```
host    DBNAME  IP_ADDRESS  ADDRESS_MASK  AUTH_TYPE  [AUTH_ARGUMENT]
hostssl DBNAME  IP_ADDRESS  ADDRESS_MASK  AUTH_TYPE  [AUTH_ARGUMENT]
local   DBNAME  AUTH_TYPE  [AUTH_ARGUMENT]
```

A pg_hba.conf file can contain three different kinds of records. host records are used to restrict or allow the access of remote machines connecting to PostgreSQL via TCP/IP. First, the name of the database you want to restrict or allow has to be defined. If you want to define a setting affecting all databases, you can use the keyword all. In the next field the IP address of a host or an IP range has to be defined. In the fourth column, a netmask has to be defined to tell PostgreSQL how big a network is. AUTH_TYPE tells PostgreSQL what kind of authentication has to be used. In the last column, arguments can be passed to the database.

Let's take a closer look at the kinds of user authentication that are supported by PostgreSQL:

- trust—No user authentication is required. Every valid user will be accepted.
- password—A user has to use a password to access the database. The password is sent to the server as plain text and won't be encrypted. A name of a file can be passed to PostgreSQL as AUTH_ARGUMENT. If a file is used, the users and passwords are taken from this file and all entries in pg_shadow will be overwritten.
- md5—In contrast to password, encrypted passwords are sent over the network. md5 can use usernames stored in secondary password files but not secondary passwords.
- crypt—This option is equal to md5 but it is used in combination with clients prior to 7.2.
- ident—Ident servers send the name a user is logged in on a machine to PostgreSQL. This way it is not necessary to pass the user to the database because it is automatically determined by ident.
- krb4—Kerberos 4 authentication.
- krb5—Kerberos 5 authentication.
- reject—Rejects the establishment of a connection to the database.
- pam—Authentication is done by PAM (Pluggable Authentication Modules). If you want to use this feature, PostgreSQL must be compiled using --with-pam.

The same ways of authentication can be used in combination with hostssl instead of host.

local records are equal to host and hostssl records, but the IP address and the netmask do not have to be defined because PostgreSQL uses Unix sockets instead of TCP/IP.

Now that you have seen which methods and flags are provided by PostgreSQL, it is time to have a look at some examples:

```
local     all                                        trust
host      all      127.0.0.1     255.255.255.255     trust
```

In the default configuration the local machine can access all databases without user authentication. local means that all connections are established via Unix sockets and not via TCP/IP. In the second line you can see that local connections using the loopback device are allowed as well. If you want to allow remote users to connect to the database, some lines have to be added:

```
local     all                                        trust
host      all      127.0.0.1       255.255.255.255   trust
host      phpbook  212.186.25.254  255.255.255.255   password
host      phpbook  192.168.1.0     255.255.255.0     crypt
```

In this example two lines have been added to the configuration. The third line tells PostgreSQL to allow users at 212.186.25.254 to connect to the database called phpbook using a password. In addition, the entire network 192.168.1.x can access phpbook as well using passwords. In this case the passwords will be sent to the server in an encrypted way.

Before you try to connect to the database, you can define the password of the user called hs:

```
phpbook=> ALTER USER hs UNENCRYPTED PASSWORD 'mypasswd';
ALTER USER
```

Let's try to connect to the database located on 212.186.25.254:

```
[postgres@athlon pgdb]$ psql -h 212.186.25.254 -d phpbook
psql: could not connect to server: Connection refused
        Is the server running on host 212.186.25.254 and accepting
        TCP/IP connections on port 5432?
```

Although you have changed pg_hba.conf, you cannot connect to the database. To solve the problem, you can restart the server. In the first step, the server is shut down:

```
[postgres@athlon pgdb]$ pg_ctl -D /var/pgdb/ stop
waiting for postmaster to shut down......done
postmaster successfully shut down
```

If no errors occurred, PostgreSQL can be started:

```
[postgres@athlon pgdb]$ pg_ctl -D /var/pgdb/ -o "-i" start
postmaster successfully started
DEBUG:  database system was shut down at 2001-12-09 01:12:14 CET
DEBUG:  checkpoint record is at 0/FE5174
DEBUG:  redo record is at 0/FE5174; undo record is at 0/0; shutdown TRUE
DEBUG:  next transaction id: 3300; next oid: 26077
DEBUG:  database system is ready
```

Don't forget the -i flag to make PostgreSQL listen to TCP/IP connections.

When starting the server, PostgreSQL reads the configuration file and uses the new settings. Therefore you can connect to the database now:

```
[postgres@athlon pgdb]$ psql -h 212.186.25.254 -d phpbook -U hs
Password:
Welcome to psql, the PostgreSQL interactive terminal.

Type:  \copyright for distribution terms
       \h for help with SQL commands
       \? for help on internal slash commands
       \g or terminate with semicolon to execute query
       \q to quit


phpbook=>
```

A password must be passed to PostgreSQL, and if it is correct, you will be in the interactive shell.

When I am teaching, people are always asking me about the behavior of PostgreSQL when the pg_hba.conf file is not definite. Because this is an important point, I have decided to include a practical example here:

```
local    all                                              trust
host     all         127.0.0.1        255.255.255.255     trust
host     phpbook     212.186.25.254   255.255.255.255     password
host     phpbook     212.186.25.254   255.255.255.255     reject
```

In the third line, it says that phpbook on 212.186.25.254 can be accessed. In the fourth line, the exact opposite is defined. What is PostgreSQL going to do?

After restarting the server, you can easily find the answer:

```
[postgres@athlon postgres]$ psql -h 212.186.25.254 -d phpbook -U hs
Password:
Welcome to psql, the PostgreSQL interactive terminal.

Type:  \copyright for distribution terms
       \h for help with SQL commands
       \? for help on internal slash commands
       \g or terminate with semicolon to execute query
       \q to quit


phpbook=>
```

You can connect to the database just as you have done before: PostgreSQL takes the settings in the third line because the first line is the first one to configure `212.186.25.254`.

If the third and the fourth line are switched, the situation will be different:

```
local     all                                                     trust
host      all          127.0.0.1        255.255.255.255           trust
host      phpbook      212.186.25.254   255.255.255.255           reject
host      phpbook      212.186.25.254   255.255.255.255           password
```

After restarting the server, PostgreSQL will tell you that you are not allowed to access the database because the first line defining `212.186.25.254` contains `reject`:

```
[postgres@athlon postgres]$ psql -h 212.186.25.254 -d phpbook -U hs
psql: FATAL 1:  No pg_hba.conf entry for host 212.186.25.254, user hs,
database phpbook
```

It is necessary to know how PostgreSQL treats ambiguous configuration files because otherwise the configuration you have built might not be enough. If you are in doubt, we always recommend that you check your configuration using an IP spoofer.

10.3.3 Advanced Authentication and SSL

Configuring business-critical and huge systems demands additional features. Business-critical applications especially demand a high level of security, so it can be useful to work with things like Secure Socket Layer (SSL) to transmit data over a network in a secure way.

In addition to secure transmission, a more complex and more flexible authentication system can be used. This section will provide a brief overview of the most important ways of authenticating.

10.3.3.1 Using SSL

To achieve a higher level of security, PostgreSQL can be used in combination with OpenSSL, which is natively supported by PostgreSQL. For using SSL some basic steps have to be taken. The first thing to do is to add the appropriate entries to pg_hba.conf:

```
local     all                                              trust
host      all       127.0.0.1       255.255.255.255        trust
hostssl   phpbook   212.186.25.254  255.255.255.255        password
```

```
[postgres@athlon tmp]$ pg_ctl -D /var/pgdb/ -o "-i -l" start
postmaster successfully started
/usr/local/postgresql/bin/postmaster: failed to load server certificate
(/var/pgdb//server.crt): No such file or directory
```

To use PostgreSQL with SSL keys, certificates have to be generated. The algorithm used by OpenSSL is based on a public and a private key. In this section you will not learn about how to use SSL in detail because this is beyond the scope of this book. The only thing you will see is how to generate a self-signed certificate fast. Let's see how it works:

```
[postgres@athlon tmp]$ openssl req -new -text -out cert.req
Using configuration from /usr/share/ssl/openssl.cnf
Generating a 1024 bit RSA private key
.++++++
..++++++
writing new private key to 'privkey.pem'
Enter PEM pass phrase:
Verifying password - Enter PEM pass phrase:
-----
You are about to be asked to enter information that will be incorporated
into your certificate request.
What you are about to enter is what is called a Distinguished Name or a DN.
There are quite a few fields but you can leave some blank
For some fields there will be a default value,
If you enter '.', the field will be left blank.
-----
Country Name (2 letter code) [AU]:AT
State or Province Name (full name) [Some-State]:Vienna
Locality Name (eg, city) []:Vienna
Organization Name (eg, company) [Internet Widgits Pty Ltd]:www.cybertec.at
Organizational Unit Name (eg, section) []:Marketing
Common Name (eg, your name or your server's hostname) []:athlon
Email Address []:hs@cybertec.at
```

```
Please enter the following 'extra' attributes
to be sent with your certificate request
A challenge password []:iloveyou
An optional company name []:
```

Just enter the command at the beginning of the listing and answer all questions you are asked. The key will be passphrase-protected. To remove the passphrase, which is necessary to start the postmaster automatically, run the following command:

```
[postgres@athlon tmp]$ openssl rsa -in privkey.pem -out cert.*pem*
read RSA key
Enter PEM pass phrase:
writing RSA key
```

In the next step, the certificate has to be turned into a self-signed certificate:

```
[postgres@athlon pgdb]$ openssl req -x509 -in cert.req -text -key cert.pem
-out cert.cert
Using configuration from /usr/share/ssl/openssl.cnf
```

Finally, the only thing left to do is to copy the key to the directory where the postmaster will look for it. In this scenario the directory will be the root directory of the database cluster the postmaster has been started for:

```
[postgres@athlon pgdb]$ cp cert.pem /var/pgdb/server.key
[postgres@athlon pgdb]$ cp cert.cert /var/pgdb/server.crt
```

Now that the certificates are ready, you can start the postmaster:

```
[postgres@athlon pgdb]$ pg_ctl -D /var/pgdb/ -o "-i -l" start
postmaster successfully started
DEBUG:  database system was shut down at 2001-12-09 17:20:47 CET
DEBUG:  checkpoint record is at 0/16FC92C
DEBUG:  redo record is at 0/16FC92C; undo record is at 0/0; shutdown TRUE
DEBUG:  next transaction id: 45517; next oid: 36086
DEBUG:  database system is ready
```

No errors occurred, and you can start working with PostgreSQL safely via SSL:

```
[postgres@athlon pgdb]$ psql -d phpbook -h 212.186.25.254 -U hs
Password:
Welcome to psql, the PostgreSQL interactive terminal.

Type:  \copyright for distribution terms
       \h for help with SQL commands
```

```
\? for help on internal slash commands
\g or terminate with semicolon to execute query
\q to quit
```

```
SSL connection (cipher: DES-CBC3-SHA, bits: 168)
```

```
phpbook=>
```

When starting the front end, PostgreSQL will mention that the connection has been established via SSL.

10.3.3.2 Kerberos Authentication

Kerberos is a standard way of performing secure authentication across a public network. Kerberos is a protocol designed for authentication. Nowadays it is used by many commercial products as well as open source products. In PostgreSQL, Kerberos 4 and Kerberos 5 are supported, but only one version can be enabled at a time.

Networks are insecure and it is not recommended to transmit information as plain text without using encryption. Some people try to secure their networks using firewalls, but in many cases the potential threat comes from both inside and from somewhere outside. Therefore those parts that are considered to be secure are sometimes more insecure than others. This problem is addressed by Kerberos whose protocol makes heavy use of cryptography.

Kerberos can be used as a security solution for entire companies and also works reliably in combination with PostgreSQL.

10.4 Preparing the Database for the Web

Open source databases play a major role in today's Web environments. Especially for complex Web applications, PostgreSQL is a good choice. To use PostgreSQL efficiently, the database should be configured to satisfy the demands of a modern IT environment. Depending on the kind of application you want to run, the best settings for your database might vary.

In this section a few basic rules will be presented.

10.4.1 Memory

Tuning PostgreSQL's memory management is an important task. The first thing is to find out if the applications you are going to run contain complex queries or a set of simple queries. If you run only a few complex queries, it won't be necessary to change the maximum number of connections allowed, but it will be necessary to increase the memory PostgreSQL is allowed to use for internal sorts. Sort buffers are a tricky thing because if many concurrent sorts are running on the system, a lot of memory could be allocated, and no memory would be left for other operations. On the other hand, small sort buffers will reduce the performance of your system because a lot of I/O power is needed.

In general, the more memory your computer has, the better it is for your database. Caching can make a database perform really fast, so it is recommended to use a lot of cache and many shared buffers. However, make sure that the system does not swap because swapping is much slower than working with temporary sort files. This is an important point, and many people think that the operating system is always faster than the database, which is not true.

To monitor the memory that is currently used by your system, we recommend working with tools like top and free (these tools are available on Linux; if you are using other operating systems, check out the manual).

10.4.2 Configuring the Linux Kernel for PostgreSQL

After PostgreSQL has been configured, it is recommended to change the configuration of the Linux kernel as well. When the database is working under heavy load, some operating system resource limits can easily be exceeded and problems occur because of wrong configuration of the underlying operating system. These problems can easily be avoided by changing the most important settings of the kernel. In this book only the kernel settings of Linux operating systems will be covered because configuring other systems is beyond the scope of this book and how to change parameters can be looked up in the manual of the operating system.

Table 10.1 shows the basic values that can be defined and a reasonable estimation of these parameters.

TABLE 10.1   Linux Kernel Parameters

Name	Description	Reasonable Values
SHMMAX	Maximum size of shared memory segment (bytes)	250kB + 8.2kB * shared_buffers + 14.2kB * max_connections or infinity
SHMMIN	Minimum size of shared memory segment (bytes)	1
SHMALL	Total amount of shared memory available (bytes or pages)	If bytes, same as SHMMAX; if pages, ceil(SHMMAX/PAGE_SIZE)
SHMSEG	Maximum number of shared memory segments per process	Only 1 segment is needed, but the default is much higher
SHMMNI	Maximum number of shared memory segments systemwide	Like SHMSEG plus room for other applications
SEMMNI	Maximum number of semaphore identifiers (that is, sets)	>= ceil(max_connections / 16)

TABLE 10.1   Continued

Name	Description	Reasonable Values
SEMMNS	Maximum number of semaphores systemwide	ceil(max_connections / 16) * 17 + room for other applications
SEMMSL	Maximum number of semaphores per set	>= 17
SEMMAP	Number of entries in semaphore map	
SEMVMX	Maximum value of semaphore	>= 255 (The default is often 32767; don't change unless asked to.)

Table 10.1 has been taken from the developers docs of PostgreSQL.

All parameters of the Linux kernel can be changed at runtime and don't require a reboot.

To change a parameter, a simple echo command can be used:

```
[root@notebook root]# echo 1 > /proc/sys/kernel/shmmni
```

Simply redirect the output of the echo command to the appropriate location in the proc filesystem and the changes will be made immediately.

10.4.3 General Recommendations

When running PostgreSQL as a Web database, we recommend changing some default settings. Keep in mind that these changes are not required, but daily work with the database has proven that it can be useful to make these changes:

- **Run VACUUM periodically**—Use cron to run VACUUM periodically to free disk space and to rebuild the optimizer statistics.

- **Turn sequential scans off**—If you use PostgreSQL as a Web database, it can be useful to turn off sequential scans. This will in many cases lead to slightly lower performance because index scans are used even if a sequential scan is faster. However, in some case indexes are useful when PostgreSQL decides to perform sequential scans. In this cases a lot of speed is gained and it is less likely that timeouts will occur (at least if enough indexes have been defined).

- **Use fsync**—Fsync helps you to raise the security of your data because buffers are flushed to disk immediately.

- **Tuning memory**—Try to tune PostgreSQL by modifying the memory setting.

Depending on your system, additional changes might be useful. In many situations the settings that have just been described have been useful.

10.5 Summary

Administering PostgreSQL is an easy task. In general two configuration files are essential for working with the database: `pg_hba.conf` contains the network configuration, and `postgresql.conf` contains the runtime parameters of the database.

PostgreSQL provides an easy-to-use yet powerful security and user authentication system. To transfer data in an encrypted way, you can use SSL.

PART III

PHP/PostgreSQL Interaction

IN THIS PART

11

Writing Database-Driven Applications

After 10 hard chapters about either PHP or PostgreSQL, it's time to write the first applications based on PHP and PostgreSQL as a team. The goal of this chapter is to introduce you to the basics of PHP/PostgreSQL interaction and to learn how to send SQL statements to the database server. In addition, you will learn what you have to take care of when working with PostgreSQL and PHP.

11.1 Connecting to the Database

The first thing you have to do when working with PHP and PostgreSQL is to connect to the database. Just as when you're working with a file, you need a handle to identify a connection and to interact with it. To generate this handle, you must use pg_connect. pg_connect establishesa connection to the database and returns a database handle. The connect string sent to the database is the same string you'd use in a C program. This is an important point because PHP's PostgreSQL interface is built on C, so the behavior of PHP is easy to understand if you are familiar with the C interface. However, to work with this book, you don't have to be familiar with C.

Let's see how to establish a connection to the database:

```php
<?php
        $connstr = "dbname=phpbook user=postgres
host=localhost port=5432";
        $dbh = pg_connect($connstr);

        if      ($dbh)
        {
```

```
                echo "the connection to the database has been established<br>";
        }
        else
        {
                echo "no connection has been established<br>";
        }
?>
```

First, a connect string is defined that contains the name of the database you want to connect to, and the host the database can be found on. In addition, the port has been specified. This string is passed to `pg_connect` and a database handle is returned. If the database handle is returned correctly, a message is displayed.

Several things can cause PHP to return a wrong database handle:

- PHP or PostgreSQL have been installed the wrong way.

- You have defined a wrong database, name, host, user, port, or password.

- PostgreSQL has run out of connections because too many users are connected to the database.

- The database cannot be reached via the network. Maybe you have not started the postmaster using `-i`.

If you have configured PHP and PostgreSQL properly, and if the database exists on the system, it should not be a problem to connect to the database.

The syntax we have just discussed is the new syntax of `pg_connect`. The old system is still available but should not be used any more:

```
int pg_connect (string host, string port, string options, string tty, string
dbname)
```

Now that you have seen how to open a database connection, it is time to see how to close a connection at the end of a script:

```
<?php
        $connstr = "dbname=phpbook user=postgres host=localhost port=5432";
        $dbh = @pg_connect($connstr);

        if      ($dbh)
        {
                echo "the connection to the database has been established<br>";
        }
```

```
$status = pg_close ($dbh);
if      ($status == TRUE)
{
        echo "Connection terminated successfully<br>";
        echo "Status: $status<br>";
}
?>
```

First, a connection to the database is established and the script checks whether everything has been done correctly. If an error occurs, the error will be suppressed by the @ symbol. This can be very important because in real-world applications it can be fatal if a user can see error messages on the screen. On the one hand, it does not look professional if a site displays errors, and on the other hand, it can be a potential security threat if certain information is displayed.

Now that you have seen how to connect to the database, take a closer look at the connect string—what happens if not all components of the string are defined? For every parameter that is not defined, the default value of that parameter will be used. Here's an example:

```
<?php
        $connstr = "dbname=phpbook user=postgres";
        $dbh = pg_connect($connstr);
        if ($dbh) {echo "connection to phpbook established ...<br>";}

        $connstr = "user=postgres";
        $dbh = pg_connect($connstr);
        if ($dbh) {echo "connection to postgres established ...<br>";}
?>
```

The first connect string does not contain a hostname. This will make PHP connect to PostgreSQL to the local using Unix sockets. In this case no TCP/IP will be used. In addition, the default port is not necessary because Unix sockets don't need a port. Because the database and the user exist, the connection can be established successfully. The next connect string does not contain the name of the database you want to connect to. In this case PostgreSQL will assume that the name of the database is the same as the user—in this example, PostgreSQL assumes that the name of the database is postgres as well. When the script executes, an error will be displayed:

```
connection to phpbook established ...

Warning: Unable to connect to PostgreSQL server: FATAL 1: Database "postgres"
does not exist in the system catalog. in /var/www/html/connect.php on line 7
```

There is no database called `postgres` on the system, so an error is displayed by the PHP interpreter.

After a connection has been established, it might be necessary to find out which parameters have been used in order to establish the connection to PostgreSQL. Therefore PHP provides a set of functions for retrieving that information:

```php
<?php
        $connstr = "dbname=phpbook user=postgres host=localhost";
        $dbh = @pg_connect($connstr);

        if      ($dbh)
        {
                echo "Handle exists<br>";
        }

        echo "Host: ".pg_host($dbh)."<br>";
        echo "Database: ".pg_dbname($dbh)."<br>";
        echo "Port: ".pg_port($dbh)."<br>";
        echo "tty: ".pg_tty($dbh)."<br>";
?>
```

`pg_host` returns the host you are connected to. `pg_dbname` returns the name of the data, `pg_port` returns the number of the port PostgreSQL is listening to, and `pg_tty` returns the current `tty`. If you execute the script in the preceding listing, the result could look like this:

```
Handle exists
Host: localhost
Database: phpbook
Port: 5432
tty:
```

We recommend using these functions only if you are connected to PostgreSQL via TCP/IP. In the case of Unix sockets, it seems as if PHP is not that stable yet. In version 4.06, PHP core dumps when calling `pg_host` if the connection has been established via Unix sockets.

After establishing the connection, it is closed explicitly by using `pg_close`. Closing database handles is not necessary because the backend process associated with a connection is destroyed automatically at the end of a PHP script. However, in applications that are implemented properly, database handles are closed explicitly. In this scenario you have seen how to work with nonpersistent connections. How to use persistent connections will be covered in Chapter 13, "Working with Persistent Database Connections."

Let's execute the script and see what is displayed on the screen:

```
the connection to the database has been established
Connection terminated successfully
Status: 1
```

The connection has been started and terminated successfully.

11.2 Inserting and Retrieving Data

Connecting to the database is just not enough. In this section you will learn how to communicate with the database, how to create tables, and how to insert and retrieve data.

The first thing to do is to create a new table. Therefore you can write a short PHP script:

```php
<?php
        $connstr = "dbname=phpbook user=postgres host=localhost";
        $dbh = pg_connect($connstr);
        if ($dbh) {echo "connection to phpbook established ...<br>";}

        $sql = "CREATE TABLE person (id serial, name text, location text)";
        $stat = pg_exec($dbh, $sql);
        if      ($stat)
        {
                echo "The table has successfully been created<br>\n";
        }
        else
        {
                echo "creating the table failed<br>\n";
        }
        pg_close($dbh);
?>
```

After connecting to the database, a string containing the SQL code is generated. In the next step the query is sent to the server. pg_exec returns a status code that can be checked. Two parameters have to be passed to pg_exec: The first parameter is the connection handle and the second parameter contains the SQL statement you want to execute. If the statement has been executed successfully, the following text will be displayed:

```
connection to phpbook established ...
The table has successfully been created
```

To see if the table is really in the database, you can use psql and \d:

```
phpbook=# \d person
                             Table "person"
  Attribute |  Type  |                   Modifier
 -----------+--------+-------------------------------------------------
  id        | integer | not null default nextval('"person_id_seq"'::text)
  name      | text   |
  location  | text   |
 Index: person_id_key
```

Now that you have created a table, you can start inserting records. The next example shows how one record can be added to the table:

```php
<?php
        $connstr = "dbname=phpbook user=postgres host=localhost";
        $dbh = pg_connect($connstr);
        if ($dbh) {echo "connection to phpbook established ...<br>";}

        $sql = "INSERT INTO person (name, location) VALUES ('Paul', 'Vienna')";
        $stat = pg_exec($dbh, $sql);
        if      ($stat)
        {
                echo "The record has been inserted successfully<br>\n";
        }
        else
        {
                echo "creating the table failed<br>\n";
        }
        pg_close($dbh);
?>
```

As you can see, adding records to the table works the same way as adding tables or executing any other SQL statement. In this regard, PHP is flexible and easy to use.

The text displayed by PHP is not surprising:

```
connection to phpbook established ...
The record has been inserted successfully
```

Now that the table contains some data, you can retrieve some records. Retrieving data is slightly more complex than inserting data or making other changes. To retrieve data, you must execute the query first. In the next step, the number of records in the result can be computed. Finally, the data can be retrieved using a simple loop as shown in the next listing:

```php
<?php
        $connstr = "dbname=phpbook user=postgres host=localhost";
        $dbh = pg_connect($connstr);
        if ($dbh) {echo "connection to phpbook established ...<br>";}

        $sql = "SELECT id, name, location FROM person";
        $stat = pg_exec($dbh, $sql);
        if      ($stat)
        {
                $rows = pg_numrows($stat);
                echo "$rows lines returned by PostgreSQL<br>\n";
        }
        else
        {
                echo "an error has occurred while processing ($sql)<br>\n";
        }
        pg_close($dbh);
?>
```

For computing the number of lines returned by a query, you can use pg_numrows. In the scenario shown in the preceding listing, the number of lines is displayed on the screen:

```
connection to phpbook established ...
1 lines returned by PostgreSQL
```

In the next example you can see how the lines returned by a query can be retrieved and displayed:

```php
<?php
        $connstr = "dbname=phpbook user=postgres host=localhost";
        $dbh = pg_connect($connstr);
        if ($dbh) {echo "connection to phpbook established ...<br>";}

        $stat = pg_exec($dbh, "SELECT id, name, location FROM person");
        $rows = pg_numrows($stat);

        for      ($i = 0; $i < $rows; $i++)
        {
                $data = pg_fetch_row($stat, $i);
                echo "data: $data[0], $data[1], $data[2]<br>\n";
        }
        pg_close($dbh);
?>
```

After computing the number of lines, a loop goes through all records and retrieves the data in the result. To extract one line of data, the command `pg_fetch_row` has to be used. The command returns an array that can easily be processed and displayed on the screen using `echo`:

```
connection to phpbook established ...
data: 1, Paul, Vienna
```

In this example, a fixed number of columns is used and displayed on the screen. In many cases, however, a dynamic number of columns has to be displayed. Therefore the number of columns has to be computed at runtime. The next example shows how this can be done and how data can be displayed:

```php
<?php
        $connstr = "dbname=phpbook user=postgres host=localhost";
        $dbh = pg_connect($connstr);
        if ($dbh) {echo "connection to phpbook established ...<br>";}

        $stat = pg_exec($dbh, "SELECT id, name, location FROM person");
        $rows = pg_numrows($stat);
        $cols = pg_numfields($stat);
        echo "rows: $rows; columns: $cols<br>\n";
        for     ($i = 0; $i < $rows; $i++)
        {
                $data = pg_fetch_row($stat, $i);
                for     ($j = 0; $j < $cols; $j++)
                {
                        echo "$data[$j] ";
                }
                echo "<br>\n";
        }
        pg_close($dbh);
?>
```

`pg_numfields` is used to retrieve the number of columns in the result. Just like the result of `pg_numrows`, it is used by a loop. The output of the script is not surprising:

```
connection to phpbook established ...
rows: 1; columns: 3
1 Paul Vienna
```

One line of data is displayed.

In the past few examples, data has been retrieved using `pg_fetch_row`. The next example shows how the same result can be achieved by using `pg_fetch_array`:

```php
<?php
        $connstr = "dbname=phpbook user=postgres host=localhost";
        $dbh = pg_connect($connstr);
        if ($dbh) {echo "connection to phpbook established ...<br>";}

        $stat = pg_exec($dbh, "SELECT id, name, location FROM person");
        $rows = pg_numrows($stat);
        echo "rows: $rows<br>\n";
        for     ($i = 0; $i < $rows; $i++)
        {
                $data = pg_fetch_array($stat, $i);
                echo $data["id"]." ".$data["name"]." ".$data["location"];
                echo "<br>\n";
        }
        pg_close($dbh);
?>
```

This time the data can be accessed by using the name of the column. As you can
easily imagine, this is far better than working with indexes because the columns in
the result cannot be mixed up. The output of the script is similar to the one you
have already seen:

```
connection to phpbook established ...
rows: 1
1 Paul Vienna
```

An important point when working with pg_fetch_array is to see how you can work
with aliases:

```php
<?php
        $connstr = "dbname=phpbook user=postgres host=localhost";
        $dbh = pg_connect($connstr);
        if ($dbh) {echo "connection to phpbook established ...<br>";}

        $stat = pg_exec($dbh, "SELECT cos(id) AS a FROM person");
        $rows = pg_numrows($stat);
        echo "rows: $rows<br>\n";
        for     ($i = 0; $i < $rows; $i++)
        {
                $data = pg_fetch_array($stat, $i);
                echo "data: ".$data["a"]."<br>\n";
        }
        pg_close($dbh);
?>
```

An alias is used for the field called cos, which contains the cosine of the id. To extract the data from the result, you have to access the alias in order to find the correct result. As you can see in the next listing, it works perfectly:

```
connection to phpbook established ...
rows: 1
data: 0.54030230586814
```

In many cases, you need to retrieve information about the result itself. You have already seen how to compute the number of rows returned by a query. In the next example you will see how to obtain some additional information:

```php
<?php
        $connstr = "dbname=phpbook user=postgres host=localhost";
        $dbh = pg_connect($connstr);
        if ($dbh) {echo "connection to phpbook established ...<br><br>";}

        $stat = pg_exec($dbh, "SELECT id, name, location FROM person");

        $myid = pg_fieldname($stat, 0);
        echo "field number 1 is called $myid<br>\n";

        $myname = pg_fieldnum($stat, "name") + 1;
        echo "'name' is field number $myname<br>";

        $myloc = pg_fieldsize($stat, 2);
        echo "the third field is $myloc bytes long<br>";

        pg_close($dbh);
?>
```

To find the name of a column, you can use pg_fieldname. Just pass the name of the result and the index of the column to the function, and PHP and PostgreSQL will do the rest for you. To find the id of a certain column, PHP offers the pg_fieldnum function. This time the name of the result and the name of the column have to be passed to the function.

The last function discussed in this example is pg_fieldsize, which returns the length of a column. In the case of a variable length, the function will return -1 because the length cannot be computed precisely.

The next listing shows the output when the script is executed:

```
connection to phpbook established ...

field number 1 is called id
'name' is field number 2
the third field is -1 bytes long
```

Complex operations with a lot of data involved might use a lot of memory. If many memory-consuming requests have to be processed simultaneously, your Web server might run out of memory and the performance of your system could decrease significantly because of swapping and inefficient behavior. To reduce the amount of memory used during complex operations, PHP provides a command called pg_freeresult. If the result of a query is not needed any more, this command will help you to free the memory allocated by PHP to store the result returned by PostgreSQL. Normally the memory allocated by PHP is freed at the end of the script automatically. pg_freeresult can be used to free it earlier in the process. Let's take a look at an example:

```php
<?php
        $connstr = "dbname=phpbook user=postgres host=localhost";
        $dbh = pg_connect($connstr);
        if ($dbh) {echo "connection to phpbook established ...<br>";}

        $result = pg_exec($dbh, "SELECT cos(id) AS a FROM person");
        for     ($i = 0; $i < pg_numrows($result); $i++)
        {
                $data = pg_fetch_array($result, $i);
                echo "data: ".$data["a"]."<br>\n";
        }

        $stat = pg_freeresult($result);
        if      ($stat)
        {
                echo "memory freed successfully<br>\n";
        }
        pg_close($dbh);
?>
```

In this example the memory is freed manually and the script checks whether the command has been successful:

```
connection to phpbook established ...
data: 0.54030230586814
memory freed successfully
```

No errors were displayed and the script terminated without any problems.

In many cases, the functions you have just seen are essential, and they are the basis of many sophisticated applications.

11.3 Error Handling and Monitoring

Error handling is one of the most important things—not only when working with databases. PHP and PostgreSQL have error-handling mechanisms that are easy to use and reliable.

Let's create a table for storing telephone numbers:

```
phpbook=# CREATE TABLE phone (id serial, name text, phone text NOT NULL);
NOTICE:  CREATE TABLE will create implicit sequence 'phone_id_seq' for SERIAL
column 'phone.id'
NOTICE:  CREATE TABLE/UNIQUE will create implicit index 'phone_id_key' for
table 'phone'
CREATE
```

The last column has been defined as NOT NULL, which means that a value has to be added to the column. In the next step you can try to write a script that tries to insert some data into the table:

```php
<?php
        $connstr = "dbname=phpbook user=postgres host=localhost";
        $dbh = pg_connect($connstr);
        if ($dbh) {echo "connection to phpbook established ...<br>";}

        $stat = pg_exec($dbh, "INSERT INTO phone (name) VALUES ('Susan')");
        if      ($stat)
        {
                echo "data inserted successfully<br>\n";
        }
        else
        {
                echo "<br>an error has occurred<br>\n";
                echo pg_errormessage($dbh)."<br>";
        }
        pg_close($dbh);
?>
```

After connecting to the database, an INSERT statement is executed. Because no telephone number has been passed to the database, an error will occur that can be displayed on the screen using pg_errormessage. The database handle, not the return value of the execute statement, has to be passed to the function—this is an important point.

Let's see what the output is when the script is executed:

```
connection to phpbook established ...

Warning: PostgreSQL query failed: ERROR: ExecAppend: Fail to add null value in
not null attribute phone in /var/www/html/createtab.php on line 6

an error has occurred
ERROR: ExecAppend: Fail to add null value in not null attribute phone
```

First pg_exec displays an error. After the error message you have displayed, the result of pg_errormessage has been printed on the screen. As you can see, PostgreSQL complains that a NULL value cannot be added to the table because the third column has been declared as NOT NULL.

Take a look at an additional example:

```php
<?php
        $connstr = "dbname=phpbook user=postgres host=localhost";
        $dbh = pg_connect($connstr);
        if ($dbh) {echo "connection to phpbook established ...<br>";}

        echo "first attempt<br>\n";
        $stat = pg_exec($dbh, "INSERT INTO phone (name) VALUES ('Susan')");

        echo "<br>second attempt<br>\n";
        $stat = pg_exec($dbh, "INSERT INTO phone (name, phone) VALUES
                ('Susan', '3432434')");
        if      ($stat)
        {
                echo "data inserted successfully<br>\n";
                echo "correct: ".pg_errormessage($dbh)."<br>";
        }
        else
        {
                echo "<br>an error has occurred<br>\n";
                echo "wrong: ".pg_errormessage($dbh)."<br>";
        }
        pg_close($dbh);
?>
```

The first SQL statement sent to the server violates the constraint defined on the third column. The second SQL statement is correct and the data will be added to the table. The most important thing in this example is to see that pg_errormessage does not return an error if the previous SQL statement has been executed successfully. This looks obvious but it isn't: In some database systems, functions always retrieve the most recent error even if a correct statement has been executed after the error has occurred.

Let's take a look at the listing generated by the PHP script:

```
connection to phpbook established ...
first attempt

Warning: PostgreSQL query failed: ERROR: ExecAppend: Fail to add null value
in not null attribute phone in /var/www/html/createtab.php on line 7

second attempt
data inserted successfully
correct:
```

Sometimes you need to find out how many rows have been affected by a query. Especially when performing UPDATE operations, this can be useful to find out what has happened inside the database. The command used to extract the number of rows affected by a SQL statement is called pg_cmdtuples. You can see how this command works in the next listing:

```php
<?php
        $connstr = "dbname=phpbook user=postgres host=localhost";
        $dbh = pg_connect($connstr);
        if ($dbh) {echo "connection to phpbook established ...<br>";}

        $stat = pg_exec($dbh, "UPDATE phone SET phone='123456'
                WHERE name='Susan'");

        if      ($stat)
        {
                echo "UPDATE successful<br>\n";
                echo pg_cmdtuples($stat)."<br>";
        }
        pg_close($dbh);
?>
```

In this scenario the phone number of Susan is updated. In our database Susan has been inserted once, so pg_cmdtuples has returned 1.

Let's see what is being displayed on the screen when the script is executed:

```
connection to phpbook established ...
UPDATE successful
1
```

The result is in no way surprising.

Error handling is an easy task when working with PHP and PostgreSQL. As you have seen in this section, it takes only a few commands to perform almost all kinds of exception handling.

11.4 Handling Huge Amounts of Data

If you have to work with more than just a few records, using INSERT is far too slow. As you have already learned, PostgreSQL provides a command called COPY, which you can use to insert more than just one record into a table at once.

In this section the PHP functions related to the COPY command will be discussed. You will also learn about the performance impact of using COPY.

Using COPY works slightly differently than working with a set of INSERT commands. Here's the next example:

```php
<?php
        $connstr = "dbname=phpbook user=postgres host=localhost";
        $dbh = pg_connect($connstr);
        if ($dbh) {echo "connection to phpbook established ...<br>";}

        echo "starting process ...<br>\n";
        echo "begin: ".date('Y-m-d H:i:s')."<br>\n";
        $result = pg_exec($dbh, "COPY testdata FROM stdin");
        for     ($i = 0; $i < 40000; $i++)
        {
                $stat = pg_put_line($dbh, "$i\t".(cos($i))."\n");
                if      (!$stat)
                {
                        echo "an error has occurred<br>\n";
                }
        }
        pg_put_line($dbh, "\\.\n");
        pg_end_copy($dbh);
        echo "end: ".date('Y-m-d H:i:s')."<br>\n";
        pg_close($dbh);
        echo "ending process ...<br>\n";
?>
```

Before running the script you have to create a table like that:

```
CREATE TABLE testdata (idx int4, val numeric(9,8));
```

After connecting to the database, the head of the COPY command is sent to the server. After that, PostgreSQL is waiting for data until \. can be found. Every line of data is submitted to the database by using the pg_put_line command. The table you want to add data to consists of two columns. The first column contains a number and the second column contains the cosine of that number. After the data has been sent to PostgreSQL, the COPY command is terminated by using pg_end_copy. To see how fast the COPY command works, the current time is displayed on the screen as well:

```
connection to phpbook established ...
starting process ...
begin: 2001-12-12 21:57:34
end: 2001-12-12 21:57:38
ending process ...
```

The entire COPY command takes not longer than four seconds, which is fast (the demo has been run on a 466Mhz laptop). Because the entire set of data is added to the table in just one transaction, there is hardly any overhead.

Let's delete the records from the table:

```
phpbook=# DELETE FROM testdata;
DELETE 40000
```

To understand why the COPY command should be used, the next listing shows how the same result can be achieved by using INSERT commands:

```php
<?php
        $connstr = "dbname=phpbook user=postgres host=localhost";
        $dbh = pg_connect($connstr);
        if ($dbh) {echo "connection to phpbook established ...<br>";}

        echo "starting process ...<br>\n";
        echo "begin: ".date('Y-m-d H:i:s')."<br>\n";
        for    ($i = 0; $i < 40000; $i++)
        {
                $stat = pg_exec($dbh, "INSERT INTO testdata VALUES
                        ($i, '".(cos($i))."')");
                if     (!$stat)
                {
                        echo "an error has occurred<br>\n";
```

```
                }
        }
        echo "end: ".date('Y-m-d H:i:s')."<br>\n";
        pg_close($dbh);
        echo "ending process ...<br>\n";
?>
```

Remember, using COPY took about four seconds to insert 40,000 records. The next listing shows how long it takes when INSERT is used:

```
connection to phpbook established ...
starting process ...
begin: 2001-12-12 22:00:03
end: 2001-12-12 22:13:20
ending process ...
```

It takes more than 13 minutes, which is significantly slower. This impressive example shows how much overhead you can save with the help of COPY.

The more data you have to process, the more performance you can gain. Technically, pg_put_line does nothing more than send a NULL terminated string to the backend process handling the connection to PostgreSQL. After sending the data to the database, the backend and the frontend process have to be synchronized, which can be done by using pg_end_copy.

11.5 Retrieving Objects from the Database

When working with object-oriented PHP, it can be helpful to retrieve data from the table as objects. Therefore PHP provides a command called pg_fetch_object, which can be used like pg_fetch_array and pg_fetch_row. To see how the command works, first create a table and insert some data:

```
phpbook=# CREATE TABLE plant(id int4, name text, color text);
CREATE
phpbook=# INSERT INTO plant VALUES (1, 'Sambucus nigra', 'yellow');
INSERT 116394 1
phpbook=# INSERT INTO plant VALUES (2, 'Abies', 'green');
INSERT 116395 1
phpbook=# INSERT INTO plant VALUES (3, 'Colchicum autumnale', 'pink');
INSERT 116396 1
```

If no error occurred, you have created a table containing information about three plants and their colors. In the next step, the data should be retrieved as objects.

The next example shows `pg_fetch_object` in action:

```php
<?php
        $connstr = "dbname=phpbook user=postgres host=localhost";
        $dbh = pg_connect($connstr);

        $sql = "SELECT id, name, color FROM plant WHERE id=1";
        $result = pg_exec($dbh, $sql);
        $data = pg_fetch_object($result, 0);

        echo "If you have the flu drink some tea made of $data->name<br>\n";
        echo "Take the $data->color parts of the plant and boil it.<br>\n";

        pg_close($dbh);
?>
```

To access the various components of the object, the `->` operator must be used. The only difference between using an array and using objects lies in the syntax you have to use.

Let's take a look at the output of the script:

```
If you have the flu drink some tea made of Sambucus nigra
Take the yellow parts of the plant and boil it.
```

The data is displayed just as if you were using arrays.

11.6 Tracing a PostgreSQL Connection

Especially for debugging purposes, tracing a connection to a PostgreSQL server can be useful. Tracing a connection means that the data transmitted from and to the back end is monitored and can be used to see what PostgreSQL does internally. In general, the information generated by a trace is only useful if you are familiar with PostgreSQL's internal protocol. However, we need to see how tracing can be turned on and off.

Take a look at the next example:

```php
<?php
        $dbh = pg_connect("host=localhost user=postgres dbname=phpbook");
        if      (!$dbh) { echo "error while connecting.<br>\n"; }

        $status = pg_trace("/tmp/trace.log");
        $result = pg_exec($dbh, "SELECT id, name, color FROM plant LIMIT 1");
        $rows = pg_numrows($result);
```

```
for      ($i = 0; $i < $rows; $i++)
{
        $data = pg_fetch_row($result, $i);
        echo "$data[0], $data[1], $data[2]<br>\n";
}
?>
```

The target is to select one record from the table called plant and to store the tracing information in /tmp/trace.log. To turn on tracing, PHP provides a function called pg_trace. Let's see what will be displayed on the screen when the script is executed:

```
1, Sambucus nigra, yellow
```

One line is displayed on the screen. In addition, the logfile has been created and a number of lines have been added to it:

```
To backend> Q
To backend> SELECT id, name, color FROM plant LIMIT 1
From backend> P
From backend> "blank"
From backend> T
From backend (#2)> 3
From backend> "id"
From backend (#4)> 23
From backend (#2)> 4
From backend (#4)> -1
From backend> "name"
From backend (#4)> 25
From backend (#2)> 65535
From backend (#4)> -1
From backend> "color"
From backend (#4)> 25
From backend (#2)> 65535
From backend (#4)> -1
From backend> D
From backend (1)> à
From backend (#4)> 5
From backend (1)> 1
From backend (#4)> 18
From backend (14)> Sambucus nigra
From backend (#4)> 10
From backend (6)> yellow
From backend> C
From backend> "SELECT"
```

```
From backend> Z
From backend> Z
To backend> X
```

As you can see, a lot of logging information has been written into the file. To use the logging information effectively, you must take a closer look at PostgreSQL's internals.

To turn off tracing again, `pg_untrace` must be used.

11.7 Locking

If you are writing software for a frequently used Web server, you'll need to take a closer look at locking. Usually locking is done by PostgreSQL internally. However, it is possible to influence locking explicitly. In many situations this is necessary, and it can help you to get around problems easily.

The most important thing when working with explicit locking is to see how concurrent PHP scripts treat locking.

In general, working with locks is easy. Everything can be done using just one command:

```
phpbook=# \h LOCK
Command:    LOCK
Description: explicitly lock a table
Syntax:
LOCK [ TABLE ] name [, ...]
LOCK [ TABLE ] name [, ...] IN lockmode MODE

where lockmode is one of:

        ACCESS SHARE | ROW SHARE | ROW EXCLUSIVE | SHARE UPDATE EXCLUSIVE |
        SHARE | SHARE ROW EXCLUSIVE | EXCLUSIVE | ACCESS EXCLUSIVE
```

As you can see, LOCK provides many different options for defining how to lock a table. One important point is how PHP and PostgreSQL treat locks that are not released explicitly. In the next example you will see how this works:

```php
<?php
        $dbh = pg_connect("host=localhost user=postgres dbname=phpbook");
        if      (!$dbh) { echo "error while connecting.<br>\n"; }

        execute("INSERT INTO plant VALUES (4, 'pines', 'green')");
```

```
        execute('LOCK plant IN EXCLUSIVE MODE');
        execute("INSERT INTO plant VALUES (5, 'rose', 'red')");

function execute($sql)
{
        global $dbh;
        echo "start: ".date('Y-m-d H:i:s')." --- $sql<br>\n";
        $status = pg_exec($dbh, $sql);
        echo "end: ".date('Y-m-d H:i:s')." --- $sql<br>\n";
        if      (!$status)
        {
                echo "an error has occurred when executing ($sql)<br>\n";
        }
}

}

?>
```

The function called `execute` combines the execution of a SQL statement with error handling. This is helpful because error handling has to be implemented only once. In addition, the starting time and the finishing time of the SQL statements is displayed. This information is necessary to see what effects locking has.

First one record is added to the table. In the next step the table is locked exclusively and an additional record is added to the table. The lock is not released, and the question now is: How will this affect the further treatment of the table?

After executing the script the first time, two additional values can be found in `plant`:

```
phpbook=# SELECT * FROM plant;
 id |        name        | color
----+--------------------+--------
  1 | Sambucus nigra     | yellow
  2 | Abies              | green
  3 | Colchicum autumnale | pink
  4 | pines              | green
  5 | rose               | red
(5 rows)
```

The logging information displayed by the script contains nothing special:

```
start: 2001-12-14 10:06:25 --- INSERT INTO plant VALUES (4, 'pines', 'green')
end: 2001-12-14 10:06:25 --- INSERT INTO plant VALUES (4, 'pines', 'green')
start: 2001-12-14 10:06:25 --- LOCK plant IN EXCLUSIVE MODE
end: 2001-12-14 10:06:25 --- LOCK plant IN EXCLUSIVE MODE
```

```
start: 2001-12-14 10:06:25 --- INSERT INTO plant VALUES (5, 'rose', 'red')
end: 2001-12-14 10:06:25 --- INSERT INTO plant VALUES (5, 'rose', 'red')
```

Everything has been processed in one second. Let's see what will be displayed when the script is executed a second time:

```
start: 2001-12-14 10:06:55 --- INSERT INTO plant VALUES (4, 'pines', 'green')
end: 2001-12-14 10:06:55 --- INSERT INTO plant VALUES (4, 'pines', 'green')
start: 2001-12-14 10:06:55 --- LOCK plant IN EXCLUSIVE MODE
end: 2001-12-14 10:06:55 --- LOCK plant IN EXCLUSIVE MODE
start: 2001-12-14 10:06:55 --- INSERT INTO plant VALUES (5, 'rose', 'red')
end: 2001-12-14 10:06:55 --- INSERT INTO plant VALUES (5, 'rose', 'red')
```

The lock does not affect the scripts started after the first one has been terminated. The reason for that is simple: When the connection to PostgreSQL is closed by PHP automatically, all locks made by this connection will be released automatically. However, PHP scripts that are accessing plant between the time the first PHP script has locked the table and the script has been terminated have to wait until the lock is released. If the script takes a long time to succeed, this will decrease the performance of your system significantly.

11.8 PHP and Transactions

Transactions and locks are strongly related to each other. After you have seen how locks can be treated, you can take a closer look at PHP and transactions. Usually working with transactions is an easy task. However, a closer look is necessary to find out what happens to uncommitted transactions. The next example shows what happens with transactions that are not committed manually:

```php
<?php
        $dbh = pg_connect("host=localhost user=postgres dbname=phpbook");
        if      (!$dbh) { echo "error while connecting.<br>\n"; }

        execute("BEGIN;");
        execute("INSERT INTO plant VALUES (6, 'cactus', 'green')");

function execute($sql)
{
        global $dbh;
        $status = pg_exec($dbh, $sql);
        if      (!$status)
        {
```

```
                echo "an error has occurred when executing ($sql)<br>\n";
        }
}

?>
```

First a transaction is started. In the next step one value is added to the table, but the transaction is not committed manually. Therefore, the new value cannot be found in the table:

```
phpbook=# SELECT * FROM plant WHERE id=6;
 id | name | color
----+------+-------
(0 rows)
```

When the script has been executed, PHP closes the connection to PostgreSQL and the database performs an implicit ROLLBACK. This way, no data from uncommitted transactions will pollute your data.

The situation differs when the transaction is ended explicitly:

```
<?php
        $dbh = pg_connect("host=localhost user=postgres dbname=phpbook");
        if      (!$dbh) { echo "error while connecting.<br>\n"; }

        execute("BEGIN;");
        execute("INSERT INTO plant VALUES (6, 'cactus', 'green')");
        execute("COMMIT;");

function execute($sql)
{
        global $dbh;
        $status = pg_exec($dbh, $sql);
        if      (!$status)
        {
                echo "an error has occurred when executing ($sql)<br>\n";
        }
}

?>
```

This time the record can be found in the table because the transaction has been committed correctly.

```
phpbook=# SELECT * FROM plant WHERE id=6;
 id |  name  | color
----+--------+-------
  6 | cactus | green
(1 row)
```

If you are not using BEGIN and COMMIT explicitly, every command will be executed as one separate transaction. This is an important point because you don't have to deal with transactions explicitly. As you have seen in this section, PHP does not provide onboard tools for handling transactions. Everything is done by executing ordinary SQL statements.

11.9 Summary

PHP's programming interface to PostgreSQL is based on PostgreSQL's C library, and therefore the PHP interface is similar to the C interface of PostgreSQL.

Inserting, retrieving, and selecting data can be done by sending SQL statements to the database. To extract data from the result, PostgreSQL provides various methods. Depending on what you like best, data can be retrieved as rows, records, or objects.

12

Working with BLOBs

Every highly developed database supports a method for storing entire files in the database. This can be essential for content management tools. However, some people prefer to store files in the filesystem, not in the database. Instead of uploading a file into the database, you only have to store the name of the file in the database. The problem with this algorithm is that the consistency of the data in the database and the filesystem needs to be checked. In addition, you have to back up the files and the database individually, and it is not as easy as dumping a database including BLOBs (Binary Large Objects).

This chapter is dedicated to all people who want to store their files in a database efficiently. You will also see how file uploads can be handled with PHP.

12.1 Working with PostgreSQL BLOBs Using SQL

The first topic in this chapter is PostgreSQL's SQL interface to BLOBs. PostgreSQL provides a set of easy-to-use functions for working with BLOBs. Using these functions is not difficult because most of these functions are only SQL counterparts of widely used C functions.

First of all, a BLOB is not stored in a table but as an object in the database. A BLOB must be accessed via a so-called object id, which is a unique identifier of an object in a database. The object id of a BLOB can then be stored in a table so that it does not get lost in the database.

Let's create a table for storing object ids and a description of the files the object id is pointing to:

```
phpbook=# CREATE TABLE ext4(file_oid oid, description text);
CREATE
```

The first column of the table contains the object id of the file you want to reference. The second column contains the description of the file.

When creating a new table containing object ids, you should keep in mind that a column should not be called oid:

```
phpbook=# CREATE TABLE ext5(oid oid, description text);
ERROR:  name of column "oid" conflicts with an existing system column
ERROR:  name of column "oid" conflicts with an existing system column
```

Internally, PostgreSQL uses a column for storing the object id of a row in a table. If an additional column is called oid, there will be a conflict as you saw in the preceding listing. To retrieve the object id from the table, you must add oid to the list of columns you want to display.

```
phpbook=# SELECT oid, * FROM ext4;
  oid  | file_oid |          description
-------+----------+------------------------------
 44294 |    44293 | file used to store user data
 44296 |    44295 | hostnames
```

Since PostgreSQL 7.2, it is possible to create tables without having a column containing an object id:

```
phpbook=# CREATE TABLE ext5(oid oid, description text) WITHOUT OIDS;
CREATE
```

Just add WITHOUT OIDS to the CREATE TABLE statement, and there will be no conflicts if the names of the columns are duplicated:

```
phpbook=# \d ext5
         Table "ext5"
   Column    | Type | Modifiers
-------------+------+-----------
 oid         | oid  |
 description | text |
```

As you can see, the table has been created successfully.

Let's get back to the first example you saw in this section. To import a file into the database, you can use lo_import:

```
phpbook=# SELECT lo_import('/etc/passwd');
 lo_import
-----------
     44293
(1 row)
```

As you can see, the function returns an object id—the file has been stored in the database but it has not been imported into a table.

To insert the object id returned by lo_import into the table, you can use an INSERT statement.

```
phpbook=# INSERT INTO ext4 VALUES (44293, 'file used to store user data');
INSERT 44294 1
```

However, using two commands is not the best way to perform this kind of operation. To import a file and add a record to the table, you can also write a SQL statement as shown in the next listing:

```
phpbook=# INSERT INTO ext4 VALUES (lo_import('/etc/hosts'), 'hostnames');
INSERT 44296 1
```

To see if the record has been generated successfully, you can query the table:

```
phpbook=# SELECT * FROM ext4;
 file_oid |          description
----------+------------------------------
    44293 | file used to store user data
    44295 | hostnames
(2 rows)
```

Two records have been added to the table, and that's the way you want it to be.

Now that you have seen how to import data, it's time to see how to export BLOBs. To export a BLOB, PostgreSQL provides a command called lo_export:

```
phpbook=# SELECT lo_export(44293, '/tmp/tmpfile.txt');
 lo_export
-----------
         1
(1 row)
```

The first parameter passed to the function is the object id of the file. The second parameter defines the filename you want to export the BLOB to. Keep in mind that after a file has been imported into a PostgreSQL database, the original filename is lost—PostgreSQL does not need it because the new identification in the database is just an object id. When exporting the file again, you must assign a name to the file.

Let's take a look at the content of the new file. With the help of head -n3, the first three lines of the file can be displayed:

```
[hs@athlon hs]$ head /tmp/tmpfile.txt -n3
root:x:0:0:root:/root:/bin/bash
bin:x:1:1:bin:/bin:
daemon:x:2:2:daemon:/sbin:
```

The file has been exported successfully.

The next example shows how one object including the entry of the object id in ext4 can be removed:

```
phpbook=# BEGIN;
BEGIN
phpbook=# SELECT lo_unlink(44295);
 lo_unlink
-----------
         1
(1 row)

phpbook=# DELETE FROM ext4 WHERE file_oid=44295;
DELETE 1
phpbook=# COMMIT;
COMMIT
```

We recommend performing the operation in a single transaction so that concurrent operations do not affect your work on the database. lo_unlink removes a BLOB—keep in mind that this does not mean that the object id is automatically removed from ext4 because this must be done by a separate DELETE statement.

In addition to the functions you have just seen, PostgreSQL provides additional functions for handling BLOBs, such as lo_open and lo_write. However, in most cases you will not use these functions as SQL commands because PHP provides an easy-to-use interface for handling BLOBs as well.

12.2 Working with PostgreSQL BLOBs Using PHP

PHP's functions related to PostgreSQL and BLOBs are comfortable and easy to use. Functions are available for all important operations such as importing, exporting, creating a new object, or writing data into an object. As we have already seen, SQL offers counterparts to the functions provided by PHP. However, in this section you will learn to use PHP's onboard functions.

The next example shows how a file is imported into a database and deleted again:

```php
<?php
        $dbh = pg_connect("host=localhost user=postgres dbname=phpbook");
        if      (!$dbh) { echo "error while connecting.<br>\n"; }

        pg_exec($dbh, "BEGIN");
        $oid = pg_loimport('/etc/passwd', $dbh);
        if      (!$oid)
        {
                echo "an error has occurred while importing<br>\n";
                exit;
        }
        echo "Object id: $oid<br>\n";
        $status = pg_lounlink($dbh, $oid);
        if      (!$status)
        {
                echo "the file could not be deleted<br>\n";
        }
        pg_exec($dbh, "COMMIT");
?>
```

PHP's functions for dealing with BLOBs can only be used inside a transaction. Therefore, a transaction is started before the file is inserted into the database by using pg_loimport. Just pass the name of the file you want to import and the connection handle to the function; if you are inside a transaction, the operation will succeed unless there is an error with user rights or things like that.

pg_loimport returns the object id of the new object, which is displayed on the screen using an echo command. Finally, the new object is deleted:

```
Object id: 44322
```

When working with multimedia data, it is often necessary to send data in a file stored in a PostgreSQL database directly to the browser. Therefore PHP provides a command called pg_loreadall. To use this function, the file must be opened first using pg_loopen:

```php
<?php
        $dbh = pg_connect("host=localhost user=postgres dbname=phpbook");
        if      (!$dbh) { echo "error while connecting.<br>\n"; }

        pg_exec($dbh, "BEGIN");
        $oid = pg_loimport('/etc/passwd', $dbh);
        if      (!$oid)
        {
                echo "an error has occurred while importing<br>\n";
                exit;
        }

        $file = pg_loopen($dbh, $oid, "rw");
        pg_loreadall($file);

        $status = pg_lounlink($dbh, $oid);
        if      (!$status)
        {
                echo "the file could not be deleted<br>\n";
        }
        pg_exec($dbh, "COMMIT");
?>
```

pg_loreadall returns void and does not return the data as a variable—the content of the BLOB is sent to the browser directly. Figure 12.1 shows what the result will look like.

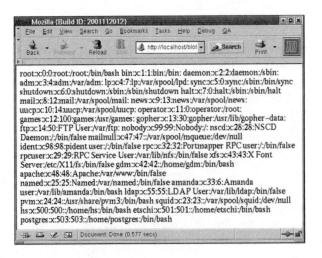

FIGURE 12.1   The /etc/passwd file.

You can import and export files, but that's not all you can do. In many situations, the BLOB must be modified. Therefore, PHP and PostgreSQL provide functions that are similar to C functions used for interacting with files. To create an empty object, check out pg_locreate. To write data to the BLOB, pg_lowrite must be used. The next example shows how the word SUSI is added to an empty BLOB:

```php
<?php
        $dbh = pg_connect("host=localhost user=postgres dbname=phpbook");
        if      (!$dbh) { echo "error while connecting.<br>\n"; }

        pg_exec($dbh, "BEGIN");
        $oid = pg_locreate($dbh);
        if      (!$oid)
        {
                echo "an error has occurred while creating object<br>\n";
                exit;
        }

        echo "object id: $oid<br>\n";
        $file = pg_loopen($dbh, $oid, "rw");
        pg_lowrite($file, "SUSI");
        pg_loclose($file);
        pg_exec($dbh, "COMMIT");
?>
```

Let's see what data can be found in the file. The BLOB must be exported to a file:

```
phpbook=# SELECT lo_export(44336, '/tmp/test_lowrite.txt');
 lo_export
-----------
         1
(1 row)
```

cat lists the content of the file on the screen:

```
[postgres@athlon html]$ cat /tmp/test_lowrite.txt; echo \
SUSI
```

SUSI has been added to the BLOB and the file has been closed correctly.

To retrieve the data from the BLOB, it is also possible to write a short PHP script:

```php
<?php
        $dbh = pg_connect("host=localhost user=postgres dbname=phpbook");
        if      (!$dbh) { echo "error while connecting.<br>\n"; }
```

```
        pg_exec($dbh, "BEGIN");
        $file = pg_loopen($dbh, 44336, "r");
        $data = pg_loread($file, 4);
        echo "data: $data<br>\n";
        pg_loclose($file);
        pg_exec($dbh, "COMMIT");
?>
```

First the BLOB is opened and four bytes of data are retrieved from the BLOB using pg_loread. Then this data is displayed on the screen:

data: SUSI

As you can see, the BLOB has been processed successfully.

12.3 Managing File Uploads

File uploads can be done with every RFC-1867–compliant browser, such as Mozilla and Netscape. File uploading means that you can store a file on a Web server where it can be used for further treatment. It does not matter if the file is in binary or ASCII format because the file is processed as a unit byte by byte. Usually files are uploaded with the help of a POST request, as shown in the next listing:

```
<html>
<head>
<title>Title</title>
</head>
<body>

<h1>Working With File Uploads</h1>
<form id="data" method="post" action="input_file.php"
        enctype="multipart/form-data">
<p>
Choose a file: <br>
<input name="testfile" type="file" size="50" maxlength="100000"><br>
<input name="submit" type="submit">
</p>
</form>

</body>
</html>
```

After things like the header and title, a form starts. The first field in the form uses `file` as type. This field will be used for the file upload. As you can see, many parameters can be defined. One of these parameters is `maxlength`, which defines the maximum size of the file being uploaded. The next field contains the Submit Query button for starting the `POST` request. After the Submit Query button, the form and the HTML file are terminated. To see what the HTML document looks like in a browser, take a look at Figure 12.2.

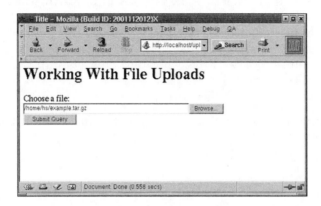

FIGURE 12.2 File uploads.

What happens if somebody selects a file and wants to process the file? The file responsible for managing the file uploaded by the user is called `input_file.php`. Take a look at the code of this file:

```php
<?php
    if      ($testfile)
    {
            if      (is_uploaded_file($testfile))
            {
                    echo "userfile: $testfile<br>\n";
                    echo "userfile_name: $testfile_name<br>\n";
                    echo "userfile_size: $testfile_size<br>\n";
            }
            else
            {
                    echo "no file uploaded";
            }
    }
    else
    {
```

```
                    echo "a problem has occurred" ;
        }
?>
```

The field in the HTML file responsible for performing the upload is called `testfile`. PHP automatically defines a variable having the same name as the field in the HTML file. This variable can be checked and if it is defined, you can try to find out if a file has been uploaded correctly. If so, some variables are displayed, which you can use to retrieve information about the file that has been processed. `$testfile` contains the name of the file on the Web server. `$testfile_name` contains the original name of the file on the user's machine. When uploading, the file won't have the original name on the Web server because this could cause problems with identical names. In addition to `$testfile` and `$testfile_name`, `$testfile_size` has been defined, which contains the size of the file in bytes.

If you select a file and click on the Submit Query button, the result might look like this:

```
userfile: /tmp/phpTdZESc
userfile_name: example.tar.gz
userfile_size: 7194
```

As you can see, the content of `$testfile` is rather cryptic, but the advantage is that the filenames generated by PHP are always unique.

12.4 Storing Files as Toasted Text

Up to now you have seen how binary data can be stored without using PHP's and PostgreSQL's BLOB interface. Many people don't like to work with BLOBs, so it is necessary to find a different solution. In the case of PHP and PostgreSQL, data can be converted to hex code and stored in a text variable. Up to PostgreSQL 7.0, the size of text variables was limited to the size of one page, which is usually 8192 bytes. With the arrival of PostgreSQL 7.1, things have changed and text is a so-called toasted data type now, which means that one field can be larger than one page used by PostgreSQL internally. Currently, a field can have a size of up to 1GB. In many cases this will be enough. If you want to work with fields larger than 1GB, you have to use PostgreSQL's BLOB interface.

In the next example you will see how the content of a file can be stored in a text column. Therefore a table for storing files is created:

```
phpbook=> CREATE TABLE filesystem(name text, data text, tstamp timestamp);
CREATE
```

In the next step you can write a simple demo application you can use to import one file into the database. The next scenario shows how the file called /etc/passwd can be imported into the table you have just seen:

```php
<?php
        # name of file you want to import
        $filename = '/etc/passwd';

        $dbh = pg_connect("host=localhost user=postgres dbname=phpbook");
        if      (!$dbh) { echo "error while connecting.<br>\n"; }

        # open file and retrieve information about it
        $fp = fopen($filename, "r");
        $fstats = fstat($fp);
        $data = fread($fp, $fstats[6]);

        # converting data to hex data
        $hexdata = bin2hex($data);

        # inserting data into database
        $sql = "INSERT INTO filesystem VALUES
                ('$filename', '$hexdata', now())";
        $stat = pg_exec($dbh, $sql);
        if      (!$stat)
        {
                echo "data cannot be added to the table<br>\n";
                exit;
        }
        else
        {
                echo "data has been added to the table<br>\n";
        }
?>
```

After connecting to the database, the file is opened for reading using fopen. The file handle returned by fopen will be needed by fstats. With the help of fstats, information about the file such as size and inode can be retrieved. You will need the size of the file in order to find out how much data you have to read from the file using fread. As you can see, these PHP functions are similar to the C functions for performing system calls. After the data is read, it is encoded using bin2hex. $hexdata is then inserted into the database and a message is displayed on the screen.

If you have a look at the content of filesystem, you will see that the data has been imported successfully:

```
phpbook=# SELECT name, length(data), tstamp FROM filesystem;
    name     | length |            tstamp
-------------+--------+-------------------------------
 /etc/passwd |   2400 | 2001-12-15 23:42:53.644758+01
(1 row)
```

The filename is stored in the first column. The content of the second column is not listed completely because it is no use to display hexadecimal data. As you can see, the field has a total size of 2400 bytes. If you take a look at /etc/passwd, you will see that the amount of storage needed has doubled:

```
[hs@athlon hs]$ ls -l /etc/passwd
-rw-r--r--   1 root     root          1200 Dez 15 01:13 /etc/passwd
```

Exporting the data is as simple as importing the data, and the next listing shows how this can be done:

```php
<?php
        # name of the file you want to retrieve
        $filename = '/etc/passwd';

        # connecting to the database
        $dbh = pg_connect("host=localhost user=postgres dbname=phpbook");
        if      (!$dbh) { echo "error while connecting.<br>\n"; }

        # selecting data
        $sql = "SELECT name, data, tstamp FROM filesystem
                WHERE name='$filename'";
        $result = pg_exec($dbh, $sql);
        $data = pg_fetch_row($result, 0) or
                exit ("an error has occurred<br>");
        $bindata = hex2bin($data[1]);

        # comparing data
        $fp = fopen($filename, "r");
        $fstats = fstat($fp);
        $data = fread($fp, $fstats[6]);

        if      ($bindata == $data) { echo "the data is the same<br>\n"; }
        else    { echo "the data differs<br>\n"; }
```

```
function hex2bin($data)
{
        $len = strlen($data);
        return pack("H" . $len, $data);
}
?>
```

First, the record containing the file you need is retrieved from the database. In the next step, the content of the second column is transformed to the original format by a function called hex2bin. At the end of the PHP program, you can see how hex2bin works: First, the length of the string passed to the function is computed, and then the decoded string is returned to the main program. Now $bindata contains the original data, and this data is compared with the data in the original /etc/passwd file. We show how this works so that you can see that the data extracted from the database is the same data you have imported before.

If you execute the PHP script, it is not surprising that the data matches:

```
the data is the same
```

Working with PHP's BLOB functions is easy, and it takes little effort to build a powerful application.

12.5 An Example of a Simple Image Management Tool

In this section you will see a simplified example of a file management tool that works with images. The basic features have been implemented. The idea is to show you how data can be extracted to the database and how it can be sent to the browser directly. Keep in mind that this is a prototype application.

First, a table for storing information about the pics must be generated:

```
CREATE TABLE pic_db (
        id serial,              -- id of pic
        name text,              -- name of the pic
        picoid oid,             -- object id of pic
        added timestamp DEFAULT now()
);
```

The next listing contains a piece of HTML code you can use for uploading files:

```
<html>
<head>
<title>Title</title>
</head>
<body>
```

```php
<?php
        echo "<b>List of pictures in the table</b><br>\n";

        # connecting to the database
        $dbh = pg_connect("dbname=phpbook user=postgres");
        if      (!$dbh)
        {
                echo "cannot open connection to the database<br>";
                exit;
        }

        $result = pg_exec($dbh, "SELECT id, name, picoid, added FROM pic_db");
        $rows = pg_numrows($result);
        for      ($i = 0; $i < $rows; $i++)
        {
                $data = pg_fetch_row($result, $i);
                echo $data[0].' - <a href="detail.php?id='.$data[0].
                        '" target="_blank"'.">$data[1]</a><br>";
        }
?>


<br><br><hr>
<b>File Upload:</b>
<form id="data" method="post" action="input_file.php"
        enctype="multipart/form-data">
<p>
Choose a file: <br>
<input name="testfile" type="file" size="50" maxlength="100000"><br>
<input name="submit" type="submit">
</p>
</form>

</body>
</html>
```

After the header is displayed, a PHP script starts. A connection to the database is established and the information about the pics that are already in the database is displayed. Every filename is displayed and a link to detail.php is generated. detail.php will contain the code for extracting the picture. After generating the links, a form is displayed. This form can be used for uploading additional files.

Figure 12.3 shows what the entire screen looks like.

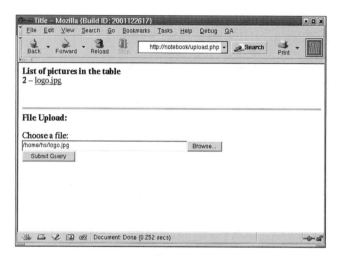

FIGURE 12.3   File uploads after a file has been added.

input_file.php is called as soon as somebody clicks the Submit Query button. A connection to the database is opened and the file that has been uploaded by the user is imported into the database. If the file has been imported successfully, a message is displayed. Let's have a look at input_file.php:

```php
<?php
    # connecting to the database
    $dbh = pg_connect("dbname=phpbook user=postgres");
    if      (!$dbh)
    {
            echo "cannot open connection to the database<br>";
            exit;
    }

    # checking for uploaded file
    if      ($testfile)
    {
            if      (is_uploaded_file($testfile))
            {
                    chmod($testfile, 0777);

                    $sql = "INSERT INTO pic_db (name, picoid) VALUES ";
                    $sql .= "('$testfile_name', lo_import('$testfile'))";
                    $stat = pg_exec($dbh, $sql);
                    if      (!$stat)
                    {
```

```
                                echo "the picture cannot be added<br>";
                                exit;
                    }
                    else
                    {
                                echo "the picture has been added
                                        successfully<br>";

                    }
            }
            else
            {
                    echo "no file uploaded";

            }
        }

        pg_close($dbh);
?>
```

The script called detail.php is used to display a picture on the screen:

```
<?php
        # connecting to the database
        $dbh = pg_connect("dbname=phpbook user=postgres");
        if      (!$dbh)
        {
                echo "cannot open connection to the database<br>";
                exit;
        }

        $sql = "SELECT id, name, picoid, added FROM pic_db WHERE id=$id";
        $result = pg_exec($dbh, $sql);
        $data = pg_fetch_row($result, 0);
        if      (!$data)
        {
                echo "undefined picture<br>";
        }
        else
        {
                Header ("Content-type: image/jpg");
                pg_exec($dbh, "BEGIN");
                $ofp = pg_loopen($data[2], "r");
                if      (!$ofp)
                {
```

```
            echo "cannot open BLOB<br>\n";
        }
        $img = pg_loreadall($ofp);
        print $img;
        pg_loclose($ofp);
        pg_exec($dbh, "END");
    }
?>
```

A connection to the database is established. Then the object id of the picture you want to see is retrieved. To open the BLOB, a transaction must be started. This is an important part because without starting a transaction, it is not possible to interact with the BLOB. pg_loopen returns a handle that can be used for further operations such as reading the data from the BLOB. Finally, all handles as well as transactions are closed. In addition, the data is sent to the browser. Figure 12.4 shows what the result looks like.

FIGURE 12.4   Watching the pics.

12.6 Summary

PostgreSQL is capable of handling Binary Large Objects (BLOBs). Entire files can be stored in the database. Internally a file is represented by an object id. PostgreSQL provides a set of functions for interacting with BLOBs. Most of these functions are similar to their C counterparts.

PHP provides functions for working with PostgreSQL's BLOBs as well. In addition to the functions related to BLOBs, you can work with hexadecimal data, which can be stored in ordinary text variables.

13

Working with Persistent Database Connections

Persistent database connections are a core feature of PHP. For many years PHP has been famous for this feature, and many people rely on it in order to gain speed and to write more efficient database applications. In this chapter you will learn about the advantages and dangers of persistent connections. We will try to dispel the myth surrounding persistent connections, and you will learn what persistent database connections are not about.

13.1 The Concept of Persistent Database Connections

This section examines the concepts related to persistent database connections in PHP.

Many people think that persistent connections can be used to have one database connection during an entire session. In other words, you connect to the database when you enter an online shop and quit it when you leave the shop. This is *not* what persistent connections are all about. HTTP is not a connection-oriented protocol, so it is not possible to use the same database handle across more than just one screen. In addition, database handles are automatically destroyed at the end of a PHP script, so it is not possible to pass the database handle to the next screen. This is a very important point that you must keep in mind when working with PHP.

The main idea of persistent database connections is that the time needed for user authentication is reduced significantly. This goal can be achieved by "connection recycling." What does connection recycling mean? PHP keeps an internal pool of open connections related to a certain database, user, and host. Every time a user wants to connect to the database, PHP looks to see if there is a spare open connection in the pool and assigns it to the new user. If no spare connection is available, PHP attempts to establish a new connection to the database. As soon as the user disconnects, the connection won't be terminated, but it will be available in the pool of free connections again. With the help of this algorithm, many user authentication processes are saved, so a lot of performance can be gained. For users working with persistent instead of nonpersistent connections, this makes no difference in most cases. However, you will learn in this chapter that there are some things you have to take care of.

13.2 An Example

Now that we've reviewed the theoretical background of persistent database connections with PHP and PostgreSQL, it's time to take a look at some practical examples.

If you are a user of PostgreSQL 7.2, you will see that two processes are running at startup time. You can easily find this out by piping the content of the process table to grep:

```
[hs@athlon html]$ ps ax | grep postgres
21647 pts/4    S      0:00 postgres: stats buffer process
21649 pts/4    S      0:00 postgres: stats collector process
 4338 pts/4    S      0:00 grep postgres
```

Let's write a script that does nothing but connect to the database and display a message:

```php
<?php
        $dbh = pg_connect("host=localhost user=postgres dbname=phpbook");
        if      (!$dbh)
        {
                echo "error while connecting.<br>\n";
        }
        else
        {
                echo "connection established<br>\n";
        }
?>
```

As you can see in the next listing, the number of processes running has not changed, although the connection to the database has not been closed explicitly:

```
[hs@athlon html]$ ps ax | grep postgres
21647 pts/4    SW      0:00 postgres: stats buffer process
21649 pts/4    SW      0:00 postgres: stats collector process
 4344 pts/4    S       0:00 grep postgres
```

All processes started by PHP have been removed without any problems. In the next step you can modify the PHP script you just saw by changing the command used for connecting to the database to pg_pconnect:

```php
<?php
        $dbh = pg_pconnect("host=localhost user=postgres dbname=phpbook");
        if      (!$dbh)
        {
                echo "error while connecting.<br>\n";
        }
        else
        {
                echo "connection established<br>\n";
        }
?>,
```

The script still does the same thing, but this time a persistent connection to the database is established. If you take a look at all active PostgreSQL processes now, the situation will look different:

```
[hs@athlon html]$ ps ax | grep postgres
21647 pts/4    S       0:00 postgres: stats buffer process
21649 pts/4    S       0:00 postgres: stats collector process
 4347 pts/4    S       0:00 postgres: postgres phpbook 127.0.0.1 idle
 4349 pts/4    S       0:00 grep postgres
```

One active connection is still in memory because it has not been closed at the end of the PHP script. If you execute the PHP script more often than once, PostgreSQL will not always create a new backend process because running backends can be reused, and this will save time and reduce the load on your database.

13.3 Persistent Connections and Performance

After giving you a slight insight into PHP's internals and after you have seen what processes are running, it's time to have a look at what effects on speed persistent database connections have.

The next example shows a script that connects and disconnects to the database 25,000 times. In addition, the average time needed to connect to a database once is computed:

```php
<?php
        $number = 25000;                        # Number of connections

        $begin = time();                        # Starting time
        for     ($i = 0; $i < $number; $i++)
        {
                $dbh = pg_pconnect("host=localhost
                        user=postgres dbname=phpbook");
                if      (!$dbh)
                {
                        echo "error while connecting.<br>\n";
                }
                pg_close($dbh);
        }
        $end = time();                          # Ending time
        $diff = $end - $begin;                  # Overall time
        $tpconn = $diff / $number;              # Time per connection

        # displaying result
        echo "Begin: $begin<br>\n";
        echo "End: $end<br>\n";
        echo "Overall time: $diff<br>\n";
        printf("Time per connection: %9.8f<br>\n", $tpconn);
?>
```

At the beginning of the script the time before connecting to the database is computed. The time is returned in seconds since January 1, 1970. In the next step the connections to the database are established. In this scenario, persistent connections are established.

After that, the time is retrieved again and computations are performed. Finally, the values are displayed on the screen:

```
Begin: 1008540275
End: 1008540276
Overall time: 1
Time per connection: 0.00004000
```

As you can see, 25,000 connections can be established in about one second if a pool of connections is already in memory. The time needed for establishing one connection is extremely low because PHP does not have to ask PostgreSQL for user authentication.

With nonpersistent connections, the situation is different. Every time a connection has to be established, a backend process has to be started and PostgreSQL has to check for things like database, user, password, and so forth. In other words, it is a lot of work to establish a connection to the database. Depending on what kind of authentication you are using (trust, password, Kerberos, and so forth), the time needed for authentication will vary significantly.

In the next scenario we try to connect to the same database using the same script. This time, nonpersistent connections are used. To reduce the time of the script, we have used 250 connections instead of 25,000 connections. The next listing shows what comes out when running this scenario:

```
Begin: 1008541909
End: 1008541917
Overall time: 8
Time per connection: 0.03200000
```

It takes 8 seconds to establish 250 connections, which means that it takes .03 seconds to establish one connection. Keep in mind that the connection is established to the local machine where all users are trusted users.

Let's modify pg_hba.conf and run the script using the official IP of the machine. Here is a modified version of pg_hba.conf:

```
local    all                                                trust
host     all        127.0.0.1       255.255.255.255         trust
hostssl  phpbook    212.186.25.254  255.255.255.255         crypt
```

To activate the changes, you can restart PostgreSQL (don't forget to activate SSL using the postmaster's -l flag as you saw in Chapter 10, "PostgreSQL Administration"). To understand the pg_hba.conf file, take a look at Chapter 10 again.

In addition to changing pg_hba.conf, a new user can be created:

```
phpbook=# CREATE USER testuser WITH PASSWORD 'mypasswd';
CREATE USER
```

In the next step you can use the script in the next listing to connect to the database:

```php
<?php
        $number = 250;                                  # Number of connections

        $begin = time();                                # Starting time
        for     ($i = 0; $i < $number; $i++)
        {
                $dbh = pg_connect("host=212.186.25.254 port=5432
                        user=testuser password=mypasswd dbname=phpbook");
                if      (!$dbh)
                {
                        echo "error while connecting.<br>\n";
                }
                pg_close($dbh);
        }
        $end = time();                                  # Ending time
        $diff = $end - $begin;                          # Overall time
        $tpconn = $diff / $number;                      # Time per connection

        # displaying result
        echo "Begin: $begin<br>\n";
        echo "End: $end<br>\n";
        echo "Overall time: $diff<br>\n";
        printf("Time per connection: %9.8f<br>\n", $tpconn);
?>
```

This time the authentication process takes much longer because you have connected to the database using SSL:

```
Begin: 1008544555
End: 1008544581
Overall time: 26
Time per connection: 0.10400000
```

In this scenario, working with persistent database connections is about 2600 times faster than working with nonpersistent SSL connections. Of course, persistent connections can hardly be compared with nonpersistent SSL connections, but it shows how much performance can be gained by using persistent database connections. When working with databases for building dynamic Web sites, the time needed to connect to the database is often underestimated. However, authentication is a crucial point and should be taken into consideration when planning high-performance systems.

13.4 Dangers and Hardware Issues

Up to now you have seen that persistent connections can be used to gain a lot of performance, which is positive. However, persistent database connections can also be a dangerous thing to use. In this section you will learn about these dangers and you will take a closer look at some other aspects such as memory consumption and system configuration.

13.4.1 Operating System Issues

When working with persistent database connections, it can easily happen that the standard configuration of your system is not enough. With persistent connections, the number of open connections, in many cases, is higher than when working with nonpersistent connections. This will lead to higher consumption of filehandles, memory, and other system resources. In some cases, the configuration of your system needs to be changed in order to achieve higher performance and to keep the system up and running. If you have to change system overall settings, check out Chapter 10 to see how the most important settings can be changed. Keep in mind that in the event of failure, the problem might have nothing to do with PostgreSQL but could be caused by the configuration of the underlying operating system. In that case, it is important to find the bottleneck and to reconfigure your system.

13.4.2 Transactions

Persistent database connections and transactions are a crucial point. If your application is not fully debugged, you can easily run into severe problems that are difficult to solve. Let's take a look at a simple scenario.

First you can create a table:

```
phpbook=# CREATE TABLE course (id int4, name text, description text);
CREATE
```

In the listing, you can see a script using explicit transactions:

```
<?php
        $dbh = pg_pconnect("user=postgres dbname=phpbook");
        if      (!$dbh) { echo "cannot connect to database<br>\n"; }

        $stat = pg_exec($dbh, "BEGIN");
        if      (!$stat) { echo "Transaction cannot be started<br>\n"; }

        echo "attempting to insert data<br>\n";
        $sql = "INSERT INTO course VALUES (9, 'C Programming', NULL)";
```

```
$stat = pg_exec($dbh, $sql);
if      (!$stat) { echo "Cannot insert data<br>\n"; }

echo '<a href="data2.php">continue</a>';
pg_close($dbh);
?>
```

First a transaction is started and then a record is added to the table. The first time the script is executed, no problems occur:

```
attempting to insert data
continue
```

However, when executing the same script again, errors might occur. It is not certain that this error will occur (it depends on what you have done with the database before). Let's see what PHP will display:

```
Transaction cannot be started
attempting to insert data
Cannot insert data
continue
```

The transaction cannot be started because a transaction is already in progress. Recall that persistent database connections are recycled connections, which means that no new backend process has been started when executing the script the second time. Therefore the transaction is still open, and because PostgreSQL does not support nested transactions, an error occurs.

After executing the scripts twice, let's take a look at the content of the table:

```
phpbook=# SELECT * FROM course;
 id | name | description
----+------+-------------
(0 rows)
```

No records have been inserted into the table, but the bigger problem is that the system is in a way locked. There is no script committing the transaction and the backend process is not killed automatically. Therefore the entire system cannot be used any more unless the problem is solved by restarting the database.

When you're working with nonpersistent connections, a transaction is automatically rolled back at the end of a PHP file when the backend process related to a connection is destroyed. With persistent connections, this does not happen, so open transactions will be in your system if your applications have not been implemented properly.

13.5 Summary

Persistent database connections are an important and widely used feature of PHP. In combination with PostgreSQL, powerful and fast applications can be built because almost all overhead caused by authentication can be avoided. However, persistent database connections can in many cases be dangerous due to hardware and software issues.

When working with transactions, it is important to keep in mind that open transactions might stay in memory after a script has terminated. Therefore, errors that are difficult to find can occur.

PART IV

Advanced Technologies

IN THIS PART

14

Managing Regular Expressions

Today almost every high-level programming language provides tools for working with patterns and retrieving complex sequences of characters. Usually pattern matching is performed by using so-called regular expressions. In PHP, a library for handling regular expressions is provided. With the help of this library, it is possible to develop a completely new view of the data and to solve complex operations efficiently.

Regular expressions are essential, especially if you have to search for imprecise data. In some cases, you might not know exactly what you are looking for. Imagine a table for storing products. Somebody asks you to look for the product, but the only thing he knows about the product is that the product id starts with "5" and ends with "98." With the help of a simple regular expression, it is an easy task to find the appropriate product with just one line of code. With the propagation of Perl, regular expressions became more and more popular. Nowadays almost every high-level programming language available on Unix machines is capable of handling regular expressions that allow you to build powerful applications fast, easily, and reliably. When you are familiar with regular expressions, you don't want to live without them.

Depending on the software you are planning to use, the syntax and the meaning of a regular expression will vary. Every software package has a slightly different flavor of regular expressions, and this can make things confusing. In this chapter you will deal with regular expressions for PHP and SQL. Both PHP and SQL have strong capabilities for pattern matching and can be used efficiently. However, some major differences have to be taken into consideration.

14.1 Perl Style

PHP provides two major interfaces for working with regular expressions. One of these interfaces supports Perl-style regular expressions. For many years Perl has been known as the big player in the regular expression business. Because many people like Perl's way of dealing with pattern matching, a set of functions has been implemented into PHP as well.

14.1.1 `preg_match` and Regular Expression Fundamentals

In this section, the `preg_match` function and regular expression fundamentals will be discussed, and you will take a closer look at the most important pattern modifiers.

14.1.1.1 Pattern Modifiers

The first important function is called `preg_match` and it can be used to see whether a certain pattern can be found in a string. Let's take a look at an example:

```php
<?php
        $string = "Welcome to the chapter about regular expressions";
        if      (preg_match("/chapter/i", $string))
        {
                echo "substring can be found<br>\n";
        }
?>
```

First the string is defined. In the next line the script checks whether the string chapter can be found in $string. If so, a message is displayed. As you can see, preg_match accepts two parameters. The first parameter contains the pattern you are looking for. The second parameter contains the variable you want to check. Let's take a closer look at the first parameter: The regular expression has to start with a slash. After the slash the pattern will be listed. At the end of the pattern, a slash has to be added to tell PHP that the string containing the pattern is over. After the slash some options can be defined. In this example the option i is used, which means that PHP will not distinguish between uppercase and lowercase patterns. If chapter is spelled with uppercase letters, the script will still find the pattern:

```php
<?php
        $string = "Welcome To The Chapter About Regular Expressions";
        if      (preg_match("/chapter/i", $string))
        {
                echo "substring can be found<br>\n";
        }
?>
```

Another important pattern modifier supported by Perl-style regular expressions is the
m modifier. Normally ^ defines the beginning of a string. If the string contains a
newline character, ^ still defines the beginning of a string. If the m pattern modifier is
used, ^ matches every beginning of a line defined by a newline character. m works
the same way when working with $, which defines the end of a string. So that you
can understand how things work, we have included an example:

```php
<?php
    $string = "Welcome To\nThe Chapter About\nRegular Expressions";
    if      (preg_match("/^Th/m", $string))
    {
            echo "1: substring can be found<br>\n";
    }

    if      (preg_match("/^Th/", $string))
    {
            echo "2: substring can be found<br>\n";
    }
?>
```

The first regular expression matches the string because m tells PHP to look for the
substring Th after every newline character. The second regular expression does not
match because the beginning of the string is not Th. Therefore the output of the
script contains just one line:

```
1: substring can be found
```

Another important modifier that is also supported by Perl is s (PCRE_DOTALL). If s is
used, dots also match newline characters. If s is not enabled, dots do not match
newlines. Let's take a look at an example:

```php
<?php
    $string = "Welcome To\nThe Chapter About\nRegular Expressions";
    if      (preg_match("/To.The/s", $string))
    {
            echo "1: substring can be found<br>\n";
    }

    if      (preg_match("/To.The/", $string))
    {
            echo "2: substring can be found<br>\n";
    }
?>
```

The first regular expression matches because s is used and therefore dots match newline characters.

14.1.1.2 Metacharacters

Regular expressions support a set of metacharacters. Every metacharacter has a special meaning. Table 14.1 contains an overview of all important metacharacters.

TABLE 14.1   An Overview of Metacharacters

Symbol	Meaning
\	Escapes a character
^	Matches beginning of a string or a line (depending on whether m is set)
$	Matches end of a string depending on whether m is set
.	Matches one character
[	Starts character class definition
]	Ends character class definition
|	Starts alternative branch
(	Starts subpattern
)	Ends subpattern
?	Matches zero or one character
*	Matches 0 times or more often
+	Matches one time or more often
{	Starts min/max quantifier
}	Ends min/max quantifier

After you have seen which metacharacters are defined, it's time to take a closer look at some practical examples where you can see how these metacharacters can be used.

Escaping special characters is one of the most important things when working with regular expressions and PHP in general. To escape a character, you can use back-slashes. The next example shows how a bracket can be escaped:

```php
<?php
    $string = 'this is a bracket: ) ';
    if    (preg_match("/\)/", $string))
    {
            echo "substring can be found<br>\n";
    }
?>
```

The regular expression starts with a slash. In the next step a backslash is passed to the function to escape the bracket that comes after the backslash. Finally the regular expression is terminated by a slash. If the backslash is removed from the regular expression, an error will be displayed:

Warning: Compilation failed: unmatched parentheses at offset 0 in
/var/www/html/regexp.php on line **3**

One question that is often asked is how backslashes can be escaped when working
with regular expressions. The answer to this question is simple because escaping
backslashes is as simple as escaping any other metacharacter. The next example
shows how to escape two backslashes:

```php
<?php
        $string = 'these are two backslashes: \\ ';
        if      (preg_match("/\\\\/", $string))
        {
                echo "substring can be found<br>\n";
        }
?>
```

Four backslashes are needed to escape two backslashes. The reason is obvious: Two
backslashes are needed for obtaining one backslash. Therefore four backslashes make
two backslashes.

^ matches the beginning of a string. The counterpart of ^ is the $ metacharacter,
which matches the end of a string. The next example shows a way to look for the
string `hello`:

```php
<?php
        $string = 'hello';
        if      (preg_match("/^hello$/", $string))
        {
                echo "substring can be found<br>\n";
        }
?>
```

In many cases, regular expressions are used to search for data you do not know
precisely. Imagine a situation where you are looking for the string `hello` but you
don't know how it is spelled. This example might seem ridiculous, but in real-world
applications it is not. Most databases contain records that have been inserted by
users, and as you probably know, users make mistakes. Therefore, the data in the
database might not be what you have been looking for. Typos will lower the quality
of your data, but with the help of regular expressions it is possible to retrieve at least
some of the words that are not spelled correctly.

Let's take a look at the next example:

```php
<?php
        $string = "hello";
```

```
if      (preg_match("/hel.o/", $string))
{
        echo "1: substring can be found<br>\n";
}

$string = "helllllo";
if      (preg_match("/hel.*o/", $string))
{
        echo "2: substring can be found<br>\n";
}
?>
```

The first regular expression matches the string hello. The dot in the regular expression matches exactly one character. In this example the second l in hello is missing, but the regular expression still matches. Dots match exactly one character occurring exactly once. If you don't know if a character is in a string, the * metacharacter might be useful for you. The second regular expression in the script means that any set of characters can be found after the substring hel. At the end of the string there has to be an o. * matches zero or more than zero characters. In contrast, + matches one or more characters.

? is an additional metacharacter. It matches one character zero or one time.

Sometimes it is necessary to check whether entire sequences of characters occur more than a predefined number of times. Brackets can be used to combine a list of characters into one block. Then this block is treated just like one single character. In the next example you can see how this works:

```
<?php
        $string = "amadeus, amadeus, rock me amadeus";
        if      (preg_match("/(amadeus, )+/", $string))
        {
                echo "substring can be found<br>\n";
        }
?>
```

The string amadeus followed by a comma and a blank matches if it occurs once or more often. In this example the + tells PHP to treat the entire string as one symbol.

In the preceding scenario, you saw how + can be used. If a string should match two to three times, it is necessary to work with curly brackets as shown in the following listing:

```php
<?php
    $string = "amadeus, amadeus, rock me amadeus";
    if      (preg_match("/(amadeus, ){2,3}/", $string))
    {
        echo "substring can be found<br>\n";
    }
?>
```

The string is treated as one symbol again, but this time curly brackets are used instead of ?, +, or *.

If a block of characters has to match more than a certain number of times, one edge of the interval has to be omitted as shown in the next listing:

```php
<?php
    $string = "amadeus, amadeus, rock me amadeus";
    if      (preg_match("/(amadeus, ){3,}/", $string))
    {
        echo "substring can be found<br>\n";
    }
?>
```

In this example the regular expression does not match because the string in brackets can only be found twice, not three times.

Sometimes you are looking for words that are spelled slightly differently. An example is the words back and pack. The meaning of the two words is totally different, but the difference between the two words is only one letter. Both words can be retrieved by using just one regular expression:

```php
<?php
    $string = ' "back" does not mean "pack" ';
    if      (preg_match("/[bp]/", $string))
    {
        echo "substring can be found<br>\n";
    }
?>
```

With the help of square brackets, a list of characters can be defined. If one of the characters matches, the condition will be fulfilled. In this example the regular expression matches if either b or p can be found.

If you are looking for a set of characters such as the entire alphabet, it is not recommended to list every character. With regular expressions, it is possible to define a range of characters:

```php
<?php
        $string = 'Hello Pinky';
        if      (preg_match("/^[A-Za-z]/", $string))
        {
                echo "substring can be found<br>\n";
        }
?>
```

The regular expression in the listing matches if the string starts with a character, whether or not it is spelled in uppercase letters. However, in case-insensitive searching, it is also possible to use the i pattern-modifier instead of working with [A-Za-z]:

```php
<?php
        $string = 'Hello Pinky';
        if      (preg_match("/^[a-z]/i", $string))
        {
                echo "substring can be found<br>\n";
        }
?>
```

The script will return the same data as the script you have seen before, but the regular expression is shorter and written more efficiently.

Intervals can be seen as various branches. In some cases branches are used for checking entire blocks of records instead of a list of records:

```php
<?php
        $string = 'Hello Pinky';
        if      (preg_match("/(Pinky)|(Brain)/i", $string))
        {
                echo "substring can be found<br>\n";
        }
?>
```

The regular expression in the script matches the substrings Pinky and Brain. With the help of the | (pipe) symbol, it is possible to tell PHP to select the appropriate value from the list.

14.1.1.3 Special Symbols
Special data like line feeds, tabs, or hex values have to be escaped using a backslash. You have already seen that things like dollar signs and brackets must be escaped. In this section you will see that many other characters need special treatment. Table 14.2 contains an overview of all important special characters escaped by using a backslash.

TABLE 14.2   Special Symbols

Symbol	Meaning
\a	System bell (hex 07)
\cx	"Control + character", where x is any character
\e	Escape (hex 1B)
\f	Formfeed (hex 0C)
\n	Newline (hex 0A)
\r	Carriage return (hex 0D)
\t	Tab (hex 09)
\xhh	Character with hex code hh
\ddd	Character with octal code ddd, or backreference
\040	A space character
\40	Is the same, provided there are fewer than 40 previous capturing subpatterns
\7	Back reference
\11	Might be a back reference, or another way of writing a tab
\011	Tab
\0113	A tab followed by 3
\113	Is the character with octal code 113
\377	Is a byte consisting entirely of 1 bits
\81	Either a back reference, or a binary zero followed by the two characters "8" and "1"
\d	Any decimal digit
\D	Any character that is not a digit
\s	Any whitespace character
\S	Any character that is not a whitespace character
\w	Any word
\W	Any non-word character
\b	Word boundary
\B	Not a word boundary
\A	Start of subject
\Z	End of subject or newline at end
\z	End of subject independent of multiline mode

14.1.2 `preg_match_all`

To perform a global pattern match, PHP provides a command called `preg_match_all`. Let's take a look at the next example and see what the function can be used for:

```php
<?php
        $string = 'Hello Frank Drebin, Hello Frank Johnston';
        preg_match_all("/Hello Frank [DJ][a-z]*/i", $string, $out);
        print "pattern: ".$out[0][0]." --- ".$out[0][1]."<br>\n";
?>
```

The pattern matches two parts of the string passed to `preg_match_all`. The substrings found in $string will be stored in the array called $out. Let's execute the string and see what comes out:

```
pattern: Hello Frank Drebin --- Hello Frank Johnston
```

Every cell contains exactly one value.

You might already have wondered why $out is a two-dimensional and not a one-dimensional array. `preg_match_all` supports subpatterns that can be defined using brackets. These subpatterns can be retrieved as well. Let's take a look at an example:

```php
<?php
        $string = 'Hello Frank Drebin, Hello Frank Johnston';
        preg_match_all("/(Hello) Frank ([DJ][a-z]*)/i", $string, $out);
        print "zero: ".$out[0][0]." --- ".$out[0][1]."<br>\n";
        print "one: ".$out[1][0]." --- ".$out[1][1]."<br>\n";
        print "two: ".$out[2][0]." --- ".$out[2][1]."<br>\n";
?>
```

The first subpattern in the regular expression is `Hello`. The second subpattern is (`[DJ][a-z]*`). The second element on the first axis of the array will contain a substring matching the first subpattern. The third element on the first axis of the array will contain the substring matching the second subpattern, and so on. To make PHP's behavior clearer, it is worth looking at the output of the script:

```
zero: Hello Frank Drebin --- Hello Frank Johnston
one: Hello --- Hello
two: Drebin --- Johnston
```

$out[0] contains the two substrings ($out[0][0] and $out[0][1]) matching the entire regular expression. $out[1] contains the two substrings matching the first subpattern. The same applies to $out[2]. With the help of subpatterns, it is possible to build brief yet powerful and flexible applications. The advantage of subpatterns is that you need just one regular expression to retrieve multiple patterns, which is more efficient than working with a set of regular expressions.

14.1.3 `preg_replace`

Up to now you have seen how to retrieve data from a string. In the next step you will learn how strings can be modified to your needs using regular expressions. The command for replacing patterns is called `preg_replace` and works as shown in the next example:

```
<?php
        $string = 'Hello Frank Drebin, Hello Frank Johnston';
        $string = preg_replace("/Hello/i", "Welcome", $string);
        print $string;
?>
```

The string Hello should be replaced by Welcome. To perform the task, three parameters have to be passed to preg_replace. The first parameter defines the pattern you
are looking for, the second parameter contains the new string, and the third parameter contains the string you want to process. If the script is executed, the desired
result will be displayed:

```
Welcome Frank Drebin, Welcome Frank Johnston
```

Sometimes it is useful to perform more than one substitution at once. This will save
you a lot of execution time and make your code shorter. The next example shows
how two patterns are substituted for new values:

```
<?php
        $string = 'Jeanny, quit living on dreams';
        $pattern = array("/Jeanny/", "/dreams/");
        $newvals = array("Carlos", "a prayer");

        $string = preg_replace($pattern, $newvals, $string);
        print $string;
?>
```

Jeanny is substituted for Carlos and dreams will be changed to the string a prayer:

```
Carlos, quit living on a prayer
```

In this section you have seen that PHP has always substituted all patterns found in
the string. This is not always the way you want it to be. Therefore, PHP provides a
method for defining how often a pattern must be substituted for. The next script
shows how only the first pattern found in the string can be substituted for a new
value:

```
<?php
        $string = 'Jeanny oh Jeanny quit living on dreams';

        $string = preg_replace("/Jeanny/", "Carlos", $string, 1);
        print $string;
?>
```

Just add thenumber of substitutions you want PHP to perform to the function. In this scenario only one change has been made:

```
Carlos oh Jeanny quit living on dreams
```

As you can see, it is an easy task to perform multiple changes, and it is easy to write complex applications with just a few lines.

14.1.4 preg_split

Splitting a string with the help of regular expressions is one of the most important tasks. You have already seen in Chapter 3, "PHP Basics," how strings can be split using other strings. In this section you will learn to work with regular expressions.

In the next example a list of words should be extracted and transformed to an array. The string called $string contains four names that are separated by commas and a variable number of whitespace characters:

```php
<?php
        $string = 'Jeanny, Carlos,Amadeus,   Falco';

        $result = preg_split("/,\s*/", $string);
        foreach ($result as $x)
        {
                print "x: $x<br>";
        }
?>
```

In this example it does not matter if two words are divided by a blank or any other whitespace character because \s has been used. If the script is executed, all four names will be retrieved and displayed utilizing a loop:

```
x: Jeanny
x: Carlos
x: Amadeus
x: Falco
```

In some cases it might be useful to extract only the first few words of a string. Therefore, preg_split provides a parameter that defines the number of components you want in the result:

```php
<?php
        $string = 'Jeanny, Carlos,Amadeus,   Falco';

        $result = preg_split("/,\s*/", $string, 2);
```

```
        foreach ($result as $x)
        {
                print "x: $x<br>";
        }
?>
```

This time the result will only be two lines long because the input string has been divided into two parts:

```
x: Jeanny
x: Carlos,Amadeus, Falco
```

If all components should be retrieved, it is either possible to omit the third parameter or to use -1 instead:

```
<?php
        $string = 'Jeanny, Carlos,,Amadeus,   Falco';

        $result = preg_split("/,\s*/", $string, -1);
        foreach ($result as $x)
        {
                print "x: $x<br>";
        }
?>
```

The result will be the same as if you had not used a parameter. Five lines will be displayed as shown in the next listing:

```
x: Jeanny
x: Carlos
x:
x: Amadeus
x: Falco
```

As you can see, in the third line of the result PHP retrieves empty fields as well. In many cases this can be a problem because you might only want to have those fields that are not empty. Therefore, PHP provides a parameter:

```
<?php
        $string = 'Jeanny, Carlos,,Amadeus,   Falco';

        $result = preg_split("/,\s*/", $string, -1, PREG_SPLIT_NO_EMPTY);
        foreach ($result as $x)
        {
```

```
        print "x: $x<br>";
    }
?>
```

PREG_SPLIT_NO_EMPTY makes PHP return all nonempty fields:

```
x: Jeanny
x: Carlos
x: Amadeus
x: Falco
```

As you can see, the empty field is neglected and will not be displayed in the output.

14.1.5 preg_quote

In this chapter you already saw that special characters must be escaped in order not to be mixed up with other characters. With complex strings this can be uncomfortable. To get around the problem, you can use a function called preg_quote. Just pass the string to the function and the result will be returned:

```
<?php
    $result = preg_quote("$ + $ = $");
    print $result;
?>
```

In this example the symbols $, +, and = have to be escaped. Therefore the result contains a lot of backslashes:

```
\$ \+ \$ \= \$
```

By default the characters in the input string are escaped to match regular expression syntax. Sometimes it is necessary to escape additional characters. In the next example you can see how the a characters can be escaped:

```
<?php
    $result = preg_quote("Heaven is a place on earth", "a");
    print $result;
?>
```

In the result, all as have been escaped using a backslash:

```
He\aven is \a pl\ace on e\arth
```

14.1.6 `preg_grep`

To scan entire arrays for patterns, PHP provides a function called `preg_grep`. The result of the function is an array containing all matches in the array:

```php
<?php
        $string[0] = "Hello Austria";
        $string[1] = "Hello Vienna";
        $string[2] = "Welcome to Paris";

        $result = preg_grep("/Hello [AV][a-z]+/", $string);
        foreach ($result as $str)
        {
                echo "$str<br>";
        }
?>
```

First, an array is defined. In the next step, `preg_grep` is called and all fields matching the regular expression are stored in `$result`. When you execute the script, two lines will be returned:

```
Hello Austria
Hello Vienna
```

14.2 POSIX Style

In addition to Perl-style regular expressions, PHP supports POSIX-style regular expressions. Depending on which style you like best, you can decide whether you want to use Perl-style or POSIX-style regular expressions.

PHP supports a set of functions related to regular expressions:

- `ereg`—Looks for matches

- `ereg_replac`—Performs substitutions

- `eregi`—Performs case-insensitive matching

- `eregi_replac`—Performs substitutions based on case-insensitive matching

- `split`—Splits a string based on regular expressions

- `spliti`—Splits a string based on regular expressions based on case-insensitive matching

- `sql_regcase`—Creates a regular expression matching the string passed to the function

After you have seen which functions are provided by PHP, you will see how these functions can be used.

14.2.1 ereg

If a substring matches a regular expression, true is returned. In POSIX-style regular expressions, no slashes are needed to mark the beginning and the end of a regular expression, as you can see in the next example:

```php
<?php
        $string = "Regular expressions are cool";

        if      (ereg("cool", $string))
        {
                echo "Yeah, regular expressions are cool<br>";
        }
?>
```

The regular expression matches the string, so the echo command will be executed.

In many cases it can be useful to retrieve the substrings matching the regular expression. Therefore, you must define a parameter defining the name of the array, which you want the matching substrings to be stored in. This way it is possible to find out how many components have been retrieved from the string:

```php
<?php
        $string = "Regular expressions are cool";

        if      (ereg("cool", $string, $regs))
        {
                echo "Yeah, regular expressions are cool<br>";
                echo "Matches: $regs[0]<br>";
        }
?>
```

In this scenario only one word matches the regular expression:

```
Yeah, regular expressions are cool
Matches: cool
```

As you can see, the result is stored in the array defined by the third parameter of the ereg function.

14.2.2 `ereg_replace`

Searching for substrings is not enough. The power of regular expressions lies in the ability to change strings satisfying an expression. With the help of the `ereg_replace` command, substitutions can be performed:

```php
<?php
        $string = "Regular expressions are cool";

        $string = ereg_replace("cool", "great", $string);
        echo "String: $string<br>";
?>
```

When you execute the script, one line will be displayed:

```
String: Regular expressions are great
```

14.2.3 `eregi`

The `eregi` function does the same sort of searching as the `ereg` function, but `eregi` performs case-insensitive searching instead of case-sensitive searching.

The next example shows how you can find out if `$string` contains the word BEER:

```php
<?php
        $string = "Epi is looking for free beer";

        if      (eregi("BE{2}R", $string))
        {
                echo "Epi seems to like beer ...<br>";
        }
?>
```

Although the word BEER is spelled in uppercase letters, the string matches the regular expression. If the script is executed, you will find out that Epi seems to like beer.

```
Epi seems to like beer ...
```

14.2.4 `eregi_replace`

The `eregi_replace` function is the counterpart of the `ereg_replace` function. In contrast to the `ereg_replace` function, `eregi_replace` performs case-insensitive searching.

Let's take a look at an example:

```php
<?php
        $string = "Epi is looking for free beer";
        $string = eregi_replace("ep+i", "Hans", $string);
        echo "$string<br>";
?>
```

In the string processed by the regular expression, Epi has been spelled in uppercase letters. In the regular expression, the E in Epi is spelled in lowercase letters. However, $string matches the regular expression because eregi_replace performs case-insensitive pattern matching.

14.2.5 sql_regcase

To generate a regular expression matching a string, you can use the function sql_regcase. The regular expression generated by the function performs case-insensitive matching and can be used directly by calling almost any other function related to POSIX-style regular expressions. The next example shows how a string can be transformed into a regular expression matching the string itself:

```php
<?php
        $string = "check out www.postgreql.at";
        $result = sql_regcase($string);
        echo "result: $result<br>\n";
?>
```

sql_regcase is called with just one parameter. Let's see what comes out when the script is executed:

```
result: [Cc][Hh][Ee][Cc][Kk] [Oo][Uu][Tt] [Ww][Ww][Ww].[Pp][Oo][Ss][Tt][Gg]
[Rr][Ee][Qq][Ll].[Aa][Tt]
```

As you can see, a simple regular expression has been generated.

14.3 Regular Expressions and SQL

Database-driven applications have to process huge amounts of data. If pattern matching with the help of regular expressions is performed by PHP, the entire data has to be transferred to the Web server where the PHP interpreter is running. With huge amounts of data, this is not a good solution because a large amount of memory and network bandwidth is wasted. Therefore, it can be useful to utilize regular expressions on the database level. PostgreSQL is capable of working with regular expressions. In some cases this is the more efficient way because of less overhead.

In this section you will learn about regular expressions and SQL.

14.3.1 Getting Started with SQL Regular Expressions

Working with SQL-style regular expressions is easy. However, it is important to understand the basic differences and specifics.

Let's create a table and insert some records into it:

```
CREATE TABLE product (
        id int4,              -- product id
        name text,            -- name of product
        prodtype text,        -- type of product
        price numeric(9,2),   -- price of product
        instock int4          -- number of products available
);


COPY product FROM stdin USING DELIMITERS ';';
34543532;The Pinky and the Brain in Vienna;Video;23.99;982
34543533;The Pinky and the Brain meet Elvis;Video;23.99;546
44545432;PostgreSQL Developer's Handbook;Book;44.99;40
44545433;PHP and PostgreSQL;Book;44.99;654
65665490;Falco Cybershow: Soundtrack;CD;23.49;60
65665491;Manifold Live;CD;23.69;129
\.
```

A table for storing products has been created and some records have been added to it using the COPY command. To see what is in the table, you can execute a simple SELECT statement:

```
phpbook=# SELECT * FROM product;
    id    |                name                | prodtype | price | instock
----------+------------------------------------+----------+-------+---------
 34543532 | The Pinky and the Brain in Vienna  | Video    | 23.99 |     982
 34543533 | The Pinky and the Brain meet Elvis | Video    | 23.99 |     546
 44545432 | PostgreSQL Developer's Handbook    | Book     | 44.99 |      40
 44545433 | PHP and PostgreSQL                 | Book     | 44.99 |     654
 65665490 | Falco Cybershow: Soundtrack        | CD       | 23.49 |      60
 65665491 | Manifold Live                      | CD       | 23.69 |     129
(6 rows)
```

The target of the next query is to retrieve only those records containing the string PostgreSQL. Therefore the ~ can be used. ~ performs case-sensitive substring matching and returns all records satisfying the expression:

```
phpbook=# SELECT * FROM product WHERE name ~ 'PostgreSQL';
     id    |               name                | prodtype | price | instock
----------+-----------------------------------+----------+-------+---------
 44545432 | PostgreSQL Developer's Handbook   | Book     | 44.99 |      40
 44545433 | PHP and PostgreSQL                | Book     | 44.99 |     654
(2 rows)
```

In this example two records have been returned. If postgresql is spelled in lowercase letters, no records will be found:

```
phpbook=# SELECT * FROM product WHERE name ~ 'postgresql';
 id | name | prodtype | price | instock
----+------+----------+-------+---------
(0 rows)
```

The ~ is case-sensitive, so no records match the expression. To perform case-insensitive pattern matching, PostgreSQL provides the ~* operator:

```
phpbook=# SELECT * FROM product WHERE name ~* 'postgresql';
     id    |               name                | prodtype | price | instock
----------+-----------------------------------+----------+-------+---------
 44545432 | PostgreSQL Developer's Handbook   | Book     | 44.99 |      40
 44545433 | PHP and PostgreSQL                | Book     | 44.99 |     654
(2 rows)
```

Two records have been found.

Sometimes it is necessary to find all records that do not match a regular expression. Therefore, PostgreSQL provides the !~ operator. Just like when working with the ~ operator, PostgreSQL performs case-sensitive pattern matching:

```
phpbook=# SELECT * FROM product WHERE name !~ 'PostgreSQL';
     id    |               name                | prodtype | price | instock
----------+-----------------------------------+----------+-------+---------
 34543532 | The Pinky and the Brain in Vienna | Video    | 23.99 |     982
 34543533 | The Pinky and the Brain meet Elvis| Video    | 23.99 |     546
 65665490 | Falco Cybershow: Soundtrack       | CD       | 23.49 |      60
 65665491 | Manifold Live                     | CD       | 23.69 |     129
(4 rows)
```

All four records that do not contain PostgreSQL are retrieved.

To perform case-insensitive matching, you can use the !~* operator:

```
phpbook=# SELECT * FROM product WHERE name !~* 'postgresql';
    id     |              name               | prodtype | price | instock
-----------+---------------------------------+----------+-------+---------
 34543532  | The Pinky and the Brain in Vienna | Video  | 23.99 |     982
 34543533  | The Pinky and the Brain meet Elvis | Video | 23.99 |     546
 65665490  | Falco Cybershow: Soundtrack     | CD       | 23.49 |      60
 65665491  | Manifold Live                   | CD       | 23.69 |     129
(4 rows)
```

Sometimes it is necessary to see if the beginning of a string matches a certain pattern. In this case you can include the ^ symbol in the regular expression. ^ matches the beginning of a string as shown in the next example:

```
phpbook=# SELECT * FROM product WHERE name ~* '^postgresql';
    id     |            name             | prodtype | price | instock
-----------+-----------------------------+----------+-------+---------
 44545432  | PostgreSQL Developer's Handbook | Book | 44.99 |      40
(1 row)
```

One record has been found because there is only one product whose name starts with PostgreSQL. The counterpart of ^ is the $ symbol, which matches the end of a string. Let's take a look at an example:

```
phpbook=# SELECT * FROM product WHERE name ~* 'elvis$';
    id     |              name               | prodtype | price | instock
-----------+---------------------------------+----------+-------+---------
 34543533  | The Pinky and the Brain meet Elvis | Video | 23.99 |     546
(1 row)
```

Only one record has been retrieved because the Pinky and the Brain videotape is the only one about Elvis.

If you don't know how to spell Pinky correctly, you can use square brackets to tell PostgreSQL that one of the characters in brackets is the correct one. In this scenario you don't know whether to spell Pinky with b or p:

```
phpbook=# SELECT * FROM product WHERE name ~* '[bp]inky';
    id     |              name               | prodtype | price | instock
-----------+---------------------------------+----------+-------+---------
 34543532  | The Pinky and the Brain in Vienna | Video  | 23.99 |     982
 34543533  | The Pinky and the Brain meet Elvis | Video | 23.99 |     546
(2 rows)
```

Two records have been found; both contain the string Pinky.

As you have already seen in the sections about Perl-style and POSIX-style regular expressions, the * symbol is used for working with repeatable characters or subpatterns. The * symbol is also supported by SQL-style regular expressions:

```
phpbook=# SELECT * FROM product WHERE name ~* 'handbo*k';
    id     |             name              | prodtype | price | instock
-----------+-------------------------------+----------+-------+---------
  44545432 | PostgreSQL Developer's Handbook | Book     | 44.99 |      40
(1 row)
```

In the following scenario, the word handbook can be spelled with zero or more os. One record matches the regular expression. To define a subpattern, brackets can be used. The syntax is the same as you have already seen when dealing with Perl- and POSIX-style regular expressions:

```
phpbook=# SELECT * FROM product WHERE name ~* 'handb(o)*k';
    id     |             name              | prodtype | price | instock
-----------+-------------------------------+----------+-------+---------
  44545432 | PostgreSQL Developer's Handbook | Book     | 44.99 |      40
(1 row)
```

The same record has been returned. In addition to the * symbol, PostgreSQL supports + and ? as well, as shown in the next two examples:

```
phpbook=# SELECT * FROM product WHERE name ~* 'handbo+k';
    id     |             name              | prodtype | price | instock
-----------+-------------------------------+----------+-------+---------
  44545432 | PostgreSQL Developer's Handbook | Book     | 44.99 |      40
(1 row)
```

```
phpbook=# SELECT * FROM product WHERE name ~* 'handboo?k';
    id     |             name              | prodtype | price | instock
-----------+-------------------------------+----------+-------+---------
  44545432 | PostgreSQL Developer's Handbook | Book     | 44.99 |      40
(1 row)
```

14.3.2 Escaping Characters

Escaping characters is important when working with SQL-style regular expressions. The syntax is the same as the one you already saw when dealing with Perl- and POSIX-style regular expressions.

One way to escape a character is to use a backslash:

```
phpbook=# SELECT * FROM product WHERE name ~* 'Developer\'s';
    id    |              name               | prodtype | price | instock
----------+---------------------------------+----------+-------+---------
 44545432 | PostgreSQL Developer's Handbook | Book     | 44.99 |      40
(1 row)
```

The single quote in `Developer's` is escaped and this way the entire string can be retrieved easily. An additional method to escape a single quote would be to use two single quotes:

```
phpbook=# SELECT * FROM product WHERE name ~* 'Developer''s';
    id    |              name               | prodtype | price | instock
----------+---------------------------------+----------+-------+---------
 44545432 | PostgreSQL Developer's Handbook | Book     | 44.99 |      40
(1 row)
```

This syntax is already familiar to you—when working with PL/pgSQL, you use the same syntax.

14.3.3 LIKE

LIKE is oneof the most widespread keywords when dealing with regular expressions on a database level. The idea of LIKE is to have a keyword for working with regular expressions rather than having a set of operators.

The way LIKE works differs slightly from the regular expressions you have just seen. Let's take a look at an example:

```
phpbook=# SELECT * FROM product WHERE name LIKE 'handboo?k';
 id | name | prodtype | price | instock
----+------+----------+-------+---------
(0 rows)
```

No values are returned because LIKE looks for complete matches and does not perform substring searching. To tell PostgreSQL that some characters might be found before and after the string Handbook, you have to add a % symbol:

```
phpbook=# SELECT * FROM product WHERE name LIKE '%Handbook%';
    id    |              name               | prodtype | price | instock
----------+---------------------------------+----------+-------+---------
 44545432 | PostgreSQL Developer's Handbook | Book     | 44.99 |      40
(1 row)
```

This way a record will be retrieved. With the help of LIKE, case-sensitive matching is performed: If the string Handbook is spelled with lowercase letters, no records will be returned.

```
phpbook=# SELECT * FROM product WHERE name LIKE '%handbook%';
 id | name | prodtype | price | instock
----+------+----------+-------+---------
(0 rows)
```

This is an important point that is often forgotten. To get around the problem, you can use the lower function:

```
phpbook=# SELECT * FROM product WHERE lower(name) LIKE '%handbook%';
    id     |               name               | prodtype | price | instock
-----------+----------------------------------+----------+-------+---------
  44545432 | PostgreSQL Developer's Handbook  | Book     | 44.99 |      40
(1 row)
```

lower computes the lowercase of a string. This way it does not matter that LIKE performs case-sensitive matching. Another way to solve the problem is to use operators instead of LIKE. The ~~ is equal to the LIKE statement:

```
phpbook=# SELECT * FROM product WHERE lower(name) ~~ '%handbook%';
    id     |               name               | prodtype | price | instock
-----------+----------------------------------+----------+-------+---------
  44545432 | PostgreSQL Developer's Handbook  | Book     | 44.99 |      40
(1 row)
```

The case-insensitive counterpart of the ~~ operator is the ~~* operator. The next example shows how the same target can be achieved without using the lower function:

```
phpbook=# SELECT * FROM product WHERE name ~~* '%handbook%';
    id     |               name               | prodtype | price | instock
-----------+----------------------------------+----------+-------+---------
  44545432 | PostgreSQL Developer's Handbook  | Book     | 44.99 |      40
(1 row)
```

To find all values that do not match a LIKE clause, you can use NOT LIKE:

```
phpbook=# SELECT * FROM product WHERE name NOT LIKE '%Handbook%';
    id     |               name               | prodtype | price | instock
-----------+----------------------------------+----------+-------+---------
  34543532 | The Pinky and the Brain in Vienna | Video   | 23.99 |     982
  34543533 | The Pinky and the Brain meet Elvis | Video  | 23.99 |     546
```

```
44545433 | PHP and PostgreSQL               | Book   | 44.99 |   654
65665490 | Falco Cybershow: Soundtrack      | CD     | 23.49 |    60
65665491 | Manifold Live                    | CD     | 23.69 |   129
(5 rows)
```

LIKE is widely used by many SQL programmers and it is an easy task to get used to working with the command. However, in some cases it is more flexible to work with PostgreSQL's operators than with LIKE.

14.3.4 Regular Expressions and Performance

Although regular expressions are a tremendous advantage, there are some conditions that can lead to real trouble in real-time systems. When the amount of data processed by your application grows, the situation might become dangerous for various reasons.

The key to high performance is to have the right indexes defined on the appropriate columns. Let's define two indexes:

```
phpbook=# CREATE INDEX idx_product_id ON product(id);
CREATE
phpbook=# CREATE INDEX idx_product_name ON product(name);
CREATE
```

The target of the index is to optimize the query looking for the word postgresql:

```
phpbook=# SELECT * FROM product WHERE name ~* 'postgresql';
   id    |              name               | prodtype | price | instock
---------+---------------------------------+----------+-------+---------
44545432 | PostgreSQL Developer's Handbook | Book     | 44.99 |      40
44545433 | PHP and PostgreSQL               | Book     | 44.99 |     654
(2 rows)
```

To find out what PostgreSQL does internally, you can take a look at the execution plan of the query. As you can see, PostgreSQL performs a sequential scan, which means that the entire table is read:

```
phpbook=# EXPLAIN SELECT * FROM product WHERE name ~* 'postgresql';
NOTICE:  QUERY PLAN:

Seq Scan on product  (cost=0.00..1.07 rows=1 width=87)

EXPLAIN
```

Sometimes sequential scans are performed—even if they are not absolutely necessary. To make PostgreSQL use an index whenever possible, sequential scans can be turned off temporarily:

```
phpbook=# SET enable_seqscan TO off;
SET VARIABLE
```

After turning off sequential scans, you can use EXPLAIN again to see if something has changed:

```
phpbook=# EXPLAIN SELECT * FROM product WHERE name ~* 'postgresql';
NOTICE:  QUERY PLAN:

Seq Scan on product  (cost=100000000.00..100000001.08 rows=1 width=87)

EXPLAIN
```

PostgreSQL still performs a sequential scan. Even if you are looking for PostgreSQL at the beginning of the cell, the situation won't change:

```
phpbook=# EXPLAIN SELECT * FROM product WHERE name ~* '^postgresql';
NOTICE:  QUERY PLAN:

Seq Scan on product  (cost=100000000.00..100000001.08 rows=1 width=87)

EXPLAIN
```

The reason for PostgreSQL's behavior is clear and easy to understand. When scanning an index, the database checks whether the value you are looking for and the data in the index match. This operation is a simple comparison of two strings. Because a regular expression is much more complex than a string, there is no way of scanning an index to find a value matching a regular expression. This is an important point that you have to keep in mind when working with regular expressions. As long as the amount of data is comparatively low, this won't be a problem, but if you are looking for values in a table that consists of millions of tables, it will take a long time and the overall performance of your system will decrease.

In most cases there is no way to get around the problem, so regular expressions should be avoided if a lot of data has to be checked within a short period of time or in the case of a lot of concurrent queries.

14.4 Summary

Regular expressions are an old and hence reliable feature of PHP and PostgreSQL. The power of regular expressions helps you to retrieve complex strings with just a few lines of code.

One problem when working with regular expressions is that no indexes can be used. Especially when dealing with large amounts of data, this can be a problem.

15

Session Management

If you want to build applications such as Web shops, it is necessary to pass information from one screen to another. Up to now you have seen that data can be submitted using buttons. However, if the amount of information that must be sent across multiple screens grows, forms and hidden fields won't be enough to satisfy your demands. In this chapter, you will see how to implement sophisticated solutions easily.

15.1 Managing Sessions with Cookies

One way to identify users and to store data is to use cookies. For a long time cookies were the only solution for storing session data permanently, and they are still widely used today.

15.1.1 Cookie Fundamentals

HTTP is not a connection-oriented protocol, so cookies can be used to fake some sort of permanent interaction with the server. The idea of a cookie is to store information directly on the client. Whenever a site is called, the information in the appropriate cookie is sent to the server automatically. Keep in mind that the server does not look for the cookie—the information is sent to the server by the browser automatically. Let's look at a simple example:

```php
<?php
        setcookie ("YourName", "Hans-Jürgen Schönig");
        header("Content-type: text/html");

        echo "Your name has been added to the
cookie<br>\n";
?>

<a href="checkcookie.php">Go to next page</a>
```

The scriptsets a cookie that is called `YourName`. The value of the cookie is `Hans-Jürgen Schönig`, which is the name of the author of this book. Note that the cookie has been set before sending the header to the client. After that, a string and a link are displayed. If you click on the link, you will get to the script called `checkcookie.php`, which is shown in the next listing:

```php
<?php
        echo "Displaying information stored in cookie:<br>\n";
        if      ($YourName)
        {
                echo "Data stored in the cookie: $YourName<br>\n";
        }
        else
        {
                echo "no data has been stored in the cookie<br>\n";
        }
?>
```

The script checks whether `$YourName` exists. If the variable exists, its content is displayed onscreen. Otherwise the script will display an error. As you saw in the preceding listing, the name of the cookie is `YourName` as well. Note that there is no submit button, but the data in the cookie is still available in the second screen. If you click on the link, two lines will be displayed:

```
Displaying information stored in cookie:
Data stored in the cookie: Hans-Jürgen Schönig
```

The second line contains the data stored in the cookie.

The following list shows the components a cookie can have:

- `name`—Defines the name of a cookie
- `value`—Contains the value of a cookie
- `expires`—Defines the time the cookie will expire
- `domain`—Defines the domains the cookie is valid for
- `path`—Defines the path the cookie is valid for
- `secure`—Restricts cookie transmission to secure channels

In the preceding example, you saw how a cookie can be generated that lasts forever. In some cases this is not useful; if you want to use the cookie only for storing the content of a shopping cart, you don't want the data to stay in the cookie forever.

You can define the time a cookie is valid. In the next example you can see how to do this:

```php
<?php
        $t = time()+3600*24;
        setcookie("yourname","Shelley",$t,"/","postgresql.at");

        header("Content-type: text/html");
        echo "Your name has been added to the cookie<br>\n";
?>


<a href="checkcookie.php">Go to next page</a>
```

This time the current time is computed by calling PHP's time function. Then 24 hours are added to this timestamp and this value is taken to tell the cookie when to expire. In addition, we tell the cookie that it is valid for the entire domain called postgresql.at.

The machine the example has been tested on does not belong to the domain postgresql.at, so no data will be available in the script when you click on the link:

```
Displaying information stored in cookie:
no data has been stored in the cookie
```

In the preceding example you saw how to generate a cookie and how then to access the value of a cookie. In the next example, you will learn how to delete a cookie:

```php
<?php
        if      ($yourname)
        {
                $t = time()-1000;
                setcookie("yourname","",$t);

                header("Content-type: text/html");
                echo "deleting cookie ...<br>\n";
                echo "value of cookie was: $yourname<br>\n";
        }
        else
        {
                $t = time()+3600*24;
                setcookie("yourname","Shelley",$t);

                header("Content-type: text/html");
                echo "setting cookie ...<br>\n";
        }
```

```
        echo '<a href="main.php">Reload page</a>';
?>
```

The preceding script does nothing except generate a cookie if no cookie has been set, and delete the cookie if a cookie has been set already. As you can see in the `if` branch, a cookie can be deleted by setting the third parameter to a previous date. This way a cookie is marked as expired and will be deleted automatically. If you execute the script twice, the result will look like this:

```
deleting cookie ...
value of cookie was: Shelley
Reload page
```

15.1.2 Dangers

Cookies are easy to use, but when you use them extensively, there are also some problems you have to take care of. One thing is that many users have disabled cookies for security reasons. Another point is that problems can easily occur in combination with secure and insecure HTTP connections. In the next example you can see which problems can occur when you are working with secure and insecure connections.

Imagine a script called setcookie.php located at `http://www.cybertec.at/test/setcookie.php`. `http` means that the data is not transmitted via a secure channel. Let's look at the script:

```php
<?php
        $t = time()+3600*24;
        setcookie("yourname","Shelley",$t);

        echo "cookie has been set in insecure area<br>\n";
        echo '<a href="https://bachata.cybertec.at/test/secure.php">
                secure.php</a>';
?>
```

A cookie is set and a link to `https://bachata.cybertec.at/test/secure.php` is displayed. As you can see, this URL points to a secure HTTP area. However, both sites, `www.cybertec.at` and `https://bachata.cybertec.at`, are located on the same machine and they are in the same domain. Here's the script located in the secure area:

```php
<?php
        echo "secure area ...<br>\n";
        if      ($yourname)
```

```
        {
                echo "the cookie is still valid<br>\n";
        }
        else
        {
                echo "no cookie available<br>\n";
        }
?>
```

The script checks whether a cookie has been set. However, no data can be found:

```
no cookie available
```

The reason is that one script is located in the secure area, and the second script is in the insecure area. This can present a problem when working with online shops, because you might easily have to face a mixture of secure and insecure areas. This can be painful when writing applications, and therefore we don't recommend using cookies extensively.

15.2 Session Management

PHP's concept of session management is more sophisticated than working with cookies. With the help of sessions, it is possible to track a user without working with hidden fields or cookies explicitly. This has significant advantages. You gain a lot of flexibility, and working with sessions will help you to implement components much more efficiently.

Let's take a look at the basic concepts of session management. When a user visits a Web site, a unique id is assigned to the user. The session id is either stored in a cookie or is passed to the next script via the URL.

In addition to using a session id, you can register variables. These variables can easily be extracted again, and so it is a fairly easy task to pass information from one form to another.

15.2.1 Session Ids

Before working with registered variables, take a look at a basic example where sessions are used.

```
<?php
        @session_start();
        $sid = session_id();
```

```
        echo "Hello from a.php<br>\n";
        echo "This is your session id: $sid<br>\n";
?>
```

The first thing to do is to start a session. This can be compared to some sort of registration. In the next step the session id is generated. In this example, the script does nothing other than display the information onscreen:

```
Hello from a.php
This is your session id: 37f7c4e2a52c3c63b8b318b1d17fa810
```

As you can see, a session id is displayed. If you execute the script more than just once, the session id will be the same. If you understand why this happens, you understand the concept of session handling.

The next scenario consists of two parts. The file a.php is the starting point. The file b.php is the second file in the scenario. Let's start with a.php:

```php
<?php
        @session_start();
        $sid = session_id();

        echo "Hello from a.php<br>\n";
        echo "This is your session id: $sid<br><br>\n";

        echo "Let's go to b.php: ";
        echo '<a href="b.php">b.php</a>';
?>
```

As you can see, a link to b.php has been added to the scenario. Here's the code for b.php:

```php
<?php
        @session_start();
        $sid = session_id();

        echo "Hello from b.php<br>\n";
        echo "This is your session id: $sid<br><br>\n";

        echo "Let's go to a.php: ";
        echo '<a href="a.php">a.php</a>';
?>
```

The code in the file is almost the same as the one you just saw. If you go to a.php, you will see a session id. If you go to b.php, the same session id will be displayed again. If you go back to a.php, you will still have the same session id. No matter what you are doing, you will always have the same session id. However, if you close the browser and start it again, the session id will be different. This is an important point because it helps you to find out when a session is terminated.

Let's modify b.php again:

```php
<?php
        setcookie(session_name(),"","","/");
        @session_start();
        $sid = session_id();

        echo "Hello from b.php<br>\n";
        echo "This is your session id: $sid<br><br>\n";

        echo "Let's go to a.php: ";
        echo '<a href="a.php">a.php</a>';

        echo "<br>name of session: ".session_name()."<br>\n";
?>
```

As you have already seen, sessions can be cookie-driven. In this case a cookie is set. This cookie has the same name as the current session. Therefore a session can easily be deleted by setting the cookie to an invalid value as in this example. When you run the script now, you will see that the session id changes when calling a.php.

PHP offers a function called session_destroy(). However, this function does not do the same as what you have just seen. You must keep in mind that the session can be passed to the next screen using the URL as well, and you must take this into consideration when deleting a session.

15.2.2 Registering Variables

Passing data from one screen to another is an important task. PHP's session library provides an easy way to store variables across multiple screens. Variables can be registered within a session. These variables will be available automatically and can be used by the user safely.

Again, you will see a scenario consisting of two files. Let's have a look at a.php:

```php
<?php
        @session_start();
        $sid = session_id();
```

```
        echo "Hello from a.php<br>\n";
        echo "This is your session id: $sid<br><br>\n";
        echo "message: $message<br>\n";

        $message = "Registered in a.php<br>\n";
        session_register("message");

        echo "Let's go to b.php: ";
        echo '<a href="b.php">b.php</a>';
?>
```

After a session starts, the session id is displayed. In addition, a variable called $message will be displayed on screen. In the next step, $message is registered in the session. Finally a link to b.php is displayed:

```
<?php
        @session_start();
        $sid = session_id();

        echo "Hello from b.php<br>\n";
        echo "This is your session id: $sid<br><br>\n";
        echo "message: $message<br>\n";

        $message = "Registered in b.php<br>\n";
        session_register("message");

        echo "Let's go to a.php: ";
        echo '<a href="a.php">a.php</a>';
?>
```

It is the exact counterpart of a.php. It displays $message and registers it again. When you run the script, you will see that a variable will be available in the next script when you click on the link. In a.php, $message, which has been registered in b.php, will be displayed. In b.php, the variable defined in a.php will be displayed.

The output of b.php might look like this:

```
Hello from b.php
This is your session id: 963d468e5e21042a6175af7a53f0cc95

message: Registered in a.php

Let's go to a.php: a.php
```

The example shows quite well what working with registered variables is all about.
The only thing you have to do is to tell PHP which variables must be passed to the
next sheet. This will help you to avoid dozens of hidden fields, and it will save a lot
of overhead because the entire system works reliably.

Let's modify b.php again:

```php
<?php
        @session_start();
        $sid = session_id();

        echo "Hello from b.php<br>\n";
        echo "This is your session id: $sid<br><br>\n";
        echo "message: $message<br>\n";

        echo "Let's go to a.php: ";
        echo '<a href="a.php">a.php</a>';
?>
```

This time no variable is registered in b.php. In this case the content of $message will
always be "Registered in a.php". This is an important point because no data can
get lost when registering variables across multiple screens.

In the next step, you can see what happens to arrays and objects:

```php
<?php
        @session_start();
        $sid = session_id();

        $message = unserialize($x);
        echo "message 0: ".$message[0]."<br>";
        echo "message 1: ".$message[1]."<br>";

        $message[0] = "field number one\n";
        $message[1] = "field number two\n";
        $x = serialize($message);
        echo "serialized version: <br> $x<br>\n";
        session_register("x");

        echo "<br>Let's restart a.php: <br>";
        echo '<a href="a.php">a.php</a>';
?>
```

The most important point when you're working with arrays is to serialize them before calling `session_register`; otherwise, the system won't work. Serialization means that an object or an array is transformed to a string. This way it can be processed just like any other string. This is the fastest way to pass objects from one screen to another. To make an object out of a serialized string again, you can use `unserialize`.

Let's have a look at the output of the script shown in the preceding listing. You have to run it twice in order to see what happens:

```
message 0: field number one
message 1: field number two
serialized version:
a:2:{i:0;s:17:"field number one ";i:1;s:17:"field number two ";}

Let's restart a.php:
a.php
```

As you can see in the listing, the values are available. In addition, the serialized string has been displayed. It contains all the information you will need.

If you want to find out if a variable has already been registered, you can use the `session_is_registered` command. The next example shows how to use this command:

```php
<?php
        @session_start();
        $sid = session_id();

        $message = unserialize($x);
        $message[0] = "field number one\n";
        $message[1] = "field number two\n";
        $x = serialize($message);

        session_register("x");
        $val = session_is_registered("x");
        echo "val: $val<br>\n";

        session_unregister("x");
        $val = session_is_registered("x");
        echo "val: $val<br>\n";

        echo "<br>Let's restart a.php: <br>";
        echo '<a href="a.php">a.php</a>';
    ?>
```

The next listing shows what happens if you execute the script twice:

```
val: 1
val:

Let's restart a.php:
a.php
```

The first time, session_is_registered returns 1 because $x has been registered the line before. In the next step, $x is unregistered, so session_is_registered does not return 1 any more.

15.2.3 Additional Features

PHP's session library provides some additional features such as caching. However, these functions are not as important as the functions you have just dealt with. To avoid confusion, these functions won't be discussed here.

15.3 Summary

PHP offers two ways for working with sessions. One way is to use cookies. Cookies have some significant disadvantages over the second method, PHP's session library. Sessions can be used to store data across multiple screens and to track users. With the help of just a few simple functions, it is possible to simulate a connection-oriented protocol.

16

Working with Dynamic Documents, Images, and Movies

The main idea of every scripting language optimized for the Web is to generate dynamic documents. Dynamic documents are not just text or HTML documents; it is also possible to generate images, movies, or any other kind of document.

In the beginning, people built static Web sites. With the arrival of interfaces such as the CGI interface, people started developing dynamic Web sites. Building a dynamic Web site also means that in some situations it might be useful to generate dynamic images or movies.

PHP has been designed to satisfy all these demands and you will learn about dynamic documents generated by PHP and PostgreSQL in this chapter.

16.1 Creating Dynamic Images

PHP supports many functions for generating or modifying images on-the-fly. These functions are mostly built on the GD library, which you can download from `http://www.boutell.com/gd`. In most binary distributions of PHP, the GD module is included. If you are compiling your binaries yourself, the GD module has to be enabled at compile time using `--with-gd` when running `configure`. In addition, support for JPG should be enabled.

After you have compiled PHP to your needs, you can start working with the module. In this section you will learn to perform all basic operations when working with images and you will also see how text can be processed efficiently.

16.1.1 Basic Operations

The first thing to do when generating a picture is to create it. With PHP, this can easily be done with the help of the `ImageCreate` function. Just define the size of the image and a handle will be returned. This handle is used for all other operations.

The second thing to do is to allocate colors. This is an important point and you will see why allocating a color is a critical operation. To allocate a color, pass the handle of the image as well as the definition of the color to the function. Finally, the image has to be sent to the browser or stored in a file. The next example shows how to create an image. The background color of the image is set to black:

```php
<?php
        $image = ImageCreate (300, 300);
        if      (!$image)
        {
                echo "picture cannot be generated<br>\n";
        }
        else
        {
                header ("Content-type: image/png");
                $white = ImageColorAllocate($image, 255, 255, 255);
                $black = ImageColorAllocate($image, 0, 0, 0);
                $red = ImageColorAllocate($image, 255, 0, 0);
                $blue = ImageColorAllocate($image, 0, 0, 255);

                $status = imagefill($image, 1, 1, $black);
                ImagePng($image);
        }
?>
```

When executing the script, the image will be displayed by the browser directly. The reason for that is the header information. As you can see, the header tells the browser to treat the data from the Web server as an image. If other data is sent to the browser, it will not be treated as HTML because the browser is prepared for receiving a PNG file.

Sometimes it is necessary to load a picture from a file and to perform some modifications before sending it to the browser. Therefore PHP provides a list of functions such as `ImageCreateFromJpeg`. This function reads the image and returns a handle to it. In the next step the image can be displayed or modified. The following listing shows how an image can be read and sent to a file:

```php
<?php
    $image = ImageCreateFromJpeg ('author_hans.jpg');
    if    (!$image)
    {
        echo "picture cannot be loaded<br>\n";
    }
    else
    {
        header ("Content-type: image/jpeg");
        ImageJpeg($image);
    }
?>
```

This time the function for displaying the image is not ImagePng but ImageJpeg because a JPEG file has been read. In Figure 16.1 you can see what the result might look like.

FIGURE 16.1   The author of this chapter.

PHP supports not only PNG and JPEG, but in addition to these two image formats, PHP supports GD, GD2, GIF, WBMP, XBM, and XPM.

To find out which types of images your current PHP installation supports, you can use the ImageTypes function as shown in the next listing:

```php
<?php
    if (ImageTypes() & IMG_PNG) { echo "PNG is supported<br>"; }
    if (ImageTypes() & IMG_GIF) { echo "GIF is supported<br>"; }
    if (ImageTypes() & IMG_JPG) { echo "JPG is supported<br>"; }
    if (ImageTypes() & IMG_WBMP) { echo "WBMP is supported<br>"; }
?>
```

In this example three lines will be displayed because GIF has been compiled into your PHP binaries:

```
PNG is supported
JPG is supported
WBMP is supported
```

The installation you are currently working on might return different values. The output of this script depends greatly on your specific installation and distribution.

To find out how many colors the palette of your image contains, PHP provides the ImageColorsTotal function:

```php
<?php
        $image = ImageCreateFromJpeg ('author_hans.jpg');
        echo "Number of colors in the picture: ".ImageColorsTotal($image);
?>
```

In this scenario 256 is returned:

```
Number of colors in the picture: 256
```

To retrieve the color of a certain pixel in the image, you can use a script like the next one:

```php
<?php
        $image = ImageCreateFromJpeg ('author_hans.jpg');
        echo "Color at 100/100: ".imagecolorat($image, 100, 100);
?>
```

PHP returns 98, which is the position of the color in the palette:

```
Color at 100/100: 98
```

Sometimes it is necessary to retrieve information about the size of a picture. Just think of an application that adds text at the center of an image. You will need the size of the image to compute the center of the image and to locate the text correctly. To gather the size of a picture, PHP supports the getimagesize function as shown in the next listing:

```php
<?php
        $data = getimagesize('author_hans.jpg');
        echo "x-coordinates: $data[0]<br>\n";
        echo "y-coordinates: $data[1]<br>\n";
?>
```

$data contains two values. The first field contains the number of pixels in the x coordinate. The second value contains information about the y-axis:

```
x-coordinates: 169
y-coordinates: 255
```

In this example 169 and 255 are returned. If you try this on your machine, the values might differ because of different pictures used as input. You can achieve the same result with the help of imagesx and imagesy:

```
<?php
        $image = ImageCreateFromJpeg ('author_hans.jpg');
        echo "width: ".imageSX($image)."<br>";
        echo "height: ".imageSY($image)."<br>";
?>
```

The output of the script contains the same values:

```
width: 169
height: 255
```

Now that you have seen how to perform basic operations, it is time to see how you can copy parts of a picture with the help of PHP's GD interface. Let's take a look at the code of the next sample application:

```
<?php
        $source = ImageCreateFromJpeg ('author_hans.jpg');
        $destination = ImageCreate(200, 200);
        $white = ImageColorAllocate($destination, 255, 255, 255);
        imagefill($destination, 199, 199, $white);

        $stat = ImageCopy($destination, $source, 0, 0, 50, 50, 100, 100);

        header ("Content-type: image/png");
        ImagePng($destination);
?>
```

First the image is loaded. The handle of that image is called $source because this is the source file where the data we are going to copy will be taken from. In the next step a new picture is created and the background of the picture is painted white. To copy a part of the source picture into the picture you have just created, you can use the ImageCopy command. The first parameter defines the destination picture. The second parameter tells PHP where to take the data from. The third and the fourth parameter define the coordinates where the image will be placed. Parameters number five and six specify the size of the fragment you want to copy. Finally the last two parameters define the coordinates from which the image should be copied.

At the end of the script the fragment is displayed. In Figure 16.2 you can see what the result looks like.

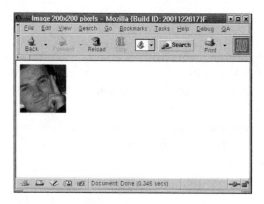

FIGURE 16.2   A piece of the author's picture.

The next thing that is often important is PHP's ability to merge pictures. In more complex operations, one picture might have to be put on top of another picture. You can easily perform operations like that using the `ImageCopyMerge` function. Let's take a look at the next piece of code:

```php
<?php
        header ("Content-type: image/jpeg");

        $one = ImageCreateFromJpeg ('author_hans.jpg');
        $two = ImageCreateFromJpeg ('logo.jpg');

        $stat = ImageCopyMerge($one, $two, 0, 120,
                0, 0, imagesx($two), imagesy($two), 50);

        ImageJpeg($one);
?>
```

First two pictures are opened. The first picture is already familiar to you. The second picture is shown in Figure 16.3.

FIGURE 16.3   Logo.jpg—Europe's new currency.

The two pictures should be merged. Therefore `ImageCopyMerge` is called with a list of parameters. The next listing shows the parameters and their meaning in the same order they occur in the function call:

- `src_im`—Defines the source image.

- `dst_im`—Defines the destination image (the picture containing the output).

- `dst_x` and `dst_y`—Defines the position of the graphics in the destination image.

- `src_x` and `src_y`—Defines the location to take the image from.

- `src_w` and `src_h`—Defines the size of the image merged by the command.

- `pct`—This parameter defines the percentage of the image being merged. A setting of 100% means the same as `copy`—in this case the underlying image cannot be seen any more.

If you execute the script, you can see that the Euro symbol lies on top of the author, which might be a good omen for the book. The output is shown in Figure 16.4.

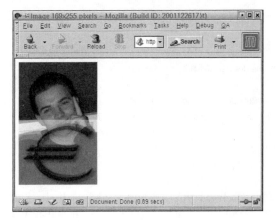

FIGURE 16.4   Merging two pictures.

In this example the pictures are merged without taking the colors of the two images into consideration. The next example shows how the second image can be used as a grayscale picture:

```php
<?php
        header ("Content-type: image/jpeg");

        $one = ImageCreateFromJpeg ('author_hans.jpg');
        $two = ImageCreateFromJpeg ('logo.jpg');

        $stat = ImageCopyMergeGray($one, $two, 0, 120,
                0, 0, imagesx($two), imagesy($two), 50);

        ImageJpeg($one);($image);
?>
```

The result will look slightly different because of the grayscale merging.

16.1.2 Drawing Components

In this section you will learn to draw simple geometric objects. For many applications this is essential. Just think of an application that draws graphs. A graph consists of many components such as lines, text, or polygons. Every component of the graph can easily be added to the scenery using PHP scripts.

Before you can start building applications that are that complex, you will take a look at some examples. Let's start with the first piece of code:

```php
<?php
        header ("Content-type: image/jpeg");

        $image = ImageCreate(200, 200);

        $white = ImageColorAllocate($image, 255, 255, 255);
        $black = ImageColorAllocate($image, 0, 0, 0);

        $stat = ImageFill($image, 0, 0, $white);
        $stat = ImageLine($image, 0, 0, 199, 199, $black);

        ImageJpeg($image);
?>
```

After creating an image, two colors are allocated and the background of the image is painted white. Finally a black line is displayed on the screen before sending the picture to the browser. The line is drawn from the left-upper edge to the lower-right edge of the picture. PHP uses the default style for lines. To modify these settings a variety of functions are provided. However, most of these functions are only available on systems with GD 2.01 or higher installed. The problem with GD 2.01 is that it has some bugs when working with anti-aliasing. Therefore we strongly recommend not using this version of the GD module. In most Linux distributions GD 1.x is still included, so GD 2 is not that widely used yet (at the time this book was written). Figure 16.5 shows the output of the preceding script.

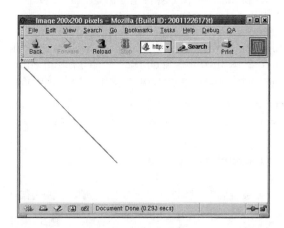

FIGURE 16.5   A line.

It's boring to draw nothing but lines, but take a look at some more objects that can be created using simple PHP functions:

```php
<?php
        header ("Content-type: image/jpeg");

        $image = ImageCreate(200, 200);

        $white = ImageColorAllocate($image, 255, 255, 255);
        $black = ImageColorAllocate($image, 0, 0, 0);
        $stat = ImageFill($image, 0, 0, $white);

        # drawing parts of an ellipse
        imagearc($image, 100, 50, 80, 40, 20, 300, $black);

        # drawing a circle
        imagearc($image, 100, 150, 60, 60, 00, 360, $black);
```

```
# drawing a polygon
$points = array(0,0, 0,199, 199,199, 199,0);
ImagePolygon($image, $points, 4, $black);

ImagePng($image);
?>
```

After allocating some color and painting the background of the image, as you have already seen, the script starts with displaying a part of an ellipse. The second and third parameters define the location of the ellipse. The fourth parameter tells PHP the width of the ellipse, and the fifth parameter contains the height of the object. Finally the starting angle and the ending angle as well as the color are defined. This way it is possible to draw incomplete ellipses as well as full ellipses. To draw a circle, the command parameters have to be modified to satisfy the demands of a circle.

The `ImagePolygon` function draws a polygon. To define the polygon nonambiguously, the handle to the image, an array of points, the number of points, and the color have to be defined.

Figure 16.6 shows the result of the script.

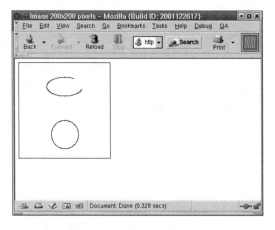

FIGURE 16.6   A set of objects.

To draw an ellipse, you can also use `imageellipse`, but it is only available on systems where GD 2.02 or higher is installed.

To draw rectangles, PHP provides a function called `imagefilledrectangle`. It draws a filled rectangle—it is not possible to draw a rectangle without filling it. The next example shows how to draw rectangles:

```php
<?php
        header ("Content-type: image/jpeg");

        $image = ImageCreate(200, 200);

        $white = ImageColorAllocate($image, 255, 255, 255);
        $black = ImageColorAllocate($image, 0, 0, 0);
        $stat = ImageFill($image, 0, 0, $white);

        imagefilledrectangle ($image, 30, 30, 60, 60, $black);
        imagefilledrectangle ($image, 90, 30, 120, 60, $black);
        imagefilledrectangle ($image, 30, 100, 120, 130, $black);

        ImagePng($image);
?>
```

The `imagefilledrectangle` function needs six parameters. The first parameter points to the image you want to process. The second and third parameters define the left-upper edge of the rectangle. The next two parameters contain information about the right-lower corner of the object. The last parameter contains the color.

16.1.3 Working with Fonts

When working with dynamically generated graphics, it is often necessary to work with text. Therefore PHP provides various sets of functions capable of processing text fast and efficiently. However, these groups of functions have advantages and disadvantages. Depending on what you need, you have to decide which group of functions to use.

One set of functions to work with is PostScript 1 functions. These functions must be enabled at compile time. By setting the two flags `--with-ttf[=DIR]` and `--with-t1lib[=DIR]` when running `configure`, you can enable TrueType. If it is not enabled at compile time, an error like the one in the next listing is displayed:

`Warning: ImagePsLoadFont: No T1lib support in this PHP build in`

In this book you will not learn about FreeType 1 functions, but you will take a closer look at functions based on FreeType 2.

To enable FreeType 2 at compile time, you have to use the `--enable-gd-native-ttf` and the `--with-freetype-dir` flags.

If you have compiled the code correctly, you can run the script in the next listing. If you are using a binary distribution of PHP, you have to run the phpinfo function to find out if FreeType 2 is supported. All these things sound complicated, but keep in mind that PHP does not natively support graphics—PHP is just a framework for a list of functions.

Let's take a look at some code:

```php
<?php
        $image = ImageCreate(350, 150);

        $white = ImageColorAllocate($image, 255, 255, 255);
        $black = ImageColorAllocate($image, 0, 0, 0);
        $stat = ImageFill($image, 0, 0, $white);

        $font = "/usr/share/fonts/default/TrueType/timb____.ttf";
        $text = "Check out";
        $pos = imagettftext($image, 30, 0, 30, 50, $black, $font, $text);
        $text = "www.postgresql.at";
        $pos = imagettftext($image, 30, 0, 30, 90, $black, $font, $text);
        if      (!$pos)
        {
                echo "cannot use Freetype 2<br>\n";
        }
        else
        {
                header ("Content-type: image/png");
                ImagePng($image);
        }
?>
```

The imagettftext function does everything you need. Just define the place where you want the text to be displayed (parameters four and five), the size of the text (parameter number two), the angle (parameter number three), the color, the font, and the text you want to be displayed. The application in the preceding listing displays two items of text and checks whether the text has been displayed correctly. The picture is shown in Figure 16.7.

FIGURE 16.7   Some simple text based on FreeType 2.

Sometimes you might want to display various lines of text at the center of an image.
Therefore you can use a temporary image and the return values of imagettftext.
Let's take a look at the next piece of code:

```php
<?php
        # defining size; creating images; allocating colors
        $xsize = 350;
        $ysize = 150;

        $image = ImageCreate($xsize, $ysize);
        $tmp = ImageCreate($xsize, $ysize);

        $white = ImageColorAllocate($image, 255, 255, 255);
        $black = ImageColorAllocate($image, 0, 0, 0);
        $stat = ImageFill($image, 0, 0, $white);
        $font = "/usr/share/fonts/default/TrueType/timb____.ttf";

        # drawing border
        $points = array(0,0, 0,$ysize-1, $xsize-1,$ysize-1, $xsize-1,0);
        ImagePolygon($image, $points, 4, $black);

        # writing text
        writetext("Greetings", 20, 30);
        writetext("From", 20, 75);
        writetext("Vienna", 40, 130);
```

```
            header ("Content-type: image/png");
            ImagePng($image);

function writetext($text, $size, $ypos)
{
            global $image, $tmp, $font, $black, $xsize;

            $pos = imagettftext($tmp, $size, 0, 0, 0, $black, $font, $text);
            $width = $pos[2] - $pos[0];
            $height = $pos[3] - $pos[1];
            $xpos = $xsize/2 - $pos[2]/2;

            $pos = imagettftext($image, $size, 0, $xpos, $ypos, $black,
                    $font, $text);
}
?>
```

First two images are created. One of the images will be the working image. The second one will be a temporary image for computing the size of the text written into the image. After allocating some colors and defining the fonts, a border will be drawn around the image to make it easier for you to see where the image starts and ends. When drawing the border, make sure that you subtract 1 from the right and lower coordinates of the picture because PHP starts counting the coordinates of the image with zero, so the 200th element has index number 199.

In the next step the writetext function is called. This function needs three parameters. The first one contains the text you want to be displayed. The second one defines the size of the text, and parameter number three tells the function which y coordinate to use when displaying the text.

To compute the size of the text you want to be displayed, the text is added to the temporary image. The return value of the function is then used to compute the center of the image. $pos contains the coordinates of the edge of the text added to the image. Therefore it is an easy task to compute the appropriate coordinates before adding the text to the real image. At the end of the function imagettftext is called.

writetext is called three times and after that the image is sent to the browser. The result can be seen in Figure 16.8.

FIGURE 16.8   Text at the center of the image.

Up to now you have seen that the text does not have to be angular. The next example shows how you can modify the way the text is displayed by defining an angle:

```php
<?php
        $xsize = 350; $ysize = 150;
        $image = ImageCreate($xsize, $ysize);

        $white = ImageColorAllocate($image, 255, 255, 255);
        $black = ImageColorAllocate($image, 0, 0, 0);
        $stat = ImageFill($image, 0, 0, $white);
        $font = "/usr/share/fonts/default/TrueType/timb____.ttf";

        header ("Content-type: image/png");
        $pos = imagettftext($image, 30, 20, 50, 100, $black,
                $font, "PostgreSQL");

        ImagePng($image);
?>
```

Figure 16.9 shows what comes out when the script is executed.

FIGURE 16.9   Angular text.

As you can see, processing text with the help of the GD module is not difficult. However, if you have to perform complex operations, it is worth taking a look at some alternative solutions.

16.1.4 Alternative Solutions

If the operations you want to perform with images are more complex, you cannot use GD. In this case alternative solutions have to be found. In Unix there are many ways to generate dynamic images on-the-fly. Unix is often said to be an operating system that cannot handle graphics, which is not true in many cases. The concepts of Unix make it easy to combine software products of all kinds with each other, and this makes Unix a powerful tool for almost all types of computing—including working with graphics.

In this section you will get a few hints about how to build even more powerful applications.

16.1.4.1 ImageMagick

For converting pictures from one image into another, you can use ImageMagick. ImageMagick is a robust collection of tools and libraries to read, write, and manipulate images in many image formats including popular formats such as TIFF, JPEG, PNG, PDF, PhotoCD, and GIF. All together more than 68 formats are supported. In most cases you will find the right converter or filter to achieve your target.

Another important feature of ImageMagick is its ability to combine various images into an animated GIF. When building Web sites, this can be essential and a great benefit.

Usually ImageMagick is used in combination with system calls because this is the only way to start external programs.

You can download ImageMagick from `http://www.imagemagick.org`.

16.1.4.2 Gimp

Gimp is the most powerful and most flexible piece of software ever written for working with graphics under Unix. Not only does it provide a lot of functionality, but it is also a flexible and well-designed piece of software. The flexibility of Gimp especially makes this product quite powerful, and interacting with other software is easy.

An additional advantage of Gimp is its scripting interface. You can execute entire programs performing complex operations and computations. Scripts can be executed by Gimp noninteractively, which means that you can write batch jobs performing exactly those operations you will need.

Let's take a look at the command-line parameters provided by Gimp:

```
gimp [-h] [--help] [-v] [--version] [-b] [--batch <commands>]
   [-g] [--gimprc <gim-prc>]  [-n]  [--no-interface]  [-r]
   [--restore-session]  [--no-data]  [--verbose]
   [--no-shm]   [--no-xshm]  [--display  display]
   [--no-splash]  [--no-splash-image]     [--debug-handlers]
   [--console-messages] [--system-gimprc <gimprc>]
   [filename]...
```

As you can see, the `--batch` command can be used to execute scripts.

When working with Gimp, you have to get used to some specifics of the onboard programming interfaces. In the case of the interactive Script-Fu interface, some aspects concerning computation might not be familiar to you.

Gimp's interactive shell is shown in Figure 16.10.

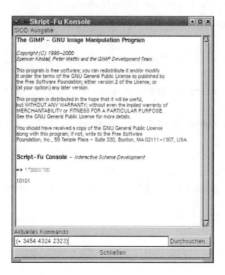

FIGURE 16.10 Gimp's interactive shell.

As you can see, Gimp can be used as a pocket calculator. Most of you won't use a graphics engine as a pocket calculator, but it shows what you can do with Gimp.

For a full reference of Gimp's functions, check out the manual, which can be found at `http://manual.gimp.org`. As a rule of thumb, you can say that everything you can do with Gimp interactively can also be done with scripts.

Feel free to experiment with the software, and you will soon see that you can generate all kinds of images on the fly efficiently.

16.2 Using Geometric Data Types

PostgreSQL providesa set of data types you can use for storing geometric information efficiently. These data types are included in PostgreSQL's core distribution and are widely used and admired by many people. In addition to the data types themselves, PostgreSQL provides an index structure based on R-trees, which are optimized for performing spatial searching.

PHP has a simple interface for generating graphics. To generate database-driven indexes, you can combine PostgreSQL and PHP. In this section you will see how to implement the "glue" between PHP and PostgreSQL.

The goal of the next example is to implement an application that extracts points from a database and displays them in an image. To store the points in the database, you can create a table:

```
phpbook=# CREATE TABLE coord (comment text, data point);
CREATE
```

Then you can insert some values into the table:

```
phpbook=# INSERT INTO coord VALUES ('no comment', '20,20');
INSERT 19873 1
phpbook=# INSERT INTO coord VALUES ('no comment', '120,99');
INSERT 19874 1
phpbook=# INSERT INTO coord VALUES ('no comment', '137,110');
INSERT 19875 1
phpbook=# INSERT INTO coord VALUES ('no comment', '184,178');
INSERT 19876 1
```

In this example four records have been added to the table. Now that some data is in the database, you can start working on a script that generates the dynamic image:

```php
<?php

include("objects/point.php");

header ("Content-type: image/png");
$im = @ImageCreate (200, 200)
    or die ("Cannot Generate Image");

$white = ImageColorAllocate ($im, 255, 255, 255);
$black = ImageColorAllocate ($im, 0, 0, 0);
ImageFill($im, 0, 0, $white);

# connecting to the database
$dbh = pg_connect("dbname=phpbook user=postgres");
if      (!$dbh)
{
        exit ("an error has occurred<br>");
}

# drawing border
$points = array(0,0, 0,199, 199,199, 199,0);
ImagePolygon($im, $points, 4, $black);

# selecting points
$sql = "SELECT comment, data FROM coord";
$result = pg_exec($dbh, $sql);
$rows = pg_numrows($result);

# processing result
for      ($i = 0; $i < $rows; $i++)
{
        $data = pg_fetch_array ($result, $i);
        $mypoint = new point($data["data"]);
        $mypoint->draw($im, $black, 3);
}

ImagePng ($im);

?>
```

First a library is included. This library will be discussed after you have gone through the main file of the script. Then an image is generated and two colors are allocated.

The background is painted white, and after that the connection to the database is established. To see where the image starts and where it ends, a rectangle is drawn that marks the borders of the image.

In the next step all records are retrieved from the table called coord. All records in the table are processed using a simple loop. In the loop a constructor is called. After the object has been created, a method called draw is called. This method adds the point to the image. Finally the image is sent to the browser.

In the next listing you can take a look at the library you will need to run the script you have just seen:

```php
<?php

# working with points
class point
{
        var $x1;
        var $y1;

        # constructor
        function point($string)
        {
                $string = ereg_replace("\(*\)*", "", $string);
                $tmp = explode(",", $string);
                $this->x1 = $tmp[0];
                $this->y1 = $tmp[1];
        }

        # drawing a point
        function draw($image, $color, $size)
        {
                imagefilledrectangle ($image,
                        $this->x1 - $size/2,
                        $this->y1 - $size/2,
                        $this->x1 + $size/2,
                        $this->y1 + $size/2,
                        $color);
        }
}
?>
```

The class called point contains two variables. $x1 contains the x coordinate of the point. $y1 contains the y coordinate of the point. Let's take a closer look at the constructor.

One parameter has to be passed to the function. This parameter contains the data returned by PostgreSQL. In the next step the data is transformed and the two coordinates of the point are extracted from the input string. Finally the two values are assigned to $this.

In addition to the constructor, a function for drawing a point has been implemented. Because a point is too small, a filled rectangle is drawn. The coordinates of the rectangle are computed based on the data retrieved from the database by the constructor. Figure 16.11 shows what comes out when running the script.

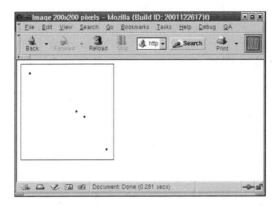

FIGURE 16.11   Dynamic points.

Points are the easiest data structure provided by PostgreSQL and therefore the PHP class you have to implement is easy as well. A more complex yet important data structure is polygons. Polygons consist of a variable number of points, so the constructor as well as the drawing functions are more complex. Before taking a look at the code, you have to create a table and insert some data into it:

```
phpbook=# CREATE TABLE mypolygon (data polygon);
CREATE
```

In the next step you can add some data to the table:

```
phpbook=# INSERT INTO mypolygon VALUES ('10,10, 150,20, 120,160'::polygon);
INSERT 19902 1
phpbook=# INSERT INTO mypolygon VALUES ('20,20, 160,30, 120,160, 90,90');
INSERT 19903 1
```

Two records have been added to the table. Let's query the table to see how the data is returned by PostgreSQL:

```
phpbook=# SELECT * FROM mypolygon;
                    data
----------------------------------------
 ((10,10),(150,20),(120,160))
 ((20,20),(160,30),(120,160),(90,90))
(2 rows)
```

The target of the next piece of code is to transform the data returned by the database and make something useful out of it. The next listing contains a class called `polygon` used for processing polygons:

```php
<?php

# working with polygons
class polygon
{
        var $x;
        var $y;
        var $number;

        # constructor
        function polygon($string)
        {
                $string = ereg_replace("\(*\)*", "", $string);
                $tmp = explode(",", $string);
                $this->number = count($tmp);
                for     ($i = 0; $i < $this->number; $i = $i + 2)
                {
                        $this->x[$i/2] = $tmp[$i];
                        $this->y[$i/2] = $tmp[$i + 1];
                }
        }



        # drawing a polygon
        function draw($image, $color)
        {
                for     ($i = 0; $i < $this->number - 1; $i++)
                {
                        imageline($image, $this->x[$i], $this->y[$i],
```

```
                                    $this->x[$i + 1], $this->y[$i + 1], $color);
                    }
                    imageline($image, $this->x[$this->number - 1],
                            $this->y[$this->number - 1], $this->x[0],
                            $this->y[0], $color);

            }
    }
?>
```

$x will be used to store a list of x coordinates and $y will contain the list of y coordinates extracted from the points defining the polygon. $number will contain the number of points a polygon consists of.

After defining the variables belonging to the polygon, the constructor has been implemented. With the help of regular expressions, the data returned by PostgreSQL is modified and can easily be transformed into an array of values. In the next step the values in the array are counted and the various coordinates are added to $this->x and $this->y.

In addition to the constructor, a function for drawing the polygon has been implemented. The function goes through all points of the polygon and adds lines to the image being generated.

Now that you have seen how to process polygons, you can take a look at the main file of the application:

```
<?php

include("objects/polygon.php");

header ("Content-type: image/png");
$im = @ImageCreate (200, 200)
    or die ("Cannot Generate Image");

$white = ImageColorAllocate ($im, 255, 255, 255);
$black = ImageColorAllocate ($im, 0, 0, 0);
ImageFill($im, 0, 0, $white);

# connecting to the database
$dbh = pg_connect("dbname=phpbook user=postgres");
if       (!$dbh)
{
        exit ("an error has occurred<br>");
}
```

```
# drawing border
$points = array(0,0, 0,199, 199,199, 199,0);
ImagePolygon($im, $points, 4, $black);

# selecting points
$sql = "SELECT data FROM mypolygon";
$result = pg_exec($dbh, $sql);
$rows = pg_numrows($result);

# processing result
for     ($i = 0; $i < $rows; $i++)
{
        $data = pg_fetch_array ($result, $i);
        $mypoly = new polygon($data["data"]);
        $mypoly->draw($im, $black);
}

ImagePng ($im);

?>
```

First the library for processing polygons is included. In the next step an image is created, colors are allocated, the background of the image is painted white, and a connection to the database is established. After drawing the borders and retrieving all records from the database, the polygons are displayed using a loop. Inside the loop the constructor is called for every record returned by PostgreSQL. After the constructor, the draw function is called, which adds the polygon to the scenery.

If you execute the script, you will see the result as shown in Figure 16.12.

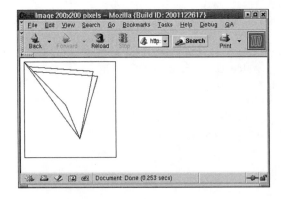

FIGURE 16.12 Dynamic polygons.

Classes can be implemented for every geometric data type provided by PostgreSQL. As you have seen in this section, implementing a class for working with geometric data types is truly simple and can be done with just a few lines of code. The major part of the code consists of basic things such as creating images, allocating colors, or connecting to the database. The code that is used for doing the interaction with the database is brief and easy to understand. This should encourage you to work with PHP and PostgreSQL's geometric data types extensively.

16.3 Creating Dynamic Flash Movies

Up to now you have seen how to generate static images or documents. However, for highly professional Web sites it can be interesting to generate Flash movies on-the-fly. Dynamic movies can be an impressive feature and will help you to sell your products easily.

16.3.1 Installation

To work with dynamic Flash movies, you can use PHP's Ming interface, which can be downloaded from `http://www.opaque.net/ming/`. In this book we used Ming 0.2a. This module is still in an early stage of development, but developers are working hard to improve the module. It is already possible to implement good-looking movies, and you can expect even better versions of Ming in the future.

To install the module, you can either download a precompiled binary or the source code of the module. After you have downloaded the binaries, you can extract them using `tar xvfz` (for Linux machines). In the next step you can copy the shared object to the directory containing the other extensions of PHP:

```
[root@duron flash]# cp php_ming.so /usr/lib/php4/ -v
»php_ming.so« -> »/usr/lib/php4/php_ming.so«
```

Now you can start working with the module. With the help of the `dl` command, you can load the module dynamically. If you want to use the module as a permanent extension, you have to edit `php.ini`. One line has to be added to the file:

```
extension=php_ming.so
```

After this change has been made, you can run Ming safely. However, keep in mind that Ming is still marked as experimental. Therefore the Ming module won't be covered in full detail.

16.3.2 Getting Started

Before you get to some more practical stuff, here's a simple yet useless example. The next listing generates an empty Flash movie, and it shows you what basic things have to be done to create a Flash movie:

```php
<?php
        dl('php_ming.so');
        header('Content-type: application/x-shockwave-flash');

        $m = new SWFMovie();
        $m->setDimension(320, 240);
        $m->setRate(12.0);
        $m->nextFrame();

        $m->output();
?>
```

In the first line the module for running Ming has to be included at runtime. This is necessary if you have not included Ming as an permanent extension to PHP. In the next step the header is sent to the browser. This header will tell the browser that the data sent to it has to be treated as a flash movie.

In the next step the movie is generated and a handle to the movie called $m is returned.

In the next step the size of the movie is defined. In this example it has a total size of 320×240 pixels. The number of pictures displayed per second is set to 12. With the help of nextFrame, a frame is added to the movie.

Now that you have seen what basic operations have to be performed, we can go on to a more impressive example. Let's take a look:

```php
<?php
        dl('php_ming.so');
        header('Content-type: application/x-shockwave-flash');

        # creating movie
        $m = new SWFMovie();
        $m->setDimension(320, 240);
        $m->setRate(12.0);

        # creating shape
        $s = new SWFShape();
        $s->setLine(5, 0xaa, 0xaa, 0xaa);
        $s->movePenTo(30, 210);
        $s->drawLineTo(290, 30);
        $m->add($s);
```

```
        # displaying output
        $m->nextFrame();
        $m->output();
?>
```

After creating the movie and defining the attributes of the movie, a shape is created. With the help of shapes you can perform some basic operations such as drawing lines, which is the target of this example. After defining the shape, the attributes of the line are defined. The first parameter of the setline function defines how thick the line should be. The next three parameters define the color of the line you are going to draw. Before the line is drawn, the position of the pen is defined. In this scenario it is located near the lower edge on the left side of the movie. In the next step a line is drawn from the current position to the point (290, 30), which is near the upper edge of the movie on the right side. Drawing the shape is not enough. To display the shape it has to be added to the scenery using the add method. Then the movie is sent to the browser. Figure 16.13 contains a screenshot of the movie.

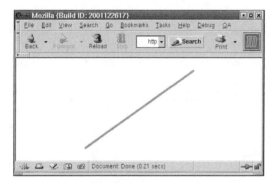

FIGURE 16.13   A line.

Up to now we have created static images instead of real movies. The next example shows how to create a real movie. In the next step you will see how to build a basic animation:

```
<?php
        dl('php_ming.so');
        header('Content-type: application/x-shockwave-flash');

        # creating movie
        $m = new SWFMovie();
        $m->setDimension(320, 320);
        $m->setRate(12.0);
```

```
# creating shape
for     ($i = 0; $i < 320; $i++)
{
        $s = new SWFShape();
        $s->setLine(5, 0xaa, 0xaa, 0xaa);
        $s->movePenTo($i, 210);
        $s->drawLineTo(290, $i);
        $m->add($s);

        $m->nextFrame();
}

# displaying output
$m->nextFrame();
$m->output();
?>
```

The script in the listing generated a set of shapes and adds them to the scenery. After adding one object to the movie, the script switches to the next frame. Finally all objects are displayed. If you execute the script, an artistic image will occur step by step. Figure 16.14 shows a snapshot taken during the execution of the script.

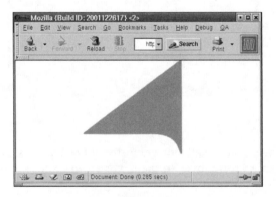

FIGURE 16.14   Building a short animation.

When building Flash movies, it is essential to know how you can work with images. In the next example you will see how an image can be loaded, modified, and moved around:

```php
<?php
    dl('php_ming.so');
    header('Content-type: application/x-shockwave-flash');

    $m = new SWFMovie();
    $m->setDimension(1024, 768);

    # adding picture to the scenery
    $pic = new SWFBitmap(fopen("beautiful.jpg", "rb"));
    $i = $m->add($pic);
    $i->moveto(512, 393);
    $m->nextFrame();

    # moving the picture
    for($j = 0; $j < 71; ++$j)
    {
        $m->nextFrame();
        $i->rotate(5);
    }

    $m->nextFrame();

    # modifying the color of an image
    for($n = 0; $n < 20; $n++)
    {
        $i->multColor(1.0 - $n /10, 0.5, 1.0);
        $i->addColor(0xff * $n /20, 0, 0);
        $m->nextFrame();
    }


    for($n = 20; $n > 0; --$n)
    {
        $i->multColor(1.0 - $n / 10, 0.5, 2.0);
        $i->addColor(0xff* $n /20, 0, 0);
        $m->nextFrame();
    }

    $m->output();
?>
```

By creating an SWFBitmap object, it is possible to load an image and to add it to the scenery. After adding the image to the movie, you have to put it into the right position. In this example the image will be located at the center of the movie. To rotate the image, you can use the rotate function. After every movement of the image, a new frame is started. In the next step the colors of the image are modified before the movie starts again. MultColor multiplies the item's color transform, and addColor adds the given color to this item's color transform.

Finally the movie is sent to the browser. Figure 16.15 contains a snapshot of the browser window.

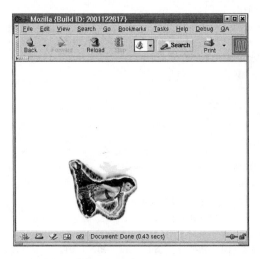

FIGURE 16.15   Moving the wonderful belly dancer.

In addition to moving images, changing colors, and drawing objects, Ming provides a set of functions for working with text, MP3s, and many other objects. There is also an interface for working with action scripts. With the help of action scripts, it is possible to build interactive Flash applications. However, the module is not that stable yet, so it is not possible to use it for building business-critical applications.

16.4 Generating PDF Files

PDF files can be generated in two ways. Depending on what you like best, you can choose whether to use LaTeX or PHP's onboard tools for working with PDF. In this section both ways will be covered extensively so that you can decide which way is the more elegant one for your application.

16.4.1 Working with LaTeX

TeX was originally developed by Donald E. Knuth, who is one of the world's most famous computer experts. He is the author of *The Art of Computer Programming*, the most commonly known book about algorithms and the most complete book on that topic ever written.

TeX has a long history. Today TeX is not used directly because it is far too complex to write a document that is based solely on TeX. LaTeX is a package of macros based on TeX, which was originally written by Leslie Lamport. When people talk about TeX, they usually mean Lamport's macro package, which is widely used today. The main advantage of TeX is its stability. For years not a single bug has been found in TeX, and you can fully rely on TeX. For business-critical applications especially, this is important because you can generate documents consisting of thousands of pages reliably and fast.

This section is not designed to be an introduction to TeX or LaTeX. This section has been designed to give you an insight into the world of professional text processing with LaTeX, PHP, and PostgreSQL. First you will see an example of a sophisticated LaTeX document including a style. After that you will learn to generate dynamic documents with the help of PHP so that you can include TeX documents in your Web applications.

16.4.1.1 An Example of LaTeX Code: A Bill

The goal of this example is that you can see how LaTeX documents are structured and what you need to generate a PDF file. When you understand how things work, it will be an easy task to generate dynamic LaTeX code.

Figure 16.16 shows what the bill will look like.

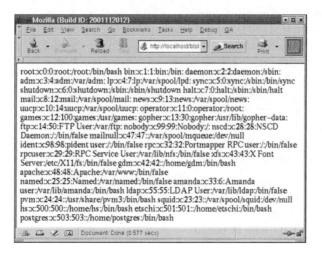

FIGURE 16.16   A bill.

Several files are needed to generate the bill. In this scenario the main file is called hon.tex. It contains the dynamic part of the document, which means that all components of the bill are compiled in this file. Let's take a look at the code of the file:

```
\documentclass[12pt,a4paper]{letter}
\usepackage{billstyle}
\input{addresses}
\sloppy
\begin{document}
\date{April, 19th 2001}
\begin{letter}{\PostgresInc}
\begin{Fee}{H}{01-07}
As we have agreed in the contract here is the bill for the
implementation of advanced replication.

\begin{Bill}{xxx 999.999,99}
\Entry{Consulting}{EUR 10.000,00}{0}
\Entry{Implementation}{EUR 69.000,00}{0}
\Entry{+ 20 \% Turnover Tax}{EUR 15.800,00}{1}
\Entry{}{EUR 94.800,00}{2}
\end{Bill}

\end{Fee}
\closing{Best regards}
\end{letter}
\end{document}
```

First the type of document is defined. In this case it is a letter. The size of the document is A4, which is the European standard format for letters. If you are American, you should use the American letter format instead. The size of the text is set to 12. In the next step, the style of the document is included so that LaTeX can understand all macros used in this document. The style of this document is called billstyle and is stored in billstyle.sty. The file addresses.tex, which is included using \input, contains some shortcuts so that you don't have to write the entire address every time you generate a new document. \begin{document} tells LaTeX that the core of the document starts here. The first thing added to the document is the date the text was written. In this example the date is April 19, 2001.

The letter will be sent to PostgresInc (a nonexistent company). addresses.tex contains the real address of the company receiving the bill. The advantage of this file is that the address can be changed globally, so only one file is affected if the address changes. Let's take a look at the file:

```
\long\def\PostgresInc{%
www.postgresql.at Inc.\\
Fünfhausgasse 20/1\\
A-1150 Vienna, Austria}

\long\def\Pine{%
Pine Networks\\
Anywherestreet 344/23\\
A-1010 Vienna, Austria}
```

As you can see, two addresses are in the file. Our bill is sent to the first company mentioned in the file.

After defining the address, a block called Fee is started. The way Fee looks is defined in the style file you will see later in this section. Fee has two parameters, which in this example are H and 01-07. The first parameter defines the type of the bill and the second parameter defines the identifier of the bill. The way bills are labeled has nothing to do with LaTeX; it is just a unique number for every bill sent to a customer.

The next two lines contain the text on the bill. Every bill contains the product a customer is charged for. In this scenario the various components of the bill are listed in the block starting with \begin{Bill}{xxx 999.999,99}. The parameter in curly brackets tells LaTeX how long the string will be. In this scenario three characters are used for the currency (for example, EUR for Euros). The rest of the characters are used for displaying the digits of the price. With the help of the \Entry command, components are added to the bill. The behavior of \Entry is defined in the style. Finally the components Bill and Fee end, a closing statement is added to the letter, and the letter is finished.

For compiling the document, a makefile is used:

```
hon.pdf :      hon.tex
        latex hon.tex
        dvips hon.dvi -o hon.ps
        ps2pdf hon.ps hon.pdf
```

The command latex generated a DVI file out of hon.tex. Dvips is used to convert the DVI file to a PostScript file, which can be transformed into a PDF file.

To be able to compile hon.tex, a style is needed. The style defines how various components of the letter look. The advantage of styles is that the way a document looks and the content of a document are separated. If you want to change the layout of all documents, you only have to change the style and recompile the documents, which is much easier than changing every single document as you would have to do when running a product such as WordPad or Notepad.

Let's take a look at the style:

```
%       Fee

\usepackage[latin1]{inputenc}
\usepackage{german}
\usepackage{graphicx}
\usepackage[dvips,usenames]{color}

\advance\topmargin by -1.5cm
\advance\textheight by 2cm
\advance\evensidemargin by -1cm
\advance\oddsidemargin by -1cm
\advance\textwidth by 2cm
\advance\headheight by 1cm
\advance\headsep by -1cm

\signature{(Hans-Jürgen Schönig)}

\renewcommand{\closing}[1]{\par\nobreak\vspace{\parskip}%
        \stopbreaks
        \noindent
        \strut\hfill\hfill
        \parbox{\indentedwidth}{\centering
                \ignorespaces #1\\[6\medskipamount]%
                \ifx\@empty\fromsig
                \fromname
                \else \fromsig \fi\strut}\hfill
        \par}

\newcommand{\Parbox}[3][c]{\fboxsep-\fboxrule\fbox{\parbox[#1]{#2}{#3}}}

\def\Hon@head{\parbox[c]{0.1\textwidth}{%
                \includegraphics[width=0.1\textwidth]{logo.eps}}
        \parbox[c]{0.6\textwidth}{\parskip0pt
        \raggedright\sloppy\sffamily
        {\Large\bfseries Cybertec Geschwinde \& Schönig\par}
        Advanced PostgreSQL and Kernel Solutions\\
        www.postgresql.at - http://kernel.cybertec.at}
        \hfill}

\def\Hon@foot{\parbox{\textwidth}{\centering\sf\footnotesize%
        Ludo-Hartmannplatz 1/14, A-1160 Vienna,
```

```
                  Phone +43/1/929 25 25/0, office@cybertec.at
              }}

\def\ps@firstpage{\let\@oddhead\Hon@head
         \let\@evenhead\Hon@head
         \let\@oddfoot\Hon@foot
         \let\@evenfoot\Hon@foot
}

\def\H@Type{H}

\def\HName{REQUEST FOR PAYMENT}
\def\RName{BILL}

\def\HEnd{Please transfer the money to: \\
         Account Number: 343-78493-43542/34 \\
         First National Austrian Bank\par}

\let\REnd\HEnd

\def\Fee#1#2{\opening{Number: #1#2}
\vskip 1cm
\centerline{\Large\bf \csname#1Name\endcsname}
\gdef\H@Type{#1}
\vskip 1cm
}

\def\endFee{\csname\H@Type End\endcsname}

%       Bill

\newbox\H@box
\newcount\H@count
\newdimen\H@width
\newdimen\H@Lwidth

\newenvironment{Bill}[1]{\settowidth{\H@width}{#1}
         \begin{quote}\rightskip \H@width}{\end{quote}\par}%

\def\H@Value#1#2{\makebox[0pt][l]{\vtop {%
         \hsize=\H@width
         \hbox to \hsize {\hfill#1}
```

```
\H@count=#2
\loop
\ifnum \H@count > 0
\vskip 2pt
\hrule
\advance \H@count by -1
\repeat }}}
```

```
\def\Entry#1#2#3{\strut#1 \dotfill\ \H@Value{#2}{#3}\\ }
\def\Entry#1#2#3{\strut
       \settowidth{\H@Lwidth}{#1}
       \ifnum \H@Lwidth > \z@
              #1 \dotfill ~
       \else
              \hfill
       \fi
       \H@Value{#2}{#3}\\ }
```

```
\dateaustrian
```

The style is already quite complex and we will not discuss it in full detail because that would be beyond the scope of this book. The only thing that is important for a PHP developer is to see what has to be done when defining a style.

The first thing to do in the style file is to tell LaTeX which packages have to be included. The second thing is to define the margins of the document, which means that you have to tell the system where the borders of the document are. In the next step various components are defined. The macros defined in this style file are called by hon.tex.

To compile the document you just have to run make, and if no errors occur, a DVI, a PostScript, and a PDF file will be generated by the system.

16.4.1.2 Generating LaTeX Code Using PHP

Now that you have seen how to build a simple LaTeX document, you can start writing a PHP script that generates documents for you. The target is to have a simple Web form that allows you to generate simple bills. Therefore we will need various forms, as shown in Table 16.1.

TABLE 16.1   Files Involved in the Process

Filename	Purpose
addresses.tex	Contains a list of addresses
billstyle_de.sty	Contains the style needed by the LaTeX document
gentex.php	Generates a LaTeX document

TABLE 16.1 Continued

Filename	Purpose
html.php	Contains HTML code
index.php	Generates the user form
tex_code.php	Contains code fragments for LaTeX

Let's start with index.php, which is the file doing most of the work. It is responsible for generating the user form. Figure 16.17 shows what the form looks like.

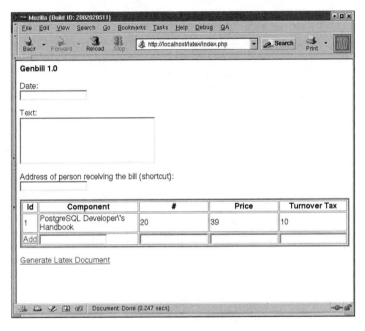

FIGURE 16.17 The user form.

```php
<?php
        include("html.php");

        # generating session and session id
        session_start();
        $sid = session_id();

        # displaying HTML header
        echo $head;
```

```php
# unserializing data
$compa = unserialize($comps);
$numbera = unserialize($numbers);
$pricea = unserialize($prices);
$taxa = unserialize($taxs);

# checking, if data has been passed to the form
if      (strlen($date) > 0)
{
        $sdate = $date;
        session_register("sdate");
}

if      (strlen($address) > 0)
{
        $saddress = $address;
        session_register("saddress");
}
if      (strlen($message) > 0)
{
        $smessage = $message;
        session_register("smessage");
}

if      ($newcomp && ($newcomp != ''))
{
        $count++;
        session_register("count");

        $compa[$count] = $newcomp;
        $comps = serialize($compa);
        session_register("comps");

        $numbera[$count] = $newnumber;
        $numbers = serialize($numbera);
        session_register("numbers");

        $pricea[$count] = $newprice;
        $prices = serialize($pricea);
        session_register("prices");
```

```php
                $taxa[$count] = $newtax;
                $taxs = serialize($taxa);
                session_register("taxs");
        }

        # drawing the table
        drawlines($count, $compa, $numbera, $pricea, $taxa);

        # generate an input line
        inputline();

        # displaying end of HTML code
        echo $tail;

# add lines containing data to the table
function drawlines($count, $compa, $numbera, $pricea, $taxa)
{
        for     ($i = 1; $i <= $count; $i++)
        {
                echo "<tr><td>$i</td><td>".$compa[$i]."</td>";
                echo "<td>".$numbera[$i]."</td><td>".$pricea[$i]."</td>";
                echo "<td>".$taxa[$i]."</td></tr>\n";
        }
}


# edit the inputline to the data
function inputline()
{
        echo '<tr><td>
                <a href="javascript: document.forms[0].submit()">Add</a>
                </td>
                <td><input type="text" name="newcomp"></td>
                <td><input type="text" name="newnumber"></td>
                <td><input type="text" name="newprice"></td>
                <td><input type="text" name="newtax"></td></tr>
        ';
}

?>
```

The first file that is included is html.php. It contains two HTML fragments ($head and $tail) you will need to build the form.

Before continuing with index.php, here is the HTML code for building the screen:

```php
<?php

$head = '
        <html>
        <body>
        <b>Genbill 1.0</b>
        <br><br>
        <form action="index.php" method="post">

        Date: <br>
        <input name="date" type="text"><br><br>

        Text: <br>
        <textarea cols="30" rows="5" name="message">
        </textarea><br><br>

        Address of person receiving the bill (shortcut):<br>
        <input name="address" type="text"><br><br>

        <table border="3">
        <tr><th>Id</th><th>Component</th><th>#</th><th>Price</th>
                <th>Turnover Tax</th></tr>
';

$tail = '
        </table><br>
        <a href="gentex.php">Generate Latex Document</a>
        </form>

        </body>
        </html>
';

?>
```

$head displays some HTML code including a user form for inserting the date, the text, and the recipient of the bill.

After starting a session, the head of the HTML document is generated. As you saw in the figure, the table consists of various columns. To store the information about these columns, variables are used. These variables are registered in the current session. Because the data is stored in arrays, serialization must be performed. At the beginning of the script, the serialized data has to be transformed to arrays again.

In the next step the script checks whether or not the variables submitted to the form should be registered. The reason for that is that after useful data has been registered, it should not be destroyed by registering empty variables.

Before drawlines is called, an if statement is processed. Inside the if-block $count is increased. It contains the number of components the bill consists of. In the case of valid input, the data is added to the arrays and a string is made out of these arrays again.

Let's take a look at the drawlines function. It has been implemented to add one line of data to the scenery. As you can see, it does nothing but generate HTML code. In addition to the data, a line containing input fields is generated. Then the HTML code for ending the screen is displayed.

As you have seen, the script adds data to the arrays storing the information every time a user clicks on the link ("Add") in the table. As soon as somebody clicks on the link at the bottom of the screen, gentex.php is called. Let's take a look at gentex.php:

```php
<?php

include("tex_code.php");

# generating session and session id
session_start();
$sid = session_id();

# checking for input
if      (strlen($date) > 2 ) { $sdate = $date; }
if      (strlen($message) > 4 ) { $smessage = $message; }
if      (strlen($address) > 2 ) { $saddress = $address; }

if      (strlen($sdate) < 3 || strlen($smessage) < 3 || strlen($saddress) < 2)
{
        echo "the data in the previous form is not complete";
        die;
}

echo "date: $sdate<br>\n";
echo "message: $smessage<br>\n";
echo "address: $saddress<br>\n";
```

```
# generating LaTex code
$tex = "$head\n";
$tex .= '\date{'.$sdate.'}'."\n";
$tex .= "\\begin{letter}{\\$saddress}\n";
$tex .= '\begin{Fee}{Bill}{}'."\n";

$tex .= "$smessage\n";
$tex .= '\\\\
\strut
\\\\
\bf Price \rm
\begin{Bill}{EUR xx.xxx,xx}
';

# adding components to the bill
$compa = unserialize($comps);
$numbera = unserialize($numbers);
$pricea = unserialize($prices);
$taxa = unserialize($taxs);

for     ($i = 1; $i <= $count; $i++)
{
        $tex .= '\Entry{'.$numbera[$i].' x '.$compa[$i].'}{\$ '.
                $pricea[$i]." per unit}{0}\n";
        $turnover += $pricea[$i] * ($taxa[$i] / 100) * $numbera[$i];
        $totprice += $pricea[$i] * (1 + $taxa[$i] / 100) * $numbera[$i];
}
$tex .= '\Entry{+ Turnover Tax}{\$ '.$turnover."}{1}\n";
$tex .= '\Entry{Total Price}{\$ '.$totprice."}{2}\n";

$tex .= $end;

# generating a temporary file and generating PDF file
$filename = tempnam ("/tmp", "phptex_");
$fp = fopen($filename.".tex", "w") or
        die ("cannot generate file $filename".".tex<br>\n");
fwrite($fp, $tex) or
        die ("cannot send data to file<br>\n");
fclose($fp);

@system("cd /tmp; latex $filename".".tex > /dev/null; dvips $filename".
        ".dvi -o $filename".".ps > /dev/null; ps2pdf $filename".
        ".ps $filename".".pdf");
```

```
checkfile($filename);
echo "<br>The file has been generated successfully.<br>\n";

# checking if a file exists
function checkfile($filename)
{
        $fp = fopen($filename.".ps", "r") or
                die ("file has not been generated<br>\n");
        $stat = fstat($fp);
        if      ($stat["size"] > 0)
        {
                # Postscript file seems to be ok
        }
        else
        {
                die ("file has not been generated<br>\n");
        }
}

?>
```

First the library containing some LaTeX code is included. After that a session is started. This is necessary to register the current script in the session that has been started when running index.php the first time. In the next step some variables are checked. The variables starting with an "s" are the ones stored in the session. However, some variables are passed to the script without using the session information. This happens when somebody inserts a date and clicks on the link for going to this script. All variables are checked, and if the user does not click on Add, the data is assigned to the variables stored in the session.

In the next step the variables are displayed using simple echo commands. Now the script starts generating the LaTeX code.

After generating the head of the document, the data in the session is unserialized and all products are processed one after the other. The turnover tax as well as the total price are computed. The total price consists of the price in the session plus the turnover tax. After the two prices have been generated, they are added to the document.

Now $tex is sent to a file. This file is processed by the LaTeX compiler and converted to a PDF file. The problem with generating the PDF file is that PHP's system call returns void. In Perl this is different because Perl's system command returns something more useful, so errors can be caught easily. In PHP this is not possible, so we have to write a function that performs some simple checks to see whether or not the file has been generated. In this example we check if the size of the PostScript file is higher than zero. This will help us to identify any errors. After a PostScript file has been generated, it is an easy and reliable task to generate the PDF file. Checking the PDF file directly is slightly more difficult because the size of an empty PDF file is not zero. This size must be checked on your local machine, so we have decided to use the more insecure PostScript version here.

Let's take a look at `tex_code.php`. It contains some LaTeX code that has been included in the document you have just generated:

```php
<?php

$head = '
\documentclass[12pt,a4paper]{letter}
\usepackage{billstyle_de}
\input{addresses}
\sloppy
\begin{document}
';

$end='
\end{Bill}
\bf Please pay within 14 days\\\\
\bf Bank\rm : xy Bank; Account Number: 432432 3424 726

\end{Fee}
\closing{Best regards,}
\end{letter}
\end{document}
';

?>
```

Finally you can take a look at `addresses.tex`:

```
\long\def\PostgresInc{%
www.postgresql.at Inc.\\
Fünfhausgasse 20/1\\
A-1150 Vienna, Austria}

\long\def\Pine{%
Pine Networks\\
Anywherestreet 344/23\\
A-1010 Vienna, Austria}
```

It contains nothing except a set of addresses. When defining the recipient of the bill, you have to use the shortcuts used in this file. If you want to send a bill to Pine Networks, you have to use `Pine` as a shortcut.

When running the Web site, the result could look like this:

```
date: July 29th, 2003
message: Thanks for buying our books.
address: Pine


The file has been generated successfully.
```

Finally you can take a look at the document that has been generated in this example. Depending on which data you add to the Web form, the result might look different (see Figure 16.18).

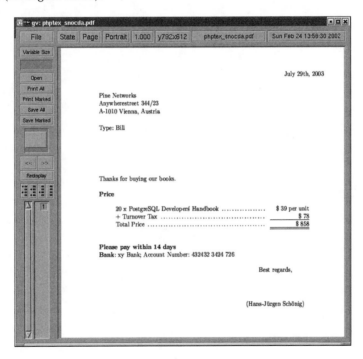

FIGURE 16.18   The output.

16.5 Summary

With the help of PHP you can build dynamic documents, images, or movies with just a few lines of code. In particular, generating dynamic images on-the-fly can be done reliably and safely. PHP provides an interface to the widely used GD module, so it is an easy task to get used to working with this interface.

In combination with PHP's Ming module, it is possible to generate Flash movies. However, the Ming module is not reliable yet, so it is better not to use it.

17

Working with Dates and Time

Working with dates and time is an important part of programming. No matter what kind of application you want to write, knowing how to treat date and time efficiently can be essential. Especially if you are writing applications that are used in many countries around the globe, the coding can be complicated because of different time zones. In this chapter you will learn to deal with dates and time in combination with SQL and PHP.

17.1 Dates and Time in SQL

PostgreSQL can easily be used to work with dates and time efficiently. In contrast to many other databases, PostgreSQL provides a set of flexible and powerful data types to handle date and time information, as well as a set of functions.

17.1.1 Data Types for Handling Dates and Time

In this section you will take a closer look at PostgreSQL's data types for handling dates and time.

17.1.1.1 `interval`

`interval` is one of the most comfortable and efficient data types supported by PostgreSQL. With the help of this data type, it is possible to store differences between two dates easily. An `interval` consists of the following components: second, minute, hour, day, week, month, year, decade, century, and millennium. Not all of these components have to be mentioned when using the data type. Let's start with some simple examples:

```
phpbook=> SELECT '4 years, 3 months, 9 hours 12 seconds'::interval;
           interval
- - - - - - - - - - - - - - - - - - - - - - -
  4 years 3 mons 09:00:12
(1 row)
```

As you can see, you just have to pass a string to the database and cast it to interval. The rest of the operations will be performed by the database. In this example you can see that the way the data is returned differs slightly from the way you have sent it to the database. PostgreSQL accepts many input formats, so it's up to you to decide which way you like best.

Here's the next example:

```
phpbook=> SELECT '4 years, 3 months, 59 hours 12 seconds'::interval;
               interval
- - - - - - - - - - - - - - - - - - - - - - - - - - - -
  4 years 3 mons 2 days 11:00:12
(1 row)
```

One of the most comfortable features of PostgreSQL is that the result is automatically transformed. In the listing you can see that 59 hours has been transformed to 2 days and 11 hours.

The next example shows more precisely how things work:

```
phpbook=> SELECT '40 hours'::interval;
  interval
- - - - - - - - - - - - -
  1 day 16:00
(1 row)
```

However, some conversions cannot be performed:

```
phpbook=> SELECT '34 days'::interval;
 interval
- - - - - - - - - -
  34 days
(1 row)
```

34 days cannot be transformed to months and days because a month does not have a fixed length. Therefore PostgreSQL decides to keep the string passed to the database as it is.

Keywords can be passed to the database as singular as well as plural words. The next example shows how centuries are treated:

```
phpbook=> SELECT '1 century 2 centuries'::interval;
 interval
-----------
 300 years
(1 row)
```

PostgreSQL recognizes that the words century and centuries have the same meaning and adds the two components. The result is 300 years because centuries are always converted to years.

17.1.1.2 date

After dealing with intervals in detail, we can take a closer look at dates. As you already saw when working with intervals, there is more than just one way to pass data to PostgreSQL. The same applies to dates. In this section you will get an overview of what you can do with dates and which input formats are accepted by PostgreSQL.

```
phpbook=> SELECT '2002/1/13'::date;
    date
-----------
 2002-01-13
(1 row)
```

First the year and the month are defined. After that, the day of the month is passed to the database. The result is January 13, 2002. Let's take a look at the next example:

```
phpbook=> SELECT '1/13/2001'::date;
    date
-----------
 2001-01-13
(1 row)
```

The date is the same again, but this time the month has been passed to the database first. Keep in mind that this format is dangerous because the result varies greatly depending on which local settings you use.

German-speaking people might prefer the German way of defining a date:

```
phpbook=> SELECT '13.12.2001'::date;
    date
-----------
 2001-12-13
(1 row)
```

The result is December 13, 2002.

In PostgreSQL, the format returned by the database will always be accepted as input as well. Therefore the next format is also valid:

```
phpbook=> SELECT '2001-1-13'::date;
    date
- - - - - - - - - - - -
 2001-01-13
(1 row)
```

Sometimes you might want to use the name of a month instead of its number. PostgreSQL provides an easy-to-use interface:

```
phpbook=> SELECT 'December 9, 2002'::date;
    date
- - - - - - - - - - - -
 2002-12-09
(1 row)
```

If you want to define explicitly that the date you are passing to the database is AD, you can add it to the string as shown in the next example:

```
phpbook=> SELECT 'December 9, 2002 AD'::date;
    date
- - - - - - - - - - - -
 2002-12-09
(1 row)
```

If you want to pass December 9, 2002 before Christ to the database, you can use BC instead of AD:

```
phpbook=> SELECT 'December 9, 2002 BC'::date;
     date
- - - - - - - - - - - - - -
 2002-12-09 BC
(1 row)
```

If you don't want to use the long version of the word December, you can use an abbreviation:

```
phpbook=> SELECT 'Dec 9, 2002'::date;
    date
- - - - - - - - - - - -
 2002-12-09
(1 row)
```

Table 17.1 contains a list of all abbreviations related to months.

TABLE 17.1 Abbreviations for Months

Month	Short Version
January	Jan
February	Feb
March	Mar
April	Apr
May	May
June	Jun
July	Jul
August	Aug
September	Sep, Sept
October	Oct
November	Nov
December	Dec

PostgreSQL supports other abbreviations besides those for months. There is also a list of abbreviations for the day of the week, as you can see in Table 17.2.

TABLE 17.2 Abbreviations for Days of the Week

Day	Short Version
Monday	Mon
Tuesday	Tue, Tues
Wednesday	Wed, Weds
Thursday	Thu, Thur, Thurs
Friday	Fri
Saturday	Sat
Sunday	Sun

Some dates are special in a way. To define these dates, PostgreSQL provides a set of keywords that can be used easily and can help you to avoid confusion. One of these keywords is epoch. epoch defines the most important point in the history of human beings, the beginning of the golden age that is also known as the century of Unix:

```
phpbook=> SELECT 'epoch'::date;
    date
- - - - - - - - - - - -
 1970-01-01
(1 row)
```

January 1, 1970 is defined as Unix starting time, and most systems perform all computations relative to epoch.

Two other important keywords are current and now. Current cannot be used with PostgreSQL 7.2 any more, so we recommend changing your applications as well. Here are two examples where current (with PostgreSQL 7.1.3) and now are used:

```
phpbook=> SELECT 'current'::date;
    date
- - - - - - - - - - -
 2002-01-10
(1 row)
```

```
phpbook=> SELECT 'now'::date;
    date
- - - - - - - - - - -
 2002-01-10
(1 row)
```

As you can see, today's date is retrieved. The same result can be achieved by using today instead:

```
phpbook=> SELECT 'today'::date;
    date
- - - - - - - - - - -
 2002-01-10
(1 row)
```

To compute yesterday's and tomorrow's date, PostgreSQL provides keywords as well:

```
phpbook=> SELECT 'tomorrow'::date;
    date
- - - - - - - - - - -
 2002-01-11
(1 row)
```

```
phpbook=> SELECT 'yesterday'::date;
    date
- - - - - - - - - - -
 2002-01-09
(1 row)
```

As you have seen, working with dates is an easy task and PostgreSQL provides various input formats.

17.1.1.3 `time [with time zone]` **and** `time [without time zone]`
To work with time, PostgreSQL provides two data types that are similar to each other. One data type is called `time with time zone`. The second one is called `time without time zone`.

Dependingon whether you want to work with time zones, you can choose which data type satisfies your demands.

Just like other data types, `time` accepts various input formats and you will learn about these in this section. Here's the first example:

```
phpbook=> SELECT '12:16'::time;
    time
 ----------
 12:16:00
(1 row)
```

Just pass the hour and the minutes to PostgreSQL as a string and cast it to `time`. The result will be what you expected it to be.

If you want to define seconds and microseconds as well, you can add that level of detail to the time easily:

```
phpbook=> SELECT '12:16:32.43'::time;
    time
 ----------
 12:16:32
(1 row)
```

In this example, you cannot see the number of microseconds in the timestamp. In the next example, the result is cast to `time with time zone`:

```
phpbook=> SELECT '12:16:32.43'::time with time zone;
    timetz
 ------------
 12:16:32+01
(1 row)
```

This time the time zone is added by PostgreSQL automatically. As you can see, the text has been written one time zone east of Greenwich Mean Time (GMT), which is Central European time (also known as Alpha time or CET).

If you need `Charlie` time (GMT+3, used in Kuwait, Moscow, Kenya, and so forth), you can change the time zone by using a + and the appropriate time zone:

```
phpbook=> SELECT '12:16:32.43+03'::time with time zone;
   timetz
------------
 12:16:32+03
(1 row)
```

If the same string is passed to the database as time without time zone, an error will be displayed:

```
phpbook=> SELECT '12:16:32.43+03'::time without time zone;
ERROR:  Bad time external representation '12:16:32.43+03'
```

In the preceding examples, you saw that the time zone is defined using a + and the offset of hours relative to Greenwich. However, the time zone can be passed to PostgreSQL differently as well; let's take a look at the next example:

```
phpbook=> SELECT '12:16 GMT'::time with time zone;
   timetz
------------
 12:16:00+00
(1 row)
```

One important point is the way EST is treated. Normally EST is short for Eastern Standard Time (Romeo, GMT–5). Let's take a look at an example:

```
phpbook=> SELECT '12:16 EST'::time with time zone;
   timetz
------------
 12:16:00-05
(1 row)
```

If you want EST to be treated as Australian time zone, you have to set a runtime parameter:

```
phpbook=> SET australian_timezones=true;
SET VARIABLE
```

This flag can be changed in postgresql.conf. If you just want to use this setting temporarily, you can use the SET command. After setting the variable, run SELECT again:

```
phpbook=> SELECT '12:16 EST'::time with time zone;
   timetz
------------
 12:16:00+10
(1 row)
```

As you see, the result differs from the one you saw before because EST has been treated as an Australian time zone.

To compute the current time, now can be used just as you saw when dealing with date:

```
phpbook=> SELECT 'now'::time with time zone;
   timetz
- - - - - - - - - - - - -
 09:57:02+00
(1 row)
```

To modify the time zone you are operating in, you can use SET again. In the following example, the time zone is set to EST:

```
phpbook=> SET TIME ZONE 'EST';
SET VARIABLE
```

Let's run now again and see that (nearly) the same data is returned, but this time a different time zone is used:

```
phpbook=> SELECT 'now'::time with time zone;
   timetz
- - - - - - - - - - - - -
 04:57:10-05
(1 row)
```

17.1.1.4 timestamp [with time zone]
The data type timestamp can be used in two ways. One way is to use timestamp with time zone. This way the values accepted by PostgreSQL range from 1903 AD to 2037 AD. The precision is 1 microsecond. If you don't have to store time zones, the range of valid data is from 4713 BC to AD 1465001. Again, the precision is 1 microsecond. If you don't have to work with time zones, the range of values is higher because internally no data is wasted for storing the time zone.

In general, timestamps are a combination of date and time—if you keep this in mind, you will find out easily how timestamps can be defined. Let's see how the data types can be used:

```
phpbook=> SELECT '24.12.2001'::timestamp;
     timestamptz
- - - - - - - - - - - - - - - - - - - - - -
 2001-12-24 00:00:00+01
(1 row)
```

In this example the German way of displaying a date is used. The format is the same as when working with dates. If no time is defined, hours, minutes, and seconds are set to zero.

If a valid time is defined, it will be displayed in the result. In addition, the time zone is mentioned:

```
phpbook=> SELECT '24.12.2001 16:34:09'::timestamp;
      timestamptz
----------------------
 2001-12-24 16:34:09+01
(1 row)
```

If you don't have to work with time zones, you can turn them off explicitly:

```
phpbook=> SELECT '24.12.2001 16:34:09'::timestamp without time zone;
      timestamp
-------------------
 2001-12-24 16:34:09
(1 row)
```

Just as when working with time, you can define a time zone using the abbreviation of the time zone you want to use. The next example shows how Japanese time can be used:

```
phpbook=> SELECT '24.12.2001 16:34:09 JST'::timestamp;
      timestamptz
----------------------
 2001-12-24 08:34:09+01
(1 row)
```

As you can see, there are nine hours of offset relative to GMT.

In addition to the German style, dates can be defined differently as well:

```
phpbook=> SELECT '2001/12/24 16:34:09 JST'::timestamp;
      timestamptz
----------------------
 2001-12-24 08:34:09+01
(1 row)
```

To define a month, strings can be used just as you saw when working with dates:

```
phpbook=> SELECT 'November 10 2002 16:34:09'::timestamp;
      timestamptz
----------------------
 2002-11-10 16:34:09+01
(1 row)
```

The year need not be defined immediately after the month. It is also possible to define the year at the end of the string:

```
phpbook=> SELECT 'November 10 16:34:09 2002'::timestamp;
     timestamptz
-----------------------
 2002-11-10 16:34:09+01
(1 row)
```

Of course, it is also possible to pass the data to the database the same way it is returned by PostgreSQL:

```
phpbook=> SELECT '2002-11-10 16:34:09+01'::timestamp;
     timestamptz
-----------------------
 2002-11-10 16:34:09+01
(1 row)
```

17.1.1.5 Time Zones

Up to now, you have seen how time zones can be used when working with SQL. In this section you will get an overview of the time zones available. Table 17.3 shows the international time zones.

TABLE 17.3   International Time Zones

GMT	Zone	Military	Civilian Time Zones	Cities
GMT	Z	Zulu	GMT: Greenwich Mean UT: Universal UTC: Universal Co-ordinated WET: Western European	London, England Dublin, Ireland Edinburgh, Scotland Lisbon, Portugal Reykjavik, Iceland Casablanca, Morocco
GMT+1	A	Alpha	CET: Central European	Paris, France Berlin, Germany Amsterdam, The Netherlands Brussels, Belgium Vienna, Austria Madrid, Spain Rome, Italy Bern, Switzerland Stockholm, Sweden Oslo, Norway

TABLE 17.3   Continued

GMT	Zone	Military	Civilian Time Zones	Cities
GMT+2	B	Bravo	EET: Eastern European	Athens, Greece
				Helsinki, Finland
				Istanbul, Turkey
				Jerusalem, Israel
				Harare, Zimbabwe
GMT+3	C	Charlie	BT: Baghdad	Kuwait
				Nairobi, Kenya
				Riyadh, Saudi Arabia
				Moscow, Russia
GMT+3:30	C*			Tehran, Iran
GMT+4	D	Delta		Abu Dhabi, UAE
				Muscat
				Tblisi
				Volgograd
				Kabul
GMT+4:30	D*			Kabul, Afghanistan
GMT+5	E	Echo		
GMT+5:30	E*			India
GMT+6	F	Foxtrot		
GMT+6:30	F*			Cocos Islands
GMT+7	G	Golf	WAST: West Australian Standard	
GMT+8	H	Hotel	CCT: China Coast	
GMT+9	I	India	JST: Japan Standard	
GMT+9:30	I*		Australian Central Standard	Darwin, Australia
				Adelaide, Australia
GMT+10	K	Kilo	GST: Guam Standard	
GMT+10:30	K*			Lord Howe Island
GMT+11	L	Lima		
GMT+11:30	L*			Norfolk Island
GMT+12	M	Mike	IDLE: International Date Line East	
			NZST: New Zealand Standard	Wellington, New Zealand
				Fiji
				Marshall Islands
GMT+13:00	M*			Rawaki Islands: Enderbury Kiribati
GMT+14:00	M±			Line Islands: Kiritimati

TABLE 17.3   Continued

GMT	Zone	Military	Civilian Time Zones	Cities
GMT–1	N	November	WAT: West Africa	Azores, Cape Verde Islands
GMT–2	O	Oscar	AT: Azores	
GMT–3	P	Papa		Brasilia, Brazil Buenos Aires, Argentina Georgetown, Guyana
GMT–3:30	P*			Newfoundland
GMT–4	Q	Quebec	AST: Atlantic Standard	Caracas La Paz
GMT–5	R	Romeo	EST: Eastern Standard	Bogota Lima, Peru New York, NY, USA
GMT–6	S	Sierra	CST: Central Standard	Mexico City, Mexico Saskatchewan, Canada
GMT–7	T	Tango	MST: Mountain Standard	
GMT–8	U	Uniform	PST: Pacific Standard	Los Angeles, CA, USA
GMT–8:30	U*			
GMT–9	V	Victor	YST: Yukon Standard	
GMT–9:30	V*			
GMT–10	W	Whiskey	AHST: Alaska–Hawaii Standard CAT: Central Alaska HST: Hawaii Standard	
GMT–11	X	X-ray	NT: Nome	
GMT–12	Y	Yankee	IDLW: International Date Line West	

17.1.2 Functions

PostgreSQL provides a set of functions for working with dates. In many cases, it is easier to use these functions than to work with PHP functions. Whether it is better to execute a function using PostgreSQL or PHP may vary, depending on how much load your database server can stand. In this section you will take a closer look at PostgreSQL's onboard functions and see how they can be used efficiently.

One function that is widely used is the now function, which computes the current timestamp:

```
phpbook=> SELECT now();
            now
--------------------------------
 2002-01-10 23:36:21.557874+01
(1 row)
```

As you can see, the current time is returned precisely and even the time zone is mentioned.

In some cases it might be useful to extract parts of the result. You can use a function called date_part. The first parameter of the function defines the component you want to retrieve. The second parameter must contain the data you want to process. Take a look at the next two examples:

```
phpbook=> SELECT date_part('year', now());
 date_part
-----------
      2002
(1 row)


phpbook=> SELECT date_part('minute', now());
 date_part
-----------
        11
(1 row)
```

First the year has been extracted. In the second example the minute has been extracted from the result. This function is a comfortable one because you need not write a function for parsing the result on an application level.

Sometimes it is not necessary to extract a component from a date, but it is necessary to cut off various parts of the data. This can be done by using the date_trunc function. The first parameter accepted by the functions defines the component having the maximum precision you want to cut off. In the next two examples you can see how this function works:

```
phpbook=> SELECT now(), date_trunc('month', now());
            now              |       date_trunc
-----------------------------+------------------------
 2002-01-12 00:12:30.346589+01 | 2002-01-01 00:00:00+01
(1 row)
```

```
phpbook=> SELECT now(), date_trunc('minute', now());
             now              |       date_trunc
------------------------------+-----------------------
 2002-01-12 00:12:44.210323+01 | 2002-01-12 00:12:00+01
(1 row)
```

First, all digits from month on are set to the lowest value. In the second example you can see that all digits from minute on are set to zero. The hour is not modified any more.

To extract data from a timestamp, PostgreSQL provides an additional method:

```
phpbook=> SELECT extract(hour from timestamp '2001-1-12 16:32');
 date_part
-----------
        16
(1 row)
```

In this example, the hour is extracted from the timestamp passed to the function. As you might have expected, the result is 16.

17.1.3 Simple Calculations

Now that you have seen which data types and functions are provided by PostgreSQL, you will take a look at some simple calculations. As you have already seen, PostgreSQL provides a powerful interface for working with dates and time. In this section you will see that performing simple computations can also be done easily and reliably.

Let's get started with an example:

```
phpbook=# SELECT now() - '2001/1/1';
     ?column?
------------------
 376 days 13:18:08
(1 row)
```

A simple subtraction has been performed. The current date is about 376 days after January 1, 2001. If you want to add two times, you will get an error:

```
phpbook=# SELECT now() + '2001/1/1';
ERROR:  Bad interval external representation '2001/1/1'
```

The addition of two times is not defined. If you think about it logically, you will find that PostgreSQL's behavior seems to be clear.

To perform additions, you can use the data type interval. In the next example you can see how 30 days can be added to the result of the now function:

```
phpbook=# SELECT now(), now() + '30 days';
            now             |         ?column?
----------------------------+--------------------------
 2002-01-12 13:20:01+01 | 2002-02-11 13:20:01+01
(1 row)
```

In this example it was not necessary to cast the string to interval explicitly. However, in some cases casting has to be done explicitly, as you can see in the next listing:

```
phpbook=# SELECT '30 days'::interval + '30 days'::interval;
 ?column?
----------
 60 days
(1 row)
```

The two components are cast to interval, so the addition can be performed easily. The result is not surprising. Because a month does not have a fixed length, the result is not displayed as months and days.

The same thing can be seen in the next example:

```
phpbook=# SELECT '1 month'::interval + '32 days'::interval;
   ?column?
---------------
 1 mon 32 days
(1 row)
```

However, in the case of hours the situation is different because the number of minutes in an hour is exactly 60, so 120 minutes make exactly two hours:

```
phpbook=# SELECT '1 day'::interval + '120 minutes'::interval;
 ?column?
-------------
 1 day 02:00
(1 row)
```

Another important point is that PostgreSQL does not distinguish between singular and plural words. In the next example you can see that PostgreSQL automatically makes plural words out of singular words:

```
phpbook=# SELECT '2 day'::interval + '120 minutes'::interval;
   ?column?
-------------
 2 days 02:00
(1 row)
```

Multiplications and divisions can be performed easily as well:

```
phpbook=# SELECT '2 hours'::interval / 10;
 ?column?
----------
 00:12
(1 row)


phpbook=# SELECT '2 hours'::interval * 12;
 ?column?
----------
 1 day
(1 row)
```

In the first example, 2 hours are divided by 10. The result is 12 minutes, which is correct. In the second example you can see that two hours are multiplied by 12. The result is 1 day.

17.2 Dates and Time in PHP

Up to now you have seen how you can work with dates and time in PostgreSQL. In this section we will see how dates and time can be treated when working with PHP's onboard functions.

17.2.1 PHP's Functions

In this section you will be guided through PHP's functions related to time.

17.2.1.1 getdate
One of the most important functions is the getdate function. It returns the current date in an array of values that can be used for further treatment. Let's take a look at an example:

```php
<?php
        $mydate = getdate();

        echo "seconds: ".$mydate['seconds']."<br>";
        echo "minutes: ".$mydate['minutes']."<br>";
```

```
        echo "hours: ".$mydate['hours']."<br>";
        echo "mday: ".$mydate['mday']."<br>";
        echo "wday: ".$mydate['wday']."<br>";
        echo "mon: ".$mydate['mon']."<br>";
        echo "year: ".$mydate['year']."<br>";
        echo "yday: ".$mydate['yday']."<br>";
        echo "weekday: ".$mydate['weekday']."<br>";
        echo "month: ".$mydate['month']."<br>";
?>
```

First the current time is computed. In the next step, the values stored in the array are displayed.

```
seconds: 2
minutes: 17
hours: 16
mday: 12
wday: 6
mon: 1
year: 2002
yday: 11
weekday: Saturday
month: January
```

17.2.1.2 date and mktime

Sometimes you want a date to be displayed in a certain format. For this purpose, you can use a function called date. Let's take a look at an example:

```
<?php
        echo date("Y-m-d H:i:s");
?>
```

The date is displayed in the same way you have already seen when dealing with PostgreSQL:

```
2002-01-12 21:38:19
```

However, with the help of date you can do even more. In general the date function is used to format a date to your needs. If you want to format any date, you pass it to the function; otherwise, the current date will be used. Let's see how this can be done:

```
<?php
        echo date("Y-m-d H:i:s", mktime(23,9,4,12,1,2002))."<br>";
        echo date("Y-m-d, h a", mktime(23,9,4,12,1,2002))."<br>";
        echo date("Y-m-d, z", mktime(23,9,4,12,1,2002))."<br>";
?>
```

The first line displays the date passed to the function by computing the result of the mktime function. mktime takes the input parameters and makes a date out of it. The result of this function can be used as input for the date function. In the first example the date including the time is displayed. In the second example you can see that 23 o'clock is equal to 11 p.m. The third example shows how many days in the year have passed until the date passed to the function.

If you execute the script, three lines will be displayed:

```
2002-12-01 23:09:04
2002-12-01, 11 pm
2002-12-01, 334
```

So far, you have seen the most important flags of the date command. The following list shows all the flags and formats accepted by date:

- a—Displays "am" (ante meridiem) or "pm" (post meridiem)
- A—Displays "AM" or "PM"
- B—Swatch Internet time (in case of 2002-12-01 23:09:04 is the result "964")
- d—Two digits defining the day of the month
- D—Displays day of week using three letters
- F—Displays month as text
- g—Displays the hour as number from 1 to 12
- G—Displays the hour as number from 0 to 23
- h—Displays the hour using two digits (01–12)
- H—Displays the hour using two digits (00–23)
- i—Displays the minutes as two digits (00–59)
- I—"1" if Daylight Savings Time, "0" otherwise
- j—Day of the month (1–31)
- l—Displays day of the week as text
- L—Boolean value defining whether a year is a leap year
- m—Displays month using two digits (01–12)
- M—Displays months using text
- n—Displays month without using leading zero
- O—Difference relative to GMT

- r—RFC-822 formatted date

- s—Displays second using two digits (00–59)

- S—Displays English ordinal suffixes

- t—Number of days in a given month

- T—Displays the time zone the local machine is in

- U—Seconds since Unix starting time (January 1, 1970)

- w—Displays day of week as number (0=Sunday; 6=Saturday)

- W—ISO-8601 week number of year, weeks starting on Monday

- Y—Displays year using 4 digits (2004)

- y—Displays year using 2 digits (99)

- z—Day of year

- Z—Time zone offset in seconds

17.2.1.3 checkdate

To find out if a date is valid, PHP provides a function called checkdate. The function accepts three parameters. The first one defines the month, the second one the day, and the third one the year of the date. When checking the date, leap years are taken into consideration.

Let's see how this function can be used:

```php
<?php
        if      (checkdate(12, 1, 2002))
        {
                echo "date valid<br>\n";
        }
        else
        {
                echo "date invalid<br>\n";
        }

        if      (checkdate(12, 1, 200200))
        {
                echo "date valid<br>\n";
        }
        else
        {
```

```
        echo "date invalid<br>\n";
    }
?>
```

The first date is valid, but the second one isn't:

```
date valid
date invalid
```

17.2.1.3 gettimeofday
The gettimeofday function returns the current date in an array. In contrast to the getdate function, gettimeofday returns microseconds, seconds, the minutes west of Greenwich, and the type of DST (Daylight Saving Time) correction. The next listing contains an example:

```
<?php
        $mydate = gettimeofday();

        echo "sec: ".$mydate['sec']."<br>\n";
        echo "usec: ".$mydate['usec']."<br>\n";
        echo "minuteswest: ".$mydate['minuteswest']."<br>\n";
        echo "dsttime: ".$mydate['dsttime']."<br>\n";
?>
```

Four lines will be displayed:

```
sec: 1010875489
usec: 567304
minuteswest: -120
dsttime: 0
```

The third line especially will be important because the content of the third field will help you when working with time zones. In this scenario we are two hours east of Greenwich (two hours in front).

17.2.1.4 gmtime
If you want a result to be displayed using GMT (Greenwich Mean Time), you can use gmtime instead of the date function. The advantage of this function is that you don't have to retrieve the current time zone and compute the offset to GMT. gmtime can do all these things for you:

```
<?php
        echo date ("M d Y H:i:s", mktime (22,39,18,12,1,2002))."<br>";
        echo gmdate ("M d Y H:i:s", mktime (22,39,18,12,1,2002))."<br>";
?>
```

If you take a look at the next example, you will find out that the second line differs from the first line:

```
Dec 01 2002 22:39:18
Dec 01 2002 21:39:18
```

17.2.1.5 gmmktime
The gmmktime function can be used to compute a Unix timestamp for a GMT date. Let's take a look at the syntax overview of the command:

```
int gmmktime (int hour, int minute, int second, int month, int day,
int year [, int is_dst])
```

To compute the number of seconds passed until Unix starting time, you can use a script like the following:

```php
<?php
        $x = gmmktime (1, 17, 53, 1, 13, 2002);
        echo "x: $x<br>\n";
?>
```

More than one billion seconds have passed since Unix starting time:

```
x: 1010884673
```

17.2.1.6 gmstrftime and strftime
To format a timestamp according to your needs, PHP provides two additional functions, which will be discussed in this section: gmstrftime and strftime. The difference between the two functions is that gmstrftime returns the data as GMT, whereas strftime uses the local settings to display the time. Let's take a look at an example:

```php
<?php
        setlocale ('LC_TIME', 'en');

        echo "GMT:<br>\n";
        echo gmstrftime ("%b %d %Y %H:%M:%S",
                mktime (23, 19, 8 ,13 ,1 ,2002))."<br><br>\n";

        echo "local settings:<br>\n";
        echo strftime ("%b %d %Y %H:%M:%S",
                mktime (23, 19, 8 ,13 ,1 ,2002))."<br>\n";
?>
```

First the local setting is defined. In the next step the date passed to the `mktime` function is formatted according to the template passed to `gmstrftime`, and `strftime` functions as the first parameter. If you execute the script, several lines will be returned as you can see in the next listing:

```
GMT:
Jan 01 2003 22:19:08

local settings:
Jan 01 2003 23:19:08
```

17.2.1.7 `localtime`

PHP's `localtime` function is similar to Perl's `localtime` function. It returns the current local time as an array consisting of all necessary components:

```php
<?php
        $mydate = localtime();

        echo "tm_sec: ".$mydate[0]."<br>\n";
        echo "tm_min: ".$mydate[1]."<br>\n";
        echo "tm_hour: ".$mydate[2]."<br>\n";
        echo "tm_mday: ".$mydate[3]."<br>\n";
        echo "tm_mon: ".$mydate[4]."<br>\n";
        echo "tm_year: ".$mydate[5]."<br>\n";
        echo "tm_wday: ".$mydate[6]."<br>\n";
        echo "tm_yday: ".$mydate[7]."<br>\n";
        echo "tm_isdst: ".$mydate[8]."<br>\n";
?>
```

The array returned by PHP can be indexed easily, so it is an easy task to retrieve the data you need. When you execute the script, the array will be displayed line by line:

```
tm_sec: 59
tm_min: 46
tm_hour: 13
tm_mday: 13
tm_mon: 0
tm_year: 102
tm_wday: 0
tm_yday: 12
tm_isdst: 0
```

17.2.1.8 `time`

PHP's `time` function returns the current Unix timestamp:

```php
<?php
        echo time();
?>
```

More than a billion seconds have passed since Unix starting time:

```
1010932663
```

17.2.1.9 `strtotime`

To convert a string to a timestamp, PHP provides a function called `strtotime`. Various input formats are accepted by the function, so almost any useful format can be converted to a timestamp. The next example shows a variety of input formats accepted by `strtotime`:

```php
<?php
        # valid dates:
        echo "January 13 2002: ".strtotime("January 13 2002")."<br>\n";
        echo "January 13 02: ".strtotime("January 13 02")."<br>\n";

        echo "2002/1/13: ".strtotime("2002/1/13")."<br>\n";
        echo "2002-1-13: ".strtotime("2002-1-13")."<br>\n";

        echo "2002/1/13 18:32:17: ".strtotime("2002/1/13 18:32:17")."<br>\n";
        echo "2002-1-13 18:32:17: ".strtotime("2002-1-13 18:32:17")."<br>\n";

        # abbreviation
        echo "3 months 12 days 29 seconds: ".
                strtotime("3 months 12 days 29 seconds")."<br>\n";

        # in valid dates:
        echo "13.1.2001: ".strtotime("13.1.2001");
?>
```

All formats but the German format you can see in the last line are accepted by PHP. As you have already seen, Unix timestamps are based on seconds. With the help of these simple formats, Unix timestamps are portable and interacting with other software products is easy. When you execute the script, you will see how the result is displayed:

```
January 13 2002: 1010876400
January 13 02: 1010876400
```

```
2002/1/13: 1010876400
2002-1-13: 1010876400
2002/1/13 18:32:17: 1010943137
2002-1-13 18:32:17: 1010943137
3 months 12 days 29 seconds: 1019742570
13.1.2001: -1
```

17.2.1.10 microtime
Retrieving the current timestamp in microseconds, you can use the `microtime` function as explained in the next listing:

```php
<?php
        $data = microtime();
        $comp = split(" ", $data);

        echo "usec: $comp[0]<br>\n";
        echo "sec: $comp[1]<br>\n";
?>
```

The result of `microtime` is one string consisting of two components. The first one contains the number of microseconds. The second component contains the seconds that have passed since Unix starting time. If you execute the script in the previous listing, the result could look like this:

```
usec: 0.94283500
sec: 1010936345
```

17.2.2 PHP and PostgreSQL as a Team
In the past two sections you have dealt with PHP and PostgreSQL in detail. However, it is important to know how the two software packages can interact with each other to build sophisticated, database-driven applications.

In this section we want to introduce you to the world of working with dates and time taken from a PostgreSQL database. As a first example, you will see how to implement a system for listing the result of a race. First, create a table:

```
phpbook=# CREATE TABLE race (id int4, competitor name, racetime time);
CREATE
```

The first column contains an id. The second column is used to store the name of a competitor, and the third column stores the time a racer needs. After creating the table, you can add some data to the table. You can use COPY:

```
phpbook=# COPY race FROM stdin;
Enter data to be copied followed by a newline.
End with a backslash and a period on a line by itself.
>> 1    Maier    00:01:53.12
>> 2    Jackson 00:02:07.43
>> 3    Bush     00:01:59.09
>> 4    Gates    00:02:43.59
>> 5    Ballmer 00:02:59.06
>> \.
```

Five records have been added to the table. To retrieve all records, you can use a simple SELECT statement as shown in the next example:

```
phpbook=# SELECT * FROM race;
 id | competitor | racetime
----+------------+----------
  1 | Maier      | 00:01:53
  2 | Jackson    | 00:02:07
  3 | Bush       | 00:01:59
  4 | Gates      | 00:02:43
  5 | Ballmer    | 00:02:59
(5 rows)
```

The problem with this result is that the number of microseconds is not returned and cannot be found in the result. To get around the problem, you can cast the third column to interval as we have done in the next listing:

```
phpbook=# SELECT id, competitor, racetime::interval as racetime FROM race;
 id | competitor | racetime
----+------------+-------------
  1 | Maier      | 00:01:53.12
  2 | Jackson    | 00:02:07.43
  3 | Bush       | 00:01:59.09
  4 | Gates      | 00:02:43.59
  5 | Ballmer    | 00:02:59.06
(5 rows)
```

Now that you have seen what is in the database, you can start writing a script that displays a list of all competitors and their delay:

```
<?php
        # connecting to the database
        $dbh = pg_connect("dbname=phpbook user=postgres");
        if      (!$dbh)
        {
```

```
                echo "connection to the database cannot be established<br>\n";
                exit;
        }

        # retrieving data
        $sql = "SELECT id, competitor, racetime::interval AS racetime
                FROM race
                ORDER BY racetime";
        $res = pg_exec($dbh, $sql);
        if      (!$res)
        {
                echo "data cannot be retrieved<br>\n";
                exit;
        }
        $rows = pg_numrows($res);
        echo "$rows competitors found<br><br>\n";

        # if no competitors -> exit
        if      ($rows == 0)
                exit;

        # retrieving time of winner and displaying information
        $winner = pg_fetch_row($res, 0);
        $winsec = postgres2php($winner[2]);
        echo "$winner[1]:<br>\n";

        # processing other competitors
        for     ($i = 1; $i < $rows; $i++)
        {
                $comp = pg_fetch_row($res, $i);
                $compsec = postgres2php($comp[2]);
                $diff = $compsec - $winsec;
                printf("%s %4.2f<br>\n", $comp[1], $diff);
        }

# transforming PostgreSQL data to PHP data
function postgres2php($data)
{
        $data = split("\.", $data);
        $sec = strtotime($data[0]) + $data[1]/100;
        return $sec;
}
?>
```

After connecting to the database, you can select the data from the table. The first record retrieved from the result is stored in $winner. To convert the data returned by PostgreSQL to a format that can be used by PHP, postgres2php is called. postgres2php has been implemented at the end of the script. First the data passed to the function is split, and in the next step, the first part of the array generated by splitting the input is converted to a timestamp. The main problem with PHP and PostgreSQL is that PHP's timestamps are not as precise as PostgreSQL's data types. Therefore you can simply add 1% of the second component in the array to the timestamp. This way it is possible to use a double instead of an integer value to store the data. The problem with dealing with dates and time this way is that a double that has been generated using the way you saw in this example cannot be used in combination with PHP's time functions. However, working with doubles is an easy way to compare various dates with each other.

After processing the first record, the rest of the data is processed with the help of a simple for loop. The delay of the various competitors is computed and the name as well as the delay are displayed on the screen. To display the number on-screen, printf is used. Some C programmers among you might already have dealt with printf in detail. printf is used to display data in a formatted way. In this scenario the first variable is displayed as string. The second variable will be treated as a floating-point number. When you execute the script, the result will be displayed on screen:

```
5 competitors found

Maier:
Bush 5.97
Jackson 14.31
Gates 50.47
Ballmer 65.94
```

As you can see, Jackson is about 14 seconds behind Maier, who has won the race.

In this example you saw that most of the computations have been performed with the help of the PHP script. However, in some cases it can be an advantage to make PostgreSQL do some things for you. The next piece of code shows how almost the same result can be computed using SQL code:

```
BEGIN;
SELECT id, competitor, NULL AS racetime, 0 AS flag
            INTO TEMPORARY tmptab
        FROM race
        WHERE racetime=(SELECT min(racetime)::interval FROM race)
```

```
UNION
SELECT id, competitor,
       racetime::interval-
               (SELECT min(racetime)::interval FROM race) AS racetime,
       1 AS flag
       FROM race
       WHERE racetime > (SELECT min(racetime)::interval FROM race);

SELECT id, competitor, racetime FROM tmptab ORDER BY flag, racetime;
COMMIT;
```

First a transaction is started. In the next step a temporary table is created that will contain the id and the name of a competitor as well as the distance between the various competitors. After creating the temporary table, all records are selected from it. The result must be ordered by `flag` and `racetime`. The `flag` field has been introduced to make sure that `Maier` is not displayed at the end of the result. Usually NULL values will be added at the end of a result—`flag` makes sure that this won't happen.

If you execute the script, you will see what comes out:

```
[hs@duron hs]$ psql phpbook < sql.sql
SELECT
 id | competitor |  racetime
----+------------+-------------
  1 | Maier      |
  3 | Bush       | 00:00:05.97
  2 | Jackson    | 00:00:14.31
  4 | Gates      | 00:00:50.47
  5 | Ballmer    | 00:01:05.94
(5 rows)
```

As we have promised, the output of the SQL batch job is pretty similar to the one you have generated with the help of PHP.

Let's take a closer look at the competitor called `Ballmer`: In the preceding listing, you can see that he is 1 minute and 5.94 seconds behind. If you take a look at the result generated by PHP, you will see that he is 65.94 seconds behind. The result is the same, but it is displayed differently. To display a result in the same way as you would with PostgreSQL is slightly more difficult when working with PHP because microseconds have to be treated differently and processed separately in order to have the opportunity to work with PHP's onboard functions. Especially when performing computations with microseconds involved, these details can be annoying.

As you have seen in this section, working with dates and time can be done with PHP as well as PostgreSQL. However, both systems have advantages but also some disadvantages. Usually it is enough to implement a set of converters to parse the date or time you have to process. In some cases, however, it can be more comfortable to perform simple calculations within the database because displaying the data is easier this way.

17.3 Summary

PHP and PostgreSQL can be used to perform a variety of complex operations for working with dates and time efficiently. Although both systems provide a set of functions, it is necessary to build bridges so that PHP and PostgreSQL can interact with each other reliably.

The major problem when combining PHP and PostgreSQL is that the precision with which dates and time are treated varies. This can cause problems when working with comparatively small time fragments.

18

Tuning

After an application has been set up, it is time for tuning to make your systems far more efficient and fast. In reality, tuning can be a complex task because many points have to be taken into consideration.

In this chapter you will learn to tune PHP and PostgreSQL. You will take a closer look at performance tuning and various runtime settings.

18.1 Tuning PostgreSQL

PostgreSQL is designed to meet the needs of a variety of different applications and requests. Depending on what you are using the database for and on which hardware you want to run, the best settings for PostgreSQL might vary significantly.

PostgreSQL offers a great deal of flexibility in the way it can be configured. You can set and modify many runtime parameters to define the behavior of the database. In addition, tuning increases the speed of your system.

In this chapter you will be guided through the fundamentals of tuning PostgreSQL. You will see what you can do to speed up your database and how PostgreSQL works internally.

When tuning databases, some important things have to be taken into consideration. In this chapter, a brief overview of all relevant topics will be provided.

18.1.1 Permanent Versus Temporary Settings

In general there are two ways of setting PostgreSQL's runtime parameters. One way is to set various variables temporarily so that only the current session or an individual query is affected. Another way is to set parameters globally so that every connection established to the database can access the same settings. Changing the global settings of PostgreSQL will help you to influence the overall speed of your database. However, in individual, complex queries that take a long time to be executed, it can be helpful to use some temporary settings as well.

In most applications, a comparatively small set of queries are responsible for most of the power needed on the machine. To get rid of or to reduce the problem, you should try to figure out the most time-consuming queries and optimize these with the help of temporary settings.

Depending on what you want to optimize, the best mixture of settings might vary.

18.1.2 The Optimizer

To tune a database and an application efficiently, it is necessary to understand the basics of how PostgreSQL processes a query. We won't go too far into detail because this would be beyond the scope of this book.

18.1.2.1 Fundamentals

The first thing to do when executing a query is to parse the statement you want PostgreSQL to process. Parsing means that the query is split up into tokens and analyzed. The syntax is checked and in the case of success, a so-called parse tree is built. This tree is used to extract the various components of the query. Now that the query has been prepared, PostgreSQL tries to find the best way through the query. Finding the best way through a query means that PostgreSQL has to decide how to execute the query best, which kind of join to use best, and the database has to decide if it is useful to use an index or not. All decisions made by PostgreSQL are based on so-called system tables, which contain statistical information about the content of a table. With the help of this data, PostgreSQL tries to compute the minimum costs to execute the query. The most important thing is that if the data in pg_statistic (the system table containing the statistical information) is not up-to-date, PostgreSQL won't be able to find the best way through a query. Therefore it is recommended to run VACUUM ANALYZE from time to time. This will make sure that the statistics are updated.

If the number of tables that have to be joined increases, the number of possible ways through the query will increase exponentially. This can be a problem because the time needed to evaluate all ways through the query will also increase, so it is fairly impossible to perform a join with dozens of tables involved. Because PostgreSQL is a highly developed database system, there is a way to get around the problem.

18.1.2.2 GEQO

GEQO is the Genetic Query Optimizer. In complex queries, GEQO is used to reduce time needed for finding the best way through a query. This is necessary because the time needed for finding the best way grows exponentially. PostgreSQL's genetic algorithm (major parts of GEQO are based on D. Whitley's Genitor algorithm) is an heuristic optimization method, which means that a good solution is found by determined, randomized searching. The list of possible solutions for the optimization problem is considered as a population of individuals. The degree of adaptation of an individual to its environment is specified by its fitness. The idea of a genetic algorithm is to check whether a mutation of an individual achieves a higher level of fitness. This way it is possible to get better solutions than just random ones. Keep in mind that the result of a genetic algorithm is based on stochastic methods ("stochastic" means "built on a probability calculus"). Therefore the way through the query computed might not be the best one, but it is still better than a random one. Don't be confused by the fact that it is a random algorithm; the result of a query is always the same. Keep in mind that this is an essential feature of PostgreSQL because otherwise it would be absolutely impossible to compute a really complex query. For mathematical reasons there is no significantly better algorithm available.

GEQO can be configured to your needs by editing the settings related to GEQO in `postgresql.conf`, but we strongly recommend sticking to the default settings unless you know extremely well what PostgreSQL is doing inside. In this book tuning GEQO won't be discussed because it takes a great deal of background information to achieve a reasonable result and in many cases it is simply not useful to change GEQO's settings. In queries that are not too complex, PostgreSQL checks possible ways through the query to find the best result and GEQO is not used.

18.1.3 Helping the Optimizer

When executing a query, it can be useful to help the optimizer in order to achieve better solutions fast. You can help the optimizer by restricting the possible steps that can be performed by the optimizer. Because this can be done temporarily, it's easy to tune PostgreSQL efficiently. In this section you will see how things can be done. You can write a simple Perl script for generating some data. You can also use PHP to write this application, but in case of slow machines or a large amount of data, it is better to use Perl for that purpose.

18.1.3.1 Generating Sample Data

The next piece of code will generate data for three tables:

```perl
#!/usr/bin/perl

open(ONE, "| psql phpbook") or die "cannot open pipe\n";
open(TWO, "| psql phpbook") or die "cannot open pipe\n";
open(THREE, "| psql phpbook") or die "cannot open pipe\n";

print ONE "CREATE TABLE one (id int4, gerade bool, modvalue int4);\n";
print TWO "CREATE TABLE two (id int4, laenge numeric(9,4));\n";
```

```
print THREE "CREATE TABLE three (id int4, modvalue int4,
        randval numeric(20,10));\n";

print ONE "COPY one FROM stdin;\n";
print TWO "COPY two FROM stdin;\n";
print THREE "COPY three FROM stdin;\n";

for     ($i = 1; $i < 100000000; $i++)
{
        $even = ($i + 1) % 2;
        $modval = $i % 23;

        print ONE "$i    $even   $modval\n";

        if      ($i % 50000 eq 0)
        {
                print "processing record: $i\n";
                $len = length($i);
                print TWO "$i    $len.0\n";
        }
        $modval = $i % 123;
        if      ($modval eq 0)
        {
                $randval = rand($i);
                printf THREE ("%s        %s        %6.3f\n",
                        $i, $modval, $randval);
        }
}

print ONE '\.';
print TWO '\.';
print THREE '\.';

close(ONE);
close(TWO);
close(THREE);
```

At the beginning of the script, three pipes to psql are opened. Every connection will be used to receive data for one table. In the next step, three tables are created and a COPY command is started for every table. Then a loop is executed 100 million times. Inside the loop $even is assigned to the result of $i%2. Every 50,000th record is added to table two. This table contains the id of the record as well as the length of the number in the first column.

For the table called three, every 123rd record is added to it. The table contains an id, $even, and a random value.

After sending the data to the server, COPY is finished and the pipes are closed. After executing the script, the database contains many records we will use for showing some basics related to tuning.

18.1.3.2 Defining Indices

After you have executed the script, the database contains three tables containing many records. To find out how many records can be found in table one, you can run a query:

```
[hs@duron data]$ time psql -c "SELECT COUNT(*) FROM one" phpbook
  count
- - - - - - - - - -
 99999999
(1 row)


real    13m54.460s
user    0m0.010s
sys     0m0.000s
```

The query has been executed using an AMD 750 CPU with 384MB of RAM and a ST320423A (20GB) hard disk. The query takes almost 14 minutes to be executed because the entire table has to be read. For the two other tables, the time needed to execute the query is significantly less:

```
[hs@duron data]$ time psql -c "SELECT COUNT(*) FROM two" phpbook
  count
- - - - - - -
  1999
(1 row)


real    0m0.645s
user    0m0.030s
sys     0m0.000s

[hs@duron data]$ time psql -c "SELECT COUNT(*) FROM three" phpbook
  count
- - - - - - - -
 813008
(1 row)
```

```
real    0m35.755s
user    0m0.000s
sys     0m0.020s
```

The reason that the queries are much faster is that the amount of data that has to be read is much smaller. In aggregation functions such as COUNT, MAX, MIN, and AVG, PostgreSQL always has to perform sequential scans because no indices can be used by the database so far.

Let's see what happens if a special value is retrieved:

```
[hs@duron data]$ time psql -c "SELECT * FROM one WHERE id=30" phpbook
 id | gerade | modvalue
----+--------+----------
 30 | t      |        7
(1 row)
```

```
real    4m48.040s
user    0m0.030s
sys     0m0.000s
```

The query takes more than four minutes, which is far too much. Imagine a production environment where dozens of concurrent users want to access the database—it would be a serious problem if every query took more than four minutes. Therefore it is necessary to find the bottlenecks of the database. The EXPLAIN command is essential for that purpose:

```
phpbook=# \h EXPLAIN
Command:     EXPLAIN
Description: Shows statement execution plan
Syntax:
EXPLAIN [ VERBOSE ] query
```

EXPLAIN can be used to display the execution plan of a query. The next listing shows the execution plan of the SQL statement we have just executed:

```
[hs@duron data]$ time psql -c "EXPLAIN SELECT * FROM one WHERE id=30" phpbook
NOTICE:  QUERY PLAN:

Seq Scan on one  (cost=0.00..22.50 rows=10 width=9)

EXPLAIN
```

```
real    0m0.620s
user    0m0.020s
sys     0m0.000s
```

As you can see, a so-called sequential scan is performed, which means that the entire table has to be read to compute the result of the query. This is far too slow, so you should consider using an index as shown in the next listing:

```
[hs@duron data]$ time psql -c "CREATE INDEX idx_one_id ON one(id)" phpbook
CREATE

real    32m17.762s
user    0m0.010s
sys     0m0.000s
```

Creating the index takes about half an hour. This is fast because building up an insert forces the database to sort the data in the table, which is a lot of work. Internally an index is a tree based on a sorted list pointing to the data in the table. Sorting about 100 million records takes a long time. Internally PostgreSQL uses the memory defined as sort memory for building up the index. In other words, in PostgreSQL's default setting 512 kilobytes of sort memory per sort process are used for sorting. If more memory is needed, the database creates temporary files on disk to perform the sort. Writing data to disk is much slower than sorting records in memory, so we recommend redefining the size of the sort buffer. Before doing this, you can take a look at how the size of the default sort buffer can be retrieved:

```
phpbook=# SHOW sort_mem;
NOTICE:  sort_mem is 512
SHOW VARIABLE
```

As you can see, 512 kilobytes of memory are used as sort buffer. If you are creating a huge index like the one you saw before, you can redefine the size of the memory temporarily as shown in the next example (don't forget to drop the old index first):

```
[hs@duron data]$ time psql -c "CREATE INDEX idx_one_id ON one(id)" phpbook
CREATE

real    26m37.654s
user    0m0.010s
sys     0m0.000s
```

As you can see, modifying the sort buffer can help you to speed up the generation of the index.

Now that the index has been created, you can take a look at the execution plan of the query so that you can see if the index is used:

```
[hs@duron data]$ psql -c "EXPLAIN SELECT * FROM one WHERE id=30" phpbook
NOTICE:   QUERY PLAN:


Seq Scan on one   (cost=0.00..1838235.99 rows=1000000 width=9)


EXPLAIN
```

As you can see, no index is used. To understand the problem, it is necessary to take a closer look at how the optimizer works.

18.1.3.3 Optimizing Queries Using Vacuum

The optimizer's results are based on statistical information that is stored in a system table called pg_statistic. If the statistical data in pg_statistic is bad, the execution plans generated by PostgreSQL are bad as well. This will lead to bad performance and long execution times. To solve these problems, PostgreSQL provides a command called VACUUM. The next listing shows the syntax overview of VACUUM:

```
phpbook=# \h VACUUM
Command:     VACUUM
Description: garbage-collect and optionally analyze a database
Syntax:
VACUUM [ FULL ] [ FREEZE ] [ VERBOSE ] [ table ]
VACUUM [ FULL ] [ FREEZE ] [ VERBOSE ] ANALYZE [ table [ (column [, ...] ) ] ]
```

With the introduction of PostgreSQL 7.2, the parameters accepted by VACUUM have grown. In particular, VACUUM FULL is an important command that tries to shrink PostgreSQL's internal consumption of storage as much as possible. With the help of VACUUM ANALYZE, PostgreSQL not only shrinks the files on disk, but it also computes the statistical information the optimizer is relying on. This leads to better execution plans and more efficient storage.

If you don't want to run VACUUM interactively, you can run vacuumdb from the command line. Here is an overview of the syntax:

```
[hs@athlon hs]$ vacuumdb --help
vacuumdb cleans and analyzes a PostgreSQL database.

Usage:
  vacuumdb [options] [dbname]
```

```
Options:
  -h, --host=HOSTNAME            Database server host
  -p, --port=PORT               Database server port
  -U, --username=USERNAME       Username to connect as
  -W, --password                Prompt for password
  -d, --dbname=DBNAME           Database to vacuum
  -a, --all                     Vacuum all databases
  -t, --table='TABLE[(columns)]' Vacuum specific table only
  -f, --full                    Do full vacuuming
  -v, --verbose                 Write a lot of output
  -z, --analyze                 Update optimizer hints
  -e, --echo                    Show the command being sent to the backend
  -q, --quiet                   Don't write any output

Read the description of the SQL command VACUUM for details.

Report bugs to <pgsql-bugs@postgresql.org>.
```

As you can see, many parameters can be defined. The most important thing is that it is possible to vacuum remote databases. Especially when working with many server machines, this can be useful because all machines can be maintained using just one machine.

Since PostgreSQL 7.2, a command called ANALYZE is provided. It can be used to gather statistical information for PostgreSQL's optimizer. Let's take a look at the syntax overview:

```
phpbook=# \h ANALYZE
Command:     ANALYZE
Description: collect statistics about a database
Syntax:
ANALYZE [ VERBOSE ] [ table [ (column [, ...] ) ] ]
```

Just define the table you want to analyze and click the button. PostgreSQL will build up the system table for you.

Now run vacuumdb to rebuild pg_statistic:

```
[hs@duron data]$ time vacuumdb -a -z
Vacuuming template1
VACUUM
Vacuuming phpbook
VACUUM
```

```
real    29m32.559s
user    0m0.040s
sys     0m0.030s
```

After executing the command, you can run a SELECT statement again to see how fast the query can be executed now:

```
[hs@duron data]$ time psql -c "SELECT * FROM one WHERE id=5000000" phpbook
   id   | gerade | modvalue
--------+--------+----------
 5000000 | t      |        7
(1 row)
```

```
real    0m0.104s
user    0m0.010s
sys     0m0.010s
```

It takes about 0.1 seconds to retrieve one value out of 100 million records, which is fast. This impressive example shows how much performance can be gained by such an operation. Execute the query a second time:

```
[hs@duron data]$ time psql -c "SELECT * FROM one WHERE id=5000000" phpbook
   id   | gerade | modvalue
--------+--------+----------
 5000000 | t      |        7
(1 row)
```

```
real    0m0.036s
user    0m0.020s
sys     0m0.010s
```

As you can see, the query has been executed even faster because of caching effects.

18.1.3.4 Optimizing Queries Using Caching

Caching means that PostgreSQL keeps some data in memory and therefore it is not necessary to read every piece of data from the hard disk every time a query is executed. To retrieve the current size of the cache, you can use the SHOW command as shown in the next listing:

```
phpbook=# SHOW effective_cache_size;
NOTICE:  effective_cache_size is 1000
SHOW VARIABLE
```

The default cache size is 1000 blocks, which is 8 megabytes. Let's see what effects caching can have on the performance of your system. You can write a simple shell script that measures the data needed to perform various queries:

```sh
#!/bin/sh

echo "1: 8mb cache"
time psql -c "SELECT COUNT(*) FROM one WHERE id<200000;
       SELECT COUNT(*) FROM one WHERE id<200000; " phpbook > /dev/null

echo "1: 160mb cache"
time psql -c "SET effective_cache_size TO 20000;
       SELECT COUNT(*) FROM one WHERE id<200000;
       SELECT COUNT(*) FROM one WHERE id<200000; " phpbook > /dev/null

echo "2: 160mb cache"
time psql -c "SELECT COUNT(*) FROM one WHERE id<100000000;
       SELECT COUNT(*) FROM one WHERE id<100000000; " phpbook > /dev/null

echo "2: 160mb cache"
time psql -c "SET effective_cache_size TO 20000;
       SELECT COUNT(*) FROM one WHERE id<100000000;
       SELECT COUNT(*) FROM one WHERE id<100000000; " phpbook > /dev/null
```

Keep in mind that these results have been computed on my machine. The absolute figures are not that important, but it is necessary to see the relationship between the various results. This will help you to understand PostgreSQL's way of caching. Let's take a look at the results:

```
1: 8mb cache

real    0m3.464s
user    0m0.020s
sys     0m0.000s
1: 160mb cache

real    0m1.674s
user    0m0.020s
sys     0m0.010s
2: 160mb cache

real    14m13.022s
user    0m0.010s
```

```
sys     0m0.000s
2: 160mb cache

real    14m40.221s
user    0m0.010s
sys     0m0.000s
```

As you can see, there is a significant difference between the first two results. The first example, which uses the standard settings, is significantly slower due to I/O. In the second example, the data needed for the executing the first query is kept in memory, so the second query can be executed much faster. This behavior seems obvious. In the third example, huge amounts of data are processed using the default settings. As you can see, the full table scan takes around 14 minutes. In the fourth example, PostgreSQL uses a lot of cache, but the queries are even slower. The reason for that is simple: Caching causes overhead. Internally PostgreSQL keeps the most recently used blocks in memory. If the cache is full and data is added to it, PostgreSQL will remove the oldest block stored in the cache, and this is exactly what happens in the case of complex queries. Caching won't help you to speed up your queries, but it can cause overhead for managing the cache. Example number four is a worst-case scenario, but it is necessary to understand what happens internally.

18.1.3.5 Joins and Helping the Optimizer

After defining an index and having a closer look at caching, it is time to see how joins are performed. The next example shows how the number of rows two tables have in common can be computed:

```
[hs@duron data]$ time psql -c "SELECT COUNT(one.id) FROM one, two WHERE
one.id=two.id" phpbook
 count
-------
  1999
(1 row)


real    0m44.202s
user    0m0.020s
sys     0m0.000s
```

As you can see, the query takes around 44 seconds to complete. But 44 seconds are quite a bit of time, so it is necessary to take a look at the execution plan of the query:

```
[hs@duron data]$ time psql -c "EXPLAIN SELECT COUNT(one.id) FROM one, two
WHERE one.id=two.id" phpbook
NOTICE:   QUERY PLAN:

Aggregate  (cost=10078.16..10078.16 rows=1 width=8)
   -> Nested Loop  (cost=0.00..10073.17 rows=1999 width=8)
        -> Seq Scan on two  (cost=0.00..32.99 rows=1999 width=4)
        -> Index Scan using idx_one_id on one  (cost=0.00..5.01 rows=1 width=4)

EXPLAIN

real    0m0.091s
user    0m0.010s
sys     0m0.010s
```

First an index scan and a sequential scan are performed. This is no problem because the second table is comparatively small. After that, a nested loop has to be done. This means that for every record in the first table, a counterpart in the second table has to be found. This takes a long time because if the number of records in the two tables doubles, it will take up to four times longer to execute the query. In the case of 10 times more data, it will take up to 100 times longer to compute the result. Therefore huge amounts of data cannot be processed this way. To join two tables, an index should be defined:

```
[hs@duron data]$ psql -c "CREATE INDEX idx_two_id ON two(id)" phpbook
CREATE
```

After defining the index, you can take a look at the execution plan of the query again:

```
[hs@duron data]$ psql -c "EXPLAIN SELECT COUNT(one.id) FROM one, two
WHERE one.id=two.id" phpbook
NOTICE:   QUERY PLAN:

Aggregate  (cost=10078.16..10078.16 rows=1 width=8)
   -> Nested Loop  (cost=0.00..10073.17 rows=1999 width=8)
        -> Seq Scan on two  (cost=0.00..32.99 rows=1999 width=4)
        -> Index Scan using idx_one_id on one  (cost=0.00..5.01 rows=1 width=4)

EXPLAIN
```

Nothing has changed. The database still performs a sequential scan. To get rid of the problem, you can either run VACUUM or tell the optimizer to use an index scan instead of a sequential scan. This can be done by using the SET command:

```
[hs@duron data]$ time psql -c "SET enable_seqscan TO off; SELECT COUNT(one.id)
      FROM one, two WHERE one.id=two.id" phpbook
 count
 -------
  1999
(1 row)


real    0m0.441s
user    0m0.010s
sys     0m0.000s
```

This time the result is computed much faster. The reason for that can easily be found in the execution plan of the query:

```
[hs@duron data]$ psql -c "SET enable_seqscan TO off;
      EXPLAIN SELECT COUNT(one.id) FROM one, two WHERE one.id=two.id" phpbook
NOTICE:  QUERY PLAN:

Aggregate  (cost=10140.18..10140.18 rows=1 width=8)
  -> Nested Loop  (cost=0.00..10135.18 rows=1999 width=8)
       -> Index Scan using idx_two_id on two  (cost=0.00..95.00 rows=1999
width=4)
        -> Index Scan using idx_one_id on one  (cost=0.00..5.01 rows=1 width=4)


EXPLAIN
```

This time two sequential scans are performed. After that a nested loop is executed to find the appropriate matches. Finally the COUNT operation is executed.

To build up the statistics the optimizer is using, you can run VACUUM for a specific table in a specific database. This can be done by using the -t flag in combination with -d:

```
[hs@duron data]$ vacuumdb -z -t two -d phpbook
VACUUM
```

After that it is not necessary any more to turn sequential scans off manually.

In many cases, setting parameters temporarily can be useful for tuning a query. However, in some cases it can be fatal to influence the optimizer. Let's take a look at the execution time of the next example:

```
[hs@duron data]$ time psql -c "SET enable_nestloop TO off;
        SELECT COUNT(one.id) FROM one, two WHERE one.id=two.id" phpbook
 count
-------
  1999
(1 row)
```

```
real    10m38.210s
user    0m0.020s
sys     0m0.000s
```

The query takes more than 10 minutes to complete. This is far too long, so it is worth taking a look at the execution plan of the query:

```
[hs@duron data]$ time psql -c "SET enable_nestloop TO off;
        EXPLAIN SELECT COUNT(one.id) FROM one, two WHERE one.id=two.id" phpbook
NOTICE:  QUERY PLAN:

Aggregate  (cost=5588303.92..5588303.92 rows=1 width=8)
  -> Hash Join  (cost=37.99..5588298.92 rows=1999 width=8)
        -> Seq Scan on one  (cost=0.00..1588235.99 rows=99999999 width=4)
        -> Hash  (cost=32.99..32.99 rows=1999 width=4)
              -> Seq Scan on two  (cost=0.00..32.99 rows=1999 width=4)

EXPLAIN
```

```
real    0m0.039s
user    0m0.020s
sys     0m0.000s
```

Two sequential scans are performed. In addition, hashes are built. This way of executing the query is far slower.

18.1.4 Performance Monitoring

To tune a database, it is necessary to know what the database is doing and how things work. One important parameter when executing a SQL statement is the time it needs to be executed by the database. The target of every tuning process is to find out which queries take too long. This can easily be done with the help of a simple function. Let's take a look at an example:

```php
<?php
        $dbh = pg_connect("user=postgres dbname=phpbook");
        if      (!$dbh) { echo "Cannot connect<br>\n"; }

        $stat = myexec($dbh, "SELECT * FROM pg_class ORDER BY relname");
        $stat = myexec($dbh, "SELECT 1+1");
        $data = pg_fetch_row($stat, 0);
        echo "1+1 makes ".$data[0]."<br>\n";

function myexec($dbh, $code)
{
        $start = split(" ", microtime());
        $stime = $start[0] + $start[1];

        $stat = pg_exec($dbh, $code);

        $endtime = split(" ", microtime());
        $etime = $endtime[0] + $endtime[1];

        echo $etime - $stime. " seconds: $code<br>\n";

        return $stat;
}

?>
```

The most important part of the example is the myexec function, which can be found at the end of the script. It measures the time needed for executing a query and prints it onscreen. The information can also be sent to a logfile, which is used solely for tuning purposes. To keep the example slim, we have decided to display the information onscreen.

Let's execute the script and see what comes out:

```
0.019946932792664 seconds: SELECT * FROM pg_class ORDER BY relname
0.0053499937057495 seconds: SELECT 1+1
1+1 makes 2
```

As you can see, three lines have been returned. The first two lines contain debugging information, and the third line contains the result of the second SQL statement. As you can see, both queries are extremely fast.

Another thing that can be important is to find out how many backend processes are running on the local machine. You can write a shell script to find that out. Let's take a look:

```
[hs@athlon data]$ ps ax | egrep -e ''postgres:''
25032 ?        S     0:00 postgres: stats buffer process
25034 ?        S     0:00 postgres: stats collector process
 4289 ?        S     0:00 postgres: postgres phpbook [local] idle
 4295 ?        S     0:00 postgres: postgres phpbook [local] idle
 4311 ?        S     0:00 postgres: postgres phpbook [local] idle
 4371 ?        S     0:00 postgres: postgres phpbook [local] idle
 4372 ?        S     0:00 postgres: postgres phpbook [local] idle
15489 pts/3    S     0:00 postgres: stats buffer process
15490 pts/3    S     0:00 postgres: stats collector process
15493 pts/3    S     0:00 postgres: hs phpbook 127.0.0.1 idle
15497 pts/4    S     0:00 egrep -e postgres:
```

ps ax returns a list of all processes on your Linux box. With the help of egrep, you can extract all processes that run on the local machine. All connections are returned. If you want to retrieve all connections that have been established via Unix sockets, you can use a different regular expression:

```
[hs@athlon data]$ ps ax | egrep -e ''postgres:.*local''
 4289 ?        S     0:00 postgres: postgres phpbook [local] idle
 4295 ?        S     0:00 postgres: postgres phpbook [local] idle
 4311 ?        S     0:00 postgres: postgres phpbook [local] idle
 4371 ?        S     0:00 postgres: postgres phpbook [local] idle
 4372 ?        S     0:00 postgres: postgres phpbook [local] idle
15445 pts/4    S     0:00 egrep -e postgres:.*local
```

As you can see, a list of processes has been returned. In addition to backend processes, you can see that egrep itself is also listed. The target of the next example is to write a SQL function that returns the number of backend processes running on your local machine and interacting with PostgreSQL via Unix sockets. You can write a simple PHP application that makes a system call and returns the data. This is not that comfortable but can be done easily.

A more elegant way is to use PL/Sh by Peter Eisentraut. PL/Sh provides access to a Unix shell from inside PostgreSQL. If you are working in a multiuser environment, you should not use it in all databases for security reasons. However, if you need it just for monitoring, you can create a separate database and PL/Sh support to it.

Check out the following Web site to download the source code:

```
http://www.ca.postgresql.org/~petere/download/
```

To install the sources, use `tar xvfz` and the name of the package. Then run `config-`
`ure` to build all makefiles. Just define the location where `configure` can find your
PostgreSQL source code. Then use `--prefix` to tell the script where your current
PostgreSQL binaries can be found. Take a look at how to do this:

```
CPPFLAGS=-I/usr/src/postgres/postgresql-7.2/src/include/ ./configure
--prefix=/usr/local/postgresql/
```

If no errors have occurred, you can run `make` and `make install` to compile and
install the package. In the next step you can add support for PL/Sh to your database.
In this example it is done for the database called `phpbook` (assume that PostgreSQL
has been installed in `/usr/local/postgresql`):

```
[hs@athlon hs]$ psql -d phpbook -f
/usr/local/postgresql/share/pgplsh/createlang_pgplsh.sql
CREATE
CREATE
```

If no error occurred, PL/Sh has been added to the database successfully. In the next
step you can write two functions. The first one returns the result of the `ps` command
you saw before. The second one returns the number of connections being established
to the local machine via Unix sockets (not via TCP/IP):

```
CREATE OR REPLACE FUNCTION "backends_list"() RETURNS "text" AS '
#!/bin/sh
ps ax | egrep -e ''postgres:.*local''
' LANGUAGE 'plsh';

CREATE OR REPLACE FUNCTION "backends_number"() RETURNS "text" AS '
#!/bin/sh
expr $(ps ax | egrep -e ''postgres:.*local'' | wc -l) - 1
' LANGUAGE 'plsh';
```

In the first function, `egrep` is used to find all processes related to PostgreSQL. In the
second function, the number of processes returned is used and reduced by one. This
is done to subtract the back end performing the calculation.

Let's execute the function and see what is happening:

```
phpbook=# SELECT backends_list();



                backends_list
```

```
--------------------------------------------------------------------
--------------------------------------------------------------------
--------------------------------------------------------------------
--------------------------------------------------------------------
--------------------------------------------------------------------
---------------------------------------------------------------
 4289 ?         S       0:00 postgres: postgres phpbook [local] idle
 4295 ?         S       0:00 postgres: postgres phpbook [local] idle
 4311 ?         S       0:00 postgres: postgres phpbook [local] idle
 4371 ?         S       0:00 postgres: postgres phpbook [local] idle
 4372 ?         S       0:00 postgres: postgres phpbook [local] idle
15408 pts/3     S       0:00 postgres: hs phpbook [local] SELECT
15419 pts/3     S       0:00 egrep -e postgres:.*local
(1 row)
```

A list of processes is returned. In this listing the egrep process is returned as well but it can easily be removed by writing a slightly more complex shell script. To compute the number of back ends, you can call backends_number:

```
phpbook=# SELECT backends_number();
 backends_number
-----------------
 6
(1 row)
```

In this example, six back end processes are running.

An additional command that can be important for you is called uptime and can be used to find out how long the system has been running and how much load your CPU has to face. Let's take a look at an example:

```
[hs@duron hs]$ uptime
 10:55pm  up 124 days, 12:10,  5 users,  load average: 1.52, 1.56, 1.54
```

In this example the machine has been up and running for 124 days since the last reboot. Currently five users have logged into the machine. The most important information for database tuners is the average load of the CPU: The first column contains the load during the last minute, the second column tells you the average load during the last 5 minutes, and the last column contains information about the last 15 minutes.

Keep in mind that the CPU load says nothing about the real load on your system. In addition, not all operating systems provide a command such as uptime.

18.1.5 Optimizations at Compile Time

A variety of settings can be changed at compile time. Depending on the compiler you are using, some basic optimizations can be done by adding or changing the default compiler flags. In this section you will get a brief insight into what you can do with the help of GCC.

One flag that can be used is the `-mcpu` flag. The following parameters are accepted by GCC 2.96: `i386`, `i486`, `i586`, `i686`, `pentium`, `pentiumpro`, `k6`, and `athlon`.

Although picking a specific CPU type will schedule things appropriately for that particular chip, the compiler will not generate any code that does not run on the `i386` without the `-march=` option being used. `i586` is equivalent to `pentium` and `i686` is equivalent to `pentiumpro`.

`-march` will help you to define the architecture. The choices for CPU type are the same as for the `-mcpu` flag. Note that specifying `-march` implies `-mcpu`. The following flags are accepted: `-m386`, `-m486`, `-mpentium`, `-mpentiumpro`.

In addition to telling GCC which CPU the binaries should be optimized for, it is possible to use various other optimization flags as shown in Table 18.1.

TABLE 18.1 Optimization Flags

`-fcaller-saves`	`-fno-function-cse`
`-fcse-follow-jumps`	`-fno-inline`
`-fcse-skip-blocks`	`-fno-peephole`
`-fdelayed-branch`	`-fomit-frame-pointer`
`-felide-constructors`	`-frerun-cse-after-loop`
`-fexpensive-optimizations`	`-fschedule-insns`
`-ffast-math`	`-fschedule-insns2`
`-ffloat-store`	`-fstrength-reduce`
`-fforce-addr`	`-fthread-jumps`
`-fforce-mem`	`-funroll-all-loops`
`-finline-functions`	`-funroll-loops`
`-fkeep-inline-functions`	`-O`
`-fmemoize-lookups`	`-O2`
`-fno-default-inline`	`-O3`
`-fno-defer-pop`	

In this section you will take a closer look at the `-O` flags.

When you use `-O` flags, compiling the binaries will take slightly more time than when not using the optimizer. In contrast, the binaries the compiler generates will be more efficient and can be executed faster. Depending on which level of optimization you use, the compiler produces more or less efficient code. By default `-O2` is used. If you want to use an even higher level of optimization, you can use the `-O3` flag, which does everything `-O2` does along with turning `-finline-functions` on. This means that the compiler is allowed to reduce the number of function calls by inlining various components of the code. The problem with this algorithm is that binaries created by using `-O3` cannot easily be debugged because small functions might be omitted by inlining them. However, if you want to get the maximum performance out of your compiler, you can try to use `-O3`. In Chapter 6 you can see how to set compiler settings.

18.2 Tuning PHP

Tuning PHP is much harder than tuning the database because scripts are always executed the same way. However, some basic things can be changed to achieve higher performance. In this section you will see what can be done to make PHP run even faster.

PHP can be used in two ways: One way is to run PHP as a Web server module so that it is called by Apache. The other way is to run PHP using the CGI interface. When you use the CGI interface, a process is started whenever a request is sent to the Web server. When the process is started, `php.ini` has to be read so that PHP can find out which parameters have been set. This takes some time and can cause significant overhead. After that the script is executed.

In the case of PHP as a module, `php.ini` does not have to be parsed and analyzed for every connection being established to the database. Therefore PHP is significantly faster when using it as a module.

18.3 Summary

After applications have been written, it is time to tune PostgreSQL as well as PHP to reach a higher level of performance. In many cases, tuning will help you to manage higher amounts of data as well as to handle more user requests.

19
XML

XML (Extensible Markup Language) is truly one of the most impressive inventions in the history of modern computing. During the past few years, it has been adopted by many people and companies around the globe. Especially for B2B solutions, XML plays a major role and is an essential component. This chapter guides you through the most important concepts of XML and shows you how to use XML in combination with PHP and PostgreSQL.

19.1 The Basic Concepts

The most important thing you have to know about XML is that XML is a metamarkup language for text documents. XML is not a programming language, which means that it is not possible to write standalone applications that need nothing other than XML—it has nothing to do with languages such as C and Perl. XML is a language like HTML or SGML and can be used to describe documents.

One of the biggest advantages of XML over other languages for describing documents is that it does not have a fixed set of tags because this would be far too inflexible. Working with a fixed set of tags would fail because the reality cannot be modeled using just a few static commands.

19.1.1 XML Technologies

Many technologies have been developed on top of XML. Let's take a look at the most important concepts and technologies you will have to deal with when working with XML and XML-based applications:

- **XLinks**—XLinks is an attribute-based syntax for hyperlinks between XML-based and non-XML-based documents. It is similar to the kind of links you have already dealt with when working with HTML but in contrast to the kind of links provided by HTML, XLinks are one-directional.

- **XSLT**—XSL is short for Extensible Stylesheet Language and can be divided into two parts. One of these is XSL Transformation. With the help of XSLT applications, it is possible to define rules you can use to transform an XML document to another. The XML file used as input is analyzed and the components of the file are compared with a stylesheet used for generating the output.

- **XPointer**—XPointers are often used in combination with XLinks. The idea of XPointers is to have a syntax for referring to parts of an XML document.

- **Xpath**—In Xpath, an XML document is seen as a tree consisting of nodes. Every document contains exactly one root node. Every element in the tree has a name, a parent node, a namespace URI, and a set of child nodes. In addition, a tree contains attributes, texts, namespaces, processing instructions, and comments. Xpath is used by XPointers, XSLT, and by a set of proposed standards for query languages based on XML.

- **Namespace**—Not all names in a document must be unique. With the help of namespaces, it is possible to distinguish various components with the same name.

- **SAX**—SAX is a simple API for working with XML. It is a Java-based programming interface that is widely used when working with XML.

- **DOM**—DOM is short for Document Object Model. It is an API that treats an XML document as a tree of nested objects having various properties and attributes.

In addition to these standard technologies, many proprietary add-ons have been developed. Most of these add-ons focus on a very specific subject. One example of an add-on is MathML (Mathematical Markup Language), which is a W3C-endorsed XML application for processing and using mathematical statements and equations in documents.

19.1.2 XML Basics

Just like HTML, XML is based on tags. In contrast to HTML, XML does not offer a fixed set of tags. This has many advantages because the user can define his own tags, so XML offers great flexibility and can easily be adapted to an application's needs.

An XML file is based on text. Unlike other file formats, XML is not a binary format, so an XML file can easily be read.

Although XML is a flexible and powerful language, it is much more strict than HTML. Tags must be placed in a certain position, or an XML document won't be valid. The reason for that is simple: XML's flexibility makes this necessary because otherwise it would be impossible to retrieve data from a document efficiently and reliably.

If a document satisfies the demands of XML, it is considered to be "well formed"; otherwise, it is not. To find out if a document is well formed, you can use a parser. Let's look at a simple XML document:

```
<?xml version="1.0"?>

<!DOCTYPE person [
<!ELEMENT person (name, birthday)>
<!ELEMENT name (academic_title, firstname, surname)>
<!ELEMENT birthday (#PCDATA)>
<!ELEMENT academic_title (#PCDATA)>
<!ELEMENT firstname (#PCDATA)>
<!ELEMENT surname (#PCDATA)>

]>

<person>
        <name>
                <academic_title>Dr. med.</academic_title>
                <firstname>John</firstname>
                <surname>Jackson</surname>
        </name>
        <birthday>1978/08/09</birthday>
</person>
```

The first thing you can do is to validate the document. The easiest way to do that is to use the XML validation tool at http://www.stg.brown.edu/service/xmlvalid/. With the help of this tool, it is possible to find out if the document you want to check is well formed. The document you have just seen is well formed, as you can see in the next listing:

```
Validation Results for file.xml
Document validates OK.
```

After this brief overview, we will take a closer look at what the content of the document is all about. First the version of XML used is specified. The syntax is similar to the syntax of HTML. The block starting with <!DOCTYPE person marks the beginning of an internal DTD. A DTD (Document Type Definition) defines the layout of an

XML document. To use the words of a database developer: With the help of DTDs, it is possible to define data structures. In most cases, data and the DTD are stored in separate files because data and definition should be separated.

In this example the data structure consists of various nested elements. The element called person consists of two further elements called name and birthday. The element called name consists of three further elements whose names are academic_title, firstname, and surname. As you probably noticed, the child elements of an element are listed in parentheses. In the next lines you can see those elements that do not have children any more. Their value is set to #PCDATA. This means that these children contain the actual data.

After the inline DTD, the data is listed. Tags are defined and the data or additional objects are listed inside a pair of tags. This way, a tree structure can be built. Every leaf of the tree contains a piece of data. Because an XML document can be seen as a tree, it contains hierarchical data. This is slightly different than the hierarchical concept, but it also has some advantages (just as a relational data structure has some advantages).

The main challenge when working with PHP, PostgreSQL, and XML is that an efficient way for extracting data from the XML file has to be found. One way to access data is DOM. PHP provides various functions for working with DOM, but these functions are still said to be experimental.

19.2 Building a Simple XML-Based Application

The standard interface for working with XML is DOM. It offers a simple way to interact with XML documents just as you would do with a tree. In PHP 4.1.1, DOM is still in beta, so we have decided not to go into detail because things can change rapidly. However, to understand the basic concepts of DOM, a simple example is helpful:

```php
<?php
        $doc = new DomDocument;
        $node = new DomNode;

        $doc = xmldocfile( "file.xml" );
        $person = $doc->root();
        $nodes = $person->children();

        print $nodes[1]->content;
?>
```

Recall the XML file you saw before. It contains various nested objects. With the help of this simple PHP script, information about a name is retrieved. First, two objects are created. The first one points to the root element of the document. The second one is used for processing one node of the document. With the help of the `xmldoc-file` function, an XML file is read and assigned to `$doc`. Then the root of the document is assigned to `$person`. In the next step, the children of `$person` are retrieved and stored in an array. This array is used to display data onscreen:

```
Dr. med. John Jackson
```

As you can see, using DOM is an easy way of retrieving data stored in an XML file. In future versions of PHP, DOM will certainly play a major role, and powerful applications will be written based on this interface.

19.3 XML and PostgreSQL

PostgreSQLis an object relational database system. Unlike databases such as Tamino, PostgreSQL is not an XML-based database. This leads to higher efficiency, but when working with XML it also has some minor disadvantages.

In this section you will learn to use PostgreSQL in combination with XML. You will see that it's easy, and the fact that PostgreSQL is an object relational database offers some significant advantages.

19.3.1 Installation

In PostgreSQL's contributed directory, you can find a directory called `xml`. This directory contains a package for working with XML inside a PostgreSQL database. To install the package, just run `make`:

```
[root@duron xml]# make
gcc -O3 -march=athlon  -Wall -Wmissing-prototypes -Wmissing-declarations
-fpic -g -I../../src/include   -c -o pgxml_dom.o pgxml_dom.c
gcc -shared -lxml2 -o pgxml_dom.so pgxml_dom.o
if [ -z "$USER" ]; then USER=$LOGNAME; fi; \
if [ -z "$USER" ]; then USER=`whoami`; fi; \
if [ -z "$USER" ]; then echo 'Cannot deduce $USER.'; exit 1; fi; \
rm -f pgxml_dom.sql; \
C=`pwd`; \
sed -e "s:_CWD_:$C:g" \
    -e "s:_OBJWD_:$C:g" \
    -e "s:_DLSUFFIX_:.so:g" \
    -e "s/_USER_/$USER/g" < pgxml_dom.source > pgxml_dom.sql
rm pgxml_dom.o
```

After compiling the source code, you can insert the functions in the package to PostgreSQL. This can easily be done with the help of psql:

```
[hs@duron xml]$ psql phpbook < pgxml_dom.sql
CREATE
CREATE
```

Two functions were added to the database. You can use these two functions to access and to validate an XML document.

19.3.2 Using the Module

In this section you will start to use PostgreSQL's XML functions. First, you can create a table for storing XML documents:

```
phpbook=# CREATE TABLE xmldocument (id serial, tstamp timestamp DEFAULT
now(), document text);
NOTICE:  CREATE TABLE will create implicit sequence 'xmldocument_id_seq'
for SERIAL column 'xmldocument.id'
NOTICE:  CREATE TABLE / UNIQUE will create implicit index
'xmldocument_id_key' for table 'xmldocument'
CREATE
```

The first column contains an id. In the second column you can see when the document has been inserted into the database. The third column is an ordinary text column. It will contain the XML documents we are going to insert into the database.

For adding an XML document to the database, you can write a simple PHP script as shown in the next listing:

```
<?php
        $xmlfile = 'file.xml';          # file containing XML code

        # connecting to the database
        $dbh = pg_connect("dbname=phpbook user=postgres host=localhost");
        if      (!$dbh)
                die ("cannot open connection to the database<br>\n");

        # reading the file
        $xml = '';                       # this var. will contain the XML file
        $data = file($xmlfile);
        foreach ($data as $tmp)
        {
                $xml .= $tmp;
        }
```

```
# escaping characters and importing file
$xml = preg_replace("/'/", "''", $xml);

$sql = "INSERT INTO xmldocument (document) VALUES ('$xml')";
$status = pg_exec($dbh, $sql);
if      (!$status)
        die ("cannot execute query<br>\n");

# disconnecting
pg_close($dbh);
?>
```

The first thing to do is to connect to the database. Now the XML file is read and a variable containing the entire document is compiled. The `file` function returns the content of the file in an array. To compile a variable containing everything, a loop has to be processed. After that, single quotes are escaped. This is necessary because otherwise inserting the data into the database might fail because of a syntax error. Escaping is done by using a simple regular expression that does nothing except make two single quotes out of one. Now that the SQL statement has been prepared, you can insert it into the database.

After running the script, you can add the file to the table:

```
phpbook=# SELECT id, tstamp, length(document) FROM xmldocument;
 id |           tstamp            | length
----+----------------------------+--------
  1 | 2002-02-05 00:56:23.66103+01 |    434
(1 row)
```

We decided to display the length of the XML document instead of the content of the column because that would lead to an extremely long output.

19.3.2.1 Validating a Document

In the next step, it is time to see if the XML document is still correct and well formed. You can use the `pgxml_parse` function. It parses the input and returns a Boolean value that tells whether the document has a syntax error. Here's an example:

```
phpbook=# SELECT pgxml_parse(document) FROM xmldocument;
 pgxml_parse
-------------
 t
(1 row)
```

In this case the XML document is well formed because true is returned. The result is correct because we have already validated the XML document in the section called "XML Basics" earlier in this chapter.

After a file has been imported into the database, its validity can be checked. However, it is better to check if an XML document is valid before adding it to the table. This will help you to prevent errors. Before creating the modified version of the table, it is necessary to delete the old table and the sequence related to it:

```
phpbook=# DROP TABLE xmldocument;
DROP
phpbook=# DROP SEQUENCE xmldocument_id_seq;
DROP
```

Then you can create a new table using a simple CREATE TABLE statement:

```
CREATE TABLE xmldocument (
        id serial,
        tstamp timestamp DEFAULT now(),
        document text CHECK (pgxml_parse(document) = 't')
);
```

A CHECK constraint has been added to the CREATE TABLE statement. This CHECK constraint makes PostgreSQL call the pgxml_parse function before adding the record to the table. This way, documents that are not well formed cannot be added to the table.

Let's run the PHP script again and see what happens inside the database:

```
phpbook=# SELECT id, tstamp, length(document) FROM xmldocument;
 id |           tstamp            | length
----+----------------------------+--------
  1 | 2002-02-05 13:51:40.619786+01 |    434
(1 row)
```

The record has been successfully added to the database. Now try to insert a random string:

```
phpbook=# INSERT INTO xmldocument (document) VALUES ('not valid');
ERROR:  ExecAppend: rejected due to CHECK constraint xmldocument_document
```

"not valid" is definitely not a well-formed XML document, so the INSERT operation fails.

19.3.2.2 Access to the Document

After documents have been added to the table, you might want to retrieve data from these XML documents. PostgreSQL offers a function called pgxml_xpath. As you can see from the name of the function, it is based on Xpath. Xpath is a language for referring to a particular part or component of an XML document. Here's an example:

```
phpbook=# SELECT pgxml_xpath(document,'//person/birthday/text()','','')
AS birthday FROM xmldocument;
  birthday
- - - - - - - - - - - -
 1978/08/09
(1 row)
```

Inside person an element called birthday can be found. The content of this element is displayed. As you can see, the syntax is similar to the one used for URLs. The variable is returned as text. To convert the result to the required format, a cast can be performed:

```
phpbook=# SELECT pgxml_xpath(document,'//person/birthday/text()','','')::date
AS birthday FROM xmldocument;
  birthday
- - - - - - - - - - - -
 1978-08-09
(1 row)
```

Now the result is returned as date.

Of course, it is also possible to access components of the documents that are deeper inside the tree structure:

```
phpbook=# SELECT pgxml_xpath(document,'//person/name/firstname/text()','','')
AS birthday FROM xmldocument;
  birthday
- - - - - - - - - -
 John
(1 row)
```

This time John has been returned. One thing that is important to know is what is returned if you refer to a nonexistent element:

```
phpbook=# SELECT pgxml_xpath(document,'//person/notthere/text()','','')
AS notthere FROM xmldocument;
  notthere
- - - - - - - - - -

(1 row)
```

An empty string is returned. Keep in mind that it is an empty string and not a NULL value. This is an important thing when checking for empty fields. The next example proves that the field is not a NULL value:

```
phpbook=# SELECT pgxml_xpath(document,'//person/notthere/text()','','')
IS NULL AS notthere FROM xmldocument;
 notthere
----------
 f
(1 row)
```

As you can see, the result is false and not true.

Sometimes it can be useful to retrieve data including some tags. PostgreSQL provides a way to do this as well. Let's take a look at the next example:

```
SELECT pgxml_xpath(document,
                   '//person/name/firstname/text()',
                   'name',
                   'firstname')
       FROM xmldocument;
```

Before taking a closer look at the SQL code in the listing, it is worth looking at the result:

```
                 pgxml_xpath
-----------------------------------------
 <name><firstname>John</firstname></name>
(1 row)
```

As you can see, tags can be found around the actual data. These tags are defined by the third and fourth parameter in the function call. Take a look at the next example:

```
phpbook=# SELECT pgxml_xpath(document, '//person/name/firstname/text()',
'name', '') FROM xmldocument;
    pgxml_xpath
-------------------
 <name>John</name>
(1 row)
```

This time there is just one tag in the result because the fourth parameter is left blank.

Up to now PostgreSQL's interface covers just a small part of XML. The module is still being developed, and we will see many additional functions in future versions of PostgreSQL's XML package. XML is an important subject, and John Gray (the father of the XML package) will certainly continue his work.

19.3.3 Problems When Working with XML

Working with XML can lead to some problems that do not occur when sticking to the relational concept.

XML files are ASCII files and they are highly redundant because of the number of tags in the code. When you're working with huge amounts of data, this can be a problem and will lead to poorly performing applications. In addition, it is not that easy to index an XML file. Usually workarounds have to be built to speed up an XML-based application. Although XML is a standard interface for exchanging data, it is just a language and not a database system. Keep this in mind when working with XML. For really fast applications, you won't find significantly faster software than some sort of (relational) database (I am not talking about proprietary software built on bitfields).

19.4 Summary

XML is a language for describing documents. It is not limited to a fixed number of tags, so it is extensible, flexible, and can be used in combination with a variety of technologies.

PHP and PostgreSQL provide interfaces to XML. However, these interfaces are still being developed and have not yet been widely used.

20
Security Issues

As the Bible tells us, "Love is patient, love is kind" (1 Corinthians 13:4). The problem is that there is not much love around when it comes to the Internet and security. Not every computer programmer is a loving one and not everybody can be trusted unreservedly. Therefore security is an important subject that you should think about when designing an IT environment or an application.

In the past few years, security has become an increasingly important issue. In the early days, only a few machines were connected to a network, so only a few machines were vulnerable. With the introduction of modern technologies such as e-business, many companies are running online stores that can be accessed by thousands of users. Can you be sure that there is not a single person who wants to harm you? Just think of Web sites such as amazon.com. Millions of people are visiting sites like that every day. One in a million is enough—if there is one professional hacker among one million people, it can be enough to make your business collapse.

Modern business sites are an interesting target. Many companies store data such as credit card information or other important information. This data can be interesting for crackers around the globe. Just think of having 300,000 credit card numbers. For many people this is an enormous treasure and it can be worth hacking a machine.

In this chapter we will discuss security in general. You will learn about the fundamentals of network security and take a look at potential threats.

20.1 Potential Threats

Today the list of potential threats can be endless. However, depending on the kind of business you are running, the most important and most dangerous threats might vary.

These are the most common dangers your systems might have to face:

- **Loss or destruction of data**—Sometimes hackers do not want to steal something; in most cases, these people want to destroy something, so destruction of data is a potential threat. Vandalism can be more dangerous than other kinds of crime because all parts of your application are potential targets— whether there is interesting data around.

- **Abuse of confidential data**—Most business applications rely on critical and confidential data. Just think of an online shop where information about thousands of customers is stored. Think of all the credit card numbers or other personal data. Think of a bank managing millions of accounts and billions of dollars. If a hacker can access this data, you can easily imagine what kind of damage can happen.

- **Modification of data**—In some cases a cracker might not be interested in deleting or stealing data. Just think of an account at a bank. It can be interesting to modify someone's account data. Modification can be more dangerous than destruction because in the case of total destruction, the problem is obvious. In the case of modification, it can take a long time to find out what has happened and see which data has been modified. The time between the intrusion of a cracker and the detection of the disaster can be used to perform all kinds of modifications.

- **Denial of Service**—Denial of service (DoS) attacks are a potential threat for everyone. Denial of service means that the offender tries to make your machine stop doing its work. DoS need not mean that your machine is hacked, but your service won't be available any more for some reason. Just think of a Web server that has been connected to the Web using a 10Mbit line. If somebody sends you more requests than your machine or your line can handle, your machine cannot be accessed any more even though it is up and running. As a rule of thumb, you can say that every machine providing some sort of service can be the victim of a DoS attack.

- **Attacks from inside**—Not all attacks must be carried out by an evil person who is operating from outside. Many attacks are done by people who are working in your company or who have access to your resources. Protecting yourself from attacks coming from inside is as important as protecting yourself against evil people threatening your business from outside.

Of course, not all applications are attractive for a hacker. If you are running a private Web server via a dial-up connection, it is rather unlikely that somebody will try to hack you. The reason for that is simple—it is no use hacking your machine. It might be fun, but this is not the ultimate benefit of hacking.

However, if you are running a huge business site, your Web server is a potential target because of all your important information. In addition, hacking famous sites is more prestigious than hacking a useless machine somewhere in the Net.

20.2 Securing Your System

In this section you will learn some basic facts about security and you will be guided through the most important principles.

20.2.1 Server Security

When talking about security, it is time to have a closer look at operating systems. What is an operating system? Well, the core of an operating system is a kernel, which is surrounded by various tools and components. The first thing you have to keep in mind is that every piece of software that has been installed on your system is a potential danger. The more packages you have installed on your machine, the more likely it is that one of these packages contains a security leak that can be used by a remote cracker to hack your system.

The network interfaces especially are security-critical. The more ports your system is listening to, the more insecure it will be. To find out which ports your system listens to, you can use a tool such as nmap. nmap is a software package for performing port scans and finding out information about a remote host. It is a perfect tool for having a look at what is up and running on your machine. Let's scan the local machine:

```
[root@duron root]# nmap localhost

Starting nmap V. 2.54BETA30 ( www.insecure.org/nmap/ )
Interesting ports on duron (127.0.0.1):
(The 1539 ports scanned but not shown below are in state: closed)
Port       State       Service
22/tcp     open        ssh
25/tcp     open        smtp
80/tcp     open        http
111/tcp    open        sunrpc
139/tcp    open        netbios-ssn
443/tcp    open        https
515/tcp    open        printer
3128/tcp   open        squid-http
```

```
5432/tcp    open        postgres
6000/tcp    open        X11
```

```
Nmap run completed -- 1 IP address (1 host up) scanned in 1 second
```

As you can see, many ports are open. Fortunately, the local machine is behind a fire-wall, so this is not a problem. With the help of nmap you can scan every host on the Internet. In this way an offender can gain information about the target and work on a strategy to hack the remote machine.

Let's take a look at a secure BSD workstation on the Net:

```
[root@duron root]# nmap bsd
```

```
Starting nmap V. 2.54BETA30 ( www.insecure.org/nmap/ )
Interesting ports on bsd (62.116.21.150):
(The 1548 ports scanned but not shown below are in state: closed)
Port        State       Service
22/tcp      open        ssh
```

```
Nmap run completed -- 1 IP address (1 host up) scanned in 9 seconds
```

Only one port is open, which is used for working with SSH. This is the far better configuration of the two because it is the more restrictive one.

Again, the less software you have installed on your system and the more restrictive your configuration is, the more secure your server will be. In addition, you should think about using firewalls. Today many powerful tools for firewalling are available. Think of all those software routers that are packed on just one floppy disk—these tools can help you to build more secure and more reliable IT environments.

However, having a restrictive configuration is not always enough to guarantee the security of your network. After a system has been installed, it takes permanent main-tenance in order to keep the system secure. Make sure that you update your system if security problems are found. It is no use running a highly restrictive system if some key components such as the Web server, Bind, or SSH have severe security leaks that haven't been discovered yet when setting up your machines. If you run a business-critical application, go through the newsgroups and Web sites related to security regularly and make sure that there are no problems with the software running on your system.

All the things I have been talking about in this section seem pretty obvious. However, most people start building secure systems and forget about security when the system is up and running. This is dangerous and security demands increase permanently. Crackers don't sleep, so there is no reason for you to sleep either.

20.2.2 Security on an Application Level

After you have secured your server, you must not forget about security on an application level. It is not enough if you take care of your server but forget about your applications.

There are some dangers you have to take care of when running PHP applications. The following scenario is not a bug in PHP, but it shows what can happen if you implement a PHP application the wrong way. You will see that this can lead to real security problems.

Let's start with a PHP program called `start.php`:

```php
<?php
        include ($includedir."inc.php");

        echo "hello $x<br>\n";
?>
```

The script does nothing except include a library and display the content of $x. If $includedir is not defined, the file called `inc.php` located in the local directory is returned. This is a flexible implementation because it is possible to change the location of your files easily. Let's take a look at `inc.php`:

```php
<?php
        $x = "Charles ...<br>\n";
?>
```

Execute the script using the following URL:

```
http://localhost/start.php
```

One line is displayed. It contains the variable in `inc.php`:

```
hello Charles ...
```

Up to now, nothing seems dangerous. However, with just four lines you have implemented a security hole. What happens if the URL is called like this:

```
http://localhost/start.php?includedir=incdir/
```

$includedir is defined by the URL, so the file in `incdir` is called instead of `inc.php`, which can be found in the local directory.

Take a look at inc.php in incdir:

```php
<?php
        $x = "from a hacker ...<br>\n";
?>
```

If you execute the script, you will get a result like this:

```
hello from a hacker ...
```

As you can see, the person using the program can modify the libraries that are included by your application. In this scenario nothing bad has happened, but what happens if libraries are included and the cracker passes the name of a library located on his machine to the script? This is extremely dangerous because now the cracker is allowed to do everything the Web server is allowed to do. He could read your source code containing all passwords; he could delete all data from the Web server if the user rights are not set properly; or he could modify the data on your Web server by loading data from his Web server on your machine. If the cracker finds out which libraries your application includes, it would be an easy task to do something very nasty to your system.

There are many potential security threats like the one you just saw, and it is necessary to think about these when building an application. Make yourself think like a hacker and try to find potential threats like the one you just saw. Never pass the name of a library to the next script via a URL. PHP is capable of retrieving libraries from a remote host, so it is an easy task to change the library your system includes. Make sure that the user rights on your system are set correctly. This means that you need not allow the Web server to write in a directory where it need not write.

This is important because all rights the Web server has are a potential security problem.

20.2.3 Database Security

After you have dealt with the server, you can start looking at PostgreSQL. PostgreSQL is a secure system and there are not so many things you have to take care of.

One important thing is that you should not turn on TCP/IP unless you really need it. If TCP/IP is turned off, PostgreSQL will work via Unix sockets. If the Web server and the database server are on the same machine, you won't need TCP/IP because everything can be done with the help of Unix sockets.

In addition, you should try to configure a restrictive database configuration. Keep in mind that if a cracker gets one of the passwords, he should not be able to delete the entire database.

When working across insecure networks, we recommend using an encrypted protocol. PostgreSQL supports SSL connections. This means that data is transmitted via a secure channel and not as plain text. The benefit is that the user need not worry that a sniffer listens to what is being transmitted to you across the network. However, using SSL will lead to a significantly slower authentication process. To get around the problem, it can be useful to establish a permanent secure tunnel so that a lot of authentication overhead can be avoided. For performance-critical systems, this is an essential advantage because if authentication takes much longer than processing the data, it can be slightly annoying.

If you have configured your database properly, PostgreSQL is a secure piece of software. Just take care of your network configuration as well as your user rights, and everything will be just fine. In addition, we recommend using firewalls. The more you protect your server, the more secure it will be and the more unlikely it is to be hacked.

20.3 User Authentication with Apache and PHP

Have you ever thought about authentication? Just think of an application consisting of dozens of screens—every user should have certain permissions and certain rights. Therefore authentication is necessary. Apache and PHP provide various methods of user authentication. In this section you will take a closer look at the most important methods for authentication. You will be guided through the principles and learn how to build a secure site.

20.3.1 Apache

The easiest way to protect your site against users who are not allowed to visit it is to use Apache's basic authentication. Basic authentication can be used easily and it provides rudimentary security for your Web site.

The next example shows a short piece of an Apache configuration file:

```
<Directory "/var/www/html">
        <Files *>
                AuthType        Basic
                AuthName        Intranet
                AuthUserFile    /etc/httpd/conf/userfile
                require valid-user
        </Files>
    Options Indexes FollowSymLinks
    AllowOverride None
    Order allow,deny
    Allow from all
</Directory>
```

As you can see, a so-called container is defined. The entire container defines attributes of the /var/www/html directory. Inside the block, a block called Files can be found. It is valid for all files in the directory and tells Apache to use basic authentication. As you can see, the type of authentication is set to Basic and a file containing the passwords is defined. A valid password is required to access the site.

After the block used for defining the type of authentication, some other options are defined. These options are not that important and won't be discussed in detail.

Figure 20.1 shows what happens when a user wants to access a site where authentication is needed.

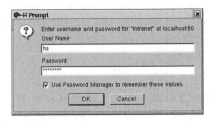

FIGURE 20.1 Basic authentication.

To administer the file containing the passwords, you can use a program called htpasswd. With the help of this program, you can add users, create new files, or change the password of a user. Let's take a look at the syntax overview of the command:

```
[root@duron root]# htpasswd
Usage:
        htpasswd [-cmdps] passwordfile username
        htpasswd -b[cmdps] passwordfile username password

        htpasswd -n[mdps] username
        htpasswd -nb[mdps] username password
 -c  Create a new file.
 -n  Don't update file; display results on stdout.
 -m  Force MD5 encryption of the password.
 -d  Force CRYPT encryption of the password (default).
 -p  Do not encrypt the password (plaintext).
 -s  Force SHA encryption of the password.
 -b  Use the password from the command line rather than prompting for it.
On Windows, TPF and NetWare systems the '-m' flag is used by default.
On all other systems, the '-p' flag will probably not work.
You have new mail in /var/spool/mail/root
```

If you want to remove a user from the password file, just call the one and only Unix editor available, Vi(m), and remove the line corresponding to a user.

If you have to build business-critical applications, it can be helpful to use secure HTTP. In contrast to HTTP, secure HTTP is an encrypted protocol. It can be used in combination with Apache and helps you to protect yourself against sniffers. Sniffing means that somebody "listens" to the data you are transmitting across a network. Because of encryption, this is not possible. Apache's SSL extensions are based on a so-called public-private key encryption algorithm (RSA). To read a message, you need a private key matching the transmission. In addition, a public key is available. If data is sent to a client, the server encrypts the data using his private and his public key. The client gets the encrypted message and decodes the message using his keys. If somebody listens to the connection, he won't be able to decode the message if he doesn't have the correct keys. Mathematically it is possible to decode the key by trying all possible keys, but there are so many possibilities that it would take millions of years to find the correct key. The algorithm used by SSL can be considered to be secure.

Apache is one of the most flexible pieces of software available. It offers tremendous power, and it is an easy task to add features to the Web server. For the purpose of securing your Web sites, Apache offers the right tools for you. Because Apache can be considered to be stable, it is a secure packet.

20.3.2 PHP

In this section you will learn about securing an application built with PHP.

In the preceding section you saw what you can do with Apache. However, sometimes you don't have the ability to change the configuration of the Web server. In addition, Apache stores the list of users and passwords in a text file. With a huge number of users, this is not very efficient. Reading an entire file can be compared to a sequential scan, which is quite slow. To get around the problem, you can use a PostgreSQL database in combination with PHP authentication to do the job. In addition to performance, it will help you to gain a lot of flexibility because modifying a database is much easier than working with flat files and htpasswd.

Before you see how to implement a database-driven authentication system, it is time to take a look at how authentication can be used in PHP. Take a look at the following script:

```
<?php
        if      (!isset($PHP_AUTH_USER))
        {
                Header("WWW-Authenticate: Basic realm=\"A Realm\"");
                Header("HTTP/1.0 401 Unauthorized");
```

```
                echo "No login\n";
                exit;
        }
        else
        {
                echo "User: $PHP_AUTH_USER<br>";
                echo "Password: $PHP_AUTH_PW<br>";
        }
?>
```

$PHP_AUTH_USER is a predefined variable. If it is not defined, a window is displayed. In Figure 20.2 you can see what this window looks like when running Mozilla.

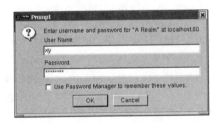

FIGURE 20.2   Authentication with PHP.

After you have passed the authentication window, the data you have passed to the screen will be displayed:

```
User: xy
Password: mypasswd
```

One important thing when dealing with authentication is that there is no way to influence the behavior of your scripts by passing parameters to the script via a URL.

Now take a look at the next listing:

```
http://localhost/auth/auth.php?PHP_AUTH_USER=John
```

Even when defining PHP_AUTH_USER, the output of the program will be the same. This is an important issue because otherwise it would be an easy task to fake a user.

Now that you have seen how to use authentication in combination with PHP, it is time to look at an example where we will use a PostgreSQL database for storing user information. Let's create a table and insert some values into the database first:

```
CREATE TABLE authentication (
        id serial,
        name text,
```

```
        passwd text
);

INSERT INTO authentication (name, passwd) VALUES ('Hans', 'hello');
INSERT INTO authentication (name, passwd) VALUES ('Epi', 'Christina');
INSERT INTO authentication (name, passwd) VALUES ('Shelley', 'Alex007');
```

The following piece of code shows how a simple system can be built:

```php
<?php
        if      (!isset($PHP_AUTH_USER))
        {
                authenticate();
        }
        else
        {
                if      (checkuser(dbconnect(), $PHP_AUTH_USER, $PHP_AUTH_PW))
                {
                        echo "authentication successful";
                }
                else
                {
                        echo "authentication failed<br>";
                }
        }

        function authenticate()
        {
                header("WWW-Authenticate: Basic realm=\"Authentication\"");
                header( "HTTP/1.0 401 Unauthorized");
        }

        # connect to database ...
        function dbconnect()
        {
                $dbh = pg_connect("dbname=phpbook user=hs")
                        or die ("cannot connect to database<br>");
                return $dbh;
        }

        # check if the user is valid ...
        function checkuser($dbh, $user, $pwd)
        {
```

```
                    $sql = "SELECT COUNT(*) FROM authentication
                            WHERE name='$user' AND passwd='$pwd'";
                    $ret = pg_exec($dbh, $sql);
                    $line = pg_fetch_row($ret, 0);
                    if      ($line[0] > 0)
                    {
                            return true;
                    }
                    else
                    {
                            return false;
                    }
            }
    ?>
```

If $PHP_AUTH_USER is not defined, the function called authenticate is started. It displays the authentication windows and quits. If the user has already logged in, checkuser is called. This function is responsible for finding out if the user is correct and if user and password are in the database. The first parameter passed to the function is a database handle, which is created by the dbconnect function. The dbconnect function is responsible for connecting to the database and returns a database handle. The second and third parameter contain the username and the password the user used for connecting to your Web site.

Let's take a look at the implementation of checkuser. First a SQL command is compiled. If there are more than zero users in the database, the user and the password are valid. The return value of checkuser will be analyzed and a string is displayed on screen.

When working with PHP authentication, you should take into consideration that authentication does not work when PHP is executed using the CGI interface. It works with mod_php but not with CGI.

20.4 Summary

Security is an important subject, and it will be even more important in the future. Making your applications and your systems resistant is a key demand of modern software development.

For adding user authentication to your Web site, Apache and PHP provide some useful features. With the help of Apache and PHP, you can define precisely who is allowed to access what. In combination with PostgreSQL, you can even build database-driven authentication systems.

PART V

Practical Examples

IN THIS PART

Web Applications

Building advanced Web applications is the core topic of this book. In this chapter you will get a close look at the most important and most widespread kinds of Web applications. You will be guided through sample code as well as various examples where you can see PHP and PostgreSQL interacting with each other.

21.1 Mail Systems

E-mail has become a everyday task. Checking your e-mail in the morning or at work is almost as important as brushing your teeth. The Internet is a fundamental tool. E-mail is essential, and not only for business processes. This section is dedicated to e-mail and what you can do with e-mail. You will learn to check your e-mail with the help of PHP and you will see how to store information about e-mail in the database.

21.1.1 Fundamentals

Before we start with some nice source code, it is necessary to take a look at the fundamentals.

In many systems text was encoded using 7-bit code. Although an ASCII character needs 8 bits, many mail systems relied on 7-bit coding. In addition to ASCII characters, it is necessary to transmit binary data. To transmit data that cannot be coded using 7-bit characters, mechanisms for encoding the data have been invented. Several standards have been defined:

- **UUencode**—Unix-To-Unix-Encode was invented for managing the communication of Unix machines. The algorithm was widespread because back in the early days Unix servers were widespread. An encoded file is about 42% larger than the original file.

- **MIME**—MIME stands for Multipurpose Internet Mail Extensions. This format was invented for transmitting attachments as well as structured messages consisting of various components. In some cases Base64 encoding is used in combination with MIME. The exact definition can be found in RFC 2045.

- **Base64**—Base64 is a standard way of transmitting attachments. The size of a Base64-encoded file is about 37% percent higher.

- **Quoted Printable**—This algorithm is used in combination with MIME. Usually it is used for non-English text. The main idea is that all characters that are not ASCII characters are escaped. Normally the size of an encoded file is 3% higher than the size of a file that is not encoded.

- **BinHex**—In Macenvironments BinHex is widespread. The encoded data is compressed, so the encoded file can even be smaller than the original file.

- **HTML**—With the arrival of modern Web technologies, HTML e-mail messages have become more and more popular. In combination with MIME, this is a simple and comfortable way. In addition, it is a standard format that can be read by every platform.

- **Binary**—Binary data is transmitted directly.

Additional methods are BTOA, BOO, or ROT-13.

Now that you have seen which algorithms are used for coding e-mail messages, it is time to see which protocols are involved when working with e-mail:

- **SMTP**—This protocol is used for the communication between various mail servers. The definition of the protocol can be found in RFC 821.

- **POP3**—In contrast to SMTP, the POP3 protocol is used for retrieving messages from the server.

- **IMAP**—IMAP is an additional protocol for retrieving messages from the server. In contrast to POP3, the mail stays on the server.

All three protocols are standard protocols and they are supported by every reasonable mail program.

21.1.2 Sending E-Mail Messages

The first thing you have to learn is how to send e-mail messages. In the case of PHP, you can send e-mail messages easily. Take a look at the following example:

```
<html>
<title>Mail ...</title>
<body bgcolor="#EEEEEE">

<b>Mail ...</b><br><br>

<form action="mail.php" method="post">
        <table>
        <tr>
                <td>Mail To: </td>
                        <td><input type="text" name="email" value=""></td>
        </tr><tr>
                <td>Subject: </td>
                        <td><input type="text" name="subject" value=""></td>
        </tr><tr>
                <td>Content: </td>
                        <td><textarea cols="50" rows="10" name="content">
                                </textarea></td>
        </tr>
        </table>

        <br>
        <td><input type="submit" name="submit" value="Send Mail"></td>

</form>

</body>
</html>
```

A form is displayed that can be used to send e-mail messages. Just enter the e-mail address of the person you want to send an e-mail to. In addition, you can insert the subject and the content of the e-mail. As soon as the button is clicked, the mail is sent to the recipient. In Figure 21.1 you can see what the form looks like.

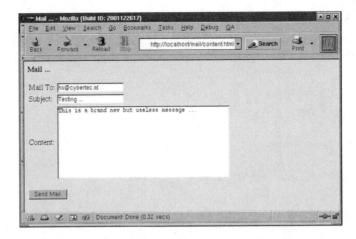

FIGURE 21.1   A simple mailing tool.

As you can see in the HTML document, clicking the button will start a script named `mail.php`. This program displays some HTML code and sends a message to the desired user:

```
<html>
<title>Mail ...</title>
<body bgcolor="#EEEEEE">

<b>Mail ...</b><br><br>

<?php
        if      (mail("$email", "$subject", "$content"))
        {
                echo "Mail has been sent successfully.";
        }
        else
        {
                echo "An error has occurred.";
        }
?>
```

If the mail cannot be sent, an error message is displayed. In the case of multiple recipients, the addresses must be separated by a comma.

21.1.3 Working with IMAP and POP3

IMAP and POP3 are the two most important protocols for accessing the data stored on a mail server. In contrast to POP3, IMAP servers store the messages on the server and the data is retrieved whenever a message is requested. Because the data is not stored on the user's machine, the owner of the mailbox is far more flexible because he can change offices whenever he or she wants to. The disadvantage of IMAP is that it can take longer to retrieve e-mail because the data has to be transmitted to the client every time the mailbox is opened. In the case of bad or slow lines, this can be a burden. In this section we will focus on IMAP because this is the better protocol for implementing Web mail systems.

21.1.3.1 Retrieving Data

In the first example in this section, you will see how to retrieve basic information about a mailbox from the mail server. Therefore we have created the e-mail address phpbook@cybertec.at on a local machine (this is not the official Cybertec server). The system is running Sendmail in combination with an IMAP daemon. One message has been sent to phpbook@cybertec.at. Let's take a look at a short PHP script retrieving information about the mailbox:

```php
<?php
        echo '<b>Displaying information about phpbook@cybertec.at</b><br><br>';

        $mbox = imap_open("{212.186.25.84}INBOX","phpbook", "test123")
                or die("cannot connect to IMAP server: ".imap_last_error());

        $testconn = imap_mailboxmsginfo($mbox);

        if      ($testconn)
        {
                echo "Date: ".$testconn->Date."<br>\n" ;
                echo "Deleted: ".$testconn->Deleted."<br>\n" ;
                echo "Driver: ".$testconn->Driver."<br>\n" ;
                echo "Mailbox: ".$testconn->Mailbox."<br>\n" ;
                echo "Messages: ".$testconn->Nmsgs."<br>\n" ;
                echo "Recent: ".$testconn->Recent."<br>\n" ;
                echo "Size: ".$testconn->Size."<br>\n" ;
                echo "Unread: ".$testconn->Unread."<br>\n" ;
        }
        else
        {
                print "An error has occurred: ".imap_last_error(). "<br>\n";
        }

        imap_close($mbox);
?>
```

At the beginning of the script, a header is displayed and a connection to the mail server is opened. In this scenario the IP address of the mail server is 212.186.25.84. The user phpbook having the password test123 is used for authentication. If the connection has been established successfully, information about the mailbox is retrieved and the various components are displayed onscreen using simple echo commands.

In the next listing, you can see what comes out when the script is executed:

```
Displaying information about phpbook@cybertec.at

Date: Sat, 9 Feb 2002 15:30:10 +0100 (CET)
Deleted: 0
Driver: imap
Mailbox: {212.186.25.84:143/imap/user="phpbook"}INBOX
Messages: 1
Recent: 0
Size: 1515
Unread: 1
```

As you can see, a lot of information is retrieved. In this scenario an IMAP server is used. The size of the message is 1515 bytes. One message is in the INBOX.

In the next step you will see how to retrieve the content of a message. Two files will be used. The file called mailserver.php will contain a library for interacting with the IMAP server. The file fetchmail.php will call the IMAP library. Let's take a look at mailserver.php first:

```php
<?php

# library for interacting with an IMAP server
class mailserver
{
        var $server;
        var $user;
        var $passwd;
        var $mbox;

        function mailserver()
        {
                $this->server = "212.186.25.84";
                $this->user = "phpbook";
                $this->passwd = "test123";
```

```php
        $this->mbox = @imap_open("{".$this->server."}INBOX",
                        $this->user, $this->passwd)
                or die("cannot connect to IMAP server: ".
                        imap_last_error());

        return $mbox;
    }

    function summary()
    {
        $headers=imap_headers($this->mbox);
        $number = count($headers);

        echo "<b>Number of messages on server: $number<br><br></b>\n";
        for    ($i = 1; $i <= $number; $i++)
        {
                $message['body'] = imap_body($this->mbox, $i);
                echo "body: ".$message['body']."<br>\n";
        }
    }
}

?>
```

After defining some variables, the constructor has been implemented. It establishes a connection to the mail server and displays an error if no valid connection handle is returned. Let's take a look at the function called summary. It retrieves the headers from the mailbox and counts the number of headers returned. Now a loop is processed that goes through all headers. The body of these messages is retrieved and displayed onscreen.

Let's take a look at fetchmail.php, which is based on the library you have just seen:

```php
<?php
    include("mailserver.php");

    $mail = new mailserver();
    $mail->summary();
    imap_close($mail->mbox);
?>
```

First the library is included and a new instance of the mail server object is generated. Now the summary is displayed and the connection to the mail server is closed.

As we have already mentioned, the mailbox of phpbook contains one message, which has been sent from hs@cybertec.at. Figure 21.2 shows what comes out when executing the script.

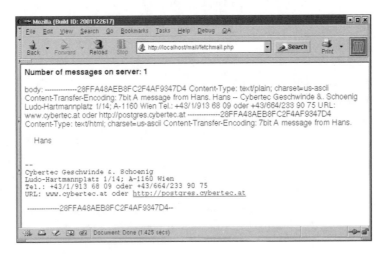

FIGURE 21.2   Watching chaos.

As you can see, the content of the mail is quite confusing. It contains bit-encoded HTML code.

Sometimes it is necessary to take a closer look at the header of messages. This is important to find out where the message comes from and to which e-mail address you have to reply. Much more information can be found in the header. The next example shows a new version of the summary function you have seen before. It displays all important parts of the header in a useful way:

```
function summary()
{
        $headers=imap_headers($this->mbox);
        $number = count($headers);

        echo "<b>Number of messages on server: $number<br></b>\n";
        for     ($i = 1; $i <= $number; $i++)
        {
                $h = imap_header($this->mbox, $i);
                echo "<br><b>Subject:</b> ".$h->subject;
                echo "<br><b>Reply to:</b> ".$h->reply_toaddress;
                echo "<br><b>Mail comes from:</b> ".$h->fromaddress;
                echo "<br><b>Cc:</b> ".$h->ccaddress;
```

```
                        echo "<br><b>Bcc:</b> ".$h->bccaddress;
                        echo "<br><b>Sender address:</b> ".$h->senderaddress;
                        echo "<br><b>Return path:</b> ".$h->return_path;
                        echo "<br><b>Second since UNIX starting time:</b> "
                                .$h->udate;
                        echo "<br><b>Fetch from:</b> ".$h->fetchfrom;
                        echo "<br><b>Fetch subject:</b> ".$h->fetchsubject;
                }
        }
```

As you can see, PHP offers a variety of functions for processing the header of an e-mail. The functions return a string that can be processed directly. Figure 21.3 shows how the result will look.

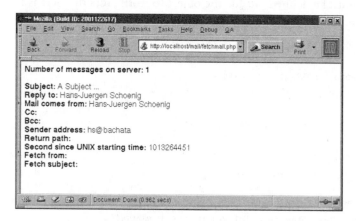

FIGURE 21.3   Processing the header.

The line "Mail comes from" is not that useful because it contains the name of the person who has sent the e-mail. This is nice but it might not be what you are looking for. Let's take a look at the next version of summary:

```
        function summary()
        {
                $headers=imap_headers($this->mbox);
                $number = count($headers);

                echo "<b>Number of messages on server: $number<br><br></b>\n";
                for     ($i = 1; $i <= $number; $i++)
                {
                        $h = imap_header($this->mbox, $i);
                        displayarray($h->to[0], "To:");
```

```
                        displayarray($h->from[0], "From:");
                        displayarray($h->cc[0], "Cc:");
                        displayarray($h->bcc[0], "Bcc:");
                        displayarray($h->reply_to[0], "Reply to:");
                        displayarray($h->sender[0], "Sender:");
                        displayarray($h->return_path[0], "Return path:");
                }
        }
```

Some of the methods you have seen in the previous version can be used to return
arrays or objects as well. In the case of "from" this is useful because more details
about the sender can be retrieved. In the listing you can see that a function called
displayarray is used. This function does nothing but display the content of an
array. It must be defined outside the object to work properly. Here is the code of the
function:

```
function displayarray($data, $text)
{
        echo "<b>$text</b><br>\n";
        while (list($key, $val) = @each($data))
        {
                echo "$key => $val<br>";
        }
        echo "<br>";
}
```

The keys as well as the values belonging to the keys are displayed. When executing
fetchmail.php, some more information is displayed:

```
Number of messages on server: 1


To:
mailbox => phpbook
host => cybertec.at

From:
personal => Hans-Juergen Schoenig
mailbox => hs
host => cybertec.at

Cc:


Bcc:
```

```
Reply to:
personal => Hans-Juergen Schoenig
mailbox => hs
host => cybertec.at

Sender:
mailbox => hs
host => bachata

Return path:
```

In the listing you can see that the name of the host is always cybertec.at. There is only one section where the name of the host is bachata instead of cybertec.at. The reason is that the mail has been sent from the internal network. The internal name of the mail server is bachata, so this name has been used instead of cybertec.at.

21.1.3.2 Attachments and Other Components of an E-mail

Up to now you have seen how to extract messages and information about these messages from the mail server. In this section you will take a closer look at how to process messages consisting of more than just one component.

You can send a second e-mail to your test mail server. In this example, I have sent an e-mail containing a picture to phpbook@cybertec.at. The goal of the next example is to find out how many messages are in the mailbox and how many parts the various messages consist of. In addition, information about these parts should be displayed.

Here is an additional version of summary that does exactly what we want it to do:

```php
function summary()
{
        $headers=imap_headers($this->mbox);
        $number = count($headers);

        echo "<b>Number of messages on server: $number<br><br></b>\n";
        for     ($i = 1; $i <= $number; $i++)
        {
                echo "<b>message number: $i</b><br>\n";
                $struct = imap_fetchstructure($this->mbox, $i);
                $data = $struct->parts;
                foreach ($data as $x)
                {
                        while (list($key, $val) = @each($x))
                        {
                                echo "$key => $val<br>";
                        }
                }
```

```
                                        echo "<br>";
                        }
                }
        }
```

The `imap_fetchstructure` function returns an object containing the structure of the e-mail. $data contains an array of all components. This array is processed and the various parts and fields of the array are displayed.

With the help of this simple function, it is possible to retrieve a lot of information about an e-mail or a set of e-mail messages. Let's see which kind of data the script displays:

```
Number of messages on server: 2

message number: 1
ifsubtype => 1
subtype => PLAIN
ifdescription => 0
ifid => 0
lines => 12
bytes => 218
ifdisposition => 0
ifdparameters => 0
ifparameters => 1
parameters => Array

ifsubtype => 1
subtype => HTML
ifdescription => 0
ifid => 0
lines => 11
bytes => 388
ifdisposition => 0
ifdparameters => 0
ifparameters => 1
parameters => Array

message number: 2
ifsubtype => 1
subtype => PLAIN
ifdescription => 0
ifid => 0
lines => 4
```

```
bytes => 52
ifdisposition => 0
ifdparameters => 0
ifparameters => 1
parameters => Array

type => 5
encoding => 3
ifsubtype => 1
subtype => JPEG
ifdescription => 0
ifid => 0
bytes => 201382
ifdisposition => 1
disposition => INLINE
ifdparameters => 1
dparameters => Array
ifparameters => 1
parameters => Array
```

As we promised, two messages are on the server. The first message consists of two components. The first component is PLAIN, which means that it is a text component. The second component consists of HTML code. Information such as the length or the number of lines a message consists of can be found in the result, and this information can easily be extracted and used by your application. When you take a look at the second message, you will find that the second part of the second message has the subtype called JPEG. In addition, the encoding is said to be 3. The message type is 5. This tells us that this part of the message is an attachment.

The next function shows a way of downloading attachments. Again, we have tried to make the function as simple and as easy to understand as possible:

```
function summary()
{
        $headers=imap_headers($this->mbox);
        $number = count($headers);

        echo "<b>Number of messages on server: $number<br><br></b>\n";
        for     ($i = 1; $i <= $number; $i++)
        {
                echo "<b>message number: $i</b><br>\n";
                $struct = imap_fetchstructure($this->mbox, $i);
```

```
$pnumber = 0;
foreach ($struct->parts as $part)
{
        $pnumber++;
        if ($part->disposition == "INLINE")
        {
                echo "size: ".$part->bytes."<br>\n";
                $fname = $part->dparameters[0]->value;
                print "filename: $filename<br>\n";

                $body = imap_fetchbody($this->mbox,
                        $i, $pnumber);
                $file = imap_base64($body);

                $fh = fopen("/tmp/".$fname, "w");
                fputs($fh, $file);
                fclose($fh);
        }
        elseif ($part->disposition == "ATTACHMENT")
        {
                # do further work ...
        }
}
}
}
```

You should already be familiar with the first few lines of the function. The most important part of the code starts after generating $struct. All components of the structure are processed one after the other. $pnumber is used to count the current part of the message being processed. This is important because this information will be needed to retrieve the correct body of the part. If $part->disposition contains INLINE, an attachment has been found. Nowadays most attachments are sent inline. This is a comfortable way of encoding e-mail and it works well. If $part->disposition was ATTACHMENT, an attachment would have been found as well. Let's go on with INLINE messages. After computing the size of the attachment, the original filename is retrieved. This is important because you will need this filename to write the file to disk. In the next step the body of the message is retrieved. It is important to retrieve the correct body because otherwise the wrong piece of data will be treated as attachment. After the data is read, the string is decoded. Because an INLINE attachment is Base64-encoded, imap_base64 can be used to regenerate the original piece of data. After retrieving and decoding, the data is written to disk. This is done with the help of fopen, fputs, and fclose.

After the script has been executed, a few lines are displayed onscreen:

```
Number of messages on server: 2

message number: 1
message number: 2
size: 201382
filename: nura.jpg
```

More important than these lines is the fact that the file has been written to disk. To check that, you can use ls:

```
[root@duron mail]# ls -l /tmp/nura.jpg
-rw-r--r--    1 apache    apache      146953 Feb 14 18:28 /tmp/nura.jpg
```

The most interesting thing is that the size of the file on disk is around 140KB. The size of the attachment is much larger (around 200KB). As we promised in the introduction to this section about Web mail systems, the encoded file is around 42% bigger than the original file.

The last thing we have to check is whether the file can be used correctly. Writing data to disk is simply not enough—you have to check whether the image can be displayed correctly. Just take a look at Figure 21.4, and if you can see a wonderful woman, everything has been done correctly.

FIGURE 21.4   The image is correct.

21.1.3.3 Retrieving Status Information

In this section you will see how to retrieve status information from an IMAP server. PHP offers a command called `imap_status`. It asks the server for some basic information. Let's take a look at a simple example:

```php
<?php
        $server = "212.186.25.84";
        $user = "phpbook";
        $passwd = "test123";

        $mbox = @imap_open("{".$server."}INBOX", $user, $passwd)
                or die("cannot connect to IMAP server: ".
                        imap_last_error());

        $status = imap_status ($mbox, "{212.186.25.84}INBOX", SA_ALL);
        if      ($status)
        {
                echo "<table>\n";
                echo "<tr><td>Messages:</td><td>".
                        $status->messages."</td><tr>\n";
                echo "<tr><td>Recent:</td><td>".
                        $status->recent."</td><tr>\n";
                echo "<tr><td>Unseen:</td><td>".
                        $status->unseen."</td><tr>\n";
                echo "<tr><td>UIDnext:</td><td>".
                        $status->uidnext."</td><tr>\n";
                echo "<tr><td>UIDvalidity:</td><td>".
                        $status->uidvalidity."</td><tr>\n";
        }
        else
        {
                echo "error: ".imap_lasterror() . "\n";
        }
?>
```

After the information has been fetched from the server, it is displayed onscreen using a table. Just access the various components of the object returned and display them onscreen. Figure 21.5 shows what comes out when you execute the script.

FIGURE 21.5   Status information.

21.1.4 E-Mail Summary

PHP provides a rich set of functions for working with e-mail messages. Whether you want to work with News, POP, or IMAP servers, PHP offers the right functions for you. Especially when working with IMAP, you can build applications easily.

Messages can consist of various parts that can contain attachments. Even files that are attached to an e-mail can be processed with the help of PHP.

21.2 Building a Web Shop

Nowadays Web shops are an essential component of every modern company's business strategy. Web shops are not built just for selling products. In many cases they are also a company's presence on the Web and will help you to present your products to a broad audience. The advantage of Web shops over other types of advertising is that people visit your Web sites to retrieve information—they are not annoyed by advertisements.

In this section you will see how to build shopping carts and how to develop personalized sites. The application consists of two screens. The first one will display the products in the database. The second script will reduce the number of products that are still in the stores, and display a list of all products a customer has bought.

21.2.1 Getting Started

Let's get started by defining a simple data structure for our shop. To keep the example small and easy to understand, we start with one table. The example is designed in a simple way. It is not intended to be a complete shop because thousands of lines of code would be far too confusing for this book:

```
CREATE TABLE product (
        id int4,                    -- unique id of a product
        name text,                  -- name of a product
        instock int4,               -- number of products in stock
        price numeric(9,2),         -- price of products
        PRIMARY KEY (id)
);

COPY product FROM stdin USING DELIMITERS ';';
1;PostgreSQL Developer's Handbook;345;41.99
2;PHP and PostgreSQL;2534;41.59
3;Python Developer's Handbook;962;39.52
4;mod_perl;0;49.99
5;PostgreSQL For UNIX Programmers;1;54.69
6;Visual C++;2;29.19
\.
```

As you can see, the table contains information about products. Every product has an id, a name, and a price. In addition, the database stores the number of products that are still in the store.

Our prototype consists of various files. Let's take a look at the files needed in this example, which are shown in Table 21.1.

TABLE 21.1   Files Needed in This Example

File	Purpose
cart.php	Creates new objects for shopping cart and session management.
cash.php	Checkout; lists the products the customer has bought and reduces the number of products that are still in the store.
error.php	Error handling.
incshop.php	Helps to get around problems concerning serialization.
ss_libcart.php	Library for working with shopping cart. It is an extension for the class called db defined in libdb.php.
libdb.php	The database library.
libhtml.php	An HTML library.
shop.php	The starting screen.
temp_cash.html	An HTML template.
temp_list.html	An HTML template for listing the products in the database.

In this section you will see various versions of these files. You will see how to build session-driven as well as cookie-driven applications. The goal of this section is to see how to separate the layout of an application from the source code. In addition, it is important to see how to pass arrays from one screen to another. You will also see how transactions are used in everyday life.

21.2.1.1 Cookie-Driven Shopping Carts

The first thing you want to implement is a cookie-based prototype. Let's take a look at libdb.php. This file contains a library for interacting with the database.

```php
<?php

class db
{
        var $conn = "host=localhost user=hs dbname=phpbook";
        var $db;
        var $res;

        function connect()
        {
                $this->db = pg_connect($this->conn);
                if      (!$this->db)
                {
                        $this->ErrorMsg('Connection failed.');
                }
        }

        function sql($statement)
        {
                if      (!$this->db)
                {
                        $this->ErrorMsg('Connect First.');
                }
                $this->res = @pg_exec($this->db, $statement);
                if      (!$this->res)
                {
                        return(0);
                }
                else
                {
                        $num = @pg_numrows($this->res);
                        return($num);
                }
        }
}
```

```
function fetch($num, $type = 3, $param = 0, $mres = 0)
{
        ($param == 1 ? $fres = $mres : $fres = $this->res);
        switch($type)
        {
                CASE 1:
                        $row = pg_fetch_row($fres, $num);
                        break;
                CASE 2:
                        $row = pg_fetch_array($fres, $num);
                        break;
                CASE 3:
                        $row = pg_fetch_object($fres, $num);
                        break;
                default:
                        $this->ErrorMsg('Query Type does not exist');
                        break;
        }
        return ($row);
}

function disconnect()
{
        @pg_close($this->db);
}

function ErrorMsg($outstr)
{
        echo ("SEVERE ERROR<br>$outstr");
        $this->sql("ROLLBACK");
        $this->disconnect();
        die();
}

}

?>
```

A db object contains three variables. $conn contains the parameters defining the connection to the database. In this example these parameters have been hard-coded to reduce the amount of code and the number of files needed for this prototype. $db contains the database handle and $res the result of a SQL statement.

The connect function establishes a connection to the database and displays an error message if no connection can be established. The function called sql can be used to execute a SQL statement. In the case of an error, the error message is suppressed. The return value of the function contains the number of records returned by a SQL statement.

To retrieve values from the result of a SQL statement, the fetch function has been implemented. Depending on what kind of result you want to retrieve, you can choose. With the help of the third parameter passed to the function, you can decide whether you want to work with arrays, objects, or rows. This is a comfortable feature because it helps you to reduce the functions in your database library without reducing the flexibility of the programmer using the library.

The disconnect function is used to destroy a connection to the database. The ErrorMsg function displays a message on the screen and makes the application quit its work.

This library will be used by the entire shop package.

The next package you will need is called ss_libcart.php. It is used to work with the shopping cart.

```php
<?php
require ("libdb.php");

class cart extends db
{
        function cartwork($id, $number, $ser_cart)
        {
                $ar_cart = unserialize($ser_cart);
                if ($number < 0)
                {
                        header("Location: shop.php?msg=2");
                        exit;
                }
                $chk = $this->checkstock($id,$number);
                if (!$chk)
                {
                        header("Location: shop.php?msg=1");
                        exit;
                }
                if ( $number < 1)
                {
                        unset ($ar_cart[$id]);
                }
```

```
            else
            {
                    $ar_cart[$id] = $number;
            }
            $ser_cart = serialize($ar_cart);
            return($ser_cart);
    }
    function checkstock($id, $number)
    {
            $chksel = "SELECT instock FROM product WHERE id=$id";
            $this->connect();
            $this->sql($chksel);
            $row = $this->fetch(0,3);
            if ($number > $row->instock)
            {
                    return(0);
            }
            return(1);
    }
}

?>
```

The first function defined in this part is called cartwork. It is needed for checking the data transmitted from one script to another. Let's have a few words on how scripts can interact with each other: To transmit data that cannot be stored in a string from one script to another, the data must be serialized. For things such as arrays or objects, this is necessary because an array or an object consists of more than just one component. Serialization makes sure that a string containing the same information as the original objects is built. This way the data can be stored in a cookie or in a session, or it can be used inside an URL.

The checkstock function is used to find out if the number of units of a certain product a customer wants to buy is available or not. If the number of products the customer wants to buy is higher than the products that are in the stores, 0 is returned. Otherwise the function will return 1. The only two parameters needed by this function are the object id and the number of products the user wants to buy. The number of units available is taken from the database.

The next file you will look at is cart.php. It is used to process the parameters passed to the payment script.

```php
<?

include ("ss_libcart.php");

@session_start();
$sid = session_id();
$keys = array_keys($HTTP_POST_VARS);
$anz = count($keys);

for ($x = 0; $x < count($keys); $x++)
{
        if ($HTTP_POST_VARS[$keys[$x]])
        {
                $id = $keys[$x];
                $number = $HTTP_POST_VARS[$keys[$x]];
                $sc = new cart();
                $ser_cart = $sc->cartwork($id, $number , $ser_cart);
        }
}
$t = time() + 50000;
setcookie("ser_cart",$ser_cart,$t,"/");
header("Location: shop.php");

?>
```

At the beginning of the script a session is started. In addition, a session id is created. After that the keys in $HTTP_POST_VARS are extracted. $HTTP_POST_VARS contains all parameters passed to the function with the help of a POST request. For every key in this array, the number of products is computed. A new cart object is created and cartwork is called. You have already seen cartwork earlier in this section.

At the end of a script a cookie is set. This cookie is needed to store the information about the shopping cart. The data is serialized, so you don't have to worry about the way the data is stored inside the cookie.

The next file in the list is called error.php. It contains a code fragment for displaying error information:

```php
<?php

if      ($msg)
{
        switch  ($msg)
        {
```

```
            CASE 1:
                    $page->add_data("MSG", "<b>Not enough products
                                          in stock!</b>");
                    break;
            case 2:
                    $page->add_data("MSG", "<b>You cannot order
                            negative numbers!</b>");
                    break;

        }
    }
?>
```

As you can see, the script checks whether $msg is defined. If it is, one $page->add_data is called and Not enough products in stock! will be added to the object containing the HTML code of the page. The object containing the code is called $page, as you will see in the next file. Let's take a look at shop.php. This file is used to display the first screen containing a list of all products a user can buy. Here is the code of the file:

```
<?php

include("ss_libcart.php");
include("libhtml.php");
include("incshop.php");

$page = new libhtml('temp_list.html');

include("error.php");

$psel = "SELECT id,name,instock,price FROM product ORDER BY name";
$con = new db();
$con->connect();
$num = $con->sql($psel);
$content = "";

for ($i = 0; $i<$num; $i++)
{
        $row = $con->fetch($i, 3);
        $content .= $page->line($row->id,
                    $row->name, $row->price, $ar_cart[$row->id]);

}
```

```
$page->add_data('CONTENT',$content);
echo $page->output();

?>
```

First the libraries needed to display the pages are included. In the next step, a new object called $page is created. This object is based on a template called temp_list.html. The code of this template is shown in the next listing:

temp_list.html:

```
<h1>Productlist</h1>
{MSG}
<form action="cart.php" method=post>
<table>
  <tr>
    <td>ID</td>
    <td>Productname  </td>
    <td>Price</td>
    <td>Quantity</td>
  </tr>
{CONTENT}
</table>
</form>
<a href="cash.php">Proceed to Checkout</a>
```

As you can see, the HTML template is fairly simple. It contains some HTML code and some keywords.

After including the libraries and creating the $page object, error.php is included. This library must be included here and not before generating the $page object because error.php relies on the existence of $page. The entire HTML code generated by this application is stored in $page before displaying it, so $page must already exist before adding code to it. Now a connection to the database is established by creating a db object. In addition, a query is executed. This query is necessary for retrieving the desired products from the database. The return value of the function called sql contains the number of rows in the result. This value is used by the loop processing every record returned by PostgreSQL. Inside the loop a function named line is called. Just like all other functions called in this block, the function has been implemented in libhtml.php:

```
<?php

class libhtml
```

```php
{
        var $page;
        var $msg;

        function libhtml($file)
        {
                $this->page = implode('', @file($file));
        }

        function add_data($field, $value)
        {
                $this->page = str_replace('{'.$field.'}', $value,$this->page);
        }

        function line($id, $name, $price, $value)
        {
                $tableline = "<tr><td>$id</td><td>$name</td><td>$price</td>";
                $tableline .= '<td>';
                $tableline .= '<input type="text" name="'.$id.'"';
                $tableline .= ' value="'.$value.'">';
                $tableline .= '</td><td>';
                $tableline .= '<input type=submit value="Buy"></td></tr>';
                return ($tableline);
        }

        function cashline($id = "", $name = "", $price = "", $value = "",
                           $sum = "")
        {
                $tableline = "<tr><td>$id</td><td>$name</td><td>$price</td>";
                $tableline .= "<td>$value</td><td>$sum</td><tr>";
                return ($tableline);

        }

        function output()
        {
                $this->page = str_replace("{MSG}", $msg, $this->page);
                return($this->page);
        }
}

?>
```

The class implemented in `libhtml.php` contains two variables. `$page` contains the entire HTML code of the page being generated. `$msg` contains important messages.

Let's take a closer look at the constructor of the object. A filename is passed to the method. This file is read and assigned to `$page`. Now the data in the file can be modified easily. To replace the variables in the files for the data you want to see, you can use add_data. It parses the files and performs simple substitutions. add_data replaces entire strings for data. However, in the case of tables this is not what you want. Therefore you need a function called `line`. This function is needed to display one line of a table. No matter which data you need, `line` will build the table for you.

The next function in the listing is called `cashline`. It is used to display data in the final sheet, which contains a list of all products a user has bought. Finally, the output function has been implemented. It performs a substitution and returns the code of the page.

As you have seen in the HTML template used by `shop.php`, the link on the bottom of the screen leads to `cash.php`. Cash.php is the file responsible for checking out. After the user has selected all the products he wants, he can buy these products, and that's exactly what he can do with the help of `cash.php`. Just like the rest of the application, the HTML code is based on templates. This time the file is called `temp_cash.html`. Let's take a look at the content of the file:

```
<h1>Payment</h1>
{MSG}
<table>
  <tr>
    <td>ID</td>
    <td>Productname  </td>
    <td>Price     </td>
    <td>Quantity</td>
    <td>Sum</td>
  </tr>
{CONTENT}
</table>
</form>
```

Two parameters are in the file. The first one is {MSG} and the second one is {CONTENT}. These two strings will be substituted for the content. This is done by `cash.php`; let's take a look at this file:

```
<?

include ("libhtml.php");
include ("libdb.php");
```

```php
include ("incshop.php");

$page = new libhtml('temp_cash.html');

$con = new db();
$con->connect();
$con->sql("BEGIN TRANSACTION");

$allsum = 0;
$keys = array_keys($ar_cart);
foreach ($keys as $element)
{
        $selcart = "SELECT id,price,name,instock
                       FROM product WHERE id=$element";
        $con->sql($selcart);
        $row = $con->fetch(0);
        if ($ar_cart[$row->id])
        {
                $sum = round($ar_cart[$row->id] * $row->price, 2);
                $allsum = $allsum + $sum;
                $content .= $page->cashline($row->id, $row->name,
                              $row->price, $ar_cart[$row->id], $sum);
                $upd = "UPDATE product SET instock =
                          instock-".$ar_cart[$row->id]." WHERE id=$row->id";
                $con->sql($upd);
        }
}
$con->sql("COMMIT");

$content .= $page->cashline("", "", "", "", $allsum);
$page->add_data('CONTENT',$content);

$t = time() - 50000;
setcookie("ser_cart", "", $t, "/");

echo $page->output();

?>
```

At the beginning of the file an object containing the HTML code is created. Just as in shop.php, the object is called $page. In the next step a connection to the database is established. In addition, a transaction is started. This is important because when removing the products from the stores, something bad must not happen in the middle of the process. If just one query fails, the number of products in the stores won't be correct any more and there is no way to solve problems like that.

In the next step the user's shopping cart is processed. For every product the user buys, a SELECT statement is performed. The data returned by the SELECT statement is used to build the final overview of the products. In addition, an UPDATE query is performed. This query reduces the products that are still in the stores.

After processing the data, the transaction is committed and additional HTML code is added to the $page object. Finally, the content of the object is displayed onscreen and the cookie is set to a negative timestamp. This means that the cookie is deleted and therefore the user's shopping cart is empty.

As you can see, it is an easy task to build a fragment of a shop. In this example the shop is based on cookies and parsing. Templates are read and strings inside these templates are substituted for the data retrieved from the database. This way it is easy to split layout and source code. It is an easy task to change the way the shop looks by changing the templates. In most cases it is not necessary to change the libraries for performing slight modifications. By splitting the code from the layout, you can save a lot of time and gain flexibility.

Now that you have seen how the application was implemented, you can take a look at the screen generated by shop.php, which is shown in Figure 21.6.

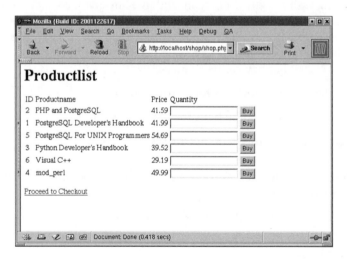

FIGURE 21.6   The main screen.

Finally, let's take a look at incshop.php:

```
<?

@session_start();
$sid = session_id();

$sel = "SELECT value FROM cart WHERE sid='$sid'";
$condb = new db();
$condb->connect();
$num = $condb->sql($sel);
if ($num)
{
        $erg = $condb->fetch(0);
        $ar_cart = unserialize($erg->value);
}
$condb->disconnect();

?>
```

21.2.1.2 Session-Driven Shopping Carts

You have already learned that cookies can have several disadvantages. Especially when working with a mixture of secure and insecure areas, cookies can be fatal because a cookie that has been set in the secure area is not valid in the insecure area. This can cause trouble and lead to a lot of work and high costs. In this section you will see how the application you have seen before can be implemented with the help of sessions. Several files have to be changed:

- cart.php—Added functions for starting sessions

- incshop.php—Added functions for starting sessions

- ss_libcart.php—Insert and update session information

The purpose of the original files is the same, but modifications have been made in order to work with sessions.

Before going to the files briefly, you can create a table:

```
CREATE TABLE "cart" (
        "sid" text,
        "value" text
);
```

This table is used for storing the information collected by the session subsystem. The first column contains the session id. The second column is used to store the values of the session.

After creating the table, you can take a look at the file we have changed for working with session information. Let's start with cart.php:

```php
<?php

include ("ss_libcart.php");

@session_start();
$sid = session_id();
$keys = array_keys($HTTP_POST_VARS);

for ($x = 0; $x < count($keys); $x++)
{
        if      ($HTTP_POST_VARS[$keys[$x]])
        {
                $id = $keys[$x];
                $number = $HTTP_POST_VARS[$keys[$x]];
                $sc = new cart();
                $sc->cartwork($id, $number);
        }
}
header("Location: shop.php");

?>
```

As you can see at the beginning of the script, a session is started. You have already seen in Chapter 15, "Session Management," how sessions can be started and how sessions can be treated. In the next step a session id is created. This id is assigned to $sid. The rest of the script works just like the cookie version of the file. The only thing you have to remove is the setcookie function and the lines related to it.

Let's go on to incshop.php:

```php
<?

@session_start();
$sid = session_id();

$sel = "SELECT value FROM cart WHERE sid='$sid'";
$condb = new db();
```

```
$condb->connect();
$num = $condb->sql($sel);
if ($num)
{
        $erg = $condb->fetch(0);
        $ar_cart = unserialize($erg->value);
}
$condb->disconnect();

?>
```

After starting a session and generating a session id, the current session id is retrieved from the database. If data is returned, the value in the second column is retrieved and `unserialize` is called. This way the session information is retrieved from the database.

Finally, take a look at the modified version of `ss_libcart.php`.

```
<?
require ("libdb.php");

class cart extends db
{
        function cartwork($id, $number)
        {
                @session_start();
                $sid=session_id();
                if ($number < 0)
                {
                        header("Location: shop.php?msg=2");
                        exit;
                }
                $con = new db();
                $con->connect();
                $chk = $this->checkstock($id,$number);
                if (!$chk)
                {
                        header("Location: shop.php?msg=1");
                        exit;
                }
                $selc = "SELECT value FROM cart WHERE sid='$sid'";
                $num=$con->sql($selc);
                if (!$num)
```

```
        {
                $ar_cart[$id] = $number;
                $ser_cart = serialize($ar_cart);
                $ins = "INSERT INTO cart(sid,value)
                        VALUES('$sid','$ser_cart')";
                $con->sql($ins);
        }
        else
        {

                $erg = $con->fetch(0);
                $ar_cart = unserialize($erg->value);
                if ($number < 1)
                {
                        unset ($ar_cart[$id]);
                }
                else
                {
                        $ar_cart[$id] = $number;
                }
                $ser_cart = serialize($ar_cart);
                $upd = "UPDATE cart SET value='$ser_cart' WHERE
                        sid='$sid'";
                $con->sql($upd);
        }
}

function checkstock($id,$number)
{
        $chksel = "SELECT instock FROM product WHERE id=$id";
        $this->connect();
        $this->sql($chksel);
        $row = $this->fetch(0,3);
        if ($number > $row->instock)
        {
                return(0);
        }
        return(1);
    }
}

?>
```

Let's start with the function called cartwork. Just as you have seen in the cookie version, the function checks whether enough products are in the stores. This is done with the help of the checkstock function that can be found at the end of this file. This function works just like the one you have already seen in the cookie version of this script. In order to work with the session database, a connection to the database must be established, which is done by creating a db object.

In the next step the records containing the session id are retrieved from the database. The content of the second field in the column is unserialized and modified before it is serialized again. Finally, the content of the database is modified.

After the application has run, some records can be found in the table called cart:

```
phpbook=# SELECT * FROM cart;
                 sid                |                    value
------------------------------------+----------------------------------------------
 1d94d8e82a893618bcfddde8b06fcf17 | a:2:{i:2;s:2:"24";i:1;s:1:"3";}
 ef495e885964545b61c10bfc6f1853fd | a:3:{i:1;s:1:"2";i:5;s:1:"1";i:2;s:1:"5";}
 9646a5abc72d26ce1975f8c389990358 | a:3:{i:1;s:1:"3";i:2;s:1:"1";i:3;s:1:"2";}
(3 rows)
```

In the first column you can see what a session id looks like; it is a 32-character long, alphanumeric string. The second column contains the serialized version of the data passed to the script called cash.php.

As you have seen in this section, working with sessions is an easy task and if an application has been implemented properly, it is an easy task to change the way sessions are managed. If all components used for working with sessions are managed by modules, you just have to change the modules you are using. In most cases this will not affect your entire application.

Finally it is time to see what the screen for the checkout looks like. Let's take a look at Figure 21.7.

The layout of the screen has been generated according to the HTML template accessed by cash.php. To change the layout, you just have to edit this template. This can be done by a designer who does not need to be able to write PHP programs. This is important because it will save costs and help you to make programmers and designers work more independently.

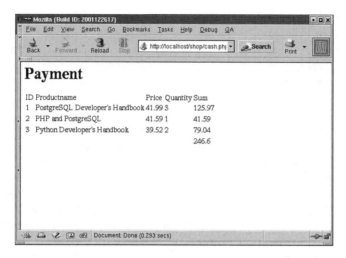

FIGURE 21.7   The checkout.

21.2.2 Collecting User Data

Collecting user data is one of the most important things when implementing business applications. The behavior of a user can be analyzed, and with the help of this data it is possible to optimize your Web site. You can find out which components are not interesting for a user and which links are used often. For marketing purposes, this is essential and it can help you to improve your business. Nearly all big players in modern e-commerce business use user tracking systems to optimize their sites. In this section we will try to implement a simple system you can use to find out what a user does inside your application. Modules like the one you will see in this section are optimized for shopping applications, but you can also use a module like this for analyzing any kind of Web site.

The key to user tracking is logging. The best thing to do is to write an object that is solely used for logging. All data collected by this object can be analyzed easily. In this section you will take a look at an object and you will see how data generated by this object can be analyzed.

Before implementing the object, you can create a table that will contain the logging information. In this example the table is called logging:

```
CREATE TABLE logging (
        id serial8,                   -- unique id of an entry
        tstamp timestamp with time zone
               DEFAULT now(),         -- timestamp
        sid varchar(32),              -- session id
        http_referer text,            -- where does the user come from
```

```
        script_filename text,          -- the name of the current script
        remote_addr inet,              -- ip address of viewer
        http_host text,                -- name of the current (virtual) host
        http_user_agent text,          -- the browser the user is using
        message text                   -- logging message
);
```

As you can see, the table contains many columns. The first one contains a unique id that will be assigned to every piece of logging information automatically. In the second column you will see when the logging information was added to the table. In addition, the table will contain the session id, the site the user comes from, the name of the script generating the logging information, the IP address of the person visiting the Web site, the name of the domain running on the machine the user is accessing, the version of the browser the user is utilizing, and a logging message. With the help of this information it is possible to track the user and to gain important information about the behavior of a user. After the table is created, the objects used for logging are implemented. In this example three objects will be shown. The object called `filelog` can be used to send logging information to a file. The `dblog` object is a database-driven logging utility. It is based on the table you have just seen. If you want to use files and a PostgreSQL database, the `log` object will be the right thing for you. It is a combination of both the `filelog` and the `dblog` object. It sends logging information to a file as well as to the database.

Let's take a look at the implementation of these three objects:

```php
<?php

# logging into a file
class filelog
{
        var $filename;
        var $fp;

        function filelog($file)
        {
                $this->filename = $file;
                $this->fp = fopen($this->filename, "a+");
        }

        function add_log($message)
        {
                setlocale("LC_TIME","en_US");
                $data = strftime("[%d/%b/%Y:%T %Z]");
```

```
                    fwrite($this->fp, "$data -- $message\n");
        }

        function logclose()
        {
                fclose($this->fp);
        }
};

# using a logging database
class dblog
{
        var $dbhost = 'localhost';
        var $dbname = 'phpbook';
        var $dbuser = 'hs';
        var $conn;

        # creating a logging object
        function dblog()
        {
                $this->conn = pg_connect("dbname=".$this->dbname.
                        " host=".$this->dbhost." user=".$this->dbuser);
                if      (!$this->conn)
                {
                        echo 'Connection failed.';
                        die;
                }
        }

        # add an entry to the logging database
        function add_log($sid, $message)
        {
                $message = str_replace("'", "''", $message);
                $message = str_replace("\\", "\\\\", $message);

                $sql = "INSERT INTO logging (sid, http_referer,
                        script_filename, remote_addr, http_host,
                        http_user_agent, message) VALUES ('$sid', '".
                        getenv('HTTP_REFERER')."', '".
                        getenv('SCRIPT_FILENAME')."', '".
                        getenv('REMOTE_ADDR')."', '".
                        getenv('HTTP_HOST')."', '".
```

```
                                getenv('HTTP_USER_AGENT')."', ".
                                "'$message')";

                    if      (pg_exec($this->conn, $sql))
                    {
                            # everything seems to work well ...
                    }
                    else
                    {
                            echo "an error in the logging library has occurred.";
                            die;
                    }
            }

            function logclose()
            {
                    pg_close($this->conn);
            }
    };

    class log
    {
            var $filelog;
            var $dblog;

            function log($file)
            {
                    $this->filelog = new filelog($file) or
                            die ("cannot create logging object (filelog,
                                $file)\n");

                    $this->dblog = new dblog() or
                            die ("cannot create logging object (dblog)\n");
            }

            function add_log($sid, $message)
            {
                    $this->filelog->add_log($message);
                    $this->dblog->add_log($sid, $message);
            }

            function logclose()
            {
```

```
        $this->filelog->logclose();
        $this->dblog->logclose();
    }
};


?>
```

The firstobject that has been implemented in `logging.php` is called `filelog`. It contains two variables. `$filename` contains the name of the file the logging information is sent to. `$fp` contains the file handle. The constructor of the objects opens a file having the name passed to the function. The next function in the list is the `add_log` function. One parameter containing the message must be passed to the function. A timestamp is compiled and the string is sent to the logfile. The last function in the code of the object is `logclose`. It does nothing but close the file containing the logging information.

Let's take a look at the `dblog` object. At the beginning of the object, three variables are initialized. The fourth variable called $conn will contain the database handle. As you can see, the constructor of the function opens a connection to the database. In this scenario the parameters taken from the header of the object are used. The `add_log` function is slightly more complex than the `add_log` function of the object you have seen before. The first thing is that special characters are escaped. This is done with the help of two regular expressions. In the next step a SQL command is built. The data is taken from the input parameters of the function as well as from predefined environment variables. These variables have been set by Apache and can be accessed using the `getenv` function. After the SQL code has been compiled, it is sent to the server.

In the case of the `dblog` function, `logclose` does nothing but close the connection to the database.

After discussing the first two objects, you can take a look at the `log` object, which combines the features of the first two objects. The constructor of the object generates two objects. These objects are assigned to the internal variables. Let's take a look at the `add_log` function. In this example it calls the `add_log` function of the two objects we have just discussed.

Now that you have seen how the objects have been implemented, it is time to take a look at an example that shows how the functions can be used:

```php
<?php
        include("logging.php");

        # starting sessions
        @session_start();
```

```
$sid=session_id();
echo "starting sessions ...<br>\n";

# creating new objects (filelog and dblog)
$filelog = new filelog ("/tmp/logfile.txt") or
        die ("cannot create logging object (1)");
$dblog = new dblog ();
echo "creating objects ...<br>\n";

# sending logging information to objects
$filelog->add_log("welcome from filelog");
$dblog->add_log($sid, "welcome from dblog");
echo "sending logging information to objects ...<br>\n";

# closing objects
$filelog->logclose();
$dblog->logclose();
echo "closing objects ...\n";
?>
```

After including the library, session information is computed. In the next step a
filelog and a dblog object are created. To see if the objects work correctly, add_log
is called.

Let's run the script and see what comes out:

```
starting sessions ...
creating objects ...
sending logging information to objects ...
closing objects ...
```

If the script has been executed successfully, you can take a look at the content of the
logfile:

```
[hs@duron shop]$ tail -n1 /tmp/logfile.txt
[11/Feb/2002:22:05:37 CET] -- welcome from filelog
```

In addition to the logfile, data has been added to the database. In this example,
more than one query is performed to display the result because otherwise the result
would not fit on one page. Let's take a look:

```
phpbook=# SELECT id, tstamp, sid FROM logging;
 id |             tstamp              |               sid
----+---------------------------------+----------------------------------
  1 | 2002-02-11 22:05:37.373493+01   | 9646a5abc72d26ce1975f8c389990358
(1 row)
```

```
phpbook=# SELECT http_referer, script_filename, remote_addr, http_host
FROM logging;
 http_referer |          script_filename           | remote_addr | http_host
--------------+------------------------------------+-------------+-----------
              | /var/www/html/shop/makelog.php | 127.0.0.1   | localhost
(1 row)

phpbook=# SELECT http_user_agent FROM logging;
                       http_user_agent
-----------------------------------------------------------------
 Mozilla/5.0 (X11; U; Linux i686; en-US; rv:0.9.7) Gecko/20011226
(1 row)

phpbook=# SELECT id, message FROM logging;
 id |      message
----+-------------------
  1 | welcome from dblog
(1 row)
```

As you can see, all information has been added to the table.

In the previous example you have seen two objects being used. In the next example you can see how almost the same goal can be reached using the log object instead of the two objects log is based on:

```php
<?php
        include("logging.php");

        # starting sessions
        @session_start();
        $sid=session_id();
        echo "starting sessions ...<br>\n";

        # creating new object
        $log = new log ("/tmp/logfile.txt") or
                die ("cannot create logging object (1)");
        $log->add_log($sid, "welcome from filelog");
        $log->logclose();
?>
```

When using this module extensively, tracking users is an easy task. Just query the table containing the logging information and with the help of the object id, you will find out who has done what inside your applications.

When implementing online shops, you can find out which products are viewed more often than others. You can try to figure out how price reductions of certain products affect the behavior of your customers and approximately how long a customer stays on one site. As an exercise, just try to add some logging information to the shop fragment you have seen in the previous section. You will see that it is easily possible to find out whether a user has removed products from the shopping cart again. You will also find out how long it takes to finish shopping.

21.3 Building a Content Management System

Building a content management system is a programmer's favorite task. This is my personal impression when talking to IT experts all around the globe. Every company focusing on Web development has implemented some sort of content management system (CMS) to speed up application development. Many different approaches and concepts for building CMS systems have been developed, and even more products have been implemented. In this section you will take a look at a basic yet powerful and easy approach to content management.

21.3.1 How to Display Data

Usually a CMS system consists of two important components. The first component is used to manage the data in the database. This part cannot be accessed by an ordinary user.

The second part of a CMS system is responsible for displaying and formatting the data in the database. In this section we will focus on this particular part, and you will see how a system like that can be implemented easily. In addition, you will see how to build systems for displaying data flexibly.

Let's get started and create a table that can be used to store simple messages. The goal of this example is to display the data in the database using HTML templates as well as configuration files. Here is the SQL code for generating the table in the database:

```
CREATE TABLE message (
        id serial,
        tstamp timestamp with time zone
                DEFAULT now(),
        who text,
        message text
);


INSERT INTO message (who, message)
        VALUES ('John', 'check out www.postgresql.at');
```

```
INSERT INTO message (who, message)
        VALUES ('Paul', 'please recompile the kernel');
INSERT INTO message (who, message)
        VALUES ('Lisa', 'who wants to dance some Salsa (LA style)?');
```

As you can see the table contains four columns. In this example three records have been added to the table.

Before going through the code of the application you can take a look at Table 21.2, which contains a list of the files involved in the process.

TABLE 21.2   Files Needed In This Example

File	Content
Config.php	Contains the configuration information of the CMS system.
temp_list.html	An HTML template.
Cms.php	The CMS library.
Testcms.php	The main file that is responsible for testing the CMS library.

With just four files, it is possible to implement a useful and flexible tool for displaying data.

The goal of the tool is to use an HTML template as well as configuration files. The HTML template contains keywords that are retrieved and substituted for data. In addition, it should be possible to retrieve data from the database and to generate tables out of it. Let's take a look at the configuration file called config.php:

```
<?php
        # static values
        $stat['TITLE'] = "Welcome To This Application";
        $stat['FILE'] = "next.php";

        # SQL code
        $sql['SQL_LISTPRODUCT'] = "SELECT tstamp, who, message FROM message";
?>
```

Two arrays have been defined. The first one contains two fields that are used to store strings. The second array contains a SQL statement that queries the table you have added to the database before. This configuration file will be included by the CMS library you will see later in this section.

Let's take a look at the HTML template we are going to use here. The file is called temp_list.html:

```
<h1>{TITLE}</h1>
<form action="{FILE}" method=post>
{SQL_LISTPRODUCT}
```

```
</form>

<br><br>
Thanks for visiting the page
```

As you can see, it contains all three strings you have used to index the two arrays in the configuration file. The strings are marked using braces. The goal of the CMS system is to substitute the strings for real data.

Let's take a look at the CMS library:

```php
<?php

class content
{
        var $template;
        var $conn;
        var $code;

        function content ($template, $cstr)
        {
                $this->conn = pg_connect($cstr);
                if      (!$this->conn)
                {
                        die ("cannot connect to database<br>\n");
                }
                $this->code = implode('', @file($template))
                        or die("cannot work with $template<br>\n");
        }

        function parsecontent($config)
        {
                include($config);

                # adding static variables to the content
                while (list ($key, $val) = each ($stat))
                {
                        $this->code = preg_replace("/\{$key\}/",
                                $val, $this->code);
                }
        }

        function dynamiccontent($config)
        {
```

```
include($config);

# adding dynamic variables to the content
while (list ($key, $val) = each ($sql))
{
        # checking if key is in the template
        if      (preg_match("/\{$key\}/", $this->code))
        {
                # retrieving data for the object
                $ret = pg_exec($this->conn, $val) or
                        die ("cannot execute query ($sql)");

                $rows = pg_numrows($ret);
                $fields = pg_numfields($ret);

                # displaying header of table
                $data .= "<table border=3><tr>\n";
                for     ($i = 0; $i < $fields; $i++)
                {
                        $data .= "<th>".
                                pg_fieldname($ret, $i)."</th>";
                }
                $data .= "</tr>\n";

                for     ($i = 0; $i < $rows; $i++)
                {
                        $data .= "<tr>";
                        $line = pg_fetch_row($ret, $i);


                        for     ($j = 0; $j < $fields; $j++)
                        {
                                $data .= "<td>";
                                $data .= $line[$j];
                                $data .= "</td>";
                        }
                        $data .= "</tr>\n";
                }

                $data .= "</table>\n";

                # adding data to document
```

```
                              $this->code = preg_replace("/\{$key\}/",
                                       $data, $this->code);
                        }
                  }

            }

            function display()
            {
                  echo $this->code;
            }
      };

?>
```

The entire library consists of just one object. This object is built on four functions that do all the work for you.

The constructor of the object connects to the database and loads the template file into memory. This is done with the help of the functions `file` and `implode`. `file` reads the data into an array and `implode` makes one string out of it. The string generated by `implode` can be processed easily.

In the configuration file you saw that two arrays have been defined. The first one is used to define static variables and constant values. Just think of variables related to the language of a file or any other value that should be configured globally. The `parsecontent` function goes through all values of the array containing the static values and substitutes the strings in the templates for the data in the configuration file. The substitution is done with the help of a simple regular expression.

After looking at the function processing the values defined in the configuration file, it is time to see how the SQL code is treated. Therefore you can take a look at the `dynamiccontent` function that has been implemented after the `parsecontent` function. It loads a configuration file as well. In this example the same configuration as in the `parsecontent` function is used. The entire array called `$sql` is processed and the system tries to find out if keys found in the array can be found in the string containing the HTML template as well. If a match is found, the SQL statement related to the key is executed, and the data retrieved from the database is formatted as table. For formatting the table, the number of rows and fields are returned. After that the header of the table is generated. As soon as the header is ready, PHP starts creating the body of the table. Therefore two loops are executed. Every line in the table is processed. The second loop generates the various columns of the table.

After you have seen the library, you can take a look at the file called testcms.php, which contains the body of the application:

```php
<?php

include("cms.php");

$page = new content("temp_list.html",
        "host=localhost dbname=phpbook user=hs");
$page->parsecontent("config.php");
$page->dynamiccontent("config.php");
$page->display();


?>
```

First the CMS library is included. In the next step an object is created. The name of the HTML template is passed to the constructor. In the next step the variables in the stat array are used by calling the parsecontent function. After this has been completed, it is time for the database to do some work. dynamiccontent is called. It performs a query and generates a table. Finally the data is sent to the browser.

Figure 21.8 shows what the HTML code generated by the application looks like when viewing it with Mozilla.

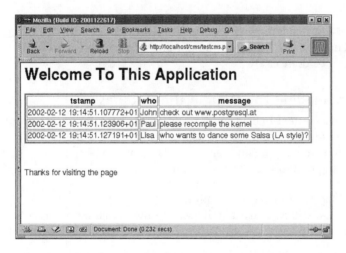

FIGURE 21.8   A simple table.

Now that you have seen what the page looks like, it is interesting to take a look at the HTML code displayed by the browser. The HTML makes clear what has happened inside the application:

```
<h1>Welcome To This Application</h1>
<form action="next.php" method=post>
<table border=3><tr>
<th>tstamp</th><th>who</th><th>message</th></tr>
<tr><td>2002-02-12 19:14:51.107772+01</td><td>John</td><td>check out
www.postgresql.at</td></tr>
<tr><td>2002-02-12 19:14:51.123906+01</td><td>Paul</td><td>please recompile
the kernel</td></tr>
<tr><td>2002-02-12 19:14:51.127191+01</td><td>Lisa</td><td>who wants to
dance some Salsa (LA style)?</td></tr>
</table>

</form>

<br><br>
Thanks for visiting the page
```

The data has been inserted into the HTML code the way it has been returned by the database. Depending on the HTML template, the result will look the way you want it to.

The advantage of a class like that is its flexibility. Just tell the person who is responsible for the layout where to place which strings, and your application will do the rest for you.

Of course, additional features must be implemented to work with things like pull-down menus. However, the most important task, which is separating layout and objects, can be done easily.

21.3.2 Managing the Data in the Database

The goal of a content management system is to manage the content of a database-driven Web site. In most cases managing the data is not the task of the user, so special screens for adding and removing data have to be built. This is exactly what you are going to deal with in this section.

21.3.2.1 Maintaining Data in Tables

In this section you will take a brief look at how to maintain data in tables. You will see a brief example that can be used to insert and to delete data from a set of tables.

Because you have already seen how data can be passed from one script to another, we will use hidden fields to do the job so that you will get a deeper insight into the basic concepts of PHP programming. The first thing to do is to remove all old tables from the database. This can be done with the help of DROP TABLE. After all tables

have been deleted, you can go on and create three new tables you will need in this
section:

```
CREATE TABLE message (
        id int4,
        tstamp timestamp with time zone
                DEFAULT now(),
        who text,
        message text
);

INSERT INTO message (id, who, message)
        VALUES (1, 'John', 'check out www.postgresql.at');
INSERT INTO message (id, who, message)
        VALUES (2, 'Paul', 'please recompile the kernel');
INSERT INTO message (id, who, message)
        VALUES (3, 'Lisa', 'who wants to dance some Salsa (LA style)?');

CREATE TABLE userinfo (
        id int4,
        name text,
        grp text,
        password text
);

CREATE TABLE groupinfo (
        id int4,
        name text
);
```

Some records have been added to the first table. The two other tables are still empty.

When building content management systems, one query must be kept in mind
because it is important for finding out which tables can be found in the system:

```
phpbook=# SELECT relname FROM pg_class WHERE relname NOT LIKE 'pg_%'
AND relkind = 'r';
  relname
- - - - - - - - - -
 message
 userinfo
 groupinfo
(3 rows)
```

As you can see, you can use the SELECT statement to retrieve the list of tables in the system that are not used by PostgreSQL itself. In other words, it retrieves all tables but PostgreSQL's system tables. The tool we are going to write will be able to modify all tables in the system, so this query will be essential.

Before going through the source code, you can take a look at the files involved in the application:

- manage.php—Displays a list of all tables in the database
- detail.php—Displays the content of the table selected in manage.php and performs INSERT operations if necessary
- action.php—Performs DELETE operations

Let's get started with manage.php. Here is the code:

```php
<?php
        echo '
                <html>
                <body>
                <h1>Content Management Tool</h1>
                Select the table you want to edit: <br>
        ';

        # connecting to the database
        $dbh = pg_connect("dbname=phpbook user=hs host=localhost");
        if      (!$dbh)
        {
                die ("cannot connect to database<br>\n");
        }

        # retrieving a list of all tables in the database
        $res = @pg_exec($dbh, "SELECT relname FROM pg_class
                WHERE relname NOT LIKE 'pg_%' AND relkind = 'r' ")
                or die ("cannot retrieve list of tables");

        # displaying list
        echo "<br><b>Tables in the database</b><br>\n";
        $rows = pg_numrows($res);
        for     ($i = 0; $i < $rows; $i++)
        {
                $line = pg_fetch_row($res, $i);
                echo '<a href="detail.php?tab='.$line[0].
                        "\">$line[0]</a><br>\n";
```

```
        }

        echo "</body></html>";
?>
```

At the beginning of the script, some HTML code is displayed. After connecting to the database, you can retrieve the list of tables you want to modify. This is done with the help of the SQL statement you have seen before. After the query executes, a list of links is displayed. These links point to `detail.php`. Every table is assigned to exactly one link and the name of the table is added to the URL of the link. In other words, `detail.php` is called with a parameter. Figure 21.9 shows what the screen looks like.

FIGURE 21.9   Select a table.

After a table has been selected, `detail.php` is started. The code of this script is shown in the next listing:

```php
<?php

        $data .= "<html>
                <body>
                <h1>Content Management Tool</h1>
                Edit the table <br>";

        # connecting to the database
        $dbh = pg_connect("dbname=phpbook user=hs host=localhost");
        if      (!$dbh)
        {
                die ("cannot connect to database<br>\n");
        }
```

```
# checking for insert
if      ($number_of_fields)
{
        $sql = "INSERT INTO $tab VALUES (";
        for     ($i = 1; $i < $number_of_fields - 1; $i++)
        {
                $sql .= "'${$i}', ";
        }
        $max = $number_of_fields - 1;
        $sql .= "'${$max}')";
        $ret = pg_exec($dbh, $sql) or
                die ("cannot execute UPDATE operation<br>\n");
}
# retrieving a list of all tables in the database
$sql = "SELECT oid, * FROM $tab";
$res = @pg_exec($dbh, $sql) or
        die ("cannot retrieve list of tables");

# displaying list
$data .= "<br><b>Details:</b><br>\n";
$rows = pg_numrows($res);
$fields = pg_numfields($res);

# displaying header of table
$table .= "<table border=3><tr>\n";
for     ($i = 1; $i < $fields; $i++)
{
        $table .= "<th>".
        pg_fieldname($res, $i)."</th>";
}
$data .= $table."<th>action</th>\n";
$data .= "</tr>\n";

# displaying data
$data .= '<form action="detail.php" method="post">';
for     ($i = 0; $i < $rows; $i++)
{
        $data .= "<tr>";
        $line = pg_fetch_row($res, $i);

        for     ($j = 1; $j < $fields; $j++)
        {
```

```
                            $data .= "<td>";
                            $data .= $line[$j];
                            $data .= "</td>";
                    }
                    $data .= '<td><a href="action.php?act=delete&oid='.
                            $line[0].'&tab='.$tab.'">Delete</a> </td> ';
                    $data .= "</tr>\n";
            }
            $data .= "</table>\n";
            $data .= "<br><b>Add data to the table</b><br>\n";

            # displaying HTML for inserting data
            $data .= $table;
            $data .= "<tr>";
            for     ($i = 1; $i < $fields; $i++)
            {
                    $data .= "<td>".
                            '<input type="text" name="'.$i.'"></td>';
            }
            $data .= "</tr>\n";
            $data .= "</table>\n";
            $data .= '<input type="hidden" name="number_of_fields" '.
                    "value=\"$fields\"><br><br>";
            $data .= '<input type="hidden" name="tab" value="'.$tab.'">';
            $data .= '<input type="submit" name="submit" >';
            $data .= "</form>\n";

            echo $data, $tail;
?>
```

Before taking a closer look at the code, we recommend taking a look at the output of
the script. Figure 21.10 shows what comes out when you select the table called
message.

In the figure you can see that the content of the table is displayed as a table. The last
column of the table contains a link. The link points to action.php and contains the
object id of the record it belongs to. The object id is a unique identifier for a record,
so it can be used safely because it cannot be changed—at least it makes no sense to
change it. On the lower end of the script, you can see a set of fields for inserting
data. When the Submit button is clicked, the data in the fields will be added to the
table.

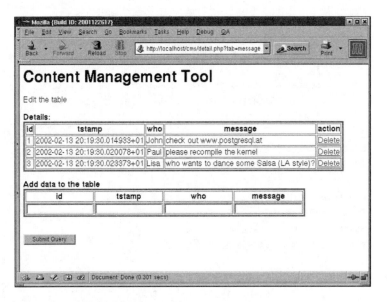

FIGURE 21.10   Results of selecting a table.

Let's take a closer look at the source code of the file. At the beginning of the script, a connection to the database is established. After that the script checks whether `$number_of_fields` is defined. If it is defined, a new record has to be added to the table. Whenever the Submit button is clicked, `$number_of_fields` will be defined. If somebody clicks on a link to delete a record, `$number_of_fields` won't be defined, so it is a good choice to find out what has to be done. The INSERT operation is simple. A SQL statement is compiled, which is sent to PostgreSQL. You will see in a minute why the algorithm works.

The next thing to do is to find out which data has to be displayed onscreen. Therefore a query is performed that retrieves all records from the table. The object id is selected as well because it is needed to identify a record. In the next step the header of the tables is created. This is done with the help of a simple loop. After displaying the head of the table, the data is added to it. The most interesting part of this component is the generation of the link for deleting records. The object id of the line and the name of the table where the record can be found are added to the link. This way no Submit button is used for calling the delete function. In the next step the table for inserting the data is added to the scenario. It consists of a dynamic number of columns, which is generated on-the-fly as well. The most important thing is that the number of the column is used as the name of the field. If your script knows how many columns your table has, it is an easy task to guess the names of the fields in the form. Of course, there are several other possibilities for extracting the names of the fields in the form, but this is one of the easiest ones.

A set of hidden fields is defined. The advantage of a hidden field is that you can use it inside a form for storing data. It is not displayed by the browser but can be used to pass data on to the next script. In this scenario the number of fields as well as the name of the table the application is all about are stored in hidden fields.

You have seen earlier in this section that the script checks whether $number_of_fields exists. With the help of a hidden field, $number_of_fields is passed to the script the form calls when the button is clicked.

At the end of the script, the data is displayed.

When the user clicks on the link, action.php is called. This file does nothing but delete the desired record and redirect the user to manage.php. Let's take a look at the code:

```php
<?php
        # connecting to the database
        $dbh = pg_connect("dbname=phpbook user=hs host=localhost");
        if      (!$dbh)
        {
                die ("cannot connect to database<br>\n");
        }

        # managing delete statements
        if      ($act == 'delete')
        {
                mydelete($dbh, $tab, $oid);
        }

# deleting a record
function mydelete($dbh, $tab, $oid)
{
        $sql = "DELETE FROM $tab WHERE oid=$oid";
        $stat = @pg_exec($dbh, $sql) or
                die ("cannot delete record $oid");

        echo '<head>
                <meta http-equiv="refresh" content="0; URL=manage.php">
                </head>
                <body>
                        Record has been deleted - you will be redirected ';
}

?>
```

As you can see, the code is easy because it does nothing but connect to the database, delete a record, and redirect the user.

21.4 Creating Stock Charts

Modern applications are not only used to store data; they also are essential for displaying data in a easy-to-understand and comfortable way. One application where displaying data plays a key role is tools for displaying information about stocks. The progression of the value of a certain stock is displayed in charts and can easily be displayed using PHP's GD interface. In this section you will see how to build a rudimentary tool for monitoring stocks. Keep in mind that you will see a rudimentary application, not a sophisticated one. The reason is that writing a complex application leads to tons of code that cannot be discussed in this book reasonably. Therefore we prefer to focus on the essential components of such an application.

The first thing to do is to create a table for storing the information you will need to generate the dynamic image. This can be done using a simple CREATE TABLE statement:

```
phpbook=# CREATE TABLE stock (name text, curdate date, curval numeric(9,2));
CREATE
```

Now that a table has been created, you can use the COPY command to insert some data into it:

```
phpbook=# COPY stock FROM stdin;
Enter data to be copied followed by a newline.
End with a backslash and a period on a line by itself.
>> Cybertec      2002/1/1        12.32
>> Cybertec      2002/1/2        12.65
>> Cybertec      2002/1/3        12.59
>> Cybertec      2002/1/4        13.00
>> Cybertec      2002/1/5        12.80
>> Cybertec      2002/1/6        12.99
>> Cybertec      2002/1/7        15.12
>> Cybertec      2002/1/8        16.89
>> \.
```

If no error occurred, the data has been added to the table successfully. In the next step you can write a user form where the user can select the stock he wants to retrieve information about as well as the interval the user wants to be displayed. The following listing shows a simple HTML form:

```
<HTML>
<HEAD>
        <META HTTP-EQUIV="CONTENT-TYPE"
                CONTENT="text/html; charset=iso-8859-15">
        <TITLE>Monitoring Tool</TITLE>
</HEAD>
<BODY>
<P><FONT FACE="Courier, monospace"><FONT SIZE=5 STYLE="font-size: 20pt">
        <B>Monitoring Tool</B>
</FONT></FONT></P>
<P><FONT FACE="Courier, monospace"><FONT SIZE=4 STYLE="font-size: 16pt">

<FORM ACTION="stock.php" METHOD="POST">
<TABLE>
        <TR><TD>Stock: </TD><TD><INPUT TYPE="TEXT" NAME="name"></TD></TR>
        <TR><TD>Beginning: </TD><TD><INPUT TYPE="TEXT" NAME="start"></TD></TR>
        <TR><TD>End: </TD><TD><INPUT TYPE="TEXT" NAME="end"></TD></TR>
        <TR><TD></TD><TD><INPUT TYPE="SUBMIT" NAME="Generate Chart"></TD></TR>
</TABLE>
</FORM>

</FONT></FONT></P>
</BODY>
</HTML>
```

The form is simple. It consists of three input fields plus one button for submitting the data. If somebody clicks the button, stock.php is called. In Figure 21.11 you can see what the form looks like.

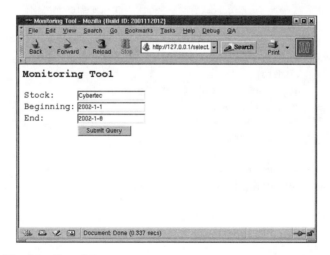

FIGURE 21.11   Inserting data.

Of course, this is just a simple form and many features can be added to it easily. Let's get to `stock.php`, which contains the code for retrieving the data from the database:

```php
<?php
        # including library for generating picture
        include("image.php");

        # connecting to the database
        $dbh = pg_connect("dbname=phpbook host=localhost user=hs");
        if     (!$dbh)
                die ("connection to the database cannot be established\n");

        # generating image
        $xsize = 400;
        $ysize = 300;
        $image = genimage($xsize, $ysize);

        # finding maximum value in chart
        $findmax = "SELECT max(curval) FROM stock WHERE name='$name'";
        $retvalue = pg_exec($dbh, $findmax);
        $retrow = pg_fetch_row($retvalue, 0);
        $max = $retrow[0];

        # computing scale
        $scale = $ysize*0.9 / $max;

        # executing query for retrieving data
        $sql = "SELECT curdate, curval FROM stock
                WHERE curdate >= '$start'
                        AND curdate <= '$end' AND name='$name'
                ORDER BY curdate";

        $data = pg_exec($dbh, $sql);
        if     (!$data)
                die ("cannot execute query<br>\n");
        $rows = pg_numrows($data);
        if     ($rows < 6)
                die("not enough data<br>\n");

        # drawing grid
        $image = drawgrid($image, $xsize, $ysize, $rows);
```

```
# retrieving data
$black = ImageColorAllocate($image, 0, 0, 0);
for     ($i = 0; $i < $rows - 1; $i++)
{
        $rescur = pg_fetch_array($data, $i);
        $resnext = pg_fetch_array($data, $i + 1);
        ImageLine($image,
                ($i + 0.5) * $xsize / $rows,
                $ysize - $rescur["curval"] * $scale,
                ($i + 1.5) * $xsize / $rows,
                $ysize - $resnext["curval"] * $scale,
                $black);
}

# displaying header and sending picture to browser
header ("Content-type: image/png");
ImagePng($image);
pg_close($dbh);

?>
```

First a file called image.php is included. This file contains a set of functions for
drawing images efficiently. You will take a closer look at this library after you have
gone through stock.php. After including the library, a connection to the database is
established. In case of an error, PHP will quit the script and an error is displayed. If
no error has occurred, the function genimage is called. This function can be found in
image.php and is used to generate an empty, white image. The return value of the
function is the image handle you will need for the steps that are still to come.

Now that a connection to the database has been established and an image has been
created, the data is selected from the database. The maximum value in the table
belonging to the stock you are interested in is selected. This is necessary in order to
compute the scale of the image. As you can see, the y coordinate of the maximum
value will be 90% of the total height of the image. No matter what the maximum
value is, it will always be at the same coordinate.

After computing the scale, the data needed to draw the graph is retrieved. As you can
see, dates are taken from the user form and are used directly without modification.
Keep in mind that the data returned by the database must be ordered by date. This is
necessary because otherwise the data might not be returned in the appropriate order.

In many real-world applications you will see that a graph is drawn on top of a grid.
In this application the grid is drawn with the help of drawgrid. Just like genimage,
this function has been implemented in image.php. After the query executes, it is

time to retrieve the data. The records are retrieved by processing a for loop. This loop is executed $rows - 1 times. You will soon see why the loop is not processed $rows times.

At the beginning of the loop, the current as well as the next record in the result are retrieved. These two records are necessary to draw a line from one point to another. Every point contains the value of the stock on a particular day. The most important part of this loop is to see how the line is drawn. In the case of $rows records in the result, it is possible to draw exactly $rows - 1 rows without using records outside the interval the user has defined. To take this into consideration, the position of the line is drawn from ($i + 0.5) * $xsize / $rows to ($i + 1.5) * $xsize / $rows. $i defines the day in the list, and $xsize defines the size of the image. By dividing the result of the multiplication by $rows, it is possible to compute the size of the slice marking one day. $i + 0.5 can be seen as the middle of the first day the user wants to take a look at.

After all lines are displayed, the result is sent to the browser. Of course it is possible to add additional text or lines to the scenario. You can do this easily by using PHP's functions for working with text. We have decided not to add text to the chart to keep the application small and simple.

After you have gone through stock.php, it is time to take a look at image.php:

```php
<?php

# library for drawing images
function genimage($xsize, $ysize)
{
        $image = ImageCreate($xsize, $ysize);
        if      (!$image)
                die("cannot create image<br>\n");

        # painting background
        $white = ImageColorAllocate($image, 255, 255, 255);
        ImageFill($image, 1, 1, $white);

        return $image;
}

# drawing a grid and borders
function drawgrid($image, $xsize, $ysize, $rows)
{
        # drawing border
        $black = ImageColorAllocate($image, 0, 0, 0);
```

```
$points = array(0,0, 0,$ysize-1, $xsize-1,$ysize-1, $xsize-1,0);
ImagePolygon($image, $points, 4, $black);

# drawing grid
$xdiff = $xsize / ($rows - 1);          # for vertical lines
$ydiff = $ysize / 5;                    # for horizontal lines

# drawing vertical lines
for     ($i = 1; $i < $rows; $i++)
{
        ImageLine($image, $xdiff * $i, 0,
                $xdiff * $i, $ysize, $black);
}

# drawing horizontal lines
for     ($i = 1; $i < 5; $i++)
{
        ImageLine($image, 0, $ydiff * $i,
                $xsize, $ydiff * $i, $black);
}

        return $image;
}

?>
```

The first function is needed to create new images. It creates an image that has the size passed to the function. If the image cannot be created, an error will occur. There are several reasons that PHP cannot create the image. The next listing contains a compilation of the most common errors as well as a list of what you have to take care of when using a function such as genimage:

- PHP does not support the GD module—If GD has not been compiled into your binaries, this function will fail. This is an important point because the GD module is an add-on to PHP.

- Negative values—ImageCreate does not return an error if negative values are passed to the function. Things like that must be checked explicitly.

- Memory limit—In the case of PHP 4.1.0 you can generate extremely large images consuming more memory than PHP is allowed to use (see memory_limit in php.ini). This happens if PHP has not been compiled using --enable-memory-limit.

The next function in the library is called drawgrid and is used to add the grid to the scenario. Depending on the number of days, you want to display information about, the number of lines will differ.

After the user inserts data into the form in select.html and clicks the button, a chart will be generated. The output is shown in Figure 21.12.

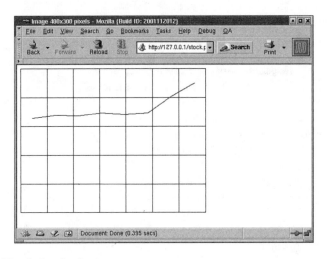

FIGURE 21.12   A simple chart.

As you have seen in this section, generating charts is easy when working with PHP and PostgreSQL. With just a few lines of code you can draw good-looking diagrams and charts. If you want to draw other kinds of diagrams, you can do that as well. The advantage of the GD module is that it is a standard interface for generating graphics, which makes it flexible and reliable.

21.5 PHP for Application Servers

Today application servers are widely used to make the development of complex, content-oriented Web sites easier. For a long time application servers were available for Java and Python (for example, Zope) only. Recently, PHP has become more and more popular as well, so a variety of application servers were introduced. In this section we will try to provide an overview of what you can do with application servers and how to use them efficiently to solve everyday problems.

21.5.1 Application Server Fundamentals

When talking about application servers, people often ask me what application servers are. Well, the answer to this question is slightly more difficult than answering the question "What is an atomic bomb?". Let's try to define the technical term *application server*: An application server can be seen as a framework that helps you to build content-oriented Web sites. Usually an application server consists of a set of classes that have a certain purpose and that fulfill certain tasks. Normally these tasks are basic operations. Imagine a table consisting of various columns. In many cases a user wants to sort the elements in a certain column. An application will most likely help you to implement this feature easily. To make it short: An application server is a set of classes. But what makes an application server an application server if it is just a set of libraries, functions, methods, and classes? Tough question. The answer is that usually libraries are limited to a certain functionality related to a certain topic. In the case of application servers, this is a little different because a variety of features are supported and all classes are optimized to work with each other. This is the main difference between a set of loose libraries and an application server.

In this chapter we will try to introduce you to some different concepts and approaches used by recent application servers based on PHP.

21.5.2 Simple Applications with PHPLens

One PHP-based application server is PHPLens, which you can download from http://www.phplens.com. PHPLens is a powerful framework for data-oriented Web sites. It is easy to use and works reliably. Although PHPLens is not free software, we have decided to include this here because it is a good example of a PHP-based application server.

21.5.2.1 Installing PHPLens

The first thing you have to do when working with PHPLens is to download the software from www.phplens.com. Several types of licenses are available. For this book Natsoft has given us a temporary advanced license. At this point, we would like to say thank you for the support we have received from the company.

After downloading and extracting the sources of PHPLens in the directory containing the HTML code (in this example we have used /usr/local/apache/htdocs/php), you can create a database:

```
[hs@duron hs]$ createdb phplens
CREATE DATABASE
```

In this example, the database is called phplens. In the next step you have to install the Zend Optimizer. This tool can be downloaded from www.zend.com. Just register on the Web site and you can get the tool free. Follow the instructions for installing the software, and within two minutes the Zend Optimizer will be up and running.

After that PHPLens must be configured to your needs. The first thing to do is to configure the database the application server should access. Therefore rename `sample-phplens.config.inc.php` in the config directory to `phplens.config.inc.php`. In this file you have to change the settings from MySQL to PostgreSQL as shown in the next listing:

```
if (!isset($PHPLENS_SESSION_DRIVER)) {
        $PHPLENS_SESSION_DRIVER='postgres';      // database driver to use
        $PHPLENS_SESSION_CONNECT='localhost';    // server address
        $PHPLENS_SESSION_USER ='hs';      // userid
        $PHPLENS_SESSION_PWD ='';         // password
        $PHPLENS_SESSION_DB ='phplens'; // database (optional for some dbs)
```

In this scenario the user who connects to the database on the local machine is called hs. As you have seen before, the database is called `phplens`. After defining the database, you can insert the data structure needed by the application server into the database. You can easily do this with the help of `psql`:

```
[hs@duron php]$ psql phplens < phplens.sql
NOTICE:  CREATE TABLE/PRIMARY KEY will create implicit index 'phplens_pkey'
for table 'phplens'
CREATE
NOTICE:  CREATE TABLE/PRIMARY KEY will create implicit index 'sessions_pkey'
for table 'sessions'
CREATE
```

If no errors occurred, a set of tables has been added to the database. In the next listing, you can see a list of these tables as well as the data structure of the new objects:

```
phplens=# \d
    List of relations
   Name    | Type  | Owner
----------+-------+-------
 phplens  | table | hs
 sessions | table | hs
(2 rows)


phplens=# \d phplens
                Table "phplens"
 Attribute |            Type           | Modifier
----------+---------------------------+----------
 id        | character(12)             | not null
 lastmod   | timestamp with time zone  | not null
 data      | text                      | not null
Index: phplens_pkey
```

```
phplens=# \d sessions
          Table "sessions"
 Attribute |      Type      | Modifier
-----------+----------------+----------
 sesskey   | character(32)  | not null
 expiry    | integer        | not null
 data      | text           | not null
Index: sessions_pkey
```

As you can see, the tables contain just a few columns. The image in Figure 21.13 shows what comes out when you execute `testlens.php`.

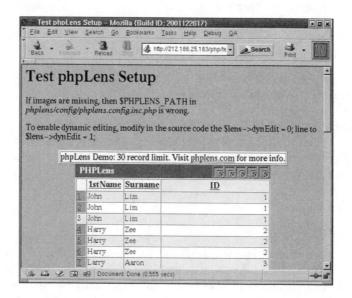

FIGURE 21.13   Testing PHPLens.

21.5.2.2 PHPLens Fundamentals and Examples
Now that you have installed PHPLens, it is time to write some code. You can create a directory so that the code of PHPLens is not mixed up with your code:

```
[hs@duron php]$ mkdir code
```

After that you can insert some data into the database. The next piece of code shows how to create a table for storing information about employees. Finally six records are added to the table:

```
CREATE TABLE employee (id int4,
        name text,
        gender char(1),
        income numeric(9,2));

COPY employee FROM stdin;
1       Peter   m       42000
2       Shelley f       59000
3       Epi     m       20000
4       Horst   m       39500
5       Ellen   f       43250
6       Kuli    m       12000
\.
```

Let's take a look at a short PHP script using PHPLens:

```
<?php
        include('../phplens.inc.php');
        session_start();
        $lens = PHPLensConnect('emplLens', 'SELECT * FROM employee',
                        'postgres', 'localhost', 'hs', '', 'phplens');
        print "state of object: ".PHPLensLastState('emplLens')."<br><br>\n";
        $lens->Render();

        $lens->Close();
?>
```

First a library is included. This is essential if you want to use PHPLens because otherwise the system won't find the libraries included in the application server. Now a session is started. This is essential as well because internally everything is done by using session variables. PHPLensConnect creates a new object and returns the handle to this object. The name of this object is emplLens. Be careful that every object has a unique name because otherwise strange things will happen. As you can see, a connection to the database is established and the result of a SELECT statement is assigned to the object. As soon as the render function is called, the HTML code generated by PHPLens is sent to the browser. Finally the connection is closed and the object is destroyed.

The image in Figure 21.14 shows what comes out when you execute the code.

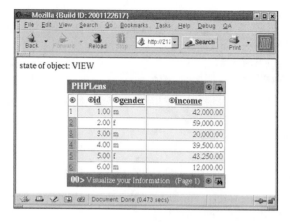

FIGURE 21.14   A simple example.

The main advantage of an application server is that many things are done by it automatically. In this example it is possible to sort the data in a column without writing a single line of code. When you click on the header of the table, you will see that the data is sorted as shown in Figure 21.15.

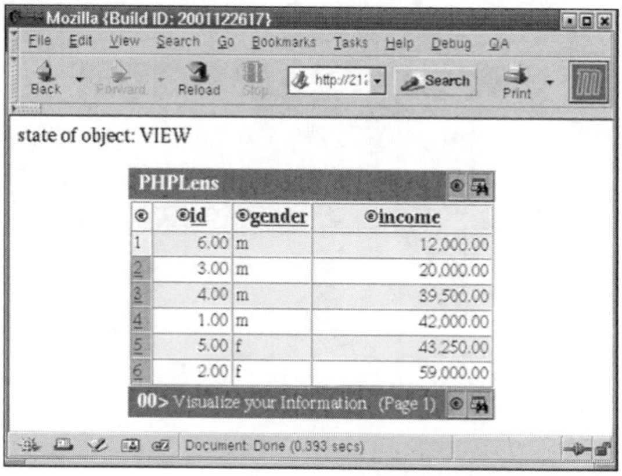

FIGURE 21.15   Sorting data.

Now that you have seen how to build a simple application with the help of PHPLens, it is time to take a look at a slightly longer application that shows the basic principles of PHPLens:

```php
<?php
    include('../phplens.inc.php');
    session_start();
```

```
$lens = PHPLensConnect('emplLens', 'SELECT * FROM employee',
                'postgres', 'localhost', 'hs', '', 'phplens');
$lens->nameLens="id^serial";
$lens->pageSize = 3;
$lens->detailLens = 'id;name;';
$lens->Render();

$lens->Close();
?>
```

Before discussing the code, it is useful to take a look at the result.

As you can see in Figure 21.16, the title of the first column in the table has changed. This is done using the nameLens method.

In the next step, the size of a page is limited to three. This way PHPLens makes sure that the result is displayed using multiple pages. One line after that, a detailed lens is created. This lens contains detailed information about the columns listed on the right side of the = symbol.

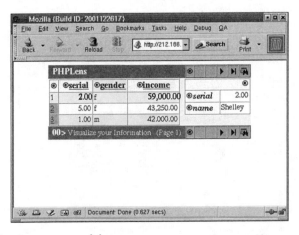

FIGURE 21.16   A more powerful screen.

The sample code you have just seen even has an additional feature. At the end of the script the data is sent to the server and the object is deleted.

As you have seen in this section, it is an easy task to write applications using PHPLens. Basic components such as tables can easily be created and modified to your needs. With just a few lines of code you can write simple yet useful applications. Although the code is only 10 lines long, it offers tremendous power. Let's click on an e in the detailed lens. The result is shown in Figure 21.17.

Many parameters can be configured to your needs.

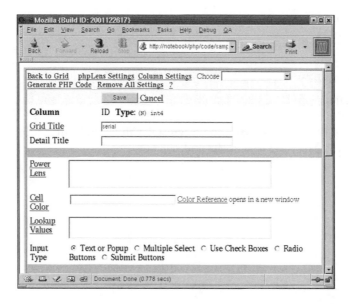

FIGURE 21.17   Configuring a lens.

21.5.3 Other Application Servers

A variety of additional application servers for PHP are available. One of the most powerful ones is called JPETO and can be downloaded from www.jpeto.com. To a large extent JPETO is built on nested objects. Here is a list of the most important features:

- Multilanguage support
- Caching objects
- WYSIWYG preview
- Session management
- Sorting objects
- Import/export functions based on XML
- Interface to any ANSI-SQL–compliant database such as PostgreSQL

JPETO can be used to build flexible and easy-to-use content management tools. For sites that require high performance, the cache manager will lead to significantly higher speed and to lower response times.

Another application server is called LXP. It is based on XML and can be used for a variety of tasks.

21.6 Summary

In this chapter you have seen that PHP and PostgreSQL can be the basis for a variety of applications. Whether you want to implement shopping systems, stock monitoring tools, or Web forums, PHP and PostgreSQL will be the perfect tool for all these purposes. You can write code easily and reliably.

22

Extending PostgreSQL

PostgreSQL is built on a flexible core that offers the programmer tremendous power and flexibility. Writing extensions to the database is an easy task, and many people have already implemented additional features and interfaces to the database. PostgreSQL's flexibility and its clear internal structure make the database a playground for every computer programmer who wants to work with a reliable and highly sophisticated DBMS. This chapter is dedicated to those who want to write simple extensions to the database. You will be guided through the basic concepts and see how extensions can be built. We won't go into too much detail because that would be beyond the scope of this book, but you can find more detail on this topic in *PostgreSQL Developer's Handbook* (Sams Publishing).

22.1 A User-Defined Data Type

Let's get started and see how you can add a user-defined data type to PostgreSQL. The standard distribution of PostgreSQL offers a set of predefined data types. In some cases these data types might not offer enough efficiency for your applications. If you have to store special information that cannot easily be modeled using standard data types, it can be useful to implement your own data type. Because this can easily be done, we have decided to provide a brief example.

The goal of this section is to implement a data type for storing information about spheres. Several files will be needed, as shown in Table 22.1.

TABLE 22.1   The Files Used in This Section

Filename	Description
Makefile	This file is used to run the compiler and to generate the SQL needed for adding the data type to the database.
Sphere.c	Sphere.c contains the C code of the data type.
Sphere.o	The object that comes out when compiling sphere.c.
Libsphere.so	The shared object that will be accessed by PostgreSQL.
Sphere.tpl	A SQL template.
Sphere.sql	Sphere.sql is generated by transforming sphere.tpl. It already contains the full path to the binaries of our data type.
Test.sql	A test suite for the data type.

Let's start with sphere.c. This file is the core of the data type sphere.c. Let's take a look at the code:

```c
#include <postgres.h>
#include <stdio.h>
#include <math.h>

#ifndef M_PI
#define M_PI      3.14159265358979323846264338327950288
#endif

typedef struct   sphere
{
        float4 x;        /* x-coordinate */
        float4 y;        /* y-coordinate */
        float4 z;        /* z-coordinate */
        float4 radius;   /* radius of sphere */
} sphere;

/* function for parsing the input */
sphere *sphere_in(char *str)
{
        float x, y, z, radius;
        sphere *mysphere;        /* creating a new object */
        mysphere = (sphere *) palloc(sizeof(sphere));
        if       (sscanf(str, " %f, %f, %f, %f ",
                &x, &y, &z, &radius) != 4)
        {
                elog(ERROR, "sphere_in: parse error in %s", str);
                return NULL;
        }
```

```
        /* checking for valid data */
        if      (x >= 0 && y >= 0 && z >= 0 && radius >= 0)
        {
                mysphere->x = x;
                mysphere->y = y;
                mysphere->z = z;
                mysphere->radius = radius;
        }
        else
        {
                elog(ERROR, "sphere_in: input not valid in %s", str);
                return NULL;
        }

        return mysphere;
}

char *sphere_out(sphere *mysphere)
{
        char *result;

        /* checking for NULL values */
        if      (mysphere == NULL)
        {
                return NULL;
        }

        /* allocate memory for storing result */
        result = (char * ) palloc(100);
           /* dangerous (buffer overflow), use snprintf if available,
              %g */
        sprintf(result, "%f, %f, %f, %f",
                mysphere->x, mysphere->y,
                mysphere->z, mysphere->radius);
        return result;
}

/* comparison function */
bool sphere_eq(sphere *one, sphere *two)
{
        if      (one->x == two->x &&
                one->y == two->y &&
```

```
                    one->z == two->z &&
                    one->radius == two->radius)
        {
                return TRUE;
        }
        return FALSE;
}


/* lower operator */
bool sphere_lt(sphere *one, sphere *two)
{
        return (one->radius < two->radius) ? TRUE : FALSE;
}


/* <= operator */
bool sphere_le(sphere *one, sphere *two)
{
        return (one->radius <= two->radius) ? TRUE : FALSE;
}


/* > operator */
bool sphere_gt(sphere *one, sphere *two)
{
        return (one->radius > two->radius) ? TRUE : FALSE;
}


/* >= operator */
bool sphere_ge(sphere *one, sphere *two)
{
        return (one->radius >= two->radius) ? TRUE : FALSE;
}


/* computing volume */
float8 *sphere_volume(sphere *one)
{
        static float8 retvalue;
        retvalue = 4./3. * M_PI * (one->radius*one->radius*one->radius);
        return &retvalue;
}
```

First a set of libraries is included. postgres.h contains the header information for all functions related to PostgreSQL. math.h is included for working with Pi (we will need this to compute the column of a sphere). Then a structure called sphere is defined. This structure contains all components of the data type.

The next step is to implement a function for reading values and one for displaying values. The function for parsing the input is called sphere_in. The goal of this function is to initialize a sphere and retrieve all values from the input. In this example sscanf is used to assign the components of a sphere to the internal structure. Now memory is allocated and the input data is checked. Notice that memory is allocated using palloc. This way PostgreSQL makes sure that no memory leaks can occur. In this scenario, the coordinates of the sphere must be positive. We have done this just for presentation purposes so that you can see how the input can be restricted.

Sphere_out is even more simple. The function is used for formatting a string that can be displayed by the back end.

In the next step a list of functions is implemented. These functions will be accessed by the operators related to the data type. The sphere_eq function, for instance, will be assigned to the = operator. As you can see, a comparison is performed that returns TRUE or FALSE.

The last function in the file can be used to compute the volume of a sphere. sphere_volume returns a float variable to the calling function. The return value of this function is float8. We recommend using float8 instead of float because what comes out when compiling the code depends on the compiler you are using.

Now that you have gone through the C file, it is time to take a look at the file you can use to create the operators and functions needed by the data type. The template for generating sphere.sql is called sphere.tpl, as shown in the next listing:

```
-- Input Function
CREATE OR REPLACE FUNCTION sphere_in(opaque)
        RETURNS sphere
        AS '%LIB%'
        LANGUAGE 'C';

-- Output Function
CREATE OR REPLACE FUNCTION sphere_out(opaque)
        RETURNS opaque
        AS '%LIB%'
        LANGUAGE 'C';

-- Creating new data type
CREATE TYPE sphere(
        internallength = 16,
        input = sphere_in,
        output = sphere_out);
```

```
/* Creating functions for operators */
CREATE OR REPLACE FUNCTION sphere_eq(sphere, sphere)
        RETURNS bool
        AS '%LIB%'
        LANGUAGE 'C';

CREATE OR REPLACE FUNCTION sphere_lt(sphere, sphere)
        RETURNS bool
        AS '%LIB%'
        LANGUAGE 'C';

CREATE OR REPLACE FUNCTION sphere_le(sphere, sphere)
        RETURNS bool
        AS '%LIB%'
        LANGUAGE 'C';

CREATE OR REPLACE FUNCTION sphere_gt(sphere, sphere)
        RETURNS bool
        AS '%LIB%'
        LANGUAGE 'C';

CREATE OR REPLACE FUNCTION sphere_ge(sphere, sphere)
        RETURNS bool
        AS '%LIB%'
        LANGUAGE 'C';

CREATE OR REPLACE FUNCTION sphere_volume(sphere)
        RETURNS float8
        AS '%LIB%'
        LANGUAGE 'C';

/* Creating operators */
CREATE OPERATOR = (
        leftarg = sphere,
        rightarg = sphere,
        procedure = sphere_eq);

CREATE OPERATOR < (
        leftarg = sphere,
        rightarg = sphere,
        commutator = >,
        procedure = sphere_lt);
```

```
CREATE OPERATOR <= (
        leftarg = sphere,
        rightarg = sphere,
        commutator = >=,
        procedure = sphere_le);

CREATE OPERATOR > (
        leftarg = sphere,
        rightarg = sphere,
        procedure = sphere_gt);

CREATE OPERATOR >= (
        leftarg = sphere,
        rightarg = sphere,
        procedure = sphere_ge);
```

In this file %LIB will be substituted for the absolute path to the C library, which will be generated using sphere.c. After adding sphere_in and sphere_out to the database, the data type can be created. The internal length is 16 bytes (four float variables). In addition, the functions used for parsing and displaying the result are defined. This is all the information PostgreSQL needs to process a rudimentary data type. All additional operators can be seen as features of this rudimentary data type.

After defining the data type, a set of functions is created. These functions will be needed for defining the operators. The first operator defined in this file is the = operator. As you can see, it has a right and a left argument. In other words, spheres can be compared with spheres as soon as this operator has been defined. The function used to compare two spheres is called sphere_eq. You have seen this function twice already. The first time it occurred in the C file, where you saw how it was implemented. The second time was in this file when a function was created. Now this function is used for defining the operator. Let's take a look at the next operator. In addition to the left operator and the right operator, the function the operator is based on has been defined. The commutator of the < operator is the > operator because it is the exact opposite of the < operator. Internally a commutator is used to help the optimizer to find the best way through the query. In addition to commutators, negators can be defined. The negator of the = operator would be the != operator, which means not equal instead of equal.

After all functions and operators have been defined, it is time to compile the code. Therefore a makefile should be used. The following listing contains a makefile you can use to compile your sources and to set up a testing environment:

```
DB=     phpbook

#       Rules
```

```
INC=      -I/usr/src/postgresql-7.2rc2/src/include
# INC=    -I/usr/include/postgresql
CFLAGS= -Wall -fPIC -O2 $(INC)
CC=       gcc

#         Libraries

OBJ=      sphere.o
LIB=      /home/hs/datatype/datatype/libsphere.so

all::    $(LIB)

clean::
          rm -f $(LIB) $(OBJ)

$(LIB): $(OBJ)
          gcc -shared -Wl,-soname,$@ -o $@ $(OBJ)

#         SQL-File

all:: sphere.sql

clean::
          rm -f sphere.sql

#         Testing

stamp_db:
          if test -f $@; then dropdb $(DB); fi
          createdb $(DB)
          touch $@

clean::
          -dropdb $(DB)
          rm -f stamp_db

run: all stamp_db sphere.sql test.sql
          psql phpbook < sphere.sql
          psql phpbook < test.sql
```

Just run make to compile the sources. The next listing shows what happens if make is used:

```
[hs@duron datatype]$ make
gcc -Wall -fPIC -O2 -I/usr/src/postgresql-7.2rc2/src/include
-c -o sphere.o sphere.c
gcc -shared -Wl,-soname,/home/hs/datatype/datatype/libsphere.so -o
 /home/hs/datatype/datatype/libsphere.so sphere.o
sed -e 's|%LIB%|/home/hs/datatype/datatype/libsphere.so|' sphere.tpl >
sphere.sql
```

The sources are compiled and a shared object called libsphere.so is generated. In addition, the SQL file is generated based on the template file sphere.sql. As you can see, sed is called to substitute %LIB for the absolute path to the shared object. This way the path need not be hard-coded in a header file or a C file. Now that sphere.sql has been generated, it is worth taking a brief look at it:

```
-- Input Function
CREATE OR REPLACE FUNCTION sphere_in(opaque)
        RETURNS sphere
        AS '/home/hs/datatype/datatype/libsphere.so'
        LANGUAGE 'C';
```

As you can see, the SQL file contains the correct settings. Now you can add the data type to the database by running make run or psql as shown in the next listing. If you decide to use make, make sure that make clean has been used before running make run:

```
psql phpbook < sphere.sql
```

make clean makes sure that trash is removed:

```
[hs@duron datatype]$ make clean -n
rm -f /home/hs/datatype/datatype/libsphere.so sphere.o
rm -f sphere.sql
dropdb phpbook
rm -f stamp_db
```

If no errors occurred during compilation, it is time to test the data type. Therefore test.sql has been implemented:

```
CREATE TABLE mysphere (data sphere);

INSERT INTO mysphere VALUES ('1, 1, 1, 3');
INSERT INTO mysphere VALUES ('1, 1, 1, 8');
INSERT INTO mysphere VALUES ('3, 9, 0, 7');
```

```
SELECT data FROM mysphere WHERE data = '3, 9, 0, 7';
SELECT data FROM mysphere WHERE data > '3, 9, 0, 7';
SELECT data FROM mysphere WHERE data <= '3, 9, 0, 7';

SELECT data, sphere_volume(data) FROM mysphere;
```

First a table is created and several lines are added to the table. Then three queries are executed and the volume of all records in the table is computed. Let's send the file to psql and see what comes out:

```
[hs@duron datatype]$ psql phpbook < test.sql
CREATE
INSERT 24944 1
INSERT 24945 1
INSERT 24946 1
                    data
-----------------------------------------
 3.000000, 9.000000, 0.000000, 7.000000
(1 row)


                    data
-----------------------------------------
 1.000000, 1.000000, 1.000000, 8.000000
(1 row)


                    data
-----------------------------------------
 1.000000, 1.000000, 1.000000, 3.000000
 3.000000, 9.000000, 0.000000, 7.000000
(2 rows)


                    data               |  sphere_volume
---------------------------------------+-----------------
 1.000000, 1.000000, 1.000000, 3.000000 | 113.097335529233
 1.000000, 1.000000, 1.000000, 8.000000 | 2144.66058485063
 3.000000, 9.000000, 0.000000, 7.000000 | 1436.75504024173
(3 rows)
```

As you can see, no errors occurred, so the data type can be used safely.

So far you have seen how to build a rudimentary data type. It is not possible to work with aggregations and index structures yet. As you can see in the next example, SUM does not work yet:

```
phpbook=# SELECT SUM(data) FROM mysphere;
ERROR:  Unable to select an aggregate function sum(sphere)
```

In addition, it is not possible to use indexes because it is necessary to add some entries to PostgreSQL's system tables. This is not as easy as implementing the C code a data type is based on. This is a book about Web development, so for our purposes, it is enough to be able to implement simple data types because you can easily build workarounds.

22.2 Building Substring Indexes

Indexes are the key to performance. If data is selected and retrieved from a table, indexes will help you to speed up your queries significantly. However, in some operations indexes cannot be used. One of these operations is substring searching. If you are working with regular expressions, PostgreSQL is not capable of using indexes. Internally an index is a tree built on a sorted list. This way data can be retrieved efficiently. In substrings it is not possible to benefit from the advantages of a sorted list. Therefore it is necessary to build a workaround. This can easily be done by using the `fulltextindex` package, which can be found in PostgreSQL's contributed section (`$PATH_TO_POSTGRES/contrib/fulltextindex`).

22.2.1 Installation

To install the package, just go to the directory containing the code and run `make` as well as `make install` as shown in the next listing:

```
[root@duron fulltextindex]# make
sed 's,MODULE_PATHNAME,$libdir/fti,g' fti.sql.in >fti.sql
gcc -O3 -march=athlon  -Wall -Wmissing-prototypes -Wmissing-declarations
-fpic -I. -I../../src/include   -c -o fti.o fti.c
gcc -shared -o fti.so fti.o
rm fti.o
[root@duron fulltextindex]# make install
/bin/sh ../../config/install-sh -c -m 644 fti.sql
/usr/local/pgsql/share/contrib
/bin/sh ../../config/install-sh -c -m 755 fti.so /usr/local/pgsql/lib
/bin/sh ../../config/install-sh -c -m 644 ./README.fti
/usr/local/pgsql/doc/contrib
/bin/sh ../../config/install-sh -c -m 755 ./fti.pl /usr/local/pgsql/bin
```

After compiling the source code of the package, you can add the package to the desired database. In this example `fti.sql` is sent to the database called `phpbook`:

```
[hs@duron fulltextindex]$ psql phpbook < fti.sql
CREATE
```

22.2.2 The Basic Concepts and an Example

The idea of PostgreSQL's substring index package is that for every column you want to index, a table for storing the substrings must exist. In this table a list of all possible substrings a string can have is stored. To use the substring index, a join must be performed. Let's create an empty table first:

```
phpbook=# CREATE TABLE word (id int4, word text);
CREATE
```

In the next step the table needed to store the substrings is created. Notice the names of the columns because these names are essential for making the system work correctly.

```
phpbook=# CREATE TABLE fti_phpbook_word (string text, id oid);
CREATE
```

Now a trigger has to be defined, which makes sure that every record added, modified, or removed is processed correctly. Every record added to the table is split up into substrings and added to the table storing the substrings. Modifications are performed in both the original and the substring table. Removing records has to be done in both tables as well. Let's take a look at the trigger:

```
CREATE TRIGGER fti_word_word_trigger
        AFTER  INSERT OR UPDATE OR DELETE ON word
        FOR EACH ROW EXECUTE PROCEDURE fti(fti_phpbook_word, word);
```

The heart of the trigger is the `fti` function. It computes the substrings needed in the substring table and adds the values to it. Now that the trigger has been created, you can try to insert a record into the table:

```
phpbook=# INSERT INTO word VALUES (1, 'PostgreSQL');
INSERT 25063 1
```

One record has been added to the table:

```
phpbook=# SELECT * FROM word;
 id |    word
----+------------
  1 | PostgreSQL
(1 row)
```

Let's see which records have been added to the table containing the substrings:

```
phpbook=# SELECT * FROM fti_phpbook_word;
   string   | id
------------+-------
 ql         | 25063
 sql        | 25063
 esql       | 25063
 resql      | 25063
 gresql     | 25063
 tgresql    | 25063
 stgresql   | 25063
 ostgresql  | 25063
 postgresql | 25063
(9 rows)
```

As you can see, nine substrings can be made out of the word PostgreSQL. Let's create three indexes:

```
phpbook=# CREATE INDEX idx_word_word ON word (word);
CREATE
phpbook=# CREATE INDEX idx_fti_oid ON fti_phpbook_word (id);
CREATE
phpbook=# CREATE INDEX idx_fti_string ON fti_phpbook_word (string);
CREATE
```

To make PostgreSQL use the indexes, whenever possible sequential scans must be turned off temporarily. This can easily be done by using the SET command:

```
phpbook=# SET enable_seqscan TO off;
SET VARIABLE
```

The basic idea of substring indexing is that only one type of regular expression can be processed using an index. If the ^ symbol is used to match the beginning of a string, it is possible to use an index but only if no other features of regular expressions, such as nested repetitions, are used. Let's take a look at the execution plan:

```
phpbook=# EXPLAIN SELECT * FROM fti_phpbook_word WHERE string ~ '^gre';
NOTICE:  QUERY PLAN:

Index Scan using idx_fti_string on fti_phpbook_word  (cost=0.00..4.68
rows=1 width=36)

EXPLAIN
```

As you can see, an index is used. To join the two tables, a join has to be performed:

```
SELECT word.*
       FROM word, fti_phpbook_word
       WHERE word.oid=fti_phpbook_word.id
             AND fti_phpbook_word.string ~ '^gresql';
```

One row is returned:

```
 id |    word
----+------------
  1 | PostgreSQL
(1 row)
```

To compute the execution plan, EXPLAIN has to be used:

```
EXPLAIN SELECT word.*
       FROM word, fti_phpbook_word
       WHERE word.oid=fti_phpbook_word.id
             AND fti_phpbook_word.string ~ '^gresql';
```

As you can see, indexes are used.

```
Hash Join  (cost=100000004.68..100000005.70 rows=1 width=44)
   -> Seq Scan on word  (cost=100000000.00..100000001.01 rows=1 width=40)
   -> Hash  (cost=4.68..4.68 rows=1 width=4)
        -> Index Scan using idx_fti_string on fti_phpbook_word
(cost=0.00..4.68 rows=1 width=4)
```

Sometimes using substring indexes is the only way to speed up queries significantly. In the case of millions of records, it can be the only chance to avoid sequential scans.

22.3 Tolerant Search Algorithms

In modern applications it is essential to use efficient algorithms for searching and retrieving data. Back in the early days, many applications offered simple search algorithms where you could look for complete components of a record (columns, cells). In some cases this will be enough. Especially if there is not much data, looking for complete components is just fine. However, if the number of records in your database grows and the data in your database is not always correct, it might be necessary to take a look at more sophisticated ways of searching for data. In this section you will be guided through some simple approaches for performing error-tolerant searching.

You have already learned about regular expressions in PHP and PostgreSQL in previous sections. You have seen that PostgreSQL is not capable of using indexes when dealing with a regular expression. This behavior seems obvious, but with huge amounts of data sequential scans can be fatal.

22.3.1 Problems Caused by Regular Expressions

Regular expressions are a flexible and powerful way of performing imprecise searching. However, in many situations regular expressions are just not what you are looking for. Imagine a situation where somebody is looking for names. Let's take a look at the following table:

```
CREATE TABLE person (id int4, name text);

INSERT INTO person VALUES (1, 'Mayr');
INSERT INTO person VALUES (2, 'Mayer');
INSERT INTO person VALUES (3, 'Mair');

INSERT INTO person VALUES (4, 'Geschwinde');
INSERT INTO person VALUES (5, 'Geschwinte');

INSERT INTO person VALUES (6, 'Schoenig');
INSERT INTO person VALUES (7, 'Schonig');
```

As you can see, there are three groups of names in the database. With the help of simple SELECT statements, any name can be selected:

```
phpbook=# SELECT * FROM person WHERE name ~* 'Ma[iy][er][r]*';
 id | name
----+-------
  1 | Mayr
  2 | Mayer
  3 | Mair
(3 rows)
```

As you can see, all possible ways of writing "mayr" that can be found in the database are retrieved. In the next example, you can see how OR can be used in combination with a regular expression:

```
phpbook=# SELECT * FROM person WHERE name = 'Mayr' OR name = 'Mayer' OR
name = 'Mair';
 id | name
----+-------
  1 | Mayr
  2 | Mayer
  3 | Mair
(3 rows)
```

The result is still the same. Let's take a look at a more impressive example. The following regular expression matches 32 transliterations of the name of the Libyan dictator. This regular expression is taken from the test suite for the GNU grep program.

```
M[ou]'?am+[ae]r.*([AEae]l[- ])? [GKQ]h?[aeu]+([dtz][dhz]?)+af[iy]
```

The next piece of SQL code contains a list of all literally correct English versions of the name:

```
INSERT INTO person VALUES (1, 'Muammar Qaddafi');
INSERT INTO person VALUES (2, 'Mo''ammar Gadhafi');
INSERT INTO person VALUES (3, 'Muammar Kaddafi');
INSERT INTO person VALUES (4, 'Muammar Qadhafi');
INSERT INTO person VALUES (5, 'Moammar El Kadhafi');
INSERT INTO person VALUES (6, 'Muammar Gadafi');
INSERT INTO person VALUES (7, 'Mu''ammar al-Qadafi');
INSERT INTO person VALUES (8, 'Moamer El Kazzafi');
INSERT INTO person VALUES (9, 'Moamar al-Gaddafi');
INSERT INTO person VALUES (10, 'Mu''ammar Al Qathafi');
INSERT INTO person VALUES (11, 'Muammar Al Qathafi');
INSERT INTO person VALUES (12, 'Mo''ammar el-Gadhafi');
INSERT INTO person VALUES (13, 'Moamar El Kadhafi');
INSERT INTO person VALUES (14, 'Muammar al-Qadhafi');
INSERT INTO person VALUES (15, 'Mu''ammar al-Qadhdhafi');
INSERT INTO person VALUES (16, 'Mu''ammar Qadafi');
INSERT INTO person VALUES (17, 'Moamar Gaddafi');
INSERT INTO person VALUES (18, 'Mu''ammar Qadhdhafi');
INSERT INTO person VALUES (19, 'Muammar Khaddafi');
INSERT INTO person VALUES (20, 'Muammar al-Khaddafi');
INSERT INTO person VALUES (21, 'Mu''amar al-Kadafi');
INSERT INTO person VALUES (22, 'Muammar Ghaddafy');
INSERT INTO person VALUES (23, 'Muammar Ghadafi');
INSERT INTO person VALUES (24, 'Muammar Ghaddafi');
INSERT INTO person VALUES (25, 'Muamar Kaddafi');
INSERT INTO person VALUES (26, 'Muammar Quathafi');
INSERT INTO person VALUES (27, 'Muammar Gheddafi');
INSERT INTO person VALUES (28, 'Muamar Al-Kaddafi');
INSERT INTO person VALUES (29, 'Moammar Khadafy');
INSERT INTO person VALUES (30, 'Moammar Qudhafi');
INSERT INTO person VALUES (31, 'Mu''ammar al-Qaddafi');
INSERT INTO person VALUES (32,
        'Mulazim Awwal Mu''ammar Muhammad Abu Minyar al-Qadhafi');
```

It is an easy task to retrieve all required values using a regular expression. However, here's the problem: How can you know which regular expression you have to use? How can anybody generate a regular expression if you don't know what you are looking for? The problem with regular expressions is that it is not possible to generate complex ones easily using nothing more than the input of the user. In addition, many flavors of regular expressions are available (this is the reason why not all records shown before will match the regular expression). Therefore other algorithms have to be used.

22.3.2 The Soundex Algorithm

The Soundex algorithm is a comfortable method for finding similar-sounding names. It was initially used by the United States Census in 1880, 1900, and 1910. It is an efficient and fast way to find similar-sounding English words. The problem with this algorithm is that it cannot be used for anything other than English words.

The idea of the algorithm is that similar-sounding words are coded using the same string. The length of the Soundex code can be defined in order to define the error tolerance of the algorithm.

22.3.2.1 Installation

Before you learn to use the Soundex algorithm, it is time to see how to install the package. To install the package you have to go to the fuzzystrmatch directory in the contributed section in the source code of PostgreSQL. There you can find several files. If you want to modify the length of your Soundex code, just modify fuzzystrmatch.h by changing the following line:

```
#define SOUNDEX_LEN 4
```

After that the only two things you have to do are to run make and make install as shown in the next listing:

```
[hs@notebook fuzzystrmatch]$ make
sed 's,MODULE_PATHNAME,$libdir/fuzzystrmatch,g' fuzzystrmatch.sql.in
>fuzzystrmatch.sql
gcc -O2 -Wall -Wmissing-prototypes -Wmissing-declarations -fpic -I.
-I../../src/include    -c -o fuzzystrmatch.o fuzzystrmatch.c
gcc -shared -o fuzzystrmatch.so fuzzystrmatch.o
rm fuzzystrmatch.o
[hs@notebook fuzzystrmatch]$ make install
mkdir /usr/local/postgresql/share/contrib
mkdir /usr/local/postgresql/doc/contrib
/bin/sh ../../config/install-sh -c -m 644 fuzzystrmatch.sql
/usr/local/postgresql/share/contrib
```

```
/bin/sh ../../config/install-sh -c -m 755 fuzzystrmatch.so
/usr/local/postgresql/lib
/bin/sh ../../config/install-sh -c -m 644 ./README.fuzzystrmatch
/usr/local/postgresql/doc/contrib
/bin/sh ../../config/install-sh -c -m 644 ./README.soundex
/usr/local/postgresql/doc/contrib
```

A file containing SQL code has been generated. This file must be sent to the database you want to use. In our scenario the database called phpbook is used:

```
[hs@notebook fuzzystrmatch]$ psql phpbook < fuzzystrmatch.sql
CREATE
CREATE
CREATE
CREATE
```

Four functions have been added to the database called phpbook:

```
CREATE FUNCTION levenshtein (text,text) RETURNS int
  AS '$libdir/fuzzystrmatch','levenshtein' LANGUAGE 'c'
       with (iscachable, isstrict);

CREATE FUNCTION metaphone (text,int) RETURNS text
  AS '$libdir/fuzzystrmatch','metaphone' LANGUAGE 'c'
       with (iscachable, isstrict);

CREATE FUNCTION soundex(text) RETURNS text
  AS '$libdir/fuzzystrmatch', 'soundex' LANGUAGE 'c'
       with (iscachable, isstrict);

CREATE FUNCTION text_soundex(text) RETURNS text
  AS '$libdir/fuzzystrmatch', 'soundex' LANGUAGE 'c';
```

The first two functions will be discussed after this section. The last two functions are related to the Soundex algorithm and will be discussed in this section.

22.3.2.2 Using Soundex
Now that you have seen how to install Soundex, it is time to take a look at how the algorithm can be used for building practical solutions.

The most important thing is to see what comes out when a string is passed to the function. In this case the name Mair is passed to soundex.

```
phpbook=# SELECT soundex('Mair');
 soundex
----------
 M600
(1 row)
```

As you can see the string has been transformed to a 4-byte string. Mayr is another name that sounds exactly the same way. Therefore the Soundex code is the same:

```
phpbook=# SELECT soundex('Mayr');
 soundex
----------
 M600
(1 row)
```

As you can see, it is an easy task to find words that sound the same. In the next example, you will see a simple piece of code. Keep in mind that you should drop tables if they already exist in your database.

```
CREATE TABLE person (
        id int4,
        name text,
        soundexcode char(4));

COPY person FROM stdin USING DELIMITERS ';';
1;John
2;Joan
3;Jon
4;Jennifer
5;Charles
6;Paul
```

If there is already a table called person in your database, you have to drop it before creating the new table. In this table you can find three names that sound like John. To retrieve all of these, you have to compare the Soundex code of the values in the table with the Soundex code of John:

```
phpbook=# SELECT name FROM person WHERE soundex(name)=soundex('John');
 name
-------
 John
 Joan
 Jon
(3 rows)
```

As you can see, three records have been returned, which is the correct result.

22.3.2.3 Soundex and Indexes

If the number of records in your table is high, it can be useful to use an index in order to speed up your database. In this section you will see how indexes can be used in combination with the soundex function.

Let's define an index on `person` and turn off sequential scans temporarily:

```
phpbook=# CREATE INDEX idx_person_name ON person (name);
CREATE
phpbook=# SET enable_seqscan TO off;
SET VARIABLE
```

Let's run the query again and see whether or not the index is used:

```
phpbook=# EXPLAIN SELECT name FROM person WHERE soundex(name)=soundex('John');
NOTICE:   QUERY PLAN:

Seq Scan on person  (cost=100000000.00..100000001.09 rows=1 width=32)

EXPLAIN
```

The database still performs a sequential scan. A sequential scan is done because the column on which we have defined an index is used inside a function call, and as you already know, there is no way to use an index in the case of functions. To get around the problem, you can use the soundexcode column, which can be found in person. Simply store the Soundex code of the second column in the third column:

```
phpbook=# UPDATE person SET soundexcode = soundex(name);
UPDATE 6
phpbook=# SELECT * FROM person;
id |   name   | soundexcode
----+----------+------------
  1 | John     | J500
  2 | Joan     | J500
  3 | John     | J500
  4 | Jennifer | J516
  5 | Charles  | C642
  6 | Paul     | P400
(6 rows)
```

As you can see, the Soundex code has successfully been inserted into the third column. Now you can define an index on this column:

```
phpbook=# CREATE INDEX idx_person_soundexcode ON person (soundexcode);
CREATE
```

By modifying the query slightly it is possible to use an index now:
```
phpbook=# EXPLAIN SELECT name FROM person WHERE soundexcode=soundex('John');
NOTICE:  QUERY PLAN:

Index Scan using idx_person_soundexcode on person   (cost=0.00..4.68 rows=1
width=32)

EXPLAIN
```

If the amount of data grows, this will be a real help and your queries will run a lot faster.

There is still one thing that must be taken into consideration. If somebody adds records to the table, it is necessary to add the Soundex code to the third column. This can easily be done with the help of a trigger. In the next example, you can see how to write a trigger:

```
CREATE OR REPLACE FUNCTION trig_person_insert_addsoundex()
      RETURNS OPAQUE AS
  '
      BEGIN
              SELECT INTO NEW.soundexcode soundex(NEW.name);
              RAISE NOTICE ''new: %'', NEW.name;
              RAISE NOTICE ''new: %'', NEW.soundexcode;
              RETURN NEW;
      END
  ' LANGUAGE 'plpgsql';
```

The first thing to do is to create a function that returns opaque. This function does nothing other than computing the Soundex code of the value in the second column and assigning it to the third column. In addition, RAISE NOTICE is called twice for displaying some useful debugging information you will need for testing the function.

Now that the function has been implemented, you can implement the trigger itself:

```
CREATE TRIGGER trig_person_insert BEFORE INSERT
      ON person FOR EACH ROW
      EXECUTE PROCEDURE trig_person_insert_addsoundex();
```

The trigger is fired before adding the record to the table. This way the Soundex code has already been computed when the data is added to the table. The trigger has to be fired for every row added to the table.

After adding the trigger to the database, you can test it by adding a record to the table:

```
phpbook=# INSERT INTO person (id, name) VALUES (7, 'Nura');
NOTICE:  new: Nura
NOTICE:  new: N600
INSERT 52909424 1
```

NOTICE is displayed twice, which shows that the trigger has been fired. To make sure that the Soundex code is in the table, you can run a query as shown in the next listing:

```
phpbook=# SELECT * FROM person WHERE id=7;
 id | name | soundexcode
----+------+-------------
  7 | Nura | N600
(1 row)
```

In addition to the trigger you have to define for INSERT operations, it is necessary to write a trigger for running UPDATE operations. Let's see how this can be done:

```
CREATE OR REPLACE FUNCTION trig_person_update_addsoundex()
        RETURNS OPAQUE AS
    '
        BEGIN
                SELECT INTO NEW.soundexcode soundex(NEW.name);
                RAISE NOTICE ''new: %'', NEW.name;
                RAISE NOTICE ''new: %'', NEW.soundexcode;
                RETURN NEW;
        END
    ' LANGUAGE 'plpgsql';

CREATE TRIGGER trig_person_update BEFORE UPDATE
        ON person FOR EACH ROW
        EXECUTE PROCEDURE trig_person_insert_addsoundex();
```

If no errors have occurred while adding the function and the trigger to the database, UPDATE operations can be performed without any problems:

```
phpbook=# UPDATE person SET name='Hans' WHERE id=6;
NOTICE:  new: Hans
NOTICE:  new: H520
UPDATE 1
```

```
phpbook=# SELECT * FROM person WHERE id=6;
 id | name | soundexcode
----+------+------------
  6 | Hans | H520
(1 row)
```

As you can see, the code for using two functions and two triggers is long and rather inflexible. Therefore we recommend writing just one function and one trigger instead of two. As you can see in the next listing, this can be done with just a few modifications:

```
CREATE OR REPLACE FUNCTION trig_person_insup_addsoundex()
        RETURNS OPAQUE AS
'
        BEGIN
                SELECT INTO NEW.soundexcode soundex(NEW.name);
                RAISE NOTICE ''new: %'', NEW.name;
                RAISE NOTICE ''new: %'', NEW.soundexcode;
                RETURN NEW;
        END
' LANGUAGE 'plpgsql';

CREATE TRIGGER trig_person_insert_update BEFORE INSERT OR UPDATE
        ON person FOR EACH ROW
        EXECUTE PROCEDURE trig_person_insup_addsoundex();
```

Don't forget to delete the old trigger before adding the new one to the database. If everything has been done correctly, the trigger will work:

```
phpbook=# UPDATE person SET name='Paul' WHERE id=6;
NOTICE:  new: Paul
NOTICE:  new: P400
UPDATE 1
```

Implementing the Soundex algorithm is an easy task, and it will help you to achieve fast and comparatively reliable results.

22.3.3 Levenshtein Distances

In addition to the Soundex algorithm, PostgreSQL provides an implementation of the Levenshtein algorithm for measuring the similarity of two strings. The Levenshtein distance of two strings defines how many transformations must be made to convert one string to another.

The algorithm was developed by the Russian scientist Vladimir Levenshtein in 1965. If you have already installed Soundex, the Levenshtein algorithm has been added to your database as well because the two algorithms are in the same contributed section.

In this section you will see how the Levenshtein distance of two strings can be used to perform error-tolerant searching. Let's take a look at a simple example and see how the algorithm can be used. The name of one of the authors' friends, Markus Kulman, is spelled the wrong way by many people.

```
phpbook=# SELECT levenshtein('Mark Kulman', 'Mark Kullman');
 levenshtein
-------------
           1
(1 row)
```

As you can see, the first parameter passed to the function contains the correct spelling of the name. The second parameter contains the wrong spelling. The result of the function is exactly 1 because one transformation has to be made to make Kulman out of Kullman. The only thing that has to be done is to remove one l from the name.

The next example shows that two operations must be performed:

```
phpbook=# SELECT levenshtein('Mark Kulman', 'Mark Kullmann');
 levenshtein
-------------
           2
(1 row)
```

The most important feature of the algorithm is that it does not matter which operations have to be performed to modify the string to your needs. The result is always the same—whether characters have to be removed or substituted:

```
phpbook=# SELECT levenshtein('Mark Kulman', 'Mark Colman');
 levenshtein
-------------
           2
(1 row)
```

The Levenshtein distance is still two because this time two substitutions have to be performed.

In real-world applications, the algorithm is used to find similar strings in a table, and this is exactly the goal of the next example (don't forget to delete `person` before running the next script if you have a table with that name in your database):

```
CREATE TABLE person (id int4, person text);
```

```
COPY person FROM stdin USING DELIMITERS ';';
1;Ewald Geschwinde
2;Markus Kulman
3;Hans-Juergen Schoenig
4;Erich Fruehstueck
```

A table has been created and several records have been inserted with the help of PostgreSQL's `COPY` command. Let's retrieve all records that are three characters away from `Ewald Gewinde`:

```
phpbook=# SELECT * FROM person WHERE levenshtein(person, 'Ewald Gewinde') <= 3;
 id |      person
----+------------------
  1 | Ewald Geschwinde
(1 row)
```

Oops, the name of the coauthor of this book has been retrieved.

The Levenshtein algorithm is a fast way of finding similar strings because the algorithm is based on just a few matrix operations. The only problem is that there is no (useful) way of using the package in combination with an index, so it is not suitable for concurrent queries on high-performance systems because there is no way to get around a sequential scan.

22.3.4 Metaphone

Metaphone is also part of the `fuzzystrmatch` package in PostgreSQL's contributed section. The goal of the `metaphone` function is to retrieve the metaphone code of an input string. Let's take a look at an example:

```
phpbook=# SELECT metaphone('Hello Reader', 10);
 metaphone
-----------
 HLRTR
(1 row)
```

The first parameter passed to the function contains the string you want to process. The problem with this string is that it can have a length of up to 255 characters only, which is not much. Therefore the algorithm cannot be used for working with text columns because text is a data type that does not have a (useful) maximum length.

The second parameter passed to the function defines the maximum length of the code returned by the function. If the metaphone code is longer than this variable, it will be cut off at the end.

22.4 Summary

Adding your own functions, operators, and data types to PostgreSQL is an easy task because PostgreSQL provides simple and powerful interfaces for interacting with the database.

PostgreSQL provides a software package for working with substring indexes. This package is based on triggers and C functions. With the help of substring indexes, it is possible to speed up queries that do not look for entire strings.

With fuzzy input parameters, PostgreSQL offers a variety of possibilities. All functions you can use for fuzzy matching are available in a package that can be found in the contributed section of PostgreSQL's source code.

23

High-Availability Systems

High availability is strongly related to security. If a system is not secure, it can hardly be considered a high-availability system as long as it is connected to a network. I want to mention this at the beginning of this chapter because it is an important point.

In this chapter you will see how high-availability systems can be designed and built. This chapter is a brief insight into the world of high availability, and the expertise you gain will help you to build more reliable systems.

23.1 An Introduction to High Availability

Let's get started with high-availability systems. The first question is what high availability means.

23.1.1 What Is High Availability?

In business-critical applications, the systems a company relies on need to be up and running 24 hours a day, 7 days a week. Every minute you lose costs money. Imagine a call center where dozens of people are working around the clock. Every minute people cannot work with the system costs money and annoys your customers, which costs money as well.

High-availability systems reduce downtime. Usually the availability of a system is measured in percent. A few years ago downtime was not as critical as it is today because a lot of recovery was done during the night while most people were sleeping. This way, a company's IT people had enough time to solve various problems during the night. With the arrival of modern Web technologies, things have changed. There is no "silent night" any more because Web applications must be available any time. Companies are global players, and European customers wouldn't be too happy if the site of an American vendor was down in the morning because at that time it is night in the U.S. In other words, having reliable systems is an important point in modern IT business. We still haven't answered the key question of this section—what is a high-availability system? There are several levels of availability, as shown in Table 23.1.

TABLE 23.1   Availability and Downtime

Type of System	Uptime	Downtime per Year
General-purpose system	99%	87 hours 36 minutes
	99.5%	43 hours 48 minutes
Most high-availability systems	99.9%	8 hours 30 minutes
"Best" high-availability today	99.95%	4 hours 23 minutes
	99.99%	53 minutes
Continuous availability system	99.999%	5 minutes

Ninety-nine percent sounds like a lot, but it isn't. Ninety-nine percent can be compared to rebooting your system after every three hours of work, and this is most likely not what you are looking for. It is important to see what 99% means, especially when talking about downtime. It means about 87 hours per year, or about 11 working days of 8 hours each. Eleven days means about two weeks. In other words: If you manage to increase the availability of your system, you can save two weeks of work. You can gain two weeks for every person working with the system. With 25 people, you can save up to 1 person simply by increasing the stability of your IT system. These numbers show you how much time you can save by using reliable software and hardware.

Today only a few systems can achieve extremely high availability (> 99.99%). Usually these systems are expensive but reliable and powerful IBM or SGI mainframe machines used by huge companies to store extremely business-critical data. In many cases these systems run proprietary software in proprietary hardware, which makes it more unlikely to get wounded by a "standard" virus. In addition, high-availability systems are protected by various security facilities. This is an important point.

23.1.2 Hardware Issues

To achieve a higher level of availability, it is important to use reliable and redundant hardware. Redundant means that every device is available at least twice. If one component fails, a second component will start doing the work of the component that has failed. This way downtime can be minimized.

In the case of storage, building redundant systems often means using Redundant Array of Independent Disks (RAID) systems. RAID systems are sophisticated tools. They combine various hard disks into an array that is redundant. If not more than a fixed number of hard disks fail, the system will work just as if no error has occurred. Hard disks especially can fail from time to time because they consist of mechanical as well as electronic components. RAID systems help to reduce the risks of errors occurring in the storage system.

One point that is often neglected is redundant electricity supply. This means that if the power supply goes down, your systems will stay up and running. From time to time (let's say once a year if you do not live in California), electricity is turned off for a few minutes for maintenance purposes. During this time it is necessary to have an external electricity supply.

Another important issue is to have a backup server. If one machine fails, you can switch to a spare machine that does the job until the primary machine has been repaired.

23.1.3 Network Issues

In addition to hardware issues, a reasonable network is essential as well. It is no use to connect an expensive IBM zSeries machine to a dial-up connection to run a Web server. If you are investing a lot of money in good reliable hardware, it is also necessary to have an eye on the quality of your connections to the Internet. For real high-availability solutions, we recommend working with two independent lines. If one fails, it is still possible to use the second line instead.

An important thing is to have a firewall that protects your production system. Keep in mind that your firewalling system should be redundant as well because otherwise your system might not be available because of a broken firewall. In this case the firewall would be a potential threat to your system.

23.2 Building Failsafe Applications

After this brief theoretical overview about high availability, it is time to see what you can do to make your PHP- and PostgreSQL-based applications work more reliably.

When building reliable solutions, a few things cannot be influenced by the programmer. The first thing is the stability of the software packages you are building your applications on. If there are bugs in PHP's core distribution, you cannot do anything about it except use the latest packages and patches. In addition, we recommend using "old" functions that have been unchanged during the last few releases. These functions will most likely be more reliable than new functions.

However, you can't totally forecast or avoid most problems with software that you haven't written. Just try to use well-known components. What can be influenced is the code you are writing, and this is exactly what we are going to deal with in this section.

In real-world IT environments, it is just not enough when an application does what it is supposed to do. The reason for that is simple. Every user is a potential threat because a user might behave the wrong way, so errors can occur. Just think of a content management system. Several people have spent days adding content to the database. Then an accidental click removes all records from the database and you can do nothing about it. This is a horror scenario, but things like that happen every day, so a lot of money is spent for recovery purposes.

In addition to downtime caused by hardware or software failures, problems caused by users can harm your applications. This can even lead to a loss of data, which cannot be repaired. Such damage is quite dangerous and very bad for your business. An additional point is that it can be useful to monitor the people working on your system.

When designing your applications properly, there is no need to allow such disasters to harm your IT environment. A possible approach to solving problems like that would be to work with rules and various flags. Do you think that all the things I have mentioned are possible with just a few lines of code? Well, I guess we have to prove it.

23.2.1 A Simple Example

The goal of this example is to implement a simple shopping application that is capable of tracking everything happening inside the database. When building up logging information, it can be useful to see which transaction has done what. Therefore it is necessary to retrieve the current transaction id. Up to now (version 7.2), there is no official function for retrieving the transaction id. Therefore it is necessary to implement a function like that quickly. Maybe we will see this feature in future versions of PostgreSQL. However, because it is truly simple to implement this feature on your own, we have decided to include it. Take a look at the following piece of C code:

```
#include "postgres.h"
#include "access/xact.h"


Datum
getxid(PG_FUNCTION_ARGS)
{
        TransactionId xid = GetCurrentTransactionId();
        PG_RETURN_INT32((int32) xid);
}
```

As you can see, it is hardly more than calling the GetCurrentTransactionId function and returning the result as a variable. In this case we have chosen int32. To compile the code and to generate a shared object out of it, you can use GCC as shown in the next listing (this time we haven't made a makefile because the code is just four lines long):

```
gcc -Wall -fPIC -O2 -I/usr/src/postgresql-7.2/src/include \
      -c -o getxid.o getxid.c
gcc -shared -Wl,-soname,/home/hs/datatype/transaction/libgetxid.so \
      -o /home/hs/datatype/transaction/libgetxid.so getxid.o
```

Just modify the paths in the code to your needs and compile the sources.

Now it is time to add the new function to your database. This can easily be done with the help of some SQL code:

```
CREATE FUNCTION getxid()
      RETURNS int4
      AS '/home/hs/datatype/transaction/libgetxid.so'
      LANGUAGE 'C';
```

If no error occurred, a function called getxid will be available, which returns the id of the current transaction. Let's see how it works:

```
phpbook=# SELECT getxid();
 getxid
--------
   1946
(1 row)
```

In this example 1946 is returned. Keep in mind that the result returned on your machine will most likely be different. Let's use the function inside a transaction:

```
phpbook=# BEGIN;
BEGIN
phpbook=# SELECT getxid();
 getxid
--------
   1947
(1 row)

phpbook=# SELECT getxid();
 getxid
--------
   1947
(1 row)
```

```
phpbook=# COMMIT;
COMMIT
```

As you can see, the same transaction id is returned twice because you are inside a transaction. In this way the transaction id can be used to identify all queries belonging to one transaction.

After the transaction is committed, the transaction id will be different because the SELECT statement is executed as one transaction:

```
phpbook=# SELECT getxid();
 getxid
--------
   1948
(1 row)
```

After implementing the fundamentals, it is time to have a look at the data structure of the shop. It consists of just two tables plus one parent table because this is enough to show you how to build a failsafe application:

```
CREATE TABLE parent (
        id serial8,                     -- id of every record in the database
        transid int4
                DEFAULT getxid(),       -- transaction id
        valid boolean DEFAULT 't',      -- record valid/yes-no
        tstamp timestamp with time zone
                DEFAULT now()           -- modification time
);

-- tables containing data
CREATE TABLE product (
        prod_id int4,                   -- id of product
        name text,                      -- name of product
        price numeric(9,2)              -- price of product
) INHERITS (parent);

CREATE TABLE sales (
        prod_id int4,                   -- id of product
        amount int4,                    -- number of products sold
        price numeric(9,2),             -- price
        customer text,                  -- customer who has bought product
        sold timestamp with time zone   -- time when product was sold
) INHERITS (parent);
```

The parent table consists of four columns that contain logging information. In the first column, an id will be used to number every record added to the table. Every record will have a unique id, so it is possible to find out in which order the records have been added to the table—even in the case of concurrent transactions. The second column, labeled `transid`, will contain the transaction id. The default value is set to the current transaction id. However, the transaction id can also be inserted explicitly. In this example a column is used to store the transaction id. This is not the only way to solve the problem, but it is an obvious one. All tables contain a hidden column called `xmin`. This column contains the transaction id and can be retrieved like the object id or another hidden column (for example, `SELECT xmin FROM table`). However, if you use the onboard transaction id, you will not be as flexible as when working with your "own" transaction id. In this example we will use a separate column to do the job.

The third column shows whether a record is still valid. Finally, the fourth column tells us the time when a record has been added to the table. Keep in mind that `now()` returns the current transaction time and not the time the `INSERT` statement has been sent to the server. This is essential because it is the most important information.

Let's take a look at the table containing the data of the shop. The first table contains the unique id of a product as well as the name and the price of a product. The second table contains a list of all sales. It stores the product id, the number of units bought, the price, which customer has bought the product, and when it was sold. Both tables, product and sales, inherit all columns from the parent table:

```
phpbook=# \d product
                              Table "product"
  Attribute |           Type           |           Modifier
 -----------+--------------------------+------------------------------
 ------------------------
  id        | bigint                   | not null default nextval
 ('"parent_id_seq"'::text)
  transid   | integer                  | default getxid()
  valid     | boolean                  | default 't'
  tstamp    | timestamp with time zone | default now()
  prod_id   | integer                  | not null
  name      | text                     |
  price     | numeric(9,2)             |
```

```
phpbook=# \d sales
                                Table "sales"
    Attribute |          Type          |              Modifier
----------+------------------------+----------------------------
--------------------
    id        | bigint                 | not null default nextval
('"parent_id_seq"'::text)
    transid   | integer                | default getxid()
    valid     | boolean                | default 't'
    tstamp    | timestamp with time zone | default now()
    prod_id   | integer                |
    amount    | integer                |
    price     | numeric(9,2)           |
    customer  | text                   |
    sold      | timestamp with time zone |
```

As you can see in the listing, the columns in the parent table have been added to the two tables automatically.

In the next step you can insert some products into the table:

```
INSERT INTO product (prod_id, name, price) VALUES
        (504532, 'cell phone', '45.39');


BEGIN;
INSERT INTO product (prod_id, name, price)
        VALUES (0815, 'MySQL tutorial', '1.15');
INSERT INTO product (prod_id, name, price)
        VALUES (0816, 'Hamburger', '2.09');
INSERT INTO product (prod_id, name, price)
        VALUES (866787, 'CPU', '199.79');
COMMIT;
```

Two transactions are processed. The first one inserted exactly one record into the table. The second transaction added three records. Let's see how to send the data to the server:

```
[hs@duron code_buch]$ psql phpbook < add_prods.sql
INSERT 49546 1
BEGIN
INSERT 49547 1
INSERT 49548 1
INSERT 49549 1
COMMIT
```

No errors occurred. The table can easily be queried. Let's see what was inserted:

```
phpbook=# SELECT id, transid, valid, tstamp::time with time zone,
prod_id, name, price FROM product;
 id | transid | valid |       tstamp        | prod_id |      name      | price
----+---------+-------+---------------------+---------+----------------+--------
  1 |    2018 | t     | 12:47:46.713663+01  |  504532 | cell phone     |  45.39
  2 |    2019 | t     | 12:47:46.836869+01  |     815 | MySQL tutorial |   1.15
  3 |    2019 | t     | 12:47:46.836869+01  |     816 | Hamburger      |   2.09
  4 |    2019 | t     | 12:47:46.836869+01  |  866787 | CPU            | 199.79
(4 rows)
```

The first few columns have been set automatically. As you can see, the last three records have the same timestamp and the same transaction id. This way you can easily identify what has happened inside your application.

For monitoring the users running applications on your system, it can also be useful to add a column for storing the name of the user to the parent table:

```
phpbook=# ALTER TABLE parent ADD COLUMN dbuser text;
ALTER
phpbook=# \d parent
                            Table "parent"
 Attribute |          Type          |            Modifier
-----------+------------------------+-----------------------------
 id        | bigint                 | not null default nextval
('"parent_id_seq"'::text)
 transid   | integer                | default getxid()
 valid     | boolean                | default 't'
 tstamp    | timestamp with time zone | default now()
 dbuser    | text                   |
Index: parent_id_key
```

Now that you have seen how to prepare the database, it is time to say an additional word about high availability.

Some of you might already have asked what all these things have to do with high availability. Well, things are more complicated than they might seem. I could tell you that you should use RAID systems or that several administrators should be around all the time. These things are essential, but they are just one part of the story. Experience has told us that most errors occur outside your software and hardware. Just think of somebody who deleted data accidentally. Think of people who want to harm your applications by adding wrong data to the database. These things can cause corrupt data and will lead to even more downtime than crashing hard disks. If you have RAID systems, these things are no problem, but problems concerning the people working on your application can only be solved by extensive monitoring and a clever design of your database. In real-world applications, this is essential and you should keep an eye on it.

23.2.2 Implementing Total Monitoring

As we have already mentioned, monitoring is the key to success. It is possible to track every customer or employee working with your applications, and you will soon find out where errors occur. In addition, it will help you to increase the efficiency of your applications. In this section we will take a closer look at monitoring. In addition to monitoring, we will try to build some sort of journaling database.

The first thing we want to do is to define a data structure in which records will never be deleted so that you can easily find out which changes have been made by the users working on the database. To do this, you must think about UPDATE and DELETE operations. If somebody performs an UPDATE operation, the old data is deleted. This is definitely not the desired behavior. In the case of DELETE, the old records should be declared invalid. To get the job done, it is necessary to implement a set of rules:

```
CREATE RULE rule_product_delete
        AS ON DELETE TO product
        DO INSTEAD (
                UPDATE parent SET valid='f'
                        WHERE id=OLD.id
);
```

The rule you have just seen redefines the behavior of a DELETE statement. Instead of deleting the record, it is set to invalid. Notice the table we use inside the rule. The value in the parent table is set to invalid. Because product inherits all columns from the parent table, the changes will also affect the table called product. Please do not update the original table here because otherwise it would not be possible to redefine UPDATE.

Let's see what happens when running DELETE. In this example the product number 815 is deleted:

```
phpbook=# DELETE FROM product WHERE prod_id=815;
UPDATE 1
```

As you can see, an UPDATE operation has been defined. Let's see if any changes have been made inside the table:

```
phpbook=# SELECT id, valid, prod_id FROM product;
 id | valid | prod_id
----+-------+----------
  1 | t     |   504532
  3 | t     |      816
  4 | t     |   866787
  2 | f     |      815
(4 rows)
```

The product number 815 has been set to invalid. It has not been deleted, and this is the most important thing.

In the next step you can write a rule for redefining UPDATE statements:

```
CREATE RULE rule_product_update
        AS ON UPDATE TO product
        DO INSTEAD (
                UPDATE parent SET valid='f'
                        WHERE id=OLD.id;
                INSERT INTO product (prod_id, name, price)
                        VALUES (NEW.prod_id, NEW.name, NEW.price)
);
```

This rule is slightly more complex. First an UPDATE is performed to set the old version of the record to invalid. Now the new version is added to the table. This way the old data is saved and the new version is added to the table. To access the new data, we have to select all valid records. If you want to access previous versions of the data, that is also possible. With the help of this algorithm, no employee will ever be able to delete your data accidentally or on purpose. With the help of the parent table, the administrator can remove or modify data from the table to reduce the amount of data in the database or to restore data. No rule has been defined on the parent table, so you can interact with the table without having to think about redefined versions of UPDATE or DELETE. We want to point out one crucial point again. If the UPDATE statement in the second rule was using the product table instead of the parent table, the rule would be called recursively or at least twice, and this wouldn't be the desired behavior.

Before testing the rule, take a closer look at the code of the rule. This is essential because it is important to know how the code works. The two SQL statements in parentheses are executed instead of the original UPDATE query. OLD contains the values before the UPDATE operation. NEW contains the new values of the rows. These values will be set by the UPDATE query. In this case all records are set to false where the id before the UPDATE was the id in the column. The INSERT statement inserts the new values into the tables. The columns can easily be accessed by using dots.

Now that you have seen how the rule works, you can start using it. Let's use it in combination with a transaction:

```
phpbook=# BEGIN;
BEGIN
phpbook=# UPDATE product SET price='1.99' WHERE name='Hamburger';
INSERT 49599 1
phpbook=# SELECT id, valid, prod_id, name, price FROM product;
 id | valid | prod_id |      name       | price
----+-------+---------+-----------------+--------
  1 | t     |  504532 | cell phone      |  45.39
  2 | t     |     815 | MySQL tutorial  |   1.15
  4 | t     |  866787 | CPU             | 199.79
  3 | f     |     816 | Hamburger       |   2.09
  5 | t     |     816 | Hamburger       |   1.99
(5 rows)

phpbook=# COMMIT;
COMMIT
```

The UPDATE query performs an INSERT operation. The result of the SELECT statement shows exactly what has happened inside your database. Two records containing Hamburger are in the listing. One of these is invalid, so the new record is the only valid record. The next query shows the recent version of the data:

```
phpbook=# SELECT id, valid, prod_id, name, price FROM product WHERE valid='t';
 id | valid | prod_id |      name       | price
----+-------+---------+-----------------+--------
  1 | t     |  504532 | cell phone      |  45.39
  2 | t     |     815 | MySQL tutorial  |   1.15
  4 | t     |  866787 | CPU             | 199.79
  5 | t     |     816 | Hamburger       |   1.99
(4 rows)
```

Of course, it is possible to define a view that only returns the recent version of the data, but this can also be overkill. It depends on whether you'd like to have a view or not.

In this section you have seen one approach to increasing the reliability of your systems, and you have seen how your data can be protected without investing any money. With the help of redundant design, many common errors can be solved, which is as important as redundant hardware.

23.4 Summary

Redundant hardware and software are essential for building high-availability solutions. The goal of building reliable solutions is to avoid downtime and to guarantee that your applications are working around the clock. High availability starts with the design of your applications and does not involve just the hardware. Often downtime is caused by loss of data. You can avoid this by building some kind of journaling database.

PART VI

Migration

IN THIS PART

24

Migration

Not all database-driven applications are based on PostgreSQL. Many people are not satisfied with their database solutions, so new solutions have to be found. PostgreSQL is the perfect database for migration. Because of its ANSI SQL compliance, its embedded languages, and its ability to work with transactions, PostgreSQL is the desired playground of every database developer.

This chapter is dedicated to those who want to migrate their applications from MySQL, Oracle, or Microsoft Access to PostgreSQL. Of course, there are many other databases that can be substituted for PostgreSQL, but that is beyond the scope of this book.

24.1 Migrating from MySQL to PostgreSQL

MySQL databases are in widespread use among Web developers. Although MySQL lacks many functions provided by sophisticated database programs such as DB2, Oracle, PostgreSQL, or many others, people like MySQL because of its simplicity.

In this section, you will see how to migrate data from MySQL to PostgreSQL.

24.1.1 A Brief Installation Guide

The first thing is to get started with MySQL. We recommend downloading a binary version of MySQL. In this section version 4.0.1 has been used. You can easily install the package using the instructions in the manual.

After installing the binaries and starting the daemon, you can use the interactive shell to connect to the database:

```
[root@duron mysql]# mysql
Welcome to the MySQL monitor.  Commands end with ; or \g.
Your MySQL connection id is 4 to server version: 4.0.1

Type 'help;' or '\h' for help. Type '\c' to clear the buffer.

mysql>
```

MySQL offers an interactive shell. It also provides some basic commands such as \h:

```
mysql> \h

MySQL commands:
Note that all text commands must be first on line and end with ';'
help     (\h)    Display this help.
?        (\?)    Synonym for `help'.
clear    (\c)    Clear command.
connect  (\r)    Reconnect to the server. Optional arguments are db and host.
edit     (\e)    Edit command with $EDITOR.
ego      (\G)    Send command to mysql server, display result vertically.
exit     (\q)    Exit mysql. Same as quit.
go       (\g)    Send command to mysql server.
nopager  (\n)    Disable pager, print to stdout.
notee    (\t)    Don't write into outfile.
pager    (\P)    Set PAGER [to_pager]. Print the query results via PAGER.
print    (\p)    Print current command.
quit     (\q)    Quit mysql.
rehash   (\#)    Rebuild completion hash.
source   (\.)    Execute a SQL script file. Takes a file name as an argument.
status   (\s)    Get status information from the server.
system   (\!)    Execute a system shell command.
tee      (\T)    Set outfile [to_outfile]. Append everything into given outfile.
use      (\u)    Use another database. Takes database name as argument.

Connection id: 3  (Can be used with mysqladmin kill)
```

As you can see, the terminal offers many functions you can use to work with the database.

In the next step, it is time to create a database. In this example the database will be called phpbook:

```
mysql> CREATE DATABASE phpbook;
Query OK, 1 row affected (0.07 sec)
```

After that the database is ready for action.

24.1.2 Migrating Data to PostgreSQL

In this section you will take a closer look at how data can be migrated from MySQL to PostgreSQL. You will need a MySQL database containing some data:

```
USE phpbook;

CREATE TABLE product (
        product_id integer NOT NULL AUTO_INCREMENT PRIMARY KEY,
        product_name varchar(200),
        description text,
        price double,
        currency char(3)
);

INSERT INTO product (product_name, description, price, currency) VALUES
        ('Hamburger', 'burger filled with meat', '1.59', 'USD'),
        ('Cheeseburger', 'burger filled with meat and cheese', '1.69', 'USD'),
        ('French Fries', 'fatty potatoes', '0.99', 'EUR'),
        ('Donut', 'somthing which makes you fat', '1.49', 'EUR');
```

The script contains one table containing four records. The goal is to migrate this database to PostgreSQL. Before doing, this you have to insert it into your MySQL database:

```
[root@duron mysql]# mysql phpbook < data.sql
```

The next listing shows that the data has been added to the database successfully:

```
mysql> SELECT * FROM product;
+------------+--------------+------------------------------------------+-------+-
----------+
| product_id | product_name | description                              | price |
currency |
+------------+--------------+------------------------------------------+-------+-
----------+
|          1 | Hamburger    | burger filled with meat                  | 1.59 |
USD      |
```

```
|           2 | Cheeseburger | burger filled with meat and cheese |   1.69 |
USD      |
|           3 | French Fries | fatty potatoes                     |   0.99 |
EUR      |
|           4 | Donut        | somthing which makes you fat       |   1.49 |
EUR      |
+-----------+--------------+------------------------------------------------+--------+-
----------+
4 rows in set (0.02 sec)
```

Just likePostgreSQL, MySQL is able to dump databases to ASCII files. This is a comfortable feature because ASCII dumps are a portable file format. To dump the database, you can use the mysqldump command.

Let's look at the dump:

```
-- MySQL dump 8.19
--
-- Host: localhost     Database: phpbook
-----------------------------------------------------------
-- Server version       4.0.1

--
-- Table structure for table 'product'
--

CREATE TABLE product (
  product_id int(11) NOT NULL auto_increment,
  product_name varchar(200) default NULL,
  description text,
  price double default NULL,
  currency char(3) default NULL,
  PRIMARY KEY  (product_id)
) TYPE=MyISAM;

/*!40000 ALTER TABLE product DISABLE KEYS */;


--
-- Dumping data for table 'product'
--
```

```
INSERT INTO product VALUES (1,'Hamburger','burger filled with meat',1.59,'USD');
INSERT INTO product VALUES (2,'Cheeseburger','burger filled with meat and
cheese',1.69,'USD');
INSERT INTO product VALUES (3,'French Fries','fatty potatoes',0.99,'EUR');
INSERT INTO product VALUES (4,'Donut','somthing which makes you fat',1.49,
'EUR');

/*!40000 ALTER TABLE product ENABLE KEYS */;
```

Now it is time to convert the MySQL database to PostgreSQL. You can use the Perl
scripts that can be found in the contributed directory of your PostgreSQL source
code. In this example, the following command is used to perform the conversion:

mysqldump phpbook | ./my2pg.pl

Simply pipe the output of the dump to `my2pg.pl`. `my2pg.pl` will take care of the
result and PostgreSQL-compliant SQL code will be generated. Do not pipe the result
to PostgreSQL directly because there could be minor errors in the PostgreSQL code.
When running this demo application, blanks were missing that led to syntax errors.
Things like that must be checked by the user migrating the data. After checking the
SQL file, you should have something like this:

```
-- My2Pg $Revision: 1.6 translated dump
--
. . . . . . . . . . . . . . . . . . . . . . . . . . . . . . . . . . . . . . . . . . . . . . . . . . . . . . . . . . . . . . . . . . . . . . .


BEGIN;


--
-- Sequences for table PRODUCT
--


CREATE SEQUENCE product_product_id_seq;

-- MySQL dump 8.19
--
-- Host: localhost    Database: phpbook
. . . . . . . . . . . . . . . . . . . . . . . . . . . . . . . . . . . . . . . . . . . . . . . . . . . . . . . . . . . .
-- Server version       4.0.1-alpha


--
-- Table structure for table 'product'
--
```

```
CREATE TABLE product (
  product_id INT4 DEFAULT nextval('product_product_id_seq'),
  product_name varchar(200) DEFAULT NULL,
  description text,
  price FLOAT8 DEFAULT NULL,
  currency char(3) DEFAULT NULL,
  PRIMARY KEY  (product_id)
);

/*!40000 ALTER TABLE product DISABLE KEYS */;


--
-- Dumping data for table 'product'
--


INSERT INTO product VALUES (1,'Hamburger','burger filled with meat',1.59,'USD');
INSERT INTO product VALUES (2,'Cheeseburger','burger filled with meat and
cheese',1.69,'USD');
INSERT INTO product VALUES (3,'French Fries','fatty potatoes',0.99,'EUR');
INSERT INTO product VALUES (4,'Donut','somthing which makes you fat',1.49,
'EUR');

/*!40000 ALTER TABLE product ENABLE KEYS */;



--
-- Sequences for table PRODUCT
--


SELECT SETVAL('product_product_id_seq',(select case when max(product_id)>0
then max(product_id)+1 else 1 end from product));

COMMIT;
```

This code can be sent to PostgreSQL now:

```
[root@duron mysql]# psql phpbook < /tmp/pgcode.sql
BEGIN
CREATE
NOTICE:  CREATE TABLE / PRIMARY KEY will create implicit index 'product_pkey'
for table 'product'
CREATE
```

```
INSERT 49615 1
INSERT 49616 1
INSERT 49617 1
INSERT 49618 1
 setval
--------
      5
(1 row)

COMMIT
```

No errors have occurred and the entire database has been converted successfully. Internally my2pg.pl does nothing except reformat the MySQL code to code that, in most cases, complies with both ANSI SQL and PostgreSQL.

Migrating data from PostgreSQL is much harder if not impossible. Because of PostgreSQL's additional features, it is impossible to port a complex application back to MySQL. The reason is that functions provided by PostgreSQL cannot be modeled with the help of MySQL because no sophisticated embedded languages are available.

24.1.3 Migrating Functions

After migrating the data, it is necessary to port the SQL code of your application to PostgreSQL. This can be a painful task because MySQL is not as ANSI-SQL–compliant as PostgreSQL, so porting SQL can be painful. Just take a look at the following example:

```
mysql> SELECT CONCAT("a", "b");
+------------------+
| CONCAT("a", "b") |
+------------------+
| ab               |
+------------------+
1 row in set (0.03 sec)
```

The CONCAT function is not ANSI-SQL–compliant. Because MySQL does not support the || operator for connecting strings, the CONCAT function was invented. When porting your application to PostgreSQL, you must make sure that functions like that are removed and replaced by proper ANSI SQL code or functions written in an embedded language.

24.2 Migrating from Oracle to PostgreSQL

In professional IT environments, databases such as DB2 and Oracle are very popular. Because of the broad variety of their functions and features, DB2 and Oracle have become widespread, and many companies around the globe are relying on DB2 and Oracle databases. There are several reasons why it can make sense to switch to PostgreSQL. One big advantage of PostgreSQL is that it is one of the most flexible databases available. It is a comparatively easy task to write extensions and to add new features to the core of the database. Because PostgreSQL supports a broad range of embedded languages, it is an easy task to use code that has already been written inside your database without having to make major changes to the code. Reusability of code is an important issue, and it can be a real advantage to make your code run as embedded software. PostgreSQL is a real open source database and this will help you when you need precise information about the internals of the database. Of course, it is not possible to use PostgreSQL for every application on earth, but you should keep in mind that the database can be administered easily and this will help you to reduce the total costs of ownership of your database environment.

In this section you will see how data can be migrated from Oracle to PostgreSQL. In most cases all data can be ported and you can use PostgreSQL as an alternative database platform.

PostgreSQL and Oracle are not totally different. Both databases support a major part of the ANSI SQL-92 standard, so as far as SQL is concerned, porting is a rather easy task.

In addition to porting the SQL code of your applications, it is necessary to port the functions based on embedded languages. In this case PostgreSQL is flexible because an entire set of embedded languages is enabled. PL/pgSQL is close to PL/SQL, so the majority of your PL/pgSQL code can be ported easily. If PL/pgSQL is not enough to port your functions, you can try to use PL/Perl or Pl/Tcl. There is no function that cannot be ported to PL/pgSQL, PL/Perl, or PL/Tcl.

For porting the data and the data structure stored in an Oracle database to PostgreSQL, we recommend using a Perl script. The easiest way to migrate data is to use ora2pg, which can be downloaded from http://www.samse.fr/GPL/ora2pg/. It is a Perl module that has been written to port data and data structures from Oracle to PostgreSQL. The module is constantly improved and provides an easy interface to Oracle and PostgreSQL. Perl programming is beyond the scope of this book, so we recommend that you check out the Web site and take a look at the latest version of the man pages, which are distributed along with the module.

24.3 Summary

Porting databases to PostgreSQL is a comparatively easy task because PostgreSQL offers great flexibility and a variety of embedded languages that can be used to model functions that are not natively supported by PostgreSQL.

For porting MySQL databases to PostgreSQL, a converter can be used. In the case of Oracle databases, you can use `ora2pg`.

Symbols

A

next command, 81

one-dimensional arrays, 75-85

range function, 80

reset command, 79

shuffle function, 80-81

sort command, 79

stacks, 81-82

two-dimensional, 301

array_diff function (PHP), 84

array_intersect function (PHP), 84-85

array_merge function (PHP), 83-84

array_multisort command (PHP), 88

array_unique function (PHP), 82-83

arsort command (PHP), 79

associative arrays (PHP), 77-78

attachments (e-mail)

downloading, 611-613

retrieving data, 609-611

attributes (objects), 124-126

authentication

Apache authentication, 591-593

PHP authentication, 593-596

PostgreSQL secure authentication, 372-375

AVG functions, 206

B

B-tree indexes (PostgreSQL), 216

Base64 (e-mail algorithm), 600

basename function (PHP), 101

BEGIN command, 268

BEGIN command (PHP), 404

BETWEEN statements, 305

binaries

installing

Debian packages, 38

RPM packages, 38

packages

installing, 151

removing, 151-152

Binary (e-mail algorithm), 600

BinHex (e-mail algorithm), 600

BLOBs (Binary Large Objects)

PHP

pg_locreate function, 411

pg_loimport function, 409

pg_loopen function, 409-410

pg_loread function, 412

pg_loreadall function, 409-410

pg_lowrite function, 411

SQL, 405-406

lo_export function, 408

lo_import function, 407

lo_unlink function, 408

pg_locreate function, 411

pg_loimport function, 409

pg_loopen function, 409-410

pg_loread function, 412

pg_loreadall function, 409-410

pg_lowrite function, 411

bool fclose function (PHP), 101

bool file_exists function (PHP), 102

bool flock function (PHP), 102

bool is_dir function (PHP), 103

bool is_executable function (PHP), 103

bool is_file function (PHP), 103

How can we make this index more useful? Email us at indexes@samspublishing.com

J – K

string readlink function, 103

string realpath function, 104

string realpath tempnam, 104

localtime function (PHP), 543

LOCK command, 273

LOCK command (PHP/PostgreSQL), 400

locking

explicit locking (PostgreSQL), 402

execute function, 401

LOCK command, 400

row-level locking, 273

table locking, 273

logical views, 139

loops

break command, 57

continue statements, 57-59

DO..WHILE loops (PHP), 56-57

endless loops, 341-342

FOR loops, 317-318

FOR loops (PHP), 59-61

WHILE loops, 320-321

WHILE loops (PHP), 55-59

lower function (PHP), 458

lo_export function, 408

lo_import function, 407

lo_unlink function, 408

ltrim function (PHP), 74

M

macaddr, 241

mailboxes (e-mail), retrieving data, 603-605

managing sessions

cookies, 463-467

registering variables, 469-473

session IDs, 467-469

mathematical functions, 222

mathematical operators, 222

MAX functions, 207

memory management (PostgreSQL), 375

merging dynamic images, 480-482

messages

Hello World messages (HTML), 44-45

Hello World messages (PHP), 43-45

adding comments, 47

assigning variables, 46

metacharacters, 438-442

metaphone function, 693-694

methods, 121-122

microtime function (PHP), 545

migration, data, 711

functions, 717

MySQL to PostgreSQL, 713-717

Oracle to PostgreSQL, 718

MIME (e-mail algorithm), 600

MIN functions, 207

Ming Web site, 499

mixed fscanf function (PHP), 102

mktime function (PHP), 539

modeling data, 144

ERMs (Entity Relationship Models), 144-146

UML (Unified Modeling Language), 146

pg_freeresult function (PHP/PostgreSQL), 391

pg_hba.conf (PostgreSQL configuration file), 369-372

pg_host function (PHP/PostgreSQL), 381-384

pg_locreate function, 411

pg_loimport function, 409

pg_loopen function, 409-410

pg_loread function, 412

pg_loreadall function, 409-410

pg_lowrite function, 411

pg_numfields function (PHP/PostgreSQL), 388

pg_numrows function (PHP/PostgreSQL), 387-388

pg_pconnect command (PHP), 425

pg_port function (PHP/PostgreSQL), 384

pg_put_line command (PHP/PostgreSQL), 396-397

pg_trace function (PHP/PostgreSQL), 399-400

pg_triggers, 334-335

pg_tty function (PHP/PostgreSQL), 384

pg_untrace function (PHP/PostgreSQL), 400

phantom reads, 272

PHP. *See also* **PHP/PostgreSQL**

Apache, installing, 16

Apache and PHP, installing, 29-31, 35

application servers, 660-661

installing PHPLens, 661-662

JPETO, 667

PHPLens, 664-666

PHPLensConnect function, 664

render function, 664

arrays, passing to functions, 90-91

authentication, 593-596

BLOBs (Binary Language Objects)

pg_locreate function, 411

pg_loimport function, 409

pg_loopen function, 409-410

pg_loread function, 412

pg_loreadall function, 409-410

pg_lowrite function, 411

classes, 122

building, 123-135

inheritance, 122, 131-135

code, debugging, 118-119

code packages, building, 108-110

command-line parameters, 47-49

commands

array_multisort command, 88

arsort command, 79

BEGIN command, 404

break command, 57

COMMIT command, 404

each command, 86-87

foreach command, 81

imap_status, 614

include commands, 106

next command, 81

pg_pconnect command, 425

preg_grep command, 449

preg_match_all command, 443-444

preg_quote command, 448

preg_replace command, 444-446

preg_split command, 446-447

reset command, 79

ROLLBACK command, 403

SAMS DEVELOPER'S LIBRARY

Cookbook   Handbook   Dictionary

PHP
DEVELOPER'S COOKBOOK

Sterling Hughes and
Andrei Zmievski

ISBN: 0-672-32325-7
$39.99 US/$59.95 CAN

PostgreSQL
DEVELOPER'S HANDBOOK

Ewald Geschwinde and
Hans–Jürgen Schönig

ISBN: 0-672-32260-9
$44.99 US/$67.95 CAN

Perl
DEVELOPER'S DICTIONARY

Clinton Pierce

ISBN: 0-672-32067-3
$39.99 US/$59.95 CAN

OTHER DEVELOPER'S LIBRARY TITLES

PHP
DEVELOPER'S DICTIONARY

R. Allen Wyke,
Michael J. Walker,
and Robert M. Cox

ISBN: 0-672-32029-0
$39.99 US/$59.95 CAN

mod_perl
DEVELOPER'S COOKBOOK

Geoffrey Young,
Paul Linder, and
Randy Kobes

ISBN: 0-672-32240-4
$39.99 US/$62.95 CAN

JavaScript
DEVELOPER'S DICTIONARY

Alexander Vincent

ISBN: 0-672-32201-3
$39.99 US/$59.95 CAN

Python
DEVELOPER'S HANDBOOK

André Lessa

ISBN: 0-672-31994-2
$44.99 US/$67.95 CAN

ALL PRICES ARE SUBJECT TO CHANGE

SAMS
www.samspublishing.com